CAMBRIDGE LIBRARY COI

Books of enduring scholarly value

History

The books reissued in this series include accounts of historical events and movements by eye-witnesses and contemporaries, as well as landmark studies that assembled significant source materials or developed new historiographical methods. The series includes work in social, political and military history on a wide range of periods and regions, giving modern scholars ready access to influential publications of the past.

The History of Jamaica

Edward Long's three-volume work marks a major turning point in the historiography of Jamaica, as the first attempt at a comprehensive description of the colony, its history, government, people, economy and geography. The son of a prominent Jamaican plantation owner, Long (1734–1813) spent twelve years running his father's property, an experience which permeates his vision of the island's past, present and future. Throughout his book, Long defends slavery as '*inevitably* necessary' in Jamaica, suggesting the institution to be implicit in the 'possession of British freedom'. Volume 2 presents a survey of the counties of Jamaica, information on religion, education and health, descriptions and racial classifications of the population, a history of the slave rebellions and details of the legal code governing slavery. This important 1774 book provides fascinating insights into eighteenth-century colonial Jamaica and the ideology of its commercial and administrative elite.

Cambridge University Press has long been a pioneer in the reissuing of out-of-print titles from its own backlist, producing digital reprints of books that are still sought after by scholars and students but could not be reprinted economically using traditional technology. The Cambridge Library Collection extends this activity to a wider range of books which are still of importance to researchers and professionals, either for the source material they contain, or as landmarks in the history of their academic discipline.

Drawing from the world-renowned collections in the Cambridge University Library, and guided by the advice of experts in each subject area, Cambridge University Press is using state-of-the-art scanning machines in its own Printing House to capture the content of each book selected for inclusion. The files are processed to give a consistently clear, crisp image, and the books finished to the high quality standard for which the Press is recognised around the world. The latest print-on-demand technology ensures that the books will remain available indefinitely, and that orders for single or multiple copies can quickly be supplied.

The Cambridge Library Collection will bring back to life books of enduring scholarly value (including out-of-copyright works originally issued by other publishers) across a wide range of disciplines in the humanities and social sciences and in science and technology.

The History of Jamaica

*Or, General Survey of the Antient and Modern
State of that Island, with Reflections on its
Situation, Settlements, Inhabitants, Climate,
Products, Commerce, Laws, and Government*

VOLUME 2

EDWARD LONG

CAMBRIDGE
UNIVERSITY PRESS

CAMBRIDGE UNIVERSITY PRESS

Cambridge, New York, Melbourne, Madrid, Cape Town, Singapore,
São Paolo, Delhi, Dubai, Tokyo

Published in the United States of America by Cambridge University Press, New York

www.cambridge.org
Information on this title: www.cambridge.org/9781108016452

© in this compilation Cambridge University Press 2010

This edition first published 1774
This digitally printed version 2010

ISBN 978-1-108-01645-2 Paperback

THE
HISTORY
OF
JAMAICA.
OR,
GENERAL SURVEY OF THE ANTIENT AND MODERN STATE
OF
THAT ISLAND:
WITH
Reflections on its Situation, Settlements, Inhabitants, Climate, Products, Commerce, Laws, and Government.

IN THREE VOLUMES.

ILLUSTRATED WITH COPPER PLATES.

VOL. II.

—— mea fuit femper hâc in re voluntas et fententia, quemvis ut hoc vellem de iis, qui effent idonei fufcipere, quàm me;—me, ut mallem, quàm neminem.

CIC. Orat. in CÆCILIUM.

LONDON:
PRINTED FOR T. LOWNDES, IN FLEET-STREET.
MDCCLXXIV.

ISLAND of
JAMAICA,
Divided into
COUNTIES, and
PARISHES,
according to the best Authorities,
By Thos. Kitchin hydrog.
Hydrographer to his MAJESTY,
1774

HANOVER

CORNWA

ST JAMES

WESTMORELAND

S. ELIZA

PURRYS TOWN

TRELAWNY TOWN

ACCOMPONGS T

MONTEGO BAY

Salt Swamp

LONG BAY

Pedro Point
Ballast Bay
Lances Bay
Cousins's Cove
Davis's Cove

GREEN ISLAND HARBOUR
Half Moon Bay
ORANGE BAY
Nth Negril Pt
Nthn NEGRIL HARB.
Booby Kay

LONG BAY

Sthn NEGRIL POINT

Westmoreland Barrack

Black Morass
Beckfords

Chapel

Morass
Morass

Johns Pt or Cabaritta Pt
Cabaritta R.
NEW CHANNEL
OLD CHANNEL

Homer's Cove
Williams Cove
Breadnut R.
SAVANNA LA MAR
Bluff for Breadnut

BLUEFIELDS BAY
Moores Reef
Crab Pond Pt

Palmeto Point
PARKERS BAY

White House
Scots Cove

Pond

Luana Point

Jacksons Valley

New Savanna Mountains

LACOVIA
Black R.

Cac Morass

GREAT MORASS

Black R. Mouth
Leewards Channel
Port of Agua alta

MAIN CHANNEL

Starvegut Point

STARVEGUT BAY
Black Spring
Billys Bay
Frenchmans Bay
GREAT PEDRO BAY

PEDRO BLUFF

Bodmans Bay
Cassava Bay
Jacks Hole
White Horses

Fynchs Vale

Efsex Va

Nassau Mountains

Nathan Mountains

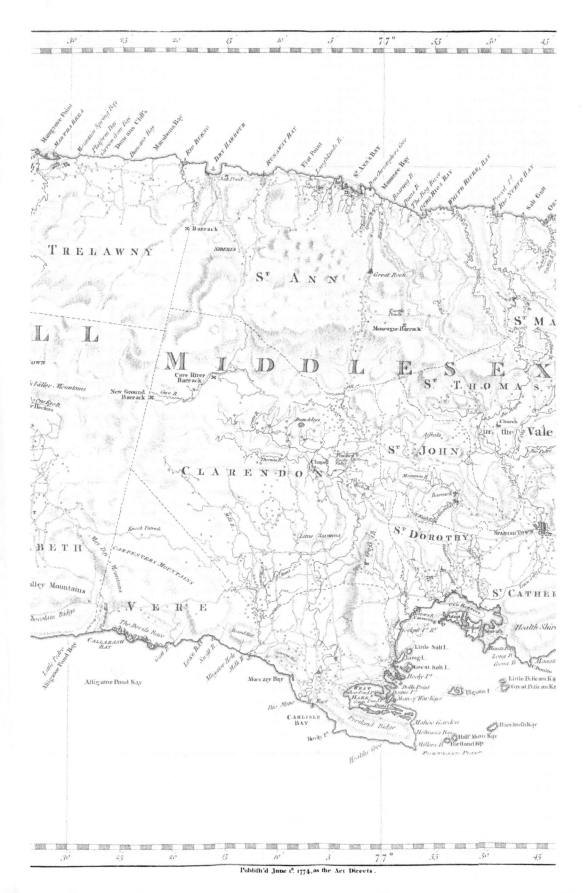

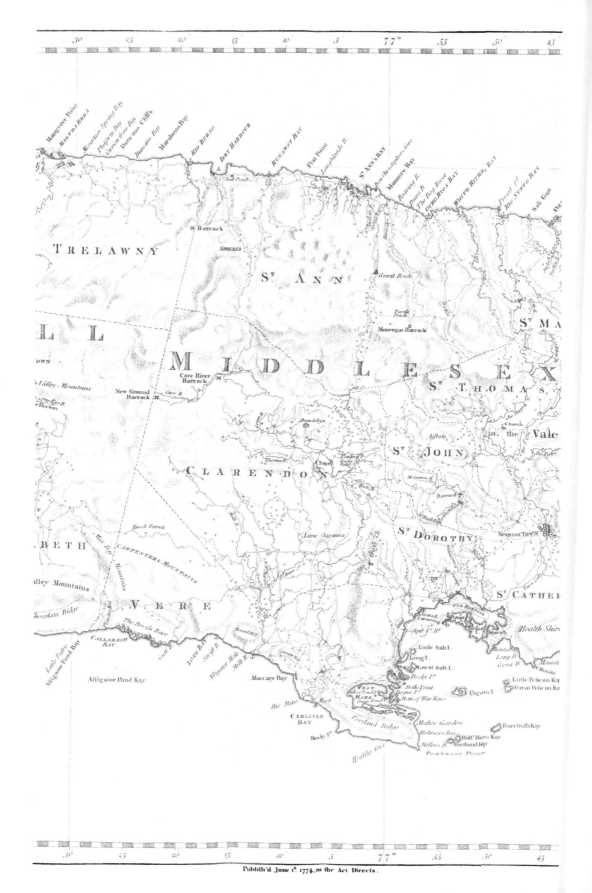

Scale of Miles.

las Hormigas

3 Fathom

EXPLANATION.

Plantations and Settlements

Churches and Chapels

Forts and Barracks

Rivers

Roads

Anchorage for Large Vessels

Anchorage for Small Vessels

Parish Boundaries

Centre of the Island

TOPOGRAPHICAL DESCRIPTION

OF

THE ISLAND.

CHAP. VII.

SECT. I.

JAMAICA is divided into three counties, Middlefex, Surry, and Cornwall. The county of Middlefex contains about 1305235 acres, and has eight parifhes, and fourteen towns and hamlets; viz.

Parifhes.	Towns.	Hamlets.
St. Catharine,	St. Jago de la Vega,	Paffage Fort.
St. Dorothy,	Old Harbour,	Market.
St. John,		
St. Thomas in the Vale.		
Clarendon,		{ Crofs, { Chapel.
Vere,		Carlifle Bay.
St. Mary,	Scots Hall Negro Town,	⌠Rio Nuevo, ⎨ Port Maria, ⌡Saltgut.
St. Anne,	St. Anne,	⌠Laughlands, ⌡Runaway Bay.

I fhall begin with an account of St. Catharine; which, having been the firft-inhabited by the Englifh, is entitled to precedence, more efpecially as it contains the antient metropolis of St. Jago de la Vega, or, as it is commonly called, Spanifh Town, the original name being chiefly ufed in acts of affembly, proclamations, and other public documents. It is fituated in about 18° 1′ North latitude, and in 76° 45' longitude, Weſt from London. It ſtands about ten miles Weſtward of Port Royal; eleven from Kingſton, by the way of Paſſage Fort; and about eighteen by the road of Halfway-Tree, in St. Andrew's. It is ſaid by ſome authors to have been founded by Chriſtopher Columbus, whoſe family took the ducal title of la Vega from it. Other accounts, with more appearance of probability, aſſert, that it was built by Diego, the ſon of Chriſtopher, about the year 1520. The accounts given us of its magnitude and opulence are ſtrongly ſuſpected of exaggeration. Some writers inform us, that it contained above two thouſand houſes, ſixteen churches and chapels, and one abbey, before the invaſion under Penn and Venables; and that the Engliſh ſoldiers exerciſed their prowefs againſt theſe edifices with ſo furious a zeal, as to leave only two churches and about five hundred houſes un-demoliſhed [a]. Other authors, with more appearance of cre-dibility, relate, that it contained one thouſand ſeven hundred houſes, two churches, two chapels, and one abbey: but even this ac-count allows pretty largely for the Spaniſh or white inhabitants; who, according to the moſt certain information of the Engliſh officers who went over with the army, and afterwards ſettled here, did not exceed fifteen hundred: ſo that, if theſe writers are to be believed, the houſes out-numbered the inhabitants. The Engliſh army eſtabliſhed their head-quarters here; and, as they had oc-caſion for moſt of the houſes that were habitable, we muſt ſuppoſe that they only pulled down thoſe of an inferior claſs, together with the religious edifices, which, as far as their ruins and tradition can afford evidence, confiſted of an abbey and two churches, the one called the Red, and the other the White Croſs. There is reaſon to believe, that, after the ſeat of government was transferred to Port Royal, the town of St. Jago became thinned of inhabitants, who

[a] This is Hickeringell's account. He was the earlieſt writer on the affairs of this iſland, and himſelf in the army at the time of the conqueſt under Venables; but it is poſſible, that he might have eſtimated the number of houſes by conjecture only, or been miſinformed. According to the beſt teſtimonies, the whole Engliſh army, at the time of their entering the town, did not conſiſt of more than about nine thouſand, including a regiment of marines. Allowing therefore ten to each houſe, when they were in quarters (which, conſidering the ſmallneſs of theſe edifices, may be reckoned full ſufficient), the number they ſpared from deſtruction may be ſuppoſed about nine hundred, for the accommodation of the officers and men.

gradually

gradually left it, either to refide at the new metropolis, or to fpread themfelves in the country: in confequence of which, a great many of the Spanifh houfes were fuffered to decay; and others were pulled down, to enlarge areas; while fome were converted into ware-houfes and ftables; fo that at prefent it does not contain more than between four and five hundred inhabited by white perfons; but, when thofe inhabited by free Negroes, Mulattoes, and flaves, are taken into account, the whole number may be eftimated at about twelve hundred. The prefent church was erected where the Spanifh Red Crofs Church formerly ftood, at the Eaftern end of the town; the White Crofs ftood at the Northern extremity, at a fmall diftance from the river, on a very agreeable fpot, which is now occupied with a handfome modern-built houfe. On digging the foundation for this houfe, feveral large pieces of wrought ftone were turned up. They appeared to be of the white lime-ftone, or fpecies of fhell-marble, fo common in the neighbouring hills, and to have been the lintels of doors or windows belonging to the old church [b]. The abbey was fituated on the South fide of the parade, where the guard-room and chapel now ftand, and extended back to the go-vernor's houfe. The bafes of two columns, which once fupported a large arch-way leading into the abbey, were vifible but a few years ago: they ftood near the South end of the public offices, were about eight feet fquare, compofed of brick-work, cemented with fo fine a mortar, that in removing them the bricks were all fhivered in pieces. I have feen in this town a great many large ftone-mouldings, for the bafes and other parts of columns; which, as well as the fculptures dug out of the ruins of Sevilla Nueva, in St. Anne's, appeared to have been executed by no mean artifts. The Spanifh ecclefiaftics (however blameable in other refpects) muft be allowed fome merit in having cultivated the elegances of archi-tecture in thefe remote parts of the world. Some of their public

[b] In blocks of this ftone, or marble, I have feen very perfect fhells of the Jamaica mufcle and pectina. In fome parts of the country, where it overfpreads the furface, and has fuffered a torrefaction from the accidental firing of the woods in dry weather, it appears pitted all over; and the little cavities, only divided from each other by fharp points, thefe have been occafioned by violent fhowers falling upon the rock when its face was foftened by fire. A gentleman's houfe built of this material, being unfortunately burnt, the walls continued ftanding till a feafon of heavy rain came on; when they fairly diffolved into a fubftrate of lime.

ftructures

ſtructures at St. Domingo, the Havannah, La Vera Cruz, Carthagena, Panama, &c. would make a noble figure even in European
cities. The fanatic rage, or heedleſs indifference, of the Engliſh
who firſt ſettled in Jamaica, occaſioned the ruin of the Spaniſh
buildings dedicated to religious uſes here; ſo that poſterity can
only form an opinion of their magnificence from ſuch fragments as
here and there are to be found in a neglected ſtate, as being of too
large dimenſions to be employed in any building of modern ſtyle.
In the ſituation of the town, the Spaniſh founder ſhewed a good
deal of judgement, but not much regularity in the diſpoſition of
the ſtreets; yet it is better laid out than moſt of thoſe in England.
That a Weſt-India town ſhould be irregularly planned is, indeed,
almoſt inexcuſable, not only on account of health, which ought
to be principally regarded, but becauſe it is formed as it were at
once. Thoſe in England had not the ſame advantage; they grew
for the moſt part from two or three ſolitary cottages, planted by
the ſide of ſome road, or at the interſection of croſs-roads, which
having been traverſed at firſt without any exactneſs, the ſame
meandring lines continued after the ſides of theſe highways were
built upon and converted into ſtreets; which name is derived with
more propriety from the word *ſtrait*, or narrow, than from *ſtraight*
or not crooked, when it is applied to the towns of England. St.
Jago ſtands on a rocky ſlope, gradually aſcending from the river
Cobre to an extenſive plain, called the Town Savannah; ſo that the
rain-water, which ſometimes falls heavily, eſpecially in the ſeaſons,
paſſes away with a free current into the river; by which means the
town is guarded from many inconveniencies. From Port Royal
harbour it is diſtant about ſix miles N. W.; and, the land having an
eaſy fall from it to the water-ſide, without any intervening moraſs,
it receives the ſea-breeze with little diminution of force or purity.
Towards the North it is about two miles from the hills, which ſink
ſo much in that direction, in compliance with the courſe of the
river, as to give a fine opening from the extenſive vale of Sixteen-
mile-walk, and admit the land-wind. The town is about a mile
in length, and ſomewhat more than a quarter in breadth, lying
longitudinally North and South; and contains about twenty ſtreets
and lanes, a ſquare, a church, a chapel, and other public buildings,

ings, which I fhall particularly fpeak of. The church is fituated in the South-Eaft quarter of the town, near the entrance coming from Paffage Fort. It is an elegant building of brick, in form of a crofs, confifting of four ailes, of which the main aile meafures one hundred and twenty-nine feet in length, and twenty-nine in breadth. As it is without a tower, the congregation is fummoned by a fmall bell hung in a wooden frame, which is erected in the church-yard; the pulpit, pews, and wainfcotting, are of cedar and mahogany; and the ailes for the moft part paved with marble. The altar-piece is handfome, and adorned with carved work; and the decalogue in gilt letters: fronting it, at the Weft end of the main aile, is a gallery fupported on columns, and furnifhed with an exceeding fine organ, which coft 440*l.* fterling, and was fet up in the year 1755. The organift has a falary of 120*l. per annum* currency, paid by the parifhioners, and receives other emoluments, his affiftance being generally required at the funeral obfequies even of the free Negroes and Mulattoes buried in this parifh. The cieling is neatly coved, and graced with two magnificent chandeliers of gilt brafs; and the walls are hung with feveral monuments of marble, plain, but well-executed. The governor's pew is diftin-guifhed from the reft by being raifed higher, and crowned with a canopy. The two chandeliers were the gift of private perfons; and part of the communion plate, I have been told, was plundered from a Roman catholic church fome years ago, at the attack of Port Louis, in Hifpaniola: it has more of grandeur than elegance in its fafhion. The building was erected in two years, at the parochial expence, on the foundation of the former one, which was irreparably damaged by the hurricane of Auguft, 1712. About the year 1762 it received a thorough repair, and at prefent yields to none in the ifland for a becoming neatnefs. The provifion made for the rector confifts of a very convenient dwelling-houfe in the town; fixty acres of rich pafture-land, within a fmall diftance of it, the donation of Mr. Edward Morgan in 1674; and upwards of five hundred acres in the neighbour-hood, patented in the fame year " for the ufe of the parifh of St. " Catharine, towards the maintenance of the minifter:" but this latter parcel has not as yet been appropriated to the original defign;

the

the different incumbents having been either unwilling or unable, by reafon of the expence, to difturb the poffeffion of thofe perfons who have occupied it; though it will fcarcely admit of a doubt, but that it was meant as a glebe to be annexed to the rectory *in perpetuum*, there being no other affigned to the purpofe. The prefent rector is Doctor Lindfay; the ftipend is 300*l.* currency *per annum*: but the whole profit of the living has been eftimated double that fum at leaft; for, as the duty is great, the occafional fees are confiderable.

The chapel ftands on the South fide of the fquare, near the governor's houfe. It is built much in the ftyle of the common-halls belonging to the inns of court in London: the walls are crowned with battlements; and on the centre of the roof is a cupola and clock. It was founded juft after the earthquake of 1692, in a religious panic, during the adminiftration of Sir William Beefton. How long it remained confecrated to pious ufes is uncertain; but the founder, as if confcious that a wicked race of people would fucceed, who, forgetful of that calamity, might incline to profane it, caufed an infcription, cut in marble, to be fixed up on one end of the building; which denounces a moft terrible imprecation againft any perfon or perfons who fhould dare to put it to any other ufe than that for which it was originally intended. Notwithftanding this, it was afterwards converted into an arfenal of fmall-arms, chiefly for the free Negroes and Mulattoes. In the year 1760, it contained two thoufand fix hundred and feventy-two ftand of firelocks, and three hundred and three brace of piftols: it generally has a ftand of about three thoufand; for keeping of which in good order, the affembly pay an annual falary to an armourer. Adjoining to this ftructure is the guard-houfe; where a party of regulars are every day on duty to attend the governor. The governor's, or, as it is more ufually called, the king's houfe occupies the whole Weft fide of the fquare. The plan of this pile was defigned and approved of under the adminiftration of lieutenant-governor Moore; but the building was not completed till the arrival of his excellency governor Lyttelton in 1762. It was erected, at the fole charge of the ifland, under the infpection of Mr. Crafkell, then engineer of Jamaica, and defigned for the ufual place of refidence

of

of the commander in chief. The expence of building and fur-
nifhing it amounted to near 30,000*l.* currency; and it is now
thought to be the nobleft and beft edifice of the kind, either in
North-America, or any of the Britifh colonies in the Weft-Indies.
The firft floor is raifed about four feet above the ground; the fecond is an Attic ftory; the length of the façade is about two hundred feet; and of the whole range, including the yard and offices,
about two hundred and fixty. The cornices, key-ftones, pediments,
copings, and quoins, are of a beautiful free-ftone, dug out of the
Hope river courfe, in St. Andrew's parifh. The entrance is by a
lofty portico, projecting from the middle of the front about fifteen
feet, fupported by twelve columns of Portland-ftone, of the Ionic
order. The pediment which rifes above the Attic ftory is fuperb,
and very properly ornamented with the imperial arms of Great-
Britain, in carved work well-executed. The pavement of the portico is of white marble, the afcent to which is by a flight of fteps
of the fame material. This portico gives an air of grandeur to the
whole building, and very happily breaks the length of the front.
Two principal entrances lead through it into the body of the
houfe; the one opens into a lobby, or ante-chamber; the other,
into the great faloon, or hall of audience, which is well-proportioned, the dimenfions being about feventy-three by thirty feet, and
the height about thirty-two: from the cieling, which is coved,
hang two brafs gilt luftres. A fcreen, of feven large Doric pillars.
divides the faloon from an upper and lower gallery of communication, which range the whole length on the Weft fide; and the
upper one is fecured with an elegant entrelas of figured iron work.
The Eaft or oppofite fide of the faloon is finifhed with Doric pilafters; upon each of which are brafs girandoles double-gilt; and
between each pilafter, under the windows of the Attic ftory, are
placed, on gilt brackets, the bufts of feveral ancient and modern
philofophers and poets, large as life; which being in bronze, the
darknefs of their complexion naturally fuggefts the idea of fo many
Negroe Caboceros, exalted to this honourable diftinction for fome
peculiar fervices rendered to the country. At the North end, over
a door which opens into the lobby, is a fmall moveable orcheftra,
made to hold a band of mufic on feftive occafions. The furniture

below

below confifts of a great number of mahogany chairs and fettees, fufficient to accommodate a large company; this room being chiefly ufed for public audiences, entertainments, balls, and the hearings of chancery and ordinary. At the South end are three folding-doors, opening into a fpacious apartment, in which, by the governor's permiffion, the council ufually meet; whence it has received the name of the council-chamber. At this end it was defigned to place full-length portraits of their prefent majefties, and likewife of the prince of Wales and his late majefty, between the pilafters; but I am informed they have not yet been obtained. Above the council-chamber is a banqueting-room, or drawing-room, of the fame fize, hung with paper, and neatly furnifhed. This room communicates with the upper gallery and a back ftair-cafe, and enjoys a view of the faloon through fome windows ranging with thofe of the Attic ftory: it is feldom ufed, except on public days, and is perfectly well-calculated for the purpofe. Thefe different apartments take up about one-half of the whole building. The room over the lobby, being fomewhat darkened by the pediment of the portico, was converted by governor Lyttelton into a chapel, for private devotions. It is neatly fitted up, and with great propriety adapted to this ufe. The Northern divifion of the houfe confifts of three large rooms below, communicating with each other, and with a long gallery; all of which are handfomely furnifhed and well-lighted: this gallery has commonly been ufed either for public fuppers, when balls were given in the hall, or as a fheltered and retired walk in wet weather. The upper ftory is difpofed in a fuite of chambers, divided by a long narrow gallery from a range of fmaller apartments or clofets, intended for lodging the governor and part of his houfhold. The two Northernmoft rooms above and below are provided with a chimney, and all the neceffary apparatus for a good fire; which in the rainy feafons is healthy and not difagreeable. In this new building are three ftair-cafes, all of which are private; a circumftance, perhaps, overlooked when the plan was drawn, and not more attended to when it came to be executed: yet there is fufficient fpace in the lobby for carrying up a very magnificent central one, anfwerable to the other parts of fo capital a ftructure; and this no doubt will, fome time or other, be

added

added, as a neceffary improvement to compleat it. Behind is a fmall fquare garden, laid out in dry walks, and planted with Seville orange, genip, and other fruit-trees, with fome flowering fhrubs intermixed; but it is not fo well cultivated as to merit a further defcription. Adjoining to it are two little fquare courts, furrounded with the old buildings, which comprehend feveral lodging-rooms, the private fecretary's office, a large fervants hall, kitchen, and other convenient offices. South of the whole is a fpacious area, environed with the ftables, coach-houfe, granary, &c. and this area communicates with the parade, or great fquare, by a large gateway. All the apartments and offices belonging to the houfe are extremely commodious and airy. In fhort, I believe there is no one of all the colonies where the commander in chief is lodged in a manner more fuitable to his convenience, and the dignity of his rank. On the oppofite fide of the parade, directly fronting the governor's houfe, is a coloffal building, erected likewife by the inhabitants of the ifland at a very great expence: it was begun about feventeen or eighteen years ago; but is not yet completed, nor probably ever will be. It puts us in mind of the gentleman's beard, defcribed by Martial, that grew under the operation of a bungling barber; the half firft-fhaved called again for the razor before the other half was finifhed. This huge pile of brick and mortar is rudely raifed into two ftories. Below is an arcade of large extent, of fixteen circular arches, and one elliptical in the centre, of ruftic work, upon the top of which is a lofty pediment raifed upon four Doric columns. The body of the building is retired, to afford an open gallery, fecured by a balluftrade, and floored with pitch pine-boards, very badly adapted to the climate, where the rain and fun are fo deftructive to wood-work thus expofed. The upper ftory is afcended by a large ftair-cafe, which divides from the firft landing into two branches, both terminating at the two ends of a fpacious lobby; the South end opens into the affembly-chamber and fpeaker's room; the other end, into the court-houfe and jury-room; and the front, into the gallery. Below are ranged the feveral offices of the ifland fecretary, provoft-marfhal, regifter in chancery, and clerks of the crown and court; for the ufe of which, as they coft fomewhat annually in repairs, thefe officers pay to the public a certain moderate rent, amounting to much lefs than they would pay, if they were obliged to hire houfes, which formerly was the cuftom. The offices being thus fo compactly difpofed, and fo contiguous to the courts of juftice, a very fignal convenience refults to all perfons having bufinefs to tranfact in them. The affembly-chamber, or commons-houfe, is about eighty feet in length by about forty. At one end of it a fort of amphitheatre is raifed, with mahogany, fome little elevation above the floor, and lined with feats for the members: the fpeaker's chair is exalted ftill higher. On the floor is a long table, at which the clerk fits; and thereon are regularly heaped, during the feffion, feveral manufcript folios of laws, minutes, and votes, the Englifh ftatutes at large, votes of the Britifh houfe of commons, with pens, ink, and paper, for the inftruction and accommodation of the fenators. The fpeaker's room is furnifhed with proper conveniences for the private committees appointed to meet in it. The cieling of the commons-houfe is lofty and vaulted, except the part of it immediately over the feats; this is boarded and flat, in order to render the debates more diftinct and audible. The court-houfe is well-defigned, and extremely commodious for the judges, jury, barrifters, and other parties that attend it. The doors of the two houfes are directly fronting each other; fo that, when the fupreme court is held during the feffion of the affembly, the fpeaker and chief-juftice are feated *vis à vis*.

Thus the judges feem tacitly admonifhed to a juft difpenfation of the law and their duty; their conduct being amenable to the inquifition and impeachment of the commons in affembly. The two bodies thus circumftanced, the one met for framing, amending, or repealing, the other for enforcing, expounding, or deciding upon, the laws, afford to the fpectators a ftriking picture of the legiflative and executive departments, as moulded by our happy conftitution (though here exhibited only in miniature), each harmonizing the other; ever acting and re-acting; various, yet concurrent. This building, which lines one entire fide of the parade or fquare, had originally a cupola on the middle of the roof, which gave an appearance of lightnefs and variety to the view; but, having afterwards been found too cumberfome, and productive of fome inconveniences, it was taken down; by which means, the front feems

too

A View of the King's House and P

Publish'd as the Act dir

J Bonner. sculp.

blic Offices at S.t Jago de la Vega.

July 1.st 1774.

too much extended, and has too heavy an aspect to please the eye. The brick columns of the arcade are much too massive and clumsy, appearing as if they were intended to sustain some enormous weight, but hitherto supporting only a slight floor, which is so leaky as not to answer the purpose of screening the offices and passengers underneath from a transient shower. The pediment in the centre, and the projection of the speaker's and jury rooms at each end, are some little relief. But, taking the whole structure together, and reflecting on the vast sums of money that have been thrown away upon it, we may justly question, whether consummate dishonesty or ignorance was the chief architect [c].

On

[c] From the grand or supreme law-court which is held here (if the *chose in action* be for a sum above 300 l. sterling), an appeal lies to the court of errors; or, if sentence of death be passed for felony, the appeal is to the governor alone, who for all such crimes, except murder and treason, can ratify or annul the judgement of the court as he pleases; but, in the two last-mentioned cases, may either respite the offender till the royal pleasure thereupon be known, or order immediate execution. The grand court is held four times a year, each session continuing three weeks. Till the year 1758, all causes of more than forty shillings throughout the island were tried in this town; when an act was passed for dividing the island into three circuits, in each of which assizes are held the like number of times in the year. From the courts that are held in Surry and Cornwall, a *venire* lies in some cases to that in Spanish Town. All informations upon actions for breach of the laws of trade and navigation, duties, customs, imports and exports, quit-rents, and escheats, are triable in the supreme court only. And, in all actions for the property in slaves or their freedom, or in ejectment, dower, partition, titles affecting lands or tenements arising in the counties of Cornwall or Surry, the judges of the supreme court may direct the issue to be tried at St. Jago de la Vega by a Middlesex jury. From the grand court the appeal goes on, as before related, to the court of errors; and, after judgement given in the court of errors, the party cast may travel with his cause before the king in council at home: he must, indeed, after the decision in the court of errors, if it affirms the sentence of the grand court, pay into the complainant's hands the amount of the action, he giving security to the defendant for re-payment of it in case the sentence should be reversed at home. It is true, that by these appeals it has been supposed that justice is more likely to be administered; but they are nevertheless highly prejudicial with regard to the immoderate delay which necessarily ensues: for, let the evidence be ever so clear and conclusive, an action of debt upon a simple bond may be brought by the defendant (after judgement has been obtained upon it in the grand court) before the governor and council in the court of errors; where it may possibly slumber a whole year, or more, before it can be heard and decided, and before the plaintiff can receive any justice or redress; for, how desirous soever the governor himself may be to hasten judgement, it is not always in his power to do it. He may advertise the holding such a court from time to time, but to very little purpose, unless a quorum of his council are pleased also to attend and assist him; who are sometimes interested in the matter in dispute, either as principals or collaterals, and consequently so far disqualified to preside upon it as judges. I have before observed on the inconveniences which attend this appeal-court; and shall therefore only add, that it has long been the sincere wish of all the inhabitants (except the partizans of knavery and litiga-

tion)

Published as the Act directs 1.st June 1774.

View of a Spanish Building.

R. B. Godfrey sculp.

in some parts lower and lower, the succeffive inhabitants of thefe
houfes were obliged to add a foundation where the water had undermined the walls, and from time to time, as the earth happened
to be fwept away ; fo that the foundations of many of thefe antient piles have in fact been laid long fince the fuperftructure. Their
houfes had no piazzas originally : the Englifh made thefe additions,
in order to render them more cool and pleafant. But they have
been attended with fome inconvenience in another refpect ; for, the
ftreets being laid out, fome of thirty, and others not exceeding
forty, feet in breadth, thefe fheds incroach fo far on each fide, that
the midway is too narrow, and liable to obftruct carriages. The
Englifh in general have copied the ichnography of the Spanifh
houfes with great uniformity [g]. They are, for the moft part,
difpofed in three divifions : the centre room is a hall, communicating at each end with a bed-chamber ; the back part, ufually a
fhed, is divided in the fame manner, and communicates with the
front, or principal hall, by an arch, which in fome houfes is wain-
fcotted with mahogany, in others covered only with plaifter. They
are fmall, and rather inconvenient for a family, efpecially when it
confifts of fix or feven perfons. Great alterations have, however,
been made by the Englifh inhabitants ; and feveral of thefe old
houfes have received very confiderable additions, which make them
more roomy and commodious. In the piazzas many families may
be faid to live the greater part of their time ; the fhade and refrefhing breeze inviting them to employ moft hours there, that are
not devoted to eating, drinking, and fleeping : nor can there be a
more agreeable indulgence enjoyed by the mafter of the houfe,
than to fit in an elbow-chair, with his feet refting againft one of
the piazza-columns ; in this attitude he converfes, fmoaks his pipe,
or quaffs his tea, in all the luxury of indolence. Almoft every
dwelling-houfe throughout the ifland is detached from the kitchen
and other offices ; which, though different from the practice in
England, is a very judicious arrangement for this climate, where
the fumes and fmoak of the kitchen, and the ftench of other neceffary offices, would be intolerable in too near a neighbourhood.
But few of the inhabitants are curious in the decorations of their

[g] See Plate IV.

apartments;

apartments: the halls are feldom adorned with any thing better than a large pier-glafs or two, a few prints, or maps: the greateft expence is beftowed upon the arch of the principal hall, which is generally of mahogany, and in fome houfes well-executed. They have for the moft part fluted pilafters, fupporting a regular entablature, ornamented with modillons, dentils, &c. But it is more frequent to behold all the orders of architecture confufedly jumbled together. The windows of the Spanifh houfes were generally made with little turned pillars, placed upright, and fhutters on the infide. However convenient thefe might have been for the conftant admiffion of air, they are at prefent almoft totally exploded, and fafhes more generally in ufe: to which are added jealoufy-fhutters, or Venetian blinds, which admit the air freely, and exclude the fun-fhine. It is but of late, that the planters have paid much attention to elegance in their habitations: their general rule was, to build what they called a *make-fhift*; fo that it was not unufual to fee a plantation adorned with a very expenfive fet of works, of brick or ftone, well-executed; and the owner refiding in a miferable, thatched hovel, haftily put together with wattles and plaifter, damp, unwholefome, and infefted with every fpecies of vermin. But the houfes in general, as well in the country-parts as the towns, have been greatly improved within thefe laft twenty years. The furniture of fome of them is extremely coftly; and others conftructed in fo magnificent a ftyle, and of fuch durable materials, as to fhew that they were not intended for a mere temporary refidence.

It might not be foreign to the fubject here to remark, that, by the general ufe of fhingle coverings throughout the Northern and Weft-India colonies, and the utter neglect of planting young trees in the room of what are cut down for this manufacture, it is very certain, that they will every year grow dearer to the fugar iflands, and that the price may increafe, till the people of Jamaica will be forced either to employ their own growth of timber for this ufe, or fall upon tile-making. The builders, therefore, of new houfes, or works, fhould confider this, and make their walls of a due thicknefs to fuftain fuch an additional weight hereafter.

SECT.

S E C T. II.

THE river Cobre, which washes the foot of the town on the East, takes its source near Luidas, and about twenty-two miles North-west from the town, rising in a cave, called River-head, and supposed by many to have a subterraneous communication with Pedro's river, which is distant from it about six miles West. The Cobre likewise buries great part of its waters, and does not form any considerable stream till it has run some distance from the cave. It is afterwards joined by the Rio Magno, Rio d'Oro, and Rio Pedro, with some smaller streams; so that, on reaching the town, it is from sixty to eighty feet in breadth, and in several places very deep, but in others generally fordable, unless swelled with the heavy rains which sometimes fall in the mountains above. Its bed, where it ranges near the town, is depressed and lowly, the water being in general not discernible beyond the verge of its banks. The current here is rapid, though almost silent. It is of unspeakable service to this neighbourhood, not only in its constant supply of water, for the use of the town, but in promoting cleanliness and health; for every day throughout the year some hundred Negroes and Mulattoes of both sexes resort to it from the town, to wash their persons and linen.

It has been imagined, that the Spaniards gave it the name of the Copper river, from its passing through a vein of that metal. But it is more probable, that they christened it after a similar name of some river in Old Spain, as they are known to have done in regard to many others, and in particular the Rio Minho, in the parish of Clarendon. Besides, although its water appears to have a fine blueish tinge, especially where it runs between the two ranges of hills proceeding from Sixteen-mile-walk, which has confirmed many in their opinion of its being tinctured with copper; yet this appearance is nothing more than a common deception, caused by the azure of the sky reflected from the surface of the water, and remarkable chiefly where it is deepest, the current most gentle, and consequently the surface extremely smooth, and therefore in the

4

fittest

fitteft ftate to reflect images; and to this effect the great height and vicinity of the inclofing ridges very much contribute [*b*]. It is ftrange, indeed, that the experiment, tried upon it fo long ago by Sir William Beefton, has not corrected this popular error; for he found, that with an infufion of galls the water acquired a deep green inclining to black [*i*]. But the moft certain teft of an in-termixture of copper is made with the cauftic *volatile alkali,* as fpirit of *fal ammon.* combined with quick lime-water; thefe, if the fmalleft particles of copper be diffolved, would caufe the whole to affume a beautiful blue colour. This experiment was tried fome years fince by Doctor Browne, without producing any fuch effect. Now, as the teft of an iron impregnation is the black or dufky co-lour it ftrikes with the vegetable aftringents, fuch as tincture of galls, and as the *foffile alkali* will give a greenifh caft, it feems pro-bable that this river is impregnated with no other metal than iron, and with a copious admixture of a calcareous earth, or lime. The purgative quality of the water, when drunk immediately from the river, is very properly conjectured by Doctor Browne to proceed from the clay with which it is in general copioufly charged; be-caufe it lofes this quality when fettled in jars and cleared of its load; which would not be the cafe if it proceeded from falts, or a folution of metals; and becaufe many other waters, of fimilar ap-pearance, poffefs the like qualities in their turbid ftate, though known to be not impregnated with metallic fubftances. Agreeably to this opinion, it is found by the inhabitants of the town, who keep this water in large jars, that, after ftanding for fome time till the fœculencies have fubfided, it entirely lofes the effect juft men-tioned, and becomes as clear, foft, and pleafant, in its depurated ftate, as any water in the world. In this ftate it was tried by an hy-droftatical apparatus, and found equal in lightnefs to Briftol Hot-well water. We may therefore fafely conclude, that it has been very unjuftly ftigmatized; and that, if the Spaniards fuppofed it impregnated with copper, they adopted this miftaken notion

[*b*] So Virgil calls the river Tyber *cœruleus,* azure, or fky-coloured. Æn. viii. v. 64.——Some have conjectured, that the original name was Rio Cobra, from the Portuguefe *cobra,* which fignifies a fnake, and might with great propriety allude to the ferpentine courfe of this river.

[*i*] An infufion of galls in water, impregnated with copper and quick lime, ftruck an orange colour inclining to reddifh.

through

through ignorance of the means by which its contents might be difcovered. In Old Spain the water is remarkably light, pure, and wholefome: to this, and the ferenity of the air, it is attributed that the Spaniards are free from the fcurvy, notwithftanding their indulgence in pork, the leaft perfpirable of all animal food. The Spaniards in America are therefore (from a national prejudice) particularly nice in the choice of their water, which forms the chief of their daily beverage. It is not improbable, what I have heard fome of the oldeft inhabitants of St. Jago relate, that the Spaniards formerly here ufed to be at the trouble of procuring water, for their common drink, from the Bridge river, fix miles Weftward from the town; and that all of them kept their drinking-water in large jars, fo many in number as to have always one fuf-ficiently clear for ufe, while others were in the courfe of depura-tion. The river Cobre, having a free current from the town to the harbour of Kingfton, uninterrupted by rocks or falls, and flowing through a pretty level, open country, might undoubtedly be made navigable up to it by means of locks; but the expence of fuch an undertaking, and the fhort diftance of land-carriage, are objections that may probably reftrain the inhabitants from ever attempting it. The river abounds with excellent mullets, mud-fifh, eels, calapever, jew-fifh, craw-fifh, and prawns. It has only one bridge, which croffes it in the road leading towards Sixteen-mile-walk. This bridge is flat, and compofed of planks on a frame of timber-work, which refts upon two fexangular piers, and two buttreffes projecting from the banks, conftructed with piles, and braces interlaced with mafonry. In great floods, the river has been known to rife feveral feet above the floor without injury, not-withftanding the vaft preffure of fo large a column of water. This is afcribed to the refiftance of the water below or under the flooring, which enables it to fuftain this weight above. In the year 1699, an arched bridge of brick was conftructed fome miles below the town, in order to keep open the communication by land with Kingfton; but, for want of a proper foundation, it was foon fwept away by a flood, and never fince re-built. Attempts have lately been made to get an act paffed for building one at the publick expence, and more conveniently fituated; but, through fame fpirit of jealoufy which I have before noticed, and the difin-clination of many to confider it as a matter of general benefit to the ifland, the fcheme was laid afide [k]. So that perfons, trav l ng by land to and from Kingfton, or the Eaftern divifion of the ifland, are obliged to ford or ferry over the river, and very frequently at the peril of their lives. Ridiculous as the prejudices of faction are in fo fmall a community, yet they are capable of producing mifchievous effects. Publick fpirit, and a liberal way of thinking, naturally tend to the ornament and improvement of every country where they refide. The contrary, or a perverfe and felfifh principle, excludes every thing that is great and generous from its narrow view, and wages eternal war againft the public welfare. I am forry to fay the latter rule of conduct has been too predominant in this ifland ; but we will hope for a time when good fenfe and rectitude of heart fhall triumph over this falfe and groveling po-licy. The ftreets of the town, I have remarked, are rendered in-conveniently narrow by piazzas added to moft of the houfes; the worft effect arifing from their want of due breadth is a great in-creafe of heat during the fultry months of the year, the wind not having fpace enough to circulate freely through them, and dif-perfe the confined air, which becomes very difagreeable from the reflection of fo many brick walls. They are repaired with pebbles brought from the river-courfe, which prevents their being clogged with mud, as fome other towns of the Weft-Indies are, and anfwer the end of a regular pavement, by not admitting the rain-water to ftagnate. They are kept tolerably clean by a publick fcavenger, paid by an annual affeffment on the houfes; and the filth collected from them is removed to certain places appointed on the outfide of the town.

The church-yard, being fituated in the windward part of the town, is very injudicioufly allotted for the common burial-ground. Dry weather occafions numberlefs chafms in it ; and the wet, which ufually fucceeds, infinuating through thefe apertures into the graves,

[k] It is true, an act was paffed in 1767, and truftees named for carrying it into execution. But, as this act only empowered them to receive 5000 l. from any perfons inclined to contribute towards it by voluntary fubfcription, it feems to have given no other power than what might have been exercifed without it.

there

there is reafon to believe, that noxious exhalations muft arife from them, which cannot fail of rendering the atmofphere unwholefome to fuch houfes as lie in a proper direction to receive them.   In the hot months, particularly June, another annoyance happens from the duft; which, by the power of the fea-breeze, generally violent at that time of the year, is blown into the houfes in fuch abundance, as to be exceedingly troublefome, and occafion fore eyes: the particles are fo fubtle, that it is very common to fee a dining-table, which has been perfectly clean before the cloth was laid, appear entirely covered with a fine powder upon removing it.   The inhabitants, if they fhut their doors and windows, are almoft fuffocated with heat; and, if they fuffer them to continue open, they are in danger of being ftifled with duft; but, neceffity obliging them to the latter expedient, they fwallow it copioufly with their food.   Thefe annoyances might attract compaffion, if they were not eafily remediable: the firft, by taking in a new burial-ground a little to leeward of the town; the next, by making ufe of water-carts, to fprinkle the ftreets, once or oftener in the day, during that time of the year when the duft has been found moft troublefome: fo fine a river gliding under the town feems, indeed, to point out this experiment to them fo obvioufly, that it is aftonifhing they have hitherto neglected it.   The air of the town has always been efteemed healthy.   But it is on the decreafe with refpect to inhabitants.   It appears, from the regifter of marriages, births, and burials, that, from 1670 to 1700, the town and parifh contained above four times more white perfons than at prefent. They have even diminifhed fince the year 1746, as will appear by the following average-table of burials from that year to 1756:

	White Refiants.	White Paupers and Tranfients.	Soldiers.	Free Blacks and Mulattoes.	Total.
Average *per annum* of Deaths,	61	$12\frac{3}{9}$	15	$16\frac{1}{9}$	$104\frac{6}{9}$

According to the above table, the whole number of Whites, exclufive of Jews, was probably about two thoufand, or near fix hundred more than the prefent. From the beft accounts it appears, that the average of marriages, baptifms, and funerals, ftands thus:

E 2

Marriages,

Marriages, — 14 ⎫
Baptisms, — 80 ⎬ *per annum.*
Funerals, — 100 ⎭

Of the baptisms, not above one-third are Whites; the marriages include all ranks and complexions; but the soldiers, paupers, tranfients, and free Blacks and Casts, make up the greatest part of the burials. Hence it appears, that the marriages, and consequently the births, are in no proportion to the deaths; and the decrease of people may from this cause be very naturally accounted for. The number of the inhabitants in this parish may be thus estimated, viz.

Resiant Christian Whites in the Town.	Ditto in the Country.	White Paupers and Transients.	Soldiers, including Wives and Children.	Jews.	Free Blacks and Casts.
700	308	176	240	350	900
Deaths annually, about } 1 in 24		1 in 22	1 in 16	1 in 26	1 in 26

Inhabitants.	In Town.	In the Country.	Total in the Parish, of all Complexions.
Christian Whites,	700	308	
Paupers and Transients,	176		
Soldiers, &c.	240		
Jews,	300	50	
Free Blacks and Casts,	800	100	
Slaves,	1960	5348	
	4176	5806	9982

The registers in this parish have, like most of the others in the island, been very incorrectly kept. They are, however, tolerably perfect from 1669 to 1702, and from 1746 to the present time. The want of due regularity prevents them in general from being useful for grounding calculations of this sort. If the several rectors had been obliged to enter attested copies of their registers once a year in the secretary's office, we should have possessed very competent information upon this subject.

The Jews here are remarkably healthy and long-lived, notwithstanding their diet is frequently salt-fish, and such kind of aliment, not generally esteemed very wholesome; and that the greater number of them deal in damaged salt-butter, herrings, beef, cheese,

and

and in train-oil; a congregation of ftinking commodities, which is enough to poifon the air of their habitations. Their fhops may be fcented at a great diftance; and, in what is called the Jew-market in this town, a whole ftreet of their houfes reeks inceffantly with thefe abominable odours. But thefe people are abftemious, and fo temperate, that a drunken Jew is rarely feen. They are particularly nice in drinking the pureft water, which moft of them ufe unmixed; and others make only a very fmall addition of rum. They are exceedingly fond of garlic, which generally has a place in all their fauces, and is known to be a great antifeptic; and they indulge in chocolate. The more luxurious among them gormondize chiefly on fifh; and no doubt but their religious fafts, of which they are very rigid obfervers, now and then interpofing, affift in freeing them from noxious redundancies. I think they may be fuppofed to owe their good health and longevity, as well as their fertility, to a very fparing ufe of ftrong liquors, their early rifing, their indulgence in garlic and fifh, their adherence to the Mofaic Ritual in the choice of found and wholefome animal food, their free ufe of fugar, chocolate, and nourifhing fruits, their religious purifications, and fafts. The free Negroes and Mulattoes fare rather harder in refpect of eating, and are not fo averfe to fpirituous liquors; for both men and women are frequently intoxicated: but their way of life is more laborious; they are more abroad in the open air, which renders them hardier; and their occupations or amufements give them fuch conftant exercife, as to keep them from fuffering by repletion: befides, their diet confifts chiefly of nourifhing broths, in which pulfe and vegetables are principal ingredients. They too are very fond of good water and chocolate; they indulge in fmoaking tobacco, devour large quantities of pepper fuch as this country produces, and feldom let a day pafs without bathing, and fcouring their fkins. Their bodies and conftitutions feem peculiarly adapted to a hot climate; yet, perhaps, they owe their health not more to this adaptation, than to their mode of living; fince it is certain, that the native Whites in this ifland, I mean fuch of them as are not addicted to drunkennefs, nor have any hereditary diftemper, are equally healthy and long-lived.

The

The greater mortality, obfervable here among the foldiers and tranfient Europeans, muft be afcribed to their importing with them the Englifh cuftoms of eating and drinking in excefs, but chiefly the latter; and their liberal indulgence in a vile fophifticated compound of new rum, pepper, and other ingredients, brewed here by the Jew-retailers; who, as they pay a tax on their licences, and a duty on the rum they retail, have recourfe to this villainous practice, in order to enhance their profit upon the miferable confumers, who are chiefly the foldiers, and meaner clafs of Whites. That this has been, and is ftill, the main caufe of bad health among the troops is evident; for, when they are in quarters not locally unwholefome, and where they cannot get at it, they are known to be very healthy. If the fpirit was even fold to them without this adulteration, it could not fail of producing fatal effects; for the Jews could not afford to keep it fo long on hand, as to become what is called old rum, and then retail it at their ufual low price. They would therefore fell it frefh from the ftill; in which ftate it is fo fiery, as to be no lefs unfit for human potation, than burning brimftone; yet fome of the foldiers have been known to drink off a bottle of it at one fitting. The officers have often attempted to check this evil, by punifhing the delinquents; but a more certain method would be by prevention. The common foldiers, employed in the Weft-India fervice, or at leaft the recruits fent over, have frequently been the very refufe of the Britifh army: thefe men cannot be broke of their fottifh habits; but, fince they muft and will have fpirituous liquor, care might be taken to provide them with fuch as, while it gratifies their inclination, may be the leaft detrimental to their health. The commanding officer (for example) in town might appropriate a certain part of their country pay, and lay in every year a ftock of the beft rum, free from all bad tafte and fmell, and permit it to be retailed by a futler to the men; taking care, that none fhould be iffued of lefs than a twelvemonth's age, and limiting the price to what they now pay the Jew-retailers, which could very well be afforded, as the foldier's rum is exempted from all duty. The futler chofen for this purpofe would no doubt be a man on whofe fobriety and honefty they could fafely depend; at leaft, fhould he be guilty of

breach

breach of his truft, he would be liable to a regimental punifhment. The terrer of this would form a fecurity for his good behaviour; the men would be much better pleafed, and beyond any doubt more healthy.

The town is partly under a civil and partly military police; a kind of *divifum imperium*, which the civil power exercifes by day, and the military by night. The civil government confifts of a *cuftos*, or chief magiftrate, and the inferior juftices of peace and conftables. The centinels here, after the day is clofed, according to an antient ufage, which has fubfifted ever fince the days of Cromwell, challenge all paffengers, as in a regular garrifon, and patrol the ftreets at certain hours, to apprehend all offenders againft the peace, and prevent robberies. It is a certain proof of the more regular lives of the families here, as well as in Kingfton, than heretofore, that at eleven o'clock at night it is very rare to fee a light in any houfe, except the taverns; and even thefe are now very feldom infefted with riots and drunken quarrels, which formerly were fo common. The town was antiently a regular garrifon, the ditch ftill remaining which was thrown up by the Spaniards towards the favannah, and terminated at a baftion flanked with a fortified building, called the Fort-houfe, the name of which is ftill preferved. The plain, of which the favannah is a part, extends, in its whole length, not lefs than twenty-two miles; but its breadth is unequal, being in fome parts ten miles, in others five, and, towards St. Dorothy's, grows more and more contracted, till it does not exceed three. After leaving this end of it, and paffing to the N. W. among the Clarendon Hills, we meet with fmaller levels here and there, as the Palmeto and Lime favannahs, till we come to St. Jago favannah, where the champaign again enlarges to the extent of about ten by fifteen miles. Thefe tracts were formerly exceeding beautiful, having only fome clumps of graceful trees irregularly fcattered over their face, which gave but little interruption to the profpect. I have been informed by an elderly gentleman, a native of the ifland, that he could remember the time when they were nearly in this ftate; but at prefent they are overfpread and disfigured in moft parts with the achaia, or American opopinax, a dwarf prickly tree, which it is found almoft impoffible to

eradicate.

eradicate. It infests the pasture-lands, and incroaches continually on the roads, to the very great annoyance of travelers, especially by night, when they cannot so well guard their faces from being scratched; so that a man, who rides among them in the dusk, is obliged to keep his whip and hands in constant employment, in order to parry the over-hanging branches. That part which bounds on the West side of the town, and called the Town sa-vannah, consisted formerly of one thousand two hundred acres, allotted for exercise, and has a common of pasture for the use of the inhabitants; but, several persons having settled upon and oc-cupied the skirts of it, the parishioners obtained an act for enabling them to lease out seven hundred acres, at 5 s. *per* acre, and foot-land at 6 d. *per* foot; and reserved the remaining five hundred to be kept open and clear, at the expence of the parish, and for ever to be held sacred to the purposes only of exercise and health. The space uninclosed is about two miles in circumference. Here the races are generally held every year in the month of March. For encou-raging a breed of large horses, one hundred pistoles are annually granted by the assembly, by way of king's plate, to be run for by any stone-horses or mares, carrying ten stone each, of fourteen pounds to the stone. There are generally two days sport, besides either bye-matches, or a subscription purse. On these occasions the concourse of people is very great; some thousands are seen assembled on the savannah; and the multitude of carriages and horses, all in motion, form a very pleasing part of the amusement. On this plain the re-gular troops, and sometimes the militia, are trained and reviewed. But its principal use is as a palestra, for the daily exercise of the inhabitants of the town in the morning and afternoon. In manner of living, the English here differ not much from their brethren at home, except in a greater profusion of dishes, a larger retinue of domestics, and in wearing more expensive cloaths. The climate obliging them to use the finer sort of fabrics, these are of course the most costly; and hence appears the great advantage to the mother-country of furnishing her West-India colonies with their cloathing. The superior fineness of manufacture is all clear gain to her artists; and the constant wear, by the effects of perspiration and washing, occasions an immense consumption. The thick, cheap, and du-rable

rable cloths, which are well-adapted to the frozen zone, will not anfwer here; and the atmofphere corrodes every kind of iron or fteel ware very quickly. The demand therefore for numberlefs products of the home induftry is (from a train of invariable caufes) likely to continue as long as thefe colonies continue to exift. Here are none of the fubftantial inhabitants who do not keep their coach or chariot with four or fix horfes. The fhop-keepers have their two-wheel chaifes, or kitereens [*l*]; and they who cannot afford a carriage, even to the pooreft free Negroe, will not be without a faddle-horfe or two. As this is an inland-town, it derives its chief fupport from the refidence of the governor and publick officers; the gentlemen of the law; the affembly and council; and the conflux of people who refort hither from the country parts on bufinefs, particularly during the fittings of the fupreme or grand court of law near four months in the year; and the feffion of the affembly, which generally lafts from the beginning of October till the Chriftmas holidays. At thefe times univerfal gaiety prevails; balls, concerts, and routs, alternately hold their reign. The governor, according to antient cuftom, gives a ball and entertainment once a year at the king's houfe, in honour of his majefty's birth-day. The appearance of company on this occafion is generally brilliant, the ladies vying with one another in the richnefs of their dreffes; every one makes a point of exhibiting a new fuit of finery; and this regulation is fo lavifhly indulged, that fuch a ball is feldom attended with lefs than three or four thoufand pounds expence to the guefts, which however is fo far excufable, as it is laid out in Britifh manufactures [*m*]. When the town is full of company, here is a very good market; at other times of the year, it is but indifferently fupplied. In general, the mutton is much better, and the beef much worfe, than in Kingfton; the latter town being furnifhed with beeves from the rich paftures of Pedro's Cockpits, where the fattened cattle are inferior to none in America. The mutton confumed in Spanifh Town is chiefly brought from the adjacent falt-pan paftures, and

[*l*] So called from the firft-imported, which came from Kettering, in Northamptonfhire.

[*m*] During one half of the year, the inhabitants enjoy all the ftillnefs and tranquillity of a country-village; and, in the other, the fcene is totally changed, and they revel in the pleafures of a town.

the penns of Vere; it is fmall, but delicioufly fweet, fat, and juicy. The market is likewife tolerably well-fupplied with fea and river fifh, black crabs, the Jamaica oyfter, poultry of all forts remarkably fine, milk, vegetables, and fruits, Weft-Indian and North-American. The flour comes for the moft part from New-York, inferior to none in the world; and the bread is excellent. The butter is imported from Cork and North-America, which cannot be much commended: the inhabitants, reconciled to it by cuftom, fhew no diflike to it, although it is fometimes fo rancid, that repeated wafhings will not fweeten it. Some few in the lowlands make a fort of frefh butter, but in fmall quantities, and commonly infipid. The vales of Pedro are capable of fup-plying the town with this article, if the penn-keepers or graziers there were encouraged to manufacture it for fale. What is ma-nufactured there for their own ufe is of a delicate flavour, and will keep good for feveral days, and even weeks. The cheapnefs of the imported butter, which is generally fold for fixpence fterling the pound, and the great plenty of it, together with a long continued habit of ufing no other, may be the reafon why the inhabitants are not very folicitous about making any change; but it would doubtlefs be attended with a confiderable faving to the ifland, and tend much more to health, if they were to promote and eftablifh fuch a manufacture among the inland penn-keepers. It is fome time before an European palate can accommodate itfelf to the rank ftuff ferved up at the tables here. On the other hand, I have known many perfons who, upon their firft arrival in Britain from Jamaica, could not endure the tafte of frefh-butter; and I have heard of a lady who, for fome years after her coming over to England, ufed to order fome firkins of the Irifh butter to be brought regularly to her from Jamaica: fo difficult it is to re-linquifh what cuftom, *altera natura,* has made agreeable to us.

As fome readers may be defirous of knowing the market-prices of provifions in this town, I fhall offer the following table, formed agreeably to the experience of fome years. It muft be underftood, however, that here, as in other places, there can be no fuch thing as a ftandard and invariable rate for thefe neceffary articles;

and

and that their rates muft vary according to the reigning plenty or fcarcity, and other predominant caufes.

	Jamaica Currency.						Reduced to Sterling.					
	s.	d.	q. to	s.	d.	q.	s.	d.	q. to	s.	d.	q.
Beef, —— —— —— per pound,	0	6	0	0	7	2	0	4	1	0	5	1
Ditto, prime parts, —— —— ditto,	1	3	0	1	10	2	0	10	3	1	4	0
Tongue, —— —— —— each,	3	1	2	3	9	0	2	2	3	2	8	1
Mutton, —— —— per pound,	1	0	0	1	3	0	0	8	2	0	10	3
Lamb, —— —— ——	1	3	0	0	0	0	0	10	3	0	0	0
Ditto, —— —— per quarter,	4	4	2	5	7	2	3	1	1	4	0	0
Calf's head, —— —— ——	6	3	0	0	0	0	4	5	3	0	0	0
Veal, —— —— per pound,	0	7	2	0	0	0	0	5	1	0	0	0
Ditto, prime parts, —— — ——	1	0	0	1	3	0	0	8	2	0	10	3
Pork, —— —— ——	0	7	2	0	0	0	0	5	1	0	0	0
Kid, —— —— ——	0	7	2	0	0	0	0	5	1	0	0	0
Turtle Calipafh, —— —— per pound,	0	7	2	0	0	0	0	5	1	0	0	0
Ditto Calipee, —— ——	1	3	0	1	6	0	0	10	3	1	0	3
Fifh large, —— —— ditto,	0	6	0	0	7	2	0	4	1	0	5	1
Ditto fmaller, per ftring of four, five, or upwards,	0	7	2	0	0	0	0	5	1	0	0	0
Ducks tame, —— per couple,	3	1	2	3	9	0	2	2	3	2	8	1
Ditto wild, —— ditto,	5	0	0	6	3	0	3	6	3	4	5	3
Teal, —— —— ditto,	5	0	0	6	3	0	3	6	3	4	5	3
Capons, —— —— ditto,	6	3	0	10	0	0	4	5	3	7	1	3
Hens, —— —— ditto,	3	9	0	5	0	0	2	8	1	3	6	3
Geefe fat, —— —— each,	7	6	0	0	0	0	5	4	1	0	0	0
Turkies fat, according to fize, —— ditto,	8	9	0	18	0	0	6	3	0	12	10	1
Chickens, —— —— ditto,	0	7	2	0	0	0	0	5	1	0	0	0
Pigeons, —— —— per pair,	1	10	2	2	6	0	1	4	0	1	9	2
Eggs, —— — fix to twelve, variable,	0	7	2	0	0	0	5	1	0	0	0	0
A roafting-pig, —— ——	5	0	0	0	0	0	3	6	3	0	0	0
A hog, —— —— about	23	9	0	0	0	0	16	11	3	0	0	0
Rabbits fat, —— —— each,	4	4	2	0	0	0	3	1	1	0	0	0
Salt-fifh, —— —— per pound, about	0	3	0	0	0	0	0	2	1	0	0	0
Shads, —— —— per barrel, about	20	0	0	0	0	0	14	3	1	0	0	0
Flour, —— —— per cwt.	17	6	0	22	6	0	12	6	0	16	1	0
Ditto, fuperfine, —— —— per ditto,	30	0	0	35	0	0	21	5	1	25	0	0
Bifcuit, —— —— per ditto,	30	0	0	32	6	0	21	5	1	23	2	3
Salt, —— —— per bufhel,	1	10	2	0	0	0	1	4	0	0	0	0
Wax-candles, —— —— per pound,	3	9	0	0	0	0	2	8	1	0	0	0
Spermaceti ditto, —— —— ditto,	2	6	0	0	0	0	1	9	2	0	0	0
Plantanes, —— —— per dozen, about,	1	3	0	0	0	0	0	10	3	0	0	0
Corn Maize, —— —— per bufhel,	5	0	0	5	7	2	3	6	3	4	0	0
Ditto, in the ears, —— — per three dozen,	0	7	2	0	0	0	0	5	1	0	0	0

Oyfters are fold in fmall bafkets, and variable in price; as are like-wife many of the articles above-mentioned; on which account, I have given their average loweft and higheft rates of feveral years. The variation of price is caufed by the occafional plenty or fcarcity

incident

incident to them. The vaft abundance of fifh caught here, and its not being a provifion that can be kept fweet for any long time, are the caufes of its cheapnefs at moft of the fea-ports. Fifh and turtle are often fold at lefs prices than are exprefled in the table; and they furnifh a confiderable part of fubfiftence to the people inhabiting thofe places. The prices in Spanifh Town are in general higher than in Kingfton, where the market is under a better regulation, and both the demand and fupply more conftant and ample. The latter town is alfo far better accommodated with vegetables of all kinds, produced in the Liguanea mountains.

By the above table, compared with the following, may be feen how much the prices of fome provifion have rifen above what they formerly were. An act of affembly, paffed in the year 1693, eftablifhed the rates thus, viz.

	Jam. Currency.			Sterling.		
	s.	d.	q.	s.	d.	q.
Beef and goat, —— —— per pound,	0	4	0	0	3	0
Mutton, —— —— —— ditto,	0	6	0	0	4	1
Veal, prime parts, —— —— ditto,	0	9	0	0	6	3
Ditto, other parts, —— —— ditto,	0	7	2	0	5	3
Hog, lamb, and turtle, —— ditto,	0	7	2	0	5	3

The fettlers in thofe days were fewer in number, yet either found means to fupply a larger quantity, or be contented with fmaller gains. In the year 1672, Doctor Blome writes, that horned cattle were fo numerous, that, although there had been every year fo many killed, yet their number feemed not much to be leffened. Hogs too he mentions were in very great plenty, as well thofe wild in the mountains, as tame in the plantations. We may conjecture, therefore, that the greater part of the beef and pork, then brought to market, were of the wild fort; for thefe animals over-ran the woods and favannahs, and were flaughtered by all perfons who chofe to go in queft of them. This probably made the fettlers fo very inattentive to the breeding of cattle, that in procefs of time, as the wild ones became diminifhed, and the plantations increafed, they began to introduce a fupply from the Spanifh Main. A dependence upon thefe importations, and the low price which they formerly coft, ftill further difcouraged the ifland-breed; and at prefent the fugar-eftates, fo vaftly increafed in their number, confume

fume a large proportion of what are bred here. There feems no remedy for this, but, by an act of legiflature, to encourage the ifland-breed, and throw gradual reftraints upon the importation; by which means, beef might poffibly, in courfe of a few years, return to a more moderate price; which would be a very defireable event to the inhabitants, and even to the breeders themfelves; to whom the certainty of demand, and largenefs of confumption, would make amends for the diminution of price; and thus might be faved many thoufand pounds now paid for foreign falted beef, which is neither fo wholefome, nutritious, nor pleafing to the white fervants, foldiers, and others, as frefh meat. The high price of fowls, and the other fmall articles, is to be lowered by the introduction of more fettlers, by encouraging a traffic in fuch articles, and particularly enlarging the annual plant of corn, the fcarcity of which is the fole caufe why eggs are in general fo cheap, and poultry fo dear; for, when corn is fcarce, fowls will devour more of it in value than they yield at the market. The greater abundance there is provided of thefe foods, the more money will be faved to the ifland in various ways; and it would confequently grow more populous and thriving, and better able to maintain families; a matter of the utmoft concern to all who wifh to fee it flourifh; marriages, the beft fource of well-peopling it, and from which fome men pretend they are at prefent deterred, from the expenfivenefs of houfekeeping, would be greatly promoted; nor would many ufeful perfons emigrate from the colony, if they could live in it at as cheap a rate in general as in Europe. To live otherwife in an ifland, fo fertile and fo capable of affording not only the comforts, but the luxuries of fuftenance, in the greateft profufion, is a reproach to induftry and policy; but to adminifter fit and practicable remedies will redound equally to the honour of legiflature, and to the public welfare. Spanifh Town covers a large extent of ground, many of the houfes having great areas, and feveral lots being vacant or unbuilt. Thefe circumftances render it the more healthy and pleafant; and a variety of trees in conftant verdure, being fcattered among the buildings, more ef-pecially in the fkirts, it has the rural appearance of a village. The town feems, however, to be rather on the decline, not having

yet

yet recovered the blow which it received during the adminiftration of governor Kn——s; who, in order to carry a favourite point againft the country, and in furtherance of this defign to gain a majority in the two other branches of the legiflature, very artfully cajoled into his intereft feveral opulent merchants and principal inhabitants of Kingfton, by hinting to them a plan of removing the feat of government, the courts of juftice, and public records, to their town. The lucrative confequences of this project were defcribed in fuch captivating terms, that they joined heart and hand with him to effect it; and at length, after a violent ftruggle which threw the whole country into commotions, they fucceeded by gaining a corrupt majority in the houfe of affembly, garbled by very iniquitous and illegal practices. The deprivation of thefe main fupports, and the uncertainty of property in a town liable to fuch mutations at the arbitrary will of a governor, reduced its inhabitants to the utmoft diftrefs: fome quitted it; and many perfons were deterred from purchafing land, or occupying houfes in it; while all thofe, who fubfifted in its neighbourhood by fupplying the market were agitated with the dread of inevitable ruin. Upon a full difcuffion of this matter before the board of trade, and a juft reprefentation fubmitted to the king in council, the fcheme appeared fo wicked and injurious to private rights, as well as public welfare, that the projector of it was recalled, and exprefs inftructions given his fucceffor to fummon a new and legitimate affembly of reprefentatives: which being complied with, they paffed a law, reinftating the feat of government, offices of record, &c. in Spanifh Town, and eftablifhing them there immutably: and this law was afterwards confirmed by the crown.

But the town has not yet recovered its former population and opulence. The proprietors of houfes and lands in and near it are fcarcely yet free from apprehenfions of another removal; and their terrors have fince been awakened, more than once, by attempts from the Kingfton quarter to repeat the blow, by purfuing the former mode of acquiring an undue majority in the houfe of affembly, for the purpofe of repealing that law. Hence has arifen a confirmed party in that branch of legiflature; and the great ftruggle at every election is, to regulate the balance of power in the new houfe.

houfe. Each fide, through a fecret jealoufy, is too apt, by an uniform fyftem of oppofition, to reject various meafures of public utility, which are greatly wanted, for the improvement and general benefit of the ifland. It is much to be regretted, that fuch animofities fhould ftill prevail; and more fo, that caufe fhould be given for keeping them alive. An artful and malevolent governor alone could wifh to foment the fpirit of difcord, with a view of turning it to his own advantage, by fiding with the ftronger party, and thus acquiring a fet of advocates ready to promote or vindicate his rapacious and unjuft proceedings. A wife and good governor will think he beft ferves the king and his fubjects by fteadily difcouraging every attempt towards re-kindling this deftructive flame.

The fituation of this town, fo centrical with refpect to the whole ifland, renders it extremely convenient for holding the chief courts of juftice; and to this end it is ftill further adapted, as being undifturbed by the noife and tumult ufual in places of great trade. The records are fafer here; becaufe, upon the invafion of an enemy, it is too diftant from the fea-coaft to be firft attacked, and there would be ample time for removing them into Sixteen-mile-walk; or, ftill further, to the inmoft receffes and fortreffes of the ifland, for their fecure prefervation. Thus, although the town might be afterwards taken and plundered, the records would be fafe; nor could an enemy follow them expeditioufly, if they may be fuppofed an object worth acquiring; the road leading to Sixteen-mile-walk being full of places proper for ambufcading, or eafily rendered impaffable by felling of trees, and throwing down fome of thofe huge rocky maffes which over-hang it. The town ferves befides as a grand ftore-houfe, or magazine, for fupplying great part of the county of Middlefex with articles of cloathing, hufbandry, falt-provifion, and other neceffaries, moft of which are brought from Kingfton, which therefore is very much benefited by this extenfion of its inland commerce; an advantage it would not, in all likelihood, enjoy without the affiftance of Spanifh Town; for, in this cafe, not only the confumption of fuch articles muft be greatly diminifhed, but many of the planters would probably rather import what they wanted, or eftablifh a new mart at Paffage Fort, as being far more convenient for their bufinefs than Kingfton. Confidered

4
alfo

alſo as a garriſon, it will appear to form a great additional ſtrength to the midland-part of the iſland, and has ſo proved in ſeveral internal diſturbances that have occurred from Negroe mal-contents; particularly in 1761, when the detachments of horſe-militia and regular troops, ordered from hence, to quell a dangerous inſurrection, which had broke out in St. Mary's pariſh, arrived there ſo expeditiouſly, as to give almoſt immediate protection to the inhabitants. A colony of ſuch extent would unqueſtionably become much ſecurer, if more towns were formed in convenient parts of it. Inſtead therefore of labouring to ruin a town ſo antient and beneficial, the men of ſenſe and fortune in the iſland ſhould rather endeavour, by ſuitable encouragements and proviſions, to found new ones in thoſe uncultivated diſtricts where congregations of people are much wanted, to add more links to the chain of communication, which ought to pervade every part of ſo fruitful and delightful a country.

The conteſt about removing the ſeat of government, before-mentioned, became the cauſe of ſetting up a printing houſe in this town; for, before that æra, the votes of aſſembly were printed at Kingſton. But the partizans of Spaniſh Town formed an aſſociation to ſupport a new preſs in their town. From this iſſues a weekly paper of intelligence, compiled moſtly from the London and North-American prints; but it is chiefly convenient to the inhabitants as a vehicle for advertiſements of different ſorts. Some occaſional pamphlets have likewiſe received their birth from it; and a new edition of the laws was lately preparing. The votes of aſſembly and the annual bills are printed here; the journals of the council are printed in Kingſton, where two preſſes are eſtabliſhed, and two weekly papers. Thus each of theſe branches of legiſlature having its ſeparate preſs, I need not remark, that, when political differences ariſe, an extraordinary employment is given to theſe machines, by appeals to the public, and the arguments on either ſide *pro* and *con:* but it is doubtful, whether theſe diſputations, carried on as they generally are with great vehemence and acrimony, do not tend more to exaſperate than to conciliate. The preſs of Spaniſh Town was devoted to a far better uſe, when the aſſociation of gentlemen before-mentioned made it ſubſervient to the intereſts of morality, and

the

the improvement of the ifland, by publifhing a weekly effay under the title of The Planter, which was fupported for a confiderable time in a lively, entertaining manner. In a garden belonging to Mrs. T——s, in this town, are two trees called baobab, or the great-cotton, defcribed by Adanfon, in his account of Guiney, from whence the feeds were brought and planted here. Some call this likewife the capot tree; of which fpecies Bofman relates, that he has feen fome capable, with their fpreading boughs, of fhading twenty thoufand men, if ranged clofe; and fo tall, that a mufquet fhot could hardly reach the top. At Axim, there is faid to be one which ten men could not grafp; and, in Prince's ifland, another, the trunk of which could not be furrounded by four and twenty men, their arms at full ftretch: not that the body itfelf is fo enormous; but the fprouts adhere in fuch a manner as to feem to form one uniform trunk. The wood is light and porous, fcarcely fit for any other ufe than making canoes. The tree bears a fpecies of cotton, ufed in Guiney by the European factors for ftuffing beds, inftead of feathers. Thefe in Spanifh Town are as yet of only a moderate bulk; but, if they fhould fpread in time into the diameter reported by thefe authors, they will require much more room than has been allotted to them. The bark and leaves are faid to poffefs fome virtues in the cure of fevers. And they deferve to be propagated; but the beft fcite would be the rich bank of fome river.

Paffage Fort, formerly called The Paffage, from its being the place of embarkation for Port-Royal, is fituated on the Weft fide of the harbour, about three quarters of a mile from the mouth of the Cobre, and fix from Spanifh Town. It was once defended by a fmall fort, of ten or twelve guns, which has long fince been demolifhed. It is at prefent a fmall village, confifting of about fifteen houfes, chiefly inhabited by wharfingers, warehoufe-keepers, and the mafters of wherries and hackney-chaifes, which conftantly ply here with paffengers to and from the towns. Thefe wherries generally put off from Paffage Fort from fix to feven o'clock in the morning, before the fea-breeze fets in, and are favoured with a gentle land-wind. On their return, they go directly before the breeze, which fometimes blows up the harbour with great violence.

They are accommodated with tilts or awnings, and navigated entirely by Negroes. This is a barquadier for Spanifh Town, and moft of the plantations in St. Catharine, St. Thomas in the Vale, and St. John. The merchant-fhips which load from hence ufually lye off the hofpital of Greenwich, where they receive their cargo out of large boats, or lighters, there not being depth of water fufficient for veffels of burthen to come nearer the wharfs. The fituation is low, and fubject to inundations from the harbour in ftorms. This place is famous in the annals of Jamaica for the landing of colonel Jackfon in 1638, and of Venables in 1655.

The firft-built town was wholly deftroyed by the great earthquake of 1692, and never thoroughly rebuilt; nor is it probable that it will ever grow again into a town. The want of fufficient depth of water, perhaps, firft induced Mr. Henderfon, an enterprizing and fpirited gentleman, to form a new and more convenient fhipping-place on the North-Eaft fide of Salt-pond hill, under cover of the Twelve-apoftle battery; this he has effected at a very large expence, and with much judgement. The depth of water admits fhips of burthen very near to the wharf, and already there appears the dawning of a new town; which, by attracting the moft confiderable part of the bufinefs, feems to forebode the fpeedy decline of Paffage Fort. This new barquadier is called at prefent by the name of Port-Henderfon; and, befides its ufe for fhipping off fugars, and other produce, with the utmoft difpatch, it has opened a ready communication on that fide of the harbour with the fquadron and Port-Royal Town; which cannot fail of proving extremely convenient, more particularly in time of war. At the back of Salt-pond hill is a remarkable cave. The adit leading into it is narrow and low; but the cave itfelf is from twenty-five to thirty feet diameter, and of good height. The floor of it is ftrewed with human bones; and there runs a tradition among the Negroes, that a white perfon many years ago collected a vaft pile and confumed it to afhes: a large quantity ftill remains; and, from the conformation of the fkulls, they are thought to have been Indian. Some have imagined that the Indians made ufe of thefe receffes as a fort of catacombs, or offuaries, for their dead. The antient Mexicans laid their dead bodies without burial on the furface

face of the earth, and environed them with ſtones or bricks. Theſe rocky chaſms and cavities, frequent in many parts of Jamaica, naturally offered as convenient and durable ſepulchres. But this conjecture, though ingenious, is not ſupported by any proof, that the Indians of this iſland were governed by the ſame cuſtom. There are better grounds for ſuppoſing, that they interred their dead; and that the bones, found in theſe places, are no other than the relicks of the laſt remnant of that unfortunate people, who periſhed here beneath the inſupportable tyranny of their conquerors, as I ſhall hereafter take occaſion to relate.

Spaniſh Town is defended on the South by a range of hill, called Healthſhire, corruptly Hellſhire, about nine miles in length, and ſix in breadth; which ſpace contains about thirty-four thouſand acres, for the moſt part ſo rocky and barren, as not to be worth inhabiting. Its chief produce is lime; which is made here in large quantities, and ſent by water to Kingſton. The air on theſe hills is extremely healthy: the rocks are concealed from view by innumerable aromatic herbs, ſhrubs, and trees, poſſeſſed of great medicinal virtues, though hitherto explored only by a few curious perſons. This whole diſtrict is filled with the larger ſpecies of mockbird, whoſe lively notes ſerve to chear its dreary vales. The curatoe and aloes grow here very luxuriantly; and ſome experiments have been made, by a gentleman who lived here, with the ſilk-graſs and grape-vines, which were found to thrive extremely well. The ſoil is alſo productive of potatoes, yams, and other Weſt-India roots, and all the melon tribe, in great perfection. There is an exceeding good fiſhery on the coaſt; but the want of water-ſprings, there being only one, that I have heard of, in the whole tract, and the few articles of profit to be gained from ſuch a ſoil, will probably be the means of its remaining for the moſt part in a ſtate of nature. The ridge of high land, part of this tract, which faces Port-Royal harbour, is called Salt-pond Hill, from a large piece of ſalt-water on the South Weſt ſide of it, covering near ſeven hundred acres. This was formerly a ſalt-work; which, with two more in the pariſh of St. David, was conducted by a captain Joſeph Noye, who made from them in one year ten thouſand buſhels, and affirmed, that he could have made as many tons, if there had been

a vent

a vent for fo much at the market. But the great manufactory of falt at Tortuga caufed this article to fall fo cheap, that it has for many years paft been difcontinued in Jamaica. This falt-pond is about four feet in depth, and moft plentifully ftocked with good fifh; which are a more profitable article of traffic to the prefent owner, who fends them daily for fale to Spanifh Town, little more than fix miles diftant.

The parifhioners of St. Catharine, St. Thomas in the Vale, and St. Dorothy, formerly exercifed a fort of right in common of making falt here, for the ufe of their families: but, during the government of Sir Thomas Lynch, they agreed with Sir Thomas Modiford, who had patented the circumjacent lands, that he fhould deliver them annually at the rate of half a bufhel of falt *per* head, including Blacks and Whites, only not to exceed five thoufand bufhels in the whole; for which they were to pay 1 *s. per* bufhel. This agreement was confirmed by an act of affembly, but has been for many years difufed.

About four miles North and North-weft from the town is another range of hills; over which is fcattered a great number of polinks, or places applied entirely to the cultivation of garden-ftuff, fruits, and fuch fort of provifion, for the town-market. The range, diftinguifhed by the name of the Red Hills, from their reddifh foil, is thought to produce the feveral Weft-India fruits, of a better flavour than almoft any other part of the ifland. Many of the town-inhabitants have little fettlements here, with good houfes, to which they occafionally retire. No part of the world can enjoy a more agreeable or healthy air. The Spaniards formerly efteemed it a Montpellier; and numbers ufed to pafs over from Cuba, in order to refide here for the re-eftablifhment of their health. From many parts of thefe hills the profpect is rich and extenfive, commanding a view of the town, the paftures adjacent, the harbour and fhipping at Port Royal, and of the veffels coming in or going out. Thefe hills are deftitute of fprings; but the inhabitants eafily fupply that want by preferving rain-water in cifterns or jars, which they find extremely pure and falubrious.

The foil of St. Catharine's parifh is various. The hills abound with lime-ftone rock; the champaign confifts chiefly of favannah

I

land,

land, or a rich brick mould; the pasture lands in the neighbourhood, and what lie adjacent to the river, are of the latter kind;
the rainy seasons have been for many years too uncertain in this
part of the country for the cultivation of the sugar-cane, to which
the nature of the soil is excellently adapted : but the richness of
their grass makes amends; and the owners draw considerable profit
by breeding cattle and sheep, and fattening for the town-markets.
Indigo once flourished in all this district. Attempts have, within
these few years, been made by one or two gentlemen to revive it;
but dry weather baffled their project, and convinced them of its
impracticability.   The well-water in these parts is in general
brackish, or containing an admixture of salt; which seems to indicate the existence of salt mines here; but none have yet been
discovered; and probably they lie at too great a depth to be of service if they are ever known.   There are other wells of a very
pure water, supplied probably by springs or subterraneous currents,
which do not pass through any strata of this fossil. That salt is
plentifully intermixed with the soil here in some places is evident
from the licks to which cattle and sheep greedily resort. I have
seen several of them in the neighbourhood of the town. These
animals are known to be extremely fond of salt; and instinct directs
them where to find it.   They experience its good effects in correcting the deleterious quality of the crude grass, produced here,
from sudden heavy rains succeeding a drowth. On these occasions,
they are subject to violent diarrhœas, which are frequently mortal.
The penn-keepers use no other remedy than mashed, pickled herrings, given them by way of a drench, which, if the disorder has
not continued too long, performs a certain cure. There is no
doubt but the salt, and not the substance of the fish, is the remedy
to which their cure is to be ascribed; and this is further confirmed
by the common observation, that sheep, pastured on the salinas,
or lands contiguous to the sea, are not afflicted with the rot; and
that the cattle, watered from a brackish well, are much less apt
to be scoured with the crude grass than others.

The air of the flat country comprehended within this parish is
esteemed in general very healthy, except after the fall of the autumnal rains; when the water, stagnating for some time on the low
grounds,

grounds, is thought with good reafon to be productive of aguifh complaints, intermittent and remittent fevers; from all which, the adjacent hills offer a certain afylum to fuch of the inhabitants whofe circumftances admit of their removal.

The following comparative table may give fome idea of the modern ftate of this parifh:

	Negroes.	Cattle.	Sugar-plantations.	Quantity of Sugar in one Year. Hogfheads.		Other Settlements.
1734,	5502	8002				
1740,	6203	8581				
1745,	6599	8043				
1761,	7016		5	350		95
1768,	7308	10402				

S E C T. III.

St. DOROTHY, in the Precinct of St. CATHARINE.

THIS parifh is bounded on the Eaft by St. Catharine; Weft, by Clarendon; North, by St. John; and South, by Old Harbour and the fea.

The town of Old Harbour contains about thirty houfes, inhabited chiefly by wharfingers and factors; this being the principal barquadier for this parifh, St. John, a part of St. Thomas in the Vale, and a part of Clarendon. It had formerly a fmall fort, or rather battery, which has not been thought of confequence enough to fupport in repair; for the harbour, or bay, lying only about feven leagues Weft from Port Royal, and about ten miles from Spanifh Town, notice might be difpatched to either of thofe places in a very fhort time upon any alarm; and as the fame breeze, which would ferve to carry a fhip of war from Port Royal to their affiftance, would prevent an enemy's veffel from getting out of the bay, no privateer will dare to venture fo far in as to give the town any annoyance: befides, the entrance into the bay is fortified with fo many cayes and fhoals, as to make the navigation very hazardous to ftrangers; and even thofe beft-acquainted with it require

day-light

day-light and a favourable land-wind to carry them out. The inner or East harbour is an inlet, or *cul de sac*, turning near six miles within land, and so sheltered on all sides, that ships have rode here with perfect safety in the most furious hurricanes. On this account, the Spaniards moored their galleons here during the stormy season ; but the channel leading to it is now so choaked with mud, that loaded ships cannot get in or out ; for which reason, the merchant-vessels, which come to take in cargoes at this port, lie further out in the bay, where vessels of almost any burthen may have sufficient depth of water and a fine anchoring-ground.

In the offing of the bay is a very good fishery, chiefly for snappers, which form a principal part of subsistence for the inhabitants at Old Harbour. At certain times of the year there is also great plenty of turtle caught upon the coast. A company of soldiers is quartered here in barracks, built at the expence of the parish. As this place contains nothing further of note, I shall pass on to the market, which is distant about two miles inland, and is so called from the Negroe market, held here regularly every Sunday fore-noon, for poultry, corn, eggs, and other small articles of provision. It is an insignificant hamlet of about twelve houses, consisting of taverns and shops, and distant about one mile from the parochial church, a small building, close by which is the rector's house, situated on a rocky eminence, which commands an agreeable pro-spect of the sea and adjacent country. From the piazza of this house the eye takes in a view of great part of St. Catharine and Li-guarea, and the sea from St. Thomas in the East to Portland Point in the West. But the flat part of St. Catharine, St. Dorothy, and Clarendon, appears to be in a manner a continued wood, from the multitude of opopinax trees which are suffered to grow in the hedge-rows and middle of the pastures ; and this detracts greatly from the beauty of the landschape. The stipend annexed to this rectory is 200*l.* *per annum* ; and, the parish not being very po-pulous, the whole income of the living is probably under 400*l.*

The only river in this parish is the Black or Bridge river, which takes its rise in a small morass about seven miles from the harbour. The excellence of its water has already been mentioned. It crosses the great Western road which leads from Spanish Town to the

leeward

leeward parts of the ifland, over a funken bridge of large timber-work and ftones. It is here but a fmall ftream; but it widens on approaching the harbour, and becomes deep enough to admit the fhips long-boats which come here for water. Near the mouth of it are caught exceeding fine jew-fifh and calipever, for the Spanifh Town market. The foil adjacent to it is extremely rich; and large tracts are capable of being watered by channels drawn from the river, and cultivated with the fugar-cane; but hitherto no fuch advantage has been made of either. The foil of this parifh in general refembles that of St. Catharine, and lies under the like misfortune of uncertain feafons; for which reafon, it has never made any confiderable figure as a fugar-parifh.

The hilly parts of it towards the North abound in pimento-trees; which fhews their foil well-adapted to this production, though it is not extenfively attended to here, for want of inhabitants. The air of the coaft is but indifferent: the interior parts are efteemed more healthy; and particularly the hills, where it is perfectly clear and temperate.

In the mountains near St. John's is an exceedingly fine chalybeate-fpring, which has performed many furprifing cures in dropfical habits; and in cafes where, by lingering and ill-managed intermittents, the patient was too relaxed and emaciated, the blood impoverifhed, and the tone of the ftomach much impaired. Some have been known to recover from a dropfy by the ufe of it, after being feveral times tapped. The eftate in which it rifes having been, a few years ago, fold by Mr. Harris, the former proprietor, the purchafer, either through ignorance, or for fome other reafon, caufed a bank to be dug down, at the foot of which it had ufed to be taken up. It now lies covered by a load of foil and rubbifh feveral feet in depth; fo that the public are at prefent unhappily deprived of this providential remedy. It is much to be lamented, that the many excellent mineral and medicinal waters in this ifland, diftributed here by the benevolent Father of mankind, on purpofe as it were to adminifter an eafy relief under fome of the moft excruciating ailments, fhould have fallen fo little under the public care, that, excepting the bath in St. Thomas, I do not know of one that has been thought worthy of the legiflative attention.

The

The aftroites, or ftar-ftones and brontiæ, hedge-hog and echini ftones, are found in great abundance on the coaft. The firft-mentioned, as well as the coral rocks, which extend from Salt-pond hill to Old Harbour, near the fhore, when calcined, make an excellent lime for building.

It feems now to be the eftablifhed opinion, founded upon anatomical obfervations, that the black complexion of Negroes proceeds entirely from a *reticulum mucofum*, or dark-coloured net-work, fpread immediately beneath the cuticle of their bodies. It is likewife prefumed, upon reafonable grounds, that the different cafts of complexion, obfervable among the different fpecies of men, derive their various tints principally, if not entirely, from the colour of their *reticula*. The offspring of two Negroe-parents, if born with a white or light-coloured *reticulum*, is called an Albinoe. A male child of this fpecies was born, a few years fince, at a polinck, in the hills between St. Catharine and this parifh, and is probably ftill living. The complexion of it was a dead, dull white, refembling that of a corpfe; its hair, or rather wool, a light-flaxen colour, ftrong, coarfe, and curling, like that of a Negroe; the features were truly of the Negroe caft; the noftrils wide, and lips thick and prominent; the eyes were a light-grey, large and full, and, when brought into a ftrong light, were in a continual, rolling motion, which gave the child the foolifh look of an idiot. If he fhould attain to manhood, and beget children, the attention of the curious will be excited to remark the colour of his progeny. A nation of thefe Albinoes are faid to inhabit fomewhere in the central parts of Africa; who are weak and of low ftature, and do not mix with the Blacks. They are called Dondos, or Mokiffes, by the natives; and are faid to have fcarcely any fight, except by moon or owl-light, and to be at continual war with the Blacks, who attack them in the day-time, when their fight is at the worft; and they take their revenge in the night, when it is beft. They are likewife faid to be educated in the fcience of prieftcraft, or witchcraft, and to fill the chief offices at Loango in all religious affairs and fuperftitious ceremonies. Some of the Negroes in Guiney are of opinion, that, although they have their males and females, like the reft of mankind, they are incapable of procreating, if not of coition. But this wants proof. Several of the fame fpecies are affirmed to have been feen in other parts of Africa, in Borneo, in India, and New Guiney.

I fhall conclude the account of this parifh with a table, as before :

| | Negroes. | Cattle. | Sugar-plantations. | Annual Produce of Sugar. | |
				Hogfheads.	Other Settlements.
1734,	2298	5341			
1740,	2515	5468			
1745,	2423	4540			
1758,	3229	4232			
1761,	3210				
1763,	3075	3899			
1766,	3713	4236			
1768,	3665	4661	12	700	56

Taking the lifts of 1768 and 1740 into comparifon, the decreafe of cattle appears to be 807, although no new fugar-plantations were formed within that time. And this falling-off, I am afraid, muft be referred chiefly to the introduction of foreign cattle, for fupplying the markets and fquadron: this proved a difcouragement to many penn-keepers in the parifh, and occafioned their deferting it; fo that feveral penns, which formerly were capital breeding-penns, are at prefent in wafte.

S E C T. IV.

St. J O H N.

This parifh has for its boundaries, on the North, St. Anne; on the South, St. Dorothy; on the Eaft, St. Thomas in the Vale; and on the Weft, Clarendon. The whole of this parifh is oc-cupied with hills, mountains, and vallies. It is watered with four rivers, of which the Rio Montando, or Mountain river, is the principal; and with the feveral fprings and ramifications which contribute to form them. The foil in general is fertile, even on the higheft ridges. It abounds with fine timber; and the

vales

vales are particularly prolific; of thefe the Vale of Luidas, diftant about twenty-one miles N. W. from Spanifh Town, is the beft-fettled. Before fugar-works were formed here, it contained only breeding-penns, whofe paftures were fo rich, that the cattle were remarkably fat, and their flefh of an exquifite flavour. Thefe penn-keepers ufed to fupply the market of Spanifh Town with veal, which Sir Hans Sloane, I think, extols very highly. The climate of this parifh is cool and temperate. Exceeding good butter has been made here by one or two families; and I have feen moft kinds of European garden ftuff, produced in the Vale of Luidas, in as great perfection as any that is brought to Covent-garden-market. The cherry, apple, quince, and peach tree, thrive and bear fruit in this vale; a fure indication of the cool temperature of the climate, and that the furrounding mountains would be found on experiment to produce them in ftill higher perfection. The air of this parifh is confequently very healthful, and has proved entirely agreeable to European conftitutions. But it is far from being well-inhabited, the roads leading from it requiring a great deal of improvement. After croffing the Red Hills, we enter a tolerably cultivated vale at Lloyd's eftate, interfperfed with a few well-built houfes, which, for want of the refidence of their proprietors, are haftening very faft to decay. From this vale we afcend Cudjve Hill; from part of which there is a South-eaft profpect over the Red Hills to Kingfton, and Weftward to Old Harbour and Goat Ifland, with a near view of fuch plantations as lie immediately below. Some miles further inland is Bolt's Hill, which rifes ftill higher; the fides of it are finely cloathed with fugar-canes; and from the fummit the Southern hills appear depreffed, and the eye takes in a boundlefs profpect over the fea, beyond Port-Royal. About the diftance of two miles further North are the barracks, which are built of ftone, and command a narrow pafs of communication be-tween the North and South fides of the ifland. This poft is ca-pable of being made exceedingly ftrong; and even now a garrifon of fifty men might hold it againft five hundred: but hitherto (as I am informed) no detachment has been cantoned in it. The bar-racks are no fooner paffed, than we difcover, at the diftance of four or five miles along a vifto between two continued chains of hills,

at

at the foot of which runs a broken gully, called Juan de Bolas (or John of the Vale), the delightful valley of Luidas, before-fpoken-of, encircled with the lofty mounds of four parifhes, St. John, Clarendon, St. Anne, and St. Thomas in the Vale. Some of thefe highlands near Juan de Bolas are faid to have rich veins of the precious ores; but no expence is fufficient to explore the profound regions in which they lie concealed. The late Sir S———n Cl———ke (who was defcended from an ancient family in Warwickfhire, and bore fome of the higheft offices in this ifland), amongft other branches of fcience, attained to confiderable knowledge in metallurgy; and, had his fuccefs been at all proportioned to his fkill, might have beftowed his application to a very profitable end: but, unhappily, after an immenfe expence and trouble in fearching for the hidden treafure, he found (too late) that his favourite purfuit had only contributed to the reduction of his fortune. The church, if not lately repaired, is in a ruinous, dilapidated ftate. The rector, however, has a good houfe and fome glebe land. His ftipend is 200*l.* and the annual value of the living fuppofed not to exceed 320*l. per annum.*

State of the Parifh:

	Negroes.	Cattle.	Sugar-plantations.	Hogfheads.	Other Settlements.
				Annual Produce.	
1734,	5242	2561			
1740,	5875	2837			
1745,	5728	2250			
1761,	5888				
1768,	5455	2726	21	2200	50

The decreafe of Negroes fhews that this parifh is not getting for-wards. Let me here remark (once for all) on the great utility of comparing the prefent and paft ftate of the parifhes together. It is the true teft by which the legiflature may judge of the ftate of the whole ifland, and where the fymptoms of a decline are manifeft; as in the example of this parifh, which is bleft with every natural advantage of a good air, a fruitful foil, and regular feafons. It may juftly be fufpected, that a retrogradation under thefe very favourable circumftances can happen no otherwife than from fome defect in the policy of internal government; perhaps nothing fo

much

much as a want of good roads, and the impoverished condition of those who have failed in their settlements, principally from this cause. But, whatever the cause may have been, it is the duty of a patriotic legiflature, when convinced of the fact, to search for the source of evil by the moft probable rules of enquiry; and, when they have difcovered it, to apply the beft remedies in their power.

SECT. V.

St. Thomas in the Vale.

THIS parifh is bounded towards the North by St. Anne, and St. Mary; towards the South, by St. Catharine; on the Eaft, by St. Andrew; and on the Weft, by St. John. It is watered by the Cobre; the D'Oro; the Rio Magno, formed by the conflux of the Tilboa and Indian rivers; and by feveral fmall rivulets which fall into them. The greater part of this parifh is comprized within the vale called Sixteen-mile-walk. This vale is about eleven miles in length by eight in width, and contains between fifty and fixty thoufand fquare acres. It is fituated Southerly, beneath the main ridge or chain of high mountains which traverfe the ifland from Eaft to Weft. It is alfo inclofed on all other fides with a circumvallation of high hills and mountains. It is neither flat nor fwampy, but diverfified throughout with gentle rifings and flopes. The foil is fertile, for the moft part a red coarfe earth mixed with clay, or a dark mould upon a whitifh marle. It is full of fprings and rivulets, which unite with the larger ftreams; and thefe, meeting together near the chafm or opening betwixt the mountains on the South fide of the vale, augment that noble river the Cobre, which continues its courfe irregularly between rocky mountains and precipices, alternately a cafcade or fmooth water, as it happens to be more or lefs impeded, exhibiting for fome miles a very romantic fcene till it reaches the plain below. At that part of the vale where it firft fhapes its courfe towards Spanifh Town, it enters between two yawning rocky hills, which ap-

peer

pear as if they had been rifted on purpofe to give it a paffage. The vale is almoft daily throughout the year overcaft with a thick fog, which begins to rife flowly on the approach of evening, grows denfer as the night advances, becomes gradual y diffufed into all the contiguous vales or inlets among the furrounding mountains, is heavieft about the dawn of day, and remains fettled until the fun has warmed and agitated the air; then it rifes higher, expanding in the atmofphere; and between the hours of eight and nine in the forenoon it begins to flow away in two principal ftreams, the one Weftward among the mountains on that fide, the other Southward, following the courfe of the river. Early in the morning it is extremely thick; and, if viewed at this time from the fummit of the mountains, it affords the moft lively reprefentation poffible of a large lake, or little fea: the feveral vales and collateral inlets appear to be arms, harbours, bays, and creeks; the elevated fpots, difperfed through it, and covered with trees, buildings, or cane-pieces, refemble fmall iflands, which here and there uplift their diminutive heads above water, combining into view the moft picturefque and delightful variety. This fog has been remarked as a fingular phænomenon almoft from the firft fettlement of the ifland. I fhall not pretend definitively to explain the phyfical caufes of it; the fubject has puzzled much abler heads: but as every one has a right to offer his conjectures; fo I may be allowed to fubmit mine, without affecting to controul the opinions of others.

The great abundance of rain that falls on the encircling mountains, their prodigious furface and fudden fteep rife from the vale on all fides, may probably occafion a vaft quantity of water to defcend inceffantly, through fubterraneous chafms, into fo low a fituation, as it were into a huge fink. The foil of the vale, which in general (as has been obferved) is a clay, may poffibly obftruct the free emergency of this water to the furface, except in particular places, where, the ftratum being thinner, the refiftance is lefs; or where gravel, fand, or mould of a loofe texture, predominate. Accordingly, we obferve it copioufly watered with feveral fprings and rivulets, which have their fource among the adjacent high lands. But although thefe currents do not burft forth in all parts, yet the fmaller globules of water may gradually be rarefied and evaporate,

affifted

affifted by the native warmth of the marle below, and the action of the folar heat above; which enable thofe globules to penetrate the furface in form of vapour. In a vale encompaffed with fuch prodigious mounds, the folar rays muft ftrike with confiderable impreffion, and fupply the earth to a certain depth with a large ftock of heat, which doth not wholly leave it for many hours after fun-fet. The ingenious Dr. Hales remarks, that fo great a heat as the fun occafions, at two feet depth under the earth's furface, muft needs have ftrong influence in raifing the moifture at that and greater depths; whereby a continual reek muft always be afcending, during a hot feafon, by night as well as by day; for the heat at two feet depth is nearly the fame night and day. The impulfe of the fun-beams giving the moifture in the earth a brifk undulating motion, thefe aqueous particles, when feparated and rarefied by heat, afcend into the atmofphere. In the day-time, the rarefaction of thefe particles is fo great, that they pafs from the earth imperceptibly: after fun-fet, the cool air, rufhing downwards from the mountains, condenfes, and renders them vifible. In this ftate the fog refts brooding over the vale, for want of heat to raife it higher, or of wind to difpel it; for the land-wind does not ufually blow here with an impetuofity fufficient to drive it over thefe lofty barriers that hem in the vale: but it is obferved, that ftrong Norths in the winter-months force it vehemently through the opening of the Southern chain, through which the Cobre flows, and difperfe it for feveral miles, even to Spanifh Town, and fometimes beyond it; but, whenever this happens, no fog is to be feen in that quarter of the vale bordering on the Northern range of mountains from which the wind then fets. Another fingularity is, that, on the approach of a rainy day, this fog does not appear the antecedent evening; the reafon of which may be, that fuch evenings being always clofe and fultry, it is probable the rarefaction continues as well by night as by day. and, the ufual condenfation not taking place, the particles are not rendered obvious to the fight, although perhaps the reek at fuch times is rather more copious than at others. So in the low lands, on the evening preceding rain, the atmofphere feels unufually clofe and moift, the thermometer does not fink after fun-fet, no perceptible vapours are

noticed,

noticed, and no dew appears on the grafs. The unaltered ftation of the thermometer is alone an evident proof, that the heat of the atmofphere is not diminifhed, and confequently, that the vapours remain uncondenfed.

Fogs are generally fuppofed detrimental to health ; but the fog of Sixteen-mile-walk by no means deferves this imputation. The inhabitants do not fcruple to expofe themfelves to it freely ; nor is it known to produce any effects injurious to them. The principal caufe of its inoffenfive quality may be, that it is not mixed with any fulphureous or noxious exhalations; at leaft, it is without any fenfible fmell ; which would moft certainly not be the cafe, if it was much impregnated with any fuch effluvia. Its good effects con-fift in the copious dew which it fheds upon the trees and herbage, and which fupports them in the drieft weather in a flourifhing ftate. Thofe long drowths therefore, which fometimes happen in this ifland, fo fatal to the eftates in general, affect the plantations in this vale but very little; the fog fupplying, in a great meafure, the want of rains, or at leaft fo far as to fave the canes from perifhing in the manner they do in other parts of the ifland.

The North-weft part of this vale is called The Maggoti, a tract of favannah lying near the foot of *Monte Diablo*. The name of this favannah gave rife to a ftory, that, whenever it rains here, the drops which fall upon any perfon's cloaths become maggots in half an hour. This wonderful metamorphofis, reported probably at firft by way of joke to fome credulous inquirer, has with all its ab-furdity been fwallowed, and retailed by feveral authors, copying one from the other, and gravely recorded by them among the *nota-bilia* of this ifland. Thefe maggots, however, never exifted, ex-cept in the brains of the inventor. The name, perhaps, was of Spanifh extraction, compounded of **Maga** (an enchantrefs), and Oteo (watching on a high place); alluding probably to the pin-nacle of *Monte Diablo*, over which the thunder-clouds fo fre-quently break, as, together with its horrid afpect, to make it feem a proper refidence for a witch, under patronage of the Devil, to whom the mountain was dedicated. The road leading from Six-teen-mile-walk to St. Anne croffes this mountain, traverfing the face of it, which is fo fteep, that few travelers venture to de-

fcend

ſcend on horſe-back. Some tradition, perhaps, remained concerning the origin of the Magotti, when a ſmall houſe of refreſhment was kept on the higheſt part of the road, many years ago, known by the ſign of Mother Red-cap; which name that part ſtill retains.

The cavern at River-head in the North-Weſt part of the vale extends near a quarter of a mile under a mountain, or perhaps more, it being impoſſible to explore the whole length, on account of the river Cobre, which occupies the inmoſt part of it, and, running for a conſiderable way, ſuddenly ſhoots through a hole in the rock on one ſide, and continues its current under ground for a conſiderable diſtance from the cave. That this river draws its origin from ſome large ſtream in the mountains, far beyond the cave, ſeems evident, by its riſing or falling in exact proportion as the rains are heavy or otherwiſe in the mountains. After very heavy rains, the river is ſo ſwelled, that, unable to vent itſelf at the hole, the ſuperfluous water diſembogues through the mouth of the cavern. An ingenious man attempted, a few years ſince, by fixing a flood-gate acroſs the hole, to force the current of the river into a regular channel by the mouth of the cavern, and conduct it from thence to turn water-mills on the neighbouring eſtates. The undertaking had all the appearance of being practicable, but was laid aſide after the death of the projector. Near the foot of the Northern ridge, at no great diſtance from the road which leads over *Monte Diablo*, is a cocoa-nut tree of very ſingular growth. About thirty feet or more above the baſe, it divides into two diſtinct ſtems, which, continuing their aſcent for ſeveral feet, at an angle thus V, and at pretty equal elevation above the main ſtem or body of the tree, are crowned with tops of beautiful foliage, and nearly of the ſame magnitude; but whether both are productive of fruit or not I could not learn. As no other of the like figure has been obſerved in the iſland, it may be regarded as a *luſus naturæ*, of a very unuſual kind. The paſs which admits a communication between Spaniſh Town and this vale ought not here to be unmentioned. After traveling about three miles from the town on a pretty level road, we come to a ſugar-plantation, formerly called by the Spaniards Los Angelos, and now The Angels. Juſt beyond this begins the entrance of the paſs. From hence to the opening into Sixteen-mile-walk, for the space of four miles and a half, is a continuation of precipice on both sides, divided only by the river, except a small elbow at the end of four miles, where a few acres of level ground at the foot of these ridges has admitted of a little sugar-work. The road cut into the side of the mountain falls by an easy descent to the bridge, and crossing the river is conducted along the remainder of the way not many feet above the surface of the water: it is therefore subject to be broken away in many places by the violence of floods; but this inconvenience is submitted to from the impracticability there appeared of carrying it higher through such immense masses of rock as form impediments the whole way. For a considerable length, the road is walled up; and, as it is so liable to damage, not only from inundations of the river, but the falling of large trees, rocks, and earth, from the impending crags and precipices under which it runs, the expence of repairing it is very great, and requires a standing body of workmen, who are employed the whole year to keep it in order. The height of the mountains on each side overshadowing it morning and afternoon, the passage is extremely cool and agreeable; every turn of the road presenting the eye with new appearances of the river, the rocks, and woods; whilst the water, sometimes roaring and foaming in its current, where it is confined to a narrow and rugged channel; at other times gliding smoothly and silently along, delights the traveler with an alternate variety. At the end of four miles, the mountain called Gibraltar opens to view a vast solid wall of rock of prodigious height, whose surface, apparently perpendicular, is nevertheless cloathed with trees and shrubs from the base to the summit; the tops of one row terminating where the roots of the next row begin, so as almost to seem growing one upon the other. After heavy rains a cataract spouts from the pinnacle of this stupendous mass, rendering it still more awful and romantic. The defile continues not far beyond this majestic object, though not widening till we enter at once the extensive and beautiful vale of Sixteen-mile-walk. The air of this vale was suspected formerly of producing the West-India colic or belly-ach; but, as that disorder does not seem at present to be particularly attached to the spot, some other cause must have made

it

it endemial: perhaps the inhabitants at this time are lefs addicted to drinking new rum, and therefore lefs afflicted with it. The air of this parifh is in general reputed healthy; and the habitations throughout the vale being for the moft part built on rifing ground, they are not fubject to damps. This tract was among the firft fettled with fugar-plantations, and what it produces now of this commodity is of an excellent quality; but the land is thought to be much worn. The truth is, that fome of the plantations here were formed upon a gritty, red, and naturally fterile foil, which, for want of regular manure, and having loft by degrees its fuperficial coat of vegetable mould, became lefs and lefs productive, till the proprietors threw them up as unfit for the fugar-cane. But others, who have purfued a better hufbandry, ftill reap advantage from it in reafonably good crops. The air of the mountains is perfectly fine and healthful. Upon one of them, near the confines of St. Catharine's, is the governor's polinck or provifion ground, which has a fmall but neat villa upon it, and was purchafed by the affembly, as an occafional retreat, during the hot months, for the commander in chief. The foil of thefe mountains is fertile; and they are chiefly appropriated to fupply the eftates in the vale with the different kinds of vegetable provifion, and lime and timber for repairing their works. This parifh contained,

	Negroes.	Cattle.	Sugar-works.	Annual produce. Hogfheads.	Other Settlements.
In 1734,	7568	4441			
1740,	8475	4813			
1745,	8239	4797			
1761,	9057				
1768,	8382	5782	41	3500	37

It appears from hence to have made little or no progrefs fince the year 1740; and the increafed number of cattle, amounting to 969, are probably the ftock brought upon thofe runs, which, after being in canes, have been converted into pafture.

S E C T. VI.

C L A R E N D O N

IS one of the largeſt, healthieſt, and beſt-ſettled pariſhes in the whole iſland. It is bounded on the Eaſt by the pariſhes of St. Dorothy and St. John ; on the Weſt, by St. Elizabeth ; on the North, by St. Anne ; and on the South, by Vere, and a part of Old Harbour Bay. It is watered with no leſs than fifteen rivers, beſides innumerable rivulets and ſprings. The names of theſe rivers are,

Green River,	Ballard's,	Rock, and
Thomas,	Pindar's,	Craal ;
Tick,	Juan de Bolas,	

whoſe ſeveral ſtreams fall into the Minho. There are likewiſe,

The Cave,	Milk,
Pedro,	Baldwin's, and
Croft's,	Bower's.

The capital of theſe is the Minho, which takes its ſource about twenty-ſix miles, in a direct line, from the ſea on the South ſide, but with its various meanders makes a courſe of fifty and upwards. I do not know if the ſhort river ſhould be added to the liſt. It lies exactly on the boundary which divides this pariſh from St. Anne. It is a large body of water, which appears in a hollow, or dell ; and, after running with great violence a little way, ſuddenly diſappears, probably to give birth to another river below ; but its ſubterraneous direction has not as yet been diſcovered. The Cave, Pedro, and Croft's rivers, are alſo remarkable for hiding themſelves under ground, after a courſe of ſome miles above. The river Minho, was probably ſo called after one of the ſame name in Portugal ; for it is to be obſerved, that the firſt ſettlers from Europe were a mixture of Spaniſh and Portugueſe. It is from this reaſon that we find in the iſland mountains and rivers named in both theſe languages. But the name was applied with great propriety to this river, as there are many circumſtances to induce a belief, that the Spaniards opened and worked a gold mine ſomewhere near its

banks.

banks. Of this I fhall hereafter fpeak more particularly under the head of mines, as I am willing to bring the whole on that head into one view, and fhall therefore add nothing further upon it for the prefent. It may be imagined, that a diftrict, watered fo plentifully as this is, muft be well calculated for fettlements: but it was not much cultivated in the time of the Spaniards; they poffeffed a few cacao-walks near the Minho, but chiefly reforted hither to hunt the wild hogs, which were always very numerous in it, and are not yet extirpated. The water in general of all the rivers and fprings is tolerably pure and wholefome, except when difturbed by land-floods. The lower part of the parifh towards the bay confifts chiefly of favannah land for about fix miles in length, here and there interfperfed with rocky hills of no great height. The hills rife gradually in height the further we advance into the heart of the parifh; yet here are few or none fo fteep or barren, as not to be fit for culture of fome fort or other. The vales between the hills and mountains are in general fpacious, watered by fome river, and enriched with fine cane-land. The conveniency of having water-mills, and the firmnefs of the roads in general, has encouraged the inhabitants to carry their fugar-plantations much farther inland than in any other diftrict of the ifland; and there are fome at no lefs diftance than twenty-two miles from the barkadier. Thefe eftates form their carriage into two ftages, fixing the termination of the firft at about midway, where they have convenient paftures and ftore-houfes, for refrefhment of their cattle, and lodgement of their goods. The foil within the mountains is inferior to none, either for the production of canes or provifions; and the woods are full of excellent timber. The rivers abound with the mullet, fo much admired for its delicious flavour. In fhort, the inhabitants have all the means of plenty in their hands from thefe fources, and the regularity of their feafons; and of courfe they are, at leaft the greater part, opulent and flourifhing. The backparts of the parifh, bordering on St. Anne and St. Elizabeth, are the worft-peopled: yet here is a great field of encouragement to invite fettlers; for the remoteft eftates hitherto formed are known to produce fugars of the beft quality. The foil of the high lands is in general either rocky, intermixed with a black fhell-mould, or

5   a fine

a fine vegetable dark mould on a clay. The lower grounds are chiefly clay, intermixed here and there with rich veins of vegetable mould, or the brick mould; the latter moftly abounds near the banks of the rivers, confifting of the fediment they have depofited, or of the finer particles wafhed down from the hills. The plantation called Carvers is one of the moft celebrated for its fertility: it is a fmall dale, furrounded with rocky hills, and fo rich, that it produces almoft invariably three hundred hogfheads of fugar *per annum*, with fo little labour to the Negroes employed upon it, that they multiply fufficiently to keep up their ftock, without having recourfe to African recruits. Near Juan de Bolas river, about fixteen miles from the coaft, the road continues towards St. Ann's, paffing by eafy traverfes up the fide of a fteep mountain, on the fummit of which we enter a favannah, or plain, of about four miles in length, called Old Woman's Savannah, from an elderly Spanifh lady, who took up her abode here after the ifland was furrendered to the Englifh, and refided here many years in a hut. This favannah is watered with feveral fine fprings; and the foil, though apparently not fertile, produces very good fugar. The air is fo pure and delightful, that many fmall fettlements have been formed here; and the inhabitants attain, for the moft part, to a good old age. The late Mr. James Dawkins made choice of this fpot for founding an academy for the inftruction of boys, natives of the ifland; and, had he lived, the project would no doubt have been brought to maturity: but of this plan I fhall hereafter give a further detail. The hamlet, or village of the Crofs, is fituated about fix miles from Old Harbour Bay, on the great roads leading, one to leeward, the other to Old Woman's Savannah. It confifts of about ten houfes, near the parifh-church, which is an handfome brick-building, of four ailes. Hard-by, likewife, ftands the fkeleton of the parfonage-houfe, which at prefent is converted into a cooper's fhop; a metamorphofis that is not at all wonderful; for the inhabitants of this hamlet, being moftly Jews and Mulattoes, afford no very agreeable neighbourhood to a Proteftant divine. The lowlands of this parifh were the firft fettled; but the inhabitants in procefs of time having found the climate of the mountains more cool, the feafons more regular, and the foil more

fertile,

fertile, removed to them, and have carried their improvements to very great perfection. The rector's ftipend is 250*l.*; but this being an extenfive and populous parifh, the living is reputed worth 600*l. per annum* at leaft, and includes about twelve Negroe flaves, who are appropriated to the ufe of the rector for the time being. The chapel is diftant about twelve miles further inland, a fmall but neat building, and furnifhed with a good organ. Divine fervice, for the convenience of the parifhioners, is alternately performed here, and at the Crofs Church : the quarter-feffion is generally held at the Chapel ; and the election of reprefentatives at the Crofs. The hamlet of the Chapel confifts of only feven or eight fcattered houfes. Here are the parifh-barracks ; in which a company of regulars is quartered, and a fmall market is held occafionally by the Negroes of the neighbourhood.

About three miles from the Crofs, the Weftern road paffes the channel of Rio Minho, which hereabouts changes its name to Dry River, becaufe it is fometimes quite dry, and at other times very broad and rapid. Weftward from this paffage, the road continues nearly the fame diftance, till it approaches Lime Savannah, where a branch diverges from it Northwards to the Chapel ; but the main road continues on to St. Jago Savannah. In the middle of this open fpace is a gentle rifing, which commands a diftant view of the whole ; and here is very properly fituated a ftarting-chair, for feeing the races, which are fometimes held, for the Vere fubfcription-purfe. Upon this favannah, which is well-ftocked with cattle of all kinds, are feveral large ponds, befides many fmall fprings and rivulets, which never lofe their water, except in times of moft unufual and long-continued drowth. The road which branches off to the Chapel, after leaving the flat country, afcends among rocky hills, till it reaches Tick Savannah. A great part of this road is truly romantic ; and the whole, from top to bottom, for the extent of two miles, is hung on either fide with the deep gloom of lofty trees, ever verdant, and rifing in wild gradation out of ftupendous rocks and chafms. The favannah receives its name from the river Tick, which runs through part of the vale juft below it. On the top of the favannah is a large piece of water, of confiderable depth, the refort of various wild-fowl. Not far from hence is the feat of

Mr. F———n,

Mr. F——n, formerly chief-juftice of the ifland; a native, and one whofe talents are fo extraordinary, that it is almoft impoffible for the moft impartial pen to do juftice to them. In this ifland alone, he has attained, by obfervation, reading, converfation, and the natural *acumen* of his genius, a more comprehenfive and accurate knowledge of places, perfons, and things, in Great-Britain, Europe, and even throughout the known world, than moft other gentlemen, who have had opportunities of being perfonally acquainted with them, or of obtaining the moft intelligent accounts of them. Though he never trod any other earth but this little fpot Jamaica, yet he is intelligent in the manners, arts, fciences, and people (fo far as have been hitherto difcovered), of the whole terreftrial globe. Nature, it is true, endued him with a retentive memory, and faculties uncommonly fagacious; but ftill it is fignally to his merit, that he has improved every advantage which fhe gave him; no one has ftudied more, nor better underftands what he has ftudied, than this gentleman, whom with the ftricteft propriety, and without the leaft particle of adulation, I may aver to be worthy of being efteemed among the firft ornaments of this country.

His houfe is delightfully placed upon a fmall rifing, in the centre of a little vale: at no great diftance from it are two craggy rocks, which peep over the fummits of two hills, and refemble the ruins of antique caftles. Immediately below it lies a little garden, filled with orange, cacao, and other trees, for ufe and pleafure. Beyond this are feveral hills, clumps of tufted wood, and natural avenues into the adjacent country.

At about one hundred paces diftance from this manfion is another of more modern and elegant conftruction. It confifts of one very large and fpacious room, upwards of fifty feet in length, about twenty wide, and twelve high. This is entered by a door-way at the North end, under a portico of about twelve or fifteen feet fquare, fupported by columns of the Tufcan order; and at the South end is a gallery, out of which the eye, over-looking a fmall garden, is carried along an avenue between two gently-rifing woods, that have a folemn, filent grandeur. Adjoining to the principal room are fmaller apartments, one of which is a library furnifhed with a collection of the beft authors. The old habitation,

though

though lefs elevated, neverthelefs commands a richer and more extenfive profpect, comprehending the fineft part of Clarendon, and of the neighbouring parifhes. The beauties of nature that are difplayed here are innumerable. In one place is feen a long, wavy furface, adorned with the lively verdure of canes, interfperfed with wind-mills and other buildings. In another are beheld feveral charming lawns of pafture-land, dotted with cattle and fheep, and watered with rivulets. In a third are Negroe villages, where (far from poverty and difcontent) peace and plenty hold their reign; a crefted ridge of fertile hills, which feparates this parifh from thofe contiguous on the North and Eaft, diftantly terminates the landfchape.

The produce of this parifh is fhipped for the moft part at Old Harbour Bay; on which there are two principal barquadiers, the one at Old Harbour Town, the other at Bower's River.

In a rocky hill, on the Northern fide of Old Woman's Savannah, is a cavern which runs a great depth under the earth. Upon examination, a few years fince, it was found to contain a great many human bones, which were probably either Indians, or the relicks of fome of the wild or rebellious Negroes, who formerly infefted this part of the country, and made it their place of concealment. Near this favannah is likewife a chalybeate-fpring, which has performed fome cures, but is not much attended to. The hills adjacent to it furnifh evident proofs of their abounding with copper ore, which one day or other may poffibly excite a ftricter inveftigation. The hard, fhining pyrites are frequently found in thefe mountains; and magnetic ftones have been picked up on this favannah, which feem to indicate the prefence of iron ore. Many of the fprings in this, as well as in St. Anne's and fome other parifhes, are remarkable for their incrufting and petrefactive qualities; forming in fome places a layer or thin cruft; in others, penetrating into wood, and other fubftances, without altering their fhape. I have feen pieces of hard wood metamorphofed, by their procefs, into ftone, fo as to anfwer the purpofe of hones for fharpening knives. In moft of the gullies bordering upon the coaft, are large quantities of agate, chiefly of the flefh-coloured, blood-coloured, and yellow kinds. But there are

others more variegated. Thefe natural productions are fo little en-
quired after here, that, I believe, they are even unknown to many:
yet the pains of collecting thofe moft in efteem might be rewarded
by the profit of vending them to Great-Britain. The moft valuable fpecies are the white-veined, the flefh-coloured, the red,
the pale-yellow, the dark-brown with black veins, and the green-
ifh-brown variegated. A few, which an ingenious gentleman of
this ifland brought with him to London, were greatly admired.
Ship-loads might be procured here at no other charge than that
of gathering them; and by breaking a few, the beft fort might
be eafily difcovered. The temperature of the air in this extenfive
parifh is various. In the lowlands it is for the moft part warm
and dry; and, among the mountains, cool, healthy, and invigorating. Some of the low grounds adjoining the rich banks of
the Minho are unwholefome, and were fo reputed by the Spaniards; for, in times of drowth, this river, about ten miles diftance
from the coaft, begins firft to bury its waters, leaving the channel
dry for a confiderable length; then rifes again; and fo continues
finking and emerging alternately until it difembogues. The mud
and weeds, thus left to ferment and turn putrid with the heat of the
fun, are fuppofed with good reafon to breed very noxious exhalations; and the known unhealthinefs of one or two eftates, which
border upon this part of it, cannot otherwife be accounted for.
The white inhabitants, or rather the proprietors of thefe eftates,
might probably be relieved from this annoyance, by removing the
dwelling houfes to fome convenient eminence; for it can never
be confiftent with health to fleep in a putrid atmofphere. The
flourifhing ftate of this parifh may be conceived from the following
table:

| | Negroes. | Cattle. | Sugar-works. | Annual Produce. | |
				Hogfheads.	Other Settlements.
1734,	10769	11027			
1740,	11575	12299			
1745,	12775	11969			
1761,	13772				
1768,	15517	14276	70	8000	180

By which it appears that, in the number of Negroes and cattle, it is
much improved; and, by the great quantity of produce, that it is

in

in a flourishing state.   The large extent of it hitherto unpeopled
will also suggest this obvious remark, that it requires many more
settlers, to bring it to a more ample state of culture, and render it
still more beneficial.   Its advantages in point of water are ob-
serveable from the number of its water-mills, there being no fewer
than fifty.   Besides sugar, ginger, and cacao, the article of coffee is
largely cultivated here ; and the annual crops of corn are so great,
that none of the parishes are better stocked with hogs and poultry.
Its low lands also abound with horses, cattle, and sheep.

SECT. VII.

VERE, in the Precinct of CLARENDON.

THIS parish, with Clarendon, forms one precinct.   It is bounded
East and North by Clarendon ; West, by St. Elizabeth ; and South,
by the sea.   The town of Carlisle, so called in honour of the earl
of that name, formerly governor of the island, was intended near
the mouth of Rio Minho ; but it is at present only an inconsiderable hamlet, of ten or twelve houses.   This place is remarkable for having been the scene of action between the French and
English in the year 1694, when Monsieur Ducasse, the governor of
Hispaniola, with a squadron of three men of war, and twenty-
three transports, having on board 1500 men, invaded the island ;
and, after some ineffectual attempts at Port Morant, Cow Bay, and
Bluefields, where he met with a repulse, anchored in Carlisle Bay
on the 18th of June.   The governor, Sir William Beeston, who
had carefully watched their motions, and conjectured their intention of making a descent on this part of the coast, immediately ordered thither two troops of horse, the St. Catharine regiment, and
part of the Clarendon and St. Elizabeth regiments of foot militia.
On the 19th in the morning, the French landed between fourteen
and fifteen hundred men, who proceeded to the attack of a breast-
work, which had been hastily thrown up, near the shore.   This
was gallantly defended for a considerable time by two hundred of
the militia; who, finding at length that they could not maintain

the

the poft, repaffed the river Minho, after killing feveral of the enemy, and the lofs of fome of their own officers. In the mean time the militia, difpatched by the governor, having arrived, advanced againft the French; and, notwithftanding the fatigue of their long march from Spanifh Town, they charged the enemy with fuch fury, as obliged them to retreat. The two following days a few flight fkirmifhes happened; and on the 22d, the French attacked a brick houfe, then occupied by a Mr. Hubbard, which was bravely defended by twenty-five men, who killed and wounded feveral of the French, among whom were fome officers of diftinction. The French retired for a while, threatening to renew the affault; and, in the mean time, a detachment from the Englifh troops, of fifty picked men, was thrown into the houfe, and an ambufcade prepared with the reft. But the enemy, intimidated with their lofs of men and officers, feeing no probability of being able to effect any further advance into the country, fuddenly retreated to the fhore, re-embarked with the utmoft expedition on board their fhips, and on the 24th, their whole fleet got under fail for Hifpaniola. The whole lofs fuftained by the French in this fhort time, by their different engagements and ficknefs, amounted to near feven hundred men. On the part of the Englifh, one hundred were killed and wounded. Captain Elliot, who had been a prifoner at Petit-Guava, and made his efcape from thence in a fmall canoe, brought the firft intelligence to Sir William Beefton of the intended invafion; for which he was afterwards recompenfed by king William III. with a gold chain and medal, of one hundred pounds value, and five hundred pounds in money.

The government of Jamaica immediately fet about framing feveral acts for better guarding the coafts; and, among others, one for enabling the inhabitants of Vere to erect a fortification for their defence; in confequence of which, Carlifle Fort was built the following year. This fortrefs, for want of repair, has been undermined by the fea, and for many years in a ruinous condition, the guns being all difmounted, and fome of them buried in the fand: nor will it probably be reftored to a proper ftate for defence till after fome future invafion; the general rule of œconomy, purfued in this ifland, having been to let the preparations for defence always

follow,

follow, inftead of preceding, the attack. The parifh-church ftands at the diftance of about two miles and a half from the fort. It is extremely well-finifhed on the infide, has an organ, and a tower. Its ftructure is low, and, being furrounded with large cotton-trees, it cannot well be feen till on a clofe approach. There is a decent rectory near it, with about feven acres of glebe, befides twelve acres more, in another part of the parifh, of very fine land. The ftipend granted by law is 200*l.* and the whole value of the living about 350*l. per annum.* About half a mile from the church, on the oppofite fide of the river Minho, is the free-fchool, founded about the year 1741, with fundry private benefactions, and calcu-lated for inftructing the poor children of the parifh in reading, writing, arithmetic, Latin, Greek, and the mathematics, under the management of truftees appointed by an act of affembly. This parifh is watered with five rivers, the Minho, Milk River, Baldwin's, Hilliard's, and Salt River; two of which, the Milk and Salt Rivers, are navigable by boats for a confiderable way up. Baldwin's and Hilliard's are only fmall branches which fall into the Milk River, which, as well as the Minho, difcharge themfelves into the fea. Long Bay, and the mouth of Milk River, are only anchoring-places for floops: the principal fhipping-places are at Carlifle Bay, and near the mouth of Salt River; which latter has its fource about a mile from an inlet on the Weft fide of Old Harbour Bay, under the foot of a rocky hill; the faltnefs of its water, from whence it takes its name, feems to indicate, that it paffes through a large bed of that foffil. The entrance into the bay of Old Harbour from Cape Boncato, or Cabarito, on the Eaft, to the Pitch of Portland, Weft, is about twelve miles and a half in the width, and the bay about twelve in depth. It is defended by fix fmall cayes, or little fandy iflands, which are low, and covered with fhrubs. The bafe of thefe iflands feems to be compofed of coral rock; over which the fea has accumulated heaps of fand and broken fhells. The reefs, extending from them very far into the bay, render the channels very dangerous to ftrangers. But the anchoring-grounds are very good in the interior parts, and capacious enough for five hundred fail of fhips. The largeft of thefe cayes is called Pigeon Ifland, from the flocks of pigeons, chiefly the bald-pate, which ufed to

frequent

frequent it formerly. On the Weſt part of the bay are, Weſt Harbour, Peake Bay, and Salt River; which are all of them commodious for ſhipping, and well-covered, either by the Ridge of Portland, or ſmall cayes; ſo that the water, where the ſhips lye to receive their loading, is generally ſmooth, and unaffected either by the wind or ſea.

The Promontory of Portland is about ten miles in length, and about two in breadth. The whole of it is extremely rocky, and contains only one ſmall ſpring. Nature has, in ſome degree, compenſated for this deficiency, by ſupplying in the ſhadier parts a great number of little baſons, or reſervoirs, formed in the cavities of rocks, and repleniſhed with rain-water; which prove of great ſervice to run-away Negroes harbouring in the woods. It has only four or five ſmall ſettlements upon it; and theſe are chiefly ſupported by the ſale of braſiletto, and ſome other valuable trees, that are found here in abundance. During the laſt war, a French privateer made a deſcent at Carliſle Bay, ſurprized two gentlemen of the pariſh, and carried them off to ſea. After having detained them for ſome time, the crew at length put them aſhore at Portland Point, with no other ſuſtenance than two or three biſcuits and a bottle of brandy. From this Point there is no road acroſs to the main land; ſo that they were obliged to keep along ſhore, for fear of loſing themſelves in the woods: but the fatigue of clambering over rocks, added to the heat and thirſt, was ſo extreme, that only one of them ſurvived this toilſome march, and returned to his family and friends; the other dropped by the way, and periſhed before any aſſiſtance could be given him. Such are too often the barbarous exploits of theſe licenſed rovers; which ſerve to aggravate the miſeries of war, by committing acts of inhumanity, from which no advantage can reſult, either to themſelves, or the ſtate that employs them! The range of hill which forms this promontory is divided, by a ſmall moraſs near the head of Salt River, from another range, called the Braſiletto Mountain, which extends Northerly into Clarendon. Theſe ridges, confining the pariſh on the South-eaſt, intercept the regular current of the ſea-breeze, and contribute to render the ſettlements Weſtward of them very hot.

The

The land on both fides the Minho in this parifh was once famous for the number of indigo works fettled upon it; all of which are now extinct. It is chiefly cultivated in canes: the almoft-level tract, which continues from the fea to the mountains of Clarendon, about fixteen miles in length, by about fourteen in width in the broadeft part (exclufive of the fugar-works), is chiefly employed in cattle and fheep paftures. The Weftern quarter of the parifh includes a range of high land called Carpenter's Mountains; on the Eaftern fide of which are fome few fettlements, but the greater part remains uninhabited: acrofs one of the higheft pitches, named May-day Hill, runs the Leeward road, by which, after paffing feveral miles of wood, we come to a good tavern, built here for the accommodation of travelers; this being the principal communication on the South fide between the windward and leeward parifhes. The air of thefe mountains is exeeedingly cool and healthy; and their foil in general very fertile; which may be judged from the ftately trees that grace each fide of the road. In fome part of thefe mountains (I do not vouch for the truth of the ftory) is faid to be a perpendicular chafm, the diameter of whofe mouth is only a few feet, and the depth of it unfathomable. The following fingular phænomenon is reported of it: that, alternately in the fpace of every twenty-four hours, it emits and inhales a ftrong body of air or vapour; and that if, at the time of the indraught, a fmall bird, or other light body, fhould be thrown within the vortex, it would be irrefiftibly drawn in, and never more make its appearance above ground. On the South of thefe mountains, the old road to Leeward paffes near the coaft from this parifh to Black River in St. Elizabeth; but it has been feldom ufed fince the track was formed acrofs May-day Hill, which is a much fafer and better way.

The low lands of Vere are, for the moft part, hot and parched; but the air is reckoned not unwholefome, except near the moraffes, which border on Peake Bay and Weft Harbour. Vere has long been famous for producing the fineft mutton, turkeys and other poultry, in the ifland; and with thefe it trafficks largely in the towns. It produces vaft annual crops of Guiney corn, and pulfe of various kinds, which form the chief part of fubfiftence for the

Negroes,

Negroes, and fmall ftock belonging to it. Near the Milk River is a hot falt-fpring, the waters of which, fome writers have not fcrupled to affirm, will coagulate the white of an egg: but this is extremely fabulous. The fpring, upon examination, was found very pellucid, but felt only milk-warm, and contained feveral little ftriped fifh of a fpecies fimilar to what are obferved in Salt River; which is an inconteftable proof, that the water is never in a ftate of ebullition. The principles of this water have not as yet been afcertained by any analyfis; but it is pretty evident, that the predominant falt is marine. It has proved very efficacious in cleanfing and healing foul ulcers, and removing cachectic fwellings of the legs and feet, externally applied.

This ifland contains the three different kinds of heights, diftinguifhed in Ireland by the words, *Knock*, fignifying an infulated hill, or one unconnected with any range; *Slieve*, a craggy mountain, gradually afcending, and continued in feveral ridges; and *Beinn*, a pinnacle, or mountain of the firft magnitude, rifing in the midft of a chain of high lands, and ending in a fharp, abrupt precipice. Of the firft fpecies, which fome authors have compared to eggs fet in falt, is the Round Hill in this parifh, formerly called by the Spaniards *Pan de Botillo*, about nine miles Weft from Carlifle, and two North from the fea. One of the like kind, refembling a fugar-loaf in its fhape, ftands near the fhore in St. David's. There are likewife feveral in Clarendon, and other parifhes.

Off the coaft there is a good fifhery; and fome marine animals, extremely curious and remarkable, have been hauled afhore here by the Negroes in their feines. Among the reft, a few years ago, a *Sierra Marina*, or fea-unicorn, was caught entangled in a net at the mouth of Swift River, and required fix ftout Negroes to drag it out of the water. It meafured, from the point of the fword to the tip of the tail, upwards of fourteen feet, and weighed near fourteen hundred pounds. Seventeen eggs, about the fize of a man's fift, were taken out of the belly; and, foon after it was brought upon the land, it difgorged fix young ones, of two feet length each, one of which, being put into the fea, fwam immediately away. From the liver were extracted about twelve gallons

of

of oil; and much more might have been obtained. The flesh was cut up into large pieces, and afforded a delicious repast to the Negroes that were employed in the capture.

The lower district of this parish, called Withywood, took its name from its having been formerly overspread with wood and withes when the English first settled upon it, and which grew so thick, that it was impossible to walk among them without a cutlass to clear the way. This is the part, which, on account of its rich soil, was afterwards filled with indigo and sugar-works, the opulence of whose owners is spoken of by several writers; and though it has been called in question by some, yet it is very certain, that more carriages of pleasure were at one time kept here, than in all the rest of the island, Spanish Town only excepted. It is, indeed, almost incredible to think what vast fortunes were made here by cultivation of this single commodity. When the act of parliament was passed with an intent to recover this branch of trade, the very art of making it was lost; few or no persons were then living in this part who were able to give instructions, and still fewer left to receive and follow them if any could have been given. The modern settlers had converted their lands into pasture, or the raising of cotton and corn; and could not be persuaded to give up a little certainty for a much greater probable advantage, where the instability of state-maxims threatened such a risque to the experimentors. The new law, which was merely temporary, instead of imposing a heavy tax, as the former law had done, allowed a small debenture in favour of every pound weight of indigo, the growth and manufacture of the British islands imported into England; yet it availed here but very little. None in this parish attempted to revive the culture of it. Three or four took it up in other parts of the island; and probably, if the law had been renewed after its expiration, with some additional bounty, it might have encouraged many more to try the effects of it.

For cattle and stock of all sorts, particularly horses and sheep, no parish in the island excels this, either in number or quality. The soil, except Main Savannah, which is a gravelly tract, and rather sterile in dry years, is of a fine brick-mould, and. were it not for the want of regular showers, it would be one of the most productive fpots in the Weft-Indies. From the fummits and fides of the hills, which almoft furround and overlook it, the appearance of it is inexpreffibly delightful, and refembling much fome of the richeft plains of England. The Round Hill before-noticed adds greatly to the elegance of the profpect; and it is enlivened every where with herds, flocks, fugar-mills, and other pleafing objects.

State of this Parifh:

	Negroes.	Cattle.	Sugar-works.	Annual Produce of Sugar.	
				Hogfheads.	Other Settlements.
1734,	3582	7194			
1740,	5370	8580			
1745,	5423	8870			
1761,	5663				
1768,	5940	7462	19	2100	131

This parifh appears to be on the decline in the article of cattle, of which it contains fourteen hundred lefs than in the year 1745; which has been owing to the laying wafte fome capital breeding penns, and the converfion of others into fugar-plantations.

S E C T. VIII.

St. M A R Y.

THIS parifh is bounded on the Eaft by St. George; Weft, by St. Anne; South, by St. Thomas in the Vale, and part of St. Andrew; and North, by that frith of the fea which feparates Cuba from this ifland. It is watered with twenty-four rivers, befides fmaller ftreams; the principal of which are the Sambre, the Nuevo, Bagnal's Waters, and Port Maria, Eafternmoft and Wefternmoft. Nearly the whole of this parifh is compofed of hill, mountain, dale, and valley. The coaft differs greatly from that of the South fide, being for the moft part iron-bound, or protected againft the fury of the North winds and furges of the fea with a wall of rocks. The foil too is different, being in general a ftiff clay on the higher grounds, and a confiderable depth of rich, black, vegetable mould in the lower. The foil is univerfally fertile; the hills and mountains

tains

tains cloathed with noble woods, full of the fineft and largeft timber-trees; and every fpot adapted to cultivation of almoft every
kind, except that the fummits of fome are thought too bleak and
chilly for the fugar-cane: this is therefore chiefly confined to the
vallies, and warmer flopes of the hills. The water is equal to
any in the world for purity and wholefomenefs; and the air is in
general extremely healthful, and agreeable to European conftitutions. About Orange River, and fome other parts of this parifh,
the quarry-ftones lie in layers, and are dug out in regular fquares,
of pretty even thicknefs, fo as to anfwer the mafon's purpofe with
very little trouble. They are of a light-brown, and yield to the
acid. The chief ports are Anotto Bay, Port Maria, Auracabeffa,
Saltgut, and Rio Nuevo; which are good anchoring-places, though
no fecurity to fhips in time of a hurricane, as they are all expofed
to the North.

Port Maria is famous for having given, as it is fuppofed, an
afylum to Columbus, when his fhip was near foundering with a
leak; and fomewhere hereabouts authors have placed the town of
Melilla, the firft which the Spaniards founded. Rio Nuevo is
likewife remarkable for the decifive victory gained there by general
D'Oyley over the Spaniards; which confirmed the Englifh
poffeffion of this ifland. The weather in this parifh is extremery
wet during great part of the year, and fo cold, that few if any of
the houfes are unfurnifhed with a chimney. Its chief productions
are fugar and rum, a little indigo, coffee, tobacco, and corn.
The land in general from its richnefs bears too luxuriant a cane:
I have feen fome here of enormous fize and length; but fuch are
unfit for making fugar, and are only ground for the ftill-houfe.
The great plenty of water and provifions are extremely favourable
to the breeding of hogs, of which there is great abundance; but
fheep and poultry do not thrive here fo well, owing to the ranknefs of the pafturage, and moifture of the atmofphere. This parifh,
having been frequently difturbed with infurrections of the Negroe
flaves belonging to it, has four barracks, at two of which there is
ufually a fmall cantonment of foldiers.

Fort Haldane, at Port Maria, ftands on an eminence commanding the entrance of the harbour, and is capable of making a good

defence.

defence. The barracks are large enough to receive fixty men. The quarters here have not proved healthy to the troops ; but the reafon, as I have been informed, is, that the men were fed too conftantly on falt provifions, which fometimes were of bad quality.

Auracabeffa has a battery, and barracks likewife for fixty men. The other barracks are, one on the Weft fide of Anotto Bay, at a place called Jack's Bay ; and one at Bagnals, near the Decoy.

The hamlets at Rio Nuevo, Port-Maria, and Saltgut, have from eight to twelve houfes each, inhabited principally by wharfingers, ftore and fhop-keepers. One of the greateft curiofities in this parifh is the Decoy, the feat of Sir Charles Price, bart. It is fituated on part of the range of mountains which border on St. Thomas in the Vale. The houfe is of wood, but well finifhed, and has in front a very fine piece of water, which in winter is commonly ftocked with wild-duck and teal. Behind it is a very elegant garden difpofed in walks, which are fhaded with the cocoanut, cabbage, and fand-box trees. The flower and kitchen-garden are filled with the moft beautiful and ufeful variety which Europe, or this climate, produces. It is decorated, befides, with fome pretty buildings ; of which the principal is an octagonal faloon, richly ornamented on the infide with luftres, and mirrors empanneled. At the termination of another walk is a grand triumphal arch, from which the profpect extends over the fine cultivated vale of Bagnals quite to the Northfide Sea. Clumps of graceful cabbage-trees are difperfed in different parts, to enliven the fcene ; and thoufands of plantane and other fruit-trees occupy a vaft tract, that environs this agreeable retreat, not many years ago a gloomy wildernefs.

The late Sir Charles [n] was extremely attached to this place, and fpent much of his time here, making it the abode of chearfulnefs

[n] This gentleman was a native of Jamaica, and endued with uncommon natural talents, which were improved by education, and polifhed by travel in the early part of his life. On his return to this ifland, his opulent fortune only ferved to make his abilities more confpicuous, and more ufeful to the community. Thefe eventually gave him the lead in public affairs. With an honeft loyalty to his fovereign, which none could furpafs, he poffeffed a truly patriotic attachment for his country ; and, though ever ready to affift and facilitate adminiftration, while conducted on the great principle of public good, he was always the fteady, perfevering, and intrepid opponent to illegal and pernicious meafures of governors. If it were at all neceffary to produce teftimonials

in

fulnefs and hofpitality: to thefe, the delightful air breathed here, and the amiable qualities of the owner of this paradife, mutually contributed. This, which I may juftly call the temple of focial enjoyments, was conftantly open to the reception of worthy men, whether of the ifland, or ftrangers: and few gentlemen of rank, whether of the army or navy, on fervice here, quitted the ifland without having paffed fome of their time at the Decoy. Among thefe was the unfortunate Mr. B—fc—n, a young officer in the fquadron, of the moft promifing abilities, and liberal accomplifh-ments; who, being on a vifit in the year 1769, went early one morning to bathe in the canal, and perifhed before affiftance could be given him. This fad accident was inexpreffibly afflicting to Sir Charles, and left fo ftrong an impreffion upon his mind, that, be-fore his own deceafe, he gave particular directions to inter his body clofe by his friend Mr. B—fc—n. The mountain on which the Decoy is fituated is a great height above the level of the fea, by fome fuppofed at leaft half a mile perpendicular. Upon digging into a marle pit here, was difcovered a vaft quantity of petrifac-tions, refembling the large conchites or cockles, or rather perhaps the efcallop kind, the edges being denticulated, but the outfide without any vifible remains of furrows, if they ever had any. I examined feveral, but could not perceive the fmalleft veftige of a teftaceous covering. They were perfectly folid maffes, hard as ftone, and compofed of very minute particles cemented together. It would be difficult to prove, that mere inert matter fhould fpon-taneoufly affume thefe regular forms, and apt imitations of marine

in juftification of this character, I might refer to the very honourable marks of approbation which were fo defervedly conferred upon him, both by the crown, and the different affemblies in which he prefided, for fo many years, as fpeaker, with an integrity, candour, and dignity, that were almoft unexampled. In private life, his complacency of manners, accomplifhed knowledge of books and men, and delicacy of humour, rendered him the polite, inftructive, and entertaining companion: here he fhone the inflexible lover of truth, the firm friend, and the generous patron. His mind was amply ftored with the treafures of liberal erudition. But theology feemed his favourite fci-ence; and the Great Author of nature, the chief object of his ftudy. Though qualified in all refpects to have made a refpectable figure on a more extenfive theatre, he preferred a refidence in this ifland; which as he enriched and embellifhed by the diffufion of his income, and tafte for improvements, fo he benefited by an inceffant attention to its welfare. Jamaica loft one of its beft friends, when he breathed his laft, which happened in June, 1772, after he had attained to a good old age. I fhall only add, that few men in any country have attracted more general veneration while living, or more general regret when dead.

2   fhells.

fhells. But it is almoft as difficult to difcover, by what means they were brought into a fituation at that height above the fea, and at fuch a diftance from it. Nature is faid to have done nothing in vain; but an original creation of fuch whimfical refemblances could anfwer no wife purpofe. This globe carries every prefumptive evidence of having undergone very extraordinary changes, and particularly by earthquakes; and, as we cannot tell by what imperceptible paffages the water of the ocean may permeate even below the bafe of iflands; fo we cannot pofitively deny, but it may force its way to a very confiderable elevation, in confequence of violent eruptions, which attend thefe commotions of the earth; carrying with it fhells and fand, and perhaps leaving maffes of falt depofited as it recedes, which may afterwards impregnate rivers, as we find in fome parts of the South fide of Jamaica. Doctor Brookes fpeaks rationally on this fubject: " We cannot," fays he, " determine " whether there has ever been an univerfal earthquake or not, " which has changed the primitive form of our world. However, " this is certain, that a great many fubftances, which feem to have " been proper only to the fea, are now found in the bowels of the " earth; and which have perhaps been petrified by degrees, by the " infinuation of water, falts, and exceeding fmall cryftalline or " ftony particles, proper to fill up their pores, without alteration " of their fhape. To this all the productions which fome have " looked upon as *lufus naturæ*, or fports of nature, are evidently " owing. Befides the bones of crocodiles, the fkeletons of fea- " horfes, the entire bodies of petrified fifh, there are almoft every " where found fea-fhells of all kinds, and all forts of the parts of " fea-animals, converted into ftone; fome very wonderful, with " regard to their fituation; and others, with regard to the oddnefs " of their fhapes." The petrifactions found at the Decoy feem to come neareft in fimilitude to Sir Hans Sloane's *Pecten Jamacienfis ftriis levibus,* Vol. II. fol. 256. N° I. which is frequent on the fhores of the ifland.

As the fettlement of this parifh was not entered upon heartily until about the year 1736, it may ftill be deemed in its infancy, and will no doubt invite new planters by degrees, as its wood-land comes to be cleared; for at prefent not one-fourth of it is brought

into

into cultivation. In the South-eaft angle of it is a Negroe town, called Scot's Hall, inhabited by a party of the Maroons, who came in upon terms.

On the road paffing from Guy's Hill to the Decoy is a quarry of black marble, with white veins. The rock appears confiderably above the level of the road in large maffes. It has never yet been worked, as it would probably anfwer little other purpofe in this country, except for making lime, or flabs for dining-apartments. The diftance from the fea renders the carriage difficult and too expenfive at prefent; but in time perhaps, when the roads are more improved, and this part of the ifland more populous, it may anfwer for exportation, either to Europe or North-America.

The State of St. Mary :

	Negroes.	Cattle.	Sugar-works.	Annual Produce.	
				Hogfheads.	Other Settlements.
1734,	2938	2182			
1740,	4484	2972			
1745,	5631	3304			
1761,	9318				
1768,	12159	7996	49	5500	56

This parifh is evidently improving faft. And we may venture to foretell, that the North fide, though labouring under the misfortune of being the laft-fettled, will in time become the moft populous, as it is naturally the healthieft divifion of the ifland. The foil, by reafon of its exceeding richnefs, does not make immediate good returns in fugar; but the proportion of rum is far greater than on the South fide; and the excellence of the land affures a permanent, and perhaps inexhauftible, fertility.

SECT. IX.

St. ANNE.

THE parifh of St. Anne is bounded on the Eaft by St. Mary; on the Weft, by St. James; South, by Clarendon and St. Thomas in the Vale; and North, by the fea. It is watered with twelve rivers,

rivers, the principal of which are Rio Rueno, St. Anne's Great-River, Roaring and White Rivers. Its ports are St. Anne's Bay, Dry Harbour [o], Rio Bueno, Ocho Rios, and Runaway Bay. At the former of these was the town of Sevilla Nueva. The bay of St. Anne is defended by a reef of rocks, which stretches almost across its entrance, leaving only one small channel for the ships to go in or out. This barrier so effectually breaks the surge of the sea, that the bason in which the ships lie at anchor is at all times perfectly smooth: it is likewise sheltered by two points of land, projecting on each side the bay like the horns of a crescent. The drift of the waves being towards the Westward, they form a current over the breakers which are lowest on that side of the bay. This current sweeps through the harbour with a direction towards the ship-channel, which is on the Eastern side; whence it happens, that, when the sea-breeze blows, which gives the water this direction, the vessels at anchor here ride with their sterns to the wind.

The harbour is deep, insomuch that the largest ships that load here with sugars, lay their broad-side close to the wharf, which is not many feet in length. It is defended by a battery of twelve embrazures; and at a small distance are the barracks, elegantly built, in which a company of regulars are stationed. The town of St. Anne consists of about thirty or forty houses, straggling along the beach, and chiefly inhabited by shop-keepers. On the West side of the bay is the parish-church, a very handsome building. The harbour has somewhat the appearance of the letter E capital, placed horizontally thus ⌣⌣⌣, the coast projecting into the centre of it, and making a semi-circular sweep on each side. Sevilla Nueva was built upon an easy eminence, rising from this centre. The situation is extremely delightful. By the projection of the land, it commands a very fine and extensive view of the country for many miles to the East and West, bounded by distant moun-

[o] This place has lately commenced a trading port, and some houses are erected at it as the *exordia* of a future town. This will probably succeed, in consequence of a road now forming from it to Cave River, in Clarendon, the distance twenty miles, about fourteen of which extend over a woody, uncultivated district. The road, when compleated, will doubtless contribute to the speedy settlement of this tract of country, and has the peculiar merit of opening a communication through these almost unoccupied parts, without crossing one river.

tains,

tains, and having the bay, buildings, shipping, and sea in front. From hence, as well as other elevated spots on the North side, some of the high lands in Cuba, called the Copper Mountains, are frequently discerned at one hundred miles distance in the months of October and November, and during some of the succeeding months. They appear of an azure cast to the eye, like the Blue Mountains; and the sight of them is esteemed a certain prognostic of approaching North winds, which usually set in about that time of the year. Several rivulets fall into this bay; and close adjoining to the spot where Seville once stood is a fine quarry of white free-stone, which is soft when first dug up, but hardens after exposure to the air. A place could not have been more happily selected than this by the Spaniards for building a town. Here was plenty of excellent materials for architecture, abundance of good water, a fertile soil in the neighbourhood, the woods filled with the greatest variety of large and valuable timber-trees, the sea and rivers stored with innumerable fish, a safe and spacious port, and the distance not remote from their island of Cuba. With all these advantages of situation and a fine air they abandoned it, because the Southside ports were more convenient for the galleons and other transient vessels passing between St. Domingo and Carthagena; and their traffic was chiefly confined to the supplying these visitors with provisions, and a few other necessaries.

It is not to be doubted, but that under the genius of Peter Martir, who was abbot of the collegiate church founded here, the public buildings would have risen with an elegance unusual in the new world. Several fragments of carved work in stone, such as mouldings, festoons, cherubs, &c. are still to be seen here, that would be thought no mean ornaments in an European church. The ruins of two edifices, one said to have been a castle, the other dedicated to religious use (probably the collegiate church), are still remaining; the walls of which are several feet in thickness, and compacted with an exceedingly hard cement. It is the property of the lime made from the shell-marble, so common in this island, to contract with age all the closeness and solidity of stone; and I have seen some plaister taken from an old Spanish tank, or cistern, which could scarcely be broken with an hammer. The battery which defends

fends the port is conftructed with materials taken from thefe venerable fabrics, and ftands in the place of an ecclefiaftical fanctuary. The poffeffion of this city fell to the fhare of captain Heming, an officer in the Oliverian army fent hither; and his pofterity ftill enjoy it.

The caftle and church, being almoft half a mile afunder, may give us fome idea of the intended extent and grandeur of this place; but, the old walls before-mentioned being every day diminifhed, for the fake of the materials which are ufed in repairing the buildings on the eftate, it is probable that in a few years more there will be fcarcely any veftige left of this celebrated city. But the ground about the church being fuppofed confecrated, is ftill preferved as a burial place. As for the ruins of the caftle, they are not only leveled to, but confiderably funk below, the prefent furface of the earth. In the year 1764 were dug up two pilafters of about feven feet length, of no particular order, but fomewhat refembling the Ionic. They appeared to have belonged to the portal, or veftibule, of fome large building, as there were alfo feveral concave ftones proper for an arched roof. Upon thefe pilafters were fome rude carvings in *alto. relievo.* Four or five coarfe images were likewife found; one of which refembled a fphynx; another, an alligator; and the reft were creatures of the mafon's fancy. The manfion-houfe on this eftate ftands on the fummit of a rifing lawn, nearly equidiftant from the fea and the mountains; a fituation which makes it both healthy and agreeable. Before the front of it is a battery of eighteen fmall guns *en barbette*; which is intended as a protection to the eftate, and to the harbour itfelf in war-time againft privateers. The garden on the Eaft fide of the houfe is prettily laid out; and decorated with a ftone-temple, elegantly defigned in the modern tafte.

The Spanifh habitations have long ago been demolifhed, and the ground whereon they ftood converted into cane-fields; but, in turning up the foil for planting, the old rubbifh continually makes its appearance, and contributes to render it lefs fertile. The ruins were more perfect in Sir Hans Sloan's time, who vifited them in 1688, and has left us the following account:

" The

" The church was not finished. It was twenty paces broad, and thirty long. There were two rows of pillars within; and over the place where the altar was intended were some carvings under the ends of the arches. The houses and foundations stand for several miles along (these were probably the houses of detached settlements, not of the streets). Captain Heming said, he sometimes found pavements under his canes three feet covered with earth, several wells, and burial-stones finely cut. There are the beginnings of a great house called a monastery; but I suppose the house was designed for the governor. There were two coats of arms lay by, not set up; a ducal one; and that of a count; belonging I suppose to the family of Columbus, proprietors of the island. There had been raised a tower, part brick, part hewn stone, as also several battlements on it; and other lower buildings unfinished. At the church lie several arched stones, to compleat it; which had never been put up, but are lodged among the canes. The rows of pillars within were for the most part unornamented. It was thought, that in the time of the Spaniards the Europeans had been cut off by the Indians; and so the church left uncompleated. When the English took the island, the ruins of this city were so overgrown with wood, that they were all turned black. Nay, I saw a mammee, or bastard mammee-tree, growing within the walls of the tower, so high as that it must have been a very large gun to kill a bird on the top of it; and the trunks of many of the trees, when felled from this place, to make room for the sugar-canes, were sixty feet or more in length. A great many wells are on this ground. The West gate of the church was of very fine work, and stands entire. It is seven feet wide, and as high to the spring of the arch. Over the door, in the centre, is our Saviour's head, with a crown of thorns, between two angels; on the right side, a small round figure of some saint, with a knife struck into his head; and on the left, a madona, her arm tied in three places after the Spanish fashion. Over the gate, and beneath a coat of arms, was this inscription :

PETRVS.

PETRVS. MARTIR. AB. ANGLERIA. ITALVS. CIVIS. MEDIOLANEN.
PROTHON. APOS. HVJVS. INSVLE. ABBAS. SENATVS. INDICI.
CONSILIARIVS. LIGNEAM. PRIVS. ÆDEM. HANC. BIS. IGNE.
CONSVMPTAM. LATERICIO. ET. QVADRATO. LAPIDE. PRIMVS.
A. FVNDAMENTIS. EXTRVXIT [*p*].

These words are entire, except *Mediolanensis*, which I have supplied
(says Sir Hans), because this Peter Martir, a famous man, wrote
himself " of Milan." He was author of the Decads, Epistles, and
some other books; which gave him great reputation in the world."

There is at this time in St. Domingo, as I am credibly informed,
a Spanish lady, of an old family, who takes her title from this
place, by the stile of Countess de Sevilla Nueva, in Jamaica.

The hamlets at Laughlands and Runaway Bay are too insignificant to merit description. At the former a chapel of ease was
erected some years ago; but it is at present in a ruinous condition,
and is only used for holding elections for the parish-representatives.
Between this and the Bay is Richmond, belonging to Mr. P——k.
This estate is graced with a very elegant mansion, consisting of
two stories. It is surrounded with a spacious piazza, supported by
columns of the Ionic order; at the four angles are pavilions, with
Venetian windows corresponding to each other. The only fault
belonging to this house is in point of situation; for it stands upon a
dead flat; but, being considerably raised from the foundation, it is
dry and healthy. Adjoining is a pleasant lawn, or paddock, fenced
with Chinese railing, skirted with a gravel-walk, and ornamented
with rows of cocoa-trees. The great road to St. James runs parallel to the North front, at the distance of about two hundred
yards: the passage from hence to the house leads through a pair of
handsome gates along a spacious gravel-walk. Immediately across
the road, and opposite to the same front, is a large pleasure-garden,
neatly laid out in walks, and stocked with a variety of flowers and
flowering-shrubs; of which the chief are, the English, Spanish,
and Arabian jasmines; balsams, Indian arrow, capsicums, sun-
flowers, French marigolds, jalap or four o'clock, coffee-bushes,

[*p*] In English: " Peter Martir, of Anghiera, an Italian, citizen of Milan, chief missionary,
" and abbot of this island, member of the council of the Indies, first raised from its foundation,
" with brick and squared stone, this edifice, which formerly was built of wood, and twice destroyed
" t y fire."

South-fea rofe, Barbadoes pride, Jerufalem thorn, pomegranate, paffion flower, phyfic nut, and many others. In the centre is a fountain ; and in another part a large labyrinth, inclofed principally with the wild olive, and furnifhed with commodious feats. The town of St. Anne carries on fome trade, chiefly for mules and cattle, with the Cuba Spaniards, who run over in one night's time in very fmall veffels, and not feldom in open boats. This pedling intercourfe has been productive of a very fignal mifchief, which has chiefly affected this parifh. The Negroes here, either perceiving the facility of this paffage, or (which is moft probable) inveigled by the flattering affurances of thefe ftrolling Spanifh traders, who for the greater part are a thievifh race, have taken every opportunity to defert in canoes, and withdraw to Cuba, in hopes of obtaining their freedom : fo that feveral hundreds have, within a few years paft, decamped from this and other parts of the North fide, to the great lofs of the planters. Thefe Spaniards, upon many occafions, have lain under fufpicion of not merely inveigling the Blacks with fair fpeeches, but even taking them away by force. This, indeed, has been a very old practice of theirs, and, for want of an authoritative check, is now become fo habitual, that they ufe as little ceremony in fupplying themfelves from Jamaica by thefe means, as the Portugueze and Hollanders formerly ufed towards the natives of Guiney. In the year 1719, the then governor of Jamaica fent the captain of a frigate to the alcaldes, or chief officers of Trinidado, a town in Cuba, demanding reftitution of feveral Negroes, piratically taken from the ifland. But the officers returned for anfwer, " that, as to thofe and other fugitives, " they were there as the other fubjects of their lord the king, and, " being brought voluntarily to their holy church, had received " the water of baptifm." The conclufion follows of courfe ; that, being thus adopted into the Roman Catholic faith, in virtue of the mere ceremonial of their baptifm, though without the leaft knowledge of their new religion, or the grounds or nature of their faith, they could not return, to mingle again with heretics, without peril to their immortal fouls. Such is the pretext by which thefe rogues, under the cobweb veil of their religion, detain the property of Britifh fubjects. It will not be difputed, but that the

induftry

induſtry and labour of ſo many uſeful hands, transferred by this fraudulent mode of conveyance to a foreign ſtate, are more than a loſs to their owners; they are a loſs to the whole Britiſh community. The governors of Jamaica have not been wanting to lend every aſſiſtance in their power towards recovery of theſe fugitives, or rather ſtolen goods, by ſending requiſitorial letters to the Spaniſh commanders; but with ſo little effect, that ſome Britiſh frigates, which ſince the late peace were ſent with theſe diſpatches to the Havannah and other Spaniſh ports, were ſhot at from their forts, and ordered to depart without coming to an anchor. Our flag was inſulted, but no redreſs given. Expoſtulations on this head have been made, as I have heard, to as little purpoſe in Europe. The alcaldes here, like thoſe of America, are equally bigots when the cant of religious ſophiſtry is required to ſanctify baſe actions.

A Negroe, flying from our colony to Cuba, or kidnapped thither, becomes the property of the Spaniſh crown, that is, of a Spaniſh alcalde. The ſtupid, illiterate wretch is preſently admitted into the boſom of holy mother-church, and ſtraight becomes a *bueno catholico*, and a Spaniſh ſubject. He continues, however, in a ſtate of ſervitude, and earns a weekly ſum for his maſter, who muſt pay a certain proportion of it into the royal coffers, or give him up to labour on the fortifications, until the confederate gang of Negroes there can make up a purſe for him. He then goes before another of theſe officers, and intimates that he has wherewithal to purchaſe his freedom. The owner is ſummoned; and, the ſum being fixed at a certain moderate rate, his maſter is obliged to take the money, and grant a manumiſſion. By this eaſy method, theſe deſerters ſoon acquire their freedom, and with very little pains are able, by cultivating tobacco, breeding poultry and hogs, making chip-hats, ſegars, and other trifling articles, to earn a comfortable livelihood among ſuch a ſet of haughty and indolent beings, who ſcorn to ſully their noble hands with vulgar occupations. Such being the encouragements held out to our Negroes, and the paſſage ſo eaſily made, it is only aſtoniſhing that the defection is not greater. It may be urged, that our Negroes, having once taſted the ſweets of ſo eaſy a life, and fraught with the moſt pernicious ſuperſtitions [q], would be uſeleſs, if not dangerous, if they

[q] For example, " that it is meritorious to kill heretics."

were reftored again to the ifland. This I ferioufly believe, but it is no argument to juftify the detainers of them; for, furely, if they had principle enough to do what the laws of nations, of juftice, and common honefty, require, they would either re-deliver the perfons of thefe Negroes, or a pecuniary indemnification; they themfelves not beftowing a *gratis* freedom to thefe poor people, but felling it to them for a valuable confideration, exacted in money, a part of which booty their illuftrious fovereign (or I am misinformed) difdains not to participate. What are we to think of a fociety of men, who are capable of committing fuch pious frauds under the mafk of pretended righteoufnefs! The very fame pretence might be brought by a highwayman, or pick-pocket, to juftify their malefactions. It is flagrant robbery, a breach of good faith between the two nations, and ought to be anfwered with reprifals to make good the damages fuftained by the plundered parties. The fovereign of Great-Britain holds an intereft in all the Negroes poffeffed by his colony-fubjects; for his revenue is very greatly benefited and fupported by the produce of their perfonal labour. The nation at large holds an intereft in them by the number of manufacturers fet to work; by the fhipping and mariners; by the articles neceffary to cloathe, feed, and employ thefe labourers; and by their general confumption of Britifh merchandizes. Hence, in every refpect, this grievance feems to rife into a national concern, and to deferve a powerful national interpofition, that fuch acts of perfidy and injuftice may ceafe for the future. That fome judgement may be formed of the height of infolence to which the Spaniards have carried their pretenfions, I muft not omit to mention that, fo recently as the year 1768, the affembly of the ifland addreffed his majefty; fetting forth, that numbers of their flaves were actually detained and employed in the fervice of the Catholic king, or his fubjects; and that, application having been made to the governor of St. Jago in Cuba for the delivery of fome of thofe flaves, he declared, " that although he knew many Negroes were at that " place, who had made their elopement from Jamaica, yet he " would not deliver them up; having received orders from the " court of Spain, injoining, that all Negroes coming thither from " the Britifh iflands, in what manner foever, fhould be employed

" in

" in his Catholic majefty's fervice, until further inftruttions fhould
" be given concerning them."

There needs no ftronger proof to fhew, that this thievifh practice,
fo repugnant to the good faith that ought to fubfift between two
nations in amity, fo deftructive of the Britifh commerce, fo inconfiftent with the rules of honefty, that, if it occurred between two
private individuals, the offender would juftly be deemed a felon;
there needs, I fay, no fuller evidence, that this difhonourable policy is countenanced, avowed, and defended, by the Spanifh government. It is plain, that his Catholic majefty's inftructions are
directly leveled againft all the Britifh colonies: no mention is made
of any other; and probably none other are included in them. We
may likewife obferve the latitude of the words: " coming in what
" manner foever;" under the implication of which are certainly
meant, not only thofe who voluntarily defert or run away, but all
others who are either trepanned, or violently brought away, by his
own Spanifh fubjects: and thefe Negroes are to be employed immediately in the king's fervice. Whence it is plain, that every
Spaniard muft efteem this as an encouragement to him; nay, he
muft think he performs his duty to his fovereign, as a zealous fubject ought to do, in taking all opportunities, that happen within
his power, to inveigle and fteal away Negroes from the Britifh
planters, for the benefit of his monarch's fervice. Unhappily, Jamaica lies more convenient in its fituation, than any other, for favouring thefe depredations. One would think, that fo peremptory
an avowal of what is apparently unjuftifiable in itfelf would be
fufficient to alarm a Britifh miniftry, and lead them at leaft to reflect, that the emigration of all the Negroes from Jamaica to Cuba
is at leaft *poffible*; more efpecially, as the Spaniards boldly affert their
intentions to get poffeffion of them by all poffible ways and means;
and that, after they have feduced, or ftolen away, thefe Negroes,
or only the major part of them, they will have much lefs difficulty
in gaining poffeffion of the ifland itfelf; which is an object that, we
have juft apprehenfion for believing, they have all along held in
view. If, indeed, they fhould be fuccefsful enough in difpeopling
it of the Negroes, we need not hefitate to let them take the land
into the bargain. I have heard the number of them purloined from

the

the ifland, or that have eloped and been detained in a few years paft, computed at eight hundred; the value of which, that is, the actual lofs to their owners, at the loweft calculation, cannot be rated at lefs than 40,000 *l.* Jamaica money. Had they taken a loaded fhip from us of half that value, the whole body of merchants would have rung the alarm, and the clamours of the nation would have fpeedily reached the cabinet at Madrid. Why the injury done to our planters has been lefs held in eftimation, why no redrefs has been obtained for them, for their paft loffes, nor fecurity againft the future, notwithftanding this affair has been ftrenuoufly reprefented, I am unable to difcover. Our Britifh courts of juftice, adopting the principle of Gronovius, inform us, that a Negroe, coming from one of our own colonies into Great-Britain, in what manner foever, becomes inftantly difcharged from the fervice of his owner. Perhaps a Spanifh Gronovius has been found, to affert the propriety of this kidnapping by the like rule of, " *Servus pere-* " *grinus, fimul atque terram Hifpanicam tetigerit, eodem momento* " *liber fiat;*" under this referve, however, that he is free only *quoad* his Britifh owner, but not fo *quoad* the king of Jerufalem [*r*].

But, to have done with a fubjeƈt on which perhaps I may be thought to have faid too much, I return to the parifh of St. Anne. From White River to Rio Bueno, its Eaftern and Weftern boundaries, there is a continued pretty level ground, for about twenty-four miles in length, along the coaft, extending in breadth in few places more than one mile to the foot of the hills, which rife gra-

---

[*r*] It is probable, that the ecclefiaftics derive fome pecuniary benefit from this praƈtice, as it conforms to fome of the Romifh doƈtrines; agreeably to the true fpirit of which, that canon was injoined by the pope to the bifhop of Worcefter, in the year 1497, viz. " that a man fhould be " permitted to retain the property of another perfon, by what method foever he had feized or ac- " quired it, provided he gave a certain portion thereof to the pope's commiffaries, or fubftitutes." Irenæus was the firft who broached this infamous tenet, in his argument to juftify the Ifraelites for having robbed the Egyptians of their plate and jewels. The ftale pretext of the Spaniards, founded on their zeal in the caufe of holy mother-church, and the tenor of the royal cedula, feem to correfpond exaƈtly with the fame abominable principle, and encourage the Negroes of our iflands to rob their mafters, and defert to them; who maintain, that, if a fhare of the plunder be but given to their church, the converfion from paganifm to their faith is fufficient of itfelf to extenuate all preceding crimes. Such pofitions are fuitable only to a community of thieves, or to the deluded votaries of fuch a religion. They may apply to themfelves and their difciples, with great propriety, the words of a French gentleman, mentioned by Lord Orrery: *Pour vous dire la verité, nous fommes tous des bon catholiques; mais pour la religion, nous n'en avons point.* " To fay the truth, " we are all good catholics; but, as for religion, we have none."

dually to very high mountains. This tract between the hills and the coaft is, for the moft part, a fhallow *ftratum* of mould upon a white, hot marle. Here are the fugar-plantations, which with good management bear moderate crops; but the canes in general are fhort-jointed, and, this part of the parifh being fubject to drowths (the high lands behind drawing off the rain), are often ftunted in their growth; for the foil in which they are planted is naturally fo dry and warm, as to require plentiful and frequent irrigations. Moft of the rivers here take their fource fo high, that their water might eafily be difperfed in channels through the cane-pieces. Some of the proprietors, I am informed, have lately had this in contemplation; and it would doubtlefs anfwer perfectly well. The hills contain but very few fugar-works. The mould here is extremely fuperficial; and underneath lies a deep vein of a white marle, or hard chalk. The pimento loves this kind of foil; and vaft woods of it overfpread the hills to a great diftance from the coaft. Behind this range of hills and mountains the land is diverfified with open, level favannahs, environed by rocky eminences, or with little cock-pits. The foil of the latter is cultivated fuccefsfully with Guiney grafs. The favannahs are covered with fern, and applied to no ufe. There are three principal mountain-roads which enter this parifh from the South fide. The road by *Monte Diablo*, in Sixteen-mile-walk, leads into it on the South-Eaft part, and is a mere avenue cut through the woods, there not being more than four or five fettlements on the whole road. About five miles from *Monte Diablo* is the Rio Hoja, which, running about a mile and half from its firft fpring, difcharges itfelf into a large lake of immenfe depth. Some have affigned this as the fource of the Cobre; which is not improbable, as the river-head and this body of water lie in exact meridian, North and South. The next road penetrates the centre of the parifh, by way of Old Woman's Savannah, in Clarendon, through the fettlements of Pedro, of which I have before given an account; and their number fcattered on each fide renders this by far the pleafanteft way. After leaving thefe fettlements about two miles, we come to a ftupendous hill of folid rock, perfectly bare, and unadorned with either plants or herbage. From this ftupendous mafs, to the neareft fet-

tlement

tlement on the North fide of the parifh, is about two miles further. The third road enters the Weft quarter of the parifh, by way of Clarendon. After running about five miles before it reaches any fettlement, it branches into two forks; one of which paffes on to Runaway Bay; the other, to Dry Harbour. From the entrance, by Clarendon, to the range of hills near the coaft of St. Anne, is about twelve miles; the road is enlivened with a very few human habitations, and thofe fcattered. This tract, from its being fo little inhabited, was called Siberia: yet it is not in other refpects deferving that appellation; for it is full of excellent timber, and furnifhes a vaft quantity of mahogany every year, the vifitors of this part being chiefly cutters. The diftrict of the parifh, interfected by thefe three avenues, comprehends near one hundred and eighty thoufand acres, as yet unfettled. In fo vaft a fpace there muft needs be a very great variety of foil, and numberlefs fpots of very fine cultivable land. But, exclufive of a few fern favannahs, the whole of it is in its primitive foreft, full of large cedar, mahogany, and other valuable timber-trees. The foil, over which the roads pafs, is in general a reddifh fat clay, intermixed with mould, or a black-fhell mould; and, fo far as fettlements are formed, it is experienced to be exceedingly fertile, being refrefhed with conftant dews and frequent fhowers. The rain does not defcend here in fuch violent ftreams as in the low country, but for the moft part in a fine fpray or drizzle; and the air is, during the whole year, cool, temperate, and perfectly healthful. Here then appears a defireable field for introducing new colonies of induftrious people; as a leading meafure to which, fome new roads are required, to penetrate through this defart tract, and open a communication with the parts already fettled. The air of the coaft is hot, and in general tolerably healthful.

Near Ocho Rios, or, as it is now more commonly called, Chereiras Bay, in this parifh, the road from St. Mary paffes through Walter's plantation to the Weftward, up a fteep hill. This road, having been gullied very much about eleven years ago, by a heavy fall of rain in October, the fkeleton of an Indian was laid bare to view, about five feet below the furface. The foil here is a white coarfe marle, which certainly did not poffefs the corrofive qualities

of

of lime in its compofition; for the bones were perfectly found and firm. The fkull appeared preternaturally compreffed at top, which made the *finciput* very low. There was fome appearance of a cut on the occipital bone, as if made with a fharp weapon. By the fize of the bones, they were conjectured to have belonged to a man of large ftature. At the head and feet lay two unglazed earthen pots, fhaped fomewhat like a canoe, and well wrought; one of them was broken in taking it out; but the other was preferved intire, and found to contain a fmall quantity of black earth, refembling foot. The body had probably been interred not lefs than two hundred years.

This parifh contains two remarkable cafcades. The leffer is formed by a branch of Rio Alto, which is fuppofed to re-emerge (after a fubterraneous current of feveral miles) between Roaring River Plantation and Menzie's Bog. The hills in this part are many of them compofed of a ftalactite matter; by whofe eafy folution, the waters, oozing through the rocks, are copioufly charged with it, fo that they incruftate all bodies depofited in them. This river rifes at a confiderable elevation above the fea's level, and at a great diftance from the coaft, and continues its courfe between the hills fucceffively broad or contracted, as they on each fide approach nearer, or recede further from, one another. In one of the more extended fpaces, it expands its water in a gentle defcent among a very curious group of anchovy pear-trees, whofe fpreading roots intercept the fhallow ftream in a multitude of different directions. The water, thus retarded, depofits its groffer contents, which in length of time have formed various incruftations, around as many cifterns, fpread in beautiful ranks, gradually rifing one above another, and bearing no ill refemblance to a magnificent flight of fteps in ruftic work, leading up to the enchanted palace of fome puiffant giant of romance. A fheet of water, tranfparent as cryftal, conforming to the bend of the fteps, overfpreads their furface; and, as the rays of light, or fun-fhine, play between the waving branches of the trees, it defcends glittering with a thoufand variegated tints. The incruftation in many parts is folid enough to bear the weight of a man; in others it is fo thin, that fome perfons, whofe curiofity led them to venture too far, have fuddenly found themfelves plunged up to the middle in a cold refervoir.

VIEW OF THE ROARING RIVER CASCADE.

J. Allan Pinxt

P. Mazell Sculp.

voir. Thefe accidents give it ftill more the appearance of a Fairy region. The cifterns, or refervoirs, have their fides formed by broken boughs and limbs, incrufted over and fuftained by the trunks of trees, promifcuoufly growing between them. The cifterns themfelves are always brim-full of water, which trickles from one to the other; and, although feveral of them are fix or feven feet deep, one may clearly difcern whatever lies at the bottom. The *lamina* which envelope them are in general near half an inch in thicknefs. To a fuperficial obferver their fides have the appearance of ftone; but, upon breaking any of them, there appears either a bough between the two incrufting coats, or a vacant fpace, which a bough has once filled, and by the mouldering of which in length of time a cavity has been left.

On opening feveral of thefe incruftations, not only boughs were found, but entire leaves of a muddy-green hue. Whence it may be conjectured, that a fhell, fomewhat thicker than that of an egg, may be concreted by this water in lefs than a twelvemonth.

The incrufting matter is foluble in the vinous acid, and when diffolved acquires a deep-black colour, much fimilar to what the vegetable aftringents ftrike with a chalybeate.

As the remarkable quality, refident in this water, feems not confined in its effects to any particular fubftance, it might be no unpleafant experiment to immerfe the ftuffed fkin of any animal for a fufficient time in it; fince it is probable, that the workmanfhip of nature would furpafs the happieft productions of the chiffel, and furnifh the moft animated and durable reprefentations by this eafy and unexpenfive method.

After dancing over thefe innumerable cifterns, the pellucid element forms itfelf into one or two ftreams; which afterwards, collecting other neighbouring rivulets, compofe feveral leffer, moft beautiful, falls. But defcription fails in attempting to convey any competent idea of its feveral beauties.

The other, or great cafcade, more properly a cataract, is formed by the White River, which is of confiderable magnitude, and, after a courfe of about twelve miles among the mountains, precipitates in a fall of about three hundred feet or more, obliquely meafured, with fuch a hoarfe and thundering noife, as to be heard

at

at a great diftance. Viewed from below, the Ajutage [s] appears to be a body of water, of fmall bulk, iffuing between a tuft of wood; but, as it continues its defcent, the breadth gradually increafes, until it reaches the bottom, where it forms a beautiful circular ba-fon, and then flows away in a ferpentine courfe towards the fea. Through the whole defcent it is broken and interrupted by a re-gular climax of fteps, of a ftalactic matter, incrufted over a kind of foft chalky ftone, which yields eafily to the chiffel. So vaft a difcharge of water, thus wildly agitated by the fteepnefs of the fall, dafhing and foaming from ftep to ftep, with all the impetuofity and rage peculiar to this element, exhibits an aweful, pleafing fcene. But the grandeur of it is aftonifhingly heightened by the frefh fup-plies which it receives after the rainy-feafons. At fuch times, the roaring of the flood, reverberated from the adjacent rocks, trees, and hills; the tumultuous violence of the torrent, tumbling head-long with refiftlefs fury; and the gloom of the over-hanging wood, contrafted with the foft ferenity of the fky, the filvery glitter of the fpray, the flight of birds fkimming over the lofty fummit of the mountain, and the placid furface of the bafon below; form, all to-gether, an affemblage of fubjects, the moft happily mingled, and beyond the power of painting to exprefs.

" Wide o'er the brim, with many a torrent fwell'd,
" And the mix'd ruin of its banks o'er-fpread;
" At laft the rous'd-up river pours along,
" Refiftlefs! roaring! dreadful!—Down it comes
" From the rude mountain, and the moffy wild,
" Tumbling through rocks abrupt, and founding far:—
" Then o'er the fanded valley floating fpreads,
" Calm; fluggifh; filent;—till again, conftrain'd
" Between two meeting crags, it burfts away,
" Where rocks and woods o'er-hang the turbid ftream.
" There gathering triple force, rapid and deep,
" It boils! and wheels! and foams! and thunders through!"
THOMPSON.

A beautiful intermixture of tall and ftately trees rifes gracefully from the margin on either fide; whofe bark and foliage are diverfi-

[s] See Plate V.

fied

Isaac Taylor sculp.

A View of the White River Cascade.

Published as the Act directs June 1. 1774.

fied with a variety of the lovelieft tints.   And, to complete the
picture, the bafon is ornamented with two elegant trees of the
palm kind, which fpring like ftrait columns out of the water,
placed by the hand of nature at fuch even diftance from the banks
on each fide, that art could not have done the work with more
attention to propriety and exactnefs.   The whole, indeed, has been
executed by nature in a tafte that furpaffes either defcription or imitation.   The late Sir Charles P——e, within whofe territory it lay,
would not fuffer the leaft alterations to be made to it, although fome
of the fteps might eafily be cut fo as to be rectilineal.   He preferred its natural beauties; and, in order to enjoy them, formed a
club of gentlemen, and built a range of apartments on a pretty
lawn juft fronting the cafcade.   Here they had an annual meeting,
which continued fome weeks; during which, they took the diverfion of fhooting the ring-tail pidgeons, which in this part of the
country are very numerous, and in great perfection at the proper
feafon.   If the leffer cafcade is delicate and curious, this is grand
and fublime.   The former is contemplated with delight, and this
with a pleafing and reverential wonder.   The fall is faid to exceed
in grandeur that of Tivoli, or any other in Europe, though much
inferior to that of Niagara.

The grotto in this parifh, near Dry Harbour, and about fourteen miles Weft from St. Anne's Bay, is fituated at the foot of a
rocky hill, under which it runs for a confiderable way, and then
branches into feveral adits, fome of which penetrate fo far, that no
perfon has yet ventured to difcover their ending.   The front is extremely Gothic in its appearance.   It is the perpendicular face of a
rock, having two arched entrances about twenty feet afunder,
which look as if they had anciently been door-ways, but funk by
time or accident to within two or three feet of their lintels.   In
the centre of the rock, between thefe portals, is a natural niche,
about four feet in height, and as many from the ground, which
might well be fuppofed intended for the reception of a madona, efpecially as at the foot of it is a fmall excavation, or bafon, projected a little beyond the face of the rock; which feems a very proper refervoir for holy water.   Excited by the accounts I had heard
of this celebrated curiofity, I made one among a party to vifit it.

After

After providing ourselves with several bundles of candlewood, split in small pieces, we crept on our hands and knees under the larger of the two apertures in the front of the rock, and immediately found ourselves in a circular vestibule, of about eighteen feet diameter, and fourteen in height. The cieling (an irregular concave), as well as the sides, was covered with stalactic and sparry matter, interspersed with innumerable glistening particles, which, reflecting the light of our torches from their polished surface, exhibited the most rich and splendid appearance imaginable.

This roof seemed to be supported by several columns of the same matter, concreted by length of time; whose chaptrels, and the angular arches above, appeared in the true Gothic taste. The pillars surrounded the vestibule; the open spaces between them led into avenues which diverged away into different parts of this subterraneous labyrinth. On one side we observed a rock, which, by the continual dripping of water upon it from the cieling, was covered with an incrustation, and bore a very striking resemblance of some venerable old hermit, sitting in profound meditation, wrapped in a flowing robe, his arms folded, and a beard descending to his waist. The head appeared bald, and the forehead wrinkled with age. Nothing was wanted to complete the figure, except the addition of features, which we immediately supplied, in the theatric manner, with a piece of charcoal. The graceful, easy folds and plaits of the drapery, and the wavy flow of the beard, were remarkably well expressed. Roubilliac, the rival of nature, could not have executed them in a more finished and masterly style. After we had sufficiently contemplated this reverend personage, we pursued our route through one of the largest adits. We found the passage every where of good height, in general from twelve to fifteen feet; but so totally excluded from day-light, that the gloom, together with the hollow sound of our trampling, and dismal echo of our voices, recalled to our minds the well-imagined description of Æneas's descent into the infernal regions. And this idea so strongly possessed us, that, in the enthusiasm of poetic delusion, we expected no less, at every turn, than to pop upon Cerberus, or some other horrid inhabitant of Pluto's dominion:

Spelunca

Spelunca alta fuit, vastoque immanis hiatu,
Scrupea, tuta lacu nigro, nemorumque tenebris.

Ibant obscuri solâ sub nocte per umbram,
Perque domos ditis vacuas, et inania regna.
Quale per incertam lunam sub luce malignâ
Est iter in sylvis; ubi cœlum condidit umbrâ
Jupiter, et rebus nox abstulit atra colorem.

" Deep, deep, the cavern lies, devoid of light,
" All rough with rocks, and horrible to sight.
" Its dreadful mouth is fenc'd with sable floods,
" And the brown horrors of surrounding woods.
" Now through the dismal gloom they pass, and tread
" Grim Pluto's courts, the regions of the dead ;
" As puzzled travelers bewilder'd move
" (The moon scarce glimm'ring through the dusky grove),
" When Jove from mortal eyes has snatch'd the light,
" And wrapp'd the world in undistinguish'd night."

PITT.

That the comparison might have appeared more just, I ought to
have premised, that the grotto is surrounded with a thick wood,
and that at a small distance before the entrance is a large lagoon
of stagnant water. The critic perhaps may object, that we were
not so entirely in the dark as Æneas is represented. But, if he
pleases, he may allow the dim light of our torch to bear some similitude to the glimmering of the moon above-mentioned; and
then it will seem more aptly applied. The soil beneath our feet we
perceived was deep, soft, and yielding, and had a faint, cadaverous smell. Upon examination, we imagined it to be a *congeries*
of bat's dung, accumulating perhaps for ages past; and were further confirmed in this opinion by the multitude of these creatures,
which, upon the disturbances of our torch-light, and the unusual
noise of so many visitors, flitted in numerous swarms over our
heads. It is probable this soil is strongly impregnated with nitre;
but we had not time to search for it. After walking a considerable
way, we observed many new adits branching from the sides. Our
guide informed us they led several miles under ground; and that

one half of them had never been explored by any human being. Soon after, we came all on a fudden to a little precipice, of about four or five feet; and fome of the party would have hurt them-felves very feverely, if it had not been for the foft *ftratum* of bat's dung which lay below ready to receive them. Our guide, and two or three of the foremoft, difappeared in an inftant, having tumbled one over the other; but foon recovered from their furprize, when they found themfelves unhurt. The reft, who followed at fome little diftance, being put on their guard, defcended with fomewhat lefs rapidity. We continued our walk without further interruption, till we hailed the day-light again, in an open area environed on all fides with fteep rocks covered with trees. This area, as nearly as we could conjecture, lies about a quarter of a mile from the en-trance of the grotto. We remarked feveral adits leading from different parts of this little court; but our guide was acquainted with one of them only, into which we walked, and came into a magnificent apartment, or rotunda, of about twenty-five feet diameter, and about eighteen to the dome, or vaulted cieling; from the centre of which defcended a ftrait tap-root of fome tree above, about the fize of a cable, and pretty uniform in fhape from top to bottom. This had made its way through a cleft in the rock, and penetrated downward quite into the floor of the apart-ment. On one fide was a fmall chafm, opening like the door-way of a clofet into a narrow paffage; which our guide endeavoured to diffuade us from entering, on account of a deep well, which he informed us lay a few paces within. However, we ventured in a little way with great caution, and found his account very true. The paffage grew more and more contracted, till we met with a thin, upright ledge of rock, rifing like a parapet-wall, almoft breaft-high, which feemed to decline gradually lower as we ad-vanced. We therefore thought it prudent to halt, and foon difco-vered the ledge of rock feparated us from a vaft cavernous hollow, or well. Having no line, we could not found the depth of the water, nor how far it lay beneath us; but, by the fall of fome ftones we threw in, we judged the diftance to the water about thirty or forty feet. The ftones in their fall produced a moft horrid, hoarfe noife, as loud as hell's porter uttered from his triple jaws, *primis in forcibus orci.* Our guide informed us it was unfathomable, and communicated with the sea. The latter is probable, as the entrance of the grotto is very near the coast. We returned across the area by the way that we came, only peeping into a few of the other avenues as we proceeded, which we found very little different. They had the like rude cielings incrusted with stalactites, here and there interspersed with the radical fibres of trees and plants, and their walks strewed with various seeds and fruits, particularly the bread-nut in great abundance; and even some reptiles, all curiously covered over with incrustations, but still preserving their original shapes. The structure and furniture of these various cloysters and apartments, at the same time that they excite the utmost curiosity, baffle all description. In some we saw, or fancied we saw, sparkling icicles, and beautifully-variegated foliage, gemmy canopies, festoons, thrones, rostrums, busts, skulls, pillars, pilasters, basons, and a thousand other semblances of such objects as struck our different imaginations. Most of the arches and columns seemed to be composed internally of a greyish, sonorous marble, and were extravagantly wild and curious. Some are perfect, and sustain the massy superstructure; others half formed; and some in their very infant state. Several of the apartments are cellular; others, spacious and airy, having here and there an eyelet-hole to the world above. These aërial communications are of signal service; for, although not in general large enough to admit much light, yet they introduce sufficient fresh air to expel noxious vapours, and afford a convenient respiration, except in those parts which are most recluse. The exterior summit of the cave is a greyish rock, honey-combed all over, full of crannies, and thick-set with various species of trees, whose roots having penetrated wheresoever they could find an opening, they flourish without any visible soil, an appearance which is extremely common in this island. We were anxious to investigate further: but, upon examining our stock of torch-wood, we found scarcely sufficient left for conducting us back to the entrance, and we were obliged to use dispatch in regaining it, for fear of rambling into some one of the numerous passages opening to the right and left, where, puzzled with mazes and perplexed with errors, we might have rambled on without the probability of ever finding our way out again: and in such a distressful event we could not reasonably have expected any human assistance. The famous Cretan labyrinth did not, I am persuaded, contain half the turns and windings which branch through every part of this infernal wildernefs; and which even Theseus, with the help of his clue, would have found difficult to unravel. Whoever may have the curiosity to examine these meanders with more attention, and to discover their extent and termination, ought to furnish himself with the implements necessary for striking fire, a portable mariner's compass, a proper quantity of wax tapers, and some provision for the stomach. Thus equipped, he may pervade them without fear of being lost, if he walks with due circumspection: the impression of his feet on the foft mould, which is thick-strewed in these passages, might enable him to re-trace his own tract almost without the assistance of a compass; though to avoid the possibility of being bewildered, it will be adviseable to carry one.

These are the most remarkable curiosities as yet discovered in this parish; but it may probably contain others, the grotto not having been found out, or at least generally known, till within these few years. We are uncertain whether it was known to the Spaniards; but it is supposed that run-away Negroes were not unacquainted with so convenient a hiding-place.

Moft of the houses in this parish are made defensible with loopholes; it having been the practice formerly, in war-time, for the enemy's privateers to land here, in order to plunder the inhabitants of their Negroes. Thus, in guarding against the insults of foreign enemies, they are fortified also against internal ones; the like precaution ought to have been used, in the other parts of the country, which are remote from the coast; but, either through negligence, or an imprudent contempt of danger, very few houses upon the inland settlements have been constructed in this manner.

The road which passes along the coast to St. James, is one of the best in the island, and kept in good repair.

State

State of the Parifh.

	Negroes.	Cattle.	Sugar-plantations.	Hogfheads.	Other Settlements.
				Annual Produce of Sugar.	
1734,	4441	2026			
1740,	5242	2342			
1745,	5231	2533			
1761,	7729				
1768,	8320	6207	22	1700	158

This parifh has increafed, as appears from the table, upwards of three thoufand in Negroes, and in cattle near four thoufand, from 1745 to 1768, or in twenty-three years. This is to be afcribed almoft entirely to the fettlements formed in Pedro's Cockpits: and a better proof cannot be required, to fhew the vaft benefits arifing to the ifland from a more extenfive colonization of its interior waftes; nor a ftronger reafon given for an immediate and vigorous encouragement of fuch a plan.

To recapitulate fome of the preceding matters, and bring them into one view, I fhall clofe my detail of this county with the following particulars:

County-town of MIDDLESEX.
St. JAGO de la VEGA,

where is held the fupreme court of common law on the laft Tuefday in February, May, Auguft, and November.

	Negroes.	Cattle.	Sugar-plantations.	Hogfheads.	Other Settlements.
				Annual Produce of Sugar.	
State of it in 1768,	66746	59512	239	24050	763

Rectories, and their Stipends.

	£	s.	d.
St. Catharine,	300	0	0
St. Dorothy,	200	0	0
St. John,	200	0	0
St. Thomas in the Vale,	200	0	0
Clarendon,	250	0	0
Vere,	200	0	0
St. Mary,	200	0	0
St. Anne,	200	0	0
	1750	0	0

The

The parish of St. Mary alone has no church as yet built; and consequently divine service is very seldom performed here; but, when it is performed, some private house is usually lent for the occasion. In the county are seven churches, two chapels of ease, and one synagogue. The civil government of each parish, or precinct, is under the direction of a *custos rotulorum*, and his associates, justices of the peace, who hold a quarter session; and subordinate to them are the several constables, clerk of the peace, surveyors and wardens of highways, coroner, collectors of the parochial taxes, &c.

C H A P.   VIII.

S E C T.   I.

S U R R Y

COntains about 672616 acres, and has seven parishes, and ten towns and hamlets, viz.

Parishes.	Towns.	Hamlets.
Kingston,	—— Kingston, the county-town,	
Port Royal,	—— Port Royal,	
St. Andrew,	——	Half-way Tree.
St. David,	——	Yallahs.
St. Thomas in the East,	Bath, —— ——	Morant.
Portland,	—— Titchfield and Moore, Negroe-town, —— }	Manchineel.
St. George,	—— Crawford, now Charlestown, Negroe-town.	

The parish of Kingston is bounded East by the parish of Port Royal; West and North, by St. Andrew; and South, by the harbour. The town of Kingston is situated in latitude 17° 59½′ North; longitude, 76° 34′ West. According to some geographers, the distance and bearing from London are 4080 miles; and the difference of time from the same, five hours, six minutes, West. After the repeated desolations by earthquake and fire, which drove the

inhabitants

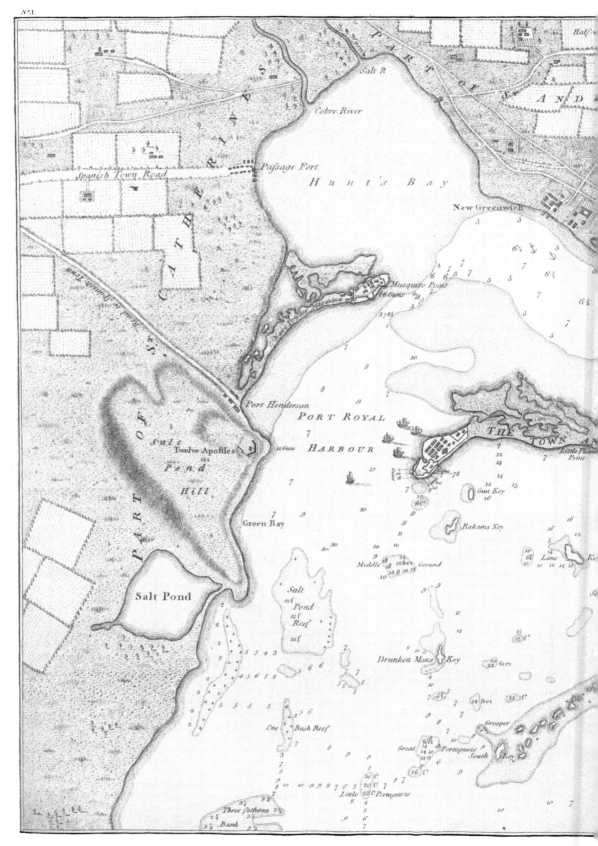

Half-

PART OF S.T ANDREW'S

THE TOWN AND

Salt R

Cobre River

Passage Fort

Hunt's Bay

New Greenwich

Spanish Town Road

New Town or Magazine

Musquite Point
6 Guns

Part of Leeward Road

PART OF ST. CATHERINE'S

Port Henderson

PORT ROYAL

HARBOUR

Twelve Apostles

6 Guns

Salt Pond Hill

Little Plumb Point

Gun Key

Green Bay

Rakams Key

Lime Key

Middle Ground

Salt Pond Reef

Salt Pond

Drunken Mans Key

One Bush Reef

Grooper

Great Portugueze

South Key

Little Portugueze

Three fathom Bank

Published as the Act

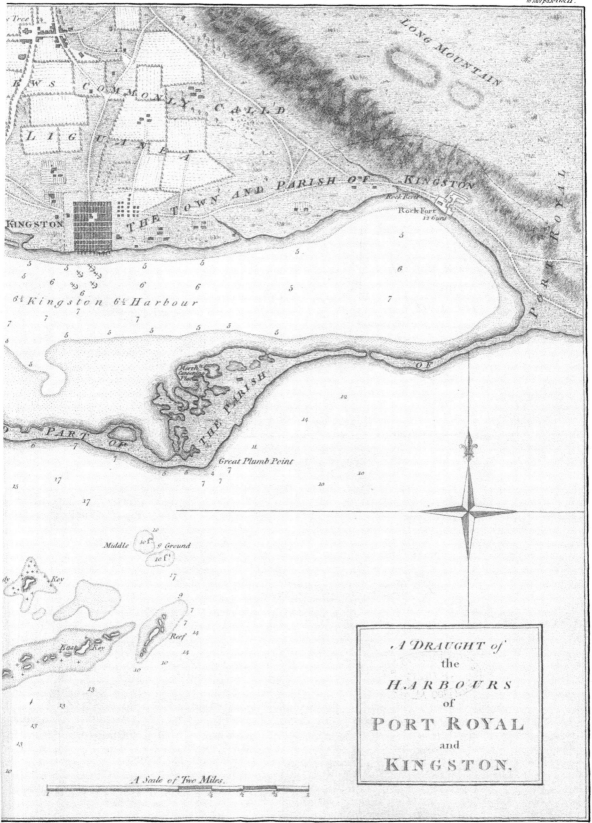

LONG MOUNTAIN

EWS COMMONLY CALL'D

LIGUANEA

KINGSTON

THE TOWN AND PARISH OF KINGSTON

Rock River
Rock Fort
12 Guns

PORT ROYAL

6¼ Kingston 6¼ Harbour

THE PARISH OF

March's Careening Place

PART OF

Great Plumb Point

Middle 10 f¹ 9 Ground
10 f¹

Key

Reef

East Key

A DRAUGHT of
the
HARBOURS
of
PORT ROYAL
and
KINGSTON.

A Scale of Two Miles.

inhabitants from Port Royal, this town was founded in the year 1693, on the North fide of the harbour, which, next to Port Royal, appeared the moft convenient part for trade. The plan of it was drawn by colonel Lilly, an experienced engineer; and in propriety of defign it is, perhaps, not excelled by any town in the world. The plan is a parallelogram, one mile in length by half a mile in breadth, regularly traverfed by ftreets and lanes, alternately croffing each other at right angles, except in the upper part of the town, where a large fquare is left. But the buildings have increafed fo rapidly, that it now extends beyond the outlines of the plan. It contains fixteen hundred and fixty-five houfes, befides Negroe houfes, and warehoufes; fo that the whole number of its buildings, including every fort, may be computed at between two and three thoufand: the number of its white inhabitants, about five thoufand; of free Negroes and Mulattoes, about twelve hundred; and of flaves, about five thoufand; making, in the whole, about eleven thoufand and upwards: thirty-five fpacious ftreets; and fixteen lanes. The harbour is formed by an inlet of the fea, which, after paffing Port Royal, divides into two branches; the Weftern, flowing to Paffage Fort and the mouth of Rio Cobre, forms a fmall bay of fhallow water; the Eaftern branch runs beyond Kingfton to Rock Fort, making a courfe this way of nine miles in length, and is two miles in width in the broadeft part; facing which the town is fituated. For a confiderable way above and below the town, the channel is deep enough to admit fhips of the greateft burthen; upwards of a thoufand fail may anchor here in perfect fafety, except from a hurricane; and the water is fo deep at the wharfs, that veffels of two hundred ton lye along-fide of them, to deliver their cargoes.

The buildings here are much fuperior to thofe of Spanifh Town. The houfes are moftly of brick, raifed two to three ftories, conveniently difpofed, and in general well-furnifhed; their roofs are all fhingled; the fronts of moft of them are fhaded with a piazza below, and a covered gallery above. The foil upon which the town is built is in fome parts gravelly; in others, a brick mould, intermixed with gravel; and the Weft part, bordering on a falina, partakes of fea-fand and ooze. From the harbour to the foot of Liguanea mountains is an eafy, gradual afcent, of about four miles and

and a half. The town, being thus fituated on a dry foil, is not in-commoded by the lodgement of water in the heavieft rains; and it is thoroughly ventilated by the daily fea-breeze. But, although the flope prevents any water from ftagnating in the town, it is at-tended with one great inconvenience; for it admits an eafy paffage to vaft torrents, which collect in the gullies at fome diftance to-wards the mountains after a heavy rain, and fometimes rufh with fo much impetuofity down the principal ftreets, as to make them almoft impaffable by wheel-carriages, and caufe a fhoal-water at the wharfs, depofiting accumulations of rubbifh and mud: by which means, the navigation of the harbour may, in procefs of time, be obftructed; for even now the channel is greatly contracted, an entire ftreet having been built on the foil thus gained upon the harbour fince the town was firft laid out. Some have propofed to remedy this inconvenience by cutting a large trench Eaft and Weft above the town, to intercept thefe floods, and conduct them into fmaller cuts, on each fide of it, quite to the harbour; by which method, the water, having a greater length of current, and not flowing fo rapidly, might depofite its foil by the way, and thus neither annoy the ftreets, nor fill up the harbour. But it may be objected to this project, that, if any ftagnant water, or a quantity of mud, fhould remain in thefe drains, the effluvia arifing from them might affect the health of the inhabitants, and fo become productive of a worfe injury than what it was calculated to pre-vent. The remarks before-made, refpecting the modern method of covering roofs in Spanifh Town, are equally applicable to King-fton. The danger from fire is very manifeft. It is true, that ac-cidents of the fort have rarely occurred in this town, the kitchens being detached buildings. But it is ftill liable to fuch a calamity from malice, as well as neglect or cafualty; and the fate of Port Royal, of Bridge Town in Barbadoes, and St. John's in Antigua, fhould ferve as horrible examples. To guard againft fuch ravages, in fome degree, here are wells and pumps in every principal ftreet, conveniently placed, and conftantly kept in good order; and in the court-houfe are fire-engines and leathern buckets. The ready af-fiftance of feamen from the fhips, which lie very near the town, would doubtlefs contribute much towards preferving it in fuch

events;

events; and the various openings formed by the ftreets and lanes may be likewife confidered as a further fafeguard againft a total conflagration. A projeƈt was once in agitation for bringing a part of Hope River into the town, and forming a refervoir in fome commodious place at the upper end, from which a certain number of conduits fhould be laid to fupply the principal ftreets. This fcheme was faid to be extremely praƈticable, and not expenfive. A want of unanimity prevented its being carried into execution. But there is no doubt it would prove of eminent benefit, in fupplying the inhabitants with a wholefome water for their common ufe; for the well-water here is in general bad; a few only are fed by fubterraneous drains from the Hope, or fome other of the mountainous ftreams; the reft are brackifh, impregnated with a muriatic falt, if not with fome mineral. They increafe thirft, inftead of flaking it; caufe a dry febrile heat, and fometimes a dyfentery in habits not much accuftomed to them. At the bottom of the town, near the water-fide, is the market place, which is plentifully fupplied with butchers meat, poultry, fifh, fruits, and vegetables of all forts. Here are found not only a great variety of American, but alfo of European, vegetables; fuch as peafe, beans, cabbage, lettuce, cucumbers, French beans, artichokes, potatoes, carrots, turnips, radifhes, celery, onions, &c. Thefe are brought from the Liguanea mountains, and are all excellent in their kind. Here are likewife ftrawberries, not inferior to the produƈtion of our Englifh gardens; grapes and melons in the utmoft perfeƈtion; mulberries, figs, and apples, exceedingly good, but in general gathered before they are thoroughly ripe. In fhort, the moft luxurious epicure cannot fail of meeting here with fufficient in quantity, variety, and excellence, for the gratification of his appetite the whole year round. The prices are but little different from thofe of Spanifh Town; but, where they difagree, they are more reafonable at Kingfton, the fupplies being more regular, and the market better fuperintended by the magiftracy. The beef is chiefly from the paftures of Pedro's, in St. Anne; the mutton, from the Salt-pan lands, in St. Catharine; what they draw from the penns in St Andrew's parifh being very indifferent meat. The fupplying of grafs for the horfes kept in this town is a very profitable article to thofe fettlements bordering on the harbour and the mouth of Rio Cobre, which are fit for no other production than the Scotch grafs: this is every day brought to the town by water, and fold in fmall bundles, a certain number for a ryal. Some of the grafs-planters have made upwards of 1500 *l.* *per annum* by this commodity. Wood is likewife another article of profit, though not fo confiderable. Near the market-place ftands the original court-houfe, which is a mean, inconvenient building, and now difufed as a feat of judicature, being fixed in the noifieft part of the town. A building erected for a free-fchool fituated in the upper diftrict of the town, being found more airy and commodious, is now made ufe of for holding the quarterly affize-court for this county. The parade is a large, handfome fquare; on the North-Weft fide of it are barracks of brick for the troops quartered here; a very well-defigned and convenient logement for two hundred men and their officers. The front, which contains apartments for the officers, makes a good appearance. The foldiers barrack ftands detached behind, in a fquare court walled round; in which are proper offices; and at one angle a powder magazine belonging to the town. On the South fide of the parade is the church; a large, elegant building, of four aifles, which has a fine organ, a tower and fpire, with a large clock. The tower is well-conftructed, and a very great ornament to the town. The rector's ftipend, as fixed by law, is only 250 *l.*; but the furplice fees are fo large, that his income is fuppofed at leaft one thoufand pounds *per annum,* Jamaica currency. The county gaol, a hofpital for tranfient fick and poor (who are fupported by an annual grant of affembly of 300 *l.*), and the free-fchool, have nothing remarkable in their ftructure. The land appropriated for the gaol was a plat of two hundred feet by one hundred and fifty; but only about fixty by fifty were inclofed a few years ago. It had only one apartment for lodging debtors, evidences, and criminals; and that of no larger extent than fifteen by fourteen feet. The walls, which enclofed it on the South-Eaft and Weft, having neither windows nor gratings, fo effectually excluded the air, that this place of confinement was rendered extremely unhealthy; and the diftempers among the prifoners became a matter of ferious concern. In 1761, upon a reprefentation of the ftate of it, the affembly made pro-

vifion

vifion for enlarging and rendering it more airy. The number of Whites ufually fhut up here is about ten; and of Negroes about one hundred. This was formerly the habitation of that ingenious and learned mathematician, Mr. Macfarlane, who built and fitted it up as an obfervatory; little fufpecting perhaps at the time, that it would be converted into a receptacle for unfortunate perfons, who are here precluded from almoft every other amufement than that of ftar-gazing.

The ftreets are all wide and regular, the houfes many of them extremely elegant, and kept very clean, confidering thefe circum- ftances, and that the foil on which they ftand is perfectly dry. It is natural to fuppofe, that the air is healthy; at leaft there appears not hitherto any local caufe affignable why it fhould be otherwife; neverthelefs, it is certain, that Kingfton has been accufed of being an unwholefome fpot. Sir Hans Sloane, indeed, obferves, that in his time, at fome plantations bordering upon this bay of Liguanea, many white perfons died, as he believed, by the ill air; fome of thefe fettlements lying in bottoms, or low fituations, contiguous to marfhes near the harbour; and, on the other hand, that plan- tations, feated high, were very healthy, and their inhabitants not fickly. The land Weftward from the town, and confining on the harbour, is, for four or five miles, very low and flat, interfperfed with lagoons, and in many places fubject to be overflown by the falt-water. The hofpital of Greenwich, fituated little more than a mile from the town, upon part of this low land, is remarkable for a bad air, and the mortality which always prevailed there. The effects of its unhealthy fituation were, that, when a patient was fent thither with only a gentle or intermitting fever, this mild difpofition was apt to be changed into either a malignant fever, a bloody flux, or fome other mortal diftemper. It was obferved, that the yellow Weft-Indian fever often reigned there, attended with the moft profufe evacuations of blood, by vomiting, ftools, and even by every pore of the body: when no fuch fymptoms di- ftreffed thofe patients whofe cafes had been fimilar, and who were permitted to remain in their fhips. The recovery of patients in that hofpital was obferved to be very tedious and uncertain: the leaft in- difcretion or irregularity brought on a relapfe. After a flux had

P 2

been

been ſtopped for ſome days, the eating of any ſort of food which had a putrid tendency, ſuch as even a meſs of broth, would ſometimes in a few hours bring on a return of the diſeaſe, accompanied with all its violent ſymptoms. Neither did this proceed from any ſource of infection in the hoſpital, or from its being too much crowded with patients. Theſe things happened even when a ſmall number of patients were lodged in the beſt-aired, and in the cleaneſt, wards. The mortality in this houſe was ſo great, and the cauſe of it ſo obvious, that there was a neceſſity for deſerting it; no more ſick were permitted to be ſent thither. During the laſt war, it was made uſe of as a place of confinement for the French priſoners, and proved fatal to ſeveral hundreds of them. Even the ſoldiers, who were ſent in good health from the garriſon at Port Royal, to mount guard there, were in a few days taken ill, and many of them died; which obliged the commanding officer to relieve the guard almoſt daily; by which means he ſaved the lives of thoſe, who, by too long a continuance on this duty, would otherwiſe have fallen a ſacrifice. The cauſe of this *endemia* has been, with great appearance of reaſon, aſcribed to the ſalt-marſhes and ſwamps, the putrid fogs or exhalations, which infeſt this part of the country, and are naturally adapted in a hot climate to produce all theſe baleful effects.

The large tract of ſalina, lying to the Northward of the hoſpital, and extending from Hunt's Bay towards Water-houſe Savannah, is frequently overflown by ſalt-water, when there happens any conſiderable ſurge in the harbour. It is alſo liable to be deluged by the brackiſh water of the Lagoon, or Ferry River. Much of this water remains afterwards ſtagnant, and becomes highly putrid. It is impoſſible not to be ſenſible of it in traveling over this ſalina to Kingſton, eſpecially at an early hour in the morning, when the ſtench of the ooze is often remarkably fœtid; and a vapour may be obſerved hovering over theſe lagoons and ſwamps, of a moſt diſagreeable ſmell. It may well therefore be ſuſpected, that a Weſterly land-wind, which ſometimes blows between the mountains behind the Ferry, eſpecially after a violent rain there, may impel theſe effluvia into the town of Kingſton. I have been informed, by an experienced phyſician, who practiſed in this town,

that

that a Wefterly wind generally brought a bad fever among the inhabitants.

Eaftward from the town, at the diftance of from twelve to fifteen miles, in the parifh of St. David's, are three large falt-ponds, and fome lagoons. At certain times of the year, when the fea-breeze, or trade, is veering either towards the Northern points, or returning from them to the South-eaft, a wind blows, known here by the name of the rock-wind, and fo called from its fweeping clofe along fhore from Eaft to Weft. Some perfons have been of opinion, that this wind drives on the putrid effluvia collected from thefe ponds and lagoons, together with what may arife from the other fmall creeks and ftagnant waters lying near the coaft, and brings them into the town : but this is merely conjectural ; and, confidering the diftance, it is not very credible. The inhabitants, it is true, refident at Yallahs, a little way leeward of thefe falt-ponds, are fenfible of an ill fmell proceeding from them, and are generally fickly. But it is doubtful whether thefe exhalations can be tranfported by the wind fo far as Kingfton, without being altered in their qualities by the many miles of atmofphere through which they muft needs pafs. To waft fuch effluvia unchanged to any diftance requires, one would fuppofe, an almoft calm ftate of the atmofphere, and the gentleft impulfe of wind. But the rock-winds are always ftrong, and therefore muft be deemed capable of difperfing exhalations, and of rendering them inoffenfive at a fmall diftance from their fource. The perfons who inhabit at Yallahs are within lefs than a mile of the two greater ponds, directly in the track of the fea-breeze, which, blowing acrofs thefe ftagnant waters, and through the lagoons that border on them, muft of courfe bring a conftant ftream of vapours upon thefe people ; for which reafon, it is no wonder that they are fickly, fince they are always involved in a peftilential atmofphere. There feem therefore, I think, no probable grounds for believing, that the air of the town is ever annoyed from the effluvia of thefe ponds. Others have imagined, that the Liguanea mountains, which are known to contain mines of lead and copper, emit continual fteams of a noxious mineral vapour, which, whenever the land and North winds blow, are precipitated down upon Kingfton, and contribute

to

to poifon its atmofphere. But there feems to be as little foundation for this conjecture, as for that already mentioned. It does not appear, that the inhabitants in the neighbourhood of mines in England are lefs healthful than thofe of other parts. The mines of Cornwall are known to emit mineral vapours very copioufly ; notwithftanding which, Mr. Borlafe affirms the air is extremely healthful ; and that the miners in particular, who are moft expofed to thefe vapours, generally live to a great age. The town of Potofi, in South-America, which is feated at the very foot of the mountain containing the famous mines, is remarkably populous and healthy [t]. With far more probability it may be alledged, that the intercourfe, which has been carried on between this town and the Spanifh ports of Carthagena and Porto Bello, has been frequently attended with fatal confequences, by introducing from that unhealthy coaft the moft malignant and deleterious diforders. The inclemency of the climate of Porto Bello is known to all Europe [u] : not only ftrangers who come thither are affected by it ; but even the natives themfelves fuffer in various manners. It deftroys the vigour of nature, and often untimely cuts the thread of life. The heat of this place is exceffive, being augmented by the fituation of the town, which is furrounded with high mountains, without any interval for the winds, whereby it might be refrefhed. The trees on the mountains ftand fo thick, as to intercept the rays of the fun, and confequently hinder them from drying the earth under their branches : hence copious exhalations, which form large clouds, and fall in violent torrents of rain. This continual inclemency, added to the fatigues of the feamen in unloading the fhips and carrying goods, and their immoderate drinking of fpirituous liquors, muft jointly deftroy the beft conftitutions, and tend to pro-

---

[t] The inhabitants about Mendip-hills, in Somerfetfhire, which contain the famous lead-mines, enjoy good health, except fuch only as are employed in fmelting the ore. But, according to fome authors, the American mines are not fo inoffenfive in all parts of the continent : and many judicious perfons fufpect, that the unhealthinefs of Kingfton muft be attributed to thefe mineral fteams, whofe *miafmata* impregnate the dews, which are carried down by the land-wind, and defcend upon the town at night; and, in confirmation of this opinion, they affert, that the inhabitants more often contract ficknefs from expofure to the night-air here, than from any other caufe whatever.

[u] Ulloa's Voyage to South-America.

duce

duce or inflame thofe terrible diforders fo common in this part of the country. The galleons and other European fhips, which ftay any time here, feldom leave it without burying half, or at leaft one third, of their men: whence this place has been termed the grave of the Spaniards; but it may, with equal propriety, be applied to thofe of other nations who vifit it. This remark is fufficiently confirmed by the havock made among the Englifh, when the fleet, under command of vice-admiral Hofier, lay before this port in 1726 for fix months. The inclemency of the air fwept away fuch numbers of his feamen, that he was obliged to bear away for Jamaica. This fleet was afterwards kept on fervice, on the coaft of Carthagena and the Baftimentos chiefly, until June 1728, when it returned to Jamaica in confequence of the peace with Spain; and it was then computed, that, from the time of admiral Hofier's arrival in June 1726, it had loft two admirals, ten captains, about fifty lieutenants, and near four thoufand fubaltern-officers and feamen; who all fell by ficknefs, and not by the hands of the enemy! But, notwithftanding this general fatality of the climate of Porto Bello, and its neighbouring coaft, to Europeans, a Spanifh fquadron, which lay here in 1730, enjoyed a good ftate of health. This happy fingularity was attributed to the ftop of the fhips at Carthagena, where the crews paffed the time of the endemia; by which their conftitutions were better adapted to the climate. So noxious is the air of this place, that even perfons born in it, if above the degree of a Mulatto, fcorn to refide here; and, for the fame reafon, the royal edict of Spain forbids the fair held annually to exceed forty days. The principal fources of this unhealthinefs, exclufive of what has been already mentioned, are, the fwampinefs of the ground on the Eaft fide of the harbour, and a black filthy mud, which at low-water is left bare, and fends forth an abominable ftench. Such a fituation muft, in any part of the Weft-Indies, render the air malignant; and it will prove fo, in a greater or lefs degree, in proportion as other caufes more or lefs concur in preventing it from being either difperfed or corrected. Upon admiral Vernon's return to Jamaica from Porto Bello and Carthagena, the crews of the men of war, and land-forces, brought with them a very contagious fever. The land-forces had been re-

duced

duced from twelve to three thoufand, more by ficknefs than in their engagements with the Spaniards. To add to the misfortune of thofe who returned, they were encamped at Greenwich; and the mortality was increafed, as well by the unwholefomenefs of that fpot, as by the rains which fell, and to which the men were inevitably expofed. The malady was foon communicated to the town of Kingfton, where it committed vaft havock. A merchant, who was here at the time, affured me, that, having dined with an intimate acquaintance one day, and left him in the evening in feeming perfect health, he was fummoned the very next day to attend his friend's funeral. He accordingly went, with five others, as a bearer; and in a few days he was left the only furvivor of the whole company, the other five having caught infection from the corpfe, as they accompanied it to the burial-place. He imputed his efcape to the precaution he took of chewing tobacco, and carrying fome in his hand, which he frequently applied to his nofe. It would be a forrowful tafk to enumerate the many fimilar cataftrophes which have befallen this town by the importation of malignant fevers from Porto Bello, Carthagena, the coaft of Guiney, and the Havannah; not omitting the gaol-fever from England: all of which in their turns have at various periods raged with a fury that threatened to depopulate it. It may be more to the purpofe (fince the town, all circumftances confidered, does not appear to be locally unhealthy) to fuggeft fome means of guarding it againft the invafion of thefe exotic difeafes; fo that, when they happen on board any of the fhips that arrive here, the infection may be debarred from extending into the town.

It would probably be one means of preferving the lives of our feamen, if the fhips, intended for Porto Bello, were difpatched at thofe times of the year when the endemia leaft prevails there. Thefe times are the months of December, January, February, and March. But, when they are unfortunately feized with thefe malignant fevers, there are no remedies which promife fo fpeedy and effectual relief as medicines of the antimonial clafs, and a removal as foon as poffible into a better air. In the year 1769, his majefty's fhip Levant being at Porto Bello, the crew were attacked with a malignant, petechial fever; but, out of feventy men who
were

were taken with this difeafe, two only died; the reft were recovered by Dr. James's well-known powder, adminiftered by the
furgeon of that fhip. From a multitude of experiments, this powder appears to be a fpecific remedy for all the Weft-India fevers of
the putrid kind; and it is but doing juftice to its merit, to fay, that
it feldom has failed of fuccefs, if given early after the firft
fymptom of the difeafe has made its appearance, and in dofes judicioufly proportioned to the patient's ftrength. When a veffel arrives at Port Royal harbour with any contagious fever on board,
fhe might be ordered to perform quarantine at the Pallifadoes. Here
a convenient lazaretto, open to the fea-breeze, might be erected at
an expence very trifling to the publick; for a boarded or plaiftered
houfe would be not only the cheapeft, but wholefomeft, kind of
building for this purpofe. Here the patients would breathe a pure,
dry, and perfectly falubrious atmofphere; and might be conftantly
fupplied with vegetables, and all other neceffaries, from the town
of Kingfton, by water-carriage. The fhips in which the infection
had raged might here be duly aired and purified for a reafonable time
before they were fuffered to approach the town. A precaution of
this nature, fo much wanted, and fo eafily to be put in practice,
feems to deferve fome attention from the legiflature of the ifland.
I think it will be allowed, that, had it been adopted fome
years ago, and continued under fit regulations ftrictly obferved,
many thoufand ufeful lives might have been redeemed from an untimely fate. Befides, thefe calamities are not confined to Kingfton alone; for, when they have raged to any confiderable degree
in this town, they have unavoidably circulated into other parts of
the ifland by means of the conftant refort to it of people from the
various diftricts. The wifdom and circumfpection of every trading
port in Europe have pointed out the utility of fuch lazarettos; and,
although the diftemper called the plague has never yet been known
in the Weft-Indies, yet the putrid fevers hatched in this climate
have at times been nearly as peftilential and mortal; chiefly fo, when
they have invaded a multitude of men pent up in the clofe atmofphere of a fhip, or the warm rooms of towns on the coaft.
To this effect is the remark of a fenfible man who refided many
years in Jamaica, cited by Dr. Lind. " He obferved the poor

" feamen in the merchant fervice to recover from the yellow fever,
" folely by having the benefit of a free and conftant admiffion of
" air into a fhip anchored at a diftance from the fhore; where
" they lay utterly deftitute of every affiftance in ficknefs, and even
" of common neceffaries; having nothing but cold water to drink,
" and not fo much as a bed to lie upon; while gentlemen newly
" arrived from England, by being fhut up in fmall, clofe, fuffo-
" cating chambers at Kingfton and Port Royal, expired with the
" whole mafs of their blood diffolved, and flowing at every pore;
" the ftifling heat of their rooms having produced a ftate of uni-
" verfal putrefaction in the body even before death." Such ftrangers, upon their arrival, are generally obliged to take up with the
common lodging-houfes; the owners of which, in order to make
the moft advantage of their bufinefs, convert every little clofet and
hole into a bed-chamber. The healthieft perfon would find it difficult to refpire freely for a whole night in one of thefe dungeons.
How improper then muft they be for thofe who are feized with a
fever, and are thus excluded from that conftant refrefhment of air
upon which their recovery fo much depends, that, without it, all
medicines are ineffectual! The houfes of towns in this climate
cannot be too airy; and on this account the jealoufy-fhutters, as they
are called, which freely admit the air, are very excellent contrivances; and no bed-chamber fhould be unfurnifhed with them;
for by their means the fmalleft apartment may be conftantly ventilated.

There are fome other remarkables in this town, which, fo far as
they appear inconfiftent with the general health, deferve to be
noticed.

The firft is, the practice of cramming fo many corpfes into a
fmall church-yard in the centre of the town; inftead of providing
a proper cemetery at a diftance, and to leeward from all the
houfes.

The fecond is, a filthy cuftom of ufing tubs, and empty butter-
firkins, inftead of vaults; and exonerating them of their contents
every day at the wharfs; by which inceffant accumulation of putrid
matter, the mud in thofe parts is rendered ftill more offenfive, and

injurious

injurious to the health of thofe who inhabit the loweft, which is the hotteft, quarter of the town.

The third is, a ftrange method of repairing their ftreets with the offals and naftinefs raked from all the dunghills about the town; inftead of gravel, or a frefh wholefome foil, of which there is great plenty in the environs.

Thefe are fo many artificial annoyances, which cannot, I think, improve the quality of the air they breathe. Natural evils, if they cannot be removed or remedied, muft be acquiefced with; but for an intelligent people to take pains to poifon themfelves in this manner can only be imputed to a liftlefs indolence, or a great de-fect of good police among them. The Mahometans can give them fome inftructions not to be flighted. The burial-places of the Turks are handfome and agreeable; which is owing chiefly to the many fine plants that grow in them, and which they carefully place over their dead. They act much more confiftently than the Chriftians, when they bury their dead without their towns, and plant over them fuch vegetables as, by their aromatic and balfamic odours, can drive away or correct the fatal exhalations with which the atmofphere of fuch places is generally loaded. By this eafy practice they efcape many misfortunes which affect Chriftians from their wandering and dwelling continually among the dead. Cypreffes and rofemary are the plants moft abundant in thefe grounds; and the Turks never, if they can avoid it, lay two bodies in the fame grave. There can be no doubt but experience taught them the rec-titude of this practice in a warm climate, fubject fo frequently to the vifitations of the plague. The contrary practice in the colder climates (Britain for example) is certainly in fome degree perni-cious, as the air even here, at certain times of the year, is in a ftate to favour the afcent of very unwholefome vapours from fuch grounds, particularly in towns, where the furrounding walls con-fine the moifture that falls within, and prevents the greater part of it from efcaping any other way than by exhalations. But our adoption of this, and fome other Britifh cuftoms, in a hot climate, is unqueftionably abfurd. Why fhould it be thought irrational to follow rather the Turkifh cuftom, and bury the dead at a fmall diftance to the North-weft of our towns in the Weft-Indies, from

which

which quarter the wind rarely fets, and plant the ground with the wild-fage, rofemary, and other aromatic fhrubs, which grow very abundant in the low lands? If there is really a wide difference be-tween a pure and a vitiated air, in regard to the effects they refpec-tively produce on the health of mankind (and that there is will be readily granted), humanity fhould unite with good fenfe to re-move thofe nuifances and erroneous cuftoms, which have too long prevailed againft the public welfare.

The Jewifh fynagogue in this town is a handfome, fpacious building; and here the principal rabbi officiates. It contains a gallery, like that in Spanifh Town, for the reception of their wo-men, who do not mingle with the other fex in their public devo-tions. The Jews are numerous in this town, being poffeffed of the greateft fhare in the Spanifh trade. They have a convenient burying-ground without the town. No public buildings having as yet been erected for the officers of the cuftoms and the receiver-general of the ifland, their offices are kept in private houfes, fitu-ated in different quarters of the town; which is a very great in-convenience to the trade. Every veffel that arrives is obliged to be entered at the poft-office, the fecretary's, the collector's, comp-troller's, naval, and receiver-general's. Thefe being all detached, and at a diftance from one another, the captains of fhips are forced to make the tour of the whole town when they attend thefe offices either to enter or clear. The Eaft fide of the parade, or fquare, in a line with the barracks, would be a very proper fpot for erecting a range of building, to include all thefe offices; but fuch an under-taking has been thought too expenfive for the town, or the county of Surry; and the other two counties are faid to have oppofed fuch a fcheme, from an apprehenfion or jealoufy that it might one day be converted into a place of refidence for the commander in chief. Moderate men, however, are of a different opinion: they wifh to fee a building erected here, fo neceffary for the accommodation and difpatch of the traders; and that an exchange, or place convenient for daily meetings of the merchants, was likewife provided; efpe-cially as no other town of fuch extent and importance is without them. In proportion as the commercial fpirit and importance are kept up among the inhabitants, they may be lefs inclined to leave

2

the

the walk of trade for party and political wranglings. The erecting
of buildings, which are really appurtenant to trade, would encourage that fpirit, and confer that importance. We may illuftrate
the argument, by fuppofing what would be the cafe, if no houfe
of refidence was provided for the governor, and no fenate-houfe for
the affembly. If the former dwelt in a private lodging, and the
latter met to tranfact all their weighty affairs in a tavern, or under
a large tree; fuch degradation would be apt to bring contempt
upon the governmental powers, and leffen the reverence and eftimation with which they ought to be regarded. But the ftrongeft
argument is, that, by bringing the commercial offices together
into one certain fpot, and affigning a certain convenient place
where traders and men of bufinefs can regularly meet, to carry on
their negociations with each other, all the fprings and movements
of the commercial machine are kept in conftant exact order, confufion and delay are avoided, every thing goes on with difpatch and
facility. Trade muft have a livelier current, where the clogs and
impediments to its free circulation are removed; and a great annual
faving made in point of time; an article upon which merchants
neceffarily fet the higheft value. In the lower part of the town is
a very pretty theatre, exceedingly well contrived, and neatly finifhed. Dramatical performances were exhibited here during the
laft war; at which time there was a confiderable quantity of prize
money in circulation; but in time of peace, the town is not able,
or not difpofed, to fupport fo coftly an amufement. The taverns
here are large and well fupplied. In the two principal ones, called
Ranelagh and Vauxhall, are long rooms for concerts, balls, and
public entertainments. A new governor is generally feafted for
three days fucceffively in Spanifh Town. Soon after which, he
makes a kind of publick entry into Kingfton; where he is again
regaled by the cuftos, or chief magiftrate of the town, and the reft
of the inhabitants, who ufually make a fubfcription-purfe for the
purpofe. In thefe feafons of feftivity there feems an emulation between the two towns, as if they contended which fhould treat him
with the moft fplendid entertainments. The tavern called Ranelagh
is a large, lofty building, commanding a fine view of the town,
harbour, and fhipping. Here the balls and concerts are ufually exhibited,

hibited; and the company are numerous and elegant in their appearance.

The principal place for taking the air is the road leading to Rock Fort, which ftands about four miles Eaftward from the town; and moft of the inhabitants who keep carriages exercife here morning and evening every day. This fort is fituated at the extremity of the long mountain, a rocky eminence, inacceffible on this part, where it projects nearly into the harbour, leaving only a fmall narrow pafs at the foot, where the fortrefs is built. It confifts of two baftions, mounting twenty-one guns (twenty-four pounders), and furnifhed with a fmall powder-magazine, and other habiliments of war neceffary for its defence. Upon the face of the hill is a little battery of fix guns, with traverfed lines that lead up to it. Outfide the walls is a wet ditch, funk lower than the furface of the water in the harbour; fo that it may be occafionally filled. The fort is provided alfo with a draw-bridge towards the Eaftern road; cafemates, for lodging the men; and a houfe for the officers. It is too fmall to admit a garrifon of more than feventy men: neverthelefs, governor Kn—l—s was fo confident of its ftrength, that he maintained it was capable of ftanding a fiege againft ten thoufand men. It defends the accefs towards the town from the Eaftward, and would undoubtedly prove a great fecurity againft an attack from that quarter; for the only way leading to it is narrow, and confined a confiderable length in a ftrait direction, expofed to the whole fire of the fort, without a poffibility of annoying it: nor could trenches be formed, to carry on a regular approach, as the road is all the way a fhallow fand clofe by the water's edge. A guard of foldiers is always kept here; but the fort is faid to be very unhealthy to the men and their officers. The caufe of this has by fome been imputed to their drinking from a brackifh ftream which runs near it. Others afcribe it to the extreme heat reverberated down upon them from the hill, which rifes like a wall above the fort. And fome have thought it proceeded from a lagoon, which lies near the mouth of Mammee River, about three miles to the Eaftward. To corroborate the latter opinion, is alledged the inftance, mentioned by Lind, of Whydaw-caftle, on the coaft of Africa; which has been rendered more unhealthy than

the

the Negroe-town in its neighbourhood by a flight circumftance un-attended to at firft. It is built on a fmall fpot of ground, which the fea-breezes cannot reach without paffing over a little, inconfi-derable brook of water, which produces fome aquatic plants always covered with a putrid flime. It is certain, from conftant expe-rience, that places adjacent to a foul fhore, or ftagnant waters, near the coaft in the Weft-Indies, are invariably unhealthful. But, whatever be the caufe, it deferves a minute enquiry of gentlemen of the faculty, in order to its difcovery ; to the end that, if it arifes from fome local evil, that cannot be remedied, the men might be lodged at night in convenient huts, erected for them upon the hill-fide ; by which means all of them, except thofe on immediate duty in the fort, might enjoy a purer air, efpecially in thofe hours when a depraved air is found to be moft pernicious ; for this is a poft of fo much importance to the town, that the men ftationed here ought neither to be difheartened by apprehenfions, nor difabled by ficknefs, from doing their regular duty. The affembly having lately granted 1500 l. for erecting barracks at this fort to contain two hundred men; if the fituation be properly attended to, the re-fult will fhew, whether the unhealthinefs of the garrifon has been owing to a peftilent quality in the air, or fome other caufe.

To conclude with Kingfton. The militia of this town, both horfe and foot, are well trained, uniformly dreffed, and well armed, at their own expence. The pains they take in learning the neceffary manœuvres, and the charges to which they are put in their equip-ment, do great honour to their public fpirit, efpecially as moft of them are independent in their circumftances. It is thought, that, upon emergency, they could mufter upwards of two thoufand effective Whites; and between four and five hundred effective free Blacks and Mulattoes. The companies of the latter caft are under the command of white officers, excellent in their difcipline, and would probably do good fervice againft an enemy, whenever called upon to give proof of it.

The parifh contains no fugar plantations, the fituation being too dry to admit of any other fettlements than grafs-penns. The fol-lowing may ferve to give fome idea of the ftate of it:

Negroes.

		Negroes.	Cattle.	Settlements.
1734,	——	3811	483	
1740,	——	4534	607	
1745,	——	7749	828	
1761,	——	6186		
1768,	——	5779	923	8

In number of Negroes it appears to be confiderably reduced; and, indeed, there feems at prefent but too much reafon for the popular opinion, that this town has paffed the zenith of its glory, having loft two fuch capital fupports of its trade, as the Negroe-con-tracts with the Spaniards, and the coafting-intercourfe with Spanifh South-America; in which it ufed, a few years ago, to employ a great number of fmall veffels. It is likewife feldom vifited by the fmall-craft, which ufed formerly to croud hither in fhoals, laden with bullion and other valuable articles. So that it has at prefent very little bufinefs but what concerns the home-confumption of the ifland; on which account, feveral of the merchants have, fince the commencement of peace, betaken themfelves to planting, as a more gainful employ than trade carried on under the prefent di-ftreffed circumftances. War, fo fatal to fome ftates, has ever been the beft friend of this town, by augmenting the confumption and demand of merchandizes; by filling it with new acceffions of people and wealth; and by laying open that profitable traffic in thefe feas which in time of peace is too ftrictly watched. From the earlieft fettlement of this ifland, its trade was ever moft flou-rifhing while war fubfifted with the Spaniards; which has admi-niftered fuch conftant opportunities of fharing in their gold and filver, as well by private commerce as by open hoftility. For this reafon, their proverbial faying of, " Peace with England, and war " with all the reft of the world," was not ill-founded. Yet I ven-ture to hope, that, by fteadily cultivating a better correfpondence with the free Indians on the Southern continent, the trade of this town is very capable of receiving a vaft enlargement; which may effectually preferve it from decay, and make it lefs dependent on a ftate of war for its fupport.

In this town are two houfes for refining fugar; but the quantity they annually confume in this manufacture I am not informed of.

The

The number of veffels which enter and clear at this port is computed at four hundred, or upwards, one year with another.
Whence it will appear to be ftill a place of very great import and export. For maintaining the harbour, feveral very excellent provifions have been made. Penalties are laid on any perfon taking materials or ballaft from the fpit of land, called the Pallifadoe, which
forms a barrier between it and the main fea; as well as on thofe
who may throw rubbifh or ballaft into the harbour. The channel
is properly marked; and the pilots under good regulation. And,
in order to prevent diforderly mooring of the fhips, a tax is laid in
the following manner:

On all veffels arriving from the Northward of the tropic of
Cancer;

	s.	d.
Three mafts, —— ——	15	0
Brig, fnow, or bilander, ——	10	0
Sloop, and fchooner, —— ——	7	6

And, on all veffels coming from between the tropics, one half the
above rates; except coafting veffels, which are taxed 2 s. 6 d. each,
payable every three months. The money arifing from this impoft
is applied to the eftablifhment of a water-bailiff; whofe bufinefs it is,
to fee that all thefe veffels fix their moorings properly and without
confufion. It feems, however, a little impolitic to throw this additional load upon the fhipping that frequent this port, from which
the other ports of the ifland are exempted; efpecially as a very moderate addition to their annual parifh-tax might have anfwered the
purpofe. The church-wardens of this town are incorporated, for
the better management of every thing relative to the parochial
taxes; the markets and ftreets are under the regulation of the
juftices and veftry; the market for butchers meat is moft plentifully
fupplied; and the fifh-market, which is kept every day from eight
in the morning till two in the afternoon, is fuperior to moft in the
world.

It is impoffible to afcertain, with precifion, either the number
of the inhabitants, or the ftate of health, from the number of burials, becaufe many feamen and ftrangers who die are confounded
with the town's people.

The number of births and deaths for feven years to the year 1771 was as follows:

Born   ——   988.
Died   ——   2085.

Deaths exceed the births — 1097.

The thermometrical heat of this town is greater than that of Spa-nifh Town, in general about three degrees upon the medium. The air is lefs elaftic; and the water, as I have before remarked, is in general of bad quality. From what has been premifed, it may be concluded, that it is not by any means fo healthful. Some have gone fo far as to compare it to a large hofpital; and to affert, that more people die in it in one year than in all the reft of the ifland in three. But this is an exaggeration; and the town is of late years become much healthier than it formerly was, when the mountain-ous tracts neareft to it were covered with woods, which have fince been pretty well cleared and laid open, and the lagoon-water more freely carried off, by cultivating the Scotch grafs, and cutting drains near Salt River. The removal of thofe annoyances which meet a ftranger's nofe upon entering the town in the morning, to-gether with the enforcing of fome other falutary regulations, might probably contribute to make the air ftill more favourable to life; yet there are many here, whofe conftitutions by long habit are inured, and who attain to a good old age, notwithftanding the inconveniences pointed out; but, in general, it muft be allowed, that this town is not fo propitious to the health of perfons newly arrived from Europe as might be wifhed.

SECT. II.

St. ANDREW.

THIS parifh is bounded on the Eaft by the parifh of Port Royal, and part of St. David; on the Weft, by part of St. Thomas in the Vale, and St. Catharine; on the North, by part of St. Anne, and St. Mary; and on the South, by the harbour and parifh of Kingfton. It is watered with fourteen rivers; the principal of
which

which are, the Wagwater, which empties itfelf into the fea on the North fide, after a courfe of about thirty miles; the Hope, which croffes the Eaft fide; the Pedro, which enters St. Thomas in the Vale on the Weft; and the Salt, which falls into the harbour on the North-weft part of Hunt's Bay. The North-weft angle of the boundary-line terminates at a large cotton-tree, on the fummit of a hill; from which there is a diftant view, in clear weather, of the fea on the North and South fides of the ifland.

The Salt River rifes about three miles above Hunt's Bay, and is joined by the Lagoon River, which divides this parifh from St. Catharine, and whofe fource is about two miles further inland. Both thefe rivers are croffed with bridges in the way leading to Spanifh Town. The Salt River Bridge has a toll-gate, granted to the proprietor; in confideration of which, he is obliged to keep them, together with about one mile of the road, in good repair, and to maintain a ferry-boat at the croffing of Rio Cobre, for the accommodation of paffengers when that river is flooded. Thefe rivers are navigated by flat-bottomed barges and canoes, which are chiefly ufed for tranfporting grafs, wood, and lime, to the town of Kingfton. A large tract of lagoon lies between their ftreams; great part of which, having been drained by cuts, which carry off the water into the rivers, is converted into good pafture-ground; and that which is more fwampy bears the Scotch grafs very luxuriantly. The road, leading from the bridge towards Kingfton, is for about a mile extremely romantic: on one fide is a range of fteep, rocky mountain, which fcarcely admits of room fufficient for carriages to pafs at the foot of it; on the other fide is a branch of the Salt River, fed here and there with fmall rivulets oozing from the bottom of the mountain. This water is exceedingly brackifh; but it affords good water-crefs, and plenty of fifh. This prey invites the alligators; which are faid to abound here, though rarely feen by any except the Negroes who navigate upon it.

The village of Half-way Tree is fituated a little more than two miles North from Kingfton, at the interfection of the three roads which lead to Spanifh Town, to St. Mary, and St. George. This village enjoys, with a good air, the moft agreeable views. Behind

R 2

are

are the majeſtic Blue Mountains, riſing above one another in gradation, till they ſeem to touch the clouds: on each ſide, lively fields
of canes, intermixed with elegant villas and paſtures: in front,
the harbours of Kingſton and Port Royal, crowded with ſhipping,
ſome at anchor, others plying in various directions: beyond theſe,
the Healthſhire hills in St. Catharine, gradually declining towards
Old Harbour: and, laſtly, the horizon cloſing on the beautiful
azure of the ocean. A number of little graſs-penns, with good
houſes on them, are diſperſed about the neighbourhood, chiefly
the property of merchants in Kingſton, who occaſionally retire to
them from the hurry of buſineſs. But its chief ornament is a very
magnificent houſe, erected here a few years ſince by Mr. Pinnock;
which may vie, in the elegance of deſign, and excellence of work-
manſhip, with many of the beſt country-ſeats in England. The
ſtone uſed about this fabrick was brought from the Hope river-
courſe: it is far more beautiful than the Portland, and of a cloſer
and finer grain. The mahogany-work and ornaments within have
been juſtly admired for their ſingular beauty, being, as I am informed, ſelected with great expence. Half-way Tree has a ſmall,
but very neat church, with a tower and organ. The emoluments
of the rectory, ariſing principally from ſix hundred acres of rich
glebe-land, leaſed advantageouſly to ſome planters, are ſaid to be
about 1400l. *per annum.* The ſtipend being only 200l. of this
country money, it may eaſily be judged that the glebe is extremely
valuable; and this is therefore conſidered as the beſt living in the
governor's preſentation. Some years ago, there was a regular
weekly aſſembly held here; but it has ſince been diſcontinued, till
lately, when it was revived, and thought inferior to none in the
iſland. The village contains about twelve or fourteen houſes.
Paſſing on from hence to the Northward about two miles, along
a road of eaſy aſcent, we come to the foot of the Liguanea Mountains: theſe are the firſt ſteps leading up to that vaſt pile of mountains which range through the iſland from Eaſt to Weſt. The
foremoſt are of moderate height, ſerving as natural buttreſſes to
ſuſtain the interior and more maſſive. As we proceed, they ſeem
to increaſe in magnitude and elevation, till we arrive at the higheſt
of all, called the Blue Mountain Ridges. The ſoil on their South
aſpect

afpect is in general a red clay; but, in other parts, it is of a coarfer, friable texture, and intermixed with fmall ftones, or a fort of grit. Where they have been cleared of wood, and cultivated, their in-fertility has been promoted by heavy rains wafhing down the finer mould. From Kingfton they appear of a reddifh caft, interfperfed with verdure here and there, and furrowed with innumerable gullies, fome of which are very deep; and at this diftance they refemble very much the South afpect of the Madeira ifland. The road af-cending into thefe lofty regions is in general fteep and irregular, incapable of admitting wheel carriages. The journey is therefore performed on horfe-back. But it is not dangerous, except in one part, where the road paffes along a precipice, and is formed on wooden ftakes driven into the fide of the mountain, and well co-vered with crofs timbers and earth, which make a kind of geome-trical bridge. But this is of no great length; and, being kept in good repair, it feems to be accompanied with more of horror than of real peril. Afcending higher, vaft numbers of the larger fwifts are feen fkimming over the mountain-tops with great velo-city; and fometimes they whiz along fo near the traveler's head, uttering their fhrill cries, as to ftartle him, if he is unprepared. The bull-finch s notes are more entertaining: they are very fingular, and of a melancholy air. The beautiful forked-tail papilio flies are feen in fwarms; they generally keep together, flitting in a di-rection with the wind; they feem ever on the wing, and fometimes venture to foar above the higheft pitch of thefe mountains. In this part of the country there is no appearance of lime ftone. The ftone obferved here is brittle and crumbling, difpofed in *lamina*, turns black in the fire, and will not ferment with *aqua fortis*. The lime made ufe of is manufactured from incruftations, which are found in fufficient abundance. The trees, for the moft part, are flender and ftunted; many of them are enveloped with mofs, and others entirely killed by it. This covering makes them appear at a fmall diftance as if they were frofted over; and the coldnefs of the air naturally caufes this deception on firft arriving from the glow of heat which broods over the lowlands about Kingfton. The thermometer here, in general, was at fixty and fixty-five degrees in the middle of the day in July; while it rofe to eighty-fix and

ninety

ninety in Kingston. The ground on the elevated spots feels, and yields to the tread, like a new carpet; it is coated all over with a deep moss. The parts I speak of are adjacent to Mr. Adams's house; for the Blue Mountain Ridge appeared from this place as much higher as this seemed to be above the low lands. Every evening a vapour descends from these summits towards the vales below, and probably adds some strength to the land-wind, which sets from this quarter after sun-set. In the morning the fog rises, and seems to creep in a regular train to the higher grounds; so that, for a great part of the day, it continues so thick, as to give the air a chill, even at noon, equal to what is felt here before sun-rise. Where it is more broken and dispersed, so as to admit the solar rays to pass freely, warm steams immediately begin to be exhaled; and the mossy ground feels to the hand like a hot bed. Upon arriving at the eminence, whereon Mr. Adams's house is built, a very beautiful scenery greets the view. Below are seen the richly-cultivated vale of Liguanea, the harbours of Kingston and Port Royal, and great part of St. Catharine, and St. Dorothy. On a sudden, the whole is excluded from sight by a dense cloud, interposing itself like a magnificent curtain. In a moment afterwards, the curtain breaks here and there in different parts, admitting only transient glances; but, when withdrawn entirely, a most luxuriant and extensive landschape opens, animated with the full splendor of sun-shine. In front are cane-fields of the liveliest verdure, pastures, and little villas intermixed; the towns and ports of Kingston and Port Royal; the shipping scattered in different groups; the forts, the hills of Healthshire, the rocky breakers, and cayes whitening with the surge; and, beyond these, a plain of ocean extending to the Southern hemisphere. To the Westward are seen the glistning meanders of the Cobre; the town of St Jago de la Vega; the bay of Old Harbour; and a vast champaign of fertile country, terminated by the lofty range of Carpenter's Mountains, at sixty miles distance.

There objects form all together a very pleasing combination. The pleasure which the mind receives from contemplating them is considerably heightened by the impenetrable gloom of thick vapours behind, which exhibits a noble contrast to the brilliant picture in front.

3

front.

front. Another fcene, not lefs magnificent, though more awful, frequently prefents itfelf in the hot months. The clouds affembling about noon gradually thicken, grow black, and defcend lower; till they appear a fpacious fea, clofing over and covering the inferior objects entirely from our view. Soon afterwards, the vapoury particles begin to condenfe and fall in rain; the lightning flafhes with great vivacity, as it traverfes along, in a variety of angular or ferpentine directions. We hear the majeftic thunder rolling at our feet, and reverberated by a thoufand echoes among the hills. This tumultuous interlude continues until the vapours, grown lighter by a plentiful difcharge of their contents, begin to re-afcend and difperfe, climbing over the ftately pinnacles of thefe mountains, like flocks of fheep retiring haftily to their fold.

Whenever the fog breaks or difperfes about noon, the fun-beams ftrike here with more power than would have been imagined at fo great an elevation. But the moffy covering of the ground, which is adapted to imbibe the warmth impreffed upon it by every ftrong gleam, and the fudden variations in the fenfible ftate of the atmofphere, by the interpofition or recefs of thefe vapours, doubtlefs affect a perfon here in like manner as the fudden tranfition in England from a cold, raw air into a heated, clofe apartment. The little pike, from whence the moft agreeable view is taken, is about half a mile from Mr. Adams's houfe, and named Catharine Hill, in honour of governor Moore's lady, who had the curiofity to pay it a vifit in the year 1760. This hill is not much lefs than a mile perpendicular height above the level of the fea. The walk to it from the houfe is not in the leaft incommodious on account of heat, even in the middle of the day. Who peregrinates into thefe regions finds every frefh afcent, however fhort, affording not only a new air, but a new fcene of nature, in regard to its profpect, its plants, and animals. The birds, the fifh, and infects, are many of them totally different from thofe we meet with in the lower fituations: and the face of things carries fo little fimilitude in appearance to what commonly occurs in other parts of the ifland, that one feems to have been tranfported by fome magic vehicle into a foreign country. This obfervation holds, it is true, in a certain degree, with refpect likewife to fome other diftricts of Jamaica;

for

for the Eaſt and Weſt ends, and the North, North-eaſt, and North-weſt ſides, are almoſt as diſſimilar, in the aſpect of the country, the weather, the plants, birds, and inſects, as if they belonged to as many differently ſituated iſlands. There are, nevertheleſs, ſeveral to be met with in theſe mountains of the ſame ſpecies as in other parts. The ring-tailed pigeons frequent them in great numbers: they are ſeen conſtantly on the wing, and generally darting along the fogs, which it is imagined they involve themſelves in, the better to conceal their flight. There are found, beſides, a ſmall martin, the whole upper parts of whoſe plumage are of a gloſſy, golden green, the inferior parts white; ſwifts, whoſe upper plumage is black, except a ring of white encircling the neck, and the parts below entirely white; blue-finches; dark-brown thruſhes; wood-peckers of various kinds; black-birds of the merops ſpecies; blue-ſparrows; long and ſhort-tailed humming-birds; blue and red-throat bull-finches; black and orange-coloured bull-finches, and brown petrils: the latter are ſaid to be very numerous on the higher parts of the Blue Mountains, where they breed in holes made in the earth. In the rivulets are found a ſqualid, yellow ſucking-fiſh, and the large common and hog-noſed freſh-water mullets. Of the quadruped reptile claſs, are the common grey lizard, a ſmall tree-frog, a ſmall galli-waſp, and rats in abundance. Of the inſect tribe, here are a ſpecies of crickets, which chirp like birds on the approach of the evening-duſk; a great variety of papilios and curculios, ſome of the latter green and gold, others grey; a large, black and yellow-ſtriped humble-bee; a fly of the cantharides kind; red and ſtinging ants; waſps; a beautiful, long forked tail butterfly, of a copperiſh and green hue. Of plants are obſerved a prodigious variety of ferns, and a ſtill greater of moſſes; black and bill-berry buſhes in abundance, large and flouriſhing; the wild-forrel; wild garden-mint, or *mentha vulgaris*; and ſeveral aromatic herbs and ſhrubs. The juniper-cedar, *agnus Scythicus*, and a yellow timber-tree, called here Mulatto-wood, are likewiſe very common, except the firſt-mentioned; it had a much ſtronger ſcent, and the wood of it was of a deeper red than the kind generally met with. The wild-forrel is as common as in England; and the garden-mint grows in wide-ſpreading tufts along the ſide of the road;

road; perhaps it has been propagated from fome plant, either cafually dropped, or put in by defign ; but it is remarkable, that it
grows, though in a very fterile foil, as luxuriantly as we find it in
any Englifh garden. The bill-berries are chiefly feen on the
higher eminences; but they are exceedingly numerous in fuch
fpots; and the black-berries not at all different from thofe of England, either in fize, or the mawkifh fweetnefs of their tafte. Cockroaches were not expected to be feen here : it is true, they are very
fcarce; and, I incline to believe, not aborigines of a region fo unfuitable to their nature, from its coolnefs; but probably brought
hither from Kingfton in fome of the packages of bottled liquor, or
provifions, which it is ufual for the parties to take with them, who
vifit this retreat for the fake of health or curiofity. That the ftate
of the atmofphere is generally very cool, I think there can be no
doubt, fince it has been found fo in the month of July; and I have
been informed, that, during the other hot months, the difference
between the thermometer here and at Kingfton is commonly twenty
to thirty degrees. The birds that were fhot did not begin to fmell
till after the fourth day. A North wind almoft conftantly blows,
and fometimes with great violence, when the vapours far below
are failing along with an Eafterly breeze, and the fhips ftanding in
for the harbour with that breeze right-aftern. The tranfition from
the heated air of the low lands caufes the chill to be the more fen-
fibly felt by thofe who remove to this elevation; the fenfation
therefore is not at all wonderful. A fire is found neceffary, even in
July, in the evening; and fome perfons have hardly been able to keep
themfelves warm enough in bed with two blankets. The butter,
which at Kingfton was in a liquified ftate, became fo firm in one
night's time, that a knife, ftuck into it, lifted the faucer in which
fome of it had been put. But the coldnefs of the air is chiefly diftreffing to the Negroes and horfes; they quickly grow fluggifh and
miferable; the latter in particular, although ftimulated by extreme
thirft, have been known to refufe tafting the fpring-water for feveral days, which was perfectly pure and tranfparent, but too
frigid for them. Exercife is attended with no fatigue; it ferves
only to keep the body in a comfortable glow. The fteep afcents
are climbed on foot in the middle of the day, without inconve-

nience; the air braces the tone of the fibres, renders the spirits lively, and creates an immoderate appetite for food, which unfortunately is not here in such abundance as to be proportionate to the demands for it.   Hence it may be supposed, that frosts are frequent on the Blue Mountain summits during the winter months, as some have positively afferted [w]   Those summits have been explored by very few persons; the air at such a height is almost too pure for human respiration.   I have been informed that some Negroes died in passing over them, some years ago, before the pacification was made with the rebels in this island.   These summits are bare of trees and shrubs, but well covered with a thick moss, which gives harbour to vast numbers of rats.   In what manner they procure subsistence in so dreary a residence, I have not been able to learn.

I must not be silent on a phænomenon, which I do not find noticed by any writer of our natural history.   I should, however, premise, that, in regard to the fact, it was communicated to me by a gentleman of such strict veracity, as not to admit a shadow of doubt.   He related it as a singularity which he could not readily account for, but had been observed by many persons living near the Yallahs and Buff Bay rivers.   During the months of November, December, January, and February, when little or no rain falls, several rivulets of water are observed to gush from the North side of the Ridges, which increase and swell the tide of these rivers very considerably : but they are not remarked at other times of the year, even after the heaviest rains.   The prodigious mantle of thick moss which cloathes these Ridges, extending over many hundreds, if not thousands of acres, receives and imbibes the water that almost continually distils upon it from the vapours that brood over their summits.   These rivulets are not seen until after the periodical North winds are set in, which usually happens in the be-

[w] According to a very accurate trigonometrical mensuration, lately taken by Dr. Alexander M'Kenzie, affisted by Mr. George Gauld, surveyor to his majesty, the results were as follow :

			Feet Height.		Mile.		
Catharine Hill,	}	above the {	5050	=	1	wanting	230 feet.
Blue Mountain Summit,	}	sea's level, {	7553	=	$1\frac{1}{2}$ ditto	367	ditto.

consequently, the mercury in the barometer (agreeably to Dr. Halley's calculations) ought to stand on the Blue Mountain at about 22 $\frac{49}{100}$ inches.

ginning

ginning of November; and they continue blowing till March, and sometimes later, but then grow more faint, and interrupted with the South-easters, or sea-breezes. The coldness and violence of these Northerly winds must be far greater at such an elevation than is ever felt below. The sun being at the same time in its Southern declination, the Northern slopes of the Ridges are shaded most part, if not all the day; and very little moisture can be exhaled from them. Is it not therefore probable, that the vehement pressure of these winds, directly against the Northern aspects, may squeeze the mossy covering as it were a sponge, so that the aqueous particles contained in it run into cohesion, and assemble in small rills; which, as they trickle downwards, are joined and augmented by others, till they form those larger rivulets, which have been observed to unite with the currents below, that lie in a convenient direction to receive them? May not the coldness of these Norths so harden the superficial soil of the Ridges, as to render it impervious to the humid particles lodged in the moss; though, in the warmer season of the year, it is sufficiently open to admit a free percolation to all that is not carried off by the sun's exhaling power? The sea-breeze has an oblique direction against the Ridges, and therefore, when most violent, blows upon them with much less pressure. It is moreover to be considered, that the moss is ranker and more luxuriant on the North aspects; and the vapours which over-hang them are, in general, denser and more constant than on the South sides. Whether the causes I have assigned are rational, or probable, must be left to the decision of abler philosophers. That judicious and benevolent writer, Dr. Lind, recommends strongly to the inhabitants of the low lands, in this and other hot climates, to retire to a hilly or mountainous residence at those times of the year when the heaviest rains fall. By their violence and continuance during the space of several successive days, the low lands are saturated with water; the exhalations from the earth are more copious than at other times; and, if any series of dry weather has preceded (which generally is the case), they are more noxious to health. Add to this, that the atmosphere is sultry and moist. These causes dispose the human body to be affected with agues and fevers (and, of the latter class, the putrid),

which

which chiefly affault perfons newly arrived from a cold Northern climate. There is no country in the torrid zone better furnifhed than Jamaica with retreats of this kind; the hills being fcattered every where very liberally near the coaft, and univerfally healthful. The inhabitants of Spanifh Town have the neighbouring Red Hills; the people of Kingfton are near the Liguanea Mountains; and in every part of thefe tracts the air is pure, temperate, and falubrious, during the whole year. The inhabitants of thefe mountains not only enjoy good health, but a fure indication of it in the frefhnefs of their complexions; and they are ftrangers to thofe deleterious diftempers which fometimes ravage the towns. The barrack at Stoney Hill in this parifh affords a ftriking proof of the goodnefs of this air. The company of foldiers quartered here were frefh from Europe, and luckily did not halt long enough at Kingfton to contract ficknefs. The whole garrifon continued in perfect health (and only one died, which happened, as I was informed, by a cafualty) till long after their arrival, when they were removed to Kingfton; where probably, not more from the change of air, than the greater facility of procuring fpirituous liquors, they grew fickly, and reduced in their number. No climate can be more propitious to European conftitutions than thefe elevated fpots; but the perfons who for the moft part emigrate to the ifland have not any choice of place for their future refidence, and of courfe they take their chance. Yet I cannot but think, that fuch as have weathered a feafoning in Kingfton, and lived there fo long as to have it in their power to chufe an occafional place of abode in a more eligible fituation here, fhould confult their own future health, and that of others fent over to their patronage and employment, and purchafe or rent a fmall fettlement fomewhere among thefe mountains, to ferve for a retreat during the moft fickly times of the year. But men educated and engaged in the buftle of commerce are too apt to defpife thefe cautions, as fpeculative and chimerical. Many are predeftinarians in their way of thinking, and will not ftep afide one inch to avoid a falling rock; and others are unwilling to lofe a fingle hour which may be employed in the purfuit of money, too inattentive to the purfuit of health, without which their labours are, in refpect to their own enjoyments, but vain and illufory. Hence

it

it happens, that we fee fo many pofting away from the ifland on their laft legs, to perifh under the icy rigours of a Northern climate; who, by occafionally withdrawing into the more temperate coolnefs of the mountains in this ifland, might have remained in the full poffeffion of good health; or, on their quitting it to re-vifit their native land, have carried with them a plenitude of bodily vigour, as well as opulence. The turf on the Ridges is fhort, and inter-mixed with a variety of wild aromatic herbs; fo that fheep, but particularly goats, might be paftured on it with great advantage to the delicacy of their flefh; and, it is probable, their milk would become in fome degree medicinal in feveral diforders. No ex-periment has yet been made to adorn the naked pikes with fome of the various fpecies of firs which are fo common in North-America; and from whence feeds, or young plants, might be had in great perfection, by reafon of the fhortnefs of the paffage. They have great beauty as well as utility, and would doubtlefs thrive extremely well on thefe eminences. The few fettlements fcattered here have gardens, which produce almoft every fort of European culinary ve-getables: thefe, indeed, are cultivated with great fuccefs at the North-fide of the ifland, and in all the interior parts. I have feen a piece of ground in one of the North fide parifhes fowed with cab-bage-feed, immediately after the wood had been cleared; and the plants it produced were beyond all comparifon much larger, firmer, and better flavoured, than any I have ever met with in England. I have feen quince-trees in a garden at Old Woman's Savannah, in Clarendon, which bore very fine, large fruit; but the apple-trees do not produce any where fo well as in the Liguanea Mountains: in the lower parts of the ifland they fhoot too much into wood, and their fruit degenerates; in thefe mountains, they appear to fructify beft on the higheft fites. The American and European peach, nectarine, and apricot, with feveral fpecies of plumbs, the raf-berry, ftrawberry, and mulberry, would hardly fail here, if planted in fituations open to the fun, and fheltered from the violence of the North winds. I have tafted nectarines which were produced in the Vale of Luidas, in St. John's. They were fmall, but re-tained all the delicious flavour peculiar to that fruit. They would certainly fucceed better in fome part of thefe mountains, where the

general

general state of air is found to approximate nearest to that of the Southern provinces of Europe.

The account I have given of these mountains is, I confess, very imperfect; no person, I believe, has hitherto visited them with the professed design of examining all their natural productions, or obtaining a regular information of the temperature of their atmosphere throughout the year, or of ascertaining their height by accurate barometrical observations. Tasks of this sort are reserved for men who are at entire leisure from the avocations of business and office; and who, to the incentives of a laudable curiosity, can join all the abilities, both of genius and fortune, that are necessary to pursue its full gratification. There is good reason to believe, that a gentleman who is duly qualified to explore them would meet with ample materials to recompense his toil; and it is greatly to be wished, that they may undergo a further scrutiny. Sir Hans Sloane possessed all that discernment and knowledge requisite for a cultivation of natural history. But he was fettered by the duties of the place he enjoyed under the duke of Albemarle; and, besides, the island was, in his time, in so rude a state, that it might have been impracticable for him to have examined much of its mountainous districts, even if he could have found sufficient leisure. And hence the many inaccuracies in his work; for he was obliged to rely chiefly on the writings and informations of other men, for want of opportunity to ground his descriptions on the result of his own personal experience. Much useful information of these interior regions might perhaps be gained, if the assembly of the island were to grant an annual pension of three or four hundred pounds sterling to some person thoroughly qualified in the branches of natural study: I mean those in particular which have relation to agriculture, husbandry, food, medicine, minerals, and commerce. The advantages to be reaped from such an appointment would depend on the ability and spirit of the person chosen. In the present age, it would not be difficult to engage one competently qualified; since there never was a period in which this study employed such numbers of ingenious men in our mother-country. This patriotic ardour for promoting science in general, and in particular natural history and husbandry, has not been confined to societies only:

private

private gentlemen have exerted their fingle efforts in fupport of it, and laudably devoted part of their fortunes to this end, inftead of wafting it in unprofitable diffipations. The ifland of Jamaica has never wanted gentlemen of diftinguifhed tafte for the fine, as well as the more ufeful and œconomical, arts; and, fince the ifland is fo opulent, that the charge of fuch an appointment would hardly be felt, what more favourable circumftances can be hoped to concur, either towards enfuring fuccefs in the undertaking, or giving the public that fatisfactory knowledge of foils, climates, and productions, that, while it gratifies the *literati*, may alfo tend to improve and people this country? The want of a liberal education, or an attention of the whole foul to get money, as if it were the only rational object of purfuit in this world, has occafioned men in general to treat the ftudy of natural hiftory, and its followers, with contempt and ridicule; all are indifcriminately confounded with the defpicable tribe of infect-hunters, and collectors of gimcracks. We fhould, however, be cautious to feparate from this drofs all thofe, whofe labours conduce to the moft ufeful purpofes of life; who not only difclofe to us the wonderful mechanifm of the creation, and the wifdom of the Deity; but exemplify his unbounded benevolence to man, while they inftruct us in the means by which our health may be preferved, our life prolonged, our agriculture improved, manufactures enlarged and multiplied, commerce and trade extended, and the public enriched. I muft confefs, that this ufeful purfuit has not been without its fautors in Jamaica. Sir Hans Sloane firft laid open a new fcene of American productions, not much known before to the learned in Europe. Yet, before his time, the fcience was cultivated in this ifland by Dr. Barham, whom Sir Hans frequently quotes, and whofe manufcripts were never publifhed. Some time afterwards, Dr. Patrick Brown undertook a fimilar work, containing many undefcribed plants and animals: this work he was enabled to publifh chiefly by the fubfcription of the gentlemen of the ifland. The late Dr. Anthony Robinfon likewife made a collection of feveral hundred figures and defcriptions of Jamaica plants and animals; the greater part of which are non-defcripts: but he unfortunately died before it could be digefted into a regular feries for publication. This

work,

work, if it fhould ever be given to the public, will be found to correct many errors in Sloane and Brown ; who, compared with him, were in various inftances very fuperficial obfervers, or ill-informed. He invented a vegetable foap, fuperior in its properties to common foap; for which difcovery, the affembly of this ifland granted him a reward of one hundred pounds fterling. He likewife prepared a fago from a fpecies of the palm, fo common in Jamaica, equal in its alimentary qualities to what comes from the Eaft-Indies. Notwithftanding thefe voluminous collections, it is certain, there ftill remains a very great number of plants and minerals in this ifland to be defcribed and claffed. And, to compleat the whole, there is required a judicious analyfis of their properties and ufe. I have been informed, that her majefty queen Anne, upon the reprefentations of Sir Hans Sloane, gave out of her privy-purfe 200 l. fterling *per annum*, to fupport and encourage a botanical profeffor in this ifland ; but her death happened foon after, and the bounty was withdrawn.

The importance of cultivating this fcience, in a part of the world fo abounding in materials, will not be denied, when we confider the immenfe fums that have been acquired in trade by the Jefuits bark, the canella, cochineal, indigo, logwood, and various other vegetable productions; whofe value might ftill have been loft to the community, and their preparations unknown, had not fome knowledge in natural hiftory revealed them. And there is very probable ground to fuppofe, that there is in this ifland a vaft variety of plants ftill to be examined; whofe fruit, gums, barks, or roots (to fay nothing of the foffile and mineral kingdoms), might be found very proper fubjects for export, or for œconomical ufes among the inhabitants. In order to promote fuch beneficial re-fearches, it is to be wifhed, that thofe planters, who fend their fons to Great-Britain for education in phyfic and furgery, would direct, that botany fhould alfo be attended to, and made a principal branch of their ftudy. Botanical knowledge feems particularly re-quifite to their practice in a country that teems with vegetable re-medies for moft of the diftempers incident to the climate. A total ignorance of this ufeful fcience is a moft contemptible defect in the practitioners here ; for what can be more reproachful than to have

it

it faid, and with truth, that many of the Negroes are well acquainted with the healing virtues of feveral herbs and plants, which a regular phyfician tramples under foot, with no other idea of them, than that they are no part of his *materia medica*, nor any better than ufelefs weeds? It will be no fmall affiftance to any perfon who may hereafter botanize in Jamaica, that Sloane and Brown have already paved the way; but, indeed, a thorough difcovery of the virtues and ufes of what have been already defcribed, feems to be more wanted at prefent than a further fcrutiny after non-defcribed plants. Superadded to this will be the endeavours of gentlemen of the ifland to introduce exotic plants and trees from the Eaft-Indian and American continents, of fuch kinds as have been moft celebrated for their medicinal, or fome other valuable qualities. No part of the ifland feems better adapted for fuch nurferies than the Liguanea or Midland Mountains. They would require fome care till their feeding time; after which, the different fpecies might eafily be propagated in other diftricts.

I return from this digreffion to clofe my account of St. Andrew's. The lower, or more level part of the parifh, comprehended under the name of Liguanea, is the quarter moft appropriated to fugar-plantations. The foil here has been chiefly formed by the fine mould wafhed down from the hills, and produces a good cane. In fome parts, the foil is mixed with a coarfe rubble, fwept by heavy torrents from the gullies. This foil requires plentiful rains (without which it is apt to burn the canes), and conftant manure. One of the Oliverian regiments firft fettled here, under the command of colonel Archbould and major Hope, who, with Sir William Beefton, poffeffed the beft and largeft fhare of this whole tract. Few of the fugar-plantations are remoter from the harbour than fix or feven miles; the interior or hilly part being chiefly employed in the cultivation of coffee and provifions. The roads here are in general firm; the fugar of excellent quality; and the carriage to and from the town fo eafy, that the eftates are juftly efteemed very valuable. The Long Mountain, which runs obliquely from Rock Fort for about four miles inland, is for the moft part compofed of lime-ftone. The end of it, which advances neareft to the harbour, fupplies large quantities of ballaft for the

fhips,

fhips, ftones for building and for lime; which are carried by water from the foot of it. But the houfes in general are of brick manu-factured from the natural foil, which is a certain proof of its fertile quality.

Near Merryman's Hill, in Liguanea, a mineral water has, not long fince, been difcovered; which is faid to contain a vitriolic acid iron, a portion of talky, argillaceous, and abforbent earths, joined to a fixed foffile alkali. Dr. Richardfon, who tried fome experi-ments upon it, acknowledges, however, that this analyfis is incom-plete, and requires further experiments, which cannot be made, except at the fountain head. This is commonly known at prefent by the name of Curtin's Spring, and probably contains a very me-dicinal quality; for which reafon, a more perfect analyfis is ex-tremely defireable, for afcertaining all its ingredients.

State of the Parifh:

	Negroes.	Cattle.	Sugar-eftates.	Annual Produce of Sugar.	
				Hogfheads.	Other Settlements.
1734,	7631	5413			
1740,	8363	5244			
1745,	8936	5001			
1761,	9024		30	2600	122
1768,	9813	4626			

This parifh is in a flourifhing ftate, and increafing in its number of fugar-plantations, though not fo rapidly as might have been ex-pected, confidering its vicinity to Kingfton. This fupinenefs may be attributed to the abfence of the chief proprietors, who refide in the mother-country, and are not folicitous about forming new eftates, which require fome money to be advanced, and perhaps the perfonal fuperintendency of the owners. The diminution in cattle has (among other caufes) proceeded from the erecting of feveral water-mills, which have rendered a lefs number neceffary. The whole ifland, indeed, has owed much of its prefent improved ftate to the extenfive introduction of thefe ufeful machines.

SECT.

View of Port Royal & Kingston Harbour.

SECT. III.

PORT ROYAL.

THIS parish is bounded on the East, by St. David; on the West, by the port, and St. Andrew; North, by Kingston harbour, and St. David; and South, by the ship channel, and sea. A part of Yallahs River forms the inland confine on the North; as the Bull Bay River does on the East. It is watered also by the Hope, and Mammee. The town, which is in 17° 57' North latitude, and 76° 37' longitude West from London, is situated on the point of a peninsula, or narrow neck of land, called the Palisadoe, which, projecting from the main land about eight miles and three quarters, forms a barrier to the harbour of Kingston against the sea. The foundation of it was first laid by general Brayne, in the year 1657. It was then called Cagua, or Cagway, a corruption probably of caragua, the Indian name for the coratoe, or great aloe, which overspreads the adjacent Saltpan Hill. The excellent anchorage in the road, where a thousand ships might lie secure from all winds except hurricanes, and the depth of water, insomuch that the largest vessels used to lay their broadsides to the wharfs, and load or unload with little trouble, made it so desireable a seat for trade, that it soon became celebrated for the number of its inhabitants, the extent of its commerce, and amazing treasures of gold and silver. In the year 1672, it contained eight hundred well-built houses, most of which were rented as high as any of that time in the heart of the city of London. Twenty years after this, the number was increased to two thousand; and it had then attained the height of its splendor. The situation was extremely incommodious in many respects. It had neither earth, wood, nor water; the soil was nothing more than a loose sand, lodged at first upon a ridge of rock, and gradually extended in breadth, as well as depth, in a long series of time, by the renditions of the sea. The natural wants, however, of so large and populous a town, proved very instrumental towards forming and encouraging plantations upon the

main

main land. The demand for fire-wood, building-timber, bricks.
flesh, corn, fruits, and other vegetable provisions, was confiderable; and this was supplied by the settlers in St. Catharine and
St. Andrew. The advantage of trade to an infant-colony, and the
mutual dependence of the merchant and planter one upon the other,
were never more conspicuous than in this example. The town
was inhabited by scarcely any other than merchants, warehouse-
keepers, vintners, and retailers of punch; the latter were very numerous, and well supported by the buccaneers, who dissipated here
whatever they got from the Spaniards. As an instance of their
profusion, it is said, that one of them has been known to squander
three thousand pieces of eight, equal to 750l. of present currency,
in less than a month. The immense riches they brought into this
town, the grand treasury of all their spoil, may partly be judged
by the sums which the armament, under Sir Henry Morgan only,
is said to have brought in during 1669 and 1670, viz.

On the capture of Puerto del Principe, —   50,000 pieces of eight.
                 Puerto Vela,   —   —   250,000
                 Maracaibo, —   —   —   250,000
                 Panama and Cruz,   —   400,000
                                   _____

            In all, 950,000 or £. 237,500
besides an immense quantity of silks, linens, gold and silver lace,
plate, jewels, and other valuable commodities; which probably
amounted to near as much more. By this means (as an historian
has observed) money grew to be in vast plenty, and returns easy
to England, into which many hundred thousand of those pieces of
eight were imported. A share of these acquisitions, however, remained in circulation among the planters, who by this time brought
their manufactures of sugar and indigo to great perfection. Their
other commodities for export were, ginger, anotto, cacao, cotton,
and pimento; fustick, mahogany, and *lignum vitæ*. All their
goods were shipped at Port Royal; and, by an act of assembly
passed in 1683, all productions of this sort, that were levied on
for payment of debts, were directed to be appraised in that town
by the church-wardens, upon their oaths, and then delivered to
the creditor, who was obliged to accept them at the appraised value,

as

as fo much money. This law, fo favourable to the planters, was likewife highly beneficial to the mother-country, by its confidering the foreign money then current here as mere merchandize, and of courfe leaving it free for exportation to England.

I am now about to defcribe the fad reverfe of fortune which this town experienced ; but, firft, it may not be improper to mention the ftate of it in the beginning of the fatal year 1692. It contained at that period upwards of three thoufand five hundred inhabitants, and two thoufand houfes ; the greater number of which were of brick, feveral ftories in height, founded clofe to the very brink of the water, on a loofe bank of fand. The fort, which then mounted fixty pieces of ordnance, and the reft of the houfes, were founded on the rocky part of the peninfula. On the 7th of June, 1692, between eleven and twelve o'clock at noon, began that terrible earthquake which, in two minutes time, produced fuch a fcene of devaftation [x]. All the principal ftreets, which were next to the water, funk at once, with the people in them ; and a high, rolling fea followed, clofing immediately over them. Not lefs than fixteen hundred were thus fwallowed up, or fhook into an

[x] The year began with very hot, dry weather, which continued till May, when there was much blowing-weather, and a great deal of rain, till the end of the month ; from which time, till the earthquake happened, it was exceffively calm, hot, and dry. The 7th of June was a very hot, clear fun-fhine-day, fcarce a cloud appearing, and not a breath of air felt. The earthquake began at forty minutes paft eleven A. M. with a very fmall trembling. The fecond fhake was fomewhat ftronger, accompanied all the while with a hollow, rumbling noife ; and, immediately after this fecond fhake, came on the third, and moft violent, which continued near a minute.

When Venables took the ifland, the point whereon Port Royal now ftands was almoft infulated, being joined to the Palifadoes only by a ridge of fand, which at that time juft began to appear above water. When Jackfon invaded St. Jago de la Vega, which was about feventeen years antecedent, it was entirely feparated by the fea. On this fandy ifthmus, which the inhabitants enlarged by driving piles, wharfing, &c. the greater part of the town was built, extending above a quarter of a mile ; and the weight of fo many large brick-houfes was juftly imagined to contribute, in a great meafure, to their downfall ; for the ground gave way as far as the houfes erected on this fandy foundation ftood, and no further.

So in the great earthquake which happened in Sicily in the following year, 1693, it was obferved, that in lefs folid ground, as chalk, fand, or loofe earth, the mifchief was beyond comparifon greater than in rocky places. And, in Syracufe, the difference was vifible in three places ; that is, in the middle of the city ; in the little ifland ; and in Zaracatti, where the antient Syracufa ftood ; in all which places, the buildings, being on a rocky foundation, remained for the moft part untouched, or only fhaken, or at leaft not quite demolifhed : whereas, on the contrary, in the reft of that territory which is not rocky, a vaft number of noble ftructures and towers lay in a heap of ruins.

heap

heap of rubbifh. Some of the ftreets were laid feveral fathoms under water; and it ftood as high as the upper rooms of fome houfes which remained. It was computed, that about two thoufand Whites and Negroes perifhed in this town alone. The harbour had all the appearance of agitation as in a ftorm; and the huge waves rolled with fuch violence, as to fnap the cables of the fhips, drive fome from their anchors, and overfet others. Among the reft, the Swan frigate, that lay by the wharf to careen, was forced over the tops of the funken houfes, and providentially enabled fome hundreds of the inhabitants to fave their lives. The fort only, and about two hundred houfes, efcaped without damage. But a part of the neck of land, communicating from the point to the Palifadoes, about a quarter of a mile in length, was entirely fubmerfed, with all the houfes, which ftood very thick upon it. The water forced its paffage through the Saltpond Hill and gufhed in torrents from its fide, at an elevation of twenty, and in fome places thirty feet above its bafe, and continued running for feveral hours afterwards. The mountains on each fide the river-road, leading from Spanifh Town to Sixteen-mile-walk, were thrown down in fuch heaps, as to obftruct the paffage of the river, and for fome time to prevent all communication between thefe two places. A great part of a rocky mountain in St. David's fell down, and buried a whole plantation lying at the foot of it. The part from which this huge fragment was detached is now a precipice of folid rock, confpicuous from its height at a great diftance, and remains a dreadful monument of that day's cataftrophe.

The fhock was not lefs violent in the mountains. Some were even of opinion, that they had funk a little; others, that the whole ifland had fomewhat fubfided; for they obferved, that feveral wells in Liguanea did not require fo long a rope, by two or three feet, as they did before the earthquake. However, it is more natural to account for this change, by fuppofing, that the water had rifen higher; for, in all thefe violent commotions of the earth, it is well known, that fprings are remarkably affected. At the North fide, above one thoufand acres of land are faid to have funk, with thirteen inhabitants. It left not a houfe ftanding at Paffage Fort; only one at Liguanea; deftroyed moft of the planters habitations

4

in

in the country; and all in St. Jago de la Vega, except what were built by the Spaniards. During these convulsions, which continued with little intermission, though in a slighter degree, for some weeks afterwards, the most offensive stenches were emitted from every fissure and opening made in the sand near the harbour; the sky became dull and reddish, which indicated a plentiful discharge of vapours from the earth; the weather grew hotter than had been observed before the shock; and such prodigious swarms of muskeetos infested the coasts, as to astonish the inhabitants; the beauty of the mountains was quite effaced, and, instead of their lively, youthful verdure, they appeared distorted with fragments, bald, and furrowed.

After this fatality, many of the inhabitants, who had survived the loss of Port Royal, removed to that part of Liguanea where Kingston now stands. Here they took refuge in miserable huts, which could not defend them from the rain. Thus destitute of suitable conveniences and medicines, they soon perished with malignant fevers. The air, empoisoned with noxious vapours, co-operating with the terror of these calamities, and the distress they occasioned, brought on a general sickness, which very few escaped in any part of the island. Not less than three thousand are computed to have died; the greater part at Kingston only, where five hundred graves were dug in a month's time, and two or three buried in a grave. What rendered the scene more tragical were the numbers of dead bodies which, after perishing in the shock at Port Royal, were seen in hundreds floating from one side of the harbour to the other. Thus fell the glory of Port Royal; and with it all the publick records; which proved a heavy loss. In the following year, the assembly taking into consideration, that the fort and many of the houses were still left standing; that it was a place so excellently adapted to carry on trade, and of great strength to resist an enemy; resolved upon rebuilding it. First, however, they endeavoured to shew the deep impression which the late misfortune had made upon their minds, by appointing every 7th of June to be observed, for the future, as a day of fasting and deprecation of the divine wrath; which still continues, and ever ought, to be religiously kept here. The sand on the South side of the town

was

was funk fo low, that it was feared the fea would encroach too faft, and endanger the houfes left ftanding on that fide. They therefore enacted that the owners of ground formerly built upon, and whofe houfes had been thrown down by the earthquake, fhould rebuild them; or, otherwife, that the lots fhould be fold on a fair valuation, and the money be paid to the owners. Some provifions were like-wife made for repairing the wall, or breaftwork, which had been built to hinder the encroachment of the fea; and the receiver-ge-neral, fecretary, and port officers, were ordered to hold their offices here, by themfelves or deputies, as heretofore.

By degrees, as the popular fears fubfided, the town increafed in buildings and inhabitants, though far fhort of its former ftate, till the year 1703, when it was deftroyed a fecond time. A terrible fire broke out among fome of the ware-houfes, which fpread with fuch fury, as to reduce moft of the houfes to afhes. It was occa-fioned, as appears from an act paffed foon after, by keeping large quantities of gun-powder, and other combuftibles, in the different quarters of the town; and its devaftation was imputed to the Northward fhingles, with which the houfes were covered. This accident produced the law, which enacts, that, as the North-Ame-rican fhingles had been found very dangerous, no perfon, inha-biting in this town, fhould for the future cover any houfe, or other building, with any fhingles brought from the Northward, nor any other than what are made and produced in this ifland, under penalty of forfeiting 100 l. and fuch houfe or building: a regula-tion fo prudent, that it is amazing it has not been extended to Kingfton, and other towns where it is equally neceffary. This ruinous accident caufed another defertion to Kingfton; which thus began to thrive by the decline of her elder fifter; fo that, two years afterwards, it was grown fo populous, that the legiflature found it convenient to eftablifh here a quarter-feffion, and court of common-pleas, and to enact feveral provifions for fecuring the na-vigation of the harbour, fettling the rates of wharfage, repairing the ftreets, and guarding againft fire. Port Royal was at this pe-riod reduced to a very low ebb, yet it was not wholly deferted. It was thought advifeable to keep it provided always with a ftrong garrifon. It ftill poffeffed fome little trade, and was the favourite

refort

refort of the feamen belonging to the men of war and privateers. But, as if Providence had decreed that it fhould never more revive to any thing like its former fplendor, what the earthquake and conflagration had fpared was nearly demolifhed by a violent hurricane, which happened on the 28th of Auguft, 1722. It began at eight in the morning, and lafted fourteen hours; during which, the rain was inceffant, and the ftorm veered all round the compafs. In Kingfton moft of the buildings were thrown down, or much fhattered. The very day preceding it was perfectly calm; but fo great a fwell at fea, that the waves broke over the breaft-work at Port Royal, and laid all the ftreets under water. The fort fuffered very much; feveral of the guns were difmounted, and fome wafhed into the fea. The church and row of houfes in the Eaft part of the town were fo battered, that there remained very little appearance of a building. In fhort, above half the town was laid in ruins; and the houfes and plantations in all parts of the ifland fuffered confiderable damage, except in St. Jago, where the Spanifh buildings ftood the fhock unhurt. Very few of the inhabitants loft their lives; but in the harbour it proved more fatal. Out of thirty-fix merchant-fhips and floops, only ten were to be feen after the ftorm; and of thefe one half were irreparably damaged. The Falkland, Swallow, and Weymouth men of war, and the floop Happy, loft all their mafts and boats; the other part of the fquadron, confifting of the Lancafter, Mermaid, and Adventure, were luckily at fea, and efcaped. The naval ftore-houfe was blown down; and moft of the powder in the magazines damaged. The Rio Cobre was obftructed for feveral miles about the Caymana's, and loft its ufual channel, by the prodigious abundance of trees and rubbifh which the wind and inundation had thrown into it; fo that the paffage from St. Jago to Kingfton by land became interrupted for fome time; and the affembly were obliged to pafs an act for clearing it. It was computed, that four hundred perfons loft their lives in the harbour, among which were two hundred Negroe flaves on board a Guiney fhip, which foundered at her anchors. In 1717, the affembly, being fenfible that the wall, or breaft-work, on the South fide of the town was of the utmoft importance to prevent the fea from breaking in, eftablifhed 150 *l. per annum* as a perpetual fund for keeping it in repair. They had, some time before, prohibited the carrying away any stones or sand from the cayes and shoals which lay in the channel, with a view to the like precaution; which was sufficiently justified in the year 1744, when another furious hurricane arose at six in the evening on the 20th of October, and continued till six the following morning. A new fort, begun at Mosquito Point, was entirely razed; many houses were blown down in the towns and other parts of the island; and all the wharfs at Port Royal, Kingston, Passage Fort, and Old Harbour, were destroyed, and most of the goods swept away. The inhabitants of Port Royal expected every moment to be swallowed up by an inundation, the streets being all laid several feet under water; but, happily, their wall withstood the shock, and saved them from utter ruin. Their dangerous situation may be imagined; for the wind, setting the whole time from the South, drove the surge full against this part of the town, and with such fury, that immense loads of stone and sand were poured over the wall. Sir Chaloner Ogle, who then had the command on this station, was fortunately at sea, with the major part of the fleet; but there were nine men of war and ninety-six merchant ships in the harbour, one hundred and four of which were stranded, wrecked, or foundered; so that only the Rippon rode it out with the loss of her masts; and a great number of mariners were drowned. Thus has this unhappy town undergone, in the space of fifty-two years, a sad succession of extraordinary disasters, by earthquake, tempest, fire, and inundation. In its present humbled condition, it has three streets, two or three lanes, and about two hundred houses. The fortification, called Fort Charles, stands on a low spot at the entrance or mouth of the harbour, and is defended by one hundred and twenty-six guns. The breast-work, or line, is also formed to guard the channel in coming in, as well as to prevent any access by the Palisadoe or land-side; so that it is now compleatly fortified. Within the fort is a small powder-magazine, and a house for the commanding officer. The barracks are capable of receiving upwards of three hundred men, exclusive of their officers; and here is a hospital for their sick. In 1734, when Sir Chaloner Ogle commanded the squadron here, a large piece of ground was taken in at the North-

East

Eaſt quarter of the town, and veſted in the crown, for the ſervice of his majeſty's ſhips; and in 1741 the yard and wharf were greatly enlarged by an act of aſſembly, paſſed for that purpoſe. Here the men of war are careened and refitted; but the greater part of the naval ſtores are kept in proper ware-houſes at Greenwich. The hoſpital for the ſeamen is a large, airy, and well-contrived building. The church is a ſmall, but neat ſtructure, with an organ, a tower, and cupola. The captain of the fort has of late years been appointed by the governor's warrant, upon the nomination of the miniſtry. His ſalary is only 109 *l.* 10 *s. per annum*; but the profits of this poſt make it far more conſiderable. By the revenue-law, paſſed in 1728, a proviſion is made of 547 *l.* 10 *s. per annum* for twelve matroſſes and gunners, who are required to be inhabitants of the town, and continually reſident in it. The holding theſe employments is an excuſe from ſervice as peace-officers, jury-men, or in the militia; and for this reaſon, the inhabitants make ſtrong intereſt to obtain warrants of appointment to theſe merely nominal commiſſions, for they gladly relinquiſh their claim to the ſalary, which of courſe becomes a perquiſite to the captain. A practice, very detrimental to trade, was formerly in uſe here; I mean the demand of a gratuity from the maſters of veſſels, importing bullion from foreign parts, for leave to paſs the fort: this, with exactions of the like nature from the governors, naval officers, &c. became ſo grievous, that theſe foreigners at length declared it to be the principal reaſon of their abandoning all further trade at this port, and of their reſort to the French at Hiſpaniola, where they are ſaid to have met with a more favourable reception, and to have made up their aſſortments full as cheap. Rapacious acts commonly begin at the top in theſe diſtant governments, and ſo deſcend to the loweſt underſtrappers.

It was unpleaſing to ſee the intereſt of a colony thus made a ſacrifice to the baſeſt principle; and more ſo, that the injured people either had not, or were not able to exert, a ſuitable remedy. But ſuch as a governor is, ſuch will be the ſubordinate miniſters within his juriſdiction. The captain of the fort takes charge of all the powder brought into the magazine purſuant to the tonnage-act, and accounts, upon oath, for its waſte and expenditure, to the

council

council and affembly when called upon; fubject, in cafe of neglect or refufal, to a penalty of 500*l.* The profits of this poft have been computed at not lefs than 1000*l.* fterling *per annum.* The expence of keeping this fort, and the barracks at Port Royal, in repair, from 1743 to 1752, paid by the public of Jamaica, amounted to 27,667*l.* which is about 3074*l. per annum.* The powder ordinarily in the magazine is about 20,500 lb.wt. and all that it is not capable of containing is lodged at Mofquito Point, and Rock Fort.

The quantity confumed in falutes, minute-guns, re-
    joicing-days, and a morning and evening-watch,
    is, *communibus annis*, about ——— ——— —— 25600 lb.wt.

The wafte, in fifting and fhifting, about —— —— 3000

                                                    28600

which, at eighteen-pence *per* pound (the price at which it is rated on being paid in), comes to 2145*l.* a charge which might be leffened, and the faving better applied to the article of repairs.

    Thefe falutes, &c. have ufually been regulated in the following manner :

                                                  N° Guns.

On the death of the governor, admiral, or the governor's
    lady, —— —— —— —— —— 61

Ditto of the king's uncle or aunt, —— —— —— 44

King's birth-day, —— —— —— —— 27

Death of the king's brother, or fifter; birth-day of any of
    the royal family, except the king's; on arrival or de-
    parture of a governor; on his vifiting or leaving the
    fort; on publifhing his commiffion; commiffioners
    of the forts vifiting, and leaving; gun-powder plot;
    St. George's day; and other publick holidays; —— 21

Salute of an admiral's flag, —— —— —— 15

Ditto a privy-counfellor of the ifland arriving, — —— 14

Ditto ditto leaving the ifland; — —— —— 13

An exact account of all the powder brought in every year to this fort, and the out-ports, would give a tolerably accurate detail of the tonnage of fhipping employed in the trade of this ifland; it
                                              would

would probably be rather under than over the truth, as their regifters feldom correfpond with exact menfuration.

The powder, expended at Fort Augufta, on Mofquito Point, is,
one year with another, about 7000 lb.wt value 525 *l.*

In the year 1760, the quantity of powder received at Fort
Charles amounted to three hundred and nine barrels, of 100 lb.wt.
each, = 30,000 lb.wt. which makes the tonnage of that year, of
the fhips that come to Kingfton harbour, thirty thoufand nine
hundred; and, fuppofing feventy tons each to be an average, the
number will be four hundred and forty-one fhips and fmaller
veffels [*y*].

For the fervice of the forts feveral Negroes are allotted; and
by the laft account there were,

At Fort Charles,	23
Fort Augufta,	13
Rock Fort,	12
Engineer for general work,	30

Total, 78

and proper canoes, either for going with difpatches, or bringing
provifions from Kingfton market, &c. The inhabitants are chiefly
fupported by the money fpent here by the garrifon and the fquadron; by the gains made by their wherries that ply for fare in the
harbour; their turtle-fifhery, which is confiderable; the pilotage
of fhips in and out; and by their votes at the election of reprefentatives; though it muft be confeffed, that, except when party-feuds
run very high in the ifland, their profits in this laft article are but
trifling: however, many perfons are proprietors of houfes in this
town, merely for the advantage of voting at thefe elections; in
the mean time letting them rent-free, on condition only, that the
tenant keeps them in tolerable repair.

Befides thefe douceurs, one inhabitant receives 400 *l.* a year for
fupplying the fort and the garrifon at Mofquito Point with frefh

[*y*] The medium quantity received, *communibus annis*, about 415, equal to 21,500 tons of
fhipping. An act has lately been paffed for levying the duty in money at 1*s.* 6*d. per* ton on all
veffels (foreign only excepted), and appropriating the proceeds as a general fund for repairing forts
and fortifications: a meafure from which, I am perfuaded, the ifland will reap very great advantage. By the fame act, the receiver-general is empowered to buy powder for fupplying them.

water,

water, brought in boats from the river Cobre; and another is paid 100 *l.* annually, for giving a dinner to the committee of the legiflature, who come hither to view the ftate of this fortrefs. Sometimes they have obtained a partial exemption from certain taxes; and, confidering the veneration and compaffion due to the town on account of its antient grandeur and prefent poverty, there feems to be juft ground for thefe eleemofynary benefactions. The air of the town has been always efteemed remarkably healthful. It is open to a free ventilation; and the wind is corrected by paffing in every direction over the fea-water. In the middle of the day it is generally very hot; for the heat of the air is greatly augmented by the fand, which retains it like a *balneum mariæ.* But rain rarely falls here. The clouds from the land have a quick drift out to fea, after being blown over the Blue Mountains; and thofe that approach from the fea generally follow the mountainous ridges, and thus are drawn away from this quarter. The inhabitants in general live to a great age; and many convalefcents repair hither from other parts of the ifland, to recruit their emaciated bodies with the purity of this atmofphere, and a regular courfe of turtle-diet, which is cooked here in the higheft perfection. The civil government of the town is, like the others, under the difpenfation of a *cuſtos,* or chief magiftrate, and his affiftants, with other peace-officers. It has alfo a quarter-feffion of the peace, and court of common-pleas, and mufters a fmall corps of militia. The rector's ftipend is 250 *l. per annum;* and, all perquifites included, does not amount to more than about 300 *l.* as I am informed.

Port Royal, as a place of defence, is defervedly valued. The fhips, in advancing towards the harbour, muft neceffarily pafs, between fhoals and rocks, through a difficult channel, in fome parts extremely narrow; and are inevitably expofed to a fevere fire, without poffibility of bringing their guns to bear. A-head they have a battery of twelve guns, moftly forty-two pounders, called the Twelve Apoftles, built on a point of Saltpan Hill (above the range of an enemy's fhot), which would rake them the whole way, till they tacked to ftand up the harbour: they are then expofed to the fire of this battery on one fide, to the fire of the fort on the other,

and

and in front to the battery of Fort Augufta. The harbour is about one mile and three quarters in breadth, but widens further-in.

The men of war anchor near the town in eight and ten fathom water. Fort Augufta ftands on Mofquito Point, which is a fandy peninfula, about two miles in length, and very narrow, projecting from the North-Eaft fide of the Saltpan Hill, and forming a kind of lunette on the Weft fide of the harbour. At the point, the fhip-channel between the harbours of Port Royal and Kingfton is not a quarter of a mile in breadth, and would probably become fhoal-water, if it was not for the Rio Cobre, which fweeps through it to the fea. The channel has from fix to eight fathom ; but on each fide of it are fand-banks, in paffing over which, the fmall wherries fometimes rub their keels. This fort mounts eighty-fix large guns, kept in excellent order. It contains a large magazine, a houfe for the commandant, barracks to contain three hundred foldiers, with all convenient offices, and cafemates. It was pro-jected to mount one hundred and fixteen guns; but it is not yet compleated. The walls and baftions are built upon piles of the palmeto or thatch-pole tree, which is endued with the property of lafting in water without being liable to erofion by the worm. Thefe were driven down through the loofe fand, until they reached a firm bed. If the fame precaution had been ufed in conftructing the houfes of Port Royal, it is probable that the greater part of the town would have furvived the earthquake. This fort con-tains an hofpital, befides habitations for the officers, and is looked upon to be an healthy garrifon. The neck of fand which joins it to the main is not above fifty or fixty feet wide in moft places, and fo low, that an enemy could not carry on approaches, on account of the water rifing near the furface ; and it is flanked by a lagoon, or inlet of water from the harbour, of fome extent; for thefe reafons, and becaufe the fhips, in paffing up the channel to-wards Kingfton, muft come within point-blank fhot of a whole line of guns, a governor of this ifland pronounced it impregnable both by land and fea. The fort is about two miles diftant from Port Royal, and about three and a half from Kingfton.

The

The broadeſt part of Port Royal peninſula is neaily oppoſite to the Eaſt quarter of Kingſton : on this part is a ſmall graſs-penn, ſtocked with ſheep and goats. The ſide next the harbour is interſected with ſeveral little ponds and inlets ; and here is the uſual careening-place for merchant-ſhips. This neck of land might be made very paſſable for horſes ; but the people of Port Royal prefer a water-carriage, which is more pleaſant, and equally expeditious. Leaving this maritime part of the pariſh, I ſhall proceed to the other diſtrict of it, which lies on the main land. It contains about fifteen thouſand acres, but very few ſettlements or inhabitants ; for the more level part bordering on the coaſt is parched, for want of rain ; and the reſt is occupied with ſteep mountains. Near the road, which leads acroſs this pariſh from the Eaſtward to Kingſton, ſtands the antient habitation of Sir James de Caſtillo, a Spaniſh gentleman ; who was knighted by king William III. for his ſervices in negociating a treaty, to furniſh the Spaniſh dominions in the Weſt-Indies with an annual number of Negroes, by the way of Jamaica [z]. This houſe was defended by ſeveral ſwivel-guns, ranged on poſts before the front ; its ſituation near the Bull Bay ſubjecting it in war-time to the danger of being attacked by the privateers, which frequently have made deſcents on this part of the country.

There is nothing further in the pariſh that merits notice, except the caſcade at Mammee River. This ſtream takes its riſe among the Blue Mountains ; and, after a winding courſe, diſcharges itſelf between two rocky hills near Bull Bay, by a fall of about two hundred feet. The direction of the fall is altered, midway, by a vaſt rock, extending from the ſide of the adjacent precipice, which breaks the ſheet of water, and cauſes it to be agitated with ſuch violence, that the ſpace below is filled with a continual miſt ; which, ſo long as the ſun ſhines upon it, exhibits a beautiful variety of fine irides : from thence the river ruſhes, foaming along between rocks, till it reaches the open ground below. Under the brow of the Eaſtern hill, above the fall, is a very large and curious cave, filled, like all the others that I have ſeen in this iſland, with

[z] He was commiſſary-general for the Aſſiento ; lived here many years ; and acquired a conſiderable property, with univerſal eſteem.

ſtalactic

ftalactic petrifactions. In many parts of the mountains are found
fimilar cavities, fome of which have adits defcending a very great
depth into the earth. It is poffible, they may have been originally
formed by earthquakes; yet, to judge from the appearance of moft
of them, they appear coeval with the ifland itfelf. On going into
one of thefe in the middle of the day to the depth of about forty
feet, the air, or vapour, grew fo hot and fuffocating, that it was
impoffible to proceed any lower. Thefe chafms, perhaps, have a
very extenfive fubterraneous communication; and, whenever the
external air is highly rarefied, the vapours rufh upwards through the
aperture in a continued ftream; on the contrary, when the external air is in a different ftate, it probably defcends with fome
violence into thefe openings: at certain times therefore, as for example in the early morning-hours, it may be practicable to go
down very low into them without inconvenience or danger. In moft
of them are found large quantities of human bones, almoft confumed by time, the teeth alone being in a tolerably perfect ftate.
Some have conjectured, that thefe places were either ufed by the
Indians as offuaries, or elfe as occafional retreats, to elude the fearch
of an enemy. The moft probable account is, that the bones belonged to thofe poor Indian natives who fell victims to the barbarity
of their Spanifh conquerors; for Efquemeling, who wrote in 1666,
and had feen great quantities of human bones lying in caves in the
ifland of Hifpaniola, tells us he was informed, by the inhabitants
of that ifland, that, when the Spaniards had refolved upon the extirpation of the Indians, they made ufe of dogs of a peculiar breed,
large, bold, and very fleet. The poor Indians having for fome
time been obliged to take refuge in their woods, thefe animals
were conftantly employed to hunt them out. The Spaniards by
this means caught a great number of them; and were content at
firft to kill feveral, quartering their bodies, and fixing their limbs
on the moft confpicuous fpots *in terrorem*, that the reft might take
warning by their fate, and fubmit at difcretion. But this horrid
cruelty, inftead of intimidating or reducing to friendly terms, only
ferved to embitter them more againft their favage invaders, and affected them with fo inveterate an abhorrence of the Spaniards, that
they determined to fly their fight for ever, and rather perifh by

famine or their own hands, than fall into the power of fo mercilefs an enemy. The greater part of them therefore retired into caves and fubterraneous privacies among the mountains; where they miferably perifhed, leaving a fad, though glorious, monument to future ages, of their having difdained to furvive the lofs of liberty and their country.

State of Port Royal Parifh:

	Negroes.	Cattle.	Sugar-works.	Annual Produce of Sugar. Hogfheads.	Settlements.
1734,	1548	106			
1740,	1546	158			
1745,	1685	35			
1761,	1203				
1768,	1432	170	1	60	11

We have here a glaring proof, that this parifh is declining very faft, and perhaps irreparably; fince there appear no means of putting the town into a more thriving way; and the inland part of the parifh is too rugged or fteep to acmit of any confiderable fettlements, while the tract adjacent to the coaft is rather fterile, and deftitute of a good fhipping-place. The only barquadier is near the mouth of Bull River, where none but fmall veffels can lie; and the anchorage is unfafe, on account of the opennefs of the bay.

S E C T. IV.

St. DAVID, in the Precinct of St. THOMAS in the EAST.

THIS parifh is bounded on the Eaft, by St. Thomas in the Eaft, and a part of Portland; on the Weft, by Port Royal parifh, and a fmall part of St. Andrew; on the North, by St. George; and on the South, by the fea. It is watered by fix rivers, the principal of which are, Collier's, Vavafor's, and Yallah's. The latter takes its firft fource in the Blue Mountains, and, after a meandring courfe of twenty-five miles, falls into the bay of the fame name, a fmall diftance from the difcharge of the others. This parifh was formerly populous: in the year 1673 it contained

eighty

eighty fettlements; but the lofs of regular feafons occafioned its defertion. The hamlet at Yallah's Bay confifts of a few fcattered houfes, near the church, which is a very fmall building, though large enough for the parifhioners ; the rector's ftipend 100*l. per annum.* The fhipping-places are, Yallah's Bay, and Cow Bay. At the former, there is anchorage for large fhips; but at the latter only fmall veffels can lie. Yallah's Bay is fheltered from the breezes and Norths by a point of land. But no fhipping can lie with fafety at either of thefe places in a ftrong Southerly wind, on account of the prodigious fwell which fets in. Cow Bay is remarkable for having been the fcene of an extraordinary action in the year 1681; when Sir Henry Morgan, the governor, having intelligence that one Everfon, a famous Dutch pirate, rid there with a floop and a barqua longa, manned with about one hundred defperate fellows, difpatched a floop with fifty men, befides officers, in queft of him. On the firft of February the governor's armed veffel attacked the pirate, and after fome refiftance, in which the Dutch captain was killed, got poffeffion of the floop. The bark cut her cable, and efcaped by outfailing her purfuer. The piratical crew, who were almoft all of them Englifh, Sir Henry fent to the governor of Carthagena, to receive punifhment for all the outrages they had committed upon the Spaniards. In this he was thought by fome to have gone too far; but he was willing perhaps to convince the Spaniards, by this facrifice, that he knew how to diftinguifh between hoftilities carried on under a lawful commiffion, and acts of lawlefs piracy; and that he was determined to keep the treaty with the Spaniards inviolate on his part. In 1694, twelve fail of the fleet, under command of Du Caffe, anchored in this bay, landed their men, and plundered and burnt all before them, for feveral miles; killed the cattle; drove whole flocks of fheep into houfes, and then fired them. They put feveral of the prifoners they took to torture, murdered others in cold blood, and committed the moft fhocking barbarities. Some days afterwards, feveral of the fleet being forced out to fea by the violence of the wind, which drove their anchors home, the commanding officer of the militia in this quarter fell npon their ftraggling parties on fhore, flew many of them, and forced the reft to take fhelter on

X 2

board

board their ſhips, leaving their proviſions behind. Soon after this action, they ſailed away.

This coaſt was always much expoſed to the inſult of privateers, until the laſt war; when a ſmall frigate was ſtationed at Morant to windward, which being only five leagues from Cow Bay, it would be very difficult for an enemy's veſſel to eſcape after making a deſcent. This pariſh has three large ponds on the coaſt, divided from the ſea only by a very narrow, ſandy bank, ſo that the waters communicate. Two of them are ſituated in the South-Eaſt ſide, between White River and Yallah's Bay; the larger is two miles and a quarter in length, and three quarters in breadth in the wideſt part; a very narrow ſlip ſeparates this from the next, which is about a mile in length. Theſe were antiently pans, formed by the Engliſh who firſt ſettled in the pariſh, for making ſalt. They were probably afterwards deſtroyed by inundations of the ſea in the great earthquake and ſubſequent hurricanes; and they have now a conſiderable depth of water in ſome places. The third lies about two miles Weſt of theſe, and is about one mile in length, and of unequal breadth. If the pariſh was crouded with ſettlements, theſe baſons might be converted to ſome advantageous ſcheme, either for maintaining a fiſhery, or opening a water-carriage from the Eaſtern part to Yallah's Bay; which would be extremely feaſible. The lower or more level range of the pariſh, lying between the hills and the ſea, was, by the failure of the regular ſeaſons, in general ſo dry, that canes would not grow here; and the ſettlements, thinly ſcattered, conſiſted only of penns and ſheep-paſtures, until within theſe few years, when a gentleman who poſſeſſes a property here conceived the idea of watering it from the neighbouring river. The experiment anſwered much beyond his expectation: he ſoon covered his formerly parched land with the verdure of cane pieces, and has now, as I am informed, made a noble eſtate of four hundred hogſheads *per annum*; the land proving moſt amazingly fertile, inſomuch that I have heard it aſſerted to have yielded him from three to four hogſheads *per* acre. This example may probably operate upon his neighbours; and, in proceſs of time, St. David will in conſequence become a populous and wealthy pariſh. The air is eſteemed healthy in all parts of it, except the neighbourhood

of

of the Saltponds, but, if the parifh fhould ever be thick-fettled, the mangrove-trees, which confine the atmofphere on the fwampy borders of thefe ponds, will be cut down, or probably fome method fallen upon, to drain them. The glades between the hills are exceedingly fertile; and the air and water perfectly good.

State of the Parifh:

	Negroes.	Cattle.	Sugar-works.	Annual produce of Sugar. Hogfheads.	Other Settlements.
1734,	1540	1165			
1740,	1628	1497			
1745,	1365	1494			
1761,	1838				
1768,	2316	1667	8	550	35

This parifh is evidently on the improving hand, having increafed both in number of Negroes and cattle. And it is to be hoped, the new fyftem of watering will pervade the lower quarter as far as may be practicable, that the greater part of that tract may be brought into cultivation.

SECT. V.

St. Thomas in the East.

THIS delightful parifh is bounded on the South and Eaft by the fea; on the North, by Portland; and on the Weft, by St. David. It is plentifully watered by upwards of twenty rivers and fmaller ftreams: the principal are, the Negroe, the Morant, and Plantain Garden rivers; the laft-mentioned of which is navigable by fmall boats for a confiderable way up. This river fweeps through the parifh from Eaft to Weft in a meandring courfe of about twenty miles from its fource, which lies among the Blue Mountains: the other two crofs it from North to South, at the diftance of about half a mile from each other. Upon entering this parifh from St. David's, the land rifes on the coaft; and the road lies along fhore near a mile, paffing under two precipitous mountains, compofed of rocks, and *ftrata* of a light-coloured friable marle, intermixed with large pebbles. Thefe cliffs are feen

a great

a great diftance from the coaft, and called by feamen " The White
Horfes." The furf fets in here very high upon the beach, and
fometimes runs up quite to the foot of the cliff; but, in general,
the fea is not fo boifterous as to prevent carriages from paffing.
On leaving the fhore, the road becomes hilly for moft part of the
way, till we come to Morant, which is about four miles to the
Eaftward. The bay of Morant is a confiderable fhipping-place.
The road in which the fhips anchor is well defended from the fea
by a reef of rocks : the fhore is lined with ftores and ware-houfes
at the bottom of a rifing ground, on which the village ftands,
which confifts of about thirty houfes, or more, as it comprehends
within its circuit the church, which is not far diftant. This village
is growing faft into a town, and indeed better deferves that appellation than fome others in the ifland : the church is a handfome
building; and adjoining is the parfonage, an exceedingly comfortable manfion: the ftipend annexed to this living is 250 *l.*; but,
confidering the extent of the parifh, the rector's income is probably
not much fhort of from five to fix hundred pounds *per annum.* There
are feveral circumftances which feem to favour the growth of a
town here. The foil is dry, the air healthy, and the water good
and in great plenty; the Eaftern branch of Morant River fall
into the fea on one fide of the bay ; and the country behind, and
all around, is well-fettled and fertile. The fhipping are defended
by a fmall battery, kept in good repair. About five miles further
Eaftward, the road brings us to Port Morant, which is one of the
largeft and moft beautiful harbours in Jamaica. It runs up the
country about two miles and a quarter; the entrance is about one
mile acrofs; but the channel dangerous to ftrangers, on account of
two reefs in the offing, which have proved fatal to feveral fhips.
On the windward-fide, the land ranges pretty high, covered with
thick wood; and, being fheltered on all fides by the main-land and
the reefs, it is always fecure, and has a good depth of water. The
entrance is defended by a fmall battery on the Eaft fide. The old
fort was erected on the oppofite fide; but it was ill-conftructed, and
efteemed not healthy [*a*]. It was in the neighbourhood of this

[*a*] Provifion has lately been made by the affembly for re-building two forts, or batteries, one
on each fide the entrance.

harbour

harbour that governor Stokes fettled in 1656, with his colony of
Nevis planters. The governor fixed himfelf about two miles and
a half from the head of the harbour, where the plantation, called
Stokes-hall, ftill commemorates him. In 1671, notwithftanding
the mortality which had fwept off many of the firft planters, there
were upwards of fixty fettlements in this neighbourhood; many of
which formed a line along the coaft Eaftward from the harbour,
where are only two or three at prefent. Point Morant, which is
the Eafternmoft end of the ifland, is diftant between nine and ten
miles from Morant Harbour. Adjacent to the Point are near eight
thoufand acres of very fine land, moftly a rich, black mould upon
a clay, at prefent in morafs, and therefore neglected; but it is capable (by draining) of being converted into rich fugar-plantations;
an example of which has been fhewn in the Northern quarter of
it, bordering upon Plantain Garden River, where an eftate, formed
out of the morafs not many years fince by this mode of improvement, was lately fold for 105,000l. and is thought to be well
worth the money. The draining of this large tract would anfwer
the further good purpofe of rendering all the fettlements, that lie
to leeward of it, more healthy; and in procefs of time this may
probably be accomplifhed [b]. The road, continuing along the
Weft fide of the harbour, and running Northwards about five
miles, terminates at the town of Bath, which is forty-four miles
diftant from Kingfton, and about fixty from Spanifh Town. The
road from Kingfton was made partly by private fubfcription, and
partly publick grants. As it paffes the whole way near the coaft,
and through a variety of flourifhing fettlements, it is cheered with
a number of moft agreeable profpects; and, to render it more commodious for travellers, there are mile-ftones fixed all along. Since
the Bath has become a place of lefs refort than formerly, this road
has been too much neglected. Some parts of it were formed

[b] About ten leagues South-eaft from the Point, or Cape of Morant, lie the two Morant
cayes, called by the French *Ranas*. The North-eaft caye is placed in latitude 17° 26′ North; and
the South-weft in 17° 20′. As they are directly in the track of fhips coming down to Jamaica
from Europe, or the Windward Iflands, great caution is ufed not to fall in with them in the nighttime. Not long fince, a Guiney-man was wrecked here. But fuch accidents have very rarely
happened. Under the South-weft caye there is good anchorage from five to eighteen fathom
water.

with

with infinite labour, being carried along the fide of a lofty precipice of folid rock, which nothing but the force of gun-powder could penetrate. This pafs is very tremendous in a wheel-carriage; from one fide of which, the eye is terrified by the view of a river foaming feveral hundred feet below; but a parapet wall is built, for the fecurity of paffengers, where any danger may be apprehended.

The Bath waters have long been known, and juftly celebrated for their falutary virtues. They are faid to have been firft difcovered by colonel Stanton, formerly a planter and inhabitant of the parifh, who was proprietor of the demefne in which they rife, and fold his right to the publick for a valuable confideration, paid him in purfuance of an act of affembly paffed in the year 1699. The diftance and trouble of coming at them prevented any experiment being made of their efficacy, till about the year 1696, when two perfons, one of whom was greatly reduced by the belly-ach, the other by the venereal difeafe, had recourfe to them for a cure: they carried proper neceffaries with them; built huts; and, by the internal and external ufe of the hot fpring, they found their health re-eftablifhed in the fpace of only ten days. The water was foon afterwards tried in the prefence of the governor, Sir William Beefton, with an infufion of galls, which in twenty-four hours gave it the tincture of Canary-wine, or old-hock; a fufficient proof that it is not impregnated with chalybeate, or at leaft in a very fmall portion.

The hot fpring iffues by feveral different rills from fiffures in the fide of a rocky cliff, the foot of which is wafhed by the Sulphur River. The fpring is in fuch a ftate of ebullition, when received immediately from the rock in a glafs, and applied to the lips, that it can only be fipped like tea. This has given occafion to fome dealers in the marvelous to affirm, that it is hot enough to boil chickens and even turkies. I have, indeed, been affured by men of veracity, that it will coagulate the white of an egg, if placed clofe to the fiffure, and held there for fome time covered from the air: and of this I have no doubt; for it is to be remarked, that at fome times it is heated to a far greater degree than at others, which depends probably on the greater or lefs effervefcence of the water within the bowels of the mountain from whence the fpring derives its fource. It is naturally light, fparkles when received in the

I

glafs,

A View of the Bath. Hot Spring.

Publish'd as the Act directs, July 1.1774.

W. Walker Sculp.

glaſs, ferments ſlightly with acids, turns ſilver black, and ſeems copiouſly charged with volatile particles, combined with a phlogiſtic, a calcareous earth, and a portion of fixible air: it has a nauſeous taſte when drunk at the rock; but this leaves it on being ſome time kept. The face of the rock over which it flows is covered with an ochrous precipitation, impregnated with ſulphur. It is remarkably beneficial in all capillary obſtructions and diſorders of the breaſt, proceeding from weakneſs, or want of the proper glandular ſecretions; in all lentors and viſcidities, proceeding from inaction; in conſumptions, and nervous ſpaſms. It reſtores the appetite, and natural action of the bowels; invigorates the circulation; warms the juices; opens the ſkin; cleanſes the urinary paſſages; ſtrengthens the nerves; and ſeldom fails to procure an eaſy ſleep at night. Externally uſed, by way of a fomentation, it has been known to heal the moſt obſtinate ulcers. In paralytic complaints it is generally ſucceſsful, and has recruited many conſtitutions that were impaired by debauch, or lingering intermittents. Numerous as its known virtues are, it ſtill requires a more thorough analyſis. Some other particulars likewiſe ought to be aſcertained, in order to make it of more general uſe. But, of the different phyſicians who have reſided here, I know of none that has been at the pains to examine it ſcientifically, or at leaſt that has favoured the public with any diſcovery of the principal purpoſes to which it is applicable in medicine, or of the methods by which it may be beſt adminiſtered, to anſwer the cure of diſeaſes; or of the ſubſtances proper to be uſed at the ſame time with it. Theſe particulars are left at preſent to the diſcretion of the patients, who drink it, for the moſt part, with very little attention to rule or meaſure; and therefore ſome of them do not reap all the advantages from the uſe of it, which, under due regulation, it might be capable of producing The general enquiries are,

1. What is the fitteſt ſtate in which the water ſhould be drank?
2. The quantity?
3. Time of the day?
4. Length of time proper for it to be continued?
5. Seaſon of the year in which it is moſt efficacious?

6. Regimen of life, and diet, whilft under the couife?

7. What medicines preparatory to, or to cooperate with, the ufe of it [c]?

In general, it is drank immediately from the fpring, beginning with one half-pint glafs, and increafing the number to three or more. It has been found to have the beft effect taken on an empty fto-mach early in the morning; but fome repeat the draught in the afternoon, befides taking a confiderable quantity, mixed with a little rum and fugar, by way of a diluent at dinner. All fruits and other acids are cautioufly abftained from, and vegetables fparingly indulged. The diet moft ufual confifts of fifh, black crabs, fowls, and the more delicate kinds of butchers meat, with puddings, and the like. At firft drinking, it diffufes a thrilling glow over the whole body; and the continued ufe enlivens the fpirits, and fome-times produces almoft the fame joyous effects as inebriation. On this account, fome notorious topers have quitted their claret for a while, and come hither, merely for the fake of a little variety in their practice of debauch, and to enjoy the fingular felicity of getting drunk with water. The cold fulphureous fpring, which rifes near Blue Mountain Valley, in this parifh, fome miles Weft-ward of the bath, is more grofs, and abundantly impregnated with fulphur, diftinguifhed by the fœtor of its fmell and inflammable fe-diment. It is efteemed more effectual than the other in all cuta-neous diforders, obftinate obftructions in the bowels, the fcurvy, and all the other difpofitions of the juices that require ftrong lixi-vious diffolvents: for thefe reafons, in fome habits, it is recom-mended to fucceed a moderate courfe of the hot fpring; but it is not much frequented, except by inhabitants of the neighbourhood. The mountains, between which the Sulphur River takes its courfe, defcend on each fide with fo precipitous a declivity, that it was found impracticable to build a town at the fpring; there is barely room to admit a bathing-houfe, and even this is inconveniently fituated on the fide oppofite the fpring; fo that, before the water can be conveyed acrofs in a wooden gutter, laid from the rock to the bathing houfe, it lofes much of its heat and volatile gas.

[c] See Falconer's treatife on the Bath-water of Somerfetfhire; which merits the perufal of any gentleman who may incline to try experiments on that of Jamaica.

This

This could not be remedied, except by uſing an iron pipe, to con-duct the water ; for a building cannot be erected on the ſame ſide as the ſpring, without being ſo remote from it, either above or below, as to be liable to equal inconvenience. This is the caſe with reſpect to a bathing-houſe for paupers, built by the river's ſide above the ſpring by a teſtamentary donation of Peter Valette, eſq; which is at too great a diſtance. This gentleman, having obſerved with re-gret that many poor and ſick white perſons, who had come from time to time to Bath for the benefit of the waters, either died, or ſuffered greatly for want of ſubſiſtence, and the common neceſſaries of life, deviſed the ſum of 100 *l. per annum,* payable during the term of ten years, from the time of his deceaſe, towards the relief and ſupport of ſuch poor perſons, not being indented ſervants, nor having any viſible way of maintaining themſelves, who might from time to time actually reſide about the Bath-ſpring; directing the phyſician there to deliver a weekly ſtipend of 7 *s.* 6 *d.* into the hands of all ſuch objects of charity; or otherwiſe to lay out the ſame for their uſe and benefit during the time of their reſidence, not exceeding three months each: and, in caſe of any overplus re-maining at the end of the year, he deſired that it might be expended in providing nurſes to attend the poor infirm people at the ſpring, or in building lodging-houſes and accommodations for them near it. His executors performed their truſt with great propriety. They built an hoſpital, provided nurſes, {ſupported upwards of one hundred paupers, who had come from different parts of the iſland at various times for relief; and in 1771, when the ten years term aſſigned by the donor expired, had a ba-lance of 96 *l.* in their hands. The aſſembly, upon their repre-ſentation, that, without the public aſſiſtance, this neceſſary relief, could no longer be continued to diſtreſſed objects reſorting to Bath, benevolently granted an aid of 70 *l. per ann.* and ordered the ſame to be paid into the hands of the phyſician there, to be expended, and accounted for, to the ſame good purpoſes, and under the ſame proviſions, as Mr. Valette's annuity. This worthy man has thus laid the foundation of a very uſeful charity, which is likely to be permanent ; ſince there is no doubt but the aſſembly will continue to ſupport it by an annual benefaction. Acts of this kind are real mo-

numents

numents of honour, which outlive the coftlieft fculpture, attract panegyric without flattery, and veneration without envy.

The patients, who defire to drink the water in the greateft perfection, take their ftand upon large flat ftones in the river-courfe, within two or three feet of the rock, and receive it immediately from the hand of the drawer. The mountain, called Carrion Crow Ridge, in which it takes its fource, is one of the higheft in this ifland, and appears from fome diftance below to have a fharper pike than moft others. The town of Bath is feated about a mile and three quarters from the fpring, on a triangular flat, wafhed on three fides by the Sulphur, Ifland, and Plantain Garden rivers; fo that it is a perfect peninfula, bounded, where it joins the main land, with a range of hills, which gradually rife one above another, till they reach the Blue Mountains. The three rivers unite their ftreams a little beyond the town, and continue their current together till they fall into the fea. This low fituation makes the town very liable to be incommoded by inundations, whenever thefe rivers happen to be fwelled by the autumnal rains. They have often endangered fome of the buildings; and feldom retire into their proper channels without committing depredation. In other refpects, the diftance from the fpring is attended with the happieft confequences to the patients, who ride on horfe-back to drink at it twice a day, and promote the efficacy of the water by joining fo wholefome an exercife with it. The road which leads to the fpring is of a romantic appearance, being conducted along the fides of very fteep mountains the whole way, whofe projections and gullies have not unaptly been compared to the folds or plaits of a man's coat. It is not in all parts of fufficient width for a wheel-carriage to pafs, nor very fecure even for horfes, if they fhould be fkittifh; for here and there it over-hangs the river at a great elevation; and thefe precipices have no other fafeguard againft fuch kind of accidents, than the trees which grow upon their face. Among thefe mountains is great abundance of iron ore. The prefence, indeed, of this metallic fubftance is, in the opinions of fome, fufficiently evidenced by the quality of the waters iffuing from them; but it is not probable they will ever be explored for the fake of obtaining it.

The

The firft vifit paid to the Hygæian fount is generally attended with fome terror; but this foon wears off; and I have known ladies, who, from a very cautious fnail's pace, proceeded gradually to a quick trot, and at laft to a hand-gallop, along this road, emboldened by habit, and animated by the infpiriting effects of the water. To prevent getting wet with fudden fhowers, which frequently defcend from the furrounding cloud-capped fummits, little fheds are erected at fhort intervals, ftretching acrofs the road, under which the bobelins may take refuge. Thefe fhowers are generally tranfient, though fometimes heavy while they laft. The hill-fide along the road, for the moft part, confifts of *ftrata* and large maffes of a brown, brittle ftone, which flides off in thin flakes, fmooth, and fhining. The foil above is a deep, rich mould, chiefly vegetable; and it abounds with fmall rills of very fine water. The extraordinary cures performed by the Bath-fpring induced the legiflature of the ifland, from motives of humanity, to take it under their fanction, and extend fo noble a remedy to thofe poor inhabitants who might want the means of procuring fubfiftence and medical advice, whilft under its operation. They formed the town into a corporation by law; granted it a public feal; directed the manner of laying out and affigning the lots of ground; caufed thirty Negroes to be purchafed, for keeping the road leading to the fpring in conftant good repair, and planting vegetable provifions for the ufe of poor perfons reforting hither; and appointed a liberal falary for a phyfician, to be refident in the town, and adminifter to the poor *gratis*. For the better accommodation of the latter, they founded an hofpital in the fquare, divided into convenient wards and apartments. The reigning fpirit of the inhabitants zealoufly feconded thefe charitable provifions. Many perfons of fortune took up lots, and began to erect houfes. The fquare was foon adorned with the hofpital, a public lodging-houfe, and a billiard-room. It became the fafhion every year for a crowd of company to affemble here from all quarters of the ifland. The powers of mufic were exerted; the card-tables were not idle; and, in fhort, from a dreary defert, it grew into a fcene of polite and focial amufements. This (alas!) was of no long continuance. The unfortunate political divifions, which afterwards prevailed during the adminiftration of a certain

2   hot-

hot-headed governor, deftroyed all that harmony between families which, while it fubfifted, had been the principal caufe of making this place an occafional retreat; where they had ufed to meet each other in friendfhip, and united their talents of pleafing. The fcene became changed; party-rage fucceeded; the partizans of the different factions could not endure the thought of mingling together under the fame roof; and the more moderate perfons grew indifferent to a place, where chearfulnefs, confidence, and mutual refpect, no longer held any fway. From this period began its decline. Moft of the houfes that were built have, from neglect and want of inhabitants, gone into decay; the half-finifhed frames of fome, which were juft beginning to rear their heads, have mouldered into duft. The billiard-room is in ruins; and, in 1768, I obferved the tattered remains of a once fuperfine green cloth, which covered the table, all befmeared with the ordure of goats and other animals, who took their nightly repofe upon it. At this time, the town was reduced to about nine or ten habitations. The hofpital was converted into a barrack for a company of the regulars. Two lodging-houfes ftill remain; but they are much in want of repair, and feem inclined to partake of the general ruin. The falutary ftream, which Providence has fo benevolently granted for the relief of human mifery, is ungratefully (I had almoft faid impioufly) fuffered to glide away neglected and unheeded to the ocean, as if it had entirely loft its former virtues. There is nothing more reproachful to the œconomy and good-fenfe of the principal men in this ifland, than fo fhameful a neglect. Will it be imputed to indolence, to caprice, or inconfiftence, that, after fo much folemnity and parade in eftablifhing the town; after fo much apparent happinefs derived from the inftitution; fuch munificent provifions for the fick poor; after advancing the plan fo far towards maturity; they have devoted their whole fabric to fubverfion? It is much to be regretted, that a fcheme attended with fo large an expence, and fo well calculated for the public health and entertainment, has been fo unaccountably dropped; when a fmall annual fund, fet apart for the purpofe, would have fupported all the buildings erected here for the general ufe or amufement. The hofpital is built of a kind of white free-ftone, of which there are feveral

I

quarries

quarries in the neighbourhood: it is of the fame quality as that which abounds in the parifhes of St. Anne and Weftmoreland; it is very foft, and eafily wrought when firft dug, but grows hard after expofure for fome time to the air. The foldiers, on their firft arrival here, became fickly. This was imputed to the conftant dampnefs of the walls; for which reafon they were afterwards plaiftered; and it was thought they grew healthier; but in the year 1768 they had no lefs than twenty-five on the fick lift; and upon enquiry it was found, that they were fubfifted on falt-fifh, falt-beef, and bifcuit, not the beft in quality; and were allowed frefh provifions only one day in the week. The falt provifion was brought from Kingfton, and came at a much dearer rate than frefh victuals, which the neighbourhood affords. Of bifcuit, for example, not more than five or fix could be bought for feven pence-halfpenny; and that quantity cannot be thought more than fufficient for a foldier's daily allowance of bread. Whereas fifty plantains were to be had at Bath for the fame money; which are more than one foldier could devour in a week. Frefh pork was to be got here cheaper than the beft falt-beef; fowls likewife, and frefh fifh, were exceedingly reafonable. The number of ladies and gentlemen, who had reforted here for the benefit of the water, amounted in two years to only fixty-fix, by many fewer than ufed to meet here at one time, when Bath was in its flourifhing æra.

Proceeding from Bath to the Eaftward, we pafs along the rich banks of Plantain Garden River, through a fucceffion of the fineft fugar-plantations in the ifland. The foil in fome parts is a black, vegetable mould, of great depth, intermixed with fhells; in other parts a deep, brick mould; and, towards the river's mouth, the land on each fide is extremely flat, which fubjects it to be overflown pretty regularly once a year by the river. Thefe floods generally lay all the canes proftrate, and cover them with a rich fediment of mud. But they fpring again after the water retires, and grow aftonifhingly luxuriant, requiring no other manure than what this river, like another Nile, fo invariably depofits. Yet the fugar produced here is commonly of a good complexion, though faineft and in greateft quantity, if the feafon continues dry during the crop.

This

This is the tract of cane-land which suffers less than any in the whole island by a long drowth; for the water is every where so near the surface, as to support a due vegetation, when the canes in other parishes are parched and destroyed for want of rain. The rich mould of Vere alone may dispute the preference with it for depth and fertility; but, I think, the land on Plantain Garden River, being happily in a more seasonable situation, must be esteemed superior; and, in short, on a general survey of this Eastern quarter of the island, it appears rather more productive, and of better staple, than the Western end. In regard to the natural productions, it contains a great many rare plants that are peculiar to it, with some others that are also observable in the West division; and the rest are such as are common to all parts of the island. Among those of the first class is the gum-tree, or *sapium* of Dr. Brown, who, by some mistake, has described the parrot gum-tree for it, which is a species of manchineel, and bears not the least affinity to the gum-tree in its parts of fructification. It is probably a new *genus*, and hitherto undescribed. It grows to a very considerable size, and yields a large quantity of a light-green, transparent, thick resin, or gum, of little smell. This is much used by the planters of the district for burning in their boiling house-lamps. They once were found here in vast abundance; but, from the continual ravage of the inhabitants, who have cut down vast numbers every year, without the least remorse, or any caution to plant a new race; it is not improbable, that, in a little time, the old stock will become extinct; for none of this class have been discovered in any other part of the country. The wood is coarse; but it supplies tolerable staves for sugar-casks: a gentleman here got as many from one tree as made one hundred hogsheads, or upwards of three thousand staves; from whence some idea may be formed of the magnitude of these trees.

The air of the hilly part of this parish is extremely healthy. At Bath it is cool during the greater part of the year; which is owing to its being shaded by the neighbouring high lands, and watered with frequent showers. The air of the low grounds near the coast, especially where they are swampy, or not drained, is by no means to be reckoned healthy. The Negroes on the plantations which border on Plantain Garden River are subject to frequent mortalities,

especially

especially if their huts are placed on the levels, which are damp, and annoyed by constant exhalations. The planters have wisely fixed their own habitations in general upon elevated spots, in order to be secure from floods, which have sometimes been so violent on the lower grounds, as to sweep away buildings, cattle, and Negroes.

State of the Parish:

	Negroes.	Cattle.	Sugar-plantations.	Annual Produce of Sugar. Hogsheads.	Other Settlements.
1734,	6176	5488			
1740,	6618	5256			
1745,	7282	5561			
1761,	12300				
1768,	14624	9007	66	9270	34

This parish, it is apparent, has increased very largely in its stock of Negroes and cattle; and now contains near one hundred settlements. From the goodness of the soil, the number of rivers, and plentiful supplies of rain, it has the promising appearance of becoming one of the most populous and opulent in the whole island.

SECT. VI.

PORTLAND.

THIS parish is bounded on the East and North by the sea; West, by St. George, and part of St. David; and on the South and South-East, by St. Thomas. The adjustment of its boundary, as the whole was formerly included in the parish of St. Thomas, has occasioned many disputes between the two parishes, both of them laying claim to the inhabitants of Manchineel, in the South-East quarter; who, though actually within the boundary of Portland, have generally paid their taxes in the parish of St. Thomas. But the law, by which Portland was first formed into a distinct parish in the year 1723, expressly makes White River the South-East boundary; and, this limitation having been ratified by clear recitals in several subsequent laws, there appears no authentic ground at prefent for controverting it. This parifh comprizes a vaft tract of fine land; but the fettlements are fcattered along the coaft; and the interior parts are as yet unoccupied, except near the Rio Grande on the North fide, where the moft diftant are not more than fix miles from the fea. It is mountainous, and fubject to almoft continual rains, which are naturally caufed by the height of the central ridges, and fo prodigious an extent of thick woods; but they would undoubtedly decreafe here, as they have done in the other diftricts, if any confiderable part of this wildernefs was cleared, and room given for a free paffage to the wind and vapours. It contains eight or nine rivers, moft of them of no great note; the principal is Rio Grande before-mentioned, which has its fource about fixteen miles from the fea, and becomes very confiderable by the acceffion of feveral ftreams which fall into it. The chief fhipping-places are, Port Antonio, formerly called St. Francis; Prieftman's Bay; and Manchineel Harbour. Port Antonio lies on the North-Eaft part of the coaft, in about 18° 11′ North latitude. It comprehends two harbours, the Eaftern and Weftern, divided from each other by a narrow peninfula, of about three miles and a half in length, on the point of which ftands Fort George. The fhip-channel leading into the Weftern harbour paffes between this point, and Lynch's, or Navy Ifland, and is about one mile over. The entrance into the Eaftern lies between the South-Eaft point of Navy Ifland and the main land, and about three miles from fhore to fhore. There is alfo a fmall channel on the Weft fide of the ifland; but it is extremely narrow, and obftructed with very extenfive fand banks; fo that the deepeft part can only admit boats. It is alfo rendered dangerous by a reef of rocks, ftretching from the North-Weft fide of the ifland, between two and three leagues towards the main land. This ifland is three miles and a half in length, by about one and a half in width, and lies in an oblique direction South-Eaft and North-Weft. Towards the fea it is inacceffible, on account of the rocks and fhoals which guard it on that fide; but on the fide next the harbour there is very deep water clofe in, fo that men of war coming in have fwept the trees with their yards. The harbours are land-locked, and capacious enough to receive a very large fleet.

This

This part of Jamaica, lying only about thirty-fix leagues from Cape Tiberon, on the Weft end of Hifpaniola; and the difficulty confidered which our men of war have fometimes encountered in turning up againft the trade-wind, and currents from Port Royal, in order to weather the Eaftern point of Jamaica; together with the commodious fituation of Port Antonio, which opens directly into the Windward Paffage; gave rife to the fcheme of fortifying and adapting it as a place of rendezvous for the fquadron in time of war. In the year 1728, the affembly paffed an act appropriating twenty acres of land on Lynch's Ifland for the conveniency of erecting ftore-houfes and wharfs for his majefty's naval ftores, and careening the fhips of war. In the year 1733, this work was in great forwardnefs; and rear-admiral Stuart, who then commanded on the ftation, finding the air of the ifland unhealthy, ordered the wood to be cut down and burnt. Unfortunately, inftead of hiring Negroes to perform this laborious tafk, it was affigned to detachments made from the crews of the Lion, Spence, and fome other fhips of war; of whofe incapacity for it Dr. Lind has given us the following melancholy account:

Many of thefe men were feized at once with a fever and delirium. This phrenzy attacked a man fo fuddenly, and with fo much fury, that with his hatchet, if not prevented, he would have cut to pieces the perfons who ftood near him. Orders were iffued, that, as foon as the men were thus feized, they fhould be bled, and immediately fent on board their refpective fhips. The confequence was, that all who were carried on board quickly recovered; whereas thofe who remained on fhore either died, or underwent a dangerous fit of ficknefs. This calamity, and the peace which not long after happened, occafioned the project to be dropped, although the government had been put to a great expence in erecting feveral ftore-houfes, and in purchafing the ifland in propriety. Thefe buildings having fince gone to decay, and the inhabitants in the neighbourhood made free to pull down and ufe fuch of the materials as were ferviceable to them. The reafons for refuming this fcheme are at prefent extremely ftrong, fince the French have laboured fo fuccefsfully in fortifying and compleating a very large town at Cape Nicola Mole; which lying only fixteen leagues and a half from the

Eafternmoft

Eafternmoft point of Cuba, they have got a key, which as effectually locks up the navigation of the Windward Paffage to the
Eaft, as the Havannah, in the hands of the Spaniards, fecures it to
the Weft by the Gulph of Florida; the confequence of which muft
neceffarily be, in any future rupture with France and Spain, that,
without a very ftrong convoy of feveral men of war, not a mer-
chant-fhip will have the leaft chance of getting home: and I think
it is evident, from all the pains and expence which the French
have been at in making their eftablifhment at the Mole, that they
defigned it as an effectual curb upon the Jamaica trade, and for no
other purpofe: becaufe the country that environs it is rocky,
barren, and unfit for plantations of any fort. It is plain, therefore, that they had not agriculture in view; and it is moft probable, that, in time of war, they will always take care to keep a
number of men of war and frigates at the Mole, or cruizing between it and Cape Maize, to intercept our homeward-bound trade,
which of courfe will fall an eafy prey, unlefs we have always fo
large a fleet on the ftation, as to be able to block up theirs, or difpute fuperiority of force with it. As a check therefore upon their
fortrefs, it would feem abfolutely neceffary, that Port Antonio
fhould be ftrengthened with fortifications, and the former plan revived of accommodating it for the reception, refitting, and careening, of his majefty's fhips: and, in order to guard againft that
havock, which the employment of felling trees, and clearing
ground, in the Weft-Indies, has never failed making among Europeans, efpecially if unfeafoned to the climate; the legiflature of
Jamaica ought, in regard to the importance of this concern to
their properties, either to purchafe fifty Negroes, or levy that number in rotation from different eftates, to be employed, under proper
white overfeers, to clear away all the wood upon the ifland, and
affift in carrying on other laborious works that may be required.
The raifing them by levy might be made very equitable, if, at the
fame time, their refpective owners were to be paid a certain juft rate
per day, for their maintenance and hire, out of the public funds;
and the expence to the ifland would be very trifling.

The

	£	s.	d.
The hire, for example, of fifty Negroes, at 6 *l. per* head *per ann.*	300	0	0
Their subsistence, at 7½ *d.* each *per* day, is, *per ann.* —	566	19	3
	866	19	3
Hire of two superintendents, or overseers, at 140 *l.* each,	280		
Cloathing and medicines, at 30 *s.* each *per ann.* (I suppose the tools to be furnished by government), —	75	0	0

Whole of one year's expence to the island is, sterling, 872 *l.* 16 *s.* 7¼ *d.*; currency, —   —   1221 19 3

It is not probable, if these Negroes were to be duly taken care of by the superintendents chosen for this purpose, that any of them would die within the twelvemonth, supposing them to be healthy and able when delivered; and none others should be accepted; but, for greater equity to the individuals to whom they belonged, they might be fairly valued by three or more disinterested magistrates before their going on service, and any deficiencies at the year's end made good by the public accordingly. In order to form a body of labourers, to be kept afterwards constantly employed in building fortifications or other works, several draughts might every year be made, from the gaols, of such slaves as are sold out for payment of their fees; and, in many cases, the sentence of death, or banishment, might be commuted for perpetual labour in the king's service; and a piece of land appropriated near the port for their provision-ground, that their subsistence might, for the future, be attended with no expence, either to the island, or to the crown. No time can be so convenient for conducting such a plan as the present interval of peace; and, being carried on with vigour, we should have in another war this sure asylum for the squadron, from whence it might sally forth to distress the enemy, defend our homeward-bound fleets, and give protection to our ships coming from Britain to Jamaica, or coasting round from the North to the South parts of the island.

When the duke of Portland was governor, a town was projected on Pattison's Point, bordering on the harbour, which was to be

called.

called Titchfield, after a manor belonging to his grace in Hamp-shire. One hundred acres were affigned by act of affembly for this purpofe; to which were added three hundred and fifty acres for a common. A quarter-feffion for the peace was to be held here four times a year; the port was made a port of entry and clearance; and the receiver-general, fecretary, and collector, were ordered to keep deputies here, who were allowed a falary of 70*l.* each *per annum*. This town was laid out, but not built; for, the project be-fore-mentioned not being carried into effect, and the parifh conti-nuing but very thinly fettled, there was not a fufficient encourage-ment to induce perfons to build; nor trade, nor manufacture to give a town fupport; fo that, at prefent, here are not above fifteen or twenty ftraggling houfes about the harbour. The making this one ftation for the fquadron would be the fureft means, not only of en-couraging a town here, but of multiplying fettlements in the neigh-bourhood, by the demand there would be for hogs, poultry, plan-tains, and other provifions; and, in regard to trade, this port lies conveniently for opening fome intercourfe with the Eaft end of Cuba, and the fmall Spanifh veffels of St. Domingo, who might fteal along fhore to the Ifle of Vache, and eafily make this port. Some beneficial traffic might likewife be occafionally carried on with the French for their indigo, in return for our Britifh hard-wares, and a few other affortments. I am not without hopes, that the legiflature of Jamaica will, in time, be rouzed into a ferious attention to the further improvement of their country, by a few eafy meafures, which require only judgement in fetting them on foot, and unabated perfeverance in conducting them to a happy ef-fect. No part of the ifland feems to claim their affiduity more, than this extenfive parifh of Portland; which, from all the reports of furveyors who have traverfed its receffes, contains immenfe tracts of very rich land, finely watered, though ftill covered with thick woods. The moft popular work they have hitherto done in it, is the road which paffes through an almoft uninhabited wild, from Bath to Port Antonio. It traverfes a tract of near fixty thou-fand acres, which has not a fingle fettlement. The former road from Titchfield to Bath through Manchineel was at leaft thirty-four miles in length. Upon a reprefentation to the houfe of af-

fembly,

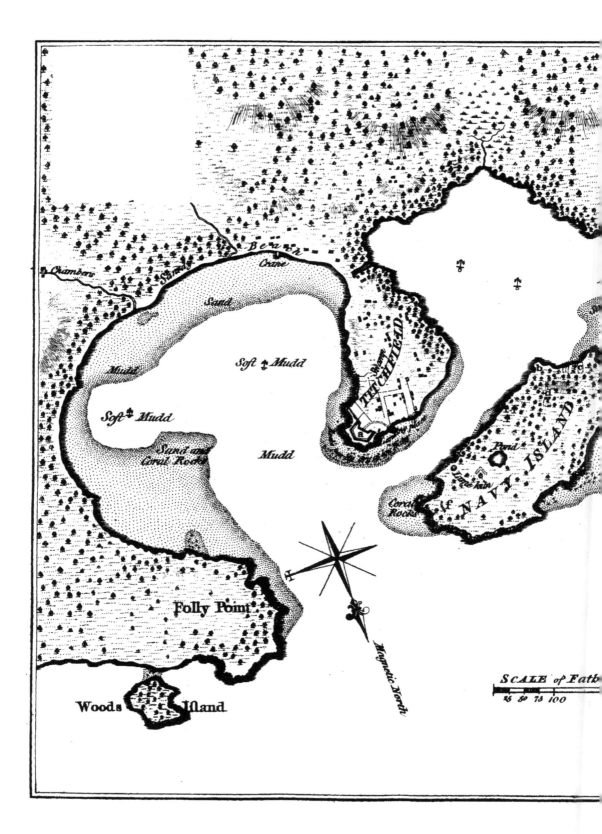

Chambers

Beaver

Crane

Sandy

Sand

Soft Mudd

Soft Mudd

Mudd

Sand and Coral Rocks

Mudd

THE CHIEFLED

NAVY ISLAND

Pond

Salt Pan

Coral Rocks

Folly Point

Magnetic North

Woods Island

SCALE of Fath

25 50 75 100

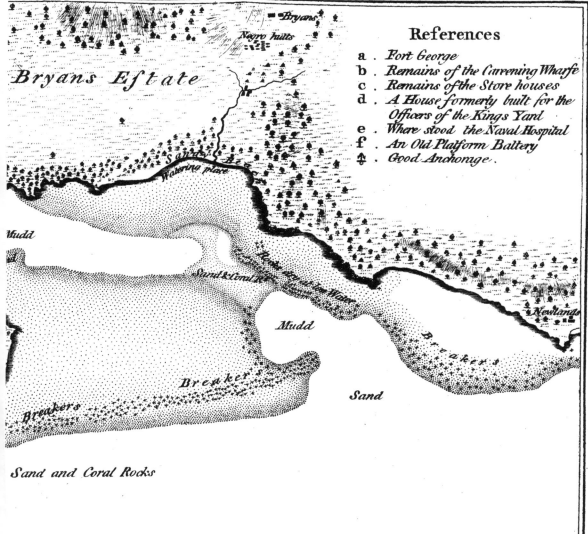

References

a . *Fort George*
b . *Remains of the Careening Wharfe*
c . *Remains of the Store houses*
d . *A House formerly built for the Officers of the Kings Yard*
e . *Where stood the Naval Hospital*
f . *An Old Platform Battery*
⚓ . *Good Anchorage.*

Bryans Estate

Bryans

Negro hutts

Sandy R.

Watering place

Mudd

Sand & Coral R.

Mudd

Breaker

Breakers

Breakers

Sand

Newlange

Sand and Coral Rocks

oms *880 to a Mile.*
200. 300. 400

PLAN
of the
HARBOURS
of
PORT ANTONIO
in the ISLAND of
JAMAICA
Surveyd A.D. 1771.
Engraved by T. Kitchin 1774.

fembly, in 1769, that a road from Titchfield through Nanny Town, and over Break-heart Hill, would be fhorter by twenty-three miles; that the lands through which it muft pafs were very fit for the culture of provifions; and that it might not only become the means of fupplying the Bath plentifully with all manner of provifions and poultry, but of fettling a large tract at that time ufelefs, and of fubfifting many poor families in Portland, then in very indigent circumftances; three hundred pounds were granted towards making it. No fum was ever voted to a better defign; but it required ftill further affiftance, to render it paffable for loaded mules, or carriages; and therefore has not yet produced all thofe advantages that the petitioners expected from it, the expence of the undertaking being rated at 1000 l. The affembly therefore have fince added 300 l. more, the parifhioners engaging to raife the remaining 400 l. by a fubfcription. I am not fond of paffing cenfures; yet I muft take leave to fay, that even in the fecurity of Port Antonio, fo ufeful a retreat for the fhipping in war-time, there has appeared a very fingular inattention. The fort, which was built here to command the channels of entrance, and which is extremely well-defigned for that intention, is a baftion of twenty-two embrazures, inclofed to the Southward from flank to flank by barracks to receive feventy men, and an apartment for the commanding officer. It was once mounted with about twelve guns, twenty-four pounders. This fortrefs, at which a company of foldiers is generally garrifoned, we fhould fuppofe to deferve full as much of the public care as the Rock Fort at Kingfton Harbour; but the condition of defence in which it was left during the late war may be judged of from the following ftate, as given in the year 1768; viz.

The guns all unfit for fervice, and without carriages.

No wadhooks, fpunges, ladles, or rammers.

The platforms for the guns entirely decayed.

No flag; the boat unfit for fervice; the roof of the magazine very leaky, and no door; the furgeon's room untenantable; the roof of the commanding officer's houfe, and barracks, wholly out of repair; the foldier's barracks without platforms; no hofpital; the guard-houfe tumbled down; and no place of confinement, &c. &c.

To

To the honour of the affembly, however, let it be mentioned, that, upon feeing this miferable catalogue of dilapidations, they immediately granted fome provifion for putting it in a better ftate; and I fhould not have quoted the report, but for the fake of re-marking the expediency there feems of having an engineer, or in-fpector-general of the barracks and fortifications all round the ifland; whofe province it fhould be, once in every year at leaft, to vifit them all, examine their ftate, take account of their ammuni-tion, ftores, and habiliments, and report them to the governor, who would regularly lay the account before the affembly.

By a method of this nature, they would be duly acquainted with the condition of thofe defences, which are too remote to admit of infpection from their own committee; and I think it will alfo be acknowledged, that their ftores would be better taken care of, and lefs wafte committed.

The road from Bath paffes by Moore Town, inhabited by the Maroon Negroes; who firft took up their refidence on the Weft fide of the parifh, bordering on St. George, at a place called Nanny Town; which they afterwards deferted. Their prefent town is much better fituated for giving fpeedy protection to the eftates on each fide the Rio Grande. The South-eaft divifion of the parifh, adjacent to Manchineel Harbour, is well-fettled, and promifes to become very populous. The harbour is capacious and fecure, de-fended by a battery of ten guns, which is not fo ftrong a fortifica-tion as it feems to require, efpecially if Port Antonio fhould not become a ftation for men of war. Between thefe two ports is another confiderable fhipping-place, at Prieftman's River. The whole number of fettlements in this parifh is between eighty and ninety; very few, in proportion to its extent. It remains for time to difcover the many natural productions and curiofities which, there is reafon to believe, are not fparingly diftributed through fo vaft a fpace of mountains and vallies, as yet but little explored. As yet we are only informed of a hot mineral fpring, which rifes on the North fide of the fame mountainous ridge that gives birth on the oppofite fide to the Bath fpring. It is reafonably conjec-tured to be only another vein proceeding from the fame refervoir;

2   there

there being, as it is faid, no perceptible difference in their heat, tafte, and medicinal operation.

State of the Parifh:

	Negroes.	Cattle.	Sugar-works.	Annual Produce.		
				Hogfheads.	Other Settlements.
1734,	640	125			
1740,	775	178			
1745,	1235	637			
1761,	2354				
1768,	2813	1651	29	1330	57

This parifh is certainly much improved. The legiflature paffed feveral acts tending to invite fettlers into it; and a confiderable part of thofe who at prefent occupy it, or their anceftors, came hither under their fanction. I have endeavoured to point out the defects in thofe acts; conceiving, that, if they had been framed upon a more effectual plan, the parifh might by this time have acquired double the number. It is fubject to fome local inconveniencies, which lay the fettlers under difficulty; for which reafon, the encouragements to beginning new plantations cannot be too great; for thefe inconveniencies will grow lefs, in proportion as it becomes more populous. The great tract of mountain covered with high woods occafions almoft inceffant rainy weather at a fmall diftance inland from the coaft; and the navigation to Kingfton for fupplies of neceffaries, or difpofal of produce, is tedious and hazardous, particularly in war-time. Their woods require, therefore, to be laid open; and a trading town is wanted. By multiplying fettlements in the interior diftrict, the firft might be gradually effected; and the fecond would naturally attend the multiplication of fettlements. The foil of the mountains, and indeed all the interior part, is extremely well-fuited to indigo; and this manufacture might be revived here, and carried on with great fuccefs and advantage. But it muft be the province of the legiflature to pave the way for it, by giving fuch aids of Negroe labourers as will leave little further to be done, by the new fettlers invited over, than to exercife their fkill in building their works, cultivating the plant, and conducting the procefs to perfection. The obtaining a colony of perfons, who are well acquainted with the whole art of managing the indigo, will, I imagine, be attended with no great difficulty, if

fuitable

suitable encouragements are given. It is certain, that, if such a manufacture should upon trial be found to answer, there is vacant land enough in this parish to furnish much more than would satisfy the confumption of Great-Britain; and the richnefs of the foil affords juft motives for expecting that indigo might be produced here of the fineft quality.

I have omitted to mention, that this parish is without a church. The incumbent's ftipend is 100 *l. per annum*; but he does not refide. The fervice is performed in fome planter's houfe, about once or twice in the year. It may appear extraordinary, that the legiflature fhould, in the example of this and fome other parifhes, have provided a ftipend for a minifter, without at the fame time providing a houfe of prayer. An act paffed here, in 1681, empowers the juftices and veftry of every parifh, at their annual meeting in January, to lay a reafonable tax on the inhabitants, for the maintenance of the minifter and poor; and for erecting convenient churches, and repairing fuch as are already made, and providing convenient feats in them. The erecting of churches is, therefore, only made a fecondary obligation, and as fuch difpenfed with by the junior parifhes, under the plea of poverty, which will probably avail them, till a more ardent zeal in the caufe of religion, than hitherto has been manifefted, fhall infpire the houfe of reprefentatives, and lead them to enquire into the merits of this pretence.

SECT. VII.

St. GEORGE, in the Precinct of St. MARY.

THIS parish is bounded on the Eaft by Portland; Weft, by St. Mary; North, by the fea; and South, by the parifhes of St. Andrew and St. David. It is watered by about fixteen rivers and principal ftreams; the largeft and moft noted are, the *Agua Alta,* or Wag-water, which forms the Weftern boundary; the Buff Bay; Anotto, Spanifh, and Swift. The former of thefe, being joined near the coaft by feveral other ftreams, forms a canal, navigable by boats from Anotto Bay (into which it difcharges), about two miles inland; which is a great conveniency to thofe fettlements that border upon it. The bay is common to this parifh and St.

2

Mary,

Mary, and is their principal fhipping-place: it is a good road, except in the time of year when the Norths prevail, to whofe violence it is too much expofed. The face of the parifh is for the moft part very hilly; and the Blue Mountain Ridge, after interfecting Portland, continues its lofty battlements from Eaft to Weft through St. George's, engroffing the whole of its Southern diftrict. The inconveniencies of much wet, and a diftant market, which have retarded the population of Portland, have likewife attended this parifh, and perhaps in a feverer degree; fo that it is ftill to be confidered in its infancy.

The lands adjacent to the coaft are not fettled for more than four miles from the fea, and in fome parts not more than one. The diftrict behind comprizes about fixty-five thoufand acres of wildernefs, whofe foil and natural productions are at prefent unknown: this vaft tract has only one road cut through it, which paffes from Kingfton through Liguanea, and, croffing the centre near the Negroe-town called New Crawford, terminates at the coaft. The land hitherto fettled in fugar-plantations turns to better account, and is lefs laborious, than what we meet with in Portland; but as yet no trial has been made with canes above the diftance of two miles from the fea. The mountainous region behind contains, probably, a very great variety of foil; which, though too rich at firft to produce fugar, would yield a large quantity of fine rum, or indigo: this latter is confidered as a great impoverifher of land, and therefore very fit to prepare a rich foil for the fugar-cane. It is pretty evident, on contemplating the face of this parifh, that it is not likely to make much further progrefs until more roads fhall be formed through fo extenfive a wood-land; for, although many thoufand acres have been patented, they were, for the greater part, forfeited, and the remainder left unfettled by the proprietors on this very account: they found it impracticable to get at their lands after they had patented, or purchafed; and of courfe were unable to make any ufe of them. The firft ftep towards further improvements here will therefore naturally commence with opening new roads of communication; which may allure the proprietors of plats on each fide to begin fettlements. It cannot be expected, that individuals will undertake this tafk, or incur fo much expence, on

the

the diftant view of profits, not to be acquired till after feveral years of diligent application, and many further charges. It muft be executed at the public coft, as it is not likely to be ever atchieved by any other means. Nor would the expence be thrown away; fince every fettlement, once eftablifhed. makes a return by adding fomewhat to the fecurity of the ifland, to its trade, opulence, and revenues. In order to prove which, let us examine the advantages of this nature which the parifh even now contributes. Here are about fixty fettlements in all, whofe quota of the poll-tax amounted to about 391 *l*. for one year; which, at an equal average, comes to 6*l*. 10*s*. each. Every new fettlement formed here may therefore be reafonably concluded to give the revenue an annuity of 6*l*. 10*s*. in that tax alone. If we affign this, on a moderate computation, as the one-half of the whole taxes levied, confifting of various branches, the annuity will appear 13*l*. *per annum*, without taking into account the confumption of tools, food, cloathing, and other articles; which to the meaneft fettler cannot be rated at lefs than 50*l. per annum*. The projecting of new fettlements therefore, and encouraging them till effectuated, when confidered in this view, feems a moft profitable adventure for the legiflature to engage in, and well deferves their moft ferious attention. To form roads which may be perfectly firm, eafy, and commodious, is doubtlefs a bufinefs of much time, labour, and charge: for thefe very reafons (if they are admitted to be true), the lefs expectation fhould be indulged, that poor families will be able, or, if able, willing to devote their induftry to road-making, inftead of agriculture. But, when the public takes this work in hand, the cafe is very different. The more perfect it caufes the road to be made, the better affured it becomes of alluring inhabitants to fix themfelves on each fide of it. The returns for thefe expenditures may be tardy; but they will be certain, and always increafing; and (what is not to be over-looked) the money, thus laid out for fuch laudable purpofes, will remain to circulate in the ifland, and give employment to many of its inhabitants, without impoverifhing the public.

There is nothing very remarkable in this parifh (at leaft that has fallen within my knowledge), except a falt lake, called Alligator Pond, extending from Fig Tree to Buff River Bay, and feparated

from

from the fea by a narrow flip of fandy land. It is near five miles in length, and about half a mile wide in the broadeft reach. There is no tradition in what manner it was formed, whether by an earthquake, or an inundation of the fea; probably both concurred. The air of this, as of all the Northfide parifhes, is in general healthy; and it may be remarked here, as at the Weft end, that the hills decline gradually towards the fea, and fwell as they recede from it towards the mid region of the ifland. The moft unwhole-fome ftate of the atmofphere in thefe parts occurs during the May rains; when the wind, fetting from the Southern points, has to pafs over an immenfe tract of woodland, before it reaches the fet-tlements on the North fide; but it rarely produces any other fe-vers than intermittents, which here are not much regarded, as they are not often attended with any dangerous confequences.

This parifh is not yet provided with a church. The incum-bent's ftipend is 100 *l. per annum*; and the living, like that of Port-land, a mere finecure.

Having no materials for a more particular account of St. George, I fhall conclude with,

The ftate of it:

	Negroes.	Cattle.	Sugar-works.	Annual Produce. Hogfheads.	Other Settlements.
1734,	1085	1485			
1740,	969	1024			
1745,	1163	1136			
1761,	2147				
1768,	2765	3421	12	1200	48

Notwithftanding the ravages committed in it by the Maroon Ne-groes before their reduction, it is apparent this parifh has made confiderable progrefs in the laft twenty years; but, as a fugar-parifh, is as yet of very fmall importance. The means by which it may be improved I have already touched upon, as the beft that offer to my judgement; and in this light only I fubmit them to the dif-cuffion of abler politicians.

To recapitulate the preceding detail of this county: it has for its metropolis, Kingfton, where the affizes are held in January, April, July, and October.

State in 1768.

Negroes.	Cattle.	Sugar-works.	Annual Produce. Hogsheads.	Other Settlements
39,542	21,465	146	15,010	314

Rectories and Stipends.

	£	s.	d.
Kingston, ——— ———	250	0	0
St. Andrew, — ———	200	0	0
Port Royal, — ———	250	0	0
St. David, ——— ———	100	0	0
St. Thomas in the East,	250	0	0
Portland, ——— ———	100	0	0
St. George, — ———	100	0	0
	1250	0	0

Churches, — 5
Chapels, — 0
Synagogue, - 1

C H A P.   IX.

C O R N W A L L

CONTAINS about 1,522,149 acres, and has five parishes, and nine towns and hamlets, viz.

Parishes.	Towns.	Hamlets.
St. Elizabeth,	Lacovia, Accompong, Negroe-Town, —— ——	Black River.
Westmoreland,	Savannah la Mar, the county-town, —	Queen's Town, *alias* Beckford Town, *alias* the Savannah.
Hanover,	Lucea.	
St. James,	Montego, Furry's, Negroe Town.	
Trelawny,	Trelawny, Negroe Town,	Marthabrae.

SECT.

SECT. I.

St. ELIZABETH.

THIS parifh is bounded on the Eaft by the parifhes of Claren-don and Vere; on the Weft, by Weftmoreland; on the North, by St. James and Trelawny; and on the South by the fea. It is watered by the Black, Y S, Hector's and Broad Rivers, and feve-ral fmall rivulets. Of thefe the two former are the moft capital. The Y S rifes, firft, in the South-Weft angle of St. James's parifh, in a very fmall ftream; and, after a courfe of about two miles, hides itfelf under-ground, and emerges at about half a mile's di-ftance in a large body of water, at about thirteen miles from the coaft; then, after a moderately winding courfe of thirteen miles and a half, falls into the Black River. The Broad River rifes in the Eaftern quarter of the parifh, about fix miles from the fea; firft emerging in a morafs, called Cafhue, through which it makes its way for about the fame number of miles, till it unites with the Black River. The latter firft emerges in the North divifion, at the di-ftance of fixteen miles from the neareft part of the coaft, and me-anders about thirty-four miles before it reaches the fea, having its ftream very much enlarged by the various tributes it receives du-ring its paffage; fo that, in moft parts, it is from one hundred and fifty to two hundred feet wide. This is the nobleft river in Ja-maica, and is navigable by boats and barges for many miles. About mid-way, and at the Forks, where it meets with the other two rivers I have mentioned, it fweeps through a large tract of morafs. The road, paffing over the May-day Hills to the Weft end, croffes this and Y S over two handfome bridges.

This great Weftern road, which leads from Spanifh Town, tra-verfes St. Jago Savannah, and the bridge of Milk River, in Cla-rendon; not far beyond which is the eftate which belonged to the late lord Ol—ph—t. Soon after leaving this, the afcent begins over May-day Hills, continuing rocky for about half a mile, till it narrows into a gloomy path between two hills, over-hung with the interwoven boughs of trees on each fide, which form an agreeable fhade. At the end of two or three miles further on is a fmall

plantation

plantation and pimento-grove; and, beyond this, the way opens suddenly upon a pretty rising lawn, on the highest part of which stands a little villa, belonging lately to Mr. W—ftn—y, who is said to be a natural son of the late duke of L—ds. This villa overlooks a diminutive vale, through which the high road passes, and extends its narrow prospect to another delightful, rising spot, of a circular form, and fringed with stately trees. A number of kids, lambs, and sheep, are pastured in the glade, or roam on the sides of the adjacent hills, which are fenced in with a wall of craggy mountains, richly cloathed with wood. In rural charms few places exceed this little spot. The road acrofs this affemblage of high lands is extremely curious in every part, and worthy the traveler's attention. There are none in England, nor I believe in Europe, refembling it. It divides the May-day Ridges, as it were, through the middle; the breadth of which, from Eaft to Weft, is upwards of fourteen miles; it is about fifty feet in width, and confined on each fide by a majeftic wood, that is almoft impervious to the fun. The lofty trees, fo clofe arranged, form a living wall; and, intermingling their leafy branches, afford a cooling fhade during the greater part of every day throughout the year. The Tavern of Knock-patrick (belonging alfo to Mr. W—ftn—y), the next fettlement we come to, ftands very commodioufly, and enjoys a moft excellent climate. The Englifh beans, peafe, and other culinary vegetables of Europe, grow here, in moft feafons of the year, to the utmoft perfection. A gentleman who fupped here could not help remarking, that the victuals were literally brought fmoaking-hot to table; a phænomenon feldom obferved in the low lands, where the air is fo much more rarefied. A fpecies of the tarantula fpider is faid to be often found in this part of the country. The woods abound with paroquets, and pigeons of various forts. The laghetto, and other ufeful trees, fuch as mahogany, cedar, pigeon-wood, &c. This tavern ftands in the midft of thefe woods, and as yet has but a very fmall tract of cleared ground about it. Every appearance of the road to the Weftward of it is fimilar to what is obferved on the approach to it from the Eaftward, till the hills begin to decline, and the parifh of St. Elizabeth breaks upon the view. From the different parts of this declivity, the

the profpects are finely variegated, and, from fome ftations, are extended not only over the champaign-country of this parifh, but into great part of Weftmoreland many miles: but one of the moft pleafing fcenes is, the fpacious tract of open land, called Labour-in-vain Savannah, which appears partly of a vivid green, and partly of a ruffet colour. One fide of it is girt about with romantic hills and woods; the other, towards the South, is wafhed by the fea; the middle fweep is graced with fcattered clumps of trees and under-wood; which objects all together combine in exhibiting a very picturefque and beautiful appearance.

    " From this the profpect varies. Plains immenfe
    " Lie ftretch'd below; interminable meads,
    " And vaft favannahs; where the wand'ring eye,
    " Unfix'd, is in a verdant ocean loft.
    " Another Flora here, of bolder hues,
    " And richer fweets, beyond our garden's pride,
    " Plays o'er the fields; and fhow'rs with fudden hand
    " Exub'rant fpring; for oft' the valleys fhift
    " Their green embroider'd robe to fiery brown,
    " And fwift to green again; as fcorching funs,
    " Or ftreaming dews and torrent-rains prevail."

One would almoft incline to think, that Thompfon, and his Pegafus, had made the tour of this region; fo appofitely has he defcribed it.

South of Effex Valley Mountains, are diftinguifhed the high lands, and fand hills near Pedro Bluff. Thefe, it is true, are fome additions to the profpect, but upon reflexion difpleafe the eye, as they are in general fo poor and barren, as to difdain all kinds of cultivation, and only yield in wet feafons a fcanty pafturage for fheep and the younger cattle. About the foot of May-day Hills, the bread-nut trees grow luxuriantly, and afford to the bordering fettlements great abundance of nourifhing fodder for their ftock.

The principal capes, or head-lands, on the coaft are Pedro Bluff, and Luana Point; the former of which gives fhelter to an anchoring-place for fmall veffels in Pedro Bay, lying to the Weftward of it. Between this and Luana Point is Black River Mouth, defended by feveral banks of fand; within them is a fine road for fhips of large burthen; and near this is therefore eftablifhed the chief barquadier for all the plantations and fettlements in the parifh [d]. The Eaftern fide retains its antient name of Palléta, or Parratee Bay. The Spaniards had a fmall village here, which was deftroyed by a detachment of the army under colonel D'Oyley. This part is fwampy, and principally inhabited by Mulattoes, Quaterons, and other Cafts; a poor, but peaceable and induftrious race, who have long been fettled here, and live by fifhing and breeding poultry. If it was not for the fhoals at the mouth of the river, there is depth and room fufficient in it to anchor, and keep afloat, a very great fleet of capital fhips. But, though it is not navigable by veffels of burthen, it is, as well as its branches, of very eminent fervice to the inhabitants of the adjacent country, by enabling them, at fmall expence and trouble, to bring their fugars, rum, and other kinds of produce, by water-carriage, down into the bay. Hector's, or One-eye River, which rifes near Wallingford-plantation, in the North-Weft diftrict, after a zig-zag courfe of about twelve miles, difcharges into Black River. The Eaftern branch of it enters into a very high ridge of mountainous land, extremely well-wooded, and filled with mahogany and other valuable timber, and difembogues again at three miles diftance. The arch-way under which it paffes is of a rude, Gothic appearance, about twenty feet in height, but rifing and falling alternately within; where it is fupported with pillars, the nuclei of which are of a very fine, white free-ftone; and in fome parts of this cavern are large *ftrata* of marble. The water deepening as we advance forwards under the mountain, it is not an eafy matter to explore this remarkable adit for any very confiderable extent; though, for a good diftance from the mouth, it does not reach much above the knees. However, it may be claffed among the more beautiful natural curiofities in the ifland, and merits a further inveftigation. This, with the Y S (fo called from the Galic word Y S, which fignifies crooked, or winding), and the other ftreams which empty themfelves into the Black River, contribute chiefly

[d] Near the mouth is often caught the manatti; which has given name to fome adjacent mountains.

to

View of a Cascade at Y S River.

Isaac Taylor sculp.

Pl.14.pa.210 Vol.III.

to its importance. The road or harbour is guarded not only by the shoals, but by two batteries; the first, a publick one, of five guns, six to nine-pounders, built on a little eminence near the sea; the other, a private property, belonging to Mr. Crutcher. Exclusive of these fortresses, the variation of the sands renders the entrance difficult, and dangerous to those who are not well acquainted with it. The barracks stand at about a quarter of a mile from the bay; are capable of receiving thirty men, and generally garrisoned with a party of regulars. The church is about the same distance from the village of Black River, a handsome edifice of brick, lately re-built. The parsonage-house stood on Middle-quarter-Mountains, in a dry, elevated, and very pleasant situation, in the centre of the glebe; but, not long since, was unfortunately burnt to the ground by an accident. The rector's stipend is 200 *l. per annum*; but he has likewise a considerable income from the labour of about twenty Negroes, which, in consequence of an act of assembly, passed in the year 1753, for disposing of sundry parcels of land belonging to the parish, were purchased with the value of the sales for the use of the rectory; and, by another act passed in 1764, all the parcels of land then undisposed of were directed to be sold, and the nett-money applied to the buying a tract of provision-ground contiguous to the old glebe, and to be annexed to it in perpetuity: so that the whole of the glebe consists of, at least, two hundred acres of fine pasture and provision-land; and the value of the living is computed to be between six and seven hundred pounds a year. By the road-side, not far from the parsonage, is a very curious object, viz. a large spreading fig-tree, whose boughs overshadow the road. It is about thirty feet in height, and out of its summit appears to grow an elegant thatch-tree, of about ten or twelve inches diameter, which has a branched top distinct from the other, and rising twelve or fifteen feet above it. The wild fig-tree is, in its infant state, only a poor, weakly, climbing plant, like the tendril of a vine, which rears itself from the ground by the friendly help of some neighbouring tree, and shoots out several delicate radicles, which entwine about the supporter, and gradually extend themselves downwards as the stem increases. This at length attains to the summit, multiplying its branches and radicles, which in pro-

cess

cefs of time reach the earth, where they foon take root, and become fo many new ftems to feed and fuftain the parent plant.
This now begins to enlarge in dimenfions, and, expanding its bark,
forms by degrees a trunk, or cafe, around its fofter tree, which,
if not compofed of very firm materials, is liable to have its vegetation entirely checked by the parafitical embrace. A fpeedy decline
is the confequence.   At laft it dies; and then ferves only to nourifh
with its duft the luxuriance of the reptile, that has fupplanted it.
The reafon why this thatch-tree has efcaped the like fate may be,
that it was probably at full-growth when it was firft invaded;
and the denfity and hardnefs of its bark, which render it almoft
impenetrable by the keeneft inftrument, have made it capable of
refifting the utmoft impreffion and efforts of its treacherous gueft.

The town of Lacovia, which ftands about feven miles inland
from the bay, between the Y S and Black rivers, has its name perhaps from a corruption of the Spanifh words *la-agua-via*, the watery way, or *lago-via*, the way by the lake; for this part of the
country, being very low and flat, is fometimes overflowed with
water, from the large morafs which furrounds it; but, as the
roads are now raifed confiderably, it is feldom, if ever, impaffable.
This town contains two good taverns, for the accommodation of
travellers, and about twelve or fourteen houfes, moftly inhabited
by Jews.   Here is alfo a court-houfe, for more conveniently holding
the quarterly feffion of the peace, petty-courts of common-pleas,
elections, and veftry-meetings, it being fituated nearly in the
middle of the parifh.

The face of the parifh is various. The Eaftern divifion is walled
in by fucceffive ridges of high mountains, diftinguifhed by the
names of Carpenter's, Don-Figuerero's, and May-day. Towards
the North, it is bounded by thofe of Edmund's Valley, and the
Blue Mountain Chain, which diffociate it from St. James and Trelawny.   Accompong and Charles Towns, inhabited by Maron
Blacks, lie among thefe mountains, in the North-weft part of the
parifh.   Befides thefe, are fmaller chains, which run in different
points; as Effex Valley Range, Eaft and Weft, near the coaft;
Top Hill, lying parallel; and the high land of Pedro Bluff, extending from the Cape, Eaftward, along the fhore. In the centre

of

of the parifh are Santa Cruz, and Burnt Savannah Mountains, lying North-weft and South-eaft. A little further back, are thofe of Naffau and Lacovia. To the South-weft of thefe, are Middle-quarter Mountains, running N. N. E. and S. S. W. and the Weftern boundary is croffed by New Savannah and Luana Mountains, tending N. W. by W. and S. E. by E. Such a multitude of eminences not only ferve to attract frequent rains, but contain refervoirs for affording the conftant fupply of water neceffary to feed the innumerable fprings, rivulets, and thofe larger collections, which are perpetually flowing through every part of the lower grounds, and fpending themfelves in the ocean. The lands between, and at the feet, of thefe different mounds, admit of a great variety of foils. In the Eaftern diftrict they confift of favannah, for the moft part dry and infertile. The moft noted are Pedro Plains, Bull, Labour-in-vain (a name perfectly defcriptive of its nature), Naffau, and Burnt Savannahs. In thefe parts there are but few fugar-plantations, though a great number of very fine penns for breeding horned cattle, horfes, mules, fheep, and goats, as well as poultry of all kinds. The foil of Middle-quarter Mountains, in the South-weft, is ftony, though not altogether fo unproductive; but the plain of Luana is a continued fand, and covered with palmeto-trees, which, though large and flourifhing, are a fure indication of its poverty. The rich veins of mould adapted to the fugar-cane are bordering upon the Y S and Black rivers; but a vaft fcope, of not lefs than twenty thoufand acres in the whole, lies fcattered in wafte morafs, which, could it be drained, might form many capital plantations. No attempt of this fort has yet been made, at leaft that I have heard of; but it promifes to yield a very great return to any of the proprietors, who fhall have fpirit, ability, and patience, fufficient for profecuting fuch an experiment. It lies in three principal divifions, each of which is pervaded by a river. The remoteft part is diftant only ten miles from the fea, and might have its products fent by water-carriage the whole way. The other two approach to the very mouth of Black River; and all of them are well circumftanced for water-mills. The land in this ifland has, from its firft fettlement, been out of all proportion too much for its average-ftock of inhabitants; but, if it fhould ever become populous, thefe neglected portions will undoubtedly be brought into culture. In the year 1764, a project indeed was talked of here for building a bridge acrofs Black River, near its mouth, in order to open a communication with the Eaft and Weft fides; by which means, it was alledged, and with great appearance of reafon, that the contiguous lands might foon be improved[e]; which at prefent they cannot well be, on account of the inconvenient and expenfive mode of paffing acrofs in a ferry-boat, for which each paffenger pays $7\frac{1}{2}d$. a time; and often it happens, that it cannot be ferried at all. The fum of 2500l. was propofed to be raifed within the parifh, for carrying this fcheme into execution; but I do not find that it has been hitherto attempted. This extenfive fpace of undrained, fwampy ground circumjacent, renders the habitations on the bay unfavourable to health. So it proved to a company of the 66th regiment, quartered here in 1764. In the month of Auguft they were attacked with putrid fevers and dyfenteries, fo fatal to them, that three men were buried in one day; an inftance of great mortality, confidering the fmall number of which the company confifted. This ravage is to be afcribed to no other caufe than the exhalations reeking from the marfhy foil around them, which, in that hot feafon of the year, imparted an evil difpofition to the atmofphere. Some of the other quarters on the coafts are not lefs unwholefome, from fimilar caufes; which I fhall occafionally fpeak of. This regiment, which was chiefly cantoned in different parts near the fea-fhore, buried in this year no lefs than one hundred and two men; whereas the 36th, whofe quarters lay moftly at Spanifh Town, Port Royal, Mofquito Fort, and Clarendon (two detachments only, I think, being pofted on the coaft in the out-parifhes; one at Old Harbour, the other at

[e] The land contiguous to the banks of this river is alledged by fome to be of an infertile nature; which they afcribe to this caufe, that the water, being uncharged with foil, affords no vegetative depofit, like moft other rivers of the ifland, when it overflows; but rather does mifchief, by leaving a petrifactive, barren fubftance behind. If this be true, it furnifhes another argument in favour of draining and embanking the adjacent grounds; by which means, the river-water, being hindered from fpreading, might be confined within the cuts. The lownefs of fituation induces a probability, that any fuch depofit is but very fuperficial, and that at a very fmall depth the natural foil is rich, and when duly turned up would become highly productive. Befides, there certainly muft have been no fmall quantity of vegetable mould accumulated in the courfe of fo many ages, by the annual decay of plants and herbage on the furface.

Port

Port Maria), loft no more than thirty men. They both arrived from Europe in the month of June. And hence may be deduced fome ufeful remarks with regard to the fituations moft proper, or moft baneful, to troops fent hither from Northern climates; which, if poffibly it can be avoided, fhould not be brought down to fwampy places near the coaft; for, in the inland barracks, they would probably enjoy their health and vigour unimpaired, and fo be in fitter condition for effective fervice; or, by the refidence of one or two years, become fo thoroughly feafoned to the climate and manner of living, as to be lefs fufceptible of malignant diftempers, in cafe of their being afterwards, upon any emergency, marched into unwholefome quarters on the coaft.

State of the Parifh:

	Negroes.	Cattle.	Sugar-plantations.	Annual Produce. Hogfheads.	Other Settlements.
1734,	7046	9184			
1740,	6641	9695			
1745,	7575	13500			
1761,	9715				
1768,	10110	16947	31	2600	150

From this view it appears to be improving; but it contains near eighty thoufand acres of land as yet unfettled; the greater part of this is mountainous, though capable of producing coffee, and other valuable commodities. The air of the low lands is hot; and they have a plentiful ftock of mofkeetos; but the hilly parts in general are temperate and pleafant.

SECT. II.

WESTMORELAND.

THIS parifh was formed in the year 1703, out of St. Elizabeth, by which and a part of St. James it is bounded on the Eaft; on the South and Weft, by the Sea; and on the North, by Hanover. Its rivers are Bluefields, in the Eaft divifion; Bonito, or Cabarito Eaft Branch; and Cabarito Weft Branch; which interfect it about the middle diftrict; and New Savannah River, which rifes further Weftward. It has likewife fome fmaller ftreams; and, on the North-eaft, the Great River, which difcharges

5

on the North fide coaſt of the iſland, makes the dividing limit. It contains ſeveral head-lands, and ſome good harbours; of the former, along its Southern ſhore, are Parkinſon's, or Palmeto Point, Crab Point, Cape Bonito or Bluff, Cabarito and Palmeto Points. From the laſt-mentioned to South Cape Negril, which is the Land's-end, is a ridge of moderately high eminences, called the Negril Hills; the ſhore iron-bound, and lined with rocks. On the Weſt end are this Cape, Cunningham's Point, and North Cape Negril, which divides this pariſh from Hanover. Bluefields Bay lies Weſtward, within Crab Point. It is ſpacious, and has ſuch excellent anchorage, with ſo fine a watering-place, that it is the conſtant rendezvous, in time of war, for the homeward-bound fleets and convoys, intending to ſteer by the way of Florida Gulph. The river, which falls into the bay, riſes ſuddenly about three quarters of a mile from the ſhore, and turns two mills in its way. Here is the ſecond great barquadier for the plantations in this pariſh. Weſt of this bay lies Savannah la Mar, latitude North about 18° 13', ſheltered on one ſide by Bluff Point; on the Weſt, by Cabarito. The road leading into Weſtmoreland from St. Elizabeth croſſes the boundary at a place called the Wells, and proceeds for eight or ten miles along a dreary, narrow lane, oppoſite Parker's Bay, till it reaches Bluefields. Near this part ſtands, on an elevated ſpot, the dwelling-houſe of Mr. Wh—e, called Bluehole, which commands an extenſive proſpect over the ſea to the Southward, and over the Weſtern diſtrict of the pariſh. This is a modern building, conſtructed with ſtone, fortified with two flankers, and loop-holes for muſquetry, and defended, beſides, towards the ſea with a barbette battery of ſix guns, nine-pounders. But, notwithſtanding theſe muniments, it was taken during the laſt war by the crew of a Spaniſh privateer, who plundered the houſe, carried away the owner and his brother priſoners, and treated them extremely ill: fortunately for them, they were re-taken, together with their enemies, upon whom the Engliſh captors did not retaliate, as they well deſerved.

From the foot of this hill, the paſſage is frequently made acroſs the bay, about four miles, to a place called the Cave, where the barquadier ſtands. This is built of timber, and projected to a conſiderable fiderable diftance into the fea, for better conveniency of fhipping goods. Here moft of the fugars, rum, mahogany-plank, and other commodities of the neighbouring eftates, are put into boats, or lighters, to be carried on board fuch fhips as are to export them, and lie either at Savannah la Mar, or the upper end of the bay. The road from hence continues rough and ftony, till it reaches Sweet River, fo called from the tranfparency and purity of its waters, which fall into the bay. After paffing this, and a long tedious lane, the face of the country opens at once upon the view, and appears truly beautiful from the continued fucceffion of well-cultivated fugar-eftates and rich paftures. The rains in this parifh being ufually heavier than in moft others on the South fide of the ifland, and the country in general flat near the fea, the roads are confequently for the moft part deep and dirty, and in the rainy feafons fcarcely paffable. Savannah la Mar, though it is the principal barquadier, has neverthelefs but a very indifferent harbour, or rather road, for the fhipping. The water is fhoal, and againft the affaults of the fea it is defended only by reefs of funken rocks, and a few fand-banks, which are apt to fhift. Nor is it much better guarded againft enemies. The fort, which coft the parifhioners upwards of fixteen thoufand pounds in building, is extremely ill-contrived, and perpetually fapped by the fea. Formerly it was mounted with eighteen or twenty guns, moftly of too fmall a calibre; and, indeed, both from its ftructure and furniture, it never could have promifed any fecurity except againft privateers. Unlefs it has very lately been repaired, it is in a very ruinous condition. It was never compleated; and, the South curtain being undermined, the wall on that fide is almoft all tumbled into the fea. As for the baftions, they are for the moft part unfinifhed. Of this fort we may juftly fay,

Vis confili expers, mole ruit fua.
" Ill-counfel'd force, by it's own native weight,
" Headlong to ruin falls."

The parifhioners thought perhaps that they had a right to lay out their money in what manner they pleafed; and therefore, confulting (as one would imagine) neither engineer, nor any other perfon better fkilled than themfelves in fortification, they refolved to throw away one half of it into the fea, and with the other erect this mif-fhapen pile, as a lafting monument to convince pofterity of the inexpertnefs of their fore-fathers in military architecture. At the entrance is a fmall magazine, and a barrack for about a dozen men. Moft of the guns are difmounted; and falutes are therefore fired from a battery of fourteen fmall pieces, ranged before the court-houfe. This building was erected in 1752, for holding a court of common-pleas in matters of debt not exceeding 100*l.*, quarter-feffions of peace, elections, and veftry-meetings. In 1758, the affize-court for the county of Cornwall was appointed by law to be holden here; in confequence of which, the jurifdiction was greatly enlarged. Two years before, this port, together with Kingfton, Montego Bay, and St. Lucia, was by act of parliament made free, for the importation of live cattle, and all other commodities except fugars, coffee, pimento, ginger, melaffes, and tobacco, the growth or produce of any foreign colony in America; and for the export of Negroes, and all other legally imported commodities in foreign floops or fchooners having only one deck. The advocates for this bill, and the fubfequent one (cap. LII. 6 Geo. III. which permits the importation of foreign melaffes, paying only a duty of one penny *per* gallon), alledged the great utility of admitting Negroes and provifions to be brought into our Weft-India iflands from the foreign colonies, and in foreign bottoms, in order that they might be plentifully and cheaply fupplied. On the other hand, it was objected, that Ireland and the North-American provinces were very able to furnifh our iflands with much more provifions than they could confume; that, if the price of Negroes is high, this may arife from fome mifmanagement in the African trade; but that it does not appear that foreigners can buy them at a cheaper rate; if they do, the trade requires to be better regulated; but, if they buy them upon equal terms, the high price is a gain to the Britifh merchants; that the capital miftake in thefe bills lay in the latitude of encouragement which they gave to the employing a greater number of foreign fhipping and feamen than are at prefent employed, and confequently diminifhing thofe of Great-Britain. Nor is this evil remedied by allowing the exportation of Negroes, and certain other commodities from our iflands, to fuch

foreign

foreign colonies, fince the fame foreign bottoms, which import provifions, melaffes, cotton-wool, and indigo, into our plantations, will undoubtedly endeavour to make bullion or fpecie the chief article of their return-cargoes. The bill therefore feems, on this prefumption, in an efpecial manner to favour the navigation and commerce of the Dutch, and fuch North-Americans as are, from the nature of their employment, adopted foreigners; who readily obtrude their veffels into an opening of this kind, and actually become the principal carriers of French fugars and coffee into the free-ports, whence they carry a return chiefly in money or bullion for the French iflands. It was faid, that, if provifions are dear in our iflands, this happens from a peculiar obftacle, namely, " that the " North-American veffels would willingly bring them as much as " they want, if they could but be fure of a back-lading; but that, " from the difficulty of procuring one, they carry their provifions " to the French iflands, and fell them cheaper than they would at " our own, becaufe they can take in at the French iflands a back-" lading of melaffes." This inconvenience was intended to be obviated, in part, by the latter of the acts mentioned, admitting the importation of French melaffes into our iflands, which may help to load back the North-American veffels: but upon this it is rightly obferved, that the importation of their fugars ought likewife to have been allowed under certain reftrictions, and for feveral ftrong reafons; viz. the North-Americans would then have no pretence, nor indeed any adequate inducement, to go to the French iflands for a back-lading; they would bring their provifions to a better market at our iflands, and be able to procure the very returns they want; for it is not to be fuppofed they refort to the French merely to take in their melaffes; the French fugars are their primary object, and furely they would rather receive them at Jamaica without rifque, than run the hazard of getting them clandeftinely from Hifpaniola. If we could become the carriers to Europe of all the fugars which the French iflands produce, it would certainly be very much for our intereft to become fuch; but, whether we are or not, their produce will find its way to the European markets, either in their own, or fome other bottoms.

We

We are then to confider, that the North-Americans are carriers every year of a certain proportion of their produce ; and in all likelihood will fo continue. The queftion therefore is, whether it would not be more advantageous for Great-Britain, that this produce fhould be firft brought into our own iflands, to be afterwards taken from thence to Europe by Britifh carriers? And it clearly appears to be fo, becaufe this double voyage tends to the employment of more Britifh fhipping. This fhipping would receive all or the greateft fhare of, the freight, which is now paid to foreigners, or to North-Americans; befides the further benefit of fupplying fugars to thofe European markets which the French and Dutch at prefent monopolize. In refpect to our iflands, they would be more plentifully furnifhed with provifions, and be able to keep up their ftock of filver fufficient for circulation, or to remit the fuperfluity to Britain, inftead of feeing it drained away to the French iflands. Nor need the planters apprehend the lowering the value of their own produce. There may be, it is true, a greater quantity and affortment of fugars at their markets; but the increafe of demand, and of fhipping, to take it off their hands, muft neceffarily be in proportion; fo that the augmentation of one will keep pace with, and prevent any mifchief from, the increafe of the other. This point is regulated by the European markets, which will ftill require to be fupplied as heretofore; and the annual quantity fupplied for their confumption cannot be at all affected, whether it is brought to them from Hifpaniola, or from Jamaica. As this confumption is permanent, fo muft be the demand; both will co-operate to relieve the ifland-markets, whilft they have fhipping enough to facilitate the carriage to Europe; and fhipping is naturally attracted by well-ftocked markets, and a certain and profitable freight.

These motives, for permitting our own fhips to carry French produce, with a view to improve our commercial dealings with the North-Americans, and re-eftablifh an export of fugars to the foreign markets in Europe, appear, I think, of fome weight, and merit ferious confideration; in order that the feveral free ports, opened in this ifland, may become of more extenfive utility to the trade of the mother-country, than in their prefent ftate they feem

capable

capable of. The act of parliament was certainly well-meant, but it has produced an effect very contrary, in some respects, to what was intended.

Of all the blunders committed by our statesmen respecting colony-trade, none perhaps have turned out more injurious, than the branding his majesty's ships and tenders, in the year 1764, with custom-house commissioners, under pretence of rigorously executing the navigation-act; in consequence of which measure, and the strict orders accompanying it, the Spanish traders were wholly proscribed from entering the ports of this island. The folly and ignorance of those who projected and abetted this French-Spanish scheme cannot be more exposed, than by shewing the loss which Great-Britain sustained in consequence of it, and which will appear from the following comparative account of the exports to Jamaica:

				Value, Sterling, £	s.	d.
1763,	(Before these regulations took place) —			584,978	o	o
1764,	—	—	—	456,528	o	o
1765,	—	—	—	415,624	o	o
1766,	—	—	—	415,524	o	o
1767,	(First year of the free-port act) — —			467,681	o	o

This loss, in actual diminution of exports, amounts, at a medium, to 146,134l. sterling *per annum*. But, when we take into the account what would have been gained on the return-cargoes, and compute the super-lucration on the prime-cost only at 30l. *per cent.* the loss in four years amounts to upwards of 700,000l. We may venture, indeed, without any exaggeration, to pronounce it near a million. And, what is worse, we have every reason to believe, that France, by the immediate translation of this trade to her colonies, gained at least the full amount of what Great-Britain lost.

Second to this enormous measure, were the orders given (rather unwisely), in a public manner, in November 1765, for the free admission of Spanish vessels into all the colonies. Little regard was paid to this invitation by the traders.

Exclusit; revocat. Redeam? Non; si me obsecret.

" He" (the minister) " kicks us out of doors; then he calls us " back. Shall we return? No; not if he should intreat us " on his knees."

4

The

The free-port act was then let go as the sheet-anchor. Great advantages would probably have resulted from this measure, if it had been thought of and tried immediately after the war, instead of commissioning cruizers to destroy the trade: and although it may have prevented a total wreck of this valuable commerce; yet it came perhaps too late, and under too many disadvantageous circumstances, to make any adequate reparation for the damages we have sustained, and are still liable to sustain.

The trading inhabitants of the island required nothing more than very strict and positive private injunctions to the governor and port-officers, not to allow or to practise exactions upon those foreigners who came hither; whereby they had at different times been much discouraged. The act of navigation, so far as regarded these particular bottoms importing live stock and bullion, was always relaxed, and never rigorously observed here; because it appeared repugnant (so far as regarded these imports) to the spirit of commence, and the plain interest of Britain. These were therefore already free-ports in every beneficial sense; and the traffic went on in silence and security. But so soon as government interfered, with a view to do no more than was already virtually done, so public a declaration of favouring this commerce, and laying open what ought to have remained clandestine, naturally awakened jealousy in the breast of that power, whose policy it has ever been to defeat and impede, as much as possible, every such attempt. Guards, cautions, and penalties, were multiplied, and held to their vigilance and execution with such unabating severity, as had never before been observed.

What would be the consequence, if the port of Boulogne, or Dunkirk, in France, was to be opened by a public arret, expressly for the importation of smuggled wool from Great-Britain? Surely, the whole British nation would take alarm, and British guarda-costas would immediately be commissioned, without number, to prevent the effect which an invitation so authoritatively given might be likely to produce. It is notorious, that large quantities of Portugal gold have been privately gleaned from Portugal, and brought into this kingdom. But, if government should, from a fond desire to swell the tide, and procure the stream to flow hither in

a publick

a publick channel, iffue proclamations for exprefsly encouraging the importation of gold coin from Portugal; is there any doubt, but every Britifh veffel, and their crews, would be fearched in the moft rigorous manner before they were fuffered to depart from Lifbon and Oporto? or may it not rather be queftioned, whether any Britifh veffel would ever be admitted to enter them again?

I have faid enough to point out the ill confequence of this meafure, and the ground of complaint among the Jamaica-traders, who are all fenfible that, inftead of being ferved by it, they have loft what perhaps may never be retrieved. And, unfortunately, things are fo circumftanced, that a repeal of the free-port law would only tend to make bad matters worfe. We muft therefore leave it to the operation of time, and the dexterous management of thofe parties who are to be reciprocal gainers by this traffic, to revive it again extenfively. It is a very juft obfervation I have fomewhere met with, that, confidering the native wants of Spain, the vaft expences fhe is at in endeavouring to prevent her colony-fubjects from fupplying themfelves with various conveniences in a clandeftine manner, which they cannot procure, at leaft in fufficient quantity, or equally cheap, by any other channel at prefent;—That, notwithftanding all thefe precautions, no lefs than fifteen millions of every annual cargo have been fuppofed to belong to foreigners; and that it is, in every view, fo much for the intereft of that nation to cultivate the friendfhip of Britain, and admit the latter to a fair and regular commerce by treaty:—Thefe circumftances confidered, it is amazing that fhe fhould rather have chofen to reject what might fettle a perpetual harmony between the two nations, and to perfift in thofe ftubborn maxims, of whofe inefficacy fhe has had fo long and uniform an experience. It is in vain for her to expect, that her numerous fubjects here will obey thofe refcripts, in the breach of which their natural wants, as well as their intereft and inclination, concur. Inftead of an equitable tariff, admitting the free importation of certain enumerated goods and manufactures from Britain; fhe has often unneceffarily infulted and provoked its vengeance: and the iffue of all her quarrels has only ended in wafte of her treafure, lofs of fhips, and the affording more convenient opportunity for the fubjects on both fides to profecute that

6

very

very intercourse which she meant to obstruct; insomuch that it never has attained to so flourishing and active a state as during the time of open war. By a different system of policy, she might have enjoyed a strict alliance with the greatest maritime power in the world, capable and ready to fight her battles, and defend her against the united forces of all the other European states; whose merchants might have largely augmented her revenue [*f*], by regular payment of the bullion-duties, and have united with her in keeping off every interloper; for it had then been their interest to put a stop to every inlet of contraband traffic, and make every return which honour, good faith, and gratitude, could prompt. Thus might Spain, instead of being one of the poorest, become one of the richest and most respectable powers in Europe; if it were not for the infatuation of those impolitic counsels which so long have kept her at variance with Great-Britain.

But it is now time to return to Savannah la Mar, hitherto the metropolis of Cornwall; though Montego Bay seems to tread close on its heels, and in a few years will probably dispute this pre-eminence. The number of vessels which enter and clear here is from sixty to seventy *per annum*; and the tonnage, exclusive of coasters, has by some been computed *per* average at eleven thousand five hundred. The town, not many years ago, possessed a very flourishing trade. It is situated commodiously for a correspondence with Truxillo, Honduras, and the Mosquito-shore; being not more than one hundred and five leagues from the bay of Honda, and the passage equally short and speedy, as the trade-wind serves both in going and returning. Near this tract lie, scattered along, the little cayes and islands of Serranilla, Quitosveno, Serrana, Roncador, Sancta Catalina or Old Providence, and St. Andreas, &c. Serrana took its name from Augustin Pedro Serrana, who was wrecked upon it, and lived here seven years. Sancta Catalina was a celebrated place of resort for the buccaneers, is about fifty leagues from Cape Gracias a Dios, and contains several good harbours; for which reason it seems a very proper station for small cruizers in war-time. The town, at present, is but small, consisting only of one tolerable street, and about fifty or sixty scattered houses. Most of the pro-

[*f*] A fifth of all the treasure shipped from their American dominions.

duce

duce of Weftmoreland, befides fome of what belongs to St. Elizabeth and Hanover, is fhipped from this port. Underneath the court-houfe, or hall of juftice, are the barracks, capable of receiving feventy men, and garrifoned with a company of the regulars. The fituation, in point of health, is by no means approvable; for to the Weftward of it lies a tract of undrained morafs, at leaft feven miles in length, which at certain times of the year cannot fail of producing mifchievous effects. It is overfpread with mangroves, and below the level of the fea, and therefore not eafily to be drained. Cabarito Eaft River difcharges its ftream into it, and contributes by this means not only to feed the lagoon-water, but in fome degree to refrefh it. Whether the river could be converted into a drain, by banking and retrieving the ground on each fide, is a point I cannot determine; but it may be worth examination. This river has two good bridges of timber acrofs it, and is navigable in boats about twelve miles inland to a public barquadier at Paul's ifland. The land on which the town is built is flat and low, fubject therefore to thofe exceffive heats and putrid vapours, which, in the months of July and Auguft, occafion fatal maladies in habits unfeafoned to fuch places of refidence. In 1768, a very neceffary act was paffed, the better to fecure this town from accidents by fire. Coopers were prohibited from making fires except within an inclofed yard, furrounded by a brick or ftone-wall of eight feet height, having only one door, and that placed to the Weftward; and the magiftrates were empowered to caufe all huts and other buildings covered with thatch to be pulled down. The hamlet of Queen's Town ftands about two miles North from Savannah la Mar. It confifts of a few houfes tolerably well built; but is a place of no note as yet. This is more ufually called Beckford Town, or Savannah, the land having been given in lots of from five to twenty acres by the late Richard Beckford, efq; and regularly laid out for ftreets, with a large fquare left in the centre for a church. At the Weft end, between the two capes of Negril, is Long Bay; where is good anchorage, and fhelter from tempeftuous winds. It is conveniently fituated for our men of war, during any rupture with Spain, to lie in wait for the Spanifh veffels paffing to or from the Havannah; and here admiral Bembow collected his fquadron in 1702, when he was looking out for Du Caffe. It is not as yet made convenient for fhipping of produce, being rendered almoft inacceffible on the land-fide by means of a large morafs, extending the whole length, comprehending upwards of fix thoufand acres, which in time may probably be drained and cultivated, as the Black Morafs which lies near the centre of the parifh has fuccefsfully been. It contains large quantities of grafs, boar-wood, Santa Maria thatch, and mountain cabbage trees; and is interfperfed with fmall iflands, full of bread-nut and other hard timber trees, and fome mahogany; which prove the foil to be very deep and rich. Three ftreams, or rivulets, take their rife in it, and empty themfelves at Negril Harbour, and Long Bay. When the wind fets hard-in upon this part of the coaft from Weft and North-Weft, they are frequently repelled; and by this means overflow the lower grounds. Yet the draining of this tract appears extremely practicable, and by means of the rivers, if proper flood-gates and banks were formed, after the method practifed on the flat coafts of Lincolnfhire and Suffex. The Eaftern range of the morafs has a fine, fubftantial clay; but the part neareft the fea is of a loofer texture, though poffibly it might become more folid, if it could be reclaimed from the water, which at prefent faps and oozes through it. It is the refort of wild pigeons, and hogs, in great abundance; and the rivulets are ftored with plenty of excellent fifh and land-turtle.

This parifh has a chapel for performing divine fervice, though fcarcely opulent and populous enough to afford a good church. The chapel is built with timber, and ftands in the favannah, about the diftance of one mile from the town of Savannah la Mar.

Some years ago, there was an exceeding good church, of white free-ftone, built in the form of a crofs, about feven miles from the bay: but the parifhioners falling into a violent difpute, whether they fhould repair it, or erect a new one at Savannah la Mar, the roof was unable to wait the iffue, but tumbled in; and, the point not having fince been brought to a final determination, it remains a ftately ruin, to add one proof more to the million of the deplorable effects which attend religious fquabbles. As the two parties could not agree, the church (which formerly was no uncommon cafe)

cafe) feems to have taken the decifion upon itfelf, and by wilful dilapidation endeavoured to convince them, that it will at leaft be the cheaper plan for them to build a new tabernacle than repair the old one. As no houfe of refidence has been provided for the rector, he receives 50 l. a year in lieu of one. The rector's ftipend is 250 l.; but his whole income has been computed at not lefs than 700 l. In the year 1710, a Mr. Thomas Manning devifed the bulk of his eftate to truftees, for the purpofes of founding a free-fchool near Beckford Town, maintaining and educating poor children of the parifh till the age of fourteen. In 1738, an act was paffed for more effectually executing this charitable bequeft. The truftees were incorporated, empowered to build a fchool-houfe, receive children, appoint tutors, and prefcribe rules and orders, under a common feal, for its better government. I fhall take occafion hereafter to offer fome remarks in regard to this and other fimilar foundations, which have not in general anfwered the good ends of their inftitution.

In the Eaft part of the parifh, near Scot's Cave, were fettled the Surinam planters in 1675, and in 1699 the remnant of the Scotch Darien colony, who may now be traced by the names of feveral fettlements hereabouts, as Culloden, Auchindown, &c. From the former, this divifion was called Surinam quarters. The favannahs, or low lands, of Weftmoreland are in general rich and fertile, but, if neglected for any time, become as much infefted with logwood as thofe in St. Catharine's are with the opopinax. The air of thefe parts is hot, but tolerably healthy, except near the fhore. The Eaft and North-eaft diftrict, being very mountainous, is not yet peopled. Towards the Weft, or land's-end, the hills diminifh. Many of the planters houfes are fituated on thefe eminences, and enjoy a very pure and healthy air, though fubject to very heavy and frequent rains, occafioned by the collection of vapours, blown hither from the Eaftward, over the whole length of the ifland, by the trade-wind: thefe are often impeded in their courfe, either by the high ridges, or Wefterly airs, and then they fall very copioufly. This plentiful irrigation, though productive of fome inconveniencies, yet conduces to the fertility of the plantations, and fecures their crops with fo much regularity and cer-

tainty,

tainty, that it may be esteemed one of the most eligible for sugar in the whole island, both in regard to quantity, and excellence of quality.

On leaving Savannah la Mar, the road to Hanover crosses Caba-rito River twice, at no great distance, by two bridges, about eight or nine feet wide, constructed with planks laid across some beams, but unprovided with any side-rails to guard passengers from tumbling over. This river takes its rise among the Hanover Mountains, a little to the Eastward of King's Valley. At Black Morass it sepa-rates into two streams, one of which empties itself into the sea at Savannah la Mar, as already mentioned; the other, a little to the Westward of it. These streams, although they run upwards of eighteen or twenty miles through the country, are neither of them navigable, except for canoes. From hence to Albany plantation the way is, in general, very flat, confined, and swampy. This brings us to the Delve barracks, which were built in consequence of the insurrection in 1761, and capable of accommodating one hundred men. They are situated near the foot of Hanover Moun-tains, tolerably well constructed, and judiciously posted. They stand on a dry spot near the dividing line of the two parishes, three or four miles distant at least from the morassy ground of Negril, and are well enough contrived to answer most of the purposes for which they were intended, being sufficiently strong to resist any force that a band of rebellious Negroes could bring against them. They are also built in a place most likely to be infested with such disturbances; for it is a part of the country where there are a great multitude of slaves, and few proprietors of estates reside; and where the neighbourhood is filled with woods and thickets, that might the oftener tempt them to mutiny, by the shelter they afford, if they were not kept in awe by these barracks, from which a small detachment might harrass and prevent their committing any ex-tensive outrages. This building is, however, defective in some respects. The hospital for the sick is only divided from the com-mon room by a boarded partition, full of chinks; by which means there is a continual passage open for malignant and noxious ef-fluvia to infect the healthy. The number of loop-holes is likewise too small, there not being more than five or six; so that very little

annoyance

annoyance can be given from it in cafe it fhould be clofely befieged. The window-fhutters are of bullet-tree-wood (fo called, becaufe an inch-board of it is bullet-proof); but, if thefe windows are to be opened in the time of attack, in order that the garrifon may fire upon their enemy, which they could not otherwife do, for want of loop holes, their bodies muft neceffarily be much expofed, and the fhutters of no ufe to fkreen them. The roads, for three miles after leaving Albany, afford a profpect delightfully variegated. Towards the North, the late commodore F—rr—ft's plantation, and feveral others, are feen ftretching along the fkirts of the Hanover Mountains, which are juft behind, and feem to over-hang them. The ground towards the South appears uneven, poor, and of a reddifh foil; full of brakes and irregular clumps of trees, and uncultivated; ferving only to feed a few young cattle that graze fcantily among the bufhes. Point Negril lies about three or four miles Weft of Albany. The moraffy land embracing it renders the air of the adjacent eftates damp and unwholefome. Eaftward, the view is terminated by another range of mountains, covered with a foreft of mahogany and other gigantic trees. Between thefe different mountainous barriers lies the road to Hanover, through the fertile glade called King's Valley, which exhibits a lively and picturefque fcene. Though not above half a mile acrofs, it is inimitably contrafted throughout. It abounds with delicious fprings and cooling rivulets, refrefhing the land through which they glide. The lofty mountains on either fide twice every day extend their grateful fhade over the whole, and veil the richly-cultivated fields below from the fun, preferving the canes from taint in times of drowth, to which the champaign lands, in many parts of the ifland, are much expofed. There are, befides, in this fequeftered vale, two or three fmooth fugar-loaf hills, that rife to confiderable elevation, and whofe ever-green and floping fides yield pafturage to numerous herds of cattle.

The whole machinery of this charming fpot is highly pleafing; for, abftracted from its natural beauties, it is decorated with fome handfome plantation-houfes; at one of which (called Glafgow) fituated on a rifing ground, is a battery which was of great ufe in protecting the eftates here during the Negroe rebellion.

From

From hence the road into Hanover is by a steep ascent, or rather pass, of about a mile in length, so narrow, that two horses can scarcely go a-breast. From the summit of it, the eye takes in, at once, a rural scene enriched with every embellishment of art and nature. The landschape is inimitably fine, and mocks description: canefields, villas, pastures, clumps, groves, and rivulets, are promiscuously spread over the whole of its swelling wavy surface. These extend two or three miles from the centre of the prospect, having about one-half filleted, as it were, with a range of hills enveloped with thickets, and a shaggy mantle of venerable trees; the other, skirted by the Western ocean. This district of the parish exceeds most others, as well in the configuration and wild arrangement of all its parts, as in the peculiar nature of its soil, which is a kind of fuller's-earth, soapy and rich; so congenial to the sugar-cane, that a long and uninterrupted culture seems not in the least to have exhausted, or even impaired, its fertility. The sugars made here most resemble those of Liguanea, remarkably fine, and inferior to none in the West-Indies. But I shall not anticipate further the description of Hanover parish.

State of the Parish:

	Negroes.	Cattle.	Sugar-plantations.	Hogsheads.	Other Settlements.
			Annual Produce.		
1734,	9081	6915			
1740,	11155	8921			
1745,	12131	8520			
1761,	15158				
1768,	15186	13750	69	8000	96

There needs no other proof, to shew how greatly it has improved of late years. It is very capable of being advanced still further in its product, if breeding-penns should ever be formed in the North-east mountains, and the lowland-penns be converted into sugar-plantations. The road, which has lately been compleated from Deane's Valley, in this parish, to the Bogue in St. James's, is skilfully conducted and well-finished, and will probably invite the proprietors of land, contiguous to it on each side, to open and settle their lots. This road is now the grand communication be-

tween

tween the two parifhes, and extremely convenient to both, as the affize-court is held at Savannah la Mar.

The natural curiofities in this parifh, hitherto difcovered, are but very few; though the want of them is, doubtlefs, compenfated by the variety of its natural beauties, in point of wood, water, and profpects. At Ricketts's Savannah, in the Weftern diftrict, two mineral fprings were difcovered not long fince. A gentleman of the faculty, who tried fome experiments upon them, affirmed, as I am told, that they were not inferior to the celebrated Geron-ftere fpa; and that, on being adminiftered, they have proved efficacious in the fame diforders which that fpa fo fuccefsfully relieves.

S E C T. III.

H A N O V E R.

THIS parifh is bounded on the Eaft by Great River, which divides it from St. James; on the Weft and North, by the fea; and on the South, by Weftmoreland. It was not formed till the year 1723; when it was taken out of the laft-mentioned parifh. It contains feveral rivers, but none of them remarkable, fcarcely any rifing more than four miles from the coaft. The principal headlands are North Negril and Pedro on the Weft, and Roundhill Bluff on the North. Proceeding from Weftmoreland, the firft fhipping-place we meet with is Orange Bay, lying within North-Negril, a capacious road, and good anchorage. About a league North from this, lies Green Ifland Harbour. But the chief barquadier is at Sancta Lucia Harbour, about ten miles further on the North coaft. Green River is navigable by boats upwards of two miles, and has many agreeable meanders, affording as many different profpects. Its banks are cloathed on each fide, either with groves of plantain, banana, and other trees, or with fugar-canes, to within about half a mile of the mouth, where the breadth expands to fifty feet at leaft; and it falls over a little fhallow bar into the bay; here the fides are moraffy, and have rather a wild and unpleafing appearance. Green Ifland Harbour and Orange Bay are the moft North-weftern parts of Jamaica. The former takes

its name from a little ifland at the offing, about half a league diftant from the main land.   On the Weft fide of the harbour is a
fmall battery of nine guns, fix-pounders, to guard the entrance,
and is kept in excellent order; but if, inftead of the battery, a fort
had been erected here, inclofing the barrack, a garrifon of forty or
fifty men might hinder any privateer, or fmall fhip of war, from
croffing the bar, and landing their crew; but, whilft it continues
open towards the Weft, it is liable to furprizes.   Befides the nine
guns mounted at the battery, there are two more at a diftance from
it, near a fmall tavern, where the main battery was firft intended;
and eleven embrazures completely built.

North-eaft from this harbour is another fmall bay, commodious
enough for fhipping; on the Weft fide of which is a ftrong battery, of feventeen or eighteen guns, built and maintained at the
private expence of Mr. J—s, whofe eftate lies contiguous.   This
battery has embrazures for twenty-one guns; and thofe already
mounted are fix and nine-pounders.

Not far from hence is Orange Cove, near Point Pedro, a part of
Hanover, beautiful beyond defcription.   So various, fo picturefque,
and admirably fine, is the combination of all the detail which
unites in forming this landfchape; and the whole fo nicely interwoven and difpofed; that it feems almoft impoffible for either
painter or hiftorian to give any thing like a faithful fketch of it.
Here has nature exerted all her plaftic powers, in laying out and
arranging the ground-work; and art has likewife put forth her
whole fkill, in vying with or affifting her in the machinery, compofed of a thoufand decorations.   Wherever the paffing eye delights to wander, it meets with a fucceffion of objects, throughout
an extent of many miles, equally new, ftriking, and lively.   In
one divifion is feen a wide plain, richly carpeted with canes of the
emerald tint, differently fhaded, and ftriped with fringes of logwood, or penguin-fence, or, inftead of this border, with rills of
cryftal water.   In another rifes a high-fwelling lawn, fmooth and
fertile, whofe gently-floping bofom is embellifhed with herds and
flocks, and whofe fummit is crowned with Negroe-villages, or
clumps of graceful trees.   Here, on a neighbouring hill, is a wind-
mill in motion; boiling-houfes, and other plantation-buildings, at
the

the foot: there, in the various duties which cultivation excites, are labourers, cattle, and carriages; all briskly employed. In addition to these animated scenes is a boundless prospect of the sea, which skirts the distant horizon towards the North; and, on the other hand, a wood-capped battlement of hills, that shuts in the Southern view. Delicious as the face of this part of the country is, it scarcely exceeds in beauty the prospect of Lucea and its environs. The harbour at the entrance is half a mile across; and, continuing its channel for about one mile inland, expands at once into a circular bason of nearly the same space in diameter every way; the anchoring-ground every where good, and depth of water from four to six fathom.

The town is inconsiderable, consisting only of one large street, and about forty or fifty scattered houses. It stands on the South-West side, upon a swampy bottom; but no part of it is seen from the road, until it is actually entered. The land behind and on each side is hilly; so that the view from it is only open towards the water. Two or three rivulets creep through it, more noisome than the antient canal of Fleet-ditch. At the bottom of the harbour, the East and West Lucea Rivers discharge their streams. Though raised to the dignity of a free port, its trade as yet is not very extensive. The number of vessels which enter and clear here may be reckoned at about fifty to sixty sail *per annum*; but the harbour is very capable of receiving three hundred top-sail ships at a time, were there but inducements to attract them. During the last war, this town carried on a very active trade; but this has been discouraged since by captures and other losses; so that at present it is far from being in a prosperous condition. The present situation is ill-chosen, and naturally unadapted for healthful residence. But the port is conveniently situated for traffic with the South-West parts of Cuba; and, enjoying as it does so fine a receptacle for shipping, it is well deserving of the public patronage. The fort, which commands the entrance, stands on the Western point, a small peninsula, and is built on a rock, rising about twenty feet above the level of the sea. It is very compleat in its defences, having embrazures for twenty-three guns, of which twenty are mounted from six to nine-pounders, and in good condition for service; so that it is capable of making a tolerable refiftance. The barracks for fifty men are at a fmall diftance to the Southward. Thefe, like the others before-fpoken of, are feparated only by a boarded partition, full of holes, from the hofpital, which is very inconfiderately placed at the windward-end; fo that a large quantity of the foul putrid air, proceeding from thofe who are unhappily affected with any virulent or epidemic diftemper, is immediately taken into the lungs, and refpired by thofe who are, and probably might otherwife long continue, in found health. The houfe defigned for accommodation of the officers is, with as little propriety, erected to leeward of the barracks, kitchen, and other neceffary offices; whence all the foetid effluvia, that reek from thefe fources, are wafted upon thofe who are ftationed here in garrifon. A want of proper regulation in thefe particulars is but too common in moft of the maritime barracks throughout the ifland; and not only the poor foldiers, but the ifland itfelf, may fuffer greatly, if it fhould not be remedied. The circumftance has been overlooked perhaps, as generally is the cafe in this country, where the genuine parents of ficknefs are not fcrupuloufly traced out. But it is to this miftaken difpofition, I am perfuaded to believe, that the unhealthinefs of the garrifon, at particular times, has been chiefly owing; for, fuppofing only one or two men to lie fick in the hofpital of a malignant fever, they may contaminate the atmofphere fo much in twenty-four hours, as to render it morbid and infectious to the healthy who are lodged in a fituation to be fufceptible of its pernicious effects. This misfortune actually befel the garrifon in 1764, compofed entirely of men newly-arrived from Europe. One or two falling fick of putrid fevers, the diforder foon grew epidemic. Thofe who probably would have efcaped (at leaft any bad fymptoms) if they could have breathed a refrefhing air, were poifoned with the ftench of the hofpital and offices; and feveral were feized with fevers of an anomalous kind, which feldom or never occur unlefs from fome fuch pre-difpofing caufe. In fact, the ficknefs fpread fo rapidly, that, in a fhort time, hardly ten men of the whole company were able to do duty. Errors of this nature, though apparently trivial in the opinion of many, ought not to be flighted, when the value of mens lives comes to be rated. And, fince the modern difcoveries of

learned

learned phyficians have taught us to confider a vitiated air as a principal agent in the acute difeafes moft common to hot climates, the publick of the ifland fhould, as far as poffible, endeavour to alleviate this inclemency, and confult the prefervation of health and vigour among thefe detachments at the out-ports. Good fenfe, humanity, and a regard to their own fecurity, all confpire to enforce this recommendation. Situated on an agreeable fpot, about half a mile from the town, and near the fort, is the church, built a few years fince by the parifhioners, at the expence of 7000*l* and upwards. It is a plain, neat building of brick, decently pewed, and provided with every convenience fuitable to the good purpofes for which it was intended, except bells, though the tower is capacious enough to hold a ring of five or fix. The living, perquifites included, is efteemed worth about 400*l*. currency. On the oppofite fide of the harbour is the Point Plantation; diftinguifhed for its fine fituation, commanding the town, fort, church, harbour, fhipping, and a diftant view continued for many miles over rich cane-fields and a country moft elegantly diverfified; fo that few parts of the ifland prefent a greater affemblage of delightful objects in one profpect.

Here, as well as at Greenwich, in the neighbourhood, and moft of the frontier plantations near the North coaft, are fmall batteries, erected at the private expence of the refpective owners of thofe plantations, which in time of war fupply the want of king's fhips, and are of ufe to intimidate the privateers from landing, to carry off Negroes, cattle, and other moveables.

The face of this parifh is, in general, hilly; and, towards Weftmoreland, it is flanked with that ridge of mountains common to both. The air is efteemed healthy, and will be more fo, when greater progrefs is made in cutting down its woods; the Eaftern and South-eaft divifion not being as yet occupied with any fettlement.

Lucea has a cuftom-houfe, under direction of a collector and comptroller.

State

State of the Parifh:

	Negroes.	Cattle.	Annual Produce.		
			Sugar-plantations.	Hogfheads.	Other Settlement
1734,	3339	1774			
1740,	4863	2631			
1745,	6351	3054			
1761,	10498				
1768,	13571	8942	71	7500	35

Confidering Hanover as a modern parifh, it has advanced fur-prizingly, and contains more fugar-works than fome of three times the extent; which is a fure proof of the fitnefs of the foil for this cultivation. There are few other in the ifland that, in the fame time (little more than thirty years), can boaft of having increafed their ftock in the proportion of four to one; which is actually the fact in refpect to Hanover; fo that it bids fair to vie with thofe efteemed the richeft in Jamaica.

SECT. IV.

St. J A M E S.

THIS parifh is bounded on the Eaft by Trelawny; Weft, by Hanover; North, by the fea; South, by St. Elizabeth. The principal rivers are Great River, on the Weftern boundary; Martha-brae, on the Eaftern; and Montego, which falls into the bay of that name. Great River rifes in the furtheft Southern extremity of the parifh, meandring a courfe of about thirty miles, and, col-lecting fome other ftreams in its way, grows pretty large where it difembogues into the fea at the Weft angle of the bay, and about five miles from the town of Montego. This river is the natural boundary between this parifh and Hanover; but, although it is pretty wide at its mouth, and penetrates fo confiderable a way into the country, it is at prefent not navigable above three or four miles, and that only for boats and canoes. At the mouth it is croffed by a ferry.

The Montego River falls into the Bay about three quarters of a mile Weft from the town. The coaft of this parifh has no head-land of any note, nor any harbour, except Montego; but this is very fufficient. The extent of the parifh from North to South being

being near twenty-four miles, it contains of courfe a large run of unfettled lands. The fettlements reach between thirteen and four-teen miles back from the fea : but there is a fpace ftill behind them of one hundred thoufand acres or upwards, yet uninhabited, ex-cept by the Maroon Negroes, of Furry's and Trelawny Towns ; who poffeffing a grant of fifteen hundred acres, there remain about ninety-eight thoufand for cultivation. This land is mountainous, but faid to be inferior to none in fertility; and, as St. James is now become the moft thriving diftrict in the ifland, fome extenfion will probably be made every year. One great fource of this flourifhing ftate has been the rapid increafe of the town and its trade from very fmall beginnings. It contains at prefent, by computation, about four hundred houfes, moftly built of brick, and fome of them inhabited by opulent merchants ; one of whom carried on the Guiney branch with fo much fuccefs, as to remit bills, in the year 1771, to Great-Britain, for near 50,000 $l.$ fterling, on account of new Negroes alone ; and, as only two of thefe bills (which were both under 300 $l.$) were protefted, we have, in this inftance, the ftrongeft indication poffible of the happy circumftances en-joyed by the planters in this part of the country. The town, fi-tuated in about 18° 30′ North latitude, ftands on the North-eaft fide of a fpacious bay, along the feet of a range of moderately hilly land, which fomewhat incommodes it by intercepting the breeze. The ftreets are laid out with tolerable exactnefs. In the bay, the water is from four to thirty fathom : the channel leading into it is guarded, on the Eaft and Weft, by a reef and funken rocks ; but far in there is excellent anchorage, and room for a large fleet of fhips. On the South-weft part of the bay is a clufter of little iflands, covered with mangroves, and other maritime trees. Be-yond thefe iflands is another fpacious harbour, but of no ufe at pre-fent; fince it is impoffible for any veffel of burthen to fail into it, on account of the fhoal-water on one fide, and the iflands on the other ; though it is affirmed, that a paffage between them might be opened at no very great expence. It is likewife fuppofed to be defended by the fort (fituated about half a mile from the town to the North-eaft, on a fmall point of land), which mounts fome guns, and may be occafionally garrifoned by a party of regulars,

for

for whofe reception the parifhioners erected barracks capable of holding one hundred men, with their officers. As the fituation of thefe barracks is high, and on a rock by the harbour-fide, they would be pleafant and healthy, if the trees and bufhes, which are fuffered to grow fo luxuriantly near them, were cut down; and if a further improvement was made in refpect to the accommodations provided for the officers, which are very inconveniently placed. The fort is, or lately was, in a ftate of decay; and fcarcely deferves to be rebuilt, as it does not, from its fituation, appear to have been ever capable of guarding the entrance; fince, at the fpot where it now ftands, the channel is fo wide, that any veffel might enter the bay without danger from its artillery, and afterwards come to anchor unmolefted. The guns (eleven in number) are of too fmall a fize to range a fufficient diftance, and (what is ftill worfe) fo honey-combed and ruft-eaten, and fo crazily mounted, as to make it dangerous to fire them; which was fatally experienced by a gunner, who was fhattered to pieces on letting off a *feu de joye* after the furrender of the Havannah to the Englifh forces. Though a more eligible fpot may be appropriated to the next fort, and though the prefent is not worthy to be rebuilt, I muft take leave to fay, that thefe ruins, like others of a fimilar kind in many defencelefs parts of the ifland, have happened chiefly for want of a trifling fum every year expended in neceffary repairs, and particularly the painting, or tarring, the guns and their carriages. In truth, the fortifications planted about the harbour of Port Royal and Kingfton, being the only ones which receive an annual vifitation from the commiffioners of forts and fortifications, are kept in better repair than any other; and, becaufe there was a time when no other part of the ifland was fortified, or of fo much importance as that diftrict, it is therefore ftill the cuftom to expend the whole fortification-fund, and feveral thoufand pounds more *per annum*, upon them; while others at the out-ports are utterly neglected, and left to be kept up at the expence of private perfons, or of the parifhes in which they have been erected, and where the inhabitants are glad, on every convenient occafion, to leffen their affeffments as much as they can, and perhaps take no thought about their forts and batteries, except in time of actual war. This proceeding of

the

the legiflative branches is much the fame as if a man, by clapping a helmet upon his head, fhould think himfelf perfectly invulnerable, though all the reft of his body remains expofed. But, in order to maintain thefe defences along the coaft, which are neceffary, not only to fuch parifhes, but to the whole ifland; the affembly, we may venture to think, might every year call for an exact and faithful report of their condition; and, if no portion can be fpared out of the fortification-fund, the juftices and veftry might at leaft be obliged, in the more opulent of thefe parifhes, to raife a fmall annual fum, by fome eafy and permanent mode, which fhould conftitute a fund to be applied folely to the repair of their refpective fortifications.

Thefe fentiments arife from confidering the improved ftate of Montego Bay; the vaft value of its trade; its buildings, rents, goods, and fhipping; the opulence which is likely to centre in it; and the hazard to which all thefe may become expofed, on any fudden revival of war, from the attacks of a few daring privateers. As it is now, with juftice, deemed the *emporium* of the Weftern part of the ifland, it certainly merits to be well guarded, and indeed feems entitled to come in for a yearly fhare of the public money, which hitherto has been partially lavifhed upon the environs of one principal port, as if they were the only quarters which an enemy could attempt, or that were worthy of the public defence.

Montego Bay, in the opinion of the beft judges, is growing very faft into a place of fo much confequence and wealth, that, in the event of a war, it will be a capital neglect of government, fhould it be left unprotected by a ftrong fort, or one or two men of war for guard-fhips.

The fhipping of every kind, that enter and clear at this port, are, one year with another, about 140 fail *per annum*, and continually on the increafe; as it not only lies fo commodious for foreign trade, but employs near about eleven thoufand tons for the products of the adjacent diftrict; this being the great mart for fupplying it with Negroes and other neceffaries, that formerly ufed to be bought at Kingfton, which has therefore fuffered a fevere blow from this new eftablifhment. For the like reafon, among others, the town o

Lucea

Lucea has made fo little progrefs ; the chief trade and bufinefs for the Northern leeward part of the ifland being engroffed and con-centered at Montego.

The eftablifhment of a trading town neceffarily attracts artificers in various branches, and other numerous dependents. Hence a great convenience refults to the fettlers around in the country-parts, from the eafy method by which they can accommodate themfelves with what they want. But a far greater advantage accrues to them from the yearly confumption of their products in fuch a town, which gives birth and fupport to a multitude of petty fettlements for cultivating provifions of different forts to anfwer that con-fumption. Such a town muft therefore add confiderably to the population of the country ; and itfelf derive a reciprocal profit from the fale of goods to, and tranfaction of bufinefs for, the more opu-lent plantations, which furnifh ftaple or exportable commodities ; and this profit will be large and durable in proportion to the fertility of the neighbouring foil. Now, the lands in this parifh being very productive, and fo many thoufand acres ftill remaining to be here-after gradually employed, here feems to be a morally certain pro-fpect, that this town, being conftituted upon the moft permanent fupports, can never decline fo long as the ftaple products of the ifland are worth any thing at the home-market.

I have elfewhere taken notice of the rapid augmentation of fet-tlements in this part of the country of late years ; which is really amazing, and will fo appear from the comparative table, that, like the foregoing, is brought down no lower than the year 1768 : but I am well informed, that at leaft twenty or more fugar-works may be added to the lift at the prefent time.

Behind the town, to the Southward, is a long range of uncul-tivated mountains, clad, like moft others in this country, with lofty trees. The road which croffes this to Montpelier is excellently conftructed, and opens an avenue into a vale behind, containing many thoufand acres of rich foil, a fmall part of which only is at prefent brought into culture. But, as improvements are moving on here at a furprizing rate, there is good reafon to believe, that the whole of this fine tract will, in a few years, be overfpread

with

with canes, and make a prodigious addition to the exports and imports of this parifh.

The land towards the Eaftern diftrict of it is of a reddifh caft, and fingularly porous quality, lying on a clayey fubftrate, excellently well adapted to the fugar-cane. Towards the Weftern parts it has more of the loamy foil, but not much lefs fertile. The produce of lands here in general is really amazing. I have been told the following anecdote in confirmation of this remark. A perfon rented a tract from the proprietor on a leafe of eleven years, conditioned to furrender it back, at the expiration of the term, compleatly planted with canes, &c. and furnifhed with proper works. But, before the term expired, the leffee is faid to have gained by the bargain a clear profit of 30,000*l*. Others, from the very meaneft and fmalleft beginnings here, have acquired very large fortunes. It is related for a fact, that a poor man and his wife, poffeffing a grant of a fmall parcel of land, planted fome part of it in canes with the labour of their own hands. From thefe, when they were ripened, they made fhift to exprefs the juice, which they boiled in an old cauldron, and manufactured a little fugar, with which they went to market. By degrees, and the inceffant application of their induftry, they augmented their produce, till they gained fufficient to purchafe a Negroe. By the fame means, they increafed their labourers, and the importance of their eftate; till, at length, they became proprietors of a valuable fugar-work, which is now enjoyed by the furvivor, and by the moft honourable title.

It is impoffible to particularize the various natural productions of this parifh, fo fmall a fection of it being as yet laid open to view; but, from what has hitherto been difcovered, it is wanting in no article conducive to the pleafure and convenience of the inhabitants. In moft parts it abounds with excellent ftone both for lime and building; and in fome, as about the neighbourhood of Montpelier, what is obtained from the quarry, refembles that of St. Anne before-defcribed, whofe texture, when firft dug, is fo foft as to be eafily worked with the faw, or the chiffel. It remains, for its further better population, to form two good roads of communication, one leading into Weftmoreland, the other to St. Elizabeth's. The former is at prefent well attended to; but the latter, by the way of Chesterfield, has been thought ill constructed, and inconvenient on other accounts, as it passes over a great deal of boggy land, and very steep hills. It has therefore been proposed to lead the road from Montego Bay, through Spring-mount estate, into Hardyman's penn; thence to Ellerslea plantation, to Nassau, the centre and most thriving part of St. Elizabeth. It is said, that the land, through which this road would go, abounds in fine materials to render it firm and durable; that it could be made fit for carriages from the bay to Ellerslea for 1600*l.* and would be the best way for travelers from Hanover and St. James to go to Spanish Town, being only a day's ride, or sixty miles extent, over level grounds, from Spanish Town to Nassau, and thirty-six from thence to Montego Bay; in all ninety-six: finally, that, by opening so easy an intercourse between the seat of government and the Western parts of the island, now advanced into so flourishing a state, a multitude of conveniences and benefits might be expected to result to the whole island; of which latter position there can be no doubt, if the former ones are as practicable as they appear plausible; since a commercial island, like the human body, will always enjoy the best health and most active vigour, when the circulation is carried on, freely and without impediment, from the heart to the extremities, and back again from these to the heart.

As St James was but recently divided into two parishes, I am obliged in the table to consider it as still indistinct, to make the detail comply with the former estimates: however, I shall endeavour also to form another state of the number of Negroes and cattle contained in it, as distinct from Trelawny.

State of the Parish:

	Negroes.	Cattle.	Sugar-works.	Annual Produce. Hogsheads.	Other Settlements.
1734,	2297	1099			
1740,	2588	1204			
1745,	4907	1961	about 20	2500	14
1761,	14729				
1768,	21749	15137	95	11000	102
1768, Proportion distinct from Trelawny by computation,	10010	7007	55	3080	36
Increase, in twenty-three years, about ———	16842	13176	75	8500	78

The

The progrefs therefore of this parifh, for the time, exceeds that of any other in the ifland; and at prefent it takes the lead of all, the annual produce of fugar being at leaft twelve or fourteen thoufand hogfheads.

The hills in general near the coaft, and to fome diftance from it, are rocky, but bear good provifions. The canes are planted in the glades and richer patches, and yield a very excellent fugar. This, being the moft Northern part of the ifland, and full of rifing grounds, enjoys an healthy air, and promifes long life to the interior fettlers, who increafe very faft. The floweft progrefs feems to be made in the Eaftern and Southern divifions, which are overfpread with ranges of mountain, requiring nothing but good roads to promote their fettlement. On this fubject I may be thought, perhaps, to have expatiated fufficiently. I fhall only further obferve, that, nature having in this and other parts of the ifland walled-in many of the richeft fpots in the world, it remains for the legiflature to make them acceffible, by opening a paffage for thofe induftrious fubjects who are willing to labour the foil, if they were but as able to get at it; and in no part of the ifland will fuch affiftance turn more beneficially to the public account than in this parifh.

In the town is a cuftom-houfe, under the direction of a collector and comptroller, deputy naval-officer, receiver-general, and fecretary. The rector's ftipend is 200 *l. per annum*; but, confidering the extent and populoufnefs of the parifh, his income cannot be eftimated at lefs than 700 *l.* A printing-prefs has lately been fet up here, furnifhed with a very beautiful type, and gives birth to a weekly paper of intelligence. There feems a ftruggle between this town and Savannah la Mar for the afcendency, fomewhat fimilar to what has happened between Spanifh Town and Kingfton; but the oftenfible object of difpute is different. Savannah la Mar having declined in proportion as Montego Town has increafed, the latter, being far more populous, and more thriving in its trade, became defirous of having the affize-court alternately held. This perhaps was confidered, by the partizans of the elder fifter, as a firft ftep towards removing the feat of juftice, and transferring it wholly to Montego Bay. It was oppofed with great warmth; and

the

the rights of feniority prevailed. But it is probable, that as the bufinefs of the court muft be in proportion to the number and opulence of the inhabitants, fo this claim of feniority will yield in
the end to the conveniency of the people of Montego and Trelawny; at leaft fo far as to eftablifh an alternate court, as firft propofed: by which means, the eafe of trade may be confulted in the
leaft partial manner, and the new eftablifhment be reafonably favoured, without ruining the older one.

It is a juft remark of Dr. Browne, that thofe towns, which,
fince the decay of the Spanifh trade, have been fupported chiefly by
ftanding courts and the calamities of the people, are rather a prejudice than an emolument to the community; while they harbour
fo many dependents in idlenefs at the expence of the induftrious,
who might have proved very ferviceable members, had they been
diftributed about the ifland, and their thoughts turned more upon
the advancement than the diftreffing of fettlements.

S E C T. V.

T R E L A W N Y.

PROCEEDING from St. James to Trelawny, the road lies,
for the moft part, along the coaft, without having any object more
pleafing to the eye than, on one fide, a profpect of the fea, and on
the other a chain of fhaggy mountains, which run along the North
fide of the ifland in one almoft uninterrupted range, except where
they are indented by creeks and bays, and cleft as it were by rivers.
In fome other parts are alfo receffes, affording room for plantations
and pafture-grounds; but, in general, their foil is good; and fuch
of them as are cultivated, produce here, as on the South fide, great
plenty of corn, plantains, coffee, pimento, yams, caffada, and
moft other forts of Weft-India provifions, as well as many kinds
of European vegetables. But although, towards the Eaft, the hills
feem retired further from the fea than in the Weftern parts of St.
James, there are few diftricts of Jamaica of a more wild and barbarous afpect than the tract which lies to the Eaftward of Long-
Bay, till the cultivated parts of Trelawny open to view. This
newly-baptized parifh is divided from St. James on the Weft by a
North

North and South line, interfecting New Canaan eftate; from St. Anne on the Eaft, by the Rio Bueno; on the North it is bounded by the Sea; and Southerly by St. Elizabeth. Its capital river is the Marthabrae, which takes its fource among the mountains, about twelve miles diftance from the coaft, as commonly fuppofed; for, there being no fettlement near the fpring-head, it is not exactly known. It ferpentines through a courfe of about thirty miles before it reaches the harbour; from whence it is navigable by canoes and boats, for fome miles, to the bridge. The depth of its water is fufficient for much larger veffels, except at the mouth, where a bar, occafioned by the fand difgorged from the ftream, and repelled by the tide, obftructs the navigation. The village of Marthabrae ftands about two miles above the mouth, on a rifing ground not far from the bridge, and confifts of about thirty houfes or more; as the late partition of St. James has of confequence tended to the eftablifhment of a new town here, which may grow in fize in proportion as the lands, at prefent unfettled in the parifh, are brought into culture. The river which glides by it abounds with fifh of various kinds; and the courfe fo delightfully twining, that its banks might be laid out in gardens, with a view to pleafure, as well as utility, which is an additional circumftance in favour of the town's increafe. The harbour is defended by a fmall fort, placed on Point Mangrove, which projects into the fea on the Weft fide. The only fault in its ftructure feems to be the narrownefs of the gorges of the baftions, and of the baftions themfelves; in which the guns cannot traverfe fo freely as they ought. The fpot whereon it ftands, and all around it, being altogether fwampy, there is reafon to fufpect that without draining thefe quarters will not be very healthy. In other refpects this fortrefs is well fituated for guarding the entrance, or channel, which runs at right angles to it about North-Eaft; narrow, and hemmed in by reefs and fhoals on either fide, for near a mile. The barracks, for the accommodation of one hundred men and officers, are at a fmall diftance.

The harbour is covered, towards the Eaft and North-Eaft, by a femicircular fweep of the main land on that fide, and by a fmall ifland; fo that within it is not only capacious, but well fheltered from the fea.

The

The country hereabouts, for a few miles, is well cultivated; but, fome miles further to the Eaftward, it ftill wears a favage afpect, though by no means unfufceptible of great improvements, and valuable plantations.   In the Eafternmoft part is a fucceffion of fine pimento walks, which continue, with little interruption, beyond Rio Bueno, the boundary between Trelawny and St. Anne, and through a confiderable extent of the laft-mentioned parifh. The beauty of thefe fpicy groves, which are likewife interfperfed with the orange, limon, ftar-apple, avogato-pear, wild cinnamon, and other favourite trees, among which fome impetuous river rolls its foaming flood, or babbling rivulet, gently trails along in glittering meanders, furnifhes a fubject worthy fome darling of the Mufes. Even paradife itfelf, defcribed by the pen of Milton, exhibits but a faint reprefentation of them, when he fays,——

" Whofe rich trees wept odorous gums and balm.
" Others, whofe fruit, burnifh'd with golden rind,
" Hung amiable—Hefperian fables true.—
" If true, here only ; and of delicious tafte.
" Betwixt them lawns or level downs, and flocks
" Grazing the tender herb, were interpos'd ;
" Or palmy hillock.   Or the flow'ry lap
" Of fome irriguous valley fpread her ftore,
" Flow'rs of all hue, and without thorn the rofe.
" Another fide, umbrageous grots and caves
" Of cool recefs.   Mean while, the murm'ring waters fall
" Down yon flope hill, difpers'd, or in a lake
" That to the fringed bank, with myrtle crown'd,
" Her cryftal mirror holds, unite their ftreams.
" The birds their choir apply.   Airs, vernal airs,
" Breathing the fmell of field and grove, attune
" The trembling leaves.   While univerfal Pan,
" Knit with the Graces and the Hours in dance,
" Led on th' eternal fpring."

The parifh extends about fifteen miles in depth, and is fettled, but imperfectly, to the diftance of fix miles only from the fea. A fpace remains behind of eighty thoufand acres, and upwards, uninhabited ; and concerning which we know nothing more at pre-

fent, except that it is very mountainous, no public road being traverfed as yet through any part of it; fo that it is almoft as much
an undifcovered country, as the regions bordering on the South
pole. But fo large a tract contains, probably, valuable timbers,
rich veins of foil, and a variety of other ftores of wealth and
curiofity.

It may be proper, as my fketch of the different parifhes is
drawing near to a clofe, that I fhould here recapitulate the feveral
parcels of fuppofed cultivated land, which have been noticed to lie
in wildernefs, and without an inhabitant.

		Acres.	Morafs.
Middlefex,	{ between St. Anne and Cla- rendon, about ———	180,000, of which	
Surry,	St. Thomas in the Eaft, —— Portland, ——— ——— ——— St. George, ——— ——— ——	133,000 —— ——	8000
Cornwall,	St. Elizabeth, —— —— Weftmoreland, ——— —— St. James, ——— —— Trelawny, ——— —— ———	284,000 ———	26,000
		597,000	34,000

exclufive of the large vacant tracts in all the other parifhes, which,
if the computation I made in treating upon this fubject be near the
truth, amount to 1,753,000 acres of plantable or cultivable acres
more. But, if the amount in all was only one million, I may
furely hope to be juftified in the propofitions which I have offered,
tending to fhew the expediency of forming roads, and of introducing fettlers, where fo vaft a fpace remains unoccupied; as well
as in the happy confequences I have deduced as necefarily attendant
upon the execution of a liberal plan of improvement; whether confidered with refpect to the ftrength, the trade, the opulence, and
falubrity, of the ifland, or to the extenfion of the commerce, manufactures, navigation, and profits, of Great-Britain.

Confiftent with the preceding order. I fhall now give a ftate of
this parifh for 1768, proportioned to the other divifion of St. James,
from which it was fo lately fevered.

	Negroes.	Cattle.	Sugar-plantations.	Annual Produce. Hogfheads.	Other Settlements.
1768,	11739	8130	40	7920	66

This

This is not to be deemed the prefent ftate, becaufe the ftock and produce may well be fuppofed to have been conftantly increafing ever fince the year mentioned. I have therefore only fubmitted this fcheme for the fake of preferving uniformity, agreeably to my firft defign of bringing the progrefs of the feveral parifhes down to 1768; beyond which, I have not been able to obtain any very exact calculation.

General State of the County of Cornwall.

County-town, Savannah la Mar, where the Affizes are held in the months of March, June, September, and December.

Negroes.	Cattle.	Sugar-plantations.	Annual Produce. Hogfheads.	Other Settlements.
60616	54776	266	29100	383

Rectories and Stipends.

	£	s.	d.
St. Elizabeth, ——	200	0	0
Weftmoreland, —	250	0	0
Hanover, ————	200	0	0
St. James, ———	200	0	0
Trelawny, ———	200	0	0
£	1050	0	0

Churches, 2;—Chapels, 2;—Synagogue, 0.

From hence will appear, that this county, though poffeffing fewer Negroes and cattle than Middlefex, is neverthelefs more productive. This may be afcribed to the greater frefhnefs of the land in general; to the greater quantity of feafonable rains, and of cane-land, fituated more conveniently with refpect to fhipping-places. The North fide parifhes labour under the inconvenience of late crops, high infurance, a voyage homewards in the moft dangerous feafon of the year, and a high freight to the Kingfton market. All thefe are attended with double charge in war-time. Notwithftanding thefe obftacles, we find that moft of them are in a flourifhing condition. The parifhes of St. George and Portland feem to be the only exceptions. The quantity of fugar produced in both of them together is not equal to the half of what is made in St. Mary's. There are natural difficulties with which the fettlers in them have to ftruggle. To thefe are added the others before-recited, to which the reft are liable in common. Perhaps a bounty

of

of twenty shillings *per* hogshead might be some encouragement to the feebler settlers; it would at least enable them to carry their sugars to the Kingston market freight-free; for it is not the least of the misfortunes attendant upon their situation, that they are obliged to pay nearly thrice as much, for the transport of a hogshead of sugar to that market, as a shipper at Old Harbour on the South side. But the pressure of this tax will appear in a more conspicuous light from the following table of

WATER-CARRIAGE from KINGSTON to the OUT-PORTS.

Out-ports.	Hhds. and Punch.	Tierces.	Barrels.	Firkins and Boxes.	Hoes and Bills.	Small Bundles.	Ginger per Cwt. or Bag.
	s. d.	s. d.	s. d.	s. d.	s. d.	s. d.	s. d.
Old Harbour and Peak Bay,	7 6	3 9	2 6	1 3	7½	7½	1 0
Withy Wood & Milk River,	8 9	3 9	2 6	1 3	7½	7½	1 0
Salt River, ——	8 9	3 9	2 6	1 3	7½	7½	1 0
Black River, —— ——	12 6	5 0	3 9	1 10½	1 3	7½	1 3
White-house, near Scot's Cove, St. Elizabeth,—	15 0	7 6	3 9	1 10½	1 10½	7½	1 3
The Hope, —— ——	16 3	8 9	5 0	2 6	1 10½	7½	1 10½
Westmoreland, ——	18 9	10 0	5 0	2 6	1 10½	7½	1 10½
Hanover and all North side,	20 0	10 0	5 0	2 6	2 6	1 3	3 9
Morant Bay, —— ——	8 9	5 0	3 9	1 10½	1 3	7½	1 0
Port Morant, —— ——	10 0	5 0	3 9	1 10½	1 10½	7½	1 0
Yallah's Bay, —— ——	8 9	4 4½	3 1½	1 3	7½	7½	1 0

WATER-CARRIAGE, as above, continued.

Out-ports.	Cotton per Cwt.	Pimento per Cwt.	Tobacco per Cwt.	Hoops, staves, bricks, per M.	Osnabrigs, per piece.	Large bundles.	Boards, and Planks.
	s. d.	s. d.	s. d.	s. d.	s. d.	s. d.	s. d.
Old Harbour and Peak Bay,	2 6	1 10½	1 10½	25 0	1 3	1 3	20 0
Withy Wood & Milk River,	3 9	2 6	2 6	25 0	1 3	1 3	23 1½
Salt River, ——	3 9	2 6	2 6	25 0	1 3	1 3	23 1½
Black River, —— ——	4 4½	3 1½	3 1½	30 0	1 10½	1 3	25 0
White-house, near Scot's Cove, St. Elizabeth,—	4 4½	3 1½	3 1½	33 9	1 10½	1 3	25 0
The Hope, —— ——	4 4½	3 1½	3 1½	33 9	1 10½	1 3	25 0
Westmoreland, ——	4 4½	3 1½	3 1½	35 0	1 10½	1 3	27 6
Hanover and all North side,	5 0	3 9	3 9	40 0	3 1½	2 6	35 0
Morant Bay, —— ——	3 9	1 10½	1 10½	25 0	1 3	1 3	23 1½
Port Morant, —— ——	3 9	1 10½	1 10½	25 0	1 3	1 3	23 1½
Yallah's Bay, —— ——	2 6	1 3	1 3	20 0	1 0	1 3	20 0

These charges are advanced, by an act of assembly, fifty *per cent.* in time of war. From hence will appear the utility of establishing Port Antonio as a place of trade; by which means the settlers in both parishes would be relieved from this heavy burthen, and put in a condition of meeting their fellow-planters of the richer districts upon a more equal footing at the British market.

It remains only for me to say, that as the perfecting those roads already struck through the interior part of the country, and opening others wherever fuch a communication is wanting, appears to be the firſt great leading meaſure towards a more compleat ſettling and peopling of this iſland; ſo I can with pleaſure bear teſtimony to the laudable ſpirit which at preſent actuates the gentlemen reſident there, who, in a late ſeſſion of aſſembly, beſtowed no leſs than 5,000*l.*, by public grant, towards forming or compleating twenty very neceſſary roads in the following pariſhes; a munificence which, faithfully applied, will redound not more to the credit of their good ſenſe, than to the general benefit of the iſland.

Weſtmoreland, from Hamberſly's Penn, to Lenox Plantation.

Ditto, from Glaſgow Eſtate, to Lucea in Hanover.

Ditto, from Dean's Valley, to Great River in St. James.

Hanover, from Lucea along the mountains, to Moſquito Cove.

St. James, from Great River, through Seven-Rivers, to Montpelier.

Ditto, from Great River, through Montpelier, to the Bogue Eſtate.

St. Elizabeth, from Moroe's Craal, to Cheſterfield.

St. Anne, from Ocho Rios Bay, to Dun's River.

Ditto, from Dry Harbour, to the Cave in Clarendon.

St. Thomas in the Vale, to St. Mary.

Ditto, to St. Anne.

Ditto, over Monte Diablo.

St. Mary, from Guy's Hill, through Bagnal's, to Rio Nuevo-Bay.

St. George, from Kingſton, through Cold Spring, to Buff-Bay.

St. David, from the head of Yallah's River, to Roger's Corner, leading to the Barquadier at Yallah's Bay.

Ditto, and Port Royal, from the conflux of the Hope and Hoghole Rivers, to Yallah's River, near its junction with Green-River.

St. Andrew, from Moore's Eſtate, to Wagwater River.

St. Thomas in the Eaſt, from Port Morant Harbour, to the Bath.

Portland, from Bath, over Break-heart Hill, to Titchfield.

Ditto, from Titchfield, to Prieſtman's River, being part of the high road from Rio Grande.

In fact, the great improvements, made in many parts of the iſland of late years, are principally to be aſcribed to the meliorated ſtate of the roads; to the more general uſe of water-mills; to an improved

proved

proved fkill in every branch of plantation-œconomy; and (in the Weftern diftrict) to the importation of Negroes immediately into the ports of Savannah la Mar and Montego; as well as to the natural excellence of the cane-land in that diftrict.

On revifing what has been faid in refpect to the fhipping which load at this ifland, and their tonnage, I perceive I fhall be thought to have greatly under-rated them. Errors on this head may very well happen, for want of an average-table, as no two fucceffive years are perhaps equal in the calculation, and as the number and quantity are yearly increafing.

Mr. Leflie, in his account publifhed in the year 1739, fuppofed the annual produce of fugar equal to feventy thoufand hogfheads, of fifteen hundred pounds weight each; which was certainly a miftake. From this *poftulatum* he endeavoured to fhew, that five hundred fail, weight fifty thoufand tons, and manned by at leaft fix thoufand feamen, were at that time loaded with the produce of the colony; and he deduces the advantages to Great-Britain in the following manner:

Seamen maintained, ———— ———— ———— ———— 6000
Perfons fubfifted in Britain by the building and outfit of
    this fhipping, ———— ———— ———— ———— 14000
Maintained and enriched by the imports into Britain, ———— 20000
Mouths fed by the return of Britifh manufactures, merchan-
    dizes, and commodities, ———— ———— ———— 40000
Ditto, by retailing thefe products, computed at ———— ———— 10000

In all (exclufive of inhabitants in the ifland), ———— ———— 90000

Whoever is well informed of the growth of Jamaica will readily difcern, that this detail, inftead of being conformable to the ftate of it at that period, was, in fact, only an anticipation of what has fince happened. But, to fpeak of the prefent time, the produce in fugar is augmented by many thoufand hogfheads; rum and melaffes in proportion. Coffee makes a very capital article of export; and indigo begins to be confpicuous. Several new ports are opened, whofe trade is in a very promifing way. The progrefs, in fhort, fince the time Mr. Leflie wrote, has been aftonifhingly great; infomuch that I do not know, whether the following computation is not ftill rather too diminutive; viz.

Shipping

Shipping employed (including Britifh and North-American, and
    exclufive of coafting veffels), —— —— —— 700 fail.
Tonnage, —— —— —— —— 90000 tons.
Seamen, —— —— — —— —— —— 10000

From which it is eafy to conceive (without minutely recapitu-
lating the fubjeƈt) how vaftly profitable this ifland is to the mother-
country in every view; whether by employing fuch multitudes of
her manufaƈturers and artificers of all kinds, or of Britifh and
American failors, fhip-builders, and all the trades and occupations
dependent upon them. Such is the value of this flourifhing colony to Britain! Whence we may rightly conclude, how enormous
and irreparable the lofs muft be, fhould it ever devolve into the
hands of any other power. In refpeƈt to the quantity of fugar
which the ifland may be capable of producing, in addition to what
it now yields, it is no eafy matter to fpeak with abfolute precifion, on account of the unequal crops obtained from different foils,
and the diverfity of fituation; thofe which are remote from the
coaft, or which have bad or indifferent roads for their carriage, or
cannot have the conveniences of wind or water-mills, requiring a
much greater traƈt of land for pafturage than others. But, in order to form fome conjeƈture on this head, let us firft confider that
the unplanted land, lying chiefly within the mountains, and diftant from the fea, muft in general be fubjeƈt, more or lefs, to the
inconveniences I have enumerated; and therefore the allowance for
pafture, or grafs-land, fhould in general be rated accordingly. Let
us fuppofe, then, a traƈt of three hundred acres compleatly fettled,
and duly apportioned in canes, provifion, pafture and grafs, wafte,
and wood for fire and repairs; and that this eftate, in the fituation
before-reprefented, yields, *communibus annis*, one hundred hogfheads
of fugar, and about forty-two puncheons of rum. Admitting
then, that here are only five hundred thoufand acres of cane-land
unplanted; thefe, according to the eftimate, are capable of producing one hundred and fixty-five thoufand hogfheads, and feventy
thoufand puncheons; the duties on which amount to 727,500 *l.*
or upwards. The computation may be eafily led on to the fhipping,
the feamen, the confumption of manufaƈtures, and other numerous
appendages, which neceffarily and invariably follow this augmented
ftate of cultivation. But all thefe are, by this time, fo obvious to

the

the apprehenfion of every reader, that I need not proceed to elucidate them any further.

Having now gone through the feveral counties and parifhes in a
manner which, though difcurfive and imperfect, I hope may be fufficient to give a tolerable idea of their ftate, in regard to fettlements,
ports, rivers, productions, advantages, and defects, it may not be
improper to exhibit a general review of the whole.

Counties.	Negroes.	Cattle.	Sugar Plantations.	Annual Prod. Hhds.	Other Settlements.	Whites Towns.	Villages and Hamlets.	Free Negroe Towns.	Forts.	Churches	Chapels.	Rector's Stipends per ann. £.	Synagogues.	Reprefen-tatives in Affembly.
Middlefex,	66746	59512	239	24050	763	3	10	1	3	7	2	1750	1	17
Surrey,	39542	21465	146	15010	314	4	4	2	5	5	0	1250	1	16
Cornwall,	60616	54776	266	29100	383	4	3	2	4	2	2	1050		10
Totals,	166904	135753	651	68160	1460	11	17	5	12	14	4	4050	2	43

A GENERAL ABSTRACT of the State of the ISLAND from the Time of OLIVER CROMWELL.

Anno	Negroes.	Cattle.	Sugar Plantations.	Annual Prod. Hhds.	Rum Puncheons.	White Inhabitants.
1658	1400					4500
1670	8000					7500
1673			70	1333	650	8564
1734	86546	76011				7644
1738	99239	84313	429	33000	13200	10080
1745	112428	88036	455	35000	14000	11330 } By conjecture.
1761	146000	122800	640	44800	22400	15330 } By conjecture.
1768	166904	135753	651	68160	27200	17000 } By conjecture.
Increafe in about 110 years.	165504					12500——The other articles proportionably.

The following table may serve to shew the comparative state of the parishes in regard to their contribution of public taxes, taking the first-mentioned as the largest contributor, and so descending in a series of diminution to the lowest, or Port Royal, whose proportion, compared with the first, is only as one to eighteen; and hence some idea may be formed of their comparative wealth:

1	St. James (including Trelawny),	11	St. Thomas in the Vale,
2	Clarendon,	12	Vere,
3	Westmoreland,	13	St. John,
4	St. Thomas in the East,	14	Kingston,
5	Hanover,	15	St. Dorothy,
6	St. Elizabeth,	16	St. George,
7	St. Mary,	17	Portland,
8	St. Andrew,	18	St. David,
9	St. Catharine,	19	Port Royal.
10	St. Anne,		

A comparative table, intended to shew the traffic carried on by captains of ships, and other transient dealers, at the different outports: and the proportion which they severally bear to Kingston; from which some judgement may be formed of the number of shipping that resort to each respectively:

Montego Bay,	One Fifth.
St. Anne, Savannah la Mar,	One Fifth.
Old Harbour,	One Ninth.
St. Lucea,	One Fifteenth.
Black River,	One Eighteenth.
Carlisle Bay,	One Twenty-second.
The others,	Not computed.

An estimate of the number of coaches, and other wheel-carriages of pleasure, kept in the several parishes:

Kingston,	500
St. Catharine,	280
St. Andrew,	170
Clarendon,	114
Westmoreland,	88
Vere,	87
St. Elizabeth,	73

St. Dorothy,

St. Dorothy,	70
St. James,	65
St. Thomas in the Vale,	25
St. Anne,	14
St. David,	7
St. Thomas in the Eaft,	4
Portland,	1
Total.	1498

The number of thefe carriages is not in exact proportion to the value of property; for it is to be confidered, that, in regard to the richer parifhes, fome of the proprietors refide more commonly in town; fome, on account of bad or hilly roads, keep no carriage in the country; but many more are abfent from the ifland, and keep theirs in Great-Britain. They are by no means to be regarded as articles of luxury in Jamaica: they are neceffary to the inhabitants for their conveniency in point of health, and in traveling from place to place; but, confidering their hafty decay in this climate, and the coftlinefs of their workmanfhip, they form no contemptible article in the lift of Britifh manufactures which this ifland confumes; and, as the roads become more and more improved, the number of them will doubtlefs increafe.

The general poft-office for the ifland is kept in the town of Kingfton. This place is in the appointment of the poft-mafter general of Great-Britain, and fuppofed worth about 1000 *l.* fterling *per annum.* With refpect to any convenience which the inhabitants at prefent derive from it, much cannot be faid; nor can, indeed, the deputy well afford to make it more ufeful to them, until the roads fhall be further improved, and the country better peopled. The feveral mails are difpatched from Kingfton but once a week; and, if a merchant there fends a letter by this conveyance to his correfpondent at Savannah la Mar, he muft wait twelve days before he can receive an anfwer. The prefent deputy, however, has had the credit of regulating the inland poft upon a better plan than any of his predeceffors.

The

The following are the diftances computed at his office; agreeably to which the poftage is demanded and paid.

South Side Poft.

From — to		Miles comp.
Kingfton	Spanifh Town,	18
Spanifh Town	Old Harbour Market,	12
Old Harbour Market	Clarendon Crofs,	12
Clarendon Crofs	Pepper St. Elizabeth,	37
Pepper St. Elizabeth	Lacovia,	13
Lacovia	Black River,	12
Black River	Savannah la Mar, Weftmoreland,	25
Savannah la Mar	Lucea,	25
		154

North Side Poft.

From — to		Miles comp.
Kingfton	Spanifh Town,	18
Spanifh Town	Salt Gut, St. Mary's,	40
Salt Gut,	St. Anne's Port,	20
St. Anne,	Rio Bueno,	20
Rio Bueno,	Marthabrae, Trelawny,	17
Marthabrae	Montego Bay, St. James,	25
		140
Kingfton,	Anotto Bay, St. Mary,	30
Anotto Bay,	Port Maria,	15
		45

Windward Poft.

From — to		Miles comp.
Kingfton	Æolus Valley, St. Thomas in the Eaft,	20
Æolus Valley	Petersfield, ditto,	6
Petersfield	Morant Bay, ditto,	5
Morant Bay	Port Morant, ditto,	7
Port Morant	Bath, ditto,	6
Bath	Amity Hall, ditto,	7
Amity Hall	Manchineal,	9
Manchineal	Port Antonio, Portland,	11
		71

Rates

Rates of the Inland-poftage, for any Diftance not exceeding fixty Englifh Miles.

	s.	d.		
Single,	o	7½	Jamaica currency, or	1 Ryal.
Double,	1	3	—— —	2 ditto.
Treble,	1	3	—— —	2 ditto.
Ounce,	1	10½	—— —	3 ditto.

For any Diftance upwards of fixty, and not exceeding one hundred Englifh Miles.

	s.	d.		
Single,	o	7½	Jamaica currency, or	1 Ryal.
Double,	1	3	—— —	2 ditto.
Treble,	1	10½	—— —	3 ditto.
Ounce,	2	6	—— —	4 ditto.

For any Diftance upwards of one hundred, and not exceeding two hundred miles.

	s.	d.		
Single,	1	3	Jamaica currency. or	2 Ryals.
Double,	1	10½	—— —	3 ditto.
Treble,	2	6	—— —	4 ditto.
Ounce,	3	9	—— —	6 ditto.

And in Proportion for every Ounce Weight.

Rates of Poftage from this Ifland to Great-Britain *per* Act 9 Anne, c. 10.

	s.	d. Sterling.		s.	d. Jamaica Currency.
Single,	—— ——	1 6	——	2	1
Double,	—— ——	3 0	——	3	4½
Treble,	—— ——	4 6	——	6	3½
Ounce,	—— ——	6 0	——	8	4¾

Merchants accounts exceeding one fheet of paper, bills of exchange, invoices, and bills of lading, are all to be rated and taxed as fo many feveral letters, *per* 6 George I.

Confidering the great and continual commerce which this ifland maintains with the mother-country, and the extenfive correfpondence carried on by letter with merchants, abfentees, and others; the frequent orders for infurance and for goods, the tranfmiffion-invoices, bills of lading, bills of exchange and accompts, with duplicates; we may suppose the revenue gains a considerable annual sum from these articles; perhaps, the clear emolument, to speak within compass, is not less than 6000*l.* sterling, or upwards. The office was first erected in Jamaica in the year 1687, and one Mr. James Wade appointed post-master. This has been produced as one example, among others, of parliamentary supremacy in the levying of internal taxes within the colonies; but, as the conveniency arising from it to trade and commerce was undoubtedly the original ground of its institution, so the sense of this conveniency gave it an easy admission into the colonies, still indulges its existence, and must continue to do so, unless the rates should be increased to a degree of oppression; in this event it must destroy itself, of which the revenue-officers are probably well satisfied.

C H A P. X.

State of the Clergy.

THE Clergy of the established church have had a footing in this island only since the Restoration of Charles II. Cromwell took care to furnish the army with spiritual as well as carnal weapons. I think there were no less than seven allotted to this service; but they were fanatical preachers; a sort of irregulars, who soon made way for more orthodox divines. It has always been a rule, in our West-India islands, to assimilate their religion, as well as laws, to those of the mother-country. It is no wonder, therefore, that popery became the favourite system in Jamaica during the reign of James II. And the character of this religion was perfectly well supported by the spirit of persecution which was let loose against all non-conformists. The Revolution under king William happily expelled or subdued these superstitions, and gave the inhabitants, at one and the same time, the enjoyment of religious and civil liberty. Recantations became frequent; industry revived; and the stubborn rage of bigotry was melted into peace and concord. Charles II, although secretly professing the Roman faith, cannot be accused of having exercised severity against its adversaries. Good sense taught him to discern the expediency of

granting

granting toleration in thefe diftant parts of his dominion; for I do not fufpect that he meant fo much to favour men of the Roman Catholic perfuafion, as to ftock thefe infant-fettlements with ufeful people. In his inftructions to the governors, he directs, " for the " encouragement of perfons, of different judgements and opinions " in matters of religion, to tranfport themfelves, with their " effects, to Jamaica; and that they may not be obftructed and " hindered under pretence of fcruples in confcience," to difpenfe with the taking the oaths of allegiance and fupremacy to thofe that fhould bear any part in the government (the members and officers of the privy council only excepted), and to find out fome other way of fecuring their allegiance; and in no cafe to let any man be molefted or difquieted in the exercife of his religion, provided he fhould be content with a quiet, peaceable enjoyment of it; not giving therein any offence or fcandal to the government. But the governors themfelves were ftrictly enjoined, in their own houfe and family, to the profeffion of the Proteftant religion, as preached in England; and to recommend it to others as far as might be confiftent with the peace of the ifland. This toleration was afterwards much narrowed by the acts of parliament affecting papifts; which are fo far admitted in force here, as to preclude them from exercifing any office, or place of truft, the oaths of abjuration and fupremacy being indifpenfably required to be taken before admiffion into any fuch office or place, or a feat in the legiflature. But men of all perfuafions are ftill received here as inhabitants; the naturalization-act, paffed in Jamaica, only obliging aliens to take the oath of allegiance: nor is any man ever queftioned here about his religious principles [g]. The bifhop of London claims this as a part of his diocefe; but his jurifdiction is renounced, and barred by the laws of the ifland, in every cafe, except fo far as relates or appertains to ecclefiaftical regimen of the clergy; which imports no higher power than that of granting orders, and giving paftoral

---

[g] In 1729, an act was paffed " for preventing dangers that may arife from difguifed, as well " as declared, Papifts." But, this not being found to anfwer the purpofes for which it was intended, and, on the contrary, having only ferved to difcourage well-affected Proteftants from coming over to fettle in the ifland, it was repealed in the year following. It is faid to have been leveled againft one particular gentleman, a member of the legiflature, and a papift; who had made himfelf offenfive to a party which at that time exifted in the houfe of affembly.

admonitions;

admonitions; for it is queſtioned, whether he can ſuſpend any clergyman here, either *ab officio*, or *a beneficio*; ſince it is expreſsly enacted, by act of aſſembly, " that no eccleſiaſtical law, or ju-" riſdiction, ſhall have power to enforce, confirm, or eſtabliſh, " any penal mulcts, or puniſhment, in any caſe whatſoever:" and, as the deprivation either of a living, or its emoluments, is virtually a mulct, and actually a puniſhment, the opinion is ſtrong againſt his right of interpoſition. The governor, as ſupreme head of the provincial church, and in virtue of the royal inſtructions, is veſted with a power of ſuſpending a clergyman here, of lewd and diſorderly life, *ab officio*, upon the petition of his pariſhioners; and I can re-member one example of this ſort. The governor inducts into the ſeveral rectories within the iſland and its dependencies; the parties firſt producing before him the teſtimonials of their being regularly in orders, and taking the uſual oaths. The cuſtom of tythes has never been in uſe here: inſtead of them, the ſeveral ſtipends are eſtabliſhed by law, and levied by the juſtices and veſtries; who are likewiſe empowered to appoint and limit the fees for chriſtening, marriage, churching, and burial. No miniſter is to demand or take his ſtipend for any longer time than he ſhall actually officiate in his pariſh, ſickneſs only excepted; ſo that a ſuſpenſion *ab officio* is, in fact, a ſuſpenſion alſo *a beneficio*. They are required to regiſter births, chriſtenings, marriages, and burials. Theſe entries are declared authentic records, to be received as ſuch in any court of juſtice; and the ſtealing, razing, or embezzling of them is made felony. Every beneficed miniſter is, *ex officio*, a freeholder to all intents and purpoſes, and accordingly admitted to vote at elections of aſſembly-members. He is alſo to be conſtantly one of the veſtry; and no veſtry can make any order, without firſt giving timely notice to the miniſter, that he may attend if he thinks fit. The ordinance reſpecting non-officiating is but vaguely expreſſed; however, it has been thought ſtrong enough to juſtify the church-wardens and veſtry in refuſing to pay the ſtipend, in caſe their rector ſhould wilfully refuſe to perform the duties of his cure. It is ſuppoſed, that non-reſidence is implied, becauſe in the rector's ab-ſence, the pariſhioners are left to bury their own dead; and a wil-ful neglect of the performance of any duty is much the ſame, in effect,

effect, as a positive denial. The statute, 21 Henry VIII. excuses from residence in three cases; 1st, the want of a dwelling-house, or the inconvenience of one too small, or mean, to receive and accommodate the rector's family: 2dly, sickness, or where, by advice of a physician, a removal into another air is, *bonâ fide*, necessary for recovery of health; 3dly, employment in the king's service. In Jamaica, the justices and vestry of each parish, where there is no parsonage-house, are required, either to hire one of 50*l. per annum* rent, or to purchase or build one of 500*l*. value. Under this limitation, which is so unequal, it may be supposed that they cannot buy or build a very convenient habitation with suitable offices. The sum allowed ought to have been 800*l*. which would have held a nearer proportion to the sum allowed for hiring; 50*l*. being little more than the annual interest of 800*l*. In general, they are well lodged, except in those parishes where the rector's immorality, or bad disposition, has created him so many enemies, that his flock would rather he should live any where than among them. The second dispensation, in regard to ill health, and change of air for recovery, has always been readily indulged here in its full latitude. As to the third, the chaplains attending the governor, or the council, or assembly, are excused; the former at all times; the two latter, during the sessions. But the same minister having usually been chaplain both to the governor and council, and holding the living of Spanish Town, where the governor resides, and the council meet, no inconvenience has hitherto resulted. But pluralities are not allowed here; and, if ever they should be attempted, the people will be greatly incensed, having severely felt the inconveniencies arising from the combination of many places in one person.

The testimonials required to be produced, before induction into any living here, are, that the candidate be qualified according to the canons of the church of England, by having taken deacon's and priest's orders; which testimonials must, after the governor's approbation, be recorded in the secretary's office. They are not to celebrate any marriage without banns have been three times published in the parish-church to which the parties belong, or without a licence from the governor, under penalty of 100*l*. By a rule

of

of the governor's court of ordinary, for better preventing furreptitious marriages of orphans, or minors; affidavits, in such cafes, are required to be filed of the guardian's confent; without which, the governor does not ufually grant a licence. Formerly, the cuftom in thefe iflands was, to be married by the juftices of the peace; for in thofe days a clergyman was not always at hand. The fame practice ftill fubfifts, as I am informed, at the Mofquito fhore, and fome of the other dependencies. And it is certain, that a marriage, celebrated in this manner in Jamaica, even now, if according to the form of words in our liturgy, would be valid in law, and fupport the right to dower or thirds. The Jamaica law reftrains none from performing the ceremony, except minifters not qualified with the teftimonials before-mentioned; and the penalty, impofed upon others who folemnize without banns or licence, does not tend to declare fuch marriages void. The chaplains of the council and affembly have a falary, of 100*l.* each, for reading prayers, every morning during feffion, previous to entering upon bufinefs. They are not called upon, as in England, to preach anniverfary fermons. Of the character of the clergy in this ifland I fhall fay but little. There have feldom been wanting fome, who were equally refpectable for their learning, piety, and exemplary good behaviour: others have been deteftable for their addiction to lewdnefs, drinking, gambling, and iniquity; having no controul, but their own fenfe of the dignity of their function, and the cenfures of the governor. The fcandalous or irreproachable demeanour of many will chiefly depend on their own quality of heart, or that of the commander in chief. If the cloth has fuffered difgrace and contempt from the actions of a few; we muft neverthelefs confider the major part, worthy the public efteem and encouragement. Some labourers of the Lord's vineyard have at times been fent, who were much better qualified to be retailers of falt-fifh, or boatfwains to privateers, than minifters of the Gofpel. It is recorded of a certain rector of one of the towns, that, having the bodies of three deceafed feamen brought to him one day for interment, he thought to make quick work of it by only one reading of the burial-fervice. The brother tars, who attended the folemnity, infifted upon three feveral readings, in honour of their comrades. The rector was obftinate. Words

grew

grew high; and at length the difpute came to blows. The parfon, the clerk, and all the congregation, engaged pell-mell. Nor long the battle raged; for divinity proved victorious, after hurling two or three of the combatants headlong into the very grave that had been prepared for their inanimate friends. Of another (a Frenchman) it is faid, that, preaching one day, in his ufual broken Englifh, on the fubject of the laft day, he entertained his audience with the comparative condition of the good and the finful; informing them, " dat dey would be feparate, de goat on de left hond, de moutons " on de right." Ridiculous characters of this ftamp fhould bring no flander on the clergy in general; they reflect difhonour alone upon thofe patrons in England, who would make no fcruple in fending over their footmen, to benefit by any employment in the colonies, ecclefiaftical or civil.

If the bifhop of London could legally exercife the right (which fome fay he claims) of infpecting the conduct of the clergy here, and fubjecting the fame, when neceffary, to ecclefiaftical cenfures and punifhment; yet his lordfhip's refidence at fo great a diftance, and the engagements of his diocefe at home, would be obftacles to his working a thorough reformation in Jamaica. His cenfures, indeed, though but fparingly inflicted, might neverthelefs produce a good effect, provided all the clergy of the ifland had been regularly trained at one of our Englifh univerfities, and early verfed in the knowledge of our religion. But, when perfons are fent hither barely qualified according to the canons of the church, and the laws of the land, as to ordination, licence, &c. and thereby entitled to the very fame privileges and favour, whether they have been bred at Cambridge, at Oxford, or St. Omer's, in an univerfity, or a cobler's fhop; whether they have been initiated in the proteftant, or in the popifh religion; whether their language is Englifh or French, or neither: I fay, fo long as the caffock is fuffered to be put on here with fo little difcrimination, not all the exhortations of all the bifhops in the world could poffibly make the clergy of this ifland a refpectable body of men. Let us, however, venture to affert in their favour, that, although fome perhaps may be found, who, in their moral conduct, would difgrace even the meaneft of mankind, there are others, and in a much greater number, who, by their ex-

6

ample

ample and their doctrine, would do honour to their profeffion in any part of England.

CHAP. XI.
MINES.

THE firft adventurers who reforted to this ifland conceived very fanguine expectations of finding gold and filver mines. They were told of a filver mine, that had been worked by the Spaniards, fomewhere in the Healthfhire Hills, in St. Catharine; but they were not able to difcover it. Still the flattering profpect encouraged two or three principal gentlemen of the ifland to folicit for an exclufive patent for working fuch mines. This they obtained, and made fome attempts; which failed of fuccefs, and brought fuch heavy expences upon them, that they were glad to relinquifh the project, and furrendered their patent. After all, the report of the Spanifh filver mine was probably no other than a fiction. However, that the mountains contain both that metal and gold is very certain, as well as that the Spaniards obtained fome of the latter from the river-courfes; in which method they were inftructed by the Indians, who, in Hifpaniola and this ifland, ufed to procure it in the fame manner. The inhabitants of Peru and Mexico purfue the fame method at this day. They dig in the angles of fome fmall brook, where by certain tokens they expect to find the grains, or particles, of gold. In order to carry off the mud, they admit a frefh ftream upon it, and keep turning it up. As foon as they perceive the gold fand, they divert the ftream into another channel, and dig up the foil with hoes or pick-axes, and convey it upon mules to certain bafons, joined together by fmall conduits. Into thefe bafons they let a fmart ftream of water, to loofen the earth, and clear away the groffer parts; the Indians ftanding all the time in the bafons, and throwing out the ftones or rubbifh. The gold ftill remains in the fediment, mixed with a black fand, and fcarcely vifible, till further depurated by more wafhings. In fome of thefe collections are gold grains, as large as bird-fhot; in others have been found lumps of it, from two or three ounces to a

5

pound

pound weight: and this way of procuring gold is juftly thought far more profitable than digging for it in the mines. In Popayan, the procefs is very little different. They ftir and dilute the mafs in the bafons till the moft ponderous parts, as little ftones, fand, and gold, remain at the bottom. They then go into the bafon, with wooden buckets, made for the purpofe, in which they take up the fediment; then moving them circularly and uniformly, at the fame time changing the waters, the lefs ponderous parts are feparated; and at laft the gold remains at the bottom of the buckets, clear from all mixture. It is generally found in grains, as fmall as thofe of fand, and, for that reafon, called *oro en polvo*; though fome-times *pepitas*, or feeds, are found amongft it, of different fizes; but generally they are fmall. The water iffuing from the firft bafon is ftopped in another, contrived a little beneath it, where it undergoes the like operation, in order to fecure any minute particles, which, from their extreme tenuity, might be carried off by the current of water, mixed with earth and other fubftances: and, laftly, this water is paffed into a third bafon; but the favings here are generally inconfiderable. The labourers moft commonly ufed are Negroe-flaves; and whilft fome are bufied in wafhing, others bring earth; fo that the wafhers are kept in continual employment. The finenefs of this gold is generally of twenty-two carats; fometimes more, even to twenty-three; fometimes indeed it is under, but very fel-dom below twenty-one [b].

There is no doubt but, by a long courfe of practice, the Spa-niards have made feveral improvements upon the original Indian procefs, which was more fimple and tedious. The Rio Minho, in Clarendon parifh, has by fome been fuppofed to derive its name from the Minho in Portugal. Others imagine it was fo called from fome mine in its neighbourhood, known to the Spanifh inhabitants; and I think there is ground for this conjecture; for, a few years ago, one of thefe lavaderos was difcovered on its bank at Longville plantation, in that parifh, which ftill remains tolerably perfect. Here is a terraffed platform, with feveral bafons chiffeled out of rock; the interftices being filled up, here and there, with a very hard cement, or mortar, to render the furface fmooth. Joined to

[b] Ulloa.

this platform is a pretty large fragment of a gutter, made for conducting the river-water into the basons. This seems to be a convincing testimony, that the bed of this river has afforded the gold sand, washed down perhaps from some of the mountains among which its course lies; and a further proof is, that bits of gold have sometimes been found after floods. The late Mr. Alderman Beckford possessed a plantation on the opposite side of the river. Many years ago, when he was in the island, the manager for this estate brought to him one day a small piece of very fine gold, which had been picked up in the sand of the river; and, at the same time, advised him to send for a skillful metallurgist, as he would probably discover a rich mine within his own land hereabouts. To this proposal Mr. Beckford made no other reply, than " whilst we " have got so profitable a mine above ground" (pointing to the cane-pieces), " we will not trouble ourselves about hunting for any " under ground." And he was certainly to be commended for the prudence of his answer; since, not to mention only the many thousand of Indians and Negroes destroyed by the Spaniards in Peru and Mexico in mining, and so little to the advantage either of individuals or their nation, how many great fortunes have there not been annihilated by undertakings of this sort, which have rarely yielded a profit in the end commensurate to the heavy expences that attended the conducting of them; and particularly in hot climates, where the subterraneous vapours are known to be of so malignant a nature, as to kill, or at least disable, very speedily the stoutest labourers! I am aware, that the manner of procuring gold by means of lavaderos is not liable to any such objection. It is neither an expensive nor unhealthy business; and therefore, if the art of discovering the river sand, in which gold has generally been found, could be revived in Jamaica, by sending for an Indian or Spaniard sufficiently intelligent, there might be no harm in trying some experiments with the sand of this river, where it has actually been found; as well as some others in the island, where it might reasonably be expected.

The mountains abound with copper ore of various species; the green and livid ore; and the shining dark ore, or vitrious copper These two kinds are the richest as yet discovered here, and thought

equal.

equal to fome of thofe that are efteemed the of firft clafs in Europe; the matrix in which they are engaged anfwering both to the hammer and fire with equal eafe. Two mines were worked for fome time in the Liguanea Mountains; but neither of them produced any thing correfpondent to the charges that attended them. The undertaking was too important for two private men of no very capital fortunes; and perhaps they required the management of perfons more experienced in the procefs. It ferved only to convince the curious, that fuch metals were to be found here; and this, I apprehend, is all the advantage that accrued, either to the proprietors, or to the publick. Yet one of thefe mines was faid to have produced; no lefs than a ton *per* week; but perhaps this was only a bubble report, or the harveft was foon at an end. Schemes of this kind are moft fuccefsfully carried on by large companies, or affociations; whofe feveral ftocks united would bear the contingent expence, till the work is brought to anfwer. But there has been fuch a multitude of frauds and knavifh practices committed, from time to time, in mining-adventures, that fuch projects are not at prefent likely to meet with any countenance. It is, however, to be regretted, that the copper and lead mines in this ifland had not been more effectually profecuted; becaufe, upon the computation that every fugar eftate, which produces one hundred hogfheads *per annum*, muft be at a certain expence of 65 *l. per annum* for copper and lead alone, it will appear, that the ifland expends 45,000 *l.*, or thereabouts, every year, in thefe articles, which might be faved. The Spaniards certainly were more intelligent, or met with better fuccefs; for the bells, which hung in the Great Church at St. Jago de la Vega when the Englifh took poffeffion, were caft of copper produced in the ifland. Lead ore likewife abounds here, richly impregnated with filver, which renders the folution of it in *aqua fortis* milky; but it is not found in any regular bodied veins, which, among other reafons, obliged the gentlemen, who had been engaged in the lead-works of Liguanea, to drop the undertaking, after they had been at a great expence in building a very compleat fet of works, and carried on the manufacture for fome time. The ore, when in fermentation with *aqua fortis*, throws up a confiderable quantity of fulphur; and hence it has been conjectured, that

fome

fome of the fulphureous fprings in the ifland derive their qualities from this fource. The varieties of the lead ore found here are the fubgranulated, linked with filver; the lamellated, fhining ore, in the fame union; the black-gloffy ore, linked with copper, and lefs impregnated with filver; and the black, lead ore, largely admixed with copper, and feldom rich; but the matrix is mellow, and eafily fluxed [i]. Stibium has been frequently found in thefe lead mines.

Iron ore has been difcovered in many parts of this ifland; but the very large quantities of black fand, which are thrown on many parts of the South fide coaft, efpecially near the mouths of rivers, having been hurried down by floods, are much more acceffible, and with little pains. This fand is obfervable almoft every where in the roads and gullies after hard rains; fo that the foil of the favannahs, as well as that of the mountains, is impregnated with it. The inhabitants ufe it in common, like what is called in England the black writing-fand. It is freely attracted by the magnet; but does not anfwer, it is faid [i], with the acid, or fire. However, it muft be referred to future experiment to difcover, whether it be not endued with the fame properties as the Virginia black fand; particularly as, upon trial of the Virginia fand fome years ago (an account of which is given in Lowthorp's Abridgement of the Philofophical Tranfactions, vol. II.), *aqua fortis* produced no ebullition, and fluxing obtained no *regulus*, nor any fubftance that would apply to the magnet, except a thin cruft, that adhered to a piece of charcoal, which dropped into the crucible during the fufion. For which reafons, this fand was imagined to be very flightly engaged with iron ore, and in fuch a manner, as that the metallic particles could not be feparated and fixed by the ufual procefs. But Mr. Horne, fufpecting thefe experiments not to be decifive, conceived that the fand was not altogether and fimply iron; but that it was ftrongly united with a very ftubborn, fixed, and permanent earth, which could not be feparated from it without fome extraordinary as well as powerful means. The ingenious artift, proceeding upon this fuppofition, fpread about eight or nine ounces of the fand, unmixed with any addition, upon an iron plate, over a ftrong fire, and gave it a very powerful torrefaction, or roafting, to try if by that means

[i] Browne.

he

he could not relax and loofen the component parts to fuch a degree, as to make the feparation and reduction of the metal more eafy, when he fhould bring it to the furnace. He then mixed it up with a flux of a very peculiar, but gentle nature, which he had before made ufe of for other purpofes with great fuccefs [*k*], and committed it to the furnace, where he urged it, by a very ftrong fire, for about three hours, and upon taking it out found the event anfwerable to his moft fanguine expectations; for in the bottom of the crucible he found rather more than half of the fand he had put in reduced to a very fine, malleable metal. Being now convinced that the fand was a very rich iron ore, he acquainted fome of his friends with the difcovery; who being largely engaged in trade with the part of the American continent from whence it was brought, he hoped the gentlemen in that part of the world would, in confequence, purfue experiments with it on a more extenfive plan. And he informs us, that Mr. G. Elliot having fince made trial of it, the event proved encouraging much beyond his expectation; infomuch that eighty-three pounds of the fand were found to produce a bar of excellent iron, weighing fifty pounds. Mr. Elliot fmelted this iron, in a common bloomary, in the fame manner as other iron ore is fmelted; excepting this difference, that the iron fand is fo pure, and fo clean wafhed, that there is not a fufficient quantity of cinder, or flagg, to perform the fmelting; and he was therefore obliged to add either the flagg which iffues from other iron ore, or elfe fome bog-mine ore, which abounds with cinder. In this way, he fays, it is capable of being wrought as bog-ore, or bog-mine. There is fo much of this fand in America, that he thinks there is more iron-ore in this form than any other. The fpecimens of iron, fent by Mr. Elliot from America, were tried by Mr. Horne, and found to poffefs all that agreeable toughnefs and ductility for which the Spanifh iron is fo defervedly famous. And he concludes with giving his opinion, that, by this difcovery, we may obtain a more pure and better kind of iron than any we have hitherto been poffeffed of [*l*].

If the experiments of thefe gentlemen are to be relied upon, the American fand yields more in value than the richeft and beft ore

[*k*] This preparation he has not communicated.   [*l*] Horne's Effays on Iron and Steel.

3

hitherto

hitherto found in Europe; for the latter ufually produces no more than from fixty to eighty pounds out of one hundred weight; and when the facility of collecting the American fand, without the labour of much digging, is taken into account, together with the difpatch and little expence of wafhing and preparing it for fufion, it will furely juftify this claim of fuperiority. It may therefore merit enquiry, whether the Jamaica fand does not contain the very fame principles which there is every reafon to believe it does; in which cafe, it may become an article of profitable export to Great-Britain, after having been too long neglected as of no value.

C H A P. XII.

S C H O O L S.

THE great importance of education, in forming the manners, enlightening the minds, and promoting the induftry and happinefs of a people, is no where more obvious than in countries where it is not attainable. It at once excites our pity and regret, that Jamaica, an ifland more valuable and extenfive than any other of the Britifh fugar-colonies, fhould at this day remain unprovided with a proper feminary for the young inhabitants to whom it gives birth. This unhappy defect may be looked upon as one of the principal impediments to its effectual fettlement.

I would by no means have it underftood, that I mean to diminifh any emoluments which Great-Britain derives from this colony: I am fenfible, that the education of the Jamaica youth is attended with an yearly gain to the mother-country. What I would fuggeft is, that the eftablifhment of one or more feminaries in Jamaica, upon a certain circumfcribed plan, would infallibly prove a means of augmenting the profits which Britain draws from thence (though not in the very fame, yet in other channels); and, if fhe is proved to gain more, it matters not in what line.

It has too long been the cuftom for every father here, who has acquired a little property, to fend his children, of whatever complexion, to Britain, for education. They go like a bale of dry goods, configned to fome factor, who places them at the fchool where he himfelf was bred, or any other that his inclination leads

him

him to prefer. The father, in the mean while, sends remittance upon remittance, or directs a liberal allowance, that his son may learn the art of squandering from his very infancy; and, not unfrequently, to gratify a little pride of heart, that little master may appear the redoubted heir to an affluent fortune. But, alas! it sometimes happens, that he sends *no* remittances: by which unlucky omission, his child is thrown upon the hands of the factor, who throws him upon the hands of the pedagogue; and, between both, the poor wretch undergoes as much neglect and ill usage, as if he was a charity-boy; and, in either case, too often comes from the feet of Gamaliel ignorant, vicious, idle, and prodigal; a disgrace to his friends, and a nuisance to his country. If suffered to remain in England, under the notion of finishing his manners, we find him, in the other view, in general rolling on the wheels of money into every species of town-debauchery; lavishing in one week what would maintain a poor family for a twelvemonth; the constant dupe of artifice; the sure gudgeon of every knave and impostor.

What a disadvantage is it to young men, of naturally strong passions and lively spirits, that they have not the watchful attention of a parent, to check their intemperate sallies, to conduct them into the ways of prudence, and habituate them in the practice of self-denial! How much to be regretted, that the fond father, whilst his son thus remains unemployed in useful pursuits during the most headstrong career of his life, is wearing himself out with incessant toil and anxiety, to no other effect than feeding the passions of an indolent or profligate spendthrift! Without a parent or monitor, at his elbow, to hold him under due awe and subordination, and gratified with plentiful supplies of money, he soon acknowledges no other governor than his own inclination, and takes pleasure for his preceptor. Few will venture to restrain him, who either doubt their authority to controul, or who suspect that such an interposition may either wear the appearance of too scrupulous a rigour, or prove detrimental, some time or other, to their interest in business.

The education of the youths *remitted* from this island is, in general, so mismanaged, that, was it not for their innate good qualities, not one in ten would ever arrive at the age of discretion, or

return

return to his native country with any other acquifition than the art of fwearing, drinking, dreffing, gaming, and wenching. It is, I own, a laudable zeal in a parent, who is folicitous to confer on his children the bleffings of liberal education. But it is furely a palpable miftake, that leads him to give their minds a wrong turn; and really pernicious to their welfare, that they fhould be brought up in a manner totally unfuitable to their future ftation. He fhould learn to diftinguifh, that to train up his fon to no profeffion is, by no means, the way to make a gentleman of him; 2dly, that, if he intends him for a profeffion, the fyftem of his education fhould be particularly adapted to it; 3dly, that to affign him a profeffion, and at the fame time leave it in his own free choice to apply to the ftudy of it or not, or to furnifh him with the inftruments of idlenefs and diffipation, when his mind fhould be engaged in the purfuits of ufeful knowledge, is no more than enjoining him to perform a tafk, and bribing him at the fame time to leave it unperformed; 4thly, that one uniform plan, or fyftem, of fcholaftic inftruction cannot be indifcriminately proper for all youths, however various their fortunes, capacities, or the refpective walks of life into which they are afterwards to pafs.

Let me now afk, what are the mighty advantages which Britain, or the colony, has gained by the many hundreds who have received their education in the former? The anfwer may be, they have fpent their fortunes in Britain, and learned to renounce their native place, their parents, and friends. Would it not have been better for both countries, that three-fourths of them had never croffed the Atlantic? Their induftry is, in general, for ever loft to the place where it might have been ufefully exerted; and they wafte their patrimony in a manner that redounds not in the leaft to the national profit, having acquired a tafte for pleafure and extravagance of every kind, far fuperior to the ability of their fortunes. Surely this can be no public acquifition, unlefs it be proved, that the kingdom is more enriched and benefited by a thoughtlefs prodigal, than by a thrifty, induftrious citizen. The education they ufually receive in Great-Britain does not qualify them for ufeful employment in Jamaica, unlefs they are bred to fome of the learned profeffions; which neverthelefs are not fuitable to all, becaufe thofe profeffions

would

would foon be overftocked in the ifland, if every youth configned from thence was to be trained to phyfick, divinity, or law, and becaufe *ex quovis ligno non fit Mercurius.* They generally leave Britain at that critical age when the blood beats high. They regret their exile from the gay delights of London, from the connections of early friendfhip, and perhaps the fofter attachments of love. The impreffions of all thefe remain lively and forcible. With this riveted prejudice againft a colony-life, it is not to be wondered at, that they embrace the firft convenient opportunity of returning to their favourite purfuits and focial intimacies. Such is often the over-fond liberality of Weft-India parents, in ordering a too large allowance for their fons in Britain, that thefe youths are not only invited by this means to neglect their ftudies, and commence men of pleafure, but are readily elevated into a deftructive opinion, that they have been fent thither merely to pafs away their time agreeably, and that it is not meant they fhould perplex themfelves with dry and abftrufe literature, as their fortune will enable them to live independent of fcience or bufinefs. Senfible therefore of their exemption from paternal reftraint, they joyoufly adhere to this conclufion, and follow the feductions of levity, caprice, and vicious indulgence, without reflection. Of the many ftudents at law, natives of Jamaica, who after compleating their terms in London have returned to affume the gown, I have not heard of one who ever gained 5 *l.* a year by his practice. This iffue we muft not afcribe to any defect of parts, but to a youth fpent in foppery, licentioufnefs, and prodigality, under a total renunciation of every other ftudy. Many I have noted, who, arriving there after having (as it is called) *finifhed their education* in England, appeared unpardonably illiterate, and poffeffed of few attainments beyond what I have already enumerated. Some I have obferved, who, being endued with tolerable genius, acquired more real knowledge and gentlemanly accomplifhments, in one twelvemonth after their arrival, than they had gained by fixteen years refidence in London; and this from being led at once into a fcene of public bufinefs, and the company and converfation of intelligent men. Having pointed out fome principal fources of that imperfect education which our young men in general receive, I fhall add a few thoughts in refpect to the other fex. If a feminary in this ifland is expedient for boys, it is ftill more fo for girls. The neceffary branches of their inftruction ufually lie within a fmall compafs. They require not the elements of Greek, Latin, or Hebrew; nor the precepts of the univerfity, nor the theory of the fciences, mechanic arts, or learned profeffions. Reading, writing, arithmetic, needlework, dancing, and mufic, will, with the additional helps of their own genius, prepare them for becoming good wives and mothers. There are many parents in this ifland, who, having a numerous family of children of both fexes, and barely able to afford their fons an education in Britain; they either fend for a governante, to inftruct their daugnters, or keep them uninftructed, except by fuch cafual tuition as may be had from itinerant mufic or dancing mafters. The utility of a boarding-fchool for thefe girls, where their number might admit of employing the ableft teachers, where they might be weaned from the Negroe dialect, improved by emulation, and gradually habituated to a modeft and polite behaviour, needs not, I think, any argument to prove it. Young ladies, fo far accomplifhed as, I think, they might be on a well-conducted plan, would infenfibly acquire, on their emerging into public life, the remaining graces and polifh which are to be attained in genteel company and converfation. They would, by this means, become objects of love to the deferving youths, whether natives or Europeans, and by the force of their pleafing attractions foon draw them, from a loofe attachment to Blacks and Mulattoes, into the more rational and happy commerce of nuptial union.

Upon enquiry, in the year 1764, into the ftate of the feveral foundations in this ifland, it appeared that confiderable fums had been given and bequeathed for the purpofe of erecting free-fchools; fome of which remained unapplied; and others had been fo illmanaged, that the public derived but very trivial advantage from them.

Thefe foundations are;

1ft. Manning's, in Weftmoreland, founded in 1710.

2d. One in Vere, by charitable donations, 1740.

3d. In Spanifh Town, by devife of Peter Beckford, efq; 1744.

4th. In Kingfton, by devife of John Woollmer, goldfmith, 1736.

2

5th. At Halfway-Tree, St. Andrew's, by devife of Sir Nicholas Laws, 1695. He gave two acres and a half of land, with a houfe for a free-fchool; conditioning, that any parifhioner, paying 5*l.* *per annum*, or 50*l.* down, towards advancement of the fchool, might fend his child thither for inftruction. This donation, by a law paffed in 1738, was eftablifhed, under the controul of governors, to make regulations, appoint teachers, &c.; but I do not find that it fucceeded.

6th. At Old Woman's Savannah, in Clarendon, by a donation of three acres of land, and fundry fubfcriptions, 1756.

7th. About 1769, or 1770, Martin Rufea, of the parifh of Hanover, devifed his eftate, confifting chiefly of perfonalty, for erecting and eftablifhing a free-fchool in that parifh; but the particular value of this donation, does not yet appear. The affembly, however, have fhewn a defire to promote it, by granting 500*l.* towards its eftablifhment.

All thefe foundations, except that at Old Woman's Savannah, were limited to receive boys of the refpective parifh in which they lay; which, together with their bad regulation, has been a principal caufe of their failing. None promifed fo well to anfwer, on a general plan, as that at Old Woman's Savannah, fituated as it was in a very healthy climate, in the centre of the ifland, and in the midft of feveral fmall fettlements. No lefs than 2000*l.* was raifed by voluntary fubfcription for carrying on the neceffary buildings. About the year 1758, it was opened, and conducted fuccefsfully for about feven years. The air was found fo healthy, that, out of eighteen youths, the difciples of the laft preceptor, not one was afflicted with any fever or acute diftemper during their refidence in it. But, at the time when this academy was brought to a tolerable ftate of maturity, it all on a fudden fell into decline under feveral impediments. The firft was the fmall allotment of land, which was not fufficient to enable the mafter to keep cows or fheep, or rear poultry, for the neceffary fubfiftence of his boarders; fecondly, the great difficulty (under this circumftance) of getting provifions; thirdly, the total want of fome certain eftablifhed fund, to afford a falary for the head-mafter, and keep the buildings in repair. The affembly, in 1764, taking into confideration the means by which

this

this feminary might be rendered more effectual, propofed to place it under the public fanction, and appoint governors and truftees by law. They likewife intended, that one hundred acres of land fhould be purchafed contiguous to the fchool; and that twenty acres fhould be cleared and fenced; and 500 *l.* be granted to truftees for this purpofe; and, being of opinion that 50*l. per annum,* though as little as could be allowed for fchooling, board, wafhing, and lodging, was too large a fum for perfons of middling fortunes and numerous families to afford, they propofed that the mafter fhould give board, wafhing, and lodging, for 30*l.* a year, and education for 20*l.*, of which no more than 5*l.* to be paid by the refpective parents, or guardians; and the remaining 15*l.* by the public. Such were their good intentions; which, if carried to effect, might have rendered this a very flourifhing inftitution. But, before any bill could be framed, the houfe became involved in a hot difpute with the governor, which was followed with feveral diffolutions, and an utter interruption of bufinefs for a year and half; after which, fuch a variety of other matters called for prefent attention, that this affair was not refumed. In the mean while, the mafter, for want of the public fupport, of which he began to defpair, found himfelf under neceffity of quitting it, and of betaking himfelf to fome other employment, that might yield him a better maintenance. In confequence of his refignation, the buildings, on which fo much money had been expended, remained without a tenant: and, in 1767, the land and buildings were vefted, by act of affembly, in truftees, with a power to fell the fame, and apply the money to the purchafe of land and erection of a fchool-houfe in fome other part of the parifh. The preamble of the act alledges, that the fituation had been found improper: but this remains to be proved.

If the affembly fhould hereafter be convinced of the very many benefits which this ifland might reap from a well-concerted plan of this nature; there is no part of it better calculated for a public fchool than this Savannah.

The principal points refpecting fituation are;

1ft, That it fhould be retired, free from the contamination of thofe vices which infeft towns and places of much public refort.

2dly, That it fhould be on a dry, healthy fpot, in an air entirely
free

free from fwampy and other noxious exhalations; and fupplied with pure and wholefome water, for drinking and culinary ufes.

3dly, That it fhould be in the near neighbourhood of feveral minor fettlements, for the convenience of procuring fmall ftock and other neceffary provifions.

4thly, That the roads leading to it fhould be good and paffable.

Every one of thefe requifites are enjoyed at Old Woman's Savannah. Nor is it in any of them liable to objection, except that the road leading to Old Harbour is fo long, as to render the carriage of goods from thence in general tedious. Yet this difficulty would eafily be furmounted, if eftablifhed prices were formed for the carriage of goods, as there are feveral teams which conftantly ufe this road; or a fhorter carriage might be opened to St. Anne's Bay. I propofe, therefore, that a fquare fhould be laid out here, about the fize of the parade in Spanifh Town. On one fide of it fhould ftand the fchool-houfe; oppofite to this, a chapel, for the regular performance of divine fervice. The Eaftern fide of the fquare fhould be occupied with the mafter's dwelling-houfe; and in each of its wings a convenient fuite of apartments, for the accommodation of boarders. Facing this range of building, fhould be difpofed fome convenient offices.

One hundred acres of land contiguous fhould be purchafed by the public; and part of it cleared, fenced, and properly laid out for pafturage and other ufes. To which fhould be added, fix cows and a fmall flock of fheep. Eight or ten Negroes fhould likewife be provided, to be under the care of a white overfeer, at 80 or 100 l. per annum wages, to clear the land, repair fences and roads, and do other neceffary work.

The mafter fhould be under the controul of a certain number of truftees, the governor for the time being to be one; a quorum of whom fhould annually meet at the fchool, to examine the condition and management of it, with full power to rectify abufes, difcharge the mafter, and appoint in his room; and to lay a ftate of their proceedings before the legiflature at their annual feffion.

For the better protection of the boys, and to guard againft any calamity likely to happen from infurrections among the Negroes,

a defenfible

a defensible barrack should be built at a convenient distance; where a party, either of soldiers or militia, should always be kept on duty. This garrison would answer a double purpose, by giving likewise a protection to this part of the country, which requires it; and would have the further advantage of being one of the healthiest cantonments in the whole island.

For the better supply of this garrison and the school, a Negroe market should be held here once a week, for poultry, hogs, and such other provisions as these people usually deal in.

A certain number of white servants should be constantly kept, in proportion to the number of boarders, that the latter might not, by a too early familiarity and intercourse with the Negroes, adopt their vices and broken English.

The articles to be taught here should be restricted to reading, writing, arithmetic (including book-keeping), the Spanish and French languages, surveying, mechanics, together perhaps with such instructions in agriculture and botany as relate to the improvement of the vegetable productions of the island. The pupils might likewise be taught music, dancing, fencing, and the military manual exercise, to qualify them the better for a course of life which requires agility and strength of body, and occasionally the use of arms. The expences of boarding, washing, lodging, and tuition, should be regulated by law upon just and equitable terms, suitable to the general price of necessaries, and the circumstances of the middling inhabitants. Nor would it be a mis-placed generosity, if the public should contribute a certain allowance towards the education of each boy; or at least certain salaries to the master and his assistants, which would enable them to carry on the undertaking on terms better suited to the ability of parents.

Restricting the scheme of education to these limits, I purposely exclude all those youths, whose fortunes qualifying them for the learned professions, or to cultivate those sublimer degrees of erudition proper to their rank, ought to pursue such studies in Europe, or North-America, because it were vain to expect that they could attain them to a due accomplishment in this island.

I confine the plan to the children of persons who do not look so high, and who would be content to see their sons virtuously trained

under

under their own eye, and at a moderate expence, to such branches of knowledge, as may qualify them to be industrious planters, surveyors, book-keepers, mechanics, useful members of this community, rather than be shipped off to Britain; from whence it is a great chance, but they might return with a thorough aversion to, or incapacity for, these or any other laudable employments. And here let me remark a little on the selfish and illiberal sentiments of those men who, in the exuberance of their contrivances for enriching the mother-country, oppose every establishment for education in the colonies, decry them as injurious to the interest of Britain, and would fain have the whole generation of infants regularly shipped home to learn their A, B, C. These politicians are not fathers, or at least have their bosoms so steeled with avarice, as to have lost all feeling for their fellow-subjects in these remote parts. The gain, made by the passage of these poor infants, is, it is true, in favour of the balance arising to Great-Britain from her freight. But let this pitiful earning be weighed against the hazard of their lives, and the extreme agony which so many tender parents must suffer at parting, through a cruel necessity, from their beloved offspring, which perhaps they never may see again. Exclusive of humanity, this circumstance must also be contemplated, in the view of social policy, as a bitter grievance, which to avoid, many persons have declined contracting marriage, lest they should thereby be driven into a distress so severe; and which has forced others, under the intolerance of such a separation, to leave the colony prematurely, instead of devoting themselves, as otherwise they would have done, to the further improvement of their estates. So that, in consequence of this local defect, the island is become far less populous and cultivated than we should find it, if provision had been made for retaining both the parents and their children within it.

I shall now suppose a seminary properly founded in the island, and happily conducted on such a plan, as that the middling families might think themselves under no such necessity of sending their children to other countries for a decent education: and because, for better illustrating the argument, we must endeavour to fix some certain number of them to be so retained in the island, let this

number

number be called two hundred. I fhall be told, that thefe boys, if fent to England, might probably expend there 30 *l.* fterling *per* head *per annum*, one with another, in cloathing, food, &c. to the amount of 6000 *l.* But, on the other hand, if we fuppofe thefe boys to remain in Jamaica, will it not be found, that Great-Britain would gain full as much by them in fimilar articles? The difference of climate will certainly require double at leaft the quantity of articles for cloathing every year, and of a much more expenfive fabric; their books, and many *items* of food and accommodation, muft be procured from Britain at an enhanced price: fo that, if any thing near an exact eftimate could be framed, it muft, I think, appear very convincingly, that thefe children would confume a much greater quantity, or value, of Britifh manufactures and products by ftaying in Jamaica, and confequently conduce more to the national profit in this way, than if they had been tranfported into Britain. But it is to be further confidered, that every one of thefe natives of the ifland will be equal to two unfeafoned Europeans in ability to undergo the fatigues of bufinefs and laborious exercifes here; be better qualified, by gradual initiation from their infancy, to underftand and execute the ufeful plans of life for which they are defigned; that they will, by habit and nature, prefer this country to every other, and therefore diligently fettle themfelves in it. The ifland, it is evident, would, in the progrefs of one generation only, contain a far greater number of families than it now poffeffes; it would be much more extenfively fettled; and Great-Britain would gain, in courfe, a proportional accefs of profit, by their confumption of manufactures, their ingenuity, and improvements. I am warranted in drawing this confequence; fince it is well known, that a family, refiding in Jamaica, confumes more of Britifh manufactures, and gives employment to many more fubjects in Great-Britain, than the fame family would do, was it tranfplanted into that kingdom [*m*]. So much for the objections

which

[*m*] We may apply, upon this occafion, what a modern writer has faid on another. Let us fuppofe a tract of country that yields a rent of 50,000 *l.* a year; the whole of which is enjoyed by one great man. In all probability, above 40 of the 50 is fpent in the capital, in a profufion of elegancies; flowing into the pockets of the induftrious, it is true, but the induftrious in what? why, the furnifhers of luxurious eatables, delicate cookery, and French wines; the exhibitors of

public

which are to be expected from that quarter. Some of more weight may arife in the ifland itfelf, by reafon of the expence attending fuch an eftablifhment; but, in fome degree to obviate this, I would propofe the confolidating of all the foundations and charity-fchools, whofe incomes united would greatly contribute to fupport the new inftitution, although, in their prefent ftate, they are of very little other ufe than the beftowing fo many annuities upon five or fix perfons under the title of fchoolmafters.

The income of Spanifh Town fchool is about £. 190 *per ann.* and		
has rarely extended to more at a time than	—	14 boys.
Woolmer's, in Kingfton, —— —— ——	300	15
Vere School, —— —— ——	300	6
Manning's (I fuppofe about the fame), ——	300	6
Of the reft I am not informed, but believe ——		—
they are entirely dropped. £.	1090	41

Not therefore to fpeak of the reft, here are four fchools, with as many different mafters; all of whom have regular falaries, although their pupils are, all together, not amounting to one half the number which one mafter in England is able enough to take charge of.

Thefe, and all other unexecuted benefactions of the like kind, being lumped into one fund, the propofed fchool fhould be open to receive as many foundation-boys from each refpective town, or parifh, as they had been ufually known to have at their refpective free-fchool, one year with another; and upon the very fame terms of board, maintenance, and inftruction: by which equitable per-miffion, no injury would accrue to thefe parifhes; but, at the fame time, it is prefumed, that the good intentions of the feveral tefta-tors, and other benefactors, would be much better fulfilled.

public fhews and entertainments; Italian fingers, and French dancers; the induftrious gentry of Newmarket and White's; in a word, in the encouragement of precifely that fpecies of induftry which is pernicious to the welfare of a kingdom. Thus the income of this tract of land is ex-pended very little to the benefit of the kingdom at large, or the fpot in particular.

Adjoining to this fpot lies another of the fame rent, but belonging to a thoufand freeholders, of 50 *l. per ann.* each, living in their neat manfions on their rents in the midft of as many, or perhaps more, tenants. What a population is here! and what a confumption of neceffary manu-factures, and home-products! What a difference to the public between the ends of fuch induftry! the one is for ever exerted to the moft beneficial purpofes; the other, to the moft pernicious ones.

POLIT. ESS.

It is aſtoniſhing to obſerve the gentlemen of this iſland ſo laviſh in ſome reſpects of public money, and ſo inattentive at the ſame time, to a matter of this intereſting concern; for what can be more ſo, than to wean the inhabitants from that detrimental habit of emigration, that unhappy idea of conſidering this place a mere temporary abode, eſpecially as ſuch numbers are, from unexpected turns in life, laid under a neceſſity of remaining in it, and bringing up a race of children, whom, for want of a ſeminary, they no ſooner begin to take delight in, than they are forced to wiſh they could eraſe from their remembrance. Theſe very people have not heſitated to diſburſe near 70,000l. in the ſpace of nine years upon fortifying the iſland, who never thought of voting a ſeventieth part of that ſum towards rendering it much more eſſentially ſecure, and much better protected, by falling on eaſy means of making it populous. The condition of the North-Americans would at this time have been deplorable indeed, if they had been equally improvident. But it is a proof of their wiſdom and regard for poſterity, that in every one of their townſhips, there is proviſion made for a ſchoolmaſter; ſo that the loweſt of their people are not left deſtitute of ſome education. For thoſe of more liberal fortune, there are colleges founded under able profeſſors; where philoſophy has already dawned with a luſtre that aſtoniſhes the oldeſt ſocieties of the learned in Europe, and commands their moſt reſpectful attention. It is ſhocking to think, that, through a defect of this generous ſpirit, or a want of ſteddineſs and reſolution, no ſuch meaſures have yet been eſpouſed in our iſland. But our hearts muſt bleed, when we reflect on the many unfortunate children who have periſhed; ſome by ſhipwreck; ſome by exploſion[n]; others by neglect after their arrival in England. To enumerate theſe fatalities, would be a melancholy recital, and perhaps only ſerve to revive paternal affliction. What bleſſings then will await that aſſembly, who ſhall patriotically reſolve to prevent this barbarous neceſſity, and theſe ſorrowful events, in future! They will, indeed, be juſtly ſtyled the fathers of their country, and merit immortal honour.

[n] Several were deſtroyed in this manner on ſhip-board, a few years ſince.

I have

I have chiefly confined my thoughts to a fchool for boys. If another for girls fhould likewife be approved, perhaps a fituation nearer one of the towns, as at Halfway-tree, in St. Andrew's, might be moft proper, in order to accommodate them eafier with the neceffary mafters. This fchool would be beft regulated under a felect committee of the principal ladies in the ifland, the governor's lady being the patronefs. Thefe fuperintendants might annually be chofen by ballot; and the legiflature no further interfere, than in fupporting the foundation, and regulating the terms of admiffion.

The expence annually attending the boys feminary cannot be exactly computed; neverthelefs, as a calculation may not only convey fome idea of what it will require, but ferve as a groundwork for concerting a regular plan of fuch an undertaking, I take the liberty to offer the following:

The head mafter, annual falary,	£. 280 to £. 300
An affiftant,	140
A Botanical profeffor,	140
A phyfician,	140
A teacher of mufick,	70
A ditto, of fencing and the manual exercife,	70
A dancing-mafter,	70
An overfeer,	80
Two white fervants, at 35l. each,	70
	1060
Neceffaries for ten Negroes *per ann.* at 60s. each,	30
	1090

A botanic garden, fituated near the fchool, might be laid out, and ftocked with thofe plants of the ifland, or of the Southern continent, moft diftinguifhed for their virtues in medicine, or value for commercial purpofes. It is certain, that nature has not only furnifhed this ifland with feveral vegetable productions ufeful in trade and manufactures, but likewife an unlimited variety of medicinal balms, barks, and roots, adapted to the cure of moft diftempers incident to the climate.

The

The perfon made choice of for mafter fhould not be allowed to follow any other avocation; which might engrofs too much of his time, to the negleft of his pupils; and for this reafon any beneficed clergyman might be unfit, becaufe his parochial duties would probably claim a great part of that attention, the whole of which ought folely to be employed in the affairs of the fchool.

My wifh to render this ifland more flourifhing far outftrips my ability to propound the means. In this cafe, the fincerity of an honeft intention muft atone for the imperfeftions of argument. The reftitude of a meafure is one thing; the means of accomplifhing it, another. Many perfons are able to difcern the former, who fearch for the other with hefitation. But, as the affembly poffeffes happily the power of conducting moft ufeful plans to effeft, I cannot but indulge the hope, that it may hold a fubjeft of this importance not unworthy its moft ferious deliberation.

C H A P. XIII.

Of the Inhabitants.

SECT. I.

THE inhabitants of this ifland may be diftinguifhed under the following claffes: Creoles, or natives; Whites, Blacks, Indians, and their varieties; European and other Whites; and imported or African Blacks.

The intermixture of Whites, Blacks, and Indians, has generated feveral different cafts, which have all their proper denominations, invented by the Spaniards, who make this a kind of fcience among them. Perhaps they will be better underftood by the following table.

DIRECT lineal Afcent from the Negroe Venter.

White Man, = Negroe Woman.
White Man, = Mulatta.
White Man, = Terceron.
White Man, = Quateron.
White Man, = Quinteron.
WHITE.

MEDIATE or STATIONARY, neither advancing nor receding.

Quateron, = Terceron.
|
Tente-enel-ayre.

RETROGRADE.

Mulatto, = Terceron.   Negroe, = Mulatta.   Indian, = Mulatta.   Negroe, = Indian.
| | | |
Saltatras.   Sambo de } = Negroe.   Meſtize.   Sambo de } = Sambo de
                Mulatta, }   Indian, }   Mulatta.
                      | |
                 NEGROE.   Givero [o].

In the Spaniſh colonies, it is accounted moſt creditable to mend
the breed by aſcending or growing whiter; inſomuch that a Quateron will hardly keep company with a Mulatto; and a Meſtize
values himſelf very highly in compariſon with a Sambo. The
Giveros lie under the imputation of having the worſt inclinations
and principles; and, if the caſt is known, they are baniſhed.
Theſe diſtinctions, however, do not prevail in Jamaica; for here
the Terceron is confounded with the Quateron; and the laws permit all, that are above three degrees removed in lineal deſcent from
the Negro anceſtor, to vote at elections, and enjoy all the privileges
and immunities of his majeſty's white ſubjects of the iſland. The
Dutch, I am informed, tranſcend the Spaniards very far in their
refinement of theſe complexions. They add drops of pure water
to a ſingle drop of duſky liquor, until it becomes tolerably pellucid. But this needs the appoſition of ſuch a multitude of drops,
that, to apply the experiment by analogy to the human race,
twenty or thirty generations, perhaps, would hardly be ſufficient to
diſcharge the ſtain.

The native white men, or Creoles, of Jamaica are in general tall
and well-ſhaped; and ſome of them rather inclined to corpulence.
Their cheeks are remarkably high-boned, and the ſockets of their
eyes deeper than is commonly obſerved among the natives of England; by this conformation, they are guarded from thoſe ill effects
which an almoſt continual ſtrong glare of ſun-ſhine might otherwiſe produce. Their ſight is keen and penetrating; which renders
them excellent markſmen: a light-grey, and black, or deep hazel,
are the more common colours of the pupil. The effect of climate
is not only remarkable in the ſtructure of their eyes, but likewiſe

[o] Perhaps from *Giſero*, a butcher.

in

in the extraordinary freedom and fuppleneſs of their joints, which enable them to move with eaſe, and give them a ſurpriſing agility, as well as gracefulneſs in dancing. Although deſcended from Britiſh anceſtors, they are ſtamped with theſe characteriſtic deviations. Climate, perhaps, has had ſome ſhare in producing the variety of feature which we behold among the different ſocieties of mankind, ſcattered over the globe: ſo that, were an Engliſhman and woman to remove to China, and there abide, it may be queſtioned, whether their deſcendants, in the courſe of a few generations, conſtantly reſiding there, would not acquire ſomewhat of the Chineſe caſt of countenance and perſon? I do not indeed ſuppoſe, that, by living in Guiney, they would exchange hair for wool, or a white cuticle for a black: change of complexion muſt be referred to ſome other cauſe. I have ſpoken only of thoſe Creoles who never have quitted the iſland; for they, who leave it in their infancy, and paſs into Britain for education, where they remain until their growth is pretty well compleated, are not ſo remarkably diſtinguiſhed either in their features or limbs. Confining myſelf to the permanent natives, or Creole men, I have this idea of their qualities; that they are in general ſenſible, of quick apprehenſion, brave, good-natured, affable, generous, temperate, and ſober; unſuſpicious, lovers of freedom, fond of ſocial enjoyments, tender fathers, humane and indulgent maſters; firm and ſincere friends, where they once repoſe a confidence; their tables are covered with plenty of good cheer, and they pique themſelves on regaling their gueſts with a profuſion of viands; their hoſpitality is unlimited; they have lodging and entertainment always at the ſervice of tranſient ſtrangers and travelers; and receive in the moſt friendly manner thoſe, with whoſe character and circumſtances they are often utterly unacquainted [p]; they affect gaiety and diverſions, which in general are cards, billiards, backgammon, cheſs, horſe-racing, hog-hunting, ſhooting, fiſhing, dancing, and muſic; the latter in particular they are formed to enjoy with the niceſt feelings; and their ear for melody is, for the moſt part, exceedingly correct. This, indeed, has alſo been remarked of the Creole Blacks, who, without being able to read a

[p] One obvious proof of this is, that there is ſcarcely one tolerable inn throughout the whole iſland, except at a great diſtance from any ſettlement.

fingle

fingle note, are known to play twenty or thirty tunes, country-dances, minuets, airs, and even fonatas, on the violin ; and catch, with an aftonifhing readinefs, whatever they hear played or fung, efpecially if it is lively and ftriking.

There are no people in the world that exceed the gentlemen of this ifland in a noble and difinterefted munificence. Such a dif-pofition deferves to be commemorated ; and I fhall therefore think it incumbent on me to give fome examples of it. After the de-ceafe of the duke of Portland, it was well known that he died in very indifferent circumftances. From the time of his death, the dutchefs and her family were provided with a regular and fplendid table, fuitable to her rank, at the public charge ; and, as fhe could not have the convenience of returning home in a man of war, the affembly caufed a fhip to be equipped for her with every proper accommodation, and added to this mark of refpect a very con-fiderable prefent in money. They have been often accufed, and very unjuftly, of wilfully feeking occafions to quarrel with their governors. On the contrary, they have never failed in liberality and a juft deference to thofe governors who have deferved well by the mildnefs and equity of their adminiftration.

They made an augmentation of 2500l. *per annum* to the go-vernor's ufual falary ; erected a magnificent houfe for his refidence ; and purchafed lands, for his better convenience, at no lefs expence than 12,000. Their gratitude to their governors would have been manifefted more frequently, if more occafions had been given for exciting it. Among other inftances of this fenfe they have of good ufage, let me mention, that, upon the death of the late worthy governor Sir William Trelawny, the affembly paid no trivial com-pliment to his merit, by giving his remains an honourable interment at the public charge ; the expence amounted to 1000l. fterling. But, what was a more confpicuous indication of their regret for the lofs of fo efteemed a man, there was not a perfon of any con-fideration, in the county where he died, who did not attend him to the grave, and with looks that befpoke the the fincerity of their affliction. But this natural propenfity to fuch actions of benevo-lence as do honour to mankind cannot fhew itfelf fo often in a public manner, as in the more filent walks of private life.

An

An officer died here, leaving his wife and feveral children in very great diftrefs. No fooner was their unfortunate condition made known, than relieved by private contributions amounting to a very large fum. Another officer's widow, in fomewhat fimilar circumftances, except that fhe was left unincumbered with a family, met with the like generous fupport. And here I muft not pafs over a ftill more ftriking anecdote of this amiable difpofition. I fhall relate it faithfully as near as I can recollect. A certain planter, having taken offence at the behaviour of his fon, refolved to difinherit him. He accordingly devifed away the whole of his eftate to a gentleman of diftinction in the country, for whom he entertained a particular efteem; and foon afterwards died. The devifee was furprized and fhocked when the will was fhewn to him. He fent for the young man; and, upon his arrival, delivered into his hands a deed which he had juft executed, reconveying to him all his paternal eftate, adding to this effect; " Your father meant to " be my friend; it is my duty to be yours. I give you back his " eftate; it is now yours by juft inheritance: go and enjoy it; and " be affured that you may always depend on my beft fervices and " advice fo long as your future conduct fhall entitle you to claim " them." An admirable example this of refined virtue and principle, untainted with felfifh or mercenary bafenefs. Though fimply no more than the effufion of a mind controuled by juftice, humanity, and moral rectitude; yet, in this age of callous venality, it deferves to be applauded as an act of felf-denial, not very commonly met with in other parts of the world. Without multiplying fuch narratives, I fhall only declare, that I know but very few natives of the ifland, among the clafs of gentlemen, who, in the like cafe, would not have acted in the fame truly noble manner.

Some years ago, feveral new fettlers, who had arrived in confequence of different acts paffed for their encouragement, were bound, by an exprefs condition, that, after the expiration of the firft feven years, they fhould be obliged to re-imburfe the treafury for the expence of their paffage, and a twelvemonth's fubfiftence advanced upon their firft coming over. In 1749, there were fifty of them found indebted to the public, on this account, no lefs

I   than

than 7479 *l.* This sum the assembly readily remitted, and discharged them entirely from the obligation [*q*].

This will be supposed an act of political generosity, and of a different nature from the examples before given; for which reason I have placed it last in my catalogue, as it is considered perhaps more referable to the spirit of patriotism, than the impulses of humanity; though to have acted otherwise would have betrayed, I confess, but a small share of either.

With all these praise-worthy qualities, the Creoles have some foibles in their disposition. They are subject to frailties in common with the rest of mankind. They are possessed with a degree of supineness and indolence in their affairs, which renders them bad œconomists, and too frequently hurts their fortune and family. With a strong natural propensity to the other sex, they are not always the most chaste and faithful of husbands. They are liable to sudden transports of anger; but these fits, like hurricanes, though violent while they last, are soon over and subside into a calm: yet they are not apt to forget or forgive substantial injuries. A lively imagination brings every circumstance present to their remembrance, and agitates them almost as much as if it had occurred but immediately before. They are fickle and desultory in their pursuits; though unshaken in their friendships. From this cause perhaps it is, that various schemes, both in pleasure and business, have been eagerly started, and then suddenly dropped, and forgotten as if they had never existed. They have some tincture of vanity, and occasionally of haughtiness; though much less of the latter than formerly. That distant carriage, which was gained here insensibly by habit, when the planters employed six times the number of white servants, whom, together with their Negroes, they might think it prudent to keep under a due awe and subordination to authority, has worn away in course of time with the causes of it. They are too much addicted to expensive living, costly entertainments, dress, and equipage. Were they but more abstemious in these respects, and more attentive to good husbandry on their plantations, there

[*q*] In 1758, was a similar act of remission of 6301 *l.* 6*s.* 8 *d.* to sixty settlers. I have not the least doubt, for my own part, but that these remissions were the pure effects of compassionate sentiments, and not the offspring of a political liberality.

are few who would not amafs confiderable fortunes, and render their pofterity opulent. But they are fond alfo of monopolizing large tracts of land, buying up all around them, and attempting to fettle new eftates before the old one is cleared of debts. By this means, and impofing on themfelves by a fpecious mode of payment, in giving their own bonds, and taking upon them the debts of other men, they become harraffed and unhappy ever after. Finding themfelves unable to depofite when the day of payment arrives, they are either reduced to be flaves for life, in hopes to redeem, or fuftain, the whole of a large territory thus acquired; or to plunge deeper and deeper in debt and diftrefs, by fubmitting to every fpecies of fraud and extortion that may gain them a little refpite; till perhaps, after a tedious conflict, they leave at their deceafe their whole fortune to be torn piece-meal, and their family turned adrift, to make room for fome worthlefs upftart, who has poffeffed cunning and villainy enough to accumulate money, or obtain credit, fufficient for becoming the proprietor. It is a fettled maxim, " that " you are not diftinguifhed, or of any note, unlefs you are in debt." In other words, you are no body, unlefs you make yourfelf literally fo. But what fort of a levee is to attend fuch pre-eminence? A banditti of creditors and deputy marfhals, who, for their own fakes, not the planter's, wifh him well for a while, that they may be the better; as a flight of vultures would rather make their repaft on a fat carcafe, than a lean one; and will pick either the one or the other to the very bones before they quit it.

Moft of the old Creole families are allied, by the inter-marriages among their anceftors before the ifland was populoufly fettled. The fame remark may be made on many other communities in the world, which have fprung from a few families; for example, the Welfh and Scotch. The natives in general prefer pure water to any other beverage. Punch feems almoft profcribed from the politer tables; though, when it is made with rum of due age, ripe fruit, and not too ftrong, it is a very pleafant, refrefhing, and wholefome drink, and one of the beft appropriated to a hot climate. Madeira wine is in more efteem than claret, not only becaufe it is cheaper, but as the greateft heat of the air only ferves to improve its flavour, and as it is not apt to ferment in the ftomach. It is generally

nerally drank here diluted with water; and in this ftate it may be regarded as a very powerful antifeptic. They are exceffively fond of chocolate, which fome drink morning and afternoon in pre-ference to tea. Formerly the men ufed to indulge in a *fiefto* in their hammocks every day after dinner. They dreffed in waiftcoats and caps; never wearing coats nor wigs, except at church, or on public occafions. Thefe modes, copied from the Spaniards, have long been difufed; and at prefent they follow the Englifh fafhions, only ftudying coolnefs and eafe. They indulge in the fruits of the country, particularly fuch as are moft nutritious; and fwallow pepper without moderation, which is alfo the principal ingredient in their olios or pepper-pots, a compofition highly efteemed here even by the Europeans.

The planters of this ifland have been very unjuftly ftigmatized with an accufation of treating their Negroes with barbarity. Some alledge, that thefe flave-holders (as they are pleafed to call them, in contempt) are lawlefs bafhaws, Weft-India tyrants, inhuman oppreffors, bloody inquifitors, and a long, &c. of fuch pretty names. The planter, in reply to thefe bitter invectives, will think it fuffi-cient to urge, in the firft place, that *he* did not make them flaves, but fucceeded to the inheritance of their fervices in the fame man-ner as an Englifh 'fquire fucceeds to the eftate of his anceftors; and that, as to his Africans, he buys their fervices from thofe who have all along pretended a very good right to fell; that it cannot be for his intereft to treat his Negroes in the manner reprefented; but that it is fo to ufe them well, and preferve their vigour and exiftence as long as he is able. The antagonifts, though willing to allow that he is felf-interefted in all he does, can hardly admit this plea; although it is evident, that the more mercenary a planter's difpofi-tion is, the ftronger muft the obligation grow upon him to treat his labourers well, fince his own profit, which he is fuppofed alone to confult, muft neceffarily prompt him to it. In proving him therefore to be fuch a mercenary wretch, they effectually confute the charge of cruel ufage; fince the one is utterly incompatible with the other [r]. " But," fays Mr. Sharpe, brandifhing his two-

edged

[r] Efquemeling, who was himfelf an indented fervant to the French Weft-India company about the year 1664, has defcribed very feelingly the difference between the condition of a Ne-

groe-

edged weapon, " the planter makes no fcruple to gain by wearing
" out his flaves with continual labour, and a fcanty allowance,
" before they have lived out half their natural days;" and he com-
pares this excefs of conftrained labour to " the mercilefs ufage
practifed in England over poft-horfes, fand-affes, &c." Soon after
this declamation, he tells us, " that the allowance of food is not
" given to a flave for his own fake, but merely for the intereft of
" his mafter; to enable the flave to continue his daily labour in the
" fame manner as the foddering a horfe, or fattening of cattle for
" flaughter, becaufe the food is given on no other confideration
" than for the profit of the owner." Then he gives us a quotation
from the learned and reverend Mr. Godwyn, " that the planter
" confiders this allowance of provifion as expedient and fit, in
" order to enable his Negroes to undergo their labour, without
" which, himfelf cannot get riches and great eftates; but nothing
" for the wretch's health and prefervation!" Now, with all fubmiffion to this profound advocate and his co-adjutor, I prefume,

groe-flave and that of a white contract-fervant, in his time, and affigned the true caufe of it.
Speaking, firft, of his countrymen at Hifpaniola, he fays, " the fervants commonly bind them-
" felves to their mafters for three years; but their mafters, having no confcience, traffic with
" their bodies as with cattle at a fair, felling them to other mafters as they do Negroes. Yet, to
" advance this trade, fome perfons go purpofely into France, and likewife to England and other
" countries, to pick up young men and boys, whom they inveigle and tranfport; and, having
" once got them into the iflands, they work them like horfes; the toil impofed upon them being
" much harder than what they enjoin the Negroes, their flaves; for thefe they endeavour to pre-
" ferve, being their perpetual bond-men; but, for their white fervants, they care not whether
" they live or die, feeing they are to ferve them no longer than three years.
" The planters of the Caribbee Ifles" (he afferts) " were ftill more cruel to their white fer-
" vants." And he names a Frenchman, at St. Chriftopher's, " who had killed above a hundred with
" ftripes and blows. In regard to the Englifh" (he fays), " they did the fame with theirs; and
" that the mildeft cruelty they exercifed towards their fervants was, that, when they had ferved fix
" years of their time (the ufual term of their contracts being feven), they ufed them fo ill, as
" forced them to beg their mafters to fell them to others, though it were to begin another fervi-
" tude of feven years; and that he had known many who had thus ferved fifteen or twenty
" years."
The low price at which thefe fervants were furnifhed by the French company to the planters,
being no more than from 4 l. 10 s. to 6 l. 15 s. fterling per head, was another caufe of their ill
ufage; fince the lofs fuftained by their death was confidered, by the purchafer, as very trifling,
and eafily to be replaced.
At prefent, it requires no argument to prove, that the enormous price of Negroe-flaves muft
procure them an indulgent and careful treatment even from owners of an inhuman difpofition;
and with fuch men, however felfifh the motive is, ftill the effect may be no lefs favourable to the
flave.

that,

that, if the enabling his Negroes to undergo their labour, by allowing them expedient food, be the true motive, as they affirm it is, for the planter's care of his Negroes; the same motive must neceſſarily induce him to be equally aſſiduous for the preſervation of their lives and health. This, indeed, is implied; ſince, if they are abandoned to ſickneſs, or ſuffered to periſh for want of his care, he muſt of courſe be deprived of the benefit of their labour, which alone (as they rightly obſerve) is the foundation of his riches. Thus the planter is affirmed to take care of the life and health of his Negroes, that he may profit by their labour; and yet to let them die through barbarity and neglect; by which he muſt eventually be a loſer of all that benefit. In one paragraph he is made to ſtarve and wear them out before they have half finiſhed their term of life; in the next he is ſaid to allow them plenty of food, to ſupport them in the continuance of their labour. How they can be hacked and ſtarved to death, like poſt-horſes, or ſand-aſſes, and yet fattened like oxen for Leadenhall-market, at one and the ſame time, is ſo far beyond the humble limits of a planter's comprehenſion, that it muſt be left to be further reconciled and explained by theſe two ſagacious writers; and the perplexing ænigma, they are deſired to ſolve, is, by what means it comes to paſs, that the planter gains equally, whether he ſtarves and deſtroys them, or whether he feeds and takes care of them?

I will aſſert, in my turn, and I hope without inconſiſtency or untruth, that there are no men, nor orders of men, in Great-Britain, poſſeſſed of more diſintereſted charity, philanthropy, and clemency, than the Creole gentlemen of this iſland. I have never known, and rarely heard, of any cruelty either practiſed or tolerated by them over their Negroes. If cruelties are practiſed, they happen without their knowledge or conſent. Some few of their Britiſh overſeers have given proofs of a ſavage diſpoſition; but inſtances are not wanting to ſhew, that, upon juſt complaint and information of inhuman uſage, the planters have puniſhed the actor as far they were able, by turning him out of their employ, and frequently refuſing a certificate that might introduce him into any other perſon's. Theſe barbarians are imported from among the liberty-loving inhabitants of Britain and Ireland. Let the reproach

then

then fall on the guilty, and not on the planter. He is to thank his mother-country for difgorging upon him fuch wretches as fome-times undertake the management of Weft-India properties; and, by wanton torture inflicted on the flaves confided to their charge (the refult of their own unprincipled hearts and abominable tem-pers), bring an unmerited cenfure on the gentlemen proprietors, who are no further culpable than in too often giving this employ-ment to the outcafts of fociety, becaufe, it may happen, they can get none better.

America has long been made the very common fewer and dung-yard to Britain. Is it not therefore rather ungenerous and unmanly, that the planter fhould be vilified, by Britifh men, for the crimes and execrable mifdeeds of Britifh refugees! It is hard upon him to fuffer this two-fold injury, firft by the wafte of his fortune in the hands of a worthlefs fervant, and next by fuch unfair imputa-tions upon his character. There is, I allow, no country exifting without fome inhuman mifcreants to difhonour it. England gives birth to fuch, as well as other ftates; but I would not, from this reafon, argue that every Englifhman is (according to Voltaire) a favage.

The planters do not want to be told, that their Negroes are hu-man creatures. If they believe them to be of human kind, they cannot regard them (which Mr. Sharpe infifts they do) as no better than dogs or horfes. But how many poor wretches, even in Eng-land, are treated with far lefs care and humanity than thefe brute animals! I could wifh the planters had not too much reafon on their fide to retort the obloquy, and charge multitudes in that king-dom with neglecting the juft refpect which they owe to their own fpecies, when they fuffer many around them to be perfecuted with unrelenting tyranny in various fhapes, and others to perifh in gaols, for want of common neceffaries; whilft no expence is thought too great to beftow on the well-being of their dogs and horfes. But, to have done with thefe odious comparifons, I fhall only add, that a planter fmiles with difdain to hear himfelf calumniated for tyran-nical behaviour to his Negroes. He would wifh the defamer might be prefent, to obferve with what freedom and confidence they ad-drefs him; not with the abject proftration of real flaves, but as

4　　　　　　　　　　　　　　　　　　　　　　　　　　　　their

their common friend and father. His authority over them is like that of an antient patriarch: conciliating affection by the mildness of its exertion, and claiming respect by the justice and propriety of its decisions and discipline, it attracts the love of the honest and good; while it awes the worthless into reformation. Amongst three or four hundred Blacks, there must be some who are not to be reclaimed from a savage, intractable humour, and acts of violence, without the coercion of punishment. So, among the whole body of planters, some may be found of naturally austere and inhuman tempers. Yet they, who act up to the dignity of man, ought not to be confounded with others, whose odious depravity of heart has degraded them beneath the rank of human beings. To cast general reflections on any body of men is certainly illiberal; but much more so, when applied to those, who, if their conduct and characters were fully known to the world, would appear so little to deserve them.

The French treat the gentlemen of their West-India settlements in a very different manner. " It is with great justice," says Bossu, " that we reckon the Creoles *noble* in France. Their sentiments " are so noble and delicate in every station of life, that they per- " fectly well merit that appellation."

I should implore pardon of the ladies, for not having given them the precedence which is their due: but I dispatched the gentlemen first, that I might pay the more attention to the lovelier sex. Feminine beauties and virtues are to be found in every clime, the growth of every soil. The Creole women are perfectly well-shaped; and many of them remarkably handsome. In general, they have exceedingly good teeth; which some have imputed to the pains they constantly take in cleaning them with the chaw-stick [s], which guards them from the scurvy. They prefer chocolate to tea; and do not drink any liquor so hot as is customary with women in England. It seems to be a vulgar error, that sugar causes the teeth to decay. It is certainly an anti-septic, and un-

[s] A species of rhamnus. It is of a bitter taste, and contains a great quantity of fixed air; both of which qualities render it a very proper corrector of any putrid slough that may happen to lodge between the interstices of the teeth. It is cut into small junks, of three or four inches in length; one extremity of which, being first soaked a little while in warm water, is soon formed into a soft brush by chawing; from whence it derives its popular name.

juftly bears that blame; which, for the moft part, fhould rather be thrown on the negle<u>ct</u> of cleanlinefs. The ladies of this ifland eat large quantities of it in fugar-cakes, or what is called *pan-fugar* [*t*], and confe<u>ct</u>ionary. I knew a man here, who was excef-fively fond of fugar and its preparations. During the crop-feafon, he not only ufed to eat plentifully of it, but mixed fyrup and water for his common beverage at meals. At the age of about eighty years, he had his teeth ftill compleat, perfe<u>ct</u>ly white and found. He informed me, that he never was affli<u>ct</u>ed with the tooth-ach in his life. His head was covered with good black hair, without any vifible intermixture of grey, or the leaft fymptom of baldnefs; and he was ftrong, hale, and lively. He imputed the foundnefs of his teeth, his unchanged hair, and a<u>ct</u>ivity, to his never having drunk malt-liquors, wine, or fpirits of any kind; his only drink being plain water, the pureft he could get, or mixed with fugar. He would probably have attained to a much greater age, if it had not been for an accident, occafioned by his own te-merity.

Kalm, accounting for the bad teeth of the ladies in Pennfylvania and other North-American provinces, oppofes the vulgar notion of bad qualities in fugar upon very probable grounds. He obferves, that women, who ufed no fugar in their tea, had equally bad teeth as the reft; that the men in general were lefs liable to this misfortune; and that the Indians, living in the fame air and country, were re-markable for good teeth. He afcribes the decay of them to their drinking tea too often, fometimes no lefs than thrice a day, and too hot. Some females may titter at the good Dr. Hales's experi-ment with a pig's tail, which being dipped into a cup of tea, heated to the degree in which it is ufually drank (viz. thirty degrees above the blood-heat), the fkin was fcalded in a minute, fo as to make the hair come off eafily. But he juftly concludes from hence, that the frequent drinking of fuch hot liquor is hurtful, agreeably to the general affertion of phyficians. And I may add, that the ableft dentifts have concurred in their teftimony, that it is particu-

[*t*] The fyrup in the tache, or laft clarifier, adheres in a thick cruft to the rim, fomewhat re-fembling brown fugar-candy. This is taken off, and paffes under the name of pan-fugar. Cakes are alfo made by mixing a little powdered ginger and cinnamon with the clarified fyrup; and, after pouring it on a plate, it hardens, and is fliced into little fquares.

larly

larly deſtructive of the enamel of the teeth. No people in the world have finer teeth than the native Blacks of Jamaica; and none devour greater quantities of ſugar. Few of the Creole ladies ſip their tea till it cools to about milk-warmth, nor oftener than once, or at the utmoſt twice, a day. But they, who have been brought up in England, where they were accuſtomed to drink it almoſt boiling-hot, and to debauch in it too freely, are many of them ſo much addicted to, and confirmed in this practice, that they cannot break themſelves of it here without much reluctance. And hence perhaps it happens, that the natives of England, and thoſe Creoles who have been educated in England, have not in general ſuch good teeth, as others who have never been out of the iſland [u].

A crooked or deformed Creole man or woman, unleſs ſuch at the time of their birth, or diſtorted by ſome miſchance, would here be a rarity to be gazed at.

The method uſed here in rearing children ſecures the graceful form of their perſons, and is a certain proof of maternal good ſenſe. From the time their infants are a month old, they are allowed no other bed than a hard matraſs, laid upon the floor; and, inſtead of a ſheet, they repoſe on a ſmooth ſheep-ſkin, which is occaſionally ſhifted, for the ſake of cleanlineſs. They are clad looſe and light, go without the incumbrance of ſtockings, are bathed regularly in water every day, and expoſed freely to the air; ſo that no part of the world can ſhew more beautiful children. The girls are not ſuffered to wear ſtays (thoſe abominable machines for the deſtruction of ſhape and health); but, as well as the boys, are indulged in ſuch a cool and unconfined attire, as admits the free extenſion of their limbs and muſcles.

[u] Some reſtrict the bad effects of ſugar entirely to what is refined, which is ſuppoſed to be impregnated with lime, uſed in the proceſs; and the corroſive power of this ſubſtance npon bones is well known. But it is ſcarcely probable, that even a ſtrong ſolution of lime in water could produce this eroſion of the teeth, unleſs they were daily rubbed with it; and even then it is far from being certain. But combine this alkali with an acid (as it is in ſugar), and ſurely its effect muſt be greatly altered. We may remark, however, the inconſiſtence of writers; ſome of whom blame the acid in the ſugar; others, the alkali of the lime; thus imputing the effect to two contrary principles. The very ſmall quantity of lime, that can remain intermixed, is certainly not anſwerable to the ſuſpicion; but, if it even ſhould be thought to deſerve it, the muſcovado, or unrefined, will ſtand clear of it.

Many of the good folks in England have entertained the strange opinion, that the children born in Jamaica of white parents turn swarthy, through the effect of the climate; nay, some have not scrupled to suppose, that they are converted into black-a-moors. The truth is, that the children born in England have not, in general, lovelier or more transparent skins, than the offspring of white parents in Jamaica. In the Southern parts of the island, they have none of that beautiful *vermeille*, so much admired in England; but, though exposed, as lively children necessarily must be, very much to the influence of sun-shine, their skins do not acquire the English tan, but in general grow pale, and of a fainter white. The genuine tan of the sun here, on faces of healthy, grown persons, who are a good deal in the open air, is a suffusion of red. The natives of both sexes are very remarkable for this kind of complexion; and it gives them the appearance of sanguine habits, and vigorous health. The brunettes, or those of a naturally thick and unperspiring skin, frequently become browner, as they advance in years, and seem to be tinged with a bilious secretion, which circulates with the blood, and lurks in the smaller vessels, instead of passing off, as it does in other habits, by the outlets of perspiration. The many Mulatto, Quateron, and other illegitimate children sent over to England for education, have probably given rise to the opinion before-mentioned; for, as these children are often sent to the most expensive public schools, where the history of their birth and parentage is entirely unknown, they pass under the general name of West-Indians; and the bronze of their complexion is ignorantly ascribed to the fervour of the sun in the torrid zone. But the genuine English breed, untainted with these heterogeneous mixtures, is observed to be equally pure and delicate in Jamaica as the mother country.

The practice of inoculation, according to the modern improvements, has been very successfully used here. I shall be forgiven, I am sure, by the ladies, for a short digression on this subject, and for introducing the following sensible remarks upon it:

" Of those who take the small-pox casually, one in seven is
" found to die. But, of fifteen hundred patients inoculated in
" England by the surgeons Ranby, Hawkins, and Middleton, three
" only

" only mifcarried, *i. e.* one in five hundred. Now, not to men-
" tion that the hazard is, by a long experience fince, reduced al-
" moft to nothing, according to this computation, which has never
" been invalidated; in every five hundred perfons inoculated, fe-
" venty lives are preferved to fociety! Let the computation be
" extended to the probable number inoculated every year, from the
" time when the practice began to obtain generally, and to thefe
" add the pofterity derived from the marriage of thefe redeemed
" perfons, as they advance to maturity; and we fhall find a pofi-
" tive and happy increafe of people, continually rifing up, and
" ftaring out of countenance all declaimers againft the prac-
" tice [*w*]."

I thought I might, without impropriety, give this quotation at
large, becaufe I have obferved fome tender mothers in the ifland led
away by vain terrors, or influenced by predeftinarian fcruples; not
confidering, that the hand of the Almighty has pointed out this
eafy method of preferving his creatures from the horrid ravages of
this difeafe, the feeds of which are probably congenial to our very
frame, and from whofe infection very few are exempted; nor perceiving the force of pofitive evidence, which, through a long courfe
of experience, has demonftrated, that inoculation is almoft an infal-
lible means of rendering it harmlefs. Nothing can be more mild
than the diforder in Jamaica, received in this manner. Infants, of
one month old, have gone through it very fafely. The working
flaves followed their ufual occupations with the puftules upon their
bodies, without inconvenience; and even bathed themfelves in the
rivers, without any ill confequence. When a preparation was ufed,
they either had no puftules, or at leaft fuch as never came to a fup-
puration. Two very moderate dofes of the mercurial medicines,
and as many gentle purgatives, with an interval of three or four
days between them, were found fufficient. With refpect to children at the breaft, care was only taken to keep their bodies gently
lax during the continuance of the eruptive fymptoms; and, after
the eruption, to correct any gripings with daily dofes of teftaceous
powder, and a few drops of *tinct. thebaic.* at night. The eruption
generally appeared, on thefe young fubjects, about the fixth day;

[*w*] Critical Review.

and,

and, in grown perfons, about the eighth or ninth. They were conftantly in a free air in the fhade, and fuffered no confinement; being reftrained only, in diet, from animal food, falt, and fpirituous liquors.

Of fifteen hundred Negroes, of all ages and habits of body, who were inoculated here by *one practitioner*, not one died. Such plain facts fhould weigh more than argument in fuppreffing groundlefs apprehenfions; and teach every mother, that the wilful confignment of her helplefs little ones to almoft certain death, when fhe might exert the probable means of faving them, is abfolute murder in effect, and little fhort of it in guilt. The infant is incapable of judging for itfelf, or of exercifing a freedom of choice. But to the parents God has imparted reafon fufficient to conduct their uninftructed charge, and protect it from impending evils. In ufing their beft endeavours for this purpofe, they manifeft a truly religious obedience to their Maker, a due affection for their offspring, and a fubmiffion to the rules of good fenfe. And, whatever the event may prove, they are confcious of having acted with the beft intentions, which will furely be moft acceptable to that Being, who

" Preferreth the upright Heart, and pure."

Whilft I render all due praife to the Creole ladies for their many amiable qualities, impartiality forbids me to fupprefs what is highly to their difcredit; I mean, their difdaining to fuckle their own helplefs offspring! they give them up to a Negroe or Mulatto wet nurfe, without reflecting that her blood may be corrupted, or confidering the influence which the milk may have with refpect to the difpofition, as well as health, of their little ones. This fhameful and favage cuftom they borrowed from England; and, finding it relieve them from a little trouble, it has gained their general fanction. How barbarous the ufage, which, to purchafe a refpite from that endearing employment fo agreeable to the humanity of their fex, fo confonant to the laws of nature, at once fo honourable and delightful to a real parent, thus facrifices the well-being of a child! Notwithftanding every precaution they take to examine the nurfe of their choice, it is a million to one but fhe harbours in her blood the feeds of many terrible diftempers. There is fcarcely one of

thefe

thefe nurfes who is not a common proftitute, or at leaft who has not commerce with more than one man; or who has not fome latent taint of the venereal diftemper, or *fcrofa*, either hereditary, or acquired, and ill-cured. The place of a nurfe is anxiouſly coveted by all of them, as it is ufually productive of various emoluments to them; and on this account they are fure to keep fecret any ailment they labour under, however detrimental to the child, rather than be turned off. The mothers in England are at leaft able to find fome healthy labourer's wife; and none of them, I venture to believe, would fend their infants to be fuckled in any of the brothels of London. It is true, the Creole ladies have not the fame advantage; they can meet with none other than unchafte nurfes; and this is another unanfwerable argument to prove the neceffity of their adminiftering their own breaft, in preference to one that they are under fo many reafons to fufpect is not equally proper.

Numberlefs have been the poor little victims to this pernicious cuftom. Many innocents have thus been murdered; and many more have fucked in difeafes, which rendered their life miferable, or fuddenly cut fhort the thread of it.

A misfortune attending moft of thefe children is, that they are extremely fubject to worm-diforders imbibed with the milk; for I have frequently feen thefe vermin difcharged from babes of three months age. But it is more ufual to fee them looking healthy and well till they reach the third year; when they frequently decline all at once, and from this caufe. They are often too much crammed with the fruits and roots of the country, which at this tender age are apt to generate a large quantity of vifcid flime in their bowels, that affords a *nidus* for the worms to depofite their eggs. The more common kinds which infeft them are the *afcarides*, and *tænia* or tape worm: both thefe forts are effectually expelled with a decoction of the *anthelmenthia*, or worm-grafs, which grows naturally in the South parts of Jamaica; and fometimes the *oleum ricini*, or nut oil, is adminiftered in fmall and frequent dofes with fuccefs.

The down of the cow-itch pods, given in the proportion of one part to three parts of honey or fyrup, to the quantity of one teafpoonful morning and evening, for a week, has been found, by

repeated

repeated trials and long experience, to be equally deſtructive to them; care being only taken to give a proper doſe of rhubarb, or other mild purgative, in order to carry off the dead worms.

An old woman here formerly performed ſeveral wonderful cures of this kind, with no other remedy than fat pork, with which ſhe fed her little patients; and, no doubt, it acted upon the worms in the like manner as the oily compoſitions frequently preſcribed, which are found to deſtroy theſe animalcules by ſtopping up their pores.

Another misfortune is, the conſtant intercourſe from their birth with Negroe domeſtics, whoſe drawling, diſſonant gibberiſh they inſenſibly adopt, and with it no ſmall tincture of their aukward carriage and vulgar manners; all which they do not eaſily get rid of, even after an Engliſh education, unleſs ſent away extremely young.

A planter of this iſland, who had ſeveral daughters, being ap-prehenſive of theſe conſequences, ſent to England, and procured a tutoreſs for them. After her arrival, they were never ſuffered to converſe with the Blacks. In ſhort, he uſed all his vigilance to preſerve their language and manners from this infection. He ſuc-ceeded happily in the deſign; and theſe young ladies proved ſome of the moſt agreeable and well-behaved in the iſland: nor could it be diſtinguiſhed from their accent, but that they had been brought up at ſome genteel boarding-ſchool in England; inſomuch that they were frequently aſked, by ſtrangers, how long they had re-ſided in that kingdom. Until a proper ſeminary can be eſtabliſhed, every maſter of a family here might purſue the like method, at leaſt with his daughters, who are generally kept more at home than boys. But a mother, who has been trained in the accuſtomed mode among a herd of Negroe-domeſtics, adopts the ſame plan, for the moſt part, with her own children, having no idea of the impropriety of it, becauſe ſhe does not diſcern thoſe ſingularities, in ſpeech or deportment, which are ſo apt to ſtrike the ears and eyes of well-educated perſons on a firſt introduction to them.

The ladies, however, who live in and about the towns, being often in company with Europeans, and others brought up in Great-Britain, copy imperceptibly their manners and addreſs; and become

better

better qualified to fill the honourable ftation of a wife, and to head their table with grace and propriety. Thofe, who have been bred up entirely in the fequeftered country parts, and had no opportunity of forming themfelves either by example or tuition, are truly to be pitied. We may fee, in fome of thefe places, a very fine young woman aukwardly dangling her arms with the air of a Negroe-fervant, lolling almoft the whole day upon beds or fettees, her head muffled up with two or three handkerchiefs, her drefs loofe, and without ftays. At noon, we find her employed in gobbling pepper-pot, feated on the floor, with her fable hand-maids around her. In the afternoon, fhe takes her *fiefto* as ufual; while two of thefe damfels refrefh her face with the gentle breathings of the fan; and a third provokes the drowfy powers of Morpheus by delicious fcratchings on the fole of either foot. When fhe rouzes from flumber, her fpeech is whining, languid, and childifh. When arrived at maturer years, the confcioufnefs of her ignorance makes her abfcond from the fight or converfation of every rational creature. Her ideas are narrowed to the ordinary fubjects that pafs before her, the bufinefs of the plantation, the tittle-tattle of the parifh; the tricks, fuperftitions, diverfions, and profligate difcourfes, of black fervants, equally illiterate and unpolifhed.

Who is there, that does not fincerely deplore the lot of this unhappy *tramontane*, and blame the inattention of the legiflature to that important article, Education! To this defect we muft attribute all that cruel ridicule and farcafm, fo frequently lavifhed upon thefe unfortunate females by others of their fex, who, having experienced the bleffings of a regular courfe of inftruction at fchool, are too oftentatioufly fond of holding in derifion what they ought to look upon with candour and concern. What ornaments to fociety might not thefe neglected women have proved, if they could have received the fame degree of liberal polifh! On the other hand, deprived thus of the means of culture and refinement, illfurnifhed as they are with capacity for undertaking the province of managing domeftic concerns, uninformed of what pertains to œconomy, order, and decency; how unfit are they to be the companions of fenfible men, or the patterns of imitation to their daughters! how incapable of regulating their manners, enlightening

their

their underſtanding, or improving their morals! Can the wiſdom of legiſlature be more uſefully applied, than to the attainment of theſe ends; which, by making the women more deſirable partners in marriage, would render the iſland more populous, and reſidence in it more eligible; which would baniſh ignorance from the riſing generation, reſtrain numbers from ſeeking theſe improvements, at the hazard of life, in other countries; and from unnaturally reviling a place which they would love and prefer, if they could enjoy in it that neceſſary culture, without which life and property loſe their reliſh to thoſe who are born, not only to inherit, but to adorn, a fortune.

The women of this iſland are lively, of good natural genius, frank, affable, polite, generous, humane, and charitable; cleanly in their perſons even to exceſs; inſomuch that they frequently bring on very dangerous complaints by the too free uſe of bathing at improper periods. They are faithful in their attachments; hearty in their friendſhips; and fond, to a fault, of their children, except in the ſingle inſtance which I am grieved to have been obliged to expatiate upon. They are temperate and abſtemious in their diet, rarely drinking any other liquor than water. They are remarkably expert at their needle, and indeed every other female occupation taught them; religious in their lives and ſentiments; and chaſte without prudery in their converſation. In horſemanſhip, dancing, and muſic, they are in general very accompliſhed: in theſe acquired qualifications they excell, more or leſs, according to the opportunities that have fallen in their way of cultivating their natural talents, which are very good, and ſuſceptible of extenſive improvements. As a foil to the brilliant part of their character, I muſt acknowledge, although with great reluctance, that they yield too much to the influence of a warm climate in their liſtleſs indolence of life. But it is chiefly the fault of the men, if they do not aſſemble till dinner is ſerved up, or retire from it with the cloth, to doze away an hour or two, or enjoy a ſeparate *tete a tete* in ſome adjoining chamber, leaving the men to their bottle. I have heard it reported of the maſter of a family, that, regularly after dinner and one circulation of the bottle, he uſed to throw out broad hints that it was time for all females in company to with-

draw;

draw; and, when this fignal was difregarded, gave fo indecent a toaft, as drove them immediately out of the room; a practice fo brutal, that it would merit the baftinadoe even among Hottentots. This unfocial cuftom, however, lofes ground, as the men are lefs attached than formerly to the pleafures of getting drunk. In the genteeler families, converfation between the two parties is kept up for a confiderable time after dinner. Tea, coffee, and cards, fupply the *paffetemps* of jovial fongs and voluptuous bumpers. They now contrive, for the moft part, to have a felect apartment, or drawing room, for rejoining the ladies after a fhort feparation; and the cuftomary intermixture in large companies, of placing the beaus and belles alternately, tends much to promote this polite intercourfe between the two fexes. Formerly the married men and bachelors ufed to carouze together almoft every day at taverns; the fpirit of gaming then prevailed to a great excefs; and the name of a *family man* was held in the utmoft derifion.

That irregular courfe of life was accompanied with innumerable evils. Many gentlemen of rank in the country impaired their fortunes, and reduced their families to the brink of ruin. It was not at all unufual to fee one of them, after lofing all his money, proceed to ftake his carriage and horfes that were waiting to carry him home; and, after lofing thefe, obliged to return on foot. Drunken quarrels happened continually between intimate friends; which generally ended in duelling. And there were very few who did not fhorten their lives by intemperance, or violence.

The prefent ftate of reformation therefore is a very happy change; which, by re-uniting the fexes, has promoted temperance, urbanity, and concord. A want of proper education and good maternal examples has rendered fome women here extravagant in their expences, and very indifferent œconomifts in their houfeold affairs. They employ too numerous a tribe of domeftic fervants, and are apt to truft too far their fidelity, which is not always proof againft ftrong temptations. From twenty to forty fervants is nothing unufual. Perhaps it may not be unpleafant to the reader, to fee a lift of one of thefe houfehold eftablifhments. I fhall therefore prefent him with the following:

1 Butler,	2 Footmen, or waiting-men,
	1 Coach-

1 Coachman,	1 Key, or ftore-keeper,
1 Poftillion,	1 Waiting-maid,
1 Helper,	3 Houfe-cleaners,
1 Cook,	3 Wafher-women,
1 Affiftant,	4 Sempftreffes.

Thefe amount all together to twenty. If there are children in the family, each child has its nurfe; and each nurfe, her affiftant boy or girl; who make a large addition to the number. Moft of thefe are on board-wages, from three to four rials *per* week, befides their cloathing; with which they feem to live very comfortably. A fpeculative writer fuppofes it very feafible, in order to increafe the number of white inhabitants, that every family fhould employ white domeftics inftead of Negroes. But he did not reflect, that even in Britain there is no one clafs of the people more infolent and unmanageable than the houfe-fervants. Their wages are enormous; the charge of maintaining them, their wilful wafte, idlenefs, profligacy, ingratitude of difpofition, and ill behaviour in general, are fo univerfally, and (I believe) with good reafon, complained of, that moft families confider them as neceffary evils, and would gladly have nothing to do with fuch plagues, if their rank or ftation in life, or their own imbecillities, could poffibly admit of their keeping none. What then muft be the cafe in Jamaica, if thefe gentry are found fo ungovernable and troublefome in Great Britain? None of them would leave home, to ferve in the colony, except for very extravagant wages: even thofe that might pafs over would foon difcover, that, by the policy of the country, there fubfifts a material diftinction between them and the Negroes. If they fhould chance to meet with any black fervants in the fame family, they would impofe every part of the drudgery of fervice upon thefe poor creatures, and commence ladies and gentlemen. The females would attend to no work, except pinning their lady's handkerchief; and the men, to no other than laying the cloth for dinner, and powdering their mafter's hair. The governors ufually bring over white fervants with them; but are very glad to get quit of them, and fall into the modes of the country. The Negroes are certainly much better fervants here, becaufe they are more orderly and obedient, and conceive an attachment to the families they ferve, far

ftronger

ftronger than may be expected from the ordinary white domeftics: at leaft, the inhabitants of the ifland feem to be of this opinion; for thofe gentlemen, whofe ample fortunes admit their affording the expence of importing and maintaining white fervants, incline univerfally to prefer the Blacks; nor will they, I believe, ever wifh to increafe population, and ftrengthen their fecurity, by the introduction of Englifh valets and friffeurs into their families; the debauched morals, and diffolute practices of this race of men, would do more hurt among the Blacks by the force of example, than their ability for defending the country could do good. The fort of men, beft qualified for increafing the number of Whites, are the fober, frugal, and induftrious artificers; together with the poorer farmers and graziers, a hardy ufeful people, and moft fit for occupying the unfettled defarts, and changing the woods and wildernefles into flourifhing paftures and plantations.

But to return to what concerns the ladies. Scandal and goffip-ing are in vogue here as well as in other countries. A natural vi-vacity and opennefs of temper are apt to betray the unguarded into little indifcretions, which are fometimes diligently aggravated and blackened with the tongue of malevolence and envy. Yet few are more irreproachable in their actions than the Creole women: they err more in trivial follies, and caprices unreftrained, than in the guilt of real vice. And, if we confider how forcibly the warmth of this climate muft co-operate with natural inftinct to rouze the paffions, we ought to regard chaftity here as no mean effort of fe-male fortitude; or, at leaft, judge not too rigidly of thofe lapfes which happen through the venial frailty and weaknefs of human nature. They have not yet learned thofe artifices and difguifes which women of the world can affume when they pleafe to veil their fentiments and conduct. Their gaiety inclines them to be fond of drefs, balls, and company; and, confidering the fmall circle of public diverfions in this ifland, it is not furprifing that they fhould feek to gratify their inclinations by every lively amufement of this fort that prefents itfelf. I muft add, that they poffefs fome fhare of vanity and pride; and that fome few join to the latter an high and over-bearing fpirit, which, not having been duly checked in their infancy, is apt to vent itfelf in turbulent fits of rage and

clamour,

clamour, to the unfpeakable difturbance of the poor animal, whofe
misfortune it may be to be linked in the nuptial bonds with fuch a
temper. Fain would I wifh to relate, that the more gentle and
efteemable fair-ones apply themfelves to repair the deficiencies of
an imperfect education, by giving fome leifure hours to the moft
approved authors, by whofe help they might add the delights of a
rational converfation to thofe abundant graces which nature has
beftowed upon them. It is a pity that fuch excellent talents fhould
lie wafte, or mifemployed, which require only cultivation to make
them fhine out with dignity and elegance. To pleafe the eye, requires only the fkill of a common mercenary harlot; but to capti-
vate the heart, and charm the mind, a woman muft diveft herfelf,
as foon as poffible, of grofs ignorance (that fofter-mother of pride),
filly prattle, and conceited airs; fhe muft endeavour, by diligent
reading and obfervation, to enlarge her notions, banifh her prejudices, and ftock her intellect with fuch improvements, as may enable her to bear her part in a fenfible converfation. By thefe eafy
means, fhe may fave many a blufh, when common fubjects are dif-
cuffed, of which fhe ought not to be ignorant; fhe will entertain
her company in a rational manner, and with correct language, and
not expofe her hufband to be hooted at, for his folly in tying himfelf for life to a pretty idiot. That audacious flanderer, Dr. Browne,
accufes fome of the ladies here of flaying their faces with the
cauftic oil of the cafhew-nut, in order to acquire a new fkin.
" The procefs" (he fays) " continues fourteen or fifteen days; du-
" ring which they fuffer the moft exquifite torture, which their
" vanity enables them to fupport with Chriftian patience." And
yet it feems to be to very little purpofe; " for" (he adds) " all
" this bliftering leaves the countenance much more deformed, than
" any fpots or freckles could have made it. Happy," (quoth he)
" had they been equally attentive to the improvement of their
" mind, which they too frequently neglect; while they bear fo
" much pain, to caft their fkins, in imitation of fnakes and
" adders."

The doctor, like many other old batchelors, had ftrange fancies
about the operations of the toilet, or (to believe the beft of him)
took a hint, from fome girlifh freak of this kind, which might
have

have come to his knowledge in the courfe of his medical practice, to infinuate that this cofmetic was in general ufe. But the women here fo univerfally underftand the cauftic nature of this oil, that they never attempt to open the nuts with their own fingers, for fear of burning them. All families have the kernels ferved up at their table in a variety of different preparations. And hence I judge it impoffible, that any woman, poffeffing two grains of fenfe, could think of befmearing her whole face with fuch a liniment, which erodes like *aqua fortis*, though fhe might ufe the kernels in emulfion. I rather fufpect the doctor's credulity was impofed upon by fome wag; and that he feized this occafion to have a fling at the ladies, who are therefore much obliged to him for fo ingenious a tale, as well as for the fting at the end of it.

It is remarked here, that the women attain earlier to maturity, and fooner decline, than in the Northern climates: they often marry very young, and are mothers at twelve years of age. They confole themfelves, however, that they can enjoy more of real exiftence here in one hour, than the fair inhabitants of the frozen, foggy regions do in two. The temperance of their life carries them on, notwithftanding, to a good old age; it being no uncommon thing to fee women here of eighty or ninety years, and upwards. A few years fince, a venerable matron died at the age of one hundred and eight; and I remember one of ninety-fix, who enjoyed all her faculties unimpaired, excepting her fight, which truly was fomewhat the worfe for wear. Many of the other fex too, who, by conftitution or from prudence, avoid ftrong liquors and hurtful exceffes, arrive at the fame periods of longevity with fewer infirmities than accompany the fame ages in England, where old folks are generally fhriveled with cold, and overwhelmed with catarrhous defluxions, the natural fruits of a raw, wet atmofphere. In Jamaica, the warmth and equable ftate of the air is friendly to age; and the nutritious quality of its foods preferves vigour and a lively flow of fpirits.

Intemperance and fenfuality are the fatal inftruments which, in this ifland, have committed fuch havoc, and fent their heedlefs votaries, in the prime of manhood, to an untimely grave. It is owing to thefe deftructive caufes, that we perceive here fuch a

number

number of young widows, who are greedily fnapped up by di-
ftreffed bachelors, or rapacious widowers, as foon as the weeds are
laid afide.   Sir Nicholas Lawes, formerly governor of the ifland,
ufed to fay, that the female art of growing rich here in a fhort
time was comprized in two fignificant words, " *marry* and *bury*."

To fum up the character of the Jamaica ladies, I fhall conclude
with this remark ; that, confidering the very great defects in their
education, and other local difadvantages, their virtues and merits
feem juftly entitled to our higheft encomium ; and their frailties and
failings to our mildeft cenfure.

S E C T. II.

THE natives of Scotland and Ireland feem to thrive here much
better than the European Englifh.   They bring founder conftitutions with them in general, and are much fooner provided for.
The national partiality, which is made an accufation againft the
gentlemen of the two former parts of the Britifh empire, is fo far
attended here with very good confequences ; for their young countrymen, who come over to feek their fortunes, are often beholden
to the benevolence of thefe patrons, who do not fuffer them to
languifh and fall into defpondence for want of employment, but
take them under friendly protection ; and, if they are well difpofed,
they are foon put into a way of doing fomething for themfelves
The gentlemen are therefore, in my opinion, very often unjuftly
cenfured for doing what humanity requires.   This hofpitable alacrity to affift and befriend their countrymen, in a place where they
might otherwife become deftitute of fupport, and fick of life, produces likewife an event very favourable to the colony, by inviting
into it frequent recruits of very able hands, who add not a little to
its population and ftrength.   The offspring of this part of Britain are extremely numerous and flourifhing in Jamaica. I have heard a computation made of no fewer than one hundred of the name of Campbel only
actually refident in it, all claiming alliance with the Argyle family.
There are likewife numbers, who, though related to other noble
ftocks of the North, deferve much more refpect from their own in-
trinfic worth, than from their illuftrious confanguinity.   Jamaica,

5   indeed,

indeed, is greatly indebted to North-Britain, as very near one third of the inhabitants are either natives of that country, or defcendants from thofe who were. Many have come from the fame quarter every year, lefs in queft of fame, than of fortunes; and fuch is their induftry and addrefs, that few of them have been difappointed in their aim. To fay the truth, they are fo clever and prudent in general, as, by an obliging behaviour, good fenfe, and zealous fervices, to gain efteem, and make their way through every ob-ftacle. The Englifh were never charged with a want of bene-volence; but, in the exercife of it, they refemble the blind god-defs Fortune, who fcatters her favours with her eyes fhut before all that happen in the way to fcramble for them. Abftracted from the line I have drawn, the extenfion of friendfhip to an undeferving man, for no other reafon but becaufe it was his lot to have been born in the fame parifh, and in preference to one of far greater merit who chanced to be born two or three hundred miles further diftant, is illiberal and unmanly, and betrays a mind enflaved, in the moft contemptible degree, to meannefs and ignorance. In this ifland no diftinctions ought to fubfift, but of good or bad citizens. They who would feem to maintain any other by their conduct, however they may affect to difdain them with their lips, are of narrow fouls, and no true friends to the intereft and peace of the ifland.

The lower order of white people (as they are called here) are, for the moft part, compofed of artificers, indented fervants, and re-fugees.

The firft live well here, and get high prices for their work [x]. Of the fecond clafs, great numbers ufed formerly to be brought

from

[x] I felect a few articles, from which fome idea may be formed of the expence of building in this ifland; and, for better comparifon with the London prices, the fums are all reduced to fterling.

	L s. d.	l. s. d.
Mafonry, *per* perch,	0 4 $5\frac{1}{4}$	
Reduced brick-work, *per* rod,	16 1 5	
Bricks, *per mill.* with carriage,	2 2 10	
Laying ditto, *per mill.*	0 14 $3\frac{1}{2}$	
Paving ditto on edge, *per* yard,	0 3 $6\frac{3}{4}$	
Ditto ditto flat, ditto,	0 1 $9\frac{1}{4}$	
Lime, *per* hogfhead,	0 3 $2\frac{1}{4}$ to	0 3 6^3
Scantling, plank, and board, *per mill.* feet,	8 11 5	

Hard

from Scotland, where they were actually kidnapped by some *man-traders*, in or near Glasgow, and shipped for this island, to be sold for four or five years term of service. On their arrival, they used to be ranged in a line, like new Negroes, for the planters to pick and chuse. But this traffic has ceased for some years, since the despotism of clanship was subdued, and trade and industry drove out laziness and tyranny from the North of Scotland. The artificers, particularly stone-masons and mill-wrights, from that part of Britain, are remarkably expert, and in general are sober, frugal, and civil; the good education, which the poorest of them receive, having great influence on their morals and behaviour. I do not know whether the overseers of plantations should be considered in a separate class: they are, for the most part, such as have passed through a regular course of service in the agriculture of this country; and, if they are sensible and thrifty, they enjoy very comfortable lives, and save enough out of their salaries to buy a settlement of their own: some of them have even become possessors, in time, of very large properties, and made a very respectable figure here. Subordinate to the overseers are the plantation book-keepers, warehouse or store-keepers, distillers, tradesmen, and drivers, or sub-overseers; but for this last office Negroes are mostly employed.

The crimp's office has supplied no small number of inferior servants. This office has the singular faculty of qualifying any man whatever for any art or mystery he inclines to follow in the colonies, and by no other magic than a common indenture; carpenters, who never handled a tool; bricklayers, who scarcely know a brick from a stone; and book-keepers, who can neither

	l.	*s.*	*d.*		*l.*	*s.*	*d.*
Hard timber, *per* hundred feet,	1	12	1½	to	1	15	8½
Best Carolina shingles, *per mill.* about	2	17	1¾		3	11	5¼
Roofing, boarding, and shingling, *per* square,	3	4	3½				
Door-frames, each,	2	17	1¾				
Window ditto,	1	15	8½				
Framing, lathing, and shingling roofs, *per* square,	2	17	1¾				
Iron work, *per* pound,	0	0	8½				
Flat and square bars, *per* pound,	0	0	8½				
Twenty-penny nails, *per mill.*	0	17	0				
Ten-penny nails, ditto,	0	10	3				
Six-penny nails, ditto,	0	5	4½				
Spike nails, *per* pound,	0	0	10¾				

write

write nor read.   Many of thefe menial fervants, who are retained for the fake of faving a deficiency, are the very dregs of the three kingdoms.   They have commonly more vices, and much fewer good qualities, than the flaves over whom they are fet in authority; the better fort of which heartily defpife them, perceiving little or no difference from themfelves, except in fkin, and blacker depravity.   By their bafe familiarity with the worft-difpofed among the flaves, thay do a very great injury to the plantations; caufing difturbances, by feducing the Negroes wives, and bringing an *odium* upon the white people in general, by their drunkennefs and profligate actions.   In fact, the better fort of Creole Blacks difdain to affociate with them, holding them in too much contempt, or abhorrence.

Although the gaol-delivery of Newgate is not poured in upon this ifland; yet it is an occafional afylum for many who have deferved the gallows.   Thefe fellows are no fooner arrived, than they cheat away to the right and left, and off again they ftart; carrying all away with them, except the infamy of their proceedings, which they leave behind, as a *memento*, to fhew the impropriety of admitting any other than honeft men to be members of an induftrious colony.

Formerly convict-felons were tranfported hither; but the inconvenience attending the admiffion of fuch mifcreants obtained the inhabitants a relief from them.   While the traffic for Scotch fervants lafted, the legiflature of the ifland lent their helping hand to give it encouragement;   and, in 1703, it was enacted, that a mafter of any fhip, importing thirty white men fervants at one time, fhould be for that voyage exempted from paying all port-charges.   If any of the fervants fo brought in fhould happen to remain undifpofed of at the expiration of thirteen days after their arrival, the receiver-general was directed to take charge of them, upon paying to the importer a certain fum *per* head.   He was then to fend them to the *cuftos* of that parifh, where the greateft deficiencies were; and the treafury was reimburfed by the perfon, or planter, on whom they were quartered.   It is curious to remark the prices which at that time were fet upon thefe fervants, and to compare them with what are paid at prefent.

Every servant, English, Scotch, Welsh, or of the islands
of Jersey, Guernsey, or Man, if in time of war, *per*
head, —— —— —— —— Currency, £ 18

If in time of peace, —— —— —— —— 14
Irish servants, in time of war, —— —— —— 15
Ditto, in time of peace, —— —— —— 12

Convicts are excepted out of this act; and none have of late
years been sent over, unless to the regiments, whose service here
is not much advanced by such recruits. The cause of this depreciation of the Irish I am not informed of; but possibly they were
more turbulent, or less skillful in work, than the others. They
are in very different estimation in South Carolina; where what
are denominated bog-trotters, or such as have been accustomed to
the boggy grounds of Ireland, are in great request for cultivating
their rice-swamps, for which work they are particularly excellent,
and generally turn out very industrious.

But to compare the different expence of indented servants in
1703 and now. At that time they were obliged, by a law of the
island, to serve seven years, if under eighteen years of age; and,
if above that age, the term of four.

The service therefore of a man, above eighteen
years old, might then be purchased for a term
of four years, in time of peace, for —— —— £ 14

Such a servant, at the present time, would contract only for four years, at from 35*l.* to 40*l.*
per annum, besides his passage. He therefore
costs the importer, for his passage, —— —— £ 14

His wages for four years, at the lowest rate of
35 *l. per annum,* —— —— —— 140   154

The difference is, —— —— —— 140

A planter therefore could, at that time, hire eleven servants at
no greater charge, for importation and service, than is now given for
one. The proportion of deficiency will stand as follows:

1703, A proprietor of 300 Negroes, 120 head of stock,
quota of servants 17; charge, —— —— —— £ 238

1770, A proprietor of 300 Negroes, 120 head of stock,
quota of servants 11; charge, —— —— —— —— 1694

It

It is no wonder, therefore, that the planters do not fupply their deficiencies as formerly, by importing indented fervants, but rather pay the penalty, which was fixed, in the year 1715, at 13 *l. per annum*, and rarely exceeds that fum now, it being feldom doubled; or elfe pick up any tranfient vagabonds that chance to fall in their way, and will ferve for 15 *l.* or 20 *l.* a year.

The firft deficiency-law, paffed in 1681, required a greater proportion. According to this, the fame proprietor muft have kept thirty-three. This may account for the greater proportion of white inhabitants in thoſe days, when fuch fervants were to be procured at the moft trifling expence, and maintained at a very cheap rate. In their condition, they were little better than flaves during their term of fervice. They were allowed yearly three fhirts, as many pair of drawers, fhoes and ftockings, and a hat or cap; which were probably of very wretched ftuff, as the penalty for not making fuch an allowance was no more than forty fhillings. Their fubfiftence was directed to be four pound weight of good flefh or fifh *per* week, with a fufficient quantity of plantation provifion, fuch as yams, &c.; and they were fubjected to various penalties for mifdemeanour; viz.

For laying violent hands on their employer; a twelvemonth's *extra* fervice.—Embezzling or wafting goods, of above 40 *s.* value; two years *extra* fervice.—Getting a fellow-fervant with child; a fervice of double the time the woman had to ferve.— Marrying without the confent of their mafter or miftrefs; two years *extra* fervice.—Abfenting from fervice without leave; one week's fervice for every day's abfence.—*Wilfully* catching the venereal, or other difeafe; or *wilfully* getting broken bones, bruifes, &c.; to ferve double the time thereby loft, and for all charges thereby occafioned, at 10 *s.* a month, after the expiration of their indentures.—Concealing a fervant, or flave; one year's fervice, or a whipping of thirty-nine lafhes, at the option of the injured party, on conviction before a juftice.—Stealing timber, or tanning-bark; 3 *l.* penalty, upon conviction.—Forging a certificate of freedom; on conviction, to be pilloried, and lofe both ears.

The only material provifions in their favour were, that they fhould not be whipped *naked*, without order of a juftice of the

P p 2

peace; nor be turned off, when grown infirm, under pretence of giving them freedom; nor be buried until the body had been viewed by a juſtice of the peace, conſtable, tything man, or two neighbours.

But the penal clauſes of theſe acts have long ſince been-extinct; and at preſent the white indented ſervants are laid under few reſtrictions, except ſo far as reſpects their ſerving out their term. And by a later law, paſſed in 1736, the miſbehaviour of ſervants during their contract, and all differences between them and their maſters (overſeers of ſugar-plantations excepted) are to be heard and determined before two juſtices of the peace, according to the nature of the caſe, and without appeal, ſave that they are to inflict no puniſhment extending to life or limb. Where they have not freſh meat, they are allowed four barrels of beef *per annum*, with flour, or bread-kind in proportion; but, in general, their allowance is not limited; and the tradeſmen and better ſort meſs with the overſeer of the reſpective plantations, unleſs he thinks proper to keep a ſeparate table for them, which is ſometimes the cuſtom on very large eſtates, where they rarely eat any ſalt-meat, except for a forenoon luncheon.

Any maſter of a ſhip attempting to carry off the iſland, or run away with another perſon's white indented ſervant, without a diſcharge from the employer, is, on conviction, to be adjudged guilty of felony, without benefit of clergy, and to ſuffer accordingly.

Many of the artificers who have come under theſe contracts, if they were ſober and diligent, have ſettled afterwards in the iſland, and acquired very handſome fortunes, particularly the Scotch. That part of Britain has likewiſe furniſhed ſome of the ableſt ſurveyors known here. There are generally twelve of theſe, who are commiſſioned by the governor, give bond in 300*l.* for the faithful execution of their office, and are put under ſeveral regulations by law. This buſineſs was formerly very profitable; and ſtill is ſo in the hands of able draughtſmen, the charges of making plans being extremely high: beſides, the ignorance and knavery of ſurveyors, formerly employed to run out the wood-lands, have cauſed ſuch errors as to breed numberleſs diſputes concerning the true fixings and boundaries even to this day; and the adjuſtment

of

of thefe contentions is a perpetual fund for employing and fupporting the profeffors of the geometric art.

The Jews were very early fettled in this ifland, attracted no lefs
by the quantity of gold and filver brought into circulation here,
than the mild difpofition of the government towards them. In
fome of the other fugar-iflands they were profcribed, by admitting
the evidence of pagan flaves againft them in the courts of juftice.
Yet, although this government was comparatively lenient, they
were oppreffed, in fome inftances, conformably to that perfecuting
fpirit which zealous Chriftians ufed antiently to manifeft towards
all thofe who differed from them in matters of faith, particularly
Jews, Turks, and Infidels. But it muft be owned, that the raf-
cally tricks, for which both antient and modern Jews have always
been diftinguifhed, may have ferved not a little to embitter the popular hatred againft them. In 1681, a law paffed in Jamaica to
prevent clipping and falfifying of coin, and debafing of gold and
filver wares. The Jews were, at that time, the principal workers
in gold and filver. Their fondnefs for this craft in all ages is remarkable, and proves the gainfulnefs of it; and it is ftill more fo,
that perhaps there feldom has been fuch a law enacted in any country, which did not abound with thefe Jewifh artifts.

I think it was in the reign of William III, that the council of
this ifland addreffed the crown to expel all the Jews from this part
of the Britifh dominions, not for the fubftantial reafon above affigned, but for a very whimfical one, viz. becaufe " they were de-
" fcended from the crucifiers of the bleffed Jefus." I need not
mention, that his majefty did not think fit to comply with their requeft. The gentlemen were not deep enough read in hiftory to
difcover, that the Romans, and not the Jews, punifhed by cruci-
fixion. But, if they fuppofed the Jews of Jamaica to be the lineal defcendents from that part of the Jerufalem mob which accufed our Saviour before the Roman governor, and, by importuning
for his execution, became *participes criminis*, and fo tranfmitted the
guilt down to their third and fourth generations; we muft admire
their fkill in pedigrees, who could thus trace the line of defcent
through a courfe of near feventeen centuries. In thefe days of ignorance, and long after, they were not taxed like other fubjects,

but

but obliged to raife among them a certain annual tribute, which the affembly varied at pleafure. During the government of Sir Thomas Lynch, they were affeffed the annual fum of 750l., befides one fhilling in the pound on their rents. In governor Molefworth's time, they began to make a confiderable figure, and were permitted to erect fynagogues, and perform divine worfhip according to their own ritual. And from this period we begin to date their deliverance out of bondage in the ifland.

It is uncertain, whether at the fame period they purchafed the intereft of a commander in chief to obtain the royal inftruction, forbidding the governor for the time being to give affent to any bill impofing this partial taxation ; but it was probable from this origin their cuftom began of prefenting every new governor, upon his arrival, with a peace-offering, confifting of a purfe of doubloons. I have heard, that the firft oblation of this fort was, for decency-fake, conveyed in a *pye*; whence it has obtained this nick-name. The fmaller douceur, prefented to a lieutenant-governor, is ftyled a *tort*; and the ftill fmaller perquifite, to the fecretary, a *tartlet* [*y*]. Oppreffion had taught them, that no argument was fo powerful as this in foliciting for protection. It muft be acknowledged, however, that thefe people have fhewn themfelves very good and ufeful fubjects upon many occafions. When the French invaded

		Piftoles.
[*y*] Their prefent to a new governor in chief has generally been, as I am told, about		200
To a lieutenant-governor,		150
To a prefident, I fuppofe the fame.		
To the governor's, &c. fecretary,		50

I fhall take the opportunity of mentioning here, what I omitted in the proper place, that the governor's fecretary has no fixed falary; nor any fees allowed by law, except a trifling fum on certificates of freedom taken out, which are renewable only once in feven years: but his income is rated by fome at about 1000l. fterling *per annum*; and by others much higher. It arifes from the gratuities he receives on all civil and military commiffions and warrants iffued by the governor, efpecially upon entrance of the latter into office; at which time it has been often the practice to renew fuch commiffions, &c. merely to put money into the fecretary's pocket. And fome governors have condefcended to take a fhare in the profits ; for they are fometimes confiderable, fifty piftoles having often been given for an honorary poft in the militia. Other emoluments accrue from let-paffes, granted to foreign veffels entering Port Royal harbour (which may be reckoned among the number of impolitic reftrictions laid upon the trade of the ifland); likewife from orders for furveying crown-lands, and *fiats*; and, in fhort, from every other inftrument vefting any office, preferment, or commiffion, within the governor's gift or appointment. But the principal harveft is gleaned, in time of war, from the grant of letters of marque, and flags of truce.

this

this ifland during the government of Sir William Beefton, they oppofed the enemy with great courage. Their knowledge of foreign languages, and intercourfe with their brethren, difperfed over the Spanifh and other Weft-India colonies, have contributed greatly to extend the trade, and increafe the wealth, of the ifland; for they have always been the chief importers of bullion : and the riches they acquire to themfelves are expanded in effect to the public welfare; for they are not mere brokers and money-holders that may remove *ad libitum*; they are allowed to purchafe lands and tenements, and actually poffefs a large fhare of both. This gives them a folid attachment to the intereft and fecurity of Jamaica; which they confider as their home. Their affection is ftill further ftrengthened by the affurance, that, under other governments, they would not be indulged with the enjoyment of the fame rights, privileges, and immunities, which they now hold undifturbed. The provincial laws, it is true, lay them under fome few reftrictions (if they can be properly called fuch, for they rather feem exemptions from burthen, than privations of any benefit).

They may not officiate, nor write, in any of the public offices. They muft fupply their deficiencies out of their own nation, and not by indented Chriftian fervants; but they are allowed to hire Chriftians for this purpofe.

Their religion neceffarily excludes them from exercifing any poft under the government above the rank of conftable; but the policy of the ifland requires all of them, without diftinction, to bear arms in the militia. If they cannot, on account of their religion, hold pofts of profit, they are neverthelefs excufed, for the fame reafon, from troublefome offices, that have no profit annexed to them, which are here exceedingly numerous: fo that the balance, upon the whole, feems much in their favour. The lenity of the laws, which tolerate them in the free exercife of their religion and cuftoms, permit them to hold landed property, protect them equally with other fubjects in the poffeffion and enjoyment of it, and load them with no partial or oppreffive taxations, altogether forms a very ample compenfation for the want of a voice in the legiflature, or courts of juftice. They are confequently contented and happy under this government; and would be more fo, if it was not for

their

1

their own little fchifms in religious matters; for they are divided into two factions, or fects; one of which, called the *Smoufe Jews*, are not acknowledged orthodox by the reft, on account of their having, through the rigours of the inquifition in the Portuguefe and Spanifh dominions, relaxed in fome indifpenfable rituals, or intermarried with Chriftians; by which abomination, they have polluted the pure Ifraelitifh blood with the corrupt ftream of the Gentiles. The *Smoufes* have therefore a diftinct conventicle, or meeting, of their own, at a private houfe, where they vociferate, to the great difturbance of the neighbourhood.

The chief men among the Jews are very worthy perfons, and ought not to be reproached for the vices and villainies of the lower rabble, fince they ftrive all in their power to put them in the way of earning their livelihood honeftly: and, although fome fraudulent bankruptcies now and then happen among the poorer and more knavifh tribe; yet there are no common beggars of their nation, the elders having an eftablifhed fund for the relief of all their poor. They traffic among the Negroes chiefly in falt-fifh, butter, and a fort of cheap pedlary wares, manufactured by their brethren in England. But among the chief men are feveral very opulent planters, and capital merchants, who are connected with great houfes in the city of London. It has been a very ftriking remark, that the multitude of them fettled in this ifland, the purchafes they are continually making both of houfes and lands, and the vaft wealth they collectively have ftaked here, are fure indications that they are delighted with the mildnefs and equity of the government, and reft fatisfied, that their property is entirely fafe, and fecurely held; from a conviction, " that a place of fuch " great importance to the mother-country will never be neglected, " nor fail of receiving all due care and protection." Some perfons have affirmed, that the Jews of this ifland are not fuch rigid obfervers of the Mofaic ritual as their brethren of other countries. Many of them have been charged with the heavy accufation of gratifying their appetites now and then with a pork dinner without licence; and others are faid to purchafe a difpenfation for it of the rabbi, after the manner of Roman catholic epicures in the Lent feafon. Indeed, the Weft-India pork is of fo exquifite a flavour,

that,

that, if Mofes had ever tafted it, he certainly would not have been fo unkind towards his followers as to include it in his catalogue of non-eatables; for I do not know any thing more likely to convert a Jew who wavers in faith in this part of the world, than the temptation of this delicious food ; and it may be owing to the juft confideration of human frailty, that the rabbis here are too politic to interdict abfolutely the moderate ufe of it to the members of their congregation, or perhaps to abftain wholly from it themfelves. In regard to other fects, fome quakers were formerly fettled here, who came principally from Barbadoes. They had a meeting-houfe in Kingfton and a burial ground, fituate Weft from the town, the walls of which are ftill remaining. They afterwards difperfed, and the greater part retired to New-England and Philadelphia. Very few here at this time openly profefs themfelves of this order. The chief inducement for their quitting Jamaica probably was no other than the indifpenfable obligation impofed by its laws, on every man in the ifland, to bear *carnal weapons* in the militia. This ordinance was incompatible with their non-refifting tenets; and all fuch as adhere to them fo rigidly, are doubtlefs very unfit inhabitants for a fugar-colony, which cannot be defended either from foreign or inteftine enemies by a flock of fheep. In 1732, there appears to have been a remnant of them in the ifland; for a law, paffed in that year, entitles them to vote at elections, proving their qualification by affirmation, inftead of oath.

A party of Moravians are fettled here, who in fome particulars feem to hold refemblance to the quakers. They are chiefly, I believe, confined to an eftate in the parifh of St. Elizabeth. In the year 1763, the freeholders of that parifh prefented a petition to the affembly, fetting forth, " that, for fome years paft, many per- " fons, who called themfelves Moravians, had arrived there ; that " they always refufed to do military duty, pleading an exemption " by act of parliament, of which they had particularly availed " themfelves during the late rebellions ; that it was conceived fuch " a pretext entirely fruftrated the ends of the deficiency-law, and " prevented a number of white perfons, capable of bearing arms, " from being employed upon the eftates where thefe drones had " met with encouragement." It does not appear that the affembly interfered at all in this matter. It was thought fufficient, perhaps, that they fhould be left to thofe penalties and articles of war, to which men of every perfuafion are liable in this ifland during martial law. The evafion of thefe fchifmatics is not founded on indifputable grounds; for the act of parliament (22 George II. cap. 30 [z]), which they fet up to fkreen themfelves, feems reftricted to the congregation of *unitas fratrum*, or Moravians, fettled in the North-American provinces. This act admits them to the privilege of making folemn affirmation, inftead of oaths or affidavits, in civil cafes; and difcharges them from perfonal fervice in a military capacity, provided they pay fuch fum of money as may be affeffed or rated on them, in lieu of perfonal fervice: and, to prevent all doubt of their being of the congregation, they muft produce a certificate of their being members of it, figned by fome bifhop of their church, or paftor, neareft to the place of their refidence; and muft likewife folemnly affirm, that they are members as before mentioned; otherwife they are not entitled to the benefit of the act. It feems pretty evident from hence, that this act does not extend to Jamaica, becaufe the laws here exempt no man from military fervice, except the council and fuperannuated perfons; and admit no fine or affeffment in lieu of any man's perfonal duty. Every proprietor of landed eftate here holds under exprefs conditions contained in his patent, that he fhall perfonally bear arms to repel invafions, and fupprefs infurrections; and his refufal to do fo would make his patent voidable. It is true, the owners of thefe Moravian properties, being non-refident, efcape from perfonal fervice; but they ought to employ fuch agents, or fervants, in the management, who will yield due obedience to the laws of the colony. That exemption cannot poffibly be legal, or juftifiable, which, if it extended to all, would endanger the ruin of the colony. What, for example, would become of it, if the feduction of their example fhould make converts of all the militia in the ifland, fo that every man of them might turn Moravian, and fet up the plea of confcience to excufe himfelf from his proper fhare of the general duty and fervice, which the very being of the ifland

[z] N. B. This act prohibits them from ferving on juries, or being evidences in criminal cafes.

I   has

has rendered indispensable to all? The consequence is evident. In order, therefore, that this sect may quietly enjoy their religious scruples, but at the same time make them inoffensive to the public weal, every Moravian proprietor ought to compound for the personal service of himself, his substitutes, and servants, who are members of the same church, by being subjected to a double deficiency-tax; which is the only fair compensation, because it leaves them the alternative of providing an equal number of servants who *will* fight, in the room of those whose hands are tied up by conscience. Nor is this repugnant to their principles; for although they refuse carrying arms, yet they profess willingness to contribute towards the pecuniary charge of war; which the quakers refuse. Of the two sects the Moravians are therefore the better citizens, since nothing can be more hateful in the present state of the world than the pusillanimous doctrine of non-resistance against an invading enemy.

The Moravians possess a large tract of land in the province of Philadelphia, where they have a settlement called Bethlem, and are very zealous in converting the Indians. They publish no creed, nor confession of faith; use musical instruments in their worship; and preach in an enthusiastical strain. The style of their hymns has such a pruriency and wantonness in it, as can scarcely be reconciled with the chaste fervour of a truly pious mind. They are said to encourage marriage among their young people, but in a strange way; for they are obliged to cast lots, in order to preserve an equality among themselves. Whether their doctrines are strictly consistent with good morality, or not, we are not particularly informed. Kalm mentions, that at Philadelphia, where they have a large meeting-house, they used to perform service, not only twice or three times every Sunday, but likewise every night after it grew dark, till they were interrupted by some wicked young fellows, who accompanied every line and stanza of their hymns with the symphony of an instrument which sounded like the note of a cuckoo. And, upon repeated serenadings of this kind, they discontinued their nocturnal conventions. We are to suppose, that nothing passed among these godly people in the dark but what was extremely decent and proper; yet the convenience which this veil

might

might adminifter to the practical performance of thofe rapturous careffes, ravifhing extafies, thrilling tranfports, with all the kiffings, pantings, fighings, dyings, which fill up the lufcious meafure of their pfalmody, might doubtlefs be apt to ftrike the imaginations of the prophane, and incline them to fufpect, that the faints behind the curtain voluptuoufly mingle a little of the fenfual with their fpiritual feelings.

These which I have mentioned are all the fchifmatics publickly avowed in Jamaica: not but there are many Roman catholics, and diffenters, who enjoy their refpective opinions in private, without feeking to form themfelves into diftinct congregations, or to put themfelves to the expence of maintaining preachers or paftors.

The laws of the ifland are favourable to the admiffion of foreigners. They empower the governor, by inftrument under the broad feal, to naturalize any alien who may come to fettle in the ifland, having firft taken the oath of allegiance: but they are required, within thirty days after their arrival, to give in their names, trades, vocations, &c. to any *cuftos*, or chief magiftrate, and apply for their letter of naturalization.

They are then declared entitled to the fame immunities, rights, laws, and privileges, of the ifland, and in as full and ample manner, as any of the king's natural-born fubjects, or as if they themfelves had been born within any of his majefty's realms or dominions. And, in order that fuch patents may be obtained at little charge, the governor is to receive five pounds currency, and his fecretary ten fhillings, each, and no more, for paffing them.

This matter is further regulated by act of parliament, paffed 13 George II.; the object whereof feems to be, that aliens, tranfporting themfelves into any of the Britifh colonies, fhould become entitled to the rights of natural-born fubjects, on condition that they remain and refide therein for a certain term of years: for a multitude of tranfient perfons, transferring their effects, perhaps for the fake of traffic, and having no fixed abode, nor making any fettlement, would add nothing to the fecurity of a colony; but, on the contrary, might do it hurt, by carrying off the profits, gained on their trade, to be fpent in a foreign dominion, and by excluding many real Britifh merchants and traders, who would

otherwife.

otherwife have fettled in the colony. It enacts, that all perfons, born out of his majefty's liegeance, who fhall refide for the fpace of feven years,. or more, in any of his American colonies; and that fhall not have been abfent from thence above two months at any one time ; and that fhall take and fubfcribe the oaths of allegiance; or, if quakers, fubfcribe the declaration ; or, if Jews, with the omiffion of fome Chriftian expreffions) ; and fhall alfo fubfcribe the profeffion of their Chriftian belief (Jews excepted), as directed by the ftatute, 1 William and Mary, before any judge of the colony they fhall refide in ; and fhall have received the facrament of the Lord's-fupper in fome proteftant or reformed congregation in Great-Britain, or in the faid colonies (quakers and Jews excepted), within three months of his or her fo qualifying, and producing a certificate thereof, figned by the minifter of the congregation, and attefted by two witneffes ; a certificate of all thefe preliminaries, having been complied with under the refpective colony feal, fhall be a fufficient proof of his or her being thereby become a natural-born fubject of Great-Britain to all intents and purpofes whatfoever : and the fecretary of the colony fhall annually tranfmit, to the board of trade and plantations, lifts of the faid perfons fo naturalized, to be regiftered in their office: provided that fuch perfons fhall not thereby be enabled to be a privy-counfellor, or a member of either houfe of parliament, or capable of taking, having, or enjoying, any office, or place of truft, within the kingdoms of Great-Britain or Ireland, either civil or military ; or taking any grant from the crown of any lands, tenements, &c. within the faid kingdoms.

In the conftruction of this act, I do not apprehend, that the abfence of two months implies any thing more than a removal to fome other dominion, or territory, of fome foreign prince. An alien, qualified as the law directs, may have his *domicile*, or fixed habitation, in one of the Britifh colonies, and neverthelefs, by reafon of his vocation, either of a merchant or feaman, be obliged, from time to time, to pafs to and fro between that and fome other Britifh colony, fo as to be abfent neceffarily above two months at one time. But, where his freehold and family are located, there is (properly fpeaking) his *domicile*, or home. And it would be in-

consistent

confiftent with the liberal fpirit and meaning of the act to fay, that an alien, having qualified in Jamaica, and purchafed a fettlement in that ifland, but making a voyage every year to the North-American continent, in the way of trade, or for health, which might caufe him to be abfent from Jamaica fomewhat more than two months, fhould therefore forfeit his acquired right of a natural-born fubject. It is more reafonable to conclude, that a refidence in any of the Britifh American colonies for the term of feven years, without having been abfent above two months from Britifh territory during that fpace, effectually meets the intention of the act.

Foreign proteftants, naturalized under the Jamaica law, poffefs all the rights of natural-born fubjects *quoad* that ifland. They may purchafe lands, or inherit, or take grants from the crown; have a right to reprefent, and be reprefented, in the affembly, if they enjoy the neceffary qualification in eftate; and may hold and exercife places of truft in the military and civil departments; for fome of them have acted under commiffion as field-officers in the militia, judges in the fupreme court and common-pleas, juftices of the peace, &c.; and the late fecretary, Mr. Ballaguire, was a naturalized German. But I do not remember any in the privy-council.

The claufe, 7 and 8 William III. § 12, enacting, " that all " places of truft, or what relates to the treafury of the Britifh " Weft-India iflands, fhall be in the hands of native-born fubjects " of England or Ireland, or of the faid iflands," feems not to exclude thofe who by naturalization are made natural-born.

The foreigners, who have taken the benefit of thefe acts, are not very numerous in Jamaica; but, if any townfhips fhould be formed in the central parts of the ifland, perhaps none would be fitter for the purpofe of inhabiting them than French proteftants.

I fhall next confider the ftate of the foldiers quartered here. The ifland ftood but little in need of regular forces, for its defence, till about the year 1730; when the depredations and outrages, committed by the Maroons (or wild Negroes, as they were called) had gone on to fuch a length, that the fettlements were in many parts deferted, and the inhabitants thrown under the oppreffion of very heavy taxes, for fupporting a continual inteftine war, which greatly interrupted the bufinefs of their plantations. Thefe motives

tives engaged governor Hunter to folicit the duke of Newcaftle (then at the head of the miniftry) for two regiments of foot; which were accordingly detached from the garrifon of Gibraltar to their affiftance. The people were told, that thefe troops would be no burthen to them, for that they were to be victualed and paid at the national expence, as they had before been at Gibraltar. However, the victualers not arriving in due time, the affembly were called upon to make fome provifion for them in the *interim*; to which they confented, and paffed a bill for this purpofe, to have a duration for fix months only. The governor had affured them, that, fo foon as the victualers fhould arrive, the provifions they brought fhould be diftributed inftantly among the troops, that the ifland might not be unneceffarily put to any further expence for their fubfiftence. But no fooner were they arrived, than he caufed the provifions to be fold, and retained the proceeds in his own hands, meanly taking advantage of the preffing neceffity which the inhabitants were under of keeping the regiments, at any rate, for their defence. This proceeding, fo difhonourable on the governor's part, firft gave rife to the country-pay, or allowance, which is now granted by annual bill. Thefe troops were, foon aftewards, difbanded here; and fuch of the men as inclined to ftay were formed into eight independent companies, and kept in pay by the ifland until the Negroes were brought to fubmiffion; which happened in the adminiftration of governor Trelawny, about the year 1739. In the year 1745, they were incorporated into a regiment, and the command given to that governor. They then became intitled to receive pay from the crown; but, neverthelefs, the affembly made an additional provifion of twenty fhillings *per* week to each officer, and five fhillings to each private. This pay has fince received confiderable augmentation; and it is at prefent upon the following eftablifhment:

	Per Week.			Per Ann.						
	£	s.	d.	£	s.	d.	£	s.	d.	
To every lieutenant-colonel, major, captain, lieutenant, or enfign, ——	1	0	0	52	0	0	116	0	0	Married officer.
Captain's lodging, ———————				25						
His wife, ————— ———		10	0	26						
Child, —— ——— ——— ——		5	0	13						
Serjeant, corporal, drum, or private, —		5	0	13						Non-commiffioned and private.
Wife, ——— ——— ———		3	9	9	15	0	29	5	0	
Child, ——— ——— ———		2	6	6	10	0				

For Lodgings.				Per Annum.
Lieutenant-colonel,	—	—	—	£ 50
Major	—	—	—	50
Lieutenant, enfign, or furgeon,	—	—	—	20

They are likewife allowed to buy their rum free of the ifland duty, which is a faving of from 1 s. to 1 s. 6 d. per gallon; an advantage purpofely given them by the legiflature, that they might be enabled to buy it of the beft quality, inftead of debauching with the balderdafh liquor, fold under the name of rum by the keepers of retail fhops.

The fubfiftence is in the three towns of St. Jago, Kingfton, and Port Royal, paid into the hands of the men; but, in the country-quarters, to their commanding officers, for the ufe of the foldiers. A diverfity of opinion has prevailed in regard to this mode of payment; as the foldiers in fome of the country quarters have, in one or two inftances, appeared to have been defrauded of their dues, or fupplied with putrid and unwholefome provifions, which were fold to them much above their prime-coft. It was argued, that, with money in their hands, the men might purchafe much better in quality, and more in quantity, of frefh meat and wholefome victuals; and that every country-barrack would attract a market for the fale of hogs, poultry, frefh fifh, fruits, and roots, which are articles produced and vended by almoft all the Negroes.

On the other hand, it was alledged, that, by paying the allowance in money to the common foldiers, they would become, in fome degree, independent of their officers; that they would diffipate it in fpirituous liquors, grow enervated with tipling, relaxed in their difcipline, and impaired in their vigour and health.

I do not take upon me to reconcile thefe different opinions; but certain it is, that all the men are not prone to drunkennefs, in particular thofe who have wives and children; that they prefer frefh meat to falt, and the many excellent roots, pulfe, and herbs, of the ifland produce, to bifcuit, which will not keep any long time undecayed in this climate; that a pound of frefh meat is far more nutritive, and will go much further in fatisfying hunger, than a pound of beef hardened with falt; that falt-beef creates an artificial thirft; and that this produces a conftant appetite for drink,

and

and therefore moft likely, either to make fots of thofe men who were not fuch before, or to confirm others more inveterately, in their drunken habits; and, laftly, that money and a demand are the only things requifite to procure a regular and well-fupplied market in a country which abounds with provifion. There is, moreover, a very great difference in the air and fituation of the different barracks; fo that, in fome of them, a diet on falt pro-vifion, concurring with any local depravity of the atmofphere, may difpofe the body to very malignant diftempers; while, in other barracks, the fame diet may prove much lefs injurious to a foldier's health. Thus, of fifty unfeafoned men, quartered at an inland barrack for three years, not one died of any diftemper; though other companies of the fame regiment, quartered on unhealthy fpots near the coaft, were fickly, and buried feveral of their men. I would not mean to infinuate any thing to the difadvantage of fo refpectable a body as the officers in general are; but fome among them are not immaculate; nor is it to be fuppofed but they are fubject, like other men, to human frailties. The worthier part of them, I am convinced, upon a due confideration of the fubject, might fall on fome plan of regulation, to the end that thefe bene-volent aids, which the inhabitants grant to the poor foldiers and their families, may not be mifapplied; that their health fhould be effectually confulted, as well by feeding them with wholefome pro-vifions, as by reftraining them from the immoderate ufe of fpi-rituous liquors.

An officer, who attends ftrictly to the health of his men in both cafes, certainly renders the moft effential fervice to the king and to the public, and makes the beft return to the good intentions of the people, by thus fupporting the ability of the troops, to give that protection in time of need, which, I conceive, is the chief defign of their being ftationed in this ifland.

By the encouragements given to the troops, the fervice here is become far lefs difagreeable than in moft other parts of the Weft-Indies. The private men, who are married, are, by living in a regular manner, more healthy than the unmarried. The children are very little burthenfome to their parents; and, when a woman has the misfortune of lofing her hufband, fhe continues but a fhort time in a state of viduity: the same reason, which in England might deter any suitors from addressing her, namely a crowd of children, is here the certain recommendation to a number of candidates for the honour of her hand; and happy is he, who succeeds, and gains her in marriage; for he enters into present possession of her children's pay, which continues even though some of them may be capable of earning an income with their own hands. And from this source, for every able-bodied soldier thus sent abroad from Great-Britain, that kingdom may possibly receive back, at the time the forces are recalled, a large stock of young recruits, to supply the losses occasioned by death during the abode of the regiments in Jamaica. But, if any stay behind, they probably acquire more riches to the nation by exerting their industry in the colony, than they could have done had they returned to the mother country.

The author of a pamphlet, entitled, " Considerations upon the " Military Establishments of Great-Britain and her Colonies," recommends to government, " that the troops, intended for garri- " soning the West-Indies, should, after passing three years at New- " York, be removed to the West-Indies; and, after three years " longer stay to garrison those parts, should be recalled home, " being first compleated to their full numbers before their return to " Britain; and such numbers to be supplied by the respective islands " and colonies." The former part of this scheme seems plausible enough, because the vicinity of New-York to the West-Indies may admit of such a remove with great expedition and facility; and because the troops, after enduring three North-American summers, which are even hotter than the same season of the year in our West-India islands, may be supposed tolerably well seasoned to the change. But their cloathing should be very different for the West-India service from what might be thought necessary in North-America; and they ought to arrive at their West-India destination in December, January, February, or March, that they might not, in separating to their country-quarters, be exposed to either the inclemency of the rainy seasons, or the great heats of the summer months. The author's proposition about recruiting the regiments on the spot is by no means admissible with respect to the West-In-

dia

dia iflands; for, if it was practicable to make fuch drains from thefe iflands, already in want of white men, for fuch a purpofe, they would occafion a very great infecurity, by wafting the fubftantial ftrength of every colony every third year, and by that means endanger our fettlements in them, without effecting any collateral benefit either to the army or nation; for fuch recruits would be of very little fervice after their emigration to Europe; the change to a damp, cold climate, and hard duty, would foon render them invalids. Befides, their inlifting of hired and indented fervants (for none other are likely to offer) would inevitably obftruct the planting bufinefs, and occafion continual quarrels and law-fuits between the planters and the military; which, in their confequences, might prove extremely embarraffing to government both abroad and at home.

The laws, for inftance, of Jamaica inflict a penalty of 200 *l.* on any captain, or commander, of any fhip, attempting to carry away a hired or indented fervant as a failor or paffenger. They make the carrying off any fuch fervant, by any perfon, felony, without benefit of clergy; and impofe a penalty likewife of 20 *l.* on every perfon hiding, hiring, or employing, a hired or indented fervant without a difcharge from his laft mafter or employer, attefted by a juftice of the peace. The parliament, no lefs attentive to the fecurity and welfare of the Weft-India iflands, in 1746, paffed an act to prevent the impreffing of mariners in thofe parts; and, in 1756, when the defence of the North-American provinces required that indented fervants fhould be inlifted, they took care to reftrain the permiffion, by the moft exprefs words, to " the Britifh colo-" nies upon the *continent* of America;" which evinces their caution, that no pretence might be made for extending this act to the Weft-India colonies.

The North-American recruits are, in general, unfit for the Weft-India fervice; for which reafon (unlefs there appears any invincible neceffity to juftify fuch an expedient), it might be more advifeable to recruit from Europe than from that continent; for the North-Americans are far lefs hardy than the Europeans, and, during the laft and former war, died in numbers whenever they were removed to a diftance from home. It is very difficult for

them

them to inure themfelves to a climate different from their own; nor do they bear tranfplanting into the Southern colonies fo well as the Britifh, Irifh, Germans, or Swifs. I cannot therefore but furmife, that fuch a project, if carried into execution, would prove in the iffue no better than a plan for facrificing triennially fo many hundred poor victims, and effentially diftreffing the fervice. In the expectation of two thoufand effective foldiers to be conftantly kept here, the inhabitants expended near 100,000*l.* in building barracks for their accommodation; which are fo difpofed among the different parifhes, that they are calculated to afford a general protection to the internal parts, and capable of holding more than that number of men, befides their officers. But, in 1764, when the 49th and 74th regiments were relieved, the people had the mortification to find, that, inftead of two regiments of one thoufand men each, they were to be protected by two of four hundred and fifty each; which was lefs than one half the complement they expected; and confequently their barracks, on which they had laid out fuch large fums of money, raifed by taxes, which fell very heavily on the planters, for three years, were left to moulder into decay, for want of being tenanted.

The fmalleft number that ought be cantoned here, for the internal fecurity of the ifland in time of peace, is an eftablifhment of one thoufand and thirty-five effectives, to be diftributed according to the plan hereafter defcribed; by which, every one of the new barracks would be garrifoned, and kept from going to decay; and the guard fo well balanced in the refpective counties and parifhes, in proportion to the danger they may feverally be expofed to from fudden infurrections, as would probably be an effectual curb upon the mutinous and difaffected. But, to form a body for this eftablifhment, either two reduced regiments fhould be raifed to five hundred and twenty-five men each; or one regiment, under the name of the Royal American, be compleated to one thoufand and thirty-five men. In time of war, if government fhould judge two regiments neceffary for the better defence of the ifland againft foreign enemies, it will appear from the following ftate of the barracks, that they are in a condition to accommodate between two and three thoufand men exclufive of their officers.

Prefent

Prefent State of the different Barracks:

County.	Parifh.	Situation of Barracks.	Number of Troops they can receive, exclufive of Officers.	
Middlefex,	St. Catharine,	St. Jago de la Vega,		300
	Ditto,	Fort Augufta,		300
	St. Dorothy,	Old Harbour,		70
	St. John,	Point Hill,		70
	St. Mary,	Bagnals,		70
	Ditto,	Port Maria,		60
	Ditto,	Auracabeffa,		60
	Ditto,	Anotto Bay,		70
	St. Anne,	Port St. Anne,		70
	Clarendon,	Chapel,		100
	Vere,	Carlifle Bay,		50
				1220
Surry,	Port Royal,	Fort Charles,		300
	Kingfton,	Kingfton,		200
	Ditto,	Rock Fort,		70
	St. Andrew,	Stony Hill,		120
	St. Thomas in the Eaft,	Morant Bay,		25
	Ditto,	Port Morant,		25
	Ditto,	Bath,		25
	Portland,	Fort George,		70
	St. George,	Gibraltar Point,		70
				905
Cornwall,	St. Elizabeth,	Black River,		30
	Weftmoreland,	Savannah la Mar,		70
	Ditto,	Delve,		100
	Hanover,	St. Lucia,		47
	St. James,	Montego Bay,		100
		Marthabrae,		100
				447
		Total in the three counties,		2572

Befides thefe, there are feveral old barracks, which were built during the war with the Marons, and are ftill kept in repair; viz. in Middlefex fix; Surry two; Cornwall three; in all, eleven; which are capable of holding a confiderable body of men, if occafion fhould ever require their being garrifoned [a]. A governor once replied, when he was folicited for a party to be quartered at one of the inland barracks, " that his majefty's troops were fent " hither to guard the coafts, not to protect the internal diftricts " from Negroe infurgents." But it is hoped that every adminiftration will not be guided by fo abfurd a policy. The men of property in this ifland pay an ample contribution, in order that it may be protected, not fo much from French or Spaniards, as againft the machinations of the many thoufand flaves, which, in proportion as the fettlements advance further and further into the heart of the

[a] Thefe would be moft convenient for receiving the corps of rangers propofed, under the head of " Militia."

country,

country, grow the more formidable from their multitude: I fpeak chiefly of imported Africans, who are the moft to be feared. Men muft firft believe their life and fortune tolerably fecure, before they will venture to fettle. But if the troops, inftead of being garrifoned in the internal parts, where the greateft danger lies, where the fettlements are few and fcattered, and incapable of defending themfelves, are ranged along the coafts, which in time of peace require no fuch guards, and at any time are leaft healthy, and too remote from the centre to afford a feafonable relief; can the inhabitants be faid to receive that degree of protection from them, to which they are entitled? It may perhaps be never prudent to leave the maritime forts without fome garrifon, to prevent furprizes; and the larger towns require a fufficiently ftrong guard, for many obvious reafons. To anfwer therefore every one of thefe purpofes, we may fuppofe the following eftablifhment of a corps, for this fervice, to confift of

Twenty companies, of fifty privates each, —— —— 1000
Two field-officers,
Twenty captains,
Twenty lieutenants,
Thirty furgeons mates,
Two furgeons in chief,
Forty ferjeants,
Twenty corporals, —— —— —— —— 134

The complement total, 1034

The offices of barrack-mafters and adjutants might be executed by fome of the *cour* of officers.

For their cantonment in time of peace, I propofe the following fcheme; by which it will appear, that the principal towns and port are well guarded, and the moft unfettled diftricts as well defended, as the number can admit on the fcale of an equal protection.

Head-

Head-quarters, St. Jago de la Vega.

County.	Parish.	Situation.	N° of each Garrison.	Total in each County.
Middlesex,	St. Catharine,	St. Jago,	100	
	Ditto,	Fort Augusta,	125	
	St. Dorothy,	Old Harbour,	25	
	St. John,	Point Hill,	50	
	St. Mary,	Port Maria,	25	
	Ditto,	Auracabessa,	12	
	Ditto,	Anotto Bay,	12	
	St. Anne,	Port St. Anne,	25	
	Clarendon,	Chapel,	50	
	Vere,	Carlisle Bay,	12	436
Surry,	Port Royal,	Port Royal,	150	
	Kingston,	Kingston and Rock Fort,	75	
	St. Andrew,	Stony Hill,	50	
	St. Thomas in the East,	Morant Bay,	12	
	Ditto,	Port Morant,	12	
	Ditto,	Bath,	25	
	Portland,	Fort George,	50	
	St. George,	Gibraltar,	50	424
Cornwall,	St. Elizabeth,	Black River,	25	
	Westmoreland,	Savannah la Mar,	25	
	Ditto,	Delve,	25	
	Hanover,	Lucea,	25	
	St. James,	Montego Bay,	50	
		Marthabrae,	25	175
		Total,		1035

The additional expence to the island for their maintenance would (by the best calculation I can make) not exceed the present annual supply more than 7000*l*., even allowing one third of men and officers to be married, and to have one child each at an average which is certainly a very large reckoning; so that the island, if it be thought necessary, is capable of supporting such an augmentation; much more so (it may be imagined) at this time than some years ago, when the assembly petitioned for a constant establishment of two thousand men, which would have brought upon them an additional charge, of at least 18,000*l. per annum*.

In regard to the state of health of the soldiers here, the following table will convey some idea of it. I have already noticed several causes of their ill health in particular cantonments, which may admit of some fit regulations for their remedy. The complement of the two regiments, landed here in June, 1764, and lately relieved, consisted, as I am informed (at four hundred and fifty each reduced establishment), of nine hundred effectives; and it is proper

to

to remark, that the 36th was kept at head-quarters and neighbour-hood; and the 66th at the out-posts.

DEATHS.

	Regiment 36th.				Regiment 66th.
1764,	30				102
5,	53				32
6,	30				30
7,	22				30
8,	27				41
9,	29				32
1770,	42				43
1771,	28				23
Totals,	261				333
Average, *per annum*,	$32\frac{5}{8}$				$41\frac{5}{8}$

According to this table, of the 36th there died, *per annum*, one in every fourteen; and, of the 66th, one in every eleven. The smallest loss of the 36th was about one in twenty; and, of the 66th, about one in nineteen. The havoc among the 66th, on the first year of their arrival, I have accounted for, in speaking of the quarters of Black River and some other out-posts. In that year a detachment was sent on the Havannah service; and the state of the troops appeared, from the return then laid before the affembly, as follows; viz.

Detachment,	500 Men
Effectives remaining,	301
In the hospital,	104
	905

Of those in hospital, the governor mentioned that several were recovered fit for duty since the last returns had been made; and that others were in a fair way.

The calculations, which Dr. Price has made, are;
Deaths, — 1 in $20\frac{3}{4}$, London; — 1 in $19\frac{1}{2}$, Vienna; — *per annum.*

Now, it is worthy experiment, whether, by proper diet of fresh meat, a moderate allowance of the best rum, and care in removing all nuisances, and sources of putrid distempers, from the several barracks in this island, the deaths might not be reduced to

the

the ftandard of London or Vienna. Let us however compare the above account (bad as it may feem) with two examples, one taken from the Eaft, and the other from the Weft-Indies. It was not long fince given in evidence, before the Houfe of Commons, that the climate of the Eaft-Indies deftroyed 700 out of 1000 men, in one campaign after their arrival. On the expedition to St. Vincent, one regiment buried 122 in one year, and 309 in three; the average of which is about 1 in every 4. The truth is, as Dr. Lind has well obferved, that every ifland in the Weft-Indies, and other parts of the world, has its healthy and unhealthy fpots. The nature and exigencies of the fervice prevent the troops, fent over to garrifon our larger iflands, from being kept on any one particular fpot, which might be felected on account of its good air; in fome cafes neceffity, in others inattention to the important evils, which originate from feemingly trifling caufes, have occafioned the erection of barracks in very improper fituations; near fwamps, the oozy banks of rivers, and ftinking lagoon waters. Sometimes an injudicious pofition of the fick wards and offices, has thrown a conftant annoyance of an impure air upon the healthy; and fometimes a tendency to ficknefs, and bad fevers, has arifen from the very materials with which the barracks have been built. Thus, the barracks in Clarendon and at Bath, being of ftone, were found infalutary to the men lodged in them, until the walls were lined with plaifter. Some fpecies of ftone are extremely porous, imbibing and tranfuding moifture freely; others are fo firm and compact in their texture, that they condenfe the watery particles in damp weather upon their furface, which trickle down the fides of walls, or pafs off again in a reek. Stone buildings, without fome precautions, are not wholefome habitations in the Weft-Indies. They ought to be furrounded with a fhed, or piazza, to keep off the beating of heavy fhowers; the walls within fhould either be lined with a facing of brickwork, plaiftered, or of boards, fet off about 1 or 2 inches, leaving a fpace behind for the free circulation of air between, in order to prevent their becoming damp. The ill contrivance of the barrack at Lucea, I have noticed in the account of Hanover parifh; if the hofpital there, the ftercorary, and kitchen, were changed to leeward of the dwelling, this barrack is in other refpects not ill fituated for health. The fame remark may be applied likewife, to fome other barracks in the ifland, which require more windows for admitting the air, proper remedies for damp walls, the draining away of ftagnant water, and removal of the fick wards and offenfive fmells, to a quarter where they may not incommode the men who are in health.

Reafon and experience point out, that men, coming from a cold into a hot climate, fhould make the change at that feafon of the year, when the degree of heat is leaft at the place of their de-ftination; by which means, the tranfition will be more gradual, and therefore productive of a lefs violent fhock to the conftitution. On their firft arrival, the change of climate moft commonly brings on a diarrhœa. If the men at this time, and during the fucceeding twelve months, are not hindered from befotting themfelves with new rum, or from dieting too conftantly upon falt fifh, falt beef or pork, and rancid butter; they will probably be feized with violent fevers of the putrid clafs, and it may be expected that many of them will die.

The moft wholefome beverage for them would be fugar and water, with or without a moderate allowance of old rum; what is ftill preferable, is the *cool drink*, prepared here by many of the free Negroe and Mulatta women, who vend it cheap to the foldiers. It is made with a mixture of fugar, guaicum chips, and ginger, infufed together in hot water, and afterwards worked into a ferment with a piece of frefh gathered chaw-ftick; which, by the quantity of fixed air contained in it, foon excites a confiderable froth, and imparts a flight bitter, of a very agreeable flavour. This drink, when cool and depurated, is racy and pleafant, extremely whole-fome, and, if taken in too large quantities, intoxicates in fome degree, but without caufing any ill effect to the conftitution. This liquor might eafily be brewed twice or oftener in the week, at the barracks, and drank by way of a change. The plantains, yams, and caffava bread, are nutritious, wholefome, and, after a little ufe, preferred by moft of the foldiers to flour bread or bifcuit at their principal meal, and are far cheaper. The potatoes and cocos are not lefs nourifhing. Half a pound of what is called in England *make-weight* beef, confifting of the coarfer parts, with fome of thefe roots, the efculent herbs of the country, fuch as the

colalu,

colalu, ocra, &c. every where to be had in ahundance, with a small seasoning of the country pepper to correct their flatulence, would make a most wholesome and strengthening mess for one or two men, and at no greater charge than about 6 *d.* or at most 7½ *d.* currency.

Particular attention ought likewise to be given to the quality of the water, with which the men are supplied. The barracks at Port Royal and Fort Augusta are served from the Rio Cobre, a person being paid about 400 *l. per annum* for this purpose: it would properly be the surgeon's duty to examine this water from time to time, left, to save a little trouble, it should be taken up too near the mouth of the river, and so be impregnated with the salt water in the harbour: it ought likewise to be suffered to settle for some time in casks or jars, that it may not be drank in a turbid state, which would probably occasion fluxes.

It was intended, some time since, to form a cistern at Port Royal, to be lined with lead, for holding water for the use of the troops quartered there: but it may not be improper to remark here, by the way, that water, standing for any time in a leaded vessel, becomes impregnated with the poisonous qualities of that metal; and from late discoveries, and many well-attested facts, has been found to produce obstinate constipations, and cholicky disorders in the bowels, and not unfrequently paralytic complaints. The water at Rock Fort is brackish and unwholesome; but the officer commanding there, being allowed a boat, and six Negroes to navigate it, might easily supply that small garrison from Kingston. At those places (if any such there are in this island) where none other than brackish water can possibly be procured, it may be rendered potable and wholesome by distillation [b]; or by suffering it to percolate through sand, with which several puncheons, open at one end, might be filled to one third of their depth.

Coolness of dress is another essential article, whenever they are on a march in the country. When lieutenant colonel Spragge

[b] Captain Wallis, of his majesty's ship Dolphin, mentions, that in 5 hours and a quarter's distillation, he obtained from 56 gallons of sea water six and thirty gallons of fresh, at an expence of nine pounds weight of wood, and sixty-nine pounds weight of coals. Thirteen gallons and two quarts remained in the still; and that which came off, had no ill taste, nor (as he had often experienced) any hurtful quality.

Voyage round the World, vol. I. p. 515.

commanded

commanded a party of the forty-ninth regiment, againſt the Maron Negroes, he provided his men with flannel jackets lined with linen ; this was their only covering over the ſhirt. In the day-time, they wore the linen next their bodies, and at night the woollen : in this dreſs, they were cool by day, ſufficiently warm at night, and went through an aſtoniſhing courſe of fatigue, without injury to their healths ; not one of the party having fallen ſick during the whole time of their being on that ſervice.

The laws of the iſland contain very few particulars relative to the regular troops. The hiring, concealing, employing, entertaining, or carrying off any ſoldier belonging to any regiment quartered here, or ſeaman belonging to any of his majeſty's ſhips on this ſtation, without a diſcharge from their commanding officer, ſubjects the offender, upon conviction, to the penalty of 50 l.; and the perſon ſo hired, &c. is admitted an evidence, and entitled to one half the fine for informing.

A ſoldier, maimed or wounded in any publick ſervice, is to be cured and maintained at the publick charge [c].

A lot of land at Bath is reſerved for erecting an infirmary for ſick ſoldiers, labouring under complaints remediable by the waters; and another lot for a burial-ground.

Contiguous to all the old country barracks, one hundred acres are allotted for the uſe of the ſoldiers, who may be poſted in them ; but as they have received no garriſons ſince the pacification with the Marons, the moſt part of theſe lands have been given up to the gentlemen poſſeſſed of plantations near them, on condition of keeping the buildings in conſtant good repair.

I ſhall cloſe this account of the white inhabitants, by obſerving on the very capital errors which ſeem to have been committed by different writers in reſpect of their number ; for ſome have not ſcrupled to aſſert that, in 1720, the iſland contained 60,000 Whites; and that, in 1740, the number was but little reduced. It is impoſſible to reconcile theſe accounts with the repreſentation made by the board of trade to the houſe of lords in 1734, when 7,644 was ſtated as the whole number of Whites at that time upon the iſland. I have ſuppoſed the preſent number (in the preceding parts of this

[c] 1681.

work)

work) about 17,000 exclufive, of tranfients, foldiers, and feamen. At
the very loweft I could not deduct more than 1000 from this calculation; for the towns, villages, and hamlets certainly contain altogether not lefs than 9000; and 7000 will not be thought too many to
allow for the fugar plantations, penns, and fmaller fettlements. In
1750, a gentleman of ability in the ifland made the computation,
that it contained 10,000 planters, merchants, fhopkeepers, hired
and indentured fervants, and artificers; or upwards. To fuppofe
therefore an advance of fix thoufand or more, fince that period, confidering the vaft multiplication of houfes and fettlements, both in the
towns and country parts, feems not at all extravagant. The account
of its population about the time of the great earthquake at Port
Royal, as cited by Dr. Browne, and put at 17,307, is evidently erroneous, having been copied from the eftimate taken when Sir
Thomas Modiford was governor, about the year 1670; which confounds the Whites with the Blacks, and claffes the whole under the
general title of the inhabitants. A more accurate lift was given, during the government of Sir Thomas Lynch, in 1673, which I have
quoted at length. This makes the Whites 8,564, and the whole
number of inhabitants, of all complexions, 18,068. We find by
Sir William Beefton's paper (in the firft book,) that in 1664 the number of regimented Whites was no more than about 3000; which,
being fuppofed one half of the whole, makes 6000, befides thofe
employed in privateering, which may be reckoned about 800;
total 6,800.

In 1670 they muftered for the militia, 2,720
And on board privateers, —— 2,500
⎯⎯⎯⎯
5,200

Allowing two fourths of that number
for women and children, or — 2,600
The whole ftock of Whites amounted to 7,800, or only 764 lefs than
in the year 1673, which gives an increafe of about 250 *per annum*.
In the year 1678, according to the fame account, the militia
muftered —— 4,526

Allowance for feamen, who were
reduced very much in number in
confequence of the American

treaty;

treaty; and betook themselves,
some to planting, and so incorporated with the land-men; and
some to piracy in other parts of
the West-Indies,   —   500
                            _____
                            5,026
Women and children   —   2,513
and the whole number appears   _____
to have been about   —   7,539; by some, computed 10,000.
Several desertions happened about this time and afterwards, in consequence of some arbitrary measures of government; which doubtless reduced the number, and retarded the increase of the colony:
the number which left the island was computed at five hundred or
upwards.

About the year 1702, the Negroes imported were 843, exported
327; so that no more than 516 remained to supply all the plantations in the island. Even in 1720, their consumption amounted to
no more than 2,249; and in 1734, to 2,904. If therefore we consider the demand for Negroes, as one sure test to judge of the in-
creasing population of a West-India colony, which it manifestly is;
and that the inhabitants were all this while kept almost perpetually
in arms, to oppose the Marons, who destroyed many infant settlements, and hindered others from being formed; I do not think, that
the number of Whites can be supposed to have risen at any time
much above 8, or 9,000, until the pacification with those disturbers.

The author of an ingenious tract (entitled "Account of the
European settlements in America") allots 25,000 Whites to Jamaica.
If he had meant all the resident Whites, and those of white extraction, he would not probably have been very wide of the true state;
but, if his estimate includes none other than the unmixed Whites,
I judge it much too high an allowance, and the rather, as he has
not favoured us with any *data*, or grounds whereby we might examine how far it should be relied on.

For a general rule of loose calculation, perhaps allowing nine
Whites to every one hundred Blacks, will come nearest to exactness.
To take one example, the board of trade represented the number
to be 7,644 in the year 1734. In that year, the number of Negroe
slaves

flaves in the ifland amounted to 86,546. Multiplying therefore 865 (the number of hundreds) by 9; the product is 7,785, or only 141 difference.

Agreeably to the fame rule, we may try what may be fuppofed the prefent number, allowing the flaves to be at this time increafed to 170,000, and they probably exceed, becaufe many new fugar-works have been formed fince the year 1768; therefore, 1700 } × } gives 15,300 Whites, or 9 } 700 only different from the loweft number I have prefumed them.

It would be more agreeable to go upon fure grounds; but where information is defective, as in this cafe, we can only take fome fpeculative line for our guide; and this appears to me to draw as near to precifion, as may be reafonably expected [d].

(d) The many nautical, or feafaring terms of expreffion, in ufe here among the planters from time out of mind, were probably introduced by the firft Englifh fettlers; who, for fome years, alternately followed privateering, and planting. I fhall enumerate a few of them, with their explanation:

Cook-room. Kitchen.

Leeward. Every place fituated to the Weftward.

Windward. The contrary.

Store-room. Warehoufe for goods.

Stoaker. The Negroe appointed to ftuff fuel into the holes under the boilers. Probably from the word *ftoaked* or ftopped as a fhip's pump.

Boatfwain of the mill. The Negroe who attends the mill-gang, or feeders.

To rig the mill. To get it ready for putting about.

Mill-tackling. The mule-traces, &c.

Sweeps. The arms or levers belonging to the *main* roller.

Skids. Poles, or levers ufed for putting cafks into a boat from the fhore.

Stanchions. Upright pieces of timber in the curing-houfe.

Gangway. Interval or fpace left for paffage through the middle of the curing-houfe.

Cot. A fettee.

Awning.

Bread-kind. Such roots and fruits of the country as are ufed inftead of bread.

To jerk. To falt meat, and fmoak-dry it.

Birth. An office, place, or employment.

Grog. } *Toddy.* } Liquors, whofe choiceft ingredient is rum. *Kill-devil.* }

Hand the mug. Carry or bring the mug.

Bowl. Inftead of cup.—As "a bowl of tea," of chocolate, or both; which term expreffes the large morning-potations of our anceftors here.

Cow. Is the bucancer term, to fignify all forts of horned cattle, &c.

SECT.

SECT III.

FREED BLACKS *and* MULATTOS.

THERE were three claffes of freed perfons here. The loweft comprehended thofe who were releafed from flavery by their owner's manumiffion, either by will or an inftrument fealed and delivered, and regiftered either in the toll-book or the fecretary's office. They were allowed no other mode of trial, than the common flaves, (*i. e.*) " by two juftices and three freeholders ;" for they were not fuppofed to have acquired any fenfe of morality by the mere act of manumiffion ; fo likewife they were not admitted evidences againft white or other free-born perfons, in the courts of juftice. nor to vote at parochial nor general elections.

The fecond clafs confifted of fuch as were free-born. Thefe were allowed a trial by jury, and might give evidence in controverfies at law with one another, and in criminal cafes ; but only in civil cafes againft white perfons, or againft freed-perfons, particularly endowed with fuperior privileges.

The third contained fuch as, by *private acts* of affembly, became entitled to the fame rights and privileges with other Englifh fubjects born of white parents, except that they might not be of the council nor affembly ; nor judges in any of the courts, nor in the public offices, nor jurymen. Some of them are likewife precluded from voting at elections of affembly-members. There are not any confiderable numbers who have enjoyed the privileges annexed to this latter clafs ; they have chiefly been granted to fuch, who were inheritors of large eftates in the ifland, bequeathed to them by their white anceftor.

The freedom of the two former claffes was much enlarged in 1748, when a law paffed, allowing the manumitted, as well as free-born, to give evidence againft any freed-perfons enjoying the liberty of white fubjects, provided, in refpect to the manumitted, they have received their freedom fix months at leaft antecedent to the time of their offering fuch evidence ; and if they fhould be

7   convicted

convicted of wilful and corrupt perjury, they are made liable to the same punishment, as the laws of England inflict on this offence.

Thus it appears, that they hold a limited freedom, similar to that of the Jews; and it has been often suggested by very sensible men, that it is too circumscribed, more especially in reference to those who have large patrimonies in the island; who, without any probable ill consequence, might be permitted to have a vote in the vestry, and at the election of members to serve in the assembly; to write as clerks in some of the offices; and hold military commissions in the Black and Mulatto companies of militia; which privileges I will not dispute: but, for many reasons, it were better to confer them on particular or select persons, of good education and morality, than to extend them by a general law to many, who, it must be confessed, are not fitly qualified for this enlargement.

The descendants of the Negroe blood, entitled to all the rights and liberties of white subjects, in the full extent, are such, who are above three steps removed in the lineal digression from the Negroe *venter* exclusive; that is to say, real *quinterons*, for all below this degree are reputed by law *Mulattos*.

The law requires likewise, in all these cases, the sacrament of baptism, before they can be admitted to these privileges. Some few other restrictions are laid on the first and second class. No one of them, except he possesses a settlement with ten slaves upon it, may keep any horses, mares, mules, asses, or neat cattle, on penalty of forfeiture. This was calculated to put a stop to the practice of slaughtering the old breed on commons, and putting their own marks upon the young.

But two justices may license any such freed-person to keep such stock, during good behaviour.

They who have not a settlement, as just mentioned, must furnish themselves with certificates of their freedom, under the hand and seal of a justice, and wear a blue cross on the right shoulder, on pain of imprisonment.

If convicted of concealing, enticing, entertaining, or sending off the island, any fugitive, rebellious, or other slave, they are to forfeit their freedom, be sold, and banished.

Thefe are the principal ordinances of the laws affecting the common freed-perfons ; whence the policy of the country may be eafily meafured.   The reftraints, fo far as they are laid upon the loweft order juft emerged from fervitude, and who have no property of any confequence, feem very juftifiable and proper ; but in refpect to the few who have received a moral and Chriftian education, and who inherit fortunes confiderable enough to make them independant, they may be thought capable of fome relaxation, without any prejudice to the general welfare of the colony ; for it deferves ferious reflection, that moft of the fuperior order (for thefe reafons) prefer living in England, where they are refpected, at leaft for their fortunes ; and know that their children can enjoy *of right* all thofe privileges, which in Jamaica are withheld from their poffeffion.

The flaves that moft commonly gain a manumiffion here from their owners, are

1. Domefticks, in reward for a long and faithful courfe of fervice.

2. Thofe, who have been permitted to work for themfelves, only paying a certain weekly or monthly fum ; many of them find means to fave fufficient from their earnings, to purchafe their freedom.

3. Thofe who have effected fome effential fervice to the public, fuch as revealing a confpiracy, or fighting valiantly againft rebels and invaders.   They have likewife generally been requited with an annuity, from the publick treafury, for life.

Some regulation feems expedient, to give the firft mentioned the means of acquiring their freedom, without the temptation of converting it into licentioufnefs.

In Antigua, every white perfon who beftows this boon upon his flave, accompanies it with fome further grant, enabling him to enjoy his new ftation with advantage to himfelf and the community. The law there compels all thefe freed-men, who have not lands wherewith to form a fettlement, to enter themfelves into the fervice of fome family. In Jamaica, where land is a cheap commodity, this is not the cafe. The Negroe receives his manumiffion, but not always a provifion for his future fubfiftence ; this defect therefore impels many of them to thefts and other illegal practices,

for

for a maintenance. A liberty of this species is baneful to society ; and it feems to be the proper object of legiflature, to make
thefe acts of private bounty fubfervient to, inftead of leaving them
fubverfive of, the publick good.

From five to ten acres of ground might very well be fpared upon
any planter's eftate. Five acres of good foil are abundantly fufficient for one fuch freed Negroe. It may be faid, that fuch a condition, tacked to thefe grants, would hinder men from rewarding their
faithful flaves with liberty ; but, on the other hand, in a publick
view, it is better that the Negroe fhould continue an honeft and induftrious flave, than to be turned into an idle and profligate free-
man. All however that is here meant is, that, in imitation of the
Antigua law, all thofe freed-men, who have neither lands to cultivate, nor trade to follow, fhould be obliged to enrol themfelves
in fome white family, as domefticks ; a lift fhould annually be taken,
and regiftered, of all the claffes, and their occupations annexed to
their names.

I come now to fpeak of the Mulattoes and other cafts, who (in
common parlance) all pafs under that appellation.   Upon enquiry of
the affembly, in the year 1762, into the devifes made by laft wills to
Mulatto children, the amount in reality and perfonalty was found in
value between two and three hundred thoufand pound. They included
four fugar eftates, feven penns, thirteen houfes, befides other lands un-
fpecified. After duly weighing the ill confequences that might befall
the colony, by fuffering real eftates to pafs into fuch hands, a bill
was paffed, " to prevent the inconveniencies arifing from exorbi-
" tant grants and devifes made by white perfons to Negroes and the
" iffue of Negroes, and to reftrain and limit fuch grants and devi-
" fes;" this bill enacted, that a devife from a white perfon, to a
Negroe or Mulatto, of real and perfonal eftate, exceeding in value
2000 l. currency, fhould be void.   It has been objected by many,
and with great warmth, to this law, " that it is oppreffive in it's
" effect, tending to deprive men of their right to difpofe of their
" own effects and acquifitions, in the manner moft agreeable to
" their inclinations".   It may not be improper, therefore, to examine a little into the fair ftate of the queftion.   That it is repugnant to the fpirit of the Englifh laws, is readily granted, and fo is

Negroe

Negroe flavery: the queftion therefore arifing from this comparifon will be, Is there or not a local neceffity for laying many reftraints in this colony, where flave-holding is legally eftablifhed, which reftraints do not exift, nor are politically expedient, in England, where flavery is not tolerated? It is a firft principle, and not to be controverted, in political and civil as well as in moral government, that if one perfon does any act, which if every other or even many others of the fame fociety were to do, muft be attended with injurious confequences to that fociety, fuch an act cannot in the nature of things be legal nor warrantable. All focieties of men, where-ever conftituted, can fubfift together only by certain obligations and reftrictions, to which all the individual members muft neceffarily yield obedience for the general good ; or they can have no juft claim to thofe rights, and that protection, which are held by all, under this common fanction.

In countries where rational freedom is moft enjoyed, as in England, the laws have affixed certain bounds to mens paffions and inclinations, in numberlefs examples; fo a fucceffion to eftates there is regulated more according to the rules of policy, and the good of the community, than to the *law of nature,* fimply confidered ; therefore, although a man may be defirous, nay thinks he has a natural right, to determine who fhall enjoy that property from time to time after his death, which he acquired by his induftry while living, the law of England, abhorring perpetuities as hurtful to the fociety, defeats this purpofe, and readily gives it's affiftance to bar fuch entails.

The right of making devifes by will was eftablifhed in fome countries much later than in others. In England, till modern times, a man could only difpofe of one third of his moveables from his wife and legitimate children ; and, in general, no will was permitted of lands till the reign of Henry the Eighth, and then only a certain portion; for it was not till after the Reftoration, that the power of devifing real property became fo univerfal as at prefent. The antient law of the Athenians directed that the ftate of the deceafed fhould always defcend to his legitimate children ; or, on failure of fuch lineal defcendants, fhould go to the collateral relations. In many other parts of Greece they were totally difcountenanced.

In

In Rome they were unknown till the laws of the twelve tables were compiled, which firſt gave the right of bequeathing; and among the Northern nations, particularly the Germans, teſtaments were not received into uſe. By the common law of England, ſince the conqueſt, no eſtate, greater than for term of years, can be diſpoſed of by teſtament, except only in Kent and in ſome antient burghs, and a few particular manors, where their Saxon immunities by particular indulgence ſubſiſted. And though the feodal reſtraint on alienations by deed vaniſhed very early, yet this on wills continued for ſome centuries after, from an apprehenſion of infirmity and impoſition on the teſtator *in extremis*; which made ſuch deviſes ſuſpicious. Every diſtinct country has different ceremonies and requiſites to make a will compleatly valid; and this variety may ſerve to evince, that the right of making wills and diſpoſing of property after death is merely a creature of the civil or municipal laws, which have permitted it in ſome countries, and denied it in others; and even where it is permitted by law, it is ſubjected to different reſtrictions, in almoſt every nation under Heaven. In England, particularly, this diverſity is carried to ſuch a length, as if it had been meant to point out the power of the laws in regulating the ſucceſſion to property; and how futile every claim muſt be, that has not it's foundation in the poſitive rules of the ſtate [*e*]. In the ſame kingdom, the inſtitution of marriage is regarded as one of the main links of ſociety, becauſe it is found to be the beſt ſupport of it. A promiſcuous intercourſe and an uncertain parentage, if they were univerſal, would ſoon diſſolve the frame of the conſtitution, from the infinity of claims and conteſted rights of ſucceſſion: for this reaſon, the begetting an illegitimate child is reputed a violation of the ſocial compacts, and the tranſgreſſors are puniſhable with corporal correction [*f*]. The civil codes were ſo rigorous, that they even made baſtards incapable, in ſome caſes, of a gift from their parents. The deteſtation in which they have been held by the Engliſh laws is very apparent, and may be inferred from the ſpirit of their ſeveral maxims: as, " Hæres *legitimus* eſt quem *nuptiæ* demonſtrant &c. [*g*]."

[*e*] Blackſtone.
[*f*] 18 Eliz. 7 Jac. I.
[*g*] A legitimate child is he that is born after wedlock.

" Cui

" *Cui pater est populus*, non habet ille patrem [*h*]". " **Qui** ex *damnato* " coitu nafcuntur, inter liberos non computentur." So they are likewife ftyled "*filii nullius* [*i*]," becaufe their real father is fuppofed to be uncertain, or unknown. The lenity however of the Englifh law at prefent, is fatisfied only with excluding them from inheritance, and with exacting a competent provifion for their maintenance, that they may not become chargeable upon the publick.

The inftitution of marriage, is doubtlefs of as much concern in the colony, as it is in the mother country: perhaps more fo; becaufe a life of celibacy is not equally hurtful in the latter, who may draw recruits to keep up her population, from the neighbouring ftates of Europe. But the civil policy of the two countries, in refpect to fucceffions to property, differ very materially; fo that, if three fourths of the nation were flaves, there can be no queftion but that the law of laft wills would be modified to a different frame, perhaps carried back again to the antient feodal doctrine of non-alienation, without confent of the lord; which reftraint was fuited to the policy of thofe times, when villeinage prevailed. A man's right of devifing his property by will ought juftly, therefore, from the conftitution of our Weft India colonies, to be more circumfcribed in them, than is fitting in the mother ftate. A fubject (for example) in Jamaica ought not to bequeath his whole perfonal eftate which may be very confiderable, to a flave; and, if he fhould do fo, it is eafy to conceive that it would be utterly repugnant to the civil policy of that ifland. The Jamaica law permits the putative father to leave, what will be thought, a very ample provifion, in order to fet his baftard forward in the world; and in all cafes where the father, having no legitimate kin to whom he may be willing to give his property, where that property is large, and his illegitimate child may be, by the polifh of a good education, and moral principles, found well deferving to poffefs it; there can be no queftion, but he might be made legitimate and capable of inheriting, by the power of an act of affembly; fince the fame thing has been done in fimilar cafes in England, by act of the parliament. It is plain, therefore, the policy of the

[*h*] The offspring of promifcuous coujunctions has no father. Marriage afcertains the father.

[*i*] Baftards are not endowed with the privilege of children. No man's children.

law

law only tends to obviate the detriment refulting to the fociety, from foolifh, and indifcriminate devifes; leaving in the breaft of the legiflature to ratify others particularly circumftanced, and which might not be fo likely to produce the fame inconveniences. It is a queftion eafily anfwered, whether (fuppofing all natural impediments of climate out of the way) it would be more for the interest of Britain, that Jamaica fhould be poffeffed and peopled by white inhabitants, or by Negroes and Mulattos?—Let any man turn his eyes to the Spanifh American dominions, and behold what a vicious, brutal, and degenerate breed of mongrels has been there produced, between Spaniards, Blacks, Indians, and their mixed progeny; and he muft be of opinion, that it might be much be better for Britain, and Jamaica too, if the white men in that colony would abate of their infatuated attachments to black women, and, inftead of being " grac'd with a *yellow offspring not their own* [*k*]," perform the duty incumbent on every good cittizen, by raifing in honourable wedlock a race of unadulterated beings. The trite pretence of moft men here, for not entering into that ftate, is " the heavy and in- " tolerable expences it will bring upon them." This, in plain Englifh, is nothing more than expreffing their opinion, that fociety fhall do every thing for them, and that they ought to do nothing for fociety; and the folly of the means they purfue, to attain this felfifh, ungrateful purpofe, is well expofed, by the profufion and mifery into which their diforderly connexions often infenfibly plunge them. Can we poffibly admit any force in their excufe, when we obferve them lavifhing their fortune with unbounded liberality upon a common proftitute? when we fee one of thefe votaries of celibacy grow the abject, paffive flave to all her infults, thefts, and infidelities; and difperfe his eftate between her and her brats, whom he blindly acknowledges for his children, when in truth they are entitled to claim twenty other fathers? It is true, the iffue of a marriage may fometimes lie under fufpicion, through the loofe carriage of the mother; but on which fide does the weight of probability reft, on the virtue of a wife, or the continence of a proftitute?

[*k*] Pitt's Virg. Æn. vi. 293.

Very

Very indigent men may indeed, with more colour of propriety, urge such an argument in their defence; but the owner of a large fortune possesses what is a visible demonstration, to prove the fallacy of his pretence. Such a man is doubtless as able to maintain a wife, as a mistress of all the vices reigning here; none are so flagrant as this of concubinage with white women, or cohabiting with Negresses and Mulattas, free or slaves. In consequence of this practice we have not only more spinsters in comparison to the number of women among the natives (whose brothers or male relations possess the greatest part of their father's patrimony) in this small community, than in most other parts of his majesty's dominions, proportionably inhabited; but also, a vast addition of spurious offsprings of different complexions : in a place where, by custom, so little restraint is laid on the passions, the Europeans, who at home have always been used to greater purity and strictness of manners, are too easily led aside to give a loose to every kind of sensual delight: on this account some black or yellow *quasheba* is sought for, by whom a tawney breed is produced. Many are the men, of every rank, quality, and degree here, who would much rather riot in these goatish embraces, than share the pure and lawful bliss derived from matrimonial, mutual love. Modesty, in this respect, has but very little footing here. He who should presume to shew any displeasure against such a thing as simple fornication, would for his pains be accounted a simple blockhead; since not one in twenty can be persuaded, that there is either sin; or shame in cohabiting with his slave. Of these men, by far the greatest part never marry after they have acquired a fortune; but usher into the world a tarnished train of beings, among whom, at their decease, they generally divide their substance. It is not a little curious, to consider the strange manner in which some of them are educated. Instead of being taught any mechanic art, whereby they might become useful to the island, and enabled to support themselves; young *Fuscus*, in whom the father fondly imagines he sees the reflected dawn of paternal genius, and Miss *Fulvia*, who mamma protests has a most delicate ear for music and French, are both of them sent early to England, to cultivate and improve the valuable talents which nature is supposed to have so wantonly bestowed, and the parents, blind with folly,

think

think they have difcovered. To accomplifh this end, no expence nor pains are fpared; the indulgent father, big with expectation of the future *eclat* of his hopeful progeny,

                        " difdains
      " The vulgar tutor, and the ruftic fchool,
      " To which the dull cit' fends his low-born fool.
      " By our wife fire to London are they brought,
      " To learn thofe arts that high-bred youths are taught;
      " Attended, dreft, and train'd, with coft and care,
      " Juft like fome wealthy duke's apparent-heir."

Mafter is fent to Weftminfter, or Eaton, to be inftructed in the elements of learning, among ftudents of the firft rank that wealth and family can give: whilft Mifs is placed at Chelfea, or fome other famed feminary; where fhe learns mufic, dancing, French, and the whole circle of female *bon ton*, proper for the accomplifhment of fine women. After much time and money beftowed on their education, and great encomiums, year after year, tranfmitted (by thofe whofe intereft it is to make them) on their very uncommon genius and proficiency, at length they return to vifit their rela- tions. From this period, much of their future mifery may be dated. Mifs faints at the fight of her relations, efpecially when papa tells her that black *Quafheba* is her own mother. The young gentleman too, after his introduction, begins to difcover that the knowledge he has gained has only contributed to make him more fufceptible of keen reflections, arifing from his unfortunate birth. He is foon, parhaps, left to herd among his black kindred, and converfe with *Quafhee* and *Mingo*, inftead of his fchool-fellows, *Sir George*, or *My Lord*; while mademoifelle, inftead of modifh French, muft learn to prattle gibberifh with her coufins *Mimba* and *Chloe*: for, however well this yellow brood may be received in England, yet here fo great is the diftinction kept up between white and mixed complexions, that very feldom are they feen to- gether in a familiar way, though every advantage of drefs or for- tune fhould centre with the latter. Under this diftinction, it is impoffible but that a well-educated Mulatta muft lead a very un- pleafant kind of a life here; and juftly may apply to her reputed father what Iphicrates faid of his, " After all your pains, you have

" made me no better than a flave; on the other hand, my mother
" did every thing in her power to render me free." On firft arriving
here, a civilized European may be apt to think it impudent and
fhameful, that even bachelors fhould publickly avow their keeping
Negroe or Mulatto miftrefles; but they are ftill more fhocked at
feeing a group of white legitimate, and Mulatto illegitimate,
children, all claimed by the fame married father, and all bred up
together under the fame roof [m]. Habit, however, and the prevailing fafhion, reconcile fuch fcenes, and leffen the abhorrence
excited by their firft impreffion.

To allure men from thefe illicit connexions, we ought to remove the principal obftacles which deter them from marriage.
This will be chiefly effected by rendering women of their own
complexion more agreeable companions, more frugal, trufty, and
faithful friends, than can be met with among the African ladies.
Of fome probable meafures to effect this defireable purpofe, and
make the fair natives of this ifland more amiable in the eyes of the
men, and more eligible partners in the nuptial ftate, I have already
ventured my fentiments. A proper education is the firft great
point. A modeft demeanour, a mind divefted of falfe pride, a
very moderate zeal for expenfive pleafures, a fkill in œconomy,
and a conduct which indicates plain tokens of good humour, fidelity, and difcretion, can never fail of making converts. Much,
indeed, depends on the ladies themfelves to refcue this truly honourable union from that fafhionable deteftation in which it feems

[m] Reafon requires, that the mafter's power fhould not extend to what does not appertain to
his fervice. Slavery fhould be calculated for utility, not for pleafure. The laws of chaftity arife
from thofe of nature, and ought in all nations to be refpected. If a law, which preferves the
chaftity of flaves, be good in thofe ftates where an arbitrary power bears down all before it, how
much more fo will it be in monarchies! and how much more ftill in republics! The law of the
Lombards has a regulation which ought to be adopted by all governments. "If a mafter debauches
" his flave's wife, the flave and his wife fhall be free;" an admirable expedient, which, without
feverity, lays a powerful reftraint on the incontinency of mafters. The Romans erred on this
head: they allowed an unlimited fcope to the mafter's luft; and, in fome meafure, denied their
flaves the privilege of marrying. It is true, they were the loweft part of the nation; yet there
fhould have been fome care taken of their morals, efpecially as, in prohibiting their marriage,
they corrupted the morals of the citizens.
So thinks the inimitable Montefquieu. And how applicable thefe fentiments are to the ftate
of things in our ifland, I leave to the difpaffionate judgement of every man there, whether married or fingle.

to be held; and one would fuppofe it no very arduous tafk to make themfelves more companionable, ufeful, and efteemable, as wives, than the Negreffes and Mulattas are as miftreffes: they might, I am well perfuaded, prove much honefter friends. It is true, that, if it fhould be a man's misfortune to be coupled with a very profligate and extravagant wife, the difference, in refpect to his fortune, is not great, whether plundered by a black or by a white woman. But fuch examples, I may hope, are unfrequent without the hufband's concur ence; yet, whenever they do happen, the mifchief they occafion is very extenfive, from the apprehenfions with which they ftrike multitudes of fingle men, the viler part of whom endeavour to increafe the number of unhappy marriages by every bafe art of feduction; while others rejoice to find any fuch, becaufe they feem to juftify their preference of celibacy, or concubinage. In regard to the African miftrefs, I fhall exhibit the following, as no unfuitable portrait. All her kindred, and moft commonly her very paramours, are faftened upon her keeper like fo many leeches; while fhe, the chief leech, confpires to bleed him *ufque ad deliquium.* In well-diffembled affection, in her tricks, cajolements, and infidelities, fhe is far more perfectly verfed, than any adept of the hundreds of Drury. She rarely wants cunning to dupe the fool that confides in her; for who " fhall teach the wily African " deceit?" The quinteffence of her dexterity confifts in perfuading the man fhe detefts to believe fhe is moft violently fmitten with the beauty of his perfon; in fhort, over head and ears in love with him. To eftablifh this opinion, which vanity feldom fails to embrace, fhe now and then affects to be jealous, laments his ungrateful return for fo fincere a paffion; and, by this ftratagem, fhe is better able to hide her private intrigues with her real favourites. I have feen a dear companion of this ftamp deploring the lofs of her deceafed cull with all the feeming fervency of an honeft affection, or rather of outrageous forrow; beating her head; ftamping with her feet; tears pouring down in torrents; her exclamations as wild, and geftures as emphatic, as thofe of an antient Roman orator in all the phrenfy of a publick harangue. Unluckily, it foon appeared, that, at this very time, fhe had rummaged his pockets and efcrutoire; and concealed his watch, rings, and money, in the

feather-bed

feather-bed upon which the poor wretch had juſt breathed his laſt. And ſuch is the mirror of almoſt all theſe conjunctions of white and black! two tinctures which nature has diſſociated, like oil and vinegar. But, as if ſome good was generally to ariſe out of evil, ſo we find, that theſe connexions have been applauded upon a principle of policy; as if, by forming ſuch alliances with the ſlaves, they might become more attached to the white people. Perhaps, the fruit of theſe unions may, by their conſanguinity with a certain number of the Blacks, ſupport ſome degree of influence, ſo far as that line of kindred extends: yet one would ſcarcely ſuppoſe it to have any remote effect; becauſe they, for their own parts, deſpiſe the Blacks, and aſpire to mend their complexion ſtill more by intermixture with the Whites. The children of a White and Quateron are called Engliſh, and conſider themſelves as free from all taint of the Negroe race. To call them by a degree inferior to what they really are, would be the higheſt affront. This pride of amended blood is univerſal, and becomes the more confirmed, if they have received any ſmattering of education; for then they look down with the more ſupercilious contempt upon thoſe who have had none. Such, whoſe mind has been a little purged from the groſſeſt ignorance, may wiſh and endeavour to improve it ſtill more; but no freed or unfreed Mulatto ever wiſhed to relapſe into the Negro. The fact is, that the opulent among them withdraw to England; where their influence, if they ever poſſeſſed any, ceaſes to be of any uſe. The middle claſs are not much liked by the Negroes, becauſe the latter abhor the idea of being ſlaves to the deſcendants of ſlaves. And as for the lower rank, the iſſue of caſual fruition, they, for the moſt part, remain in the ſame ſlaviſh condition as their mother; they are fellow-labourers with the Blacks, and are not regarded in the leaſt as their ſuperiors. As for the firſt-mentioned, it would probably be no diſſervice to the iſland, to regain all thoſe who have abandoned it. But, to ſtate the compariſon fairly, if their fathers had married, the difference would have been this; their white offspring might have remained in the colony, to ſtrengthen and enrich it: the Mulatto offspring deſert and impoveriſh it. The lower claſs of theſe mixtures, who remain in the iſland, are a hardy race, capable of undergoing equal fatigue with the Blacks,

above

above whom (in point of due policy) they ought to hold fome degree of diftinction. They would then form the centre of connexion between the two extremes, producing a regular eftablifhment of three ranks of men, dependent on each other, and rifing in a proper climax of fubordination, in which the Whites would hold the higheft place. I can forefee no mifchief that can arife from the enfranchifement of every Mulatto child. If it be objected, that fuch a plan may tend to encourage the illicit commerce of which I have been complaining; I reply, that it will be more likely to reprefs it, becaufe, although the planters are at prefent very indifferent about the birth of fuch children upon their eftates, knowing that they will either labour for them like their other flaves, or produce a good price, if their fathers fhould incline to purchafe them; yet they will difcountenance fuch intercourfes as much as lies in their power (when it fhall no longer be for their intereft to connive at them), and ufe their endeavours to multiply the unmixed breed of their Blacks. Befides, to expect that men will wholly abftain from this commerce, if it was even liable to the fevereft penalties of law, would be abfurd; for, fo long as fome men have paffions to gratify, they will feek the indulgence of them by means the moft agreeable, and leaft inconvenient, to themfelves. It will be of fome advantage, as things are circumftanced, to turn unavoidable evils to the benefit of fociety, as the beft reparation that can be made for this breach of its moral and political inftitutions. A wife phyfician will ftrive to change an acute diftemper into one lefs malignant; and his patient compounds for a flight chronic indifpofition, fo he may get relief from a violent and mortal one. I do not judge fo lightly of the prefent ftate of fornication in the ifland, as to fuppofe that it can ever be more flourifhing, or that the emancipation of every Mulatto child will prove a means of augmenting the annual number. The retrieving them from profound ignorance, affording them inftruction in Chriftian morals, and obliging them to ferve a regular apprenticefhip to artificers and tradefmen, would make them orderly fubjects, and faithful defenders of the country. It may, with greater weight, be objected, that fuch a meafure would deprive the planters of a

part

3

part of their property ; and that the bringing up fo many ~o trades and mechanic arts might difcourage white artificers.

The firft might be obviated, by paying their owners a certain rate *per* head, to be determined by the legiflature. The fecond is not infurmountable ; for few or none will be mafter-workmen ; they will ferve as journeymen to white artificers ; or do little more than they would have done, if they had continued in flavery ; for it is the cuftom on moft eftates at prefent to make tradefmen of them. But, if they were even to fet up for themfelves, no difadvantage would probably accrue to the publick, but the contrary. They would oblige the white artificers to work at more moderate rates ; which, though not agreeable perhaps to thefe artificers, would ftill leave them an ample gain, and prove very acceptable to the reft of the inhabitants ; for to fuch a pitch of extravagance have they raifed their charges, that they tax their employers juft what they think fit ; each man of them fixes a rate according to his own fancy, unregulated by any law ; and, fhould his bill be ever fo enormous or unjuft, he is in no want of brother tradefmen in the jury-box to confirm and allow it. I fhall not here prefume to dictate any entire plan for carrying this fcheme into effect. This muft be left to the wifdom of the legiflature, and be made confiftent with the abilities of the treafury. In general only I may fuppofe, that for every fuch child, on its attaining the age of three years, a reafonable allowance be paid to the owner : from that period it becomes the care of the public, and might be provided for, at a cheap rate, until of an age fit for fchool ; then be inftructed in religion ; and at the age of twelve apprenticed for the term of four years ; after this, be regimented in his refpective diftrict, perhaps fettled near a townfhip ; and, when on militia or other public duty, paid the fame fubfiftence *per* day, or week, that is now allowed to the Marons. The expediency muft be feen of having (as in the French iflands) fuch a corps of active men, ready to fcour the woods upon all occafions ; a fervice, in which the regulars are by no means equal to them. They would likewife form a proper counter-balance to the Maron Negroes ; whofe infolence, during formidable infurrections, has been moft infufferable. The beft way of fecuring the allegiance of thefe irregular people muft be by preferving the treaty

with

with them inviolate : and, at the fame time, awing them into the confervation of it on their part by fuch a powerful equipoife, compofed of men diffimilar from them in complexion and manners, but equal in hardinefs and vigour.

The Mulattos are, in general, well-fhaped, and the women well-featured. They feem to partake more of the white than the black. Their hair has a natural curl; in fome it refembles the Negroe fleece; but, in general, it is of a tolerable length. The girls arrive very early at the age of puberty ; and, from the time of their being about twenty-five, they decline very faft, till at length they grow horribly ugly. They are lafcivious ; yet, confidering their want of inftruction, their behaviour in public is remarkably decent ; and they affect a modefty which they do not feel. They are lively and fenfible, and pay religious attention to the cleanlinefs of their perfons : at the fame time, they are ridiculoufly vain, haughty, and irafcible. They poffefs, for the moft part, a tendernefs of difpofition, which leads them to do many charitable actions, efpecially to poor white perfons, and makes them excellent nurfes to the fick. They are fond of finery, and lavifh almoft all the money they get in ornaments, and the moft expenfive forts of linen. Some few of them have intermarried here with thofe of their own complexion ; but fuch matches have generally been defective and barren. They feem in this refpect to be actually of the mule-kind, and not fo capable of producing from one another as from a commerce with a diftinct White or Black. Monfieur Buffon obferves, that it is nothing ftrange that two individuals fhould not be able to propagate their fpecies, becaufe nothing more is required than fome flight oppofition in their temperaments, or fome accidental fault in the genital organs of either of thefe two individuals : nor is it furprifing, that two individuals, of different fpecies, fhould produce other individuals, which, being unlike either of their progenitors, bear no refemblance to any thing fixed, and confequently cannot produce any thing refembling themfelves, becaufe all that is requifite in this production is a certain degree of conformity between the form of the body and the genital organs of thefe different animals. Yet it feems extraordinary, that two Mulattos, having intercourfe together, fhould be unable to continue their fpecies, the

woman

woman either proving barren, or their offspring, if they have any, not attaining to maturity; when the fame man and woman, having commerce with a White or Black, would generate a numerous iffue. Some examples may poffibly have occurred, where, upon the intermarriage of two Mulattos, the woman has borne children; which children have grown to maturity: but I never heard of fuch an inftance; and may we not fufpect the lady, in thofe cafes, to have privately intrigued with another man, a White perhaps? The fufpicion is not unwarrantable, if we confider how little their paffions are under the reftraint of morality; and that the major part, nay, almoft the whole number, with very few exceptions, have been *filles de joye* before they became wives. As for thofe in Jamaica, whom I have particularly alluded to, they married young, had received fome fort of education, and lived with great repute for their chafte and orderly conduct; and with them the experiment is tried with a great degree of certainty: they produce no offspring, though in appearance under no natural incapacity of fo doing with a different connexion.

The fubject is really curious, and deferves a further and very attentive enquiry; becaufe it tends, among other evidences, to eftablifh an opinion, which feveral have entertained, that the White and the Negroe had not one common origin. Towards difproving this opinion, it is neceffary, that the Mulatto woman fhould be paft all fufpicion of intriguing with another, or having communication with any other man than her Mulatto hufband; and it then remains for further proof, whether the offspring of thefe two Mulattos, being married to the offspring of two other Mulatto parents, would propagate their fpecies, and fo, by an uninterrupted fucceffion, continue the race. For my own part, I think there are extremely potent reafons for believing, that the White and the Negroe are two diftinct fpecies. A certain philofopher of the prefent age confidently avers, that " none but the blind can doubt it." It is certain, that this idea enables us to account for thofe diverfities of feature, fkin, and intellect, obferveable among mankind; which cannot be accounted for in any other way, without running into a thoufand abfurdities.

The

The antient fathers of the Chriftian church, difliking the Co-pernican fyftem, pronounced it damnable and heretical for any one to maintain the doctrine of the antipodes, and the annual motion of the earth round the fun. According to the ecclefiaftical fyftem of thofe days, the fun was made to revolve above three hundred and twenty thoufand miles in the fpace of a minute; but it is found more rational to conclude, and more eafy to believe, that the earth makes one revolution on its own axis once in twenty-four hours; and we have living teftimonies of its having been circumnavigated, and the doctrine of antipodes confirmed beyond a doubt. The freedom of philofophic enquiry may ftill proceed to extirpate old prejudices, and difplay more and more (to the utter confufien of ignorance and bigotry) the beautiful gradation, order, and har-mony, which pervade the whole feries of created beings on this globe.

Of the number of the free Blacks and Mulattos in the ifland I have before given an eftimate. They increafe very faft. By an act, paffed in 1761, they were all required to take out certificates of their freedom, to be figned by the governor. This was a very proper method to come at the knowledge of their number. In 1762, or 1763, they were found as follows:

Middlefex.		Surry.		Cornwall.		Total in the 3 Counties.
St. Catharine,	872	Kingfton,	1093	St. Elizabeth,	228	
St. Thomas in the Vale,	44	Port Royal,	103	Weftmoreland,	189	
St. John,	67	St. Andrew,	56	Hanover,	67	
St. Dorothy,	38	St. David,	22	St. James,	26	
Clarendon,	130	St. Thomas in the Eaft,	64			
Vere,	172	Portland,	27			
St. Anne,	78	St. George,	32			
St. Mary,	100					
	1501		1397		510	3408

They are fince increafed to upwards of three thoufand feven hundred, principally in the towns; and, I think, we may reckon about one thoufand five hundred of them for fencible men, fit for able fervice in the Militia.

I fhall conclude this account of them with a hearty recommen-dation of fome plan, both for inftructing them in morality, and regimenting their fencible men, to be employed by rotation on conftant duty. I need not recapitulate my former arguments, tending to illuftrate the utility, and even neceffity, of adopting this meafure.

S E C T. IV.

M A R O N S [*l*].

WHEN the Spaniards retreated before the army under command of Venables, they had with them about one thoufand five hundred Negroes and Mulattos, many of whom were flaves. Some adhered to their mafters; while others difperfed, thirty or forty in a gang, to different parts of the mountains, chufing their own leaders; from whence they made frequent excurfions, to harrafs the Englifh foldiers, who had been reprefented to them as blood-thirfty heretics, that gave no quarter. They frequently killed ftragglers near the head-quarters; and one night grew fo bold, as to fire a houfe in the very town. Major-general Sedgewick prophefied, in his letter to Thurloe (1656), that thefe Blacks would prove thorns in our fides; living as they did in the woods and mountains, a kind of life natural and agreeable to them. He adds, that they gave no quarter to his men, but deftroyed them whenever they found opportunity, fcarce a week paffing without their flaying one or two; and, as the foldiers grew more fecure and carelefs, they became more enterprifing and bloody. "Having no *moral fenfe*," continues he, " nor underftanding what the laws and cuftoms of " civil nations mean, we neither know how to capitulate or dif- " courfe with, nor how to take, any of them. But, be affured, they " muft either be deftroyed, or brought in upon fome terms or " other; or elfe they will prove a great difcouragement to the fet- " tling of people here." What he foretold actually came to pafs. At the latter end of the fame year (1656), the army gained fome trifling fuccefs againft them; but this was foon afterwards feverely retaliated by the flaughter of forty foldiers, cut off as they were carelefsly rambling near their quarters. A party was immediately fent in queft of the enemy, came up with, and killed feven or eight

[*l*] Probably derived from the Spanifh *Marráno*, a porker, or hog of one year old. The name was firft given to the hunters of wild hogs, to diftinguifh them from the bucaniers, or hunters of wild cattle and horfes.

of

of them. The following year, they difcovered the place where
the Blacks held their ufual rendezvous, and gave them fome annoyance. But they ftill found means to hold out, until, being hard
preffed by colonel D'Oyley, who, by his final overthrow of the
Spaniards at Rio Nuevo, having taken from them all hope of future fuccour from their antient friends, they became very much
ftreightened, for want of provifions and ammunition. The main
party, under the command of their captain, Juan de Bolas (whofe
place of retreat, in Clarendon, ftill retains his name), furrendered
to the Englifh on terms of pardon and freedom. But other parties
remained in the moft inacceffible retreats within the mountainous
wilds; where they not only augmented their numbers by procreation, but, after the ifland became thicker fown with plantations,
they were frequently reinforced by fugitive flaves, and at length
grew confident enough of their force to undertake defcents upon
the interior planters, many of whom they murdered from time to
time; and, by their barbarities and outrage, intimidated the Whites
from venturing to any confiderable diftance from the fea-coaft.
One of thefe parties was called the Vermaholis Negroes; in queft
of whom captain Ballard was fent, in the year 1660, with a detachment, and took feveral of them prifoners. In 1663, the lieutenant-governor Sir Charles Lyttelton, and his council, iffued a
proclamation, offering to grant twenty acres of land *per* head, and
their freedom, to all fuch of them as would come in. But I do not
find that any of them inclined to accept the terms, or quit their
favage way of life. On the contrary, they were better pleafed
with the more ample range they poffeffed in the woods, where
their hunting-ground was not yet limited by fettlements. They
took care that none of the latter fhould be formed; and, for this
purpofe, butchered every white family that ventured to feat itfelf
any confiderable diftance inland. When the governor perceived
that the proclamation wrought no effect upon their favage minds,
Juan de Bolas, who was now made colonel of the Black regiment,
was fent to endeavour their reduction; but, in the profecution of
this fervice, he fell unfortunately into an ambufcade, and was cut
in pieces. In March, 1664, captain Colbeck, of the White militia, was employed for the fame purpofe. He went by fea to the

X x 2

North

North fide; and, having gained fome advantages over them, he returned, with one who pretended to treat for the reft. This embaffy, however, was only calculated to amufe the Whites, and gain fome refpite; for they no fooner found themfelves in a proper condition, and the white inhabitants lulled into fecurity, than they began to renew hoftilities.

Thefe Blacks poffeffed feveral fmall towns in different divifions of the country; and, about the year 1693, commenced open war, having chofen Cudjoe for their generaliffimo. They continued to diftrefs the ifland for about forty-feven years; and, during this time, forty-four acts of affembly were paffed, and at leaft 240,000 *l*. expended, for their fuppreffion. In 1730, they were grown fo formidable, that it was found expedient to ftrengthen the colony againft them by two regiments of regular troops, which were afterwards formed into independent companies, and employed, with other hired parties, and the whole body of militia, towards their reduction. In the year 1734, captain Stoddart, who commanded one of thefe parties, projected and executed with great fuccefs an attack of their windward town, called Nanny, fituated near Carrion-crow Ridge, one of the higheft mountains in the ifland, in the neighbourhood of Bath. Having provided fome portable fwivel-guns, he filently approached their quarters, and reached within a fmall diftance of them undifcovered. After halting for fome time, he began to afcend by the only path leading to their town. He found it fteep, rocky, and difficult, and not wide enough to admit the paffage of two perfons abreaft. However, he furmounted thefe obftacles; and, having gained a fmall eminence, commanding the huts in which the Negroes were lodged all faft afleep, he fixed his little train of artillery to the beft advantage, and difcharged upon them fo brifkly, that many were flain in their habitations, and feveral more, amidft the confternation which this furprize occafioned, threw themfelves headlong down precipices. Captain Stoddart purfued the advantage, killed numbers, took many prifoners, and, in fhort, fo compleatly deftroyed or routed the whole body, that they were unable afterwards to effect any enterprize of moment in this quarter of the ifland.

About

About the fame time, another party of the Blacks (having perceived that a body of the militia, ftationed at the barrack of Bagnal's Thicket, in St. Mary, under command of colonel Charlton and captain Ivy, ftrayed heedlefsly from their quarters, and kept no order) formed an ambufcade to cut them off, and, whilft the officers were at dinner, attended by very few of their men, the Marons rufhed fuddenly from the adjacent woods, and affaulted them. Several pieces were difcharged; the report of which alarmed the militia, who immediately ran to their arms, and came up in time to refcue their officers from deftruction. The Marons were repulfed, and forced to take fhelter in the woods; but the militia did not think fit to purfue them far. Some rumours of this fkirmifh reached Spanifh Town, which is diftant from the fpot about thirty miles; and, as all the circumftances were not known, the inhabitants were thrown into the moft dreadful panic, from apprehenfions that the Marons had defeated Charlton, and were in full march to attack the town. Ayfcough, then commander in chief, fell in with the popular fear, ordered the trumpets to found, the drums to beat, and in a few hours collected a body of horfe and foot, who went to meet the enemy. On the fecond day after their departure, they came up to a place, where, by the fires which remained unextinguifhed, they fuppofed the Marons had lodged the preceding night. They therefore followed the track, and foon after got fight of them. Captain Edmunds, who commanded the detachment, difpofed his men for action; but the Marons declined engaging, and fled different ways. Several, however, were flain in the purfuit, and others made prifoners. Thefe two victories reduced their ftrength, and infpired them with fo much terror, that they never after appeared in any confiderable body, nor dared to make any ftand. Indeed, from the commencement of the war till this period, they had not once ventured a pitched battle; but fkulked about the fkirts of remote plantations, furprifing ftragglers, and murdering the Whites by two or three at a time, or when they were too few to make any refiftance. By night they feized the favourable opportunity, that darknefs gave them, of ftealing into the fettlements; where they fet fire to cane-pieces and outhoufes, killed all the cattle they could find, and carried off the

flaves

flaves into captivity. By this daftardly method of conducting the war, they did infinite mifchief to the Whites, without much expofing their own perfons to danger; for they always cautioufly avoided fighting, except with a number fo difproportionately inferior to them, as to afford them a pretty fure expectation of victory. They knew every fecret avenue of the country; fo that they could either conceal themfelves from purfuit, or form ambufcades, or fhift their ravages from place to place, according as circumftances required. Such were the many difadvantages under which the Englifh had to deal with thefe defultory foes; who were not reducible by any regular plan of attack; who poffeffed no plunder to allure or reward the affailants; nor had any thing to lofe, except life and liberty.

Previous to the fucceffes above-mentioned, the diftrefs into which the planters were thrown may be collected from the fenfe which the legiflature expreffed in fome of their acts. In the year 1733, they fet forth, that thefe Blacks had within a few years greatly increafed, notwithftanding all the meafures that had then been concerted, and made ufe of, for their fuppreffion; in particular, that they had grown very formidable in the North-Eaft, North-Weft, and South-Weft diftricts of the ifland, to the great terror of his majefty's fubjects in thofe parts, who had greatly fuffered by the frequent robberies, murders, and depredations, committed by them; that, in the parifhes of Clarendon, St. Anne, St. Elizabeth, Weftmoreland, Hanover, and St. James, they were confiderably multiplied, and had large fettlements among the mountains, and leaft acceffible parts; whence they plundered all around them, and caufed feveral plantations to be thrown up and abandoned, and prevented many valuable tracts of land from being cultivated, to the great prejudice and diminution of his majefty's revenue, as well as of the trade, navigation, and confumption, of Britifh manufactures; and to the manifeft weakening and preventing further increafe of ftrength and inhabitants in the ifland. We may learn from hence what extenfive mifchief may be perpetrated by the moft defpicable and cowardly enemy. The affembly, perceiving that the employment of flying parties had proved ineffectual, by the length of their marches, the difficulty
of

of subsisting them in the woods for so long a time as the service required, and the facility with which the Marons eluded their pursuers, ordered several defensible houses, or barracks fortified with bastions, to be erected in different parts, as near as possible to the enemy's most favourite haunts: in every one of these they placed a strong garrison, who were regularly subsisted, and roads of communication were opened from one to the other. These garrisons were composed of white and black shot and baggage Negroes, who were all duly trained. Every captain was allowed a pay of 10*l.*; the lieutenants each 5*l.*; serjeants 4*l.*; and privates 2*l.*, *per* month. They were subjected to rules and articles of war; and the whole body put under the governor's immediate order, to be employed conjunctly, or separately, as he should see occasion. Their general plan of duty, as directed by the law, was to make excursions from the barracks, scour the woods and mountains, and destroy the provision-grounds and haunts of the Marons; and, that they might not return without effecting some service, they were required to take twenty days provision with them on every such expedition. Every barrack was furnished besides with a pack of dogs, provided by the church-wardens of the respective parishes; it being foreseen, that these animals would prove extremely serviceable, not only in guarding against surprizes in the night, but in tracking the enemy.

This arrangement was the most judicious hitherto contrived for their effectual reduction; for so many fortresses, stationed in the very centre of their usual retreats, well supplied with every necessary, gave them a constant and vigorous annoyance, and, in short, became the chief means of bringing on that treaty which afterwards put an end to this tiresome war.

About the year 1738, the assembly resolved on taking two hundred of the Mosquito Indians into their pay, to hasten the suppression of the Marons. They passed an act, for rendering free Negroes, Mulattos, and Indians, more useful, and forming them into companies, with proper encouragements. Some sloops were dispatched to the shore; and that number were brought into the island, formed into companies under their own officers, and allowed forty shillings a month for pay, besides shoes; and white guides were assigned to conduct them to the enemy. In this service they

gave

gave proofs of great fagacity. One of their white conductors, having fhot a wild hog whilft they were on a march, the Indians told him that was not the way to furprize the Blacks, for the noife ferved only to put them upon their guard; and that, if he wanted provifions, they could kill the game equally well with their arrows, or lances, without giving any alarm. It was their practice to obferve the moft profound filence in marching to the enemy's quarters; and, when they had once hit upon a track, they were fure to difcover the haunt to which it led. They effected confiderable fervice; and were, indeed, the moft proper troops to be employed in that fpecies of action, which is known in America by the name of *bufh-fighting*. They were well rewarded for their good conduct; and afterwards difmiffed to their own country, when the pacification took place with the Marons. In 1741, the affembly fhewed a further mark of efteem for thefe honeft Indians; for, being informed that fome traders belonging to the ifland had made a practice frequently of ftealing away, and felling their children as flaves, which occafioned the Indians of Darien and Sambla to withdraw their friendfhip from the Englifh, and embrace alliance with the Spaniards; they paffed a bill, enacting, that all Indians, imported into the ifland for fale, fhould be as free as any other aliens or foreigners; and that all fuch fales fhould, *ipfo facto*, be void; and the buyer and feller be liable to a penalty of 50*l.* each. In 1739, governor Trelawny, by the advice of the principal gentlemen of the ifland, propofed overtures of a peace with the Maron chiefs. Both parties were now grown heartily wearied out with this tedious conflict. The white inhabitants wifhed relief from the horrors of continual alarms, the hardfhip of military duty, and the intolerable burthen of maintaining an army on foot. The Marons were not lefs anxious for an accommodation: they were hemmed in and clofely befet on all fides; their provifions deftroyed; and themfelves reduced to fo miferable a condition by famine and inceffant attacks, that Cudjoe (whom I converfed with many years afterwards) declared, if peace had not been offered to them, they had no choice left but either to be ftarved, lay violent hands on one another, or furrender to the Englifh at difcretion. The extremity, however, of their cafe was not at that time known to the white inhabitants; and the articles of pacification were therefore ratified with the Maron chiefs, who were colonel Cudjoe, captains Accompong, Johnny, Cuffee, and Quaco. By these articles it was ftipulated, that they and their adherents (except fuch as had fled to them within two years preceding, and might be willing to return to their owners upon grant of full pardon and indemnity, but otherwife to remain in fubjection to Cudjoe) fhould enjoy perpetual freedom: that they fhould poffefs in fee fimple one thoufand five hundred acres of land near Trelawny-Town, in the parifh of St. James; have liberty to plant coffee, cacao, ginger, tobacco, and cotton; and breed cattle, hogs, goats, and any other ftock, and to difpofe of the fame; with liberty of hunting any where within three miles of any fettlement [n].

That they, and their fucceffors, fhould ufe their beft endeavours to take, kill, fupprefs, and deftroy, all rebels throughout the ifland, unlefs they fhould fubmit to the like terms of accommodation [o]. That they fhould repair at all times, purfuant to the governor's order, to repel any foreign invafion: that, if any white perfon fhould do them injury, they fhould apply to a magiftrate for redrefs; and in cafe any Maron fhould injure a white perfon, the offender fhould be delivered up to juftice: that Cudjoe, and his fucceffors in command, fhould wait on the governor once a year, if required: that he and his fucceffors fhould have full power to punifh crimes committed among themfelves by their own men, punifhment of death only excepted; and that, in capital cafes, the offenders fhould be brought before a juftice of peace, in order to be proceeded againft, and tried like other free Negroes: that two white men fhould conftantly refide with Cudjoe and his fucceffors, to keep up friendly correfpondence. The command of Trelawny Town was limited to Cudjoe during life; and, after his deceafe, to Accompong, Johnny, Cuffee, and Quaco; and, in remainder, to fuch perfon as the governor for the time being may think fit to

[n] One thoufand acres have likewife been affigned to Accompong's Town, in St. Elizabeth's; and due proportions to the other towns; fecured to their refpective Negroe inhabitants in perpetuity; and a penalty of 500l. ordained againft any perfon convicted of difturbing their poffeffion.

[o] This alludes to captain Quao, of the windward party, who did not come in till the following year.

appoint. Thefe are the moft material articles recognized by the law. It likewife provides, that no perfon fhall feize, cetain, or difturb, any of the Negroes in the poffeffions and privileges thereby granted, under penalty of 500 *l.*; and it allows them, for apprehending and bringing in run-away flaves, 10 *s. per* head, with a poundage of 2 *s.* 6 *d.* for money difburfed, befides mile-money, according to the diftance. Thefe were the Negroes belonging to the leeward towns, Trelawny and Accompong, the former in St. James; the other in St. Elizabeth. Some years afterwards, upon fome difference arifing among the Negroes at Trelawny, as I have heard, concerning the right of command, a fray enfued. The town divided into two factions; one of which adhered to a new chief, named Furry, and removed with him to another fpot, where they formed a new town, called after his name. In 1740, the like accommodation was entered into with Captain Quao, of the windward party; the purport of which is much the fame as the preceding, except that they are prohibited exprefsly from planting an fugar-canes, except for their hogs; and are to be tried for capital crimes, like other Negroes. The command, upon Quao's death, is fettled to devolve to Captain Thomboy; remainder to Apong, Blackwall, Clafh; and afterwards to be fupplied by the governor for the time being. It was likewife conditioned, that all fugitive flaves, who had joined Quao's party, or had been taken prifoners by them within three years antecedent fhould be delivered up to their refpective owners upon affurance of pardon and good ufage. This windward party now occupy Scot's Hall, in St. Mary; Moore Town (formed upon the defertion of Nanny Town), in Portland and Crawford; or Charles Town, in St. George.

By fubfequent laws, the premium for taking up run-aways was augmented to 3 *l. per* head [*p*], and fome other provifions enacted: viz. that any Negroes in thefe towns, committing tumult and difturbance, fhall fuffer fuch punifhment as the white fuperintendant, with four townfmen, and the captain commandant, fhall inflict, not extending to life: that the governor fhall iffue commiffions for trial of the offenders: that they fhall not abfent themfelves

[*p*] By an act paffed fince, viz. in the year 1769, the premium is reduced to 2 *l. per* head, or fo much only as the magiftrate may deem meet; and mile-money at the rate of 7½ *d. per* mile.

from

from their respective towns, without leave in writing from their respective commanding officer, under penalty, upon conviction before two justices and three freeholders, of being deprived of freedom, and transported off the island: the like penalty, for enticing slaves to run away. They are also forbidden to purchase slaves, under penalty of forfeiture, and 100 *l*. fine, to be paid by the seller, or other person concerned

These Negroes, although inhabiting more towns than at first, are diminished in their number by deaths, and cohabitation with slaves on the plantations, instead of intermixing with each other. They have been very serviceable, particularly the leeward parties, in suppressing several insurrections. Their captains are distinguished with a silver chain and medal, inscribed with their names: they wear cockades, and are regularly commissioned by the governor. It is customary for the governors to give audience to their chiefs once a year, and confer some mark of favour, such as an old laced coat or waistcoat, a hat, sword, fusee, or any other articles of the like nature, which seem most acceptable. They are pleased with these distinctions; and a trifling douceur of this sort bestowed annually, accompanied with expressions of favour, wins their hearts, and strengthens their dutiful attachment. It is probable, they would be much honester allies, and more faithful subjects, if some little pains were taken to instil a few notions of honesty and religion into their minds. The erection of a chapel in each of their towns would be attended with very small expence; and here they might regularly attend divine worship once a week. A small addition to the rector's salary would enable him to visit and discourse to them occasionally. The white residents ought to be thoroughly examined by the governor; and care be taken, that they are men of good morals, sober, and promoters of order and peace in their several towns. They should be punished with exemplary severity, whenever found guilty of oppression, or other ill usage. And the articles of treaty should never be infringed by legislature, while the Negroes conform to them on their part: but, when any deviation is made, it ought in justice to affect only the contravenors of them. Good faith, good usage, and moral instruction, as far as they may be capable of it, are the best guarantees of their firm allegiance; a

different

different meafure of conduct will neceffarily render them difcontented and troublefome.

Tedious and expenfive as the war was, which continued for fo many years before they could be brought to terms, the event was very happy for the ifland. The multitude of parties kept on foot, to inveft their quarters, led to the difcovery of various tracts of exceedingly fine land, unknown before. Many of thefe were brought into cultivation foon after they were reduced; and the roads, which were cut from time to time through the woods, for the better carrying on of military operations, were in confequence found of great ufe to the new fettlers, for carriage of their goods. The treaty, moreover, gave a fecurity to young beginners in the remote parts, even againft any machinations of their own flaves: fo that this conteft, which, while it lafted, feemed to portend nothing lefs than the ruin of the whole colony, became productive of quite contrary effects in the end; infomuch that we may date the flourifhing ftate of it from the ratification of the treaty; ever fince which, the ifland has been increafing in plantations and opulence.

Their manner of engaging with an enemy has fomething too fingular in it to be paffed over. In the year 1764, when governor Lyttelton paffed through St. James parifh on his leeward tour, the Trelawny Marons attended him at Montego Bay, to the number of eighty-four, men, women, and children. After the white militia belonging to the parifh were reviewed, the fencible men of the black party drew up, impatient to fhew their martial fkill. No fooner did their horn found the fignal, than they all joined in a moft hideous yell, or war-hoop, and bounded into action. With amazing agility, they literally ran and rolled through their various firings and evolutions. This part of their exercife, indeed, more juftly deferves to be ftyled evolution than any that is practifed by the regular troops; for they fire ftooping almoft to the very ground; and no fooner is their piece difcharged, than they throw themfelves into a thoufand antic geftures, and tumble over and over, fo as to be continually fhifting their place; the intention of which is, to elude the fhot, as well as to deceive the aim of their adverfaries, which their nimble and almoft inftantaneous change of pofition

renders

renders extremely uncertain. In fhort, throughout their whole manœuvres, they fkip about like fo many monkies [q]. When this part of their exercife was over, they drew their fwords; and, winding their horn again, they began, in wild and warlike capers, to advance towards his excellency, endeavouring to throw as much favage fury into their looks as poffible. On approaching near him, fome, with a horrid, circling flourifh, waved their rufty blades over his head, then gently laid them upon it; whilft others clafhed their arms together in horrid concert. They next brought their mufkets, and piled them up in heaps at his feet, which fome of them defired to kifs, and were permitted. By way of clofing the ceremony, their leader, captain Cudjoe, in the name of all the reft, ftood forth, and addreffed his excellency aloud, defiring the continuance of the great king George's favour and protection; and that his excellency, as his vice-gerent, would adminifter right and juftice to them, according to the happy treaty and agreement fubfifting between them and the white people of the ifland.

To this the governor replied, that they might depend upon the favour and protection of the great king George; and of his own conftant endeavours likewife, that right and juftice fhould be always done them; and alfo, that he would take care, that the good underftanding, then fo happily fubfifting between the white inhabitants and them, fhould inviolably be preferved; provided that they, on their parts, continued to be always active and ready in obeying their commanding officer, and doing whatever elfe they had, in the treaty, folemnly promifed to perform. To this they all affented; and then, having a dinner ordered for them, and a prefent of three cows, were difmiffed, and went away perfectly well fatisfied.

I have no certain account of the number of thefe Negroes in their feveral towns at prefent; but the following was the ftate of them in the year 1749 [r].

[q] A bucanier hiftorian tells us, that, having landed with a party at Cofta Rica, the toil of fhooting was fufficiently compenfated with the pleafure of killing the monkies; for at thefe they ufually made fifteen or fixteen fhot, before they could kill three or four; fo nimbly did they elude their hands and aim, even after being much wounded: and that it was *high fun* to fee the females carry their little ones on their backs, juft as the Negroes do their children.

[r] According to a late return, the Negroes of Moore Town are increafed to two hundred; but the whole number of fighting men does not exceed one hundred and fifty; and the whole number of Negroes in all the towns is not augmented much beyond the above lift of the year 1749.

Totals.

Totals.			Men.	Women.	Boys.	Girls.
276	Trelawny Town,	St. James,	112	85	40	39
85	Accompong's,	St. Elizabeth,	31	25	13	16
233	Crawford, or Charles Town,	St. George,	102	80	26	25
70	Nanny, or Moore Town,	Portland,	28	21	9	12
	N. B.					
664	{ " Scot's Hall, in St. Mary, } not then formed."		273	211	88	92
	{ " Furry's, in St. James,					

The pay to thefe Negroes, when they are upon fervice, is,

		£	s.	d.
To each captain, —— —— —— *per* day,		0	2	6
Ditto private, —— —— ——				7½

This expence is charged to the annual fund of 500 *l.* appropriated for the ufe of parties. We may add to this the following eftablifh-ment, augmented fince 1769; viz.

	£
To a fuperintendant-general, —— —— Currency,	300
To three white fuperintendants, at 200 *l.* falary each, *per ann.*	600
To one ditto, of Trelawny Town, 300 *l.* ditto, —— ——	300
To one ditto, of Scot's Hall, 100 *l.* ditto, —— ——	100
To five white refidents, 40 *l.* ditto, —— ——	200
For parties as above, brought down, —— ——	500
Total, *per annum*, £	2000

The expence of a curate, to perform divine fervice, baptize,

&c. as propofed, may be put at 50 *l.* each, —— —— £ 250
Which would be no great addition to the annual charge. And it is not to be forgotten, that all this money remains to circulate in the ifland, and is of advantage to the fhop-keepers, who fupply thefe Negroes with feveral fmall articles for their cloathing and con-fumption.

END OF THE SECOND BOOK.

THE

THE THIRD BOOK
CHAP I.
NEGROES.

I SHALL divide this people into two claffes, the native, or Creole blacks, and the imported, or Africans; but, before I come to
fpeak of thofe who inhabit Jamaica, I fhall beg to premife fome remarks upon the Negroes in general found on that part of the African
continent, called Guiney, or Negro-land. The particulars wherein
they differ moft effentially from the Whites are, firft, in refpect to their
bodies, viz. the dark membrane which communicates that black colour
to their fkins [a], which does not alter by tranfportation into other
climates,

[a] Anatomifts fay, that this *reticular membrane*, which is found between the *Epidermis* and the
fkin, being foaked in water for a long time, does not change its colour. Monfieur Barrere, who
appears to have examined this circumftance with peculiar attention, as well as Mr. Winflow,
fays, that the *Epidermis* itfelf is black, and that if it has appeared white to fome that have examined
it, it is owing to its extreme finenefs and tranfparency; but that it is really as dark as a piece of
black horn, reduced to the fame gracility. That this colour of the *Epidermis*, and of the fkin,
is caufed by the bile, which in Negroes is not yellow, but always as black as ink. The bile in
white men tinges their fkin yellow; and if their bile was black, it would doubtlefs communicate the
fame black tint. Mr. Barrere affirms, that the Negroe bile naturally fecretes itfelf upon the *Ep-
dermis*, in a quantity fufficient to impregnate it with the dark colour for which it is fo remarkable.
Thefe obfervations naturally lead to the further queftion, " why the bile in Negroes is black?"

Mr. Buffon endeavours to refolve the former part of this enquiry, by fuppofing that the heat of
climate is the principal caufe of their black colour. " That exceffive cold and exceffive heat produce
" fimilar effects on the human body, and act on the fkin by a certain drying quality, which tans it;
" that originally there was but one fpecies of men; and that difference of climate, of manner of
" living, of food, of endemical diftempers, and the mixtures of individuals, more or lefs varied,
" have produced the diftinctions that are now vifible; and that this black colour of Negroes, if they
" were tranfplanted into a cold climate, would gradually wear off and difappear in the courfe of ten
" or twelve generations."

But, to admit the force of this reafoning, we muft fuppofe the world to be much older than
has been generally believed. The Æthiopian is probably not at all blacker now than he was in the
days of Solomon. The nations of Nicaragua and Guatimala, on the American continent, who lie
under the fame parallel of latitude as the inhabitants of Guiney, have not acquired this black tincture,
although many more generations have paffed fince they were firft difcovered by the Europeans than
Mr. Buffon thinks fufficient for changing a Negroe from black to white. How many centuries muft
have revolved before that continent was difcovered, may be imagined from the populous ftate of it
in the days of Americus Vefpucius, and the prodigious length of time required for a nation or large
fociety of men to grow up, become powerful, warlike, and tolerably civilized, as the Mexicans
were!

climates, and which they never lofe, except by fuch difeafes, or cafualties, as deftroy the texture of it ; for example, the leprofy, and accidents of burning or fcalding.   Negroes have been introduced into the
North American colonies near 150 years.   The winters, efpecially at
New York and New England, are more fevere than in Europe.   Yet
the Blacks born here, to the third and fourth generation, are not at all
different in colour from thofe Negroes who are brought directly from
Africa ; whence it may be concluded very properly, that Negroes, or
their pofterity, do not change colour, though they continue ever fo
long in a cold climate.

Secondly, A covering of wool, like the beftial fleece, inftead of
hair.

Thirdly, The roundnefs of their eyes, the figure of their ears, tu-
mid noftrils, flat nofes, invariable thick lips, and general large fize of
the female nipples, as if adapted by nature to the peculiar conformation
of their childrens mouths.

Fourthly, The black colour of the lice which infeft their bodies.
This peculiar circumftance I do not remember to have feen noticed
by any naturalift ; they refemble the white lice in fhape, but in general are of larger fize.   It is known, that there is a very great variety of thefe infects ; and fome fay, that almoft all animals have their
peculiar fort.

Fifthly, Their beftial or fetid fmell, which they all have in a
greater or lefs degree ; the Congo's, Arada's, Quaqua's, and Angola's,

were! Further, as this change is fuppofed by Mr. Buffon to be gradual, fome proof of it would
doubtlefs appear in the courfe of one or two centuries.   But we do not find, that the pofterity of
thofe Europeans, who firft fettled in the hotteft parts of the Weft Indies, are tending towards this
black complexion, or are more tawny than an Englifhman might become by refiding five or fix
years in Spain, and expofing himfelf to the fun and air during his refidence.   It would likewife
happen, that the progeny of Negroes brought from Guiney two hundred years ago, and tranfplanted into a colder climate, would be comparatively lefs black than the natives of that part of
Africa, from whence their progenitors were removed ; but no fuch effect has been obferved.   And
laftly, the whole fabric of Mr. Buffon's hypothefis is fubverted at once, by the race of *Albinoes*,
in the very heart of Guiney ; who, although fubject to the fame intenfe heat of climate, which,
he fays, has caufed the black colour of Negroes, are unaccountably exempted from the influence
of this caufe, though equally expofed to it.   Without puzzling our wits, to difcover the occult
caufes of this diverfity of colour among mankind, let us be content with acknowledging, that
it was juft as eafy for Omnipotence to create black fkinned, as white-fkinned men ; or to create
five millions of human beings, as to create one fuch being.

particularly

particularly the latter, who are likewife the moft ftupid of the Negroe race, are the moft offenfive; and thofe of Senegal (who are diftinguifhed from the other herds by greater acutenefs of underftanding and mild-nefs of difpofition) have the leaft of this noxious odour.

This feent in fometof them is fo exceffively ftrong, efpecially when their bodies are warmed either by exercife or anger, that it continues in places where they have been near a quarter of an hour.

I fhall next confider their difparity, in regard to the faculties of the mind. Under this head we are to obferve, that they remain at this time in the fame rude fituation in which they were found two thoufand years ago.

In general, they are void of genius, and feem almoft incapable of making any progrefs in civility or fcience. They have no plan or fyftem of morality among them. Their barbarity to their children debafes their nature even below that of brutes. They have no moral fenfations; no tafte but for women; gormondizing, and drinking to excefs; no wifh but to be idle. Their children, from their tendereft years, are fuffered to deliver themfelves up to all that nature fuggefts to them. Their houfes are miferable cabbins. They conceive no plea-fure from the moft beautiful parts of their country, preferring the more fterile. Their roads, as they call them, are mere fheep-paths, twice as long as they need be, and almoft impaffable. Their country in moft parts is one continued wildernefs, befet with briars and thorns. They ufe neither carriages, nor beafts of burthen. They are repre-fented by all authors as the vileft of the human kind, to which they have little more pretenfion of refemblance than what arifes from their exterior form.

In fo vaft a continent as that of Afric, and in fo great a variety of climates and provinces, we might expect to find a proportionable diverfity among the inhabitants, in regard to their qualifications of body and mind; ftrength, agility, induftry, and dexterity, on the one hand; ingenuity, learning, arts, and fciences, on the other. But, on the contrary, a general uniformity runs through all thefe various regions of people; fo that, if any difference be found, it is only in degrees of the fame qualities; and, what is more ftrange, thofe of the worft kind; it being a common known proverb, that all people on the globe have fome good as well as ill qualities, except the

Africans. Whatever great perfonages this country might anciently
have produced, and concerning whom we have no information, they
are now every where degenerated into a brutifh, ignorant, idle, crafty,
treacherous, bloody, thievifh, miftruftful, and fuperftitious people,
even in thofe ftates where we might expect to find them. more
polifhed, humane, docile, and induftrious.   It is doubtful, whether
we ought to afcribe any fuperior qualities to the more ancient Africans; for we find them reprefented by the Greek and Roman authors
under the moft odious and defpicable character; as proud, lazy, deceitful, thievifh, addicted to all kinds of luft, and ready to promote
them in others, inceftuous, favage, cruel, and vindictive, devourers
of human flefh, and quaffers of human blood, inconftant, bafe, and
cowardly, devoted to all forts of fuperftition; and, in fhort, to every
vice that came in their way, or within their reach.

For the honour of human nature it were to be wifhed, that thefe
defcriptions could with juftice be accufed of exaggeration; but, in refpect to the modern Africans, we find the charge corroborated, and
fupported by a confiftent teftimony of fo many men of different nations, who have vifited the coaft, that it is difficult to believe they have
all been guilty of mifreprefenting thefe people; more efpecially, as
they tally exactly with the character of the Africans that are brought
into our plantations.   This brutality fomewhat diminifhes, when
they are imported young, after they become habituated to cloathing
and a regular difcipline of life; but many are never reclaimed, and
continue favages, in every fenfe of the word, to their lateft period.
We find them marked with the fame beftial manners, ftupidity, and
vices, which debafe their brethren on the continent, who feem to be
diftinguifhed from the reft of mankind, not in perfon only, but in
poffeffing, in abftract, every fpecies of inherent turpitude that is to be
found difperfed at large among the reft of the human creation, with
fcarce a fingle virtue to extenuate this fhade of character, differing in
this particular from all other men; for, in other countries, the moft
abandoned villain we ever heard of has rarely, if ever, been known
unportioned with fome one good quality at leaft, in his compofition
It is aftonifhing, that, although they have been acquainted with Europeans, and their manufactures, for fo many hundred years, they
have, in all this feries of time, manifefted fo little tafte for arts, or a

genius

genius either inventive or imitative. Among fo great a number of provinces on this extenfive continent, and among fo many millions of people, we have heard but of one or two infignificant tribes, who comprehend any thing of mechanic arts, or manufacture; and even thefe, for the moft part, are faid to perform their work in a very bungling and flovenly manner, perhaps not better than an *oranoutang* might, with a little pains, be brought to do.

The Chinefe, the Mexicans, the Northern Indians, are all celebrated, fome for their expert imitation of any pattern laid before them; others for their faculty of invention; and the reft for the ingenuity of their feveral fabrics. There was not a tribe of thefe Indians, from the Mexican to the Caribbean, that was not found to poffefs many amiable endowments. In the hotteft region of South America the natives were effeminate, lefs robuft and courageous than the Northern inhabitants; but none of them addicted to the brutal practices common to the Negroes, lying under the fame parallel of climate; on the contrary, thefe Indians are reprefented as a docile, inoffenfive, fagacious, and ingenious people. The Northern Indians, we know, have, ever fince they came to the knowledge of Europeans, difplayed an elevation of foul, which would do honour to the moft civilized nations. It muft be agreed, (fays *Charlevoix*) that the nearer we view them, the more good qualities we difcover in them; moft of the principles, which feem to regulate their conduct, the general maxims by which they govern themfelves, and the effential part of their character, difclofe nothing of the barbarian.

The Negroes feem to conform neareft in character to the Ægyptians, in whofe government, fays the learned Goguet, there reigned a multitude of abufes, and effential defects, authorized by the laws, and by their fundamental principles. As to their cuftoms and manners, indecency and debauchery were carried to the moft extravagant height, in all their public feafts, and religious ceremonies; neither was their morality pure. It offended againft the firft rules of rectitude and probity; they lay under the higheft cenfure for covetoufnefs, perfidy, cunning, and roguery. They were a people without tafte, without genius, or difcernment; who had only ideas of grandeur, ill underftood: knavifh, crafty, foft, lazy, cowardly, and fervile, fuperftitious in excefs, and extravagantly befotted with an abfurd and monftrous

Z z 2

theology;

theology: without any skill in eloquence, poetry, music, architecture, sculpture, or painting, navigation, commerce, or the art military. Their intellect rising to but a very confused notion, and imperfect idea, of the general objects of human knowledge. But he allows, that they invented some arts, and some sciences; that they had some little knowledge of astronomy, geography, and the mathematics; that they had some few good civil laws and political constitutions; were industrious enough adepts in judicial astrology; though their skill in sculpture, and architecture, rose not above a flat mediocrity. In these acquisitions, however imperfect, they appear far superior to the Negroes, who, perhaps, in their turn, as far transcend the Ægyptians in the superlative perfection of their worst qualities.

When we reflect on the nature of these men, and their dissimilarity to the rest of mankind, must we not conclude, that they are a different species of the same *genus*? Of other animals, it is well known, there are many kinds, each kind having its proper species subordinate thereto: and why shall we insist, that man alone, of all other animals, is undiversified in the same manner, when we find so many irresistible proofs which denote his conformity to the general system of the world? In this system we perceive a regular order and gradation, from inanimate to animated matter; and certain links, which connect the several *genera* one with another; and, under these *genera*, we find another gradation of species, comprehending a vast variety, and, in some classes, widely differing from each other in certain qualities. We ascend from mere inert matter into the animal and vegetable kingdoms, by an almost imperceptible deviation; and these two are again nearly connected by a very palpable similitude; so that, where the one ends, the other seems to begin. When we proceed to divide and subdivide the various classes of animals, we perceive the same exact subordination and close affinity between the two extremes combining all together in a wonderful and beautiful harmony, the result of infinite wisdom and contrivance. If, amidst the immense variety of all animate beings which people the universe, some animal, for example, the body of a man, be selected to serve as a criterion, with which all the other organized beings are to be compared; it will be found, that, although all these beings exist abstractedly, and all vary by differences infinitely graduated, yet, at the same time, there appears a primitive and general design, or model, that

may

may be very plainly traced, and of which the degradations are much flower than thofe of fhape, figure, and other external appearances. For, befides the organs of digeftion, circulation, and generation, belonging to all animals, and without which the animal muft ceafe to be an animal, as it could neither fubfift, nor propagate its fpecies; there is, even in the parts which principally contribute to the variety of exterior forms, a prodigious refemblance, which neceffarily reminds us of an original model, after which every thing feems to have been worked. The body of a horfe, for inftance, which, at firft fight feems fo different from that of a man, when properly compared part by part, inftead of furprizing us by the difference, fills us with aftonifhment at the fingular and almoft complete refemblance we find between them; for, take the fkeleton of a man, incline the bones of the *pelvis*, fhorten the bones of the thighs, legs, and arms, lengthen thofe of the feet and hands, connect the phalanges, extend the jaws, fhorten the frontal bone, and, laftly, lengthen the fpine; this fkeleton, inftead of refembling any longer the remains of a man, will be the fkeleton of a horfe. It may be eafily fuppofed, that, by lengthening the fpine and the jaws, the number of the *vertebræ*, the ribs and teeth are increafed at the fame time; and it is only in the number of thefe bones, which may be confidered as neceffary, and the protracting, fhortening, or junction of the others, that the fkeleton of the body of this animal differs from that of the human body. But, to carry thefe refemblances ftill further, let us feparately confider fome parts effential to the figure; the ribs, for inftance, which will be found in man, in all the quadrupeds, in birds, fifhes, and even the veftiges of them, may be traced to the very tortoife, where a delineation of them plainly appears in the futures under the fhell. Let it alfo be confidered, that the foot of a horfe, though in appearance fo different from the hand of a man, is yet compofed of fimilar bones; and that, at the extremity of each of our fingers, there is the fame horfe-fhoe fhaped little bone, which terminates the foot of that animal; let it then be decided, whether this latent refemblance be not more aftonifhing than the vifible differences; whether this conftant conformity, and continuing model, followed from man to quadrupeds; from quadrupeds to the cetaceous fpecies; from them to birds; from birds to reptiles; from reptiles to fifh, &c. in which are always found the effential parts, as the heart,

2   inteftines,

inteſtines, the ſpine, the ſenſes, &c. do not ſeem to indicate, that the Supreme Being, at the creation of animals, intended to make uſe of one model ; varying it, at the ſame time, in every poſſible manner, that man might equally admire the ſimplicity of the plan, and the magnificence of the execution [b].

When we come to examine the exterior figures of any particular claſs of animals, we find them marked with a moſt remarkable variety.   To inſtance, for example, the dog kind, who have ſome of them ſo near an affinity to the wolf and fox ; there is more difference between the maſtiff and lap-dog, than between the horſe and the aſs ; and what two animals can be more unlike, than the little black Guiney dog, of a ſmooth ſkin, without a ſingle hair upon it, and the rough ſhock dog ? From theſe let us paſs on to the monkey-kind, or anthropomorphits, ſo called by naturaliſts, becauſe they partake more or leſs of the human ſhape and diſpoſition ; we here obſerve the palpable link which unites the human race with the quadruped, not in exterior form alone, but in the intellectual quality.   The variety of them is ſo great, that a complete catalogue has never yet been made. Condamine, who traveled through the country of the Amazons, ſaw ſo many, that he affirms, it would take up ſome length of time to write out a liſt of their names.   As far however as they are yet deſcribed, we trace them from the cynocephalus, which moſt reſembles quadrupeds in the ſhape of its head, through a variety of the ape kind, which have tails and pouches, to thoſe which have ſhorter tails, and ſomewhat more of the human viſage ; to thoſe which have no tails, who have a callous breech, whoſe feet ſerve occaſionally for hands, which conſtitute them of the order of quadrumains, or four-handed animals, and who more commonly move on all-four than erect, to the cephus, or gibbon, of Buffon ; from theſe we come to the oran-outang ſpecies, who have ſome trivial reſemblance to the ape-kind, but the ſtrongeſt ſimilitude to mankind, in countenance, figure, ſtature, organs, erect poſture, actions or movements, food, temper, and manner of living.

The few which have been brought into Europe, being extremely young, were, from a popular error, denominated pigmies ; for it is affirmed on every authority, that they grow to the ordinary ſize of

[b] Buffon.

man.

man. Mr. Buffon, who has examined this curious fubject with great attention, defcribes them thus; " The oran-outang has no pouch, tail, nor callofity, on his hind parts; thefe parts, and the calves of his legs, are plump and flefhy, differing intirely from the ape and monkey. All his teeth are the fame as the human, his face is broad, naked, and taw-ney, his ears, hands, feet, breaft, and belly, are likewife without hair, and of the fame tawney complexion; the hair of his head is like that of a man, and defcends in a forelock on each temple; the hair on his back and loins is thin, and in fmall quantity; he grows from *five* to *fix* feet in height."

The nofe is flat, the breaft of the females furnifhed with two paps, and they are fubject to the periodical flux. The latter characteriftic, which is common alfo to the monkey-clafs, was not unobferved by the ancient Ægyptians, who drew a fingular advantage from it in their aftronomical regifters; for they kept the cynocephalus, and other monkies, in their temples, in order to know, with tolerable certainty, by this means, the periodical conjunctions of the fun and moon.

Lewis le Compte, in his Memoirs of China, afferts, that in the ftraits of Molucca he faw fome of *four feet* in height, that walked erect, and nad faces fhaped like thofe of the Hottentots at the Cape. They made a noife like a young child; their paffions appeared with a lively expreffion in their countenances; they feemed to be of a tender difpofition, and would kifs and embrace thofe they were fond of. Doctor Tyfon, giving an account of a young male brought from Angola (afterwards diffected), obferves, that he poffeffed the like tender-nefs of difpofition towards the failors on board fhip. He would not affociate with the monkies brought in the fame fhip, but fhunned their company. He ufed to put on his own cloaths; or, at leaft, whenever he found a difficulty in managing any part of his drefs, he would take it in his hand to fome of the company, fignifying (as it were) his defire that they fhould help him.

Mr. Noell fpeaks of apes, which he faw in Guiney, and calls *barris* (which Mr. Buffon takes to be a fynonym of the oran-outang), who walked erect, and had more gravity, and appearance of underftand-ing, than any other of the ape kind, and were paffionately fond of women.

Linnæus,

Linnæus, upon the authority of some voyage writers, affirms, that they converse together in a kind of *hiffing* dialect ; that they possess thought and reflexion, and believe the world was made for them, &c. but Mr. Buffon, with good reason, suspects that Linnæus has confounded the albinoe with the oran-outang.

The oran-outangs are said to make a kind of huts, composed of boughs interlaced, which serve to guard them from the too great heat of the sun [c].

It is also averred, that they sometimes endeavour to surprize and carry off Negroe women into their woody retreats, in order to enjoy them.

Monsieur la Brosse says, he knew a Negress at Loangs in Guiney, who had resided three years with them; he asserts that they grow to the height of *six* to *seven* feet, have vast muscular strength, and defend themselves with sticks. He bought two young ones, a male of fourteen months, and a female of twelve. They sat at table, ate of every thing without distinction, handled the knife and fork, and helped themselves, drank wine, and other liquors; made themselves understood by the cabbin boy, when they wanted any thing, and, upon the boy's refusal to give them what they seemed to desire, they shewed symptoms of violent anger and disgust. The male falling sick, was twice blooded in the right arm, which relieved him; and afterwards, whenever he found himself indisposed, he pointed to his arm, as if he knew what had done him good in his former illness. I must own, this account contains some particulars very extraordinary; for a child of the same age, in England, would be regarded as wonderfully forward, if it should exhibit the like proofs of sagacity. But, if we allow to these oran-outangs a degree of intellect not restricted wholly to instinct, but approaching, like the frame of their organs, to an affinity with the human, we may establish the credibility of this relation, by supposing that like, the human inhabitants of Guiney, they arrive three or four years earlier at the age of puberty, or maturity, than the inhabitants of Northern climates: and consequently that their faculties, in general, blossom and expand proportionably earlier.

[c] Jobson.

Mr.

Mr. Groffe reports, that two young ones, fcarcely two feet high (probably under two years of age), which he prefented to the governor of Bombay, refembled mankind in all their actions. If they were gazed at when in bed, they covered with their hands thofe parts which modefty forbids to expofe. They appeared dejected under their captivity; and the female dying on board fhip, her comrade exhibited every token of heart-felt affliction, rejected his food, and did not furvive her above two days.

Guat, fpeaking of a female which he faw at Java, fays, her ftature was *very large*; that fhe refembled ftrongly fome Hottentot women he had feen at the Cape; that fhe made her own bed every day very properly, laid her head on the pillow, and covered herfelf with the quilt. When fhe had a pain in her head, fhe bound it with a handkerchief.—Several other particulars, he fays, might be enumerated, that were very fingular; but he fufpected that thefe animals are often brought, by a habit of inftruction, to do many of thofe feats, which the vulgar regard as natural; this, however, he only gives as a matter of conjecture.

Gemelli Careri afferts to have feen one that cried like an infant, and carried a mat in its arms, which it occafionally laid down and repofed upon. Thefe apes, fays he, feem to have more fenfe than fome among mankind; for, when they are unable to find any fruits in the mountains for their fubfiftence, they come down to the fea fhore, where they catch crabs, lobfters, and fuch like. A fpecies of oyfter, called *taclovo*, frequently lie on the beach. The apes, on perceiving any of them gaping, chuck a ftone between the fhells, which hinders them from clofing, and then proceed to devour them without any apprehenfion.

Francis Pyrard reports, he found the *barris* in the province of Sierra Leon, in Guiney; that they are corpulent and mufcular, and fo docile, that, if properly inftructed while they are young, they become very good fervants.

Father Jarrie fpeaks of them in the fame terms; and the teftimony of Schoutten agrees with Pyrard on the fubject of the education of thefe animals; he fays, they are taken with nets, that they walk erect, and can ufe their feet occafionally as hands, in performing certain domeftic fervices, as rinfeing of glaffes, prefenting them to drink, turning fpits, and the like. Thefe and other examples are quoted by Mr. Buffon, who confiders thefe animals, fpoken of by voyagers under different appellations, to be only varieties of the oran-outang; and in this light he mentions the jocko, which he faw publickly fhewn at Paris. This animal always walked in an erect pofture; his carriage was rather aukward, his air dejected, his pace grave, and movements fedate; he had nothing of the impatience, caprice, and mifchief of the baboon, nor extravagancies of the monkey; he was ever ready and quick of apprehenfion; a fign or a word was fufficient to make him do what the baboon and others would not without the compulfion of the cudgel or whip. He prefented his hand to re-conduct the perfons who came to vifit him, and ftalked with a ftately gait before them. He fat at table, unfolded his napkin, wiped his lips, helped himfelf, and conveyed the victuals to his mouth with the fpoon and fork; poured the drink into a glafs, brought the tea-things to the table, put in the fugar, poured out the tea, let it ftand till it was cool enough for drinking, and all this with no other inftigation than a fign or word from his mafter, and often of his own free accord; he was of a courteous, tender difpofition; he fpent the fummer at Paris, and died the following winter at London, of a cough and confumption. He ate of every food indifferently, except that he feemed to prefer confectionary, ripe and dried fruits, and drank wine in moderation.

This creature was about 2½ feet tall, and, according to the teftimony of the perfon who brought him to Europe, not above two years old; Mr. Buffon, therefore, imagines that at his full ftature he would have attained above five feet, fuppofing his growth proportioned to that of mankind.

The pigmy defcribed, and diffected, by Dr. Tyfon, was not more than two feet in height, and ftill younger, or under two years old, for his teeth and fome other offifications were not entirely formed.

The effential differences between the body of the oran-outang and that of a man, are reduced by Mr. Buffon to two, namely, the conformation of the *os ilium*, and that of the feet; the bone of the *ilium* is more clofe or contracted than in man. He has calves, and flefhy pofteriors, which indicate that he is deftined to walk erect; but his toes are very long, and the heel preffed with difficulty to the ground: he

runs

runs with more eafe than he can walk, and requires artificial heels, more elevated than thofe of fhoes in general, to enable him to walk with-out incovenience for any length of time. Thefe are the only parts in which he bears more refemblance to the ape kind than to man; but when he is compared with the ape, baboon, or monkey, he is found to have far more conformity to man than to thofe animals. The In-dians are therefore excufable for affociating him with the human race, under the appellation of oran-outang, or *wild man*, fince he re-fembles man much more than he does the ape, or any other animal. All the parts of his head, limbs, and body, external and internal, are fo perfectly like the human, that we cannot (fays he) collate them toge-ther, without being amazed at a conformation fo parallel, and an or-ganization fo exactly the fame, although *not refulting to the fame ef-fects*. The tongue, for example, and all the organs of fpeech are the fame in both, and yet the oran-outang *does not fpeak*; the brain is abfolutely the fame in texture, difpofition, and proportion, and yet *he does not think*; an evident proof this, that mere matter alone, though perfectly organized, cannot produce thought, nor fpeech, the index of thought, unlefs it be animated with *a fuperior principle*.

His imitation and mimickry of human geftures and movements, which come fo near in femblance to the refult of thought, fet him at a great diftance from brute animals, and in a clofe affinity to man. If the effence of his nature confifts entirely in the form and organiza-tion of the body, he comes nearer to man than any other creature, and may be placed in the fecond clafs of animal beings.

If he is a creature *fui generis*, he fills up the fpace between man-kind and the ape, as this and the monkey tribe fupply the interval that is between the oran-outang and quadrupeds.

When we compare the accounts of this race, fo far as they appear credible, and to be relied on, we muft, to form a candid judgement, be of opinion that Mr. Buffon has been rather too precipitate in fome of his conclufions.

We obferve that, in their native countries, they are not thoroughly known; they live fequeftered in deep woods, poffefs great ftrength and agility of body, with probably fufficient cunning to guard againft, as well as nimblenefs to elude, furprizes. The Negroes and Indians believe them to be favage men; it is no wonder that, for the moft part,

they

they are fearful of approaching the haunts of this race ; and that from some or other of thefe caufes, none have been obtained for infpection in Europe, except very young ones, who could not efcape their purfuers.

So far as they are hitherto difcovered to Europeans, it appears that they herd in a kind of fociety together, and build huts fuitable to their climate ; that, when tamed and properly inftructed, they have been brought to perform a variety of menial domeftic fervices ; that they conceive a paffion for the Negroe women, and hence muft be fuppofed to covet their embraces from a natural impulfe of defire, fuch as inclines one animal towards another of the fame fpecies, or which has a conformity in the organs of generation.

The young ones exhibited in Europe have fhewn a quicknefs of apprehenfion, and facility of imitation, that we fhould admire very much in children of the fame tender age.

The conformation of their limbs denotes beyond all controverfy, that they are deftined to an erect pofition of body, and to move like men. The ftructure of their teeth, their organs of fecretion, digeftion, &c. all the fame as the human, prove them entitled to fubfift on the fame aliments as man. The organs of generation being alike, they propagate their fpecies, and their females fuckle their young, in the fame manner.

Their difpofition fhews a great degree of focial feeling ; they feem to have a fenfe of fhame, and a fhare of fenfibility, as may be inferred from the preceding relations ; nay, fome trace of reafon appears in that young one, which (according to Le Broffe) made figns expreffive of his idea that " bleeding in the arm had been remedial to " his diforder." Nor muft we omit the expreffion of their grief by fhedding tears, and other paffions, by modes entirely refembling the human. Ludicrous as the opinion may feem, I do not think that an oran-outang hufband would be any difhonour to an Hottentot female; for what are thefe Hottentots ?——They are, fay the moft credible writers, a people certainly very ftupid, and very brutal. In many refpects they are more like beafts than men ; their complexion is dark, they are fhort and thick-fet ; their nofes flat, like thofe of a Dutch dog ; their lips very thick and big ; their teeth exceedingly white, but very long, and ill fet, fome of them fticking out of their mouths like boars

tufks ;

tufks; their hair black, and curled like wool; they are very nimble, and run with a fpeed that is almoft incredible; they are very dif-agreeable in their perfons, and, in fhort, taking all things together, one of the meaneft nations on the face of the earth [*d*].

Has the Hottentot, from this portrait, a more manly figure than the oran-outang? I fufpect that he owes, like the oran-outang, the celerity of his fpeed to the particular conformation of his foot; this, by the way, is only my conjecture, for he has not as yet undergone anato-mical inveftigation. That the oran-outang and fome races of black men are very nearly allied, is, I think, more than probable; Mr. Buf-fon fupports his deductions, tending to the contrary, by no decifive proofs.

We can fcarcely fpeak more of the oran-outang race than we might of any newly difcovered people, the meafure of whofe facul-ties we have not yet had fufficient opportunity to examine.

We have feen their bodies hitherto in miniature only, which con-veys very little further information of their intellect than might be gained from the view of a picture, or a ftatue.

But, if we reafon about them from analogy, they poffefs all thofe organizations which indicate, according to Le Pluche [*e*], the pre-emi-nence of man over brutes, and fhew him born to govern them.

Thefe tokens of fuperiority are, 1ft, The advantages received from the erect pofition of his head and body. All the brute fpecies re-cline towards the earth, and creep upon it. Man alone walks with his head upright, and by this attitude maintains himfelf in full liberty of action, and command. 2d, The expreffion in his countenance, from the multitude of mufcles which are diftributed through the extent of his face. 3d, The liberty of governing all, and varying his actions according to the exigency of circumftances, is the firft help which man experiences from the *noble* pofition of his body. 4th, But the analogy of his fhape, with the things around him, is a new fource of eafy methods to him in making himfelf *mafter of all*. What we have juft remarked of the whole frame of the body of man, and of the exact proportion between his fhape and that univerfal fway which is alloted him, we may again obferve in his legs and arms. 5th, His legs fupport him with an air of dignity, that fets him off, and be-

[*d*] Commodore Roggewein's voyage.　　[*e*] Spectacle de la Nature.

fpeaks

fpeaks him *a mafter* : by a particular form, and by mufcles peculiar to them, they perform a multitude of actions, and fituations, adapted to the feveral exigencies of his government, but ufelefs and denied to his *flaves*, the *inferior animals* ; his legs grow lefs and lefs towards the ground, where they terminate in a bafis flattened on purpofe to fuftain the body, by giving it a *noble* and firm attitude, without clogging the freedom of its motions by the largenefs of bulk. 6th, The mufcles and nerves, which produce fo many ftretchings, retractions, jerks, flidings, turnings, and operations of all kinds, have been all collected into one bundle, neatly rounded behind the fhin-bone; this mafs becomes a commodious pillow, fit to lay and reft the tender bones upon, fo very neceffary, and fo brittle. I pafs by a great many other marks of precaution, thefe inftruments are evidently full of; but I muft not omit obferving, that the two columns of the body always afcend thicker and thicker, not only to lay the body upon a proportionable prop, but alfo that it may lie foft, when it wants to eafe itfelf of its fatigues. 7th, The arm and hand together contribute ftill more to the exercife of the authority of man. Since man has an arm, I fay, he is mafter of every thing on earth ; this muft naturally follow ; that being truly the token and inftrument of a moft effectual fovereignty. The arm of man being an univerfal inftrument, his operations and government extend as far as nature itfelf. By ftiffening, it performs the functions of a lever, or bar. When bent in the feveral articulations which divide it, it imitates the flail, the bow, and any other kind of fpring. By doubling the fift, that terminates it, it ftrikes like a mallet. When it rounds the cavity of the hand, it holds liquids like a cup, and tranfports them as a fpoon would do. By bending or joining its fingers clofe to each other, it makes hooks, nippers, and pincers of them. The two arms, ftretched out, imitate the balance ; and, when one of them is fhortened, to fupport fome great burthen, the other, extended out immediately on the oppofite fide, conftitutes an equilibrium. But it is extenuating the merits of the arm and hand, to compare them with our ordinary inftruments. In truth, the arm is both the model and the foul as it were, of all inftruments whatfoever; it is the foul of them, as the excellence of their effects does always proceed from the hand and arm that direct them; fince they are all fo many imitations, or extenfions, of its different properties.

ties. 8th, One may know the *deſtination*, and general power, of man, in the ſame manner as we know the peculiar deſtination of the eye, arm, or leg; *the proportion of theſe inſtruments, with certain effects, points out to us the intention of the Creator.* 9th, One might be apt to think, that his ſtomach confounds him with the other animals, ſince they all have a ſtomach, and digeſt as well as he does; yet his very ſtomach ſerves to evidence his general dominion. The cormorant, the diver, and the hern, have a ſtomach fitted to digeſt the fleſh of a fiſh. They are never ſeen obſerving, as the dove does, the departure of the ploughman, who has been juſt ſowing his ground. The lion and tiger have a ſtomach fit to digeſt the fleſh of terreſtrial animals; you would in vain tie them up to the rack or manger, and reduce them to a few oats, or the graſs of your meadows. The horſe overlooks the hen, that turns up the ſtraw he treads upon. The beaſts of burthen, who exhauſt their ſtrength in our ſervice, are no leſs valuable on account of the cheapneſs of their food; and in vain ſhould we attempt to reward their labour, by offering them meats of the moſt exquiſite taſte, from which they would turn away with loathing. Theſe animals are then, from the very diſpoſition of their ſtomach, tied down to a certain kind of food; but man alone is unreſtrained; and, as he has on his tongue the diſcernment of all the favours that are diſtributed among other animals, he has likewiſe in his ſtomach the faculty of digeſting whatever is wholeſome and nouriſhing. God has given him hands, that he might lay hold of, and faſhion, whatever can nouriſh, cure, and defend him; and a ſtomach capable of digeſting the foods tried by his palate. But the ſtomach of man is not the principal part of his body; *that* ſeems by its functions to have a nearer affinity with that of animals, at the ſame time that it has a degree of excellence that *raiſes it much above them.* It is the ſame with his *other organs.* 10th, The lips are the ramparts of the gums; the latter are the fence of the tongue, and of the roof of the mouth. They are a couple of true bulwarks, not only forming an incloſure round the tongue, but alſo ſerving as a baſis to the two rows of teeth. Theſe inſtruments, chiefly appointed to grind and diſſolve, are a bony ſubſtance, perfectly hard, and covered with enamel, which embelliſhes the mouth by its whiteneſs, and preſerves, by its firmneſs, thoſe precious tools from the friction of maſſy foods, and the inſinuation

2   of

of penetrating liquors. The *incifory* teeth fill the fore part; they are thin at the edge, like a wedge, and sharp as knives. The *canine* are rounded, longer than the rest, and ending in a point. All the rest have a square surface, that grows wider and wider, the further they are set within the mouth; thefe are the *molares,* or grinders. From the variety of their feveral operations, thefe teeth comprehend in abftract all the powers of cutting, dividing, and triturating, that are partially dilperfed among other animals; they accommodate to every fpecies of vegetable as well as animal food; and, together with the ftomach, fhew, that man was formed to derive his fuftenance from both or either of thefe alimentary claffes, at his pleafure. The wonders of man's organization are multiplied through every part of his body, infomuch that anatomifts confefs, that the ftructure is, to any ftrict enquirer, an abyfs, which fwallows up both our eyes and reafon.   11th, The human voice, merely as a voice, is not ex-traordinary, fince other animals have a voice as well as man. But *fpeech* puts an immenfe diftance between man and the animals. The merit of fpeech does not confift in noife, but in the variety of its inflections and univerfality of fignification. Man can exprefs his thoughts very varioufly.   If making one's felf underftood is the fame as fpeaking, we may of courfe fpeak with the foot, the eye, or the hand. A man, who feems tranfported with joy, or overwhelmed with grief, has already told us many things before he opens his mouth.   His eyes, his features, his geftures, his whole countenance, correfpond with his mind, and make it very well underftood. *He fpeaks from head to foot:* all his motions are fignificant, and his expreffions are as infinite as his thought.   But his voice takes place of thefe figns whenever he pleafes, and is not only equivalent to them, but even fufficient alone to explain diftinctly what they cannot exprefs when combined together. Speech was fuperadded to all thefe figns, that man fhould not want any means of explaining himfelf clearly.   In every thing, man alone unites the prerogatives that have been granted but fingly to any particular fpecies, and his dignity arifes from the *right ufe* to which his *reafon* enables him to apply his corporeal powers and fenfes.

If then, the pre-eminence of man over the brute creation be difplayed in the ftructure of his body, and the feveral *infignia* which the ingeni-ous author has enumerated, it follows of courfe, that the oran-outang poffeffing the fame ftructure and organization, is alfo deftined to the like precedence and authority. The fole diftinction between him and man, muft confift in the meafure of intellectual faculties; thofe faculties which the moft fkilful anatomift is incapable of tracing the fource of, and which exift *independent of the ftructure of the brain*; thefe powers are rendered vifible only in the refult they produce, through the intervention of the bodily organs. Hence it is certain, that the oran-outang, though endued with brains and organs of a ftructure not to be diftinguifhed from thofe of man by the ableft anatomifts, ftill remains very far inferior to our idea of a *perfect* human being, unlefs he alfo is endowed with the faculties of reafon and perception, adapted to direct him in the application of that mechanifm to the fame ufes as we find it applied in a rational man. According to Mr. Buffon, he has eyes, but fees not; ears has he, but hears not; he has a tongue, and the human organs of fpeech, but *fpeaks not*; he has the human brain, but does not *think*; forms no comparifons, draws no conclufions, makes no reflections, and is determined, like brute animals, by a pofitive limited inftinct. But in truth, we know not the meafure of their intellect, nor can form a competent judgement of it from one or two young animals, that were fhewn for a few months in France and England. Dogs, and fome other brutes, have been made, by dint of blows, rewards, and conftant exercife, to vary their motions in a very furprifing manner, according to the defires and fignals of their teachers; but in thefe cafes, the actual fkill has been fuppofed to refide in the teacher, and that no juft argument can be drawn from hence to prove any particular dexterity in them, much lefs any defign of theirs, or degree of perfection acquired by reafoning: the monkey tribe indeed form fome exception, who, even in their wild ftate, fhew a voluntary delight and readinefs in mimicking human actions, of which there are an infinite multitude of well-attefted proofs. When we come to view the ftructure of the oran-outang, we are forced to acknowledge, that his actions and movements would *not be natural*, unlefs they refembled thofe of *man*. To find him therefore excelling the brute animals in the dexterity of his manœuvres, and aptnefs of his imitations, does not excite our admiration, fo much as the readinefs of apprehenfion, with which, in his ftate of impuberty or childhood (if I may fo exprefs myfelf), his performances before fuch a variety of fpectators were ufually

accompanied.   How far an oran-outang might be brought to give ut-
terance to thofe European words (the fignification of whofe founds, it
is plain from Buffon, and others, he has capacity to underftand, fo as
to conform his demeanour and movements to them voluntarily at the
immature period of life, when his mental faculties are in their weakeft
ftate), remains for experiment.   If the trial were to be *impartially*
made, he ought to pafs regularly from his horn-book, through the regular fteps of pupilage, to the fchool, and univerfity, till the ufual
modes of culture are exhaufted upon him.   If he fhould be trained up
in this manner from childhood (or that early part of exiftence in
which alone he has been noticed by the learned in Europe), to the age
of 20 or 25, under fit preceptors, it might then with certainty be determined, whether his tongue is incapable of articulating human languages.   But if, in that advanced age, and after a regular procefs of
education, he fhould ftill be found to labour under this impediment,
the phænomenon would be truly aftonifhing; for if it be alledged,
that he could not produce fuch founds for want of the fentient or
thinking principle to excite the organs of fpeech to fuch an effect, ftill
we fhould expect him capable of uttering founds refembling the
human, juft as well as a natural idiot, or a parrot, can produce them
without the agency of thought.   For my own part, I conceive that
probability favours the opinion, that human organs were not given
him for nothing: that this race have fome language by which their
meaning is communicated; whether it refembles the gabbling of turkies like that of the Hottentots, or the hiffing of ferpents, is of very
little confequence, fo long as it is intelligible among themfelves: nor,
for what hitherto appears, do they feem at all inferior in the intellectual
faculties to many of the Negroe race; with fome of whom, it is credible that they have the moft intimate connexion and confanguinity.
The amorous intercourfe between them may be frequent; the Negroes
themfelves bear teftimony that fuch intercourfes actually happen; and
it is certain, that both races agree perfectly well in lafcivioufnefs of
difpofition [*f*].

But

[*f*] An ingenious modern author has fuggefted many ftrong reafons to prove, that the faculty of
fpeech is not the gift of nature to man; that articulation is the work of art, or at leaft of a habit acquired by cuftom and exercife; and that mankind are truly in their natural ftate a *mutum pecus.* He
inftances the cafe of Peter the wild youth, caught in the forefts of Hanover, who (he tells us) was
a man

But if we admit with Mr. Buffon, that with all this analogy of organization, the oran-outang's brain is a fenfelefs *icon* of the human; that it is meer matter, unanimated with a thinking principle, in any, or at leaft in a very minute and imperfect degree, we muft then infer the ftrongeft conclufion to eftablifh our belief of a natural diverfity of the human intellect, in general, *ab origine*; an oran-outang, in this cafe, is a human being, *quoad* his form and organs; but of an inferior fpecies, *quoad* his intellect; he has in form a much nearer refemblance to the Negroe race, than the latter bear to white men; the fuppofition then is well founded, that the brain, and intellectual organs, fo far as they are dependent upon meer matter, though fimilar in texture and modification to thofe of other men, may in fome of the Negroe race be fo conftituted, as *not to refult to the fame effects*; for we cannot but allow, that the Deity might, if it was his pleafure, diverfify his works in this manner, and either withhold the *fuperior principle* entirely, or in part only, or infufe it into the different claffes and races of human creatures, in fuch portions, as to form the fame gradual climax towards perfection in this human fyftem, which is fo evidently defigned in every other.

If fuch has been the intention of the Almighty, we are then perhaps to regard the oran-outang as,

> " — the lag of human kind,
> " Neareft to brutes, by God defign'd [g]."

The Negroe race (confifting of varieties) will then appear rifing progreffively in the fcale of intellect, the further they mount above the oran-outang and brute creation. The fyftem of man will feem more confiftent, and the meafure of it more compleat, and analagous to the harmony and order that are vifible in every other line of the world's ftupendous fabric. Nor is this conclufion degrading to human nature, while it tends to exalt our idea of the infinite perfections of the Deity;

a man in mind as well as body, yet was not only mute when firft caught, but continued fo for 30 years after, having never learned to fpeak, notwithftanding his conftant intercourfe with mankind during that fpace. This would feem to prove, that the want of articulation, or expreffing ideas by fpeech, does not afford a pofitive indication of a want of intellect: fince the difficulty arifing from the mechanifm of fpeech, or pronunciation, may to fome organs be infurmountable. Singular examples of this kind may happen, but they are rare. To find a whole fociety of people labouring under the fame impediment, would be really wonderful.

[g] Prior.

for how vaft is the diftance between inert matter, and matter endued with thought and reafon! The feries and progreffion from a lump of dirt to a perfect human being is amazingly extenfive; nor lefs fo, per-haps, the interval between the latter and the moft perfect angelic being, and between this being and the Deity himfelf. Let us fhake off thofe clouds with which prejudice endeavours to invelope the under-ftanding; and, exerting that freedom of thought which the Beft of Beings has granted to us, let us take a noon-tide view of the human *genus*; and fhall we fay, that it is totally different from, and lefs per-fect than, every other fyftem of animal beings? The fpecies of every other *genus* have their certain mark and diftinction, their varieties, and fubordinate claffes: and why fhould the race of mankind be fingularly indifcriminate?

> " —— In the catalogue they go for *men*,
> " As hounds and greyhounds, mongrels, fpaniels, curs,
> " Shocks, water-rugs, and demi-wolves, are 'clep'd
> " *All* by the *name of dogs*; the valued file
> " Diftinguifhes the fwift, the flow, the fubtle,
> " The houfekeeper, the hunter; every one
> " According to the gift, which bounteous nature
> " Hath in him clos'd; whereby he does receive
> " Particular addition, from the bill
> " That writes them all alike;—*And fo of men*—"

fays that faithful obferver of nature, our immortal Shakefpear; and with him fo far agrees that truly learned and fagacious naturalift Monf. Buffon, who inveftigates the marks of variation among mankind in the following manner: " Men differ from white to black, from com-pound to fimple, by the height of ftature, fize, activity, ftrength, and other bodily characteriftics; and from the genius to the dolt, from the greateft to the leaft, *by the meafure of intellect*." That there are fome phyfical diftinctions, in refpect of perfon, I think, requires no further demonftration; and that men vary ftill more in intellect, is almoft equally evident. On our entering Africa towards the European con-fine on the North, we firft meet with the Moors, a race of tawny men, who poffefs many vices, and fome virtues; they are acute, induftrious, and carry on trade and manufactures; next to thefe, are a mixture of Moors and Arabs: we then arrive at the gum coaft, or country of

Senaga,

Senaga, whofe inhabitants are an intermixture of blacks and the two former [b]. Next to thefe lie the Jaloffs, Phulis, and Mandingo Blacks; the former of whom are the moft humanized and induftrious of any on the coaft; yet they are varioufly defcribed by travelers, fome commending them for amiable qualities, others accufing them of the worft; fo that, to judge impartially, we are to fuppofe that they poffefs both, and differ only from each other in degree; but the Mandingoes are reprefented as little better than their Southern neighbours on whom they border. From hence we proceed through the different diftricts called the grain, ivory, gold, and flave coaft, to Angola; all thefe we find occupied by petty Negroe ftates, whofe character is nearly uniform, and who fcarcely deferve to be ranked with the human fpecies. The kingdoms of Angola and Benguela, having been chiefly peopled by the Giagas an interior nation, the inhabitants are faid to be favages in a fhape barely human. The Giagas were a tribe that poured out of the inland parts, ravaged and plundered almoft every country bordering on the coaft, deluging them like the Goths and Vandals of Europe, and intermixing with moft of the conquered ftates, particularly Angola and Benguela. They are defcribed as a barbarous race, hardened in idolatry, wallowers in human blood, cannibals, drunkards, practifed in lewdnefs, oppreffion, and fraud; proud and flothful, curfed with all the vices that can degrade human nature, poffeffing no one good quality, and in fhort more brutal and favage than the wild beafts of the foreft. From thefe, the Angolans borrowed their horrid cuftom of butchering a vaft number of human victims, at the obfequies of their kings and relations, as well as that of feafting upon human flefh, and preferring it to any other; infomuch, that a dead flave was of more value at their market than a living one: the former practice indeed obtained in almoft if not all the other provinces on the coaft, and has only been difcontinued by the greater advantage that offered, of felling their flaves and captives to the Euro-

[b] The Moors inhabiting on one fide of the Senaga are wanderers, removing from place to place, as they find pafturage for their cattle. The Jaloff and Phulis Negroes, fettled on the other fide of the fame river, live in villages. The Moors have fuperiors, or chiefs, of their own free election; the Negroes are in fubjection to their kings, who are vefted with a very arbitrary power. The Moors are fmall, lean, and ill-looked, but have a lively, acute genius; the Negroes are large, fat, and well-proportioned, but filly, and of a flender capacity. The country inhabited by the Moors is a barren defart, almoft deftitute of verdure; that of the Negroes is a fertile foil, abounding with pafturage, producing grain, and trees of feveral kinds. Le Maire.

3

pean.

pean traders, inſtead of putting them to death.   After leaving Benguela we arrive among the Hottentots, whoſe women are ſo remarkable for a natural callous excreſcence, or flap, which diſtinguiſhes them
from all others of the ſame ſex in the known world.   Theſe people
are of a dark nut, or dingy olive complexion, and in all other reſpeɛts,
ſave what have been noticed, are like the other Negroes in perſon.
They are a lazy, ſtupid race ; but poſſeſs benevolence, liberality, integrity, and friendſhip; they are hoſpitable and chaſte, have ſome appearance of a regular form of government among them, and the barbarities they practiſe are more the reſult of antient cuſtoms, whoſe
ſource is now unknown, than any innate cruelty of their diſpoſitions.
Theſe people have ſeveral mechanic arts among them; but their language is guttural, and inarticulate, compared by ſome to the gabbling
of enraged turkey-cocks, and by others to the rumbling of wind *a
poſteriori*.   As we approach towards Abyſſinia, the North Eaſt confine of Negro-land, we find the Blacks well ſhaped and featured, and
for the moſt part having lank black hair inſtead of wool, though not
very long.   The Abyſſinians are repreſented to be of a brown olive
complexion, tall, of regular and well-proportioned features, large
ſparkling black eyes, elevated noſes, ſmall lips, and beautiful teeth;
the charaɛter of their minds is equally favourable; they are ſober,
temperate, ſenſible, pious, and inoffenſive.

The Red Sea divides theſe people from the Arabs, who, in complexion, perſon, and intelleɛt, come ſtill nearer to the Whites or Perſians, their next neighbours, whoſe valour, quick parts, and humanity, are juſtly celebrated.

Having now compleated this tour, we are ſtruck with one very per-
tinent remark; the natives of the whole traɛt, compriſed under the
name of Negro-land, are all black, and have wool inſtead of hair;
whereas the people in the moſt torrid regions of Libya and America,
who have the ſun vertical over them, have neither the ſame tinɛture
of ſkin, nor woolly covering.   As we recede from Negro-land, this
blackneſs gradually decreaſes, and the wool as gradually changes to
lank hair, which at firſt is of a ſhort ſtaple, but is found longer, the
further we advance [*i*].   We obſerve the like gradations of the intel-
leɛtual

[*i*]   I admit there is ſome variety both in colour and feature among the different nations of the
Negroes; ſome are lighter than others by a ſhade or two, and ſome have ſmaller features; but this
diverſity

lectual faculty, from the first rudiments perceived in the monkey kind, to the more advanced stages of it in apes, in the *oran-outang*, that type of man, and the Guiney Negroe; and ascending from the varieties of this class to the lighter casts, until we mark its utmost limit of perfection in the pure White. Let us not then doubt, but that every member of the creation is wisely fitted and adapted to the certain uses, and confined within the certain bounds, to which it was ordained by the Divine Fabricator. The measure of the several orders and varieties of these Blacks may be as compleat as that of any other race of mortals; filling up that space, or degree, beyond which they are not destined to pass; and discriminating them from the rest of men, not in *kind*, but in *species*.

The examples which have been given of Negroes born and trained up in other climates, detract not from that general idea of narrow, humble intellect, which we affix to the inhabitants of Guiney. We have seen *learned horses*, *learned* and even *talking dogs*, in England; who, by dint of much pains and tuition, were brought to exhibit the signs of a capacity far exceeding what is ordinarily allowed to be possessed by those animals. The experiment has not been fully tried with the *oran-outangs*; yet, from what has hitherto been proved, this race of beings may, for aught we know to the contrary, possess a share of intellect, which, by due cultivation,

diversity only serves to strengthen my argument; there is likewise a variety in the colour of their wool, for I have seen some perfectly reddish.

The natives of the Indian peninsula, betwixt the rivers Indus and Ganges in the East Indies, have the African black complexion, the European features, and the American lank hair, but all native and genuine.

It is not a variety of climate that produces various complexions. America lies from 65 degrees North lat. to 55 deg. South lat. comprehending all the various climates of Europe, Asia, Africa, and America. The American complexion is every where permanently the same, only with more or less of a metalline lustre. Between the Tropics, and in the high Northern latitudes, they are paler; in the other parts, of a copper colour, have thin lips, jet black lank hair, and no beards; in the high Northern and Southern latitudes, they are tall and robust; between the Tropics they are short and squat. Douglas.—The greatest alteration caused by difference of climate seems to consist in enlarging or depressing the stature; relaxing or contracting the muscles, and articulations of the limbs; lengthening or shortening the bones; and, in consequence perhaps, raising or depressing, in a small degree, some particular features. The natives of Madagascar have neither such flat noses nor dark complexions as the Guiney Negroes; there are some of them said to be mere *brunets*; and most of them have long hair: they are by most travelers pronounced to be lively, intelligent, sensible of gratitude, and possessed of many amiable qualities; so that it is not without regret, that we find them treated as the most abject slaves by the French, on their settlements in Mauritius.

might

might raife them to a nearer apparent equality with the human, and make them even excel the inhabitants of *Quaqua, Angola,* and *Whidah.* Mr. *Hume* prefumes, from his obfervations upon the native Africans, to conclude, that they are inferior to the reft of the fpecies, and utterly incapable of all the higher attainments of the human mind. Mr. *Beattie,* upon the principle of philanthropy, combats this opinion; but he is unfortunate in producing no demonftration to prove, that it is either lightly taken up, or inconfiftent with experience. He likewife makes no fcruple to confound the Negroes and Mexican Indians together, and to deduce conclufions from the ingenuity of the latter, to fhew the probable ingenuity of the former. We might reafonably fuppofe, that the commerce maintained with the Europeans for above two centuries, and the great variety of fabrics and things manufactured, which have been introduced among the Guiney Negroes for fuch a length of time, might have wrought fome effect towards polifhing their manners, and exciting in them at leaft a degree of imitative induftry; but it is really aftonifhing to find, that thefe caufes have not operated to their civilization; they are at this day, if any credit can be given to the moft modern accounts, but little divefted of their primitive brutality; we cannot pronounce them infufceptible of civilization, fince even [k] apes have been taught to eat, drink, repofe, and drefs, like men; but of all the human fpecies hitherto difcovered, their natural bafenefs of mind feems to afford leaft hope

[k] The docility of many among the brute creation, is a fubject which the pride of man is not very fond of examining with a too critical inveftigation; but none is more curious; the enquiry is humiliating to thofe who would fondly confider man as poffeffing fomething of an angelic nature; they think it degrades them to allow brutes a reafoning faculty; yet there are not wanting proofs of fomewhat very like it, efpecially in thofe animals with whom we are moft converfant, and therefore have more frequent opportunities of ftudying. *Pope,* more free in his opinion, calls the *elephant* "half-reafoning;" the relations that are given of the fenfibility of this animal appear to many perfons almoft incredible.

Mr. *Toreen* affirms, that, when he was at Surat in 1751, he had an opportunity of remarking one, whofe mafter had let it out to hire for a certain fum *per* day. Its employment was, to carry timber for building, out of the river; which bufinefs it difpatched very dextroufly under the command of a boy, and afterwards laid one piece upon another in fuch good order, that no man could have done it better.

The docility of monkeys and apes is ftill fuperior. One of the latter, trained in France, was not long fince exhibited in London. He performed a variety of equilibres on the wire with as much expertnefs as the moft noted human artifts that have appeared before the public in this walk.

of

of their being (except by miraculous interpofition of the divine Providence) fo far refined as to *think*, as well as act like *perfect men*.

It has been faid, that the nature of their governments is unfavourable to genius, becaufe they tolerate flavery; but genius is
manifefted in the right frame of government: they have republics.
among them as well as monarchies, but neither have yet been known
productive of civility, of arts, or fciences. Their genius (if it can
be fo called) confifts alone in trick and cunning, enabling them,
like monkies and apes, to be thievifh and mifchievous, with a peculiar dexterity. They feem unable to combine ideas, or purfue
a chain of reafoning; they have no mode of forming calculations,
or of recording events to pofterity, or of communicating thoughts
and obfervations by marks, characters, or delineation; or by that
method fo common to moft other countries in their rude and primitive ages, by little poems or fongs: we find this practice exifted
formerly among the Ægyptians, Phœnicians, Arabians, Mexicans,
and many others. The ancient inhabitants of Brazil, Peru, Virginia, St. Domingo, and Canada, preferved, in poems of this kind,
fuch events as they thought worthy of the knowledge of future
times, and fung them at their public feftivals and folemnities. Arith-
metick, aftronomy, geometry, and mechanicks, were, in other focieties of men, among the firft fciences to which they applied themfelves.
The origin of arts and fciences in other countries has been afcribed to
their uniting in focieties, inftead of leading a gregarious life; their
neceffities, the inftitution of laws and government, and the leifure
which thefe afforded for indulging in fuch refearches. It may be
faid, that the Negroes are not affected by this neceffity which has
affected other people; that their foil is wonderfully productive;
that their country abounds with food; that the warmth of their
climate makes cloathing fuperfluous; but no fuch pretences reftrained the South Americans, and others living under the fame
parallel of climate, from cloathing themfelves.

The art of making garments was invented in the mildeft climates,
where there was the leaft need of any covering for the body; neceffity
alone therefore could not be the caufe of mens cloathing themfelves.

The Negroes live in focieties; fome of their towns (as they are
called) are even faid to be very extenfive; and if a life of idlenefs

implies leifure, they enjoy enough of it. In regard to their laws
and government, thefe may, with them, be more properly ranged
under the title of cuftoms and manners; they have no regulations
dictated by forefight: they are the fimple refult of a revengeful
felfish fpirit, put in motion by the crimes that prevail among them;
confequently their edicts are moftly vindictive, and death or flavery
the almoft only modes of punifhment; they feem to have no polity,
nor any comprehenfion of the ufe of civil inftitutions. Their punifhments are actuated either by a motive of revenge or of avarice;
they have none to balance the allurements of pleafure, nor the
ftrength of the paffions, nor to operate as incitements to induftry
and worthy actions. In many of their provinces they are often reduced to the utmoft ftraights for want of corn, of which they might
enjoy the greateft abundance, if they were but animated with the
fmalleft portion of induftry. If no rules of civil polity exift among
them, does it not betray an egregious want of common fenfe, that
no fuch rules have been formed? If it be true, that in other countries mankind have cultivated fome arts, through the impulfe of the
neceffities under which they laboured, what origin fhall we give to
thofe contrivances and arts, which have fprung up after thofe neceffities were provided for? Thefe are furely no other than the
refult of innate vigour and energy of the mind, inquifitive, inventive, and hurrying on with a divine enthufiafm to new attainments.
The jurifprudence, the cuftoms and manners of the Negroes, feem
perfectly fuited to the meafure of their narrow intellect. Laws
have juftly been regarded as the mafter-piece of human genius:
what then are we to think of thofe focieties of men, who either
have none, or fuch only as are irrational and ridiculous?

Religion and Religious Opinions among the Negroes.

They are faid to have as many religions almoft as they have
deities, and thefe are innumerable; but fome have been taught to
believe the exiftence of a fupreme God. Thefe fay that God is
partial to the Whites, and treats them as his own children. but
takes pleafure in afflicting the Blacks with a thoufand evils; that
they are indebted to him for nothing but fhowers, without which
the earth would not afford them provifions; but even in this, they

alledge

alledge he is only the undefigning caufe, and for the effect they are obliged to the fertility of the foil. Man's creation they affert to have happened in the following manner: in the beginning, black as well as white men were created; nay, if there was any difference in time, the Blacks had the priority. To thefe, two forts of favours were prefented; to the Blacks, gold; and to the Whites, the knowledge of arts and fciences. It was from choice, that the Blacks had gold for their fhare: and, to punifh their avarice, it was decreed they fhould ever be flaves to the white men; they are fully perfuaded that no country but Afric produces gold, and that Blacks can never attain the knowledge of letters [m].

The *Mocas* not only worfhip, but eat, fnakes; now adore, and prefently devour, their deity. In this however they are not unexampled by fome ftates in Europe; I mean thofe pious canibals, one effential part of whofe faith it is to believe, that they verily and fubftantially eat the flefh, and quaff the blood, of their God.

The fnake is likewife a favourite divinity among many other of the Negroe ftates, and particularly the Whidahs. In 1697, a hog that had been teazed for fome time by one of thefe reptiles, killed and gobbled it up. The marbuts, or priefts, went with their complaint in form to the king; and no one prefuming to appear as council for defendant hog, he was convicted of the facrilege, and a warrant iffued for a general maffacre of all his fpecies throughout the kingdom. A thoufand chofen warriors, armed with cutlaffes, began the bloody execution; and the whole race of fwine would have been extirpated from Whidah, if the king (who loved pork) had not put a ftop to the dreadful carnage, by reprefenting to the marbuts, that they ought to reft fatisfied with the fevere vengeance they had taken.

Of fome Cuftoms among them.

In hot climates, bathing is one of the higheft luxuries; it is no wonder then that we find their inhabitants univerfally adopt this agreeable practice, efpecially as cattle, wild beafts, and other quadruped animals, ufe it for their refrefhment. The Negroes teach their children to fwim at a very tender age; hence they become

[m] Bofman.

expert

expert divers, and are able to continue an incredible length of time under water; hence too they incline to fix their dwellings on the sea coast, or the banks of the rivers, to save themselves the trouble of a long walk.

In these climates the brute creation fly to shelter from the rain; the Negroes likewise avoid it with extreme anxiety; if they are catched in a shower they clasp their arms over their heads to defend them, run with all the speed they can to the nearest retreat, and seem to groan at every drop that falls upon them; to preserve their bodies the better from it, they rub them over with palm oil, as the aquatic birds besmear their plumage with the oily liquor expressed from the glands which nature has provided them with. Their women are delivered with little or no labour; they have therefore no more occasion for midwives, than the female oran-outang, or any other wild animal. A woman brings forth her child in a quarter of an hour, goes the same day to the sea, and washes herself. Some have even been known to bring forth twins without a shriek, or a scream; and it is seldom they are confined above two, or, at most, three days.

Immediately before her labour she is conducted to the sea side or a river, followed by a number of little children, who throw all manner of ordure and excrement at her in the way, after which she is washed with great care. Without this cleanly ceremony, the Negroes are persuaded that either the mother, the child, or one of the parents, will die during the period of lying-in. Thus they seem exempted from the curse inflicted upon Eve and her daughters, " I will greatly multiply thy sorrow; in sorrow shalt " thou bring forth children."

Medicine.

The origin of the invention of medicine is intirely unknown; some ascribe it to chance, others to observation on the couduct of brute animals; both probably combined. We know that the Northern Indians discovered that herb, which is an antidote to the venom of the rattle snake, by the latter means. Brutes are botanists by instinct; whether man in his rude state possesses any

similar

similar inſtinct we are uninformed, but probability is in the affir-
mative.

The chief medicaments among the Negroes are lime juice, car-
damoms, the roots, branches, leaves, bark, and gums of trees, and
about thirty different herbs. The latter have been experienced
in many caſes wonderfully powerful, and have ſubdued diſeaſes
incident to their climate, which have foiled the art of European
ſurgeons at the factories. However, the Negroes generally apply
them at random, without any regard to the particular ſymptoms
of the diſeaſe; concerning which, or the operation of their *materia
medica*, they have formed no theory.

Eſquemeling relates, that when he and his companions were
amuſing themſelves at Coſta Rica with ſhooting at monkies, if one
of them happened to be wounded, the reſt flocked about him,
and while ſome laid their paws upon the wound, to hinder the
blood from iſſuing forth, others gathered moſs from the trees (or
rather probably ſome ſpecies of ſtyptic *fungus*) and thruſt into the
orifice, by which means they ſtopped the effuſion. At other times
they gathered particular herbs, and, chewing them in their mouth,
applied them as a poultice; all which, ſays he, " cauſed in
" me great admiration, ſeeing ſuch ſtrange actions in thoſe irra-
" tional creatures, which teſtified the fidelity and love they had
" for one another."

From what ſource did theſe monkies derive their chirurgical ſkill
and knowledge? From the ſame, no doubt, whence the Negroes
received theirs—the hands of their Creator; who has impartially
provided all animals with means conducive to their preſervation.

Diet.

Maize, palm oil, and a little ſtinking fiſh, make up the general
bill of fare of the prince and the ſlave; except that they regale
themſelves, as often as they can, with *aqua vitæ*, and palm wine [n],
Their old cuſtom of gormandizing on human fleſh has in it ſomething ſo nauſeous, ſo repugnant to nature and reaſon, that it would
hardly admit of belief, if it had not been atteſted by a multitude
of voyagers; ſome of whom affirm to have been eye-witneſſes of it,

[n] Barbot.

and,

and, what is ſtrſnger, by report of Negroes themſelves imported from that continent into our colonies [o]. The difficulty indeed of believing it to be true, is much leſſened when we reflect on the ſanguinary, cruel temper, and filthy practices of theſe people, in other reſpects; many Negroes in our colonies have been known to drink the blood of their enemies with great apparent reliſh; and at Benin, Angola, and other kingdoms, they at this day prefer apes, monkies, dog's fleſh, carrion, reptiles, and other ſubſtances, uſually deemed improper for human food, although they abound with hogs, ſheep, poultry, fiſh, and a variety of game and wild-fowl; why ſhould we doubt but that the ſame ravenous ſavage, who can feaſt on the roaſted quarters of an ape (that *mock-man*), would be not leſs delighted with the ſight of a loin or buttock of human fleſh, prepared in the ſame manner? This opinion muſt be ſtrengthened by conſidering the idea they entertain of the ape ſpecies; for they eſteem them as ſcarcely their inferiors in humanity; and ſuppoſe they are very able to talk, but ſo cunning withal, that, to avoid working, they diſſemble their talent, and pretend to be dumb.

They are moſt brutal in their manners and uncleanly in their diet, eating fleſh almoſt raw by choice, though intolerably putrid and full of meggots. Even thoſe that inhabit the ſea coaſt, though well provided with other victuals, are ſo ravenous that they will devour the raw guts of animals. The unhealthineſs of ſome of the European factories here, has been imputed in great meaſure to the abominable cuſtom of the natives, of expoſing their fiſh to the ſun till they become ſufficiently ſtinking, fly-blown, and rotten. This cauſes a ſtench, which fills all the atmoſphere in the neighbourhood; and, though inſupportably offenſive to the Europeans, it does not

[o] The exiſtence of canibals or man-eaters is now unqueſtionably proved, by the late diſcoveries made by Mr. Banks and Dr. Solander, in their voyage to the South Sea; where they found, in the country called *New-Zealand*, a people who fed upon human fleſh. The author of "*The Origin and Progreſs of language,*" ſays, he is well informed of a nation in the inland parts of *Africa*, where human fleſh is expoſed to ſale in the market, as beef and mutton are among us; this agrees with the accounts which have been formerly given by ſome travelers, and which till lately have not met with much credit; for this incredulity, the before mentioned ingenious author aſſigns a very ſufficient reaſon. "Thoſe, ſays he, who judge of mankind only by what "they ſee of the modern nations of Europe, are not, I know, diſpoſed to believe this; but "they may as well not believe that there are men, who live without cloaths or houſes; without "corn, wine, or beer; and without planting or ſowing."

2   feem

feem to affect the Blacks with any other than the moft delicious fenfations.

At their meals they tear the meat with their talons, and chuck it by handfulls down their throats with all the voracity of wild beafts; at their politeft entertainments they thruft their hands all together into the difh, fometimes returning into it what they have been chewing. They ufe neither table-cloths, knives, forks, plates, nor trenchers, and generally fquat down upon the bare earth to their repaft.

Their hofpitality is the refult of felf-love; they entertain ftrangers only in hopes of extracting fome fervice or profit from them; and in regard to others, the hofpitality is reciprocal; by receiving them into their huts, they acquire a right of being received into theirs in turn. This in fact is a fpecies of generofity which gives no decifive evidence of goodnefs of heart, or rectitude of manners, except in thofe countries where no advantage is expected to be made by the hoft.

In fhort, their corporeal fenfations are in general of the groffeft frame; their fight is acute, but not correct; they will rarely mifs a ftanding object, but they have no notion of fhooting birds on the wing, nor can they project a ftraight line, nor lay any fubftance fquare with another. Their hearing is remarkably quick; their faculties of fmell and tafte are truly beftial, nor lefs fo their commerce with the other fex; in thefe acts they are libidinous and fhamelefs as monkies, or baboons. The equally hot temperament of their women has given probability to the charge of their admitting thefe animals frequently to their embrace. An example of this intercourfe once happened, I think, in England [p]; and if luft can prompt to fuch exceffes in that Northern region, and in defpight of all the checks which national politenefs and refined fentiments impofe, how freely may it not operate in the more genial foil of Afric, that parent of every thing that is monftrous in nature, where thefe creatures are frequent and familiar; where the paffions rage without any controul; and the retired wildernefs prefents opportunity to gratify them without fear of detection!

[p] It is faid the lady conceived by her paramour, which gave occafion to the Stat. 25 Hen. VIII. which was purpofely extended to women, as well as men.

CHAP.

C H A P. II.

GUINEY SLAVES.

THE part of the African continent whence the Negroe slaves are transported, begins at the river Senaga, and terminates at the river Quanza, in Angola; comprehending a shore of little less than 2000 leagues in extent, and including the several divisions before enumerated.

It is computed, that, for these hundred years past, not less than 40,000 have been shipped from thence every year upon an average; which, if true, makes the whole amount not less than four millions.

It is a matter of surprize to some, that so large and continual a drain has not depopulated this country. But, independent of the prodigious extent of Afric, there are many solid reasons given why this depopulation has not, and cannot happen. The state of slavery in use here does not hinder depopulation, as it doubtless would in a civilized part of the world, where liberty is highly prized. A man or woman of sensibility, that sensibility encreased by reflexion, and perhaps study, would, under the yoke of slavery, be deaf to all the calls of inclination, and refuse giving being to wretches doomed to inherit the misery their parents feel in so exquisite a manner. The idea of *slavery* is totally different in Afric. Exclusive of the entire absence of keen sensations, the slaves of a family are considered as no mean part of it; scarce any of them are sold, except for very great crimes. The owners are full as careful of bringing them up as their own children. For in the number of their slaves consist their wealth, their pride, and dignity; and therefore they shew an attention to preserve and multiply them, similar to that of an European merchant, in the care and improvement of his money.

Slaves likewise, who have any abilities, are allowed to make the most of them; by which means they grow rich, and able to purchase slaves for themselves; in this, it is said, (I know not with what truth) they meet with no interruption, provided they acknowledge their subservience from time to time, and pay a tribute,

or

or make fatisfactory prefents to their owner and his defcendants. Elegance of thinking finds no place here; the air is foft, the food ftimulating, and the paffions unreftrained. Child-birth is attended with little or no danger or difficulty. The fruitfulnefs of the foil leaves no room to fear that children will become burdenfome; and, this anxiety being removed, nature does the reft.

Many families ally themfelves by marriage as foon as the children are born, without any other ceremony than the confent of parents on both fides. Such as have made free with the paffion before marriage, are not the lefs refpected by their hufbands, or the public: on the contrary, they are efteemed the better qualified to enter into matrimony, and are accordingly often preferred to abfolute *veftals*.

Scarcely any of the prifoners taken in battle are now put to death, but are almoft all fold, and brought to fome part of the coaft. Polygamy univerfally prevails, and contributes greatly to populoufnefs. Of this we may form fome judgement from Hafflequift's account of Egypt; he informs us of a Turk, who by feveral wives had 40 children; of another who had at once in his haram feventy-feven women all with child by him; and a third who had by eight wives, in ten years, eighty children, all of whom lived to mature age. But to produce examples of the like kind among the Negroe provinces; Bofman, in his account of Whidah, mentions that he had frequently feen fathers who had upwards of two hundred children. Upon interrogating a certain captain of the king's guards concerning the number of his family, he replied with a figh, that he was unhappy in that particular, not having above feventy living. Bofman then afked him how many had died, and he anfwered feventy. Thus a family of 140 children is by no means looked upon as extraordinary [q].

Of the flaves fhipped from the coaft, not a fixth part are women; and this happens from there being fewer female criminals to be tranfported, and no female warriors to be taken prifoners. The number of females born exceeds the males, and though fome Blacks in the inland countries have ten, others an hundred wives, yet by the ftricteft enquiries from the inland merchants, it appears that no man goes without a wife from a fcarcity of women; and that

[q] Mod. Univ. Hift vol. xvi. p. 402.

although the richeſt have many wives, the pooreſt are not thereby precluded from having one or two; in ſhort, that an unpaired man or woman is ſeldom or never ſeen.

Thus of many hindrances to population in Europe, not one takes place in Afric; and ſuch is the rapidity of propagation here, that it ſhould ſeem there would be a ſuperabundance of inhabitants, if the ſlave trade did not take ſo many off. Certain it is, that in many parts of Aſia the climate and other circumſtances are ſo much more favourable than the ſoil, that whilſt the people multiply, the famines deſtroy; for this reaſon, in ſome parts of China, fathers ſell or ex-poſe their ſupernumerary children. It ſeems from hence very pro-bable, that Afric not only can continue ſupplying the Weſt Indies with the ſame quantities as hitherto; but, if neceſſity required it, could ſpare thouſands, nay millions more, and continue doing the ſame to the end of time, without any viſible depopulation.

Theſe circumſtances, together with the incurable ignorance and unſkilfulneſs of the natives, ſpread over a country of ſuch extent, abounding with gold and a multitude of other rich commodities, highly prized in Europe, ſeem to point it out as an object of moſt valuable commerce to the trading and manufacturing nations of that quarter; we find accordingly, that Britain alone employs 50,000 tons of ſhipping in it, and imports from thence to the amount of above half a million ſterling, excluſive of the ſlaves.

The populouſneſs of this country, and ſpirit of the people, make it reaſonable to ſuppoſe, that the conſtitution of ſlavery has been of ſome thouſand years exiſtence among them. Their commerce in ſlaves muſt be fixed exceeding early. Joſephus, giving an account of the trade carried on by Solomon [r] with Ophir, which he places in Africa, mentions that, " beſides gold and ſilver," there were brought to the king, " ϰ πολὺς ἐλέφας, Αἰθίοπες τε, ϰ π θηϰοὶ," " much ivory, *Blacks*, and monkeys," which are the ſame com-modities that form the chief part of their trade at this day. Solo-mon however had no occaſion for any great number of Blacks; they were bought perhaps chiefly for attending the ſeraglios of princes, high-prieſts, and other great officers of ſtate; or for adding variety to their retinues. In ſome of the ſubſequent ages, from the

[r] About the year before Chriſt 1009.

decline

decline or ruin of thofe petty kingdoms which had ufed to traffic with them, the demand grew lefs and lefs, until the Negroe provinces had no communication left, except with their neighbours, the Arabs and Moors.

The want of more extenfive vent for their fuperfluous people occafioned thofe horrid methods of diminifhing them, of which we read in hiftory, by facrificing them to their fettifhes and great men; butchering their captives in war, and, in moft of the provinces, devouring human flefh; which perhaps fupplied them with a permanent kind of food, and made it lefs neceffary for them to break through their natural abhorrence of labour, and take the pains either of cultivating the earth, or laying up provifions againft unfeafonable years. Man's flefh was then in fuch cheap eftimation among them, that they would give ten or twelve flaves for a horfe: *Labat* cites an example of one being fold for forty flaves.

The Portuguefe, who were the earlieft Europeans of the modern ages that had any intercourfe with thefe people, and firft came among them about the year 1450, found flaves an eftablifhed article of their inland commerce with one another, and hence conceived the idea of turning this local medium of traffic to account, by purchafing flaves to work their mines in South America. It is not improbable too that they thought it a meritorious act to refcue fo many human victims from fuffering death and torture, under fuch idolatrous and favage cuftoms; and thus make their private gain compatible with the fuggeftions of humanity and religion.

It was the South-weft part which the Portuguefe firft grew acquainted with. Many years paffed before the Englifh entered into the flave trade; in 1621, when captain Jobfon touched at the river Gambia in the North-weft part, the inhabitants offered him feveral flaves in exchange for goods; but he refufed, alledging " that the Englifh did not trade in them;" for a long time after, this traffic was regularly adopted by many of the different European ftates, fo abundant were flaves, and fo eager the natives to furnifh themfelves with brandy, trinkets, and other novelties, that, even in 1730, Snelgrave tells us, he purchafed a child for a bunch of beads, worth no more than half a crown. But, to fpeak of the prefent ftate of this trade, the rivalfhip of the Europeans, the bad manage-ment of fome factories, and the overbidding of others, have opened the eyes of the crafty natives to their intereft, and fuch a compe-tition being extremely favourable to their avarice, they have gra-dually raifed the price to 23 *l.* and 24 *l. per* head for able men and women; but, rating the price at 20 *l.* at medium, the annual profit to the Africans is 800,000 *l.* fterling, out of which their petty fove-reigns on the coaft draw a tribute, by way of capitation tax on all that are exported, of not lefs than 70 or 80,000 *l.*; the moft of which, if not the whole, arifes from the extrufion of thofe, who, agreeably to the primitive frame of their conftitution and ufages, would but for this trade have been put to death, and fo loft to their country, without any refulting benefit. The love of gain, which enables them the better to gratify their pride, floth, and debauched inclinations, animates them in fupplying the trade as at prefent conducted; and although it may lead to fome acts of violence and injuftice among them, yet it has leffened the number and atrocity of thefe acts, and is attended with fuch pleafing confequences to them, that it is probable they never will let it drop willingly.

The flaves in general are,

1. Such as are captived in war.

2. Such as are fold by their brutal parents, or hufbands.

3. Native flaves fold by their owners, generally for fome crime.

4. Such as are free born, but condemned to forfeiture of freedom for fome flagitious offence.

Of the latter fort there is a great number; fince to their natural vices is fuperadded, in fome provinces, a long lift of conftructive crimes, for which the punifhment affigned by their kings and great men is, a fine or flavery.

In fome places, offences of all forts, except treafon, are atonable with money; but, that being deficient, the penalty is flavery. In others all crimes and offences, great and fmall, are punifhed with flavery.

An owner here has the abfolute dominion over his flaves, their bodies, life, and goods, as the kings have over thofe of their vaffals. He may kill or fell his flaves and their children at pleafure; and

parents

parents confider their own offspring, as creatures wholly in their power, to be difpofed of juft as they think proper. The children uniformly follow the condition of their mother: if fhe is a flave, they continue fuch, though the father be free. All their work is performed by their women and flaves, and the latter are in place of beafts of burthen. Hence the chief riches among all the Negroe ftates confift in the number of their flaves. If they treat them at any time with particular indulgence, it appears to arife folely from the advantages derived from their fervice, and the fear of their elopement; but the third offence of this fort is punifhed by death, or fale to the traders, at the pleafure of their owner; their care of the children of their flaves is founded upon the fame interefted motive; for thefe are their wealth: and many breed flaves, like cattle, to make profit by the fale of them, either to the more opulent natives, or to the Black or White traders. Before the Europeans traded to this coaft, their flaves, as well as prifoners of war, ufed to be facrificed to their divinities; flaughtered or buried alive at the funerals of their princes and chief men, and at all great feafts. Slaves and prifoners were indifcriminately devoured; and in fome provinces were regular markets, at which the aged and infirm were publicly fold for thefe ufes. There is even fome reafon to believe, that in the interior countries thefe cuftoms ftill prevail in a degree, though much fewer are butchered than formerly. Indeed, the profits by felling in trade all thofe whom formerly they ufed to put to death, in fo many various modes, and for various caufes, either from revenge or fuperftition, for food or amufement, are fo great, that it is probable but very few of their flaves, prifoners, and criminals, are now put to death. As they confider their flaves merely as their neceffary beafts during life, fo they treat their bodies with no mark of humanity after their deceafe. In moft of the provinces they do not beftow even interment upon them, but throw their carcaffes in any open place, and leave them a prey to wild animals; in a few places only they cover them with earth, but without any ceremony.

The emoluments they draw from their flaves, in one way or other, operate as a perpetual incentive to their encouraging population

tion (already fo favoured in feveral local circumftances, as has been mentioned) to the utmoft of their power; in order that they may never want a fufficient number for their domeftic fervices, for agriculture, and other purpofes; befides enough of fupernumeraries, to fupport and augment their revenues arifing from trade with the Europeans. Slaves may therefore be now confidered with them, actual *ftaple products*, as much as wool and corn are to Great Britain. They have gained by this means a conftant vent for all their rogues and vagabonds; and the tranfportation of them is fo far from being a burthen to their ftates, as the cafe is with refpect to the European nations, that it is highly lucrative to them. Thus they are relieved from their vileft criminals, with a large profit into the bargain; whilft the European plantations in America are made the common receptacle of thefe abandoned outcafts; and are become as ufeful to the African provinces, as fcavengers to a dirty town, or Virginia and Maryland to Britain. It is clear, that the African ftates have juft as good right as any European power, to banifh their criminals to other parts of the world that will receive them; it is certainly agreeable to the principles of humanity, that captives alfo fhould be exiled, rather than cruelly tortured to death; and by banifhment of all thefe victims for life, they reap this fure benefit, that they are effectually prevented from returning to repeat again their former courfe of criminal or hoftile practices; nor is the indemnification for thefe practices trifling, which accrues to the refpective ftates, from the fale of their bodies to the Europeans.

In England, multitudes are hanged, and many more fent to the plantations and fold into flavery; fome for a term, others for life. Such as are executed, can no longer commit injury nor do good; but of the many hundred wretches tranfported, many find methods of returning, and generally, if not univerfally, follow the fame trade of villainy as before, till they fuffer the *ultimum jus* of hanging. It may be faid of our Englifh tranfported felons, as of the Negroe criminals, that neither of them go into a voluntary banifhment; but it muft be allowed, that the Africans may with equal juftice fell their convicts, as the Englifh fell theirs; and equally well veft a legal right to their fervice in the purchafers. The argument that fome are wrongfully punifhed in this way, is nothing to the purpofe; it holds

equally

equally refpecting each government; for how many examples have we continually, of innocent perfons condemned to death or banifh-ment in England, upon falfe evidence? and if this occurs, as it frequently does, in a country that boafts of its righteous laws, and equitable forms of juftice; we ought not to be furprized, that the fame events happen in Africa, where juftice is fo ill adminiftered through the natural barbarity of the people. Exclufive therefore of this argument, the African ftates having the power of difpenfing life or death; they are likewife empowered to regulate the condition upon which life is granted, where it has been adjudged by their forms of proceeding to be forfeited to their laws, or cuftomary ufages. It may juftly then be queftioned, whether this banifhment is to be termed involuntary; fince the parties, knowing what muft be the in-evitable penalty of their doing fo or fo, might have avoided falling under it; but by committing offences to which the penalty is annex-ed, they wilfully fubject themfelves to the confequential punifhment, which is no other than flavery, perpetual or temporary, at the pleafure of their purchafers; to whofe difcretion the fellers have left it. But although it is well known that ninety-nine out of one hundred of the flaves fhipped from Africa, are now convicted felons, whofe lives were forfeited, and whofe punifhment has been com-muted for flavery to the Europeans; this fact is denied, upon a fup-pofition, " that Africa could not have fo many felons yearly as there " are flaves thus fold." To elucidate this, let us only confider, that Great Britain has above two thoufand convicted felons yearly; Africa does not fell any thing near two hundred thoufand flaves yearly; yet that would be only in the proportion of one hundred to one; and Africa is not only one hundred, but perhaps one thoufand times larger and more populous than Great Britain. It would not be wonderful then, if from thence were to be fhipped every year two hundred thoufand convicts; thefe in fact would be juft fo many lives faved, and rendered ufeful to the community; which advantages would be wholly loft, were the flave trade univerfally given up; for as the Africans are naturally thieves and villains, though flavery is the certain punifhment now on their conviction, the breaking up of the flave trade might indeed alter the punifhment to that of death, but would not reform them; and that this would be the fure confe-

quence,

quence, may be judged from the well-attested fact, that if the slaves which the Africans bring to market are so old or blemished, that they cannot get what they think a sufficient price for them, they will cut their throats before the faces of the Europeans [s]. To abolish this trade, is therefore no other than to resign them up to those diabolical butcheries, cruelty, and carnage, which ravaged their provinces before the European commerce with them began.

It appears from the fullest evidence, that the provinces bordering upon the coast do not send any of their own natives into banishment, unless for atrocious crimes; the major part are brought from the interior parts, where these slaves are an established article of traffic; some few captives of war, the rest convicts, or criminal persons, born in a state of pure slavery; and over whom their owners exercise, agreeably to their usage and constitutions, the most absolute will and power.

We are informed, that the Black merchants travel many hundred miles, and collect them from the utmost extremities of Afric; great numbers, sold from Angola, having been brought from the interior parts of Æthiopia, on the borders of the Indian ocean; and at Sabi, and in other provinces, inland, regular markets are held, where are to be sold men, women, children, hogs, sheep, goats, &c. in common. We find therefore, that these supplies are drawn, by a variety of channels, from every part of this extensive continent; every province contributing a few; so that by the time these several quotas are assembled at the coast, or grand shipping-place, they may well amount to a very considerable multitude.

If a Negroe, so purchased, should, upon being transplanted into a country where freedom is truly understood, aspire to get free from that bondage in which he has always lived, or to which the judgement of his society has decreed him; I acknowledge there are no means of preventing his attempts, but by an exertion of *force*. Few men (except those Africans who live in their own country in a state of servility) are without the desire of enlargement. These Africans know not what freedom is, until they enter our colonies; and therefore can have no passion for a state, whose qualities they are ignorant of. In regard to other countries, and other men, the laws of

[s] Treatise on the Trade from Great Britain to Africa, 1773.

different

different ftates, aware of this *furor* for liberty, have taken care to lay reftraints upon it. In England, for example, the common labourers are obliged, by force of penal inftitutions, to remain content with a very limited portion of liberty. The felons banifhed to America would foon evade their fentence, if not conftrained to obedience by fuperior ftrength. Without this curb, no man would fuffer himfelf to be deprived of his perfonal freedom for debt; no feaman would fubmit to be preffed, no foldier to be retained in the fervice, no highwayman to be hanged. A labourer in England never confented to the laws which impofe reftrictions upon him; but there is in every government a certain fupreme controuling power, included in the focial compact, having the energy of law, or publifhed and declared as the law of the land; by which every member of the community, high and low, rich and poor, is refpectively bound: it is in truth an affociation of the opulent and the good, for better preferving their acquifitions, againft the poor and the wicked. For want, complicated with mifery and vice, generally feeks relief by plundering from thofe who are better provided. An African is as much bound by this fupreme power, as the Englifh labourer.

If then every African ftate has from the earlieft ages, as far as we can trace, not only tolerated a property in men, but afferted and exercifed a right of felling their criminals, flaves of war, and native flaves, to any one that would buy them, in this transfer is implied as much right of property in the vendee, as in the vender: no one queftions in that country, not even the criminals and flaves themfelves, this right of felling, and acquiring a property; it is univerfally acknowledged; nor is the will of the party fold, ever confulted; he admits the vender's right, as part of the law or ufage of his fociety; and this precludes all idea of *illegal durefs*, and proves that the right of perfonal property over fuch, as are purchafed out of a ftate of pure flavery, is lawfully continued to the fubfequent owners.

No one doubts, but that every contract made in Afric for the purchafe of a flave, is there underftood by the three parties, the buyer, the feller, and the perfon fold, to be perfectly firm and valid; the one knows what he buys, the other what he fells, and the third, that his fervices are thus become tranflated to his new owner; he is confcious likewife, that he himfelf would acquire the fame right, fhould he ever become a flave-holder; accordingly we are told, that in certain provinces, the flaves are permitted to grow rich enough to become themfelves the buyers and proprietors of flaves. The commencement of this bondage therefore in Afric is fo very far from being illegal, that (refpecting the laws and cuftoms of that continent) it is univerfally admitted and fanctified by publick notoriety, eftablifhed ufage, and the general full confent of all the inhabitants. Surely, a voyage from Afric to any other country, where this claim of property is continued, cannot diffolve the bargain.

In regard to captives of war, fold as flaves, it appears that they come under that ftate by an act of their own, which cannot be deemed otherwife than voluntary. It is evident, from the hiftory we have of the Negroe ftates, that the moft potent among them cannot pretend to be enfured from flavery; for it may become the lot of every one that ventures a battle. It is confiftent with every maxim of equity, reafon, and juftice, that a perfon reduced to this clafs, to which he intended reducing his conqueror, does (on the principle of enflaving, or of being enflaved) fubmit knowingly and voluntarily to the event. Among Chriftian princes at war with each other, *Grotius* obferves, that this practice of enflaving prifoners has entirely ceafed. But ftill fome fhadow remains among them of the original power, which the victors exercifed over their captives. Their perfonal liberty is reftrained, until they either bind themfelves not to refume arms, or until a valuable confideration is paid for their enlargement; this confifts either of a pecuniary ranfom, or an exchange of man for man, which is the fame as giving value for value. It is faid, that a Negroe chieftain fpares the life of his captive, which fhews (according to the civilians) that he is under no abfolute neceffity of killing him. But who is to be judge of this neceffity, the civilians or the chieftain? This proves only a commutation of the mode, by which the chieftain feeks to be rid of, and to deprive his enemy of further capacity to do him hurt. His rage and his fears ufed formerly to meet fatisfaction by two ways, either by putting him to cruel death, or by holding him in ftrict bondage; thefe both fecured him from future attacks. If he fpared his life for a time, it was only to make him drag on a miferable xiftence, under continual hard treatment; and by a lingering mifery

administer

adminifter more zeft to implacable vengeance. This was the cuftom before the Europeans vifited the coaft. But this trade diverted the thirft of blood, and the refinements of malice, into the love of gain ; and now the practice of banifhment not only gratifies this powerful incentive, but confults their fecurity equally well as the antient mode, by removing their enemies, and effectually preventing their repetition of hoftility.

They, as well as the Europeans, confider their prifoner as one who is to be redeemed with a price. They hold his body as their abfolute property ; and the prifoner, from the moment of his captivity, as well as before he was made a prifoner, knows the full latitude of that power ; he is confcious there is a price fixed upon his head ; if he is redeemed from death by his countrymen, he is fenfible that he becomes juftly their debtor, and no lefs fo if, his countrymen refufing to ranfom him, he is redeemed by others. We form an erroneous idea of the Negroes, if we fuppofe that they prefer death to life ; or that, upon the choice being offered, they would not rather be perpetual fervants to a man of tolerable humanity, than be mangled and butchered by their inhuman conquerors. But without entering into the fubtle diftinctions of civilians, which would lead us too far, it is certain, that the Negroe ftates at prefent encounter with each other, with a view chiefly to acquire as many flaves as they can : flaves being their real wealth, whether retained for their own ufe, fold to other Negroe ftates, or to foreigners ; and all parties among them well underftanding this to be, if not the motive, at leaft the fure iffue, of all the wars in which they engage, *they* cannot be faid to fuffer injuftice who meet with that fate, which they either defign for others, or have reafon to expect themfelves.

It is faid, that many are *kidnapped* into our plantations. This however is a fact which wants to be proved. The trade is not now to be eftimated by the manner in which it was originally carried on (when irregular rovers of many nations made defcents upon the coaft), but as a regularly conducted, and eftablifhed plan. Our acts of parliament, and the African company, ftrictly prohibit the buying any *panyard* or ftolen Negroe, under fevere penalties ; and the flaves bought by the factories always undergo a review of the chief men of the place, to prevent any fuch being fhipped off ; their intereft

makes

makes this caution neceffary, becaufe very difagreeable confequences might enfue to the trade, if it fhould be neglected; for, many years ago, when any violences of this nature were practifed, they not only put a ftop to commerce at the particular place where they happened, but alarmed the neighbouring diftricts; and fuch injuries were ufually retaliated upon innocent navigators, who afterwards touched there, and were often furprized and murthered by the natives. Almoft every act of this fort, perhaps, has thus been atoned for at the price of blood; and it is therefore highly improbable that, under thefe circumftances, any fuch thefts can at prefent be committed; nor would any planter knowingly purchafe Negroes obtained in that furreptitious manner, through a juft fear, that they would either fhorten their lives with pining after their friends and country, or take every opportunity of eloping from him; events which he has not equal reafon to expect from exiles, whom their country has renounced, and vomited forth.

Banifhment being now fubftituted throughout moft part of the Negroe territory in Afric, in place of death; it is not furprizing, that the convicts and captives entertain horrid notions of it, and often ftruggle for relief before they quit the coaft. Many of them, it is probable, when they have committed faults, were threatened to be fold to the Europeans; and this menace may be often ufed, as the name of Marlborough was by women in France, to frighten their children into good behaviour. Perceiving that this is the general courfe of punifhment, inflicted on very capital crimes, they naturally apprehend it to be a moft fevere and cruel penalty. This apprehenfion muft dwell upon their minds the more, as they remain ignorant of the fate which has attended the many other thoufand exiles, their predeceffors, none of whom return to tell the tale; fo that, no doubt, their imaginations paint the change in the moft terrific colours. Thefe prejudices are ftrengthened by the neceffity there is for treating them as condemned criminals and victims, from the time of their firft delivery into the hands of the Negroe merchants, by whom they are conducted through the country tied together with thongs to prevent their efcaping; at the factory they are fhackled for the like reafon, and on board fhip they meet with the like treatment. Thefe precautions are injurious to their health, and

and confequently to the intereft of the traders; but they feem inevitable. The many acts of violence they have committed, by murdering whole crews, and deftroying fhips, when they had it left in their power to do fo, have made this rigour wholly chargeable on their own bloody and malicious difpofition, which calls for the fame confinement as if they were wolves or wild boars.

Several of the Negroes imported into our colonies, having been queftioned, as foon as they had learned Englifh enough to be underftood, what opinion they had conceived in Afric of their future deftination among the white people; it appeared from their anfwer, that fome of thefe poor wretches believe that they are bought in order to be fattened, roafted, and eaten. Others fuppofe, that the Europeans buy them to make gunpowder of their bones; and *Du Pratz* fays, that the French Negroes imbibe a notion from their infancy, that the white men buy them to drink their blood; which, he tells us, is owing to this; that when the firft Negroes faw the Europeans drink red wine, they imagined it was blood; fo that nothing but experience can eradicate thefe falfe terrors: but as none of the flaves, who have had that experience, ever return to their own country, fo the fame prejudices continue to fubfift on the coaft of Guiney, where they are purchafed. Some, who are ftrangers to the manner of thinking among the Negroes, imagine, that this can be of no bad confequence. But there are many examples of the contrary, efpecially if the Negroes, on their firft arrival, meet with no other flave who can talk their dialect, and quiet their fears; for thefe have often caufed fome to hang or drown themfelves, and others to run away.

To thefe prejudices may be afcribed the reluctance they fo often manifeft, on leaving Afric. They who are fold for heinous crimes, as well as others who are fold for trivial faults, or perhaps no fault at all, are equally fufceptible of thefe apprehenfions. The merely leaving their country, can work no fuch effect on the minds of thofe who are fenfible that, if they had remained in it, or fhould return to it again, they muft inevitably fuffer death. *Snelgrave* mentions, that when he was on the coaft, in 1730, the king of Old Calabar, falling fick, caufed (by advice of his *marbuts*) a child about ten months old to be facrificed to his fetifhe, or divinity, for recovery. Snelgrave faw the child, after it was killed, hung up on the bough of a tree, and a

live

live cock tied to it, as an addition to the fpell. Being afterwards on another voyage at the fame place, he beheld the fame king fitting on a ftool under a fhady tree, and near him a little boy tied by the leg to a ftake driven into the ground, covered with flies and other vermin, and two *marbuts* ftanding by. On enquiry he learnt, it was intended to be facrificed that night to their god *Egbo*, for his majefty's profperity. Snelgrave redeemed the child at the king's own price, and carrying his bargain on board fhip, found that this infant's mother had been fold to him the very day before; whofe joy on thus meeting again with her fon, fo unexpectedly refcued from the brink of flaughter, he pathetically defcribes; adding, that the ftory coming to be known among all the Blacks on board, it difpelled their fears, and impreffed them with fo favourable an opinion of the white men, that although he had three hundred in all, they gave him not the leaft difturbance during the voyage. When their prejudices were diffipated by fo ftriking an example of humanity fhewn to a Negroe, they perceived the Whites were not fuch bugbears as they had been induced to believe, and grew happy and peaceable, on finding that a white mafter was likely to be more merciful towards them than a black one.

The objection, that many die in tranfportation to the colonies, does not bear againft the trade itfelf, but againft fome defect or impropriety in the mode of conducting it. A fimilar objection may lie againft cooping up debtors or other prifoners in a clofe unwholefome jail; fending convicts to America huddled together in fmall veffels; cramming foldiers into inconvenient tranfport fhips; or impreffed men into clofe tenders, or ill-conftructed fhips of war; by all which means vaft multitudes have perifhed, without any bead-roll taken of their number, though, it is probable, the lift would run fhockingly high. To what end are the contrivances of ventilators, &c. but the prevention or diminution of this mortality? But the mortality is *fully evinced* in point of fact, by the many expedients which have been recommended by humane perfons to render it lefs frequent.

The captains, I believe, to whofe charge they are committed, are careful of their healths to the utmoft of their power, confiftent with the fafety of their own lives; their intereft, and that of their employers, depends much upon it. But captains, and other feafaring men, are not often philofophers or phyficians; nor all as difcerning as a
Lind

Linde or a *Macbride*. The African merchants will, for their own fakes, adopt every expedient that may conduce to the good health and condition of thefe cargoes [*t*]; but even with the utmoft care it may happen, that an epidemic difeafe may break out during the paffage; probably the fmall-pox or fluxes. Accidents of this nature cannot be totally excluded; and it is fome fatisfaction to reflect, even in this cafe, that moft, or all of the poor wretches, if it were not for the trade, would have met with an untimely and more painful end in their own country; it is better furely, that a few fhould perifh by fuch cafualties, than that all fhould die by the hand of an executioner. That in the native Africans fale of Negroes to our fhipping, various frauds have been committed, and perfons improperly and unjuftly fold; that merchants of fhips have been inhuman; that planters have been wantonly cruel, may be fuppofed from the enormity of crimes feen every day in the moft civilized ftates. To thefe abufes, efficacious remedies fhould be applied; and the African merchants will own the higheft obligations to government, if by falutary laws it can alleviate any diftreffes fuffered by thofe, whofe labour fupports our colonies, and enriches our mother country. But, to fay the truth, it muft be confeffed, that the difference between the condition of the Negroes in general in Africa, and in our colonies, is fo great, and fo much happier in our colonies, that they themfelves are very fenfible of it. I once interrogated a Negroe, who had lived feveral years in Jamaica, on this fubject. I afked him if he had no defire of re-vifiting his native country?

[*t*] The benefit of ventilators in tranfport fhips has been found very great. In a Liverpool fhip which had ventilators, not one of 800 flaves died, except only a child, born in the voyage; but in feveral other flave fhips without ventilators, there died 30, 40, 50, or 60 in a fhip.

Capt. Thompfon, of the Succefs tranfport, with 200 *preffed men*, delivered out of gaol with diftempers on them, were all landed fafe in Georgia (1749), though they had been detained near a twelvemonth on board; which *uncommon good luck* the captain attributed to his ventilators.

Capt. Crammond, with 392 flaves bound to Buenos Ayres, carried all of them fafe by the fame means, except 12 only, who were ill with a flux when they came on board. In the year 1753, ventilators being put on board the French veffels in the flave trade at Bourdeaux, it was found that by the ufe of them, inftead of one-fourth lofs in long paffages from Africa to their plantations, the lofs feldom exceeded a twentieth; and one veffel faved 308 out of 312 flaves, in fpight of moft tedious calms, and a lingering paffage. So in the Nova Scotia tranfport fhips, 12 to 1 more were found to die in unventilated than in ventilated fhips. *Hales, on Ventilators.*

Thefe examples will prove, that the fhip owners of both nations have not been wanting in the exercife of means for preferving the lives and health of the flaves tranfported from Africa; but it appears obvious, that Englifh convicts and recruits fent over the water were fubject to equal mortality, till the like means were ufed for their prefervation.

his reply was to the following effect; that he would much rather live, and end his days, where he was. That he could not live so comfortably in his own country; for in Jamaica he had food and cloathing as much as he wanted, a good house, and his family about him; but that in Africa he would be destitute and helpless, without any security to his life, or any of those enjoyments which now rendered it comfortable. Although some few of these poor wretches may have inexorable tyrants for their masters, who may treat them worse perhaps than any person of humanity would treat a brute; yet, in general, the case is very different, and one thing is self-evident, that it being so opposite to the interest of any planter thus barbarously to treat, or inhumanly to work his slaves to death; if ever such instances of cruelty happen, the owner is, without doubt, either a fool or a madman.

Many of the Negroes in this island, the tradesmen, and such as are usually called House Negroes, live as well, or perhaps much better, in point of meat and drink, than the poorer class of people do in England; and not one of them, even to the plantation labourer, goes through half the work; for even those who cultivate the lands, are not without indulgence, and frequent intervals of recreation.

If, indeed, we suppose a man bred up and habituated to a state of *pure slavery* among numberless others in the same predicament, subject to the vilest species of bondage; that his life, his person, his food, and acquisitions, are all at the absolute and arbitrary disposal of his owner, as much as if he were a meer ox or sheep; and that he is in hourly peril of being damnified in some one or other of them, by the wanton cruelty or caprice of his owner: let us then imagine this unhappy wretch conveyed into another region, and among a people very different from the last, in government, manners, and disposition; where his servitude is tempered with lenity, where he is permitted to enjoy a little property undisturbed, where his life, his body, his food, and raiment, are protected and assured to him by public regulations; can we hesitate one moment to say, that his yoke is now become easy, his burthen light? and shall we not conclude, that such a being, though perhaps averse at first to the change, through erroneous impressions, and utter ignorance of his future destiny, will soon discern the more happy circumstances of his new condition, and really think, that, compared with the past, his present services are *perfect freedom.*

In

In this light, if we are impartial, we ought to examine the subject; not using slavery as an indefinite term, but considering how far just our particular idea or definition of it is, when applied to this or that set of men, who live in a different part of the world; since what is deemed slavery in one place, is far from being reputed so in another: a Briton therefore, who has always lived in fruition of a rational freedom, must not judge of every other man's feelings by his own ; because they who have never experienced the same British freedom, or any degree near to it, cannot possibly hold the same opinion of slavery that a Briton does; for they know not how to distinguish it; and with such, the servitude they live under, has neither horrors nor hardship.

Among men of so savage a disposition, as that they scarcely differ from the wild beasts of the wood in the ferocity of their manners, we must not think of introducing those polished rules and refinements, which have drawn their origin and force from the gradual civilization of other nations that once were barbarous. Such men must be managed at first as if they were beasts; they must be tamed, before they can be treated like men. Ridiculous is it, when the argument regards such men, to say, that they do not come into our colony-servitude under *regular compacts!* True, they do not; for, if they did, they would no longer be slaves, in the usual acceptation of the term. As slaves, they come into the colony from their native country ; but the difference lies in this, they were slaves, abject slaves in Africa, and so would have continued, with infinitely greater disadvantages than they experience in the colony. In the former, they were subject to all the severities of the most brutal and licentious tyranny, under men living in something worse than a state of nature. In the colony, the owner of the slave receives him with a tacit agreement that his services shall be requited with necessary food and cloathing; a just proportion and interval of rest; some leisure too for his own particular emoluments; a weather-tight and convenient habitation; a prospect of many temporary and occasional douceurs; and even of an independence, if his deserts should claim it. Add to this, that his life is protected by law, and that his owner holds not an unlimited power over him. He enjoys a more narrowed degree of liberty than some subjects in Britain, but in several respects a much larger extent than some others. Under the penal laws of Jamaica, he is (in general) entitled to equitable modes of juſtice, trial, and judgement; from other laws he derives protection, immunities, and emoluments. In his habitation, cloathing, fubfiſtence, and poſſeſſions, he is far happier and better provided for than moſt of the poor labourers, and meaner clafs, in Britain. It is not therefore a mere found, importing flavery, that makes men flaves; the Negroes here are not the more fo for the title; although the common ideas of uninformed perfons lead them to think of their condition in the very worſt fenſe which that term admits. In truth, on many plantations, and under mild maſters, if they receive not hire in money, they receive an equivalent in the neceſſaries and conveniencies of life, and the peaceable enjoyment of their private acquifitions; and, what is ſtill better, good ufage, and protection from injuries; which are a more current coin amongſt the honeſt and free-minded, than money itſelf.

It does not follow, becaufe thefe flaves are delivered into the hands of Europeans by the Negroe merchants or potentates, to be dealt with as they think proper, that the Europeans aſſert any power of inflicting cruelty upon them; or believe, there is any merit in abſtaining from mifufage of thefe poor wretches; who might poſſibly have been put to death, if they had not redeemed them.

In fact, the moſt humane of the Europeans, among whom I furely may efteem the Britiſh, hold them only in what Grotius   other authors diſtinguiſh as a legitimate, equitable ſpecies of ſervitude; including a fort of compact, by which (abſtracted from the *right* acquired by *purchafe)* one man owes to another perpetual fervices for the prefervation of his life, for his fuftenance, and other neceſſaries; and this is founded on the principles of reafon. The maſter does not extend his power over his flave beyond the bounds of natural equity, but a reciprocal obligation connects them; protection and maintenance on the one hand, fidelity and fervice on the other; this obligation has nothing in it oppreſſive, but, on the contrary, gives the flave a certainty of food and conveniencies; which others often want, who hire out their labours by the day. To this effect fays alfo Gronovius, " forafmuch as the maſter is bound to give food to his flave, fo is the flave bound to make a return or retribution by his labour; this duty is equally permanent on both fides:" and this is the kind of fervitude exifting in Jamaica; the laws of which impofe fuch an obligation upon every owner of flaves, and punifh all who fail of conforming to it.

From the furvey I have taken of the African Negroes, and the nature of the flavery exifting among them, it will not, I think, be deduced, that the people they export undergo more hardfhip or injury by the tranfition, than they would have fuffered in their own country.

The captives of war, inftead of being inhumanly flaughtered, pafs into a ftate of fervitude, it is true; but it is fuch a ftate, that, under Chriftian mafters, who, I venture to fay, are not fuch tyrants as the African flaveholders, they enjoy indulgence proportioned to, and often far tranfcending, the merits of their behaviour; the comforts, even I may add, the pleafures of life; and not a few obtain their freedom.

Such as are banifhed for crimes and mifdemeanors, have reafon to rejoice at the fentence; which reprieves them from fome horrid mode of execution, and prolongs their exiftence.

Should any be unjuftly exiled, they may think themfelves happy in being placed beyond the reach of a cruel and favage government.

If they were flaves in their own country, or had forfeited their freedom by fome crime, they have no right to repine at the want of it in the country to which they are driven. They were already flaves, and have only exchanged their owner and laws; the former, for one lefs arbitrary; the latter, for one more beneficent and gentle than they before had experience of. In general, they gain life, for death; clemency, for barbarity; comfort and convenience, for torture and mifery; food, for famine. Infomuch that, after fome trial of their new condition, under a mafter who in fact purfues his own intereft beft in treating them well, they would account it the higheft act of inhumanity to be fent back to their native country.

The choice of Negroes for different purpofes requires experience, and particular attention; for there is not only fome variety in their paffions and bent of mind, but, from the conftitution of their native climates and local manners, they inherit a variety of different diftempers. The Coromantins, and many others of the Gold Coaft flaves, are haughty, ferocious, and ftubborn. The Minnahs, timid and defponding, apt to deftroy themfelves upon the leaft, and often without any, provocation. The Mundingo Negroes are very fubject to worm diforders; the Congos to dropfies. The Ebo men are lazy, and averfe

to

to every laborious employment; the women performing almost all the work in their own country; thefe men are fullen, and often make away with themfelves, rather than fubmit to any drudgery: the Ebo women labour well, but are fubject to obftructions of the *menftrua*, often attended with fterility, and incurable. The Congos, Papaws, Conchas, Whidahs, and Angolas, in general. are good field labourers, but the laft-mentioned are moft ftupid. The Negroes brought from Senegal are of better underftanding than the reft, and fitter for learning trades, and for menial domeftic fervices. They are good commanders over other Negroes, having a high fpirit, and a tolerable fhare of fidelity: but they are unfit for hard work; their bodies are not robuft, nor their conftitution vigorous. The delicacy of their frame, perhaps, has fome effect on their minds, for they are eafier difciplined than any other of the African Blacks. The Aradas are thought to excel all the reft in knowledge of agriculture, yet their fkill is extremely incompetent. The Congos, and Gold Coaft Negroes, in general, are good fifhermen, and excel in making canoes.

It has been remarked of the Guiney Negroes, that, although they are for the greater part of ftrong, healthy bodies, they rarely live to a determinate old age in their own country. A Negroe there of fifty is reckoned a very old man indeed; and at forty they appear debilitated. This fhort fpan has been attributed to their exceffive venery: Buffon afcribes it to polygamy; but in Egypt, and the hotter parts of Afia, where polygamy prevails, the inhabitants are found to attain great ages. So, in Jamaica, if they are not far advanced in years when brought over, they have been known to attain to 80 and 90, or upwards; but 50 and 60 are extremely ufual.

C H A P. III.

Of the CREOLE SLAVES *and* AFRICAN NEGROES *in* JAMAICA

THE *general* character of our Creole flaves may be fummed up in the words of an old proverb, " Like mafter, like man." They are capable of being made diligent, and moderately faithful; or the reverfe, juft as their difpofitions happen to be worked upon. It cannot be doubted, but the far greater part of them are more inclined to a life of idlenefs and eafe, than a life of labour: yet the regular difcipline to which they are inured from their infancy, becomes habitual and natural to them, as it does to foldiers, failors, and fchool-boys; and, like the latter, their principal addrefs is fhewn in finding out their mafter's temper, and playing upon it fo artfully as to bend it with moft convenience to their own purpofes. They are not lefs ftudious in fifting their mafter's reprefentative, the overfeer; if he is not too cunning for them, which they foon difcover after one or two experiments, they will eafily find means to over-reach him on every occafion, and make his indolence, his weaknefs, or fottifhnefs, a fure prognoftic of fome comfortable term of idlenefs to them: but, if they find him too intelligent, wary, and active, they leave no expedient untried, by thwarting his plans, mifunderftanding his orders, and reiterating complaints againft him, to ferret him out of his poft: if this will not fucceed, they perplex and worry him, efpecially if he is of an impatient, fretful turn, till he grows heartily fick of his charge, and voluntarily refigns it. An overfeer therefore, like a premier minifter, muft always expect to meet with a faction, ready to oppofe his adminiftration, right or wrong; unlefs he will give the reins out of his hands, and fuffer the mobility to have things their own way; which if he complies with, they will extol him to his face, contemn him in their hearts, and very foon bring his government into difgrace. But fuch a man, if he is gifted with good-nature and humanity, will eafily get the better in every ftruggle; for thefe are qualities which the Negroes prize in their fuperiors above all others. Some overfeers, unlefs fharply looked after, have been known to play the tyrant; and where this is the cafe, we cannot blame their black fubjects for wifhing a change, nor for their zealous endeavours to effect it. The old woman was much in the right, who prayed for the life of the tyrant Dionyfius, fearing, that if he died, fhe might fall under the dominion of a fucceffor, ftill more odious and diabolical. It would be an act of humanity, reflecting the higheft honour on the legiflature of Jamaica, if the gentlemen who compofe it fhould, in imitation of the French, promulge a code of laws and ordinances refpecting the Negroes, more particularly in the treatment of them upon their plantations; reftraining and punifhing, in an exemplary manner, all fecret practices of barbarity; that thofe men, whofe callous hearts are impenetrable to the feelings of human nature, may be affected in fome degree by a dread of legal pains and penalties.

Were

Were this duly attended to, and proper encouragement given to in-formers, it would be impoffible to act fuch private oppreffions often; becaufe, out of the whole poffe of white fervants on each plantation, there might always be fuppofed one or more, who, from the abhor-rence of fuch practices, if not the allurement of reward, would quickly impeach the tyrant. At the fame time, the very apprehenfion of fuch a confequence would infallibly check the moft hardened; efpecially if, in addition to other punifhment, the law fhould difqualify the offender from ever again exercifing his profeffion, or office, within the ifland.

If every owner of a plantation refided upon it, there would be no caufe for the interpofition of legiflative authority; but it is well known, that a great many eftates belonging to different abfentees, and lying in diftant parts of the ifland, are often given up to the charge of one agent only, who cannot poffibly refide at all, nor vifit them very frequently. Matters are then left to the difcretion of overfeers, whofe chief aim it is to raife to themfelves a character as able planters, by encreafing the produce of the refpective eftates; this is too frequently attempted, by forcing the Negroes to labour beyond their abilities; of courfe they drop off, and, if not recruited inceffantly, the gentle-man fteals away like a rat from a barn in flames, and carries the credit of great planterfhip, and vaft crops, in his hand, to obtain advanced wages from fome new employer in another diftrict of the ifland. The abfentees are too often deceived, who meafure the condition of their properties by the large remittances fent to them for one or two years, without adverting to the heavy loffes fuftained in the production of them; and they find, too late, their incomes fuddenly abridged, and the finews of their eftate wafted far below their expectation. It might be of fervice to many of them, if they could bring themfelves to live more within bounds; be content with a moderate equal remittance, fuch as they know is proportioned to the ftrength of their labourers; and once, in a certain number of years, revifit their plantations, in or-der to regulate their future meafures from the plain evidence of their own eyes and ears.

When once they have fhot beyond the mark of œconomy, and become involved in England, they grow infenfible to every other confidera-tion than how to extricate themfelves; which is commonly atchieved

I

by

by exhaufting the vigour of their only fupporters ; when a little patience, retrenchment of expences, and moderate uniform crops, would probably bring about what they wifh, without any lofs to their capital. Humanity operates here like virtue ; it is its own fure reward. It is a planter's beft intereft to be humane ; and it is clearly moft conducive to his honour and peace of mind.

The great Chriftian precept " of doing unto others what we would " that they fhould do unto us," fpeaks pathetically to every rational breaft ; though few among us paufe perhaps to afk ourfelves this candid queftion : How fhould I wifh to be treated, if I was in a ftate of fervitude, like thefe my fellow creatures ? Doubtlefs we would wifh, that our mafter might be a Chriftian in practice, as well as principle, and render our condition as eafy as poffible, by a mild and compaffionate ufage. Let every overfeer and planter then only act the part of that mafter, and not be feduced, by a foolifh vanity, to plume himfelf on his happier lot, or fancy that he is created to be the tyrant, not the friend, to mankind. I fhall not attempt to give a complete defcription of all the cuftoms and manners of our Creole Negroes, fince many of them are not worth recording ; and, in confequence of their frequent intermixture with the native Africans, they differ but little in many articles.

In their tempers they are in general irafcible, conceited, proud, indolent, lafcivious, credulous, and very artful. They are excellent diffemblers, and fkilful flatterers. They poffefs good nature, and fometimes, but rarely, gratitude. Their memory foon lofes the traces of favours conferred on them, but faithfully retains a fenfe of injuries ; this fenfe is fo poignant, that they have been known to diffemble their hatred for many years, until an opportunity has prefented of retaliating ; and, in taking their revenge, they fhew a treachery, cowardice, and deliberate malice, that almoft exceed credibility. A ftupid infenfibility of danger often gives them the fpecious appearance of dauntlefs intrepidity ; though, when once thoroughly made fenfible of it, none are more arrant cowards. A blind anger, and brutal rage, with them ftand frequently in place of manly valour The impreffions of fear, naturally accompanied with cunning and warinefs, make them always averfe to any other mode of engaging with an enemy, than by ambufcades, and furprize ; and in all their boxing matches with one

another

another, one may obferve their efforts directed by malice, fo foon as their fury is raifed. When they have been employed againft the rebellious flaves, each party meeting in a wood, have difperfed in an inftant, and every man fingled out his tree, behind which he fheltered his perfon, and fired. After the firft volley, one party generally fled; but, if both ftood their ground, the next conflict was made with cutlaffes, in the management of which they are furprifingly active and fkilful, ufing either hand alternately, as they fee occafion. But they would never be brought to withftand horfe, platoons, or fcrewed bayonets; nor to engage in an open place. When they did not fucceed at the firft fire, they trufted to the lightnefs of their heels, rallied at fome diftance, if not too clofely purfued, and returned again to the bufh-fight. They are remarkable, like the North American Indians, for tracking in the woods; difcerning the veftige of the perfon, or party, of whom they are in queft, by the turn of a dried leaf, the pofition of a fmall twig, and other infignificant marks, which an European would overlook; but I have known fome white Creoles not lefs expert at this art, which they acquired, as they faid, by frequently ranging the woods after wild hogs, or runaways. The Negroes know each other's haunts and artifices, much better than the Whites; and, probably, form their conjectures, by reflecting which way they would fteer their courfe, if they were purfued themfelves. In marching through a wood they walk in *enfilade*, but do not always keep filence. Sometimes, when engaged with cutlaffes, they will fight very defperately, and ftand to it with the infenfibility of pofts, till they almoft hack one another to pieces, before either will furrender.

They are in general excellent markfmen at a ftanding fhot, their eye quick, and fight fo clear, that they feldom mifs; yet their vifion (as I have before remarked) is the worft poffible for the regular pofition of any thing. They cannot place a dining-table fquare in a room; I have known them fail in this, after numberlefs endeavours; and it is the fame in other things. So that fuch as are bred carpenters and bricklayers, are often unable, after many tedious and repeated trials with the rule and plumb-line, to do a piece of work ftraight, which an apprentice boy in England would perform with one glance of his eye in a moment. It is fomewhat unaccountable, too, that they always mount a horfe on the off-fide. Their ideas feem confined to a very

few

few objects; namely, the common occurrences of life, food, love, and drefs: thefe are frequent themes for their dance, converfation, and mufical compofitions.

The African, or imported Negroes, are almoft all of them, both men and women, addicted to the moft beftial vices, from which it is the more difficult to reclaim them, as they are grown inveterately confirmed by habit from their very infancy. In Guiney they are taught to regard a dram, as one of the chief comforts of life; they grow up in this opinion: and I have feen fome of them forcing the precious liquor down the throats of their children, or *pickaninnies*, with the fame eagernefs that indulgent mothers in England fhew, when they cram their little favourite with fugar-plumbs. In thieving they are thorough adepts, and perfectly accomplifhed. To fet eyes on any thing, and endeavour to poffefs it, is with them intirely the fame. From this caufe it happens, that, upon their being brought into the plantations, they are foon engaged in quarrels, which fometimes are attended with fatal confequences; for, when they are prompted to revenge, they purfue it againft one another with fo much malevolence and cruelty, that the punifhment exacted is generally beyond all proportion greater than the offence can poffibly merit. It is therefore moft prudent for a planter to wink at petty offences againft himfelf, but to chaftife all thofe who are found guilty of doing injury to the perfon, or property, of their fellow Blacks; by which means he will be the conftant referee and umpire of their difputes; and, by accommodating them agreeably to juftice and right, prevent his Negroes from having recourfe to open violence, or fecret vengeance, againft each other; which are too often perpetrated with a blind and unrelenting hatred; in purfuit whereof many have been killed outright, others maimed, and not a few deftroyed by the flower operation of fome poifon.

The Creoles, in general, are more exempt from ebriety, that parent of many crimes! I have known feveral, who rejected every fort of fpirituous liquor with loathing, and would drink nothing but water. If the Negroes could be reftrained intirely from the ufe of fpirits in their youth, they would probably never become very fond of dramdrinking afterwards. I have often thought, that the lower order of white fervants on the plantations exhibit fuch deteftable pictures of

G g g drunk-

drunkennefs, that the better fort of Creole Blacks have either conceived a difguft at a practice that occafions fuch odious effects, or have refrained from it out of a kind of pride, as if they would appear fuperior to, and more refpectable than, fuch beaftly white wretches. Be this as it may, there is nothing furely can more degrade a man, than this voluntary rejection of his rational faculties; deprived of which, he finks below the loweft rank of brutes. The Creole Blacks differ much from the Africans, not only in manners, but in beauty of fhape, feature, and complexion. They hold the Africans in the utmoft contempt, ftiling them, " falt-water Negroes," and " Guiney " birds;" but value themfelves on their own pedigree, which is reckoned the more honourable, the further it removes from an African, or tranfmarine anceftor. On every well-governed plantation they eye and refpect their mafter as a father, and are extremely vain in reflecting on the connexion between them. Their mafter's character and repute cafts, they think, a kind of fecondary light upon themfelves, as the moon derives her luftre from the fun; and the importance he acquires, in his ftation of life, adds, they imagine, to their own eftimation among their neighbour Negroes on the adjacent eftates. Their attachment to the defcendants of old families, the anceftors of which were the mafters and friends of their own progenitors, is remarkably ftrong and affectionate. This veneration appears hereditary, like clanfhips in the Scotch Highlands; it is imbibed in their infancy, or founded perhaps in the idea of the relation which fubfifted between, and connected them in, the bond of fatherly love and authority on the one fide, and a filial reverence and obedience on the other; nor is this effect, however it arifes, unmixed with fomewhat of gratitude, for the favours and indulgencies conferred on their predeceffors; fome fruits of which they themfelves have probably enjoyed by devife; for, even among thefe flaves, as they are called, the black grandfather, or father, directs in what manner his money, his hogs, poultry, furniture, cloaths, and other effects and acquifitions, fhall defcend, or be difpofed of, after his deceafe. He nominates a fort of truftees, or executors, from the neareft of kin, who diftribute them among the legatees, according to the will of the teftator, without any moleftation or interruption, moft often without the enquiry, of their mafter; though fome of thefe Negroes have been known to poffefs from 50*l*. to 200*l*.

at

at their death; and few among them, that are at all induſtrious and frugal, lay up leſs than 20 or 30 *l.* For in this iſland they have the greateſt part of the ſmall ſilver circulating among them, which they gain by ſale of their hogs, poultry, fiſh, corn, fruits, and other commodities, at the markets in town and country.

They in general love their children, though ſometimes they treat them with a rigour bordering upon cruelty. They ſeem alſo to feel a patriotic affection for the iſland which has given them birth; they rejoice at its proſperity, lament its loſſes, and intereſt themſelves in the affairs and politics that are the talk of the day. Whoever has ſtudied their diſpoſition and ſentiments attentively, will be of opinion, that, with mild and humane uſage, they are more likely to become the defenders than the deſtroyers of their country. As a large ſhare of vanity and pride may be obſerveable among them, ſo the better ſort appear ſenſible to ſhame. I have known a very conſiderable number of them on a plantation kept in due decorum for ſeveral years, with no other diſcipline than keen and well-timed rebukes; and my obſervations have tended to confirm me in opinion, that our Creole Blacks (for I ſpeak of them only) may, with a very moderate inſtruction in the Chriſtian rules, be kept in good order, without the whip. Raſh correction has often rendered them ſtubborn, negligent, and perverſe, when they might have been influenced chearfully to perform every thing required of them, by judiciouſly working on their vanity; by beſtowing ſeaſonable rewards and encomiums on their praiſe-worthy conduct, and by ſtinging reproaches for their miſdemeanors. There are many artifices to be practiſed with the greateſt ſucceſs; ſuch as, degrading for a while from ſome employment eſteemed among them a poſt of diſtinction, and authority; holding them up to the ridicule of their fellow Blacks, and the like. What they endure, upon theſe occaſions, has nothing in it of that ſenſe of vile abaſement, which corporal inflictions are apt to produce; and whenever corporal puniſhment is carried to extreme, it is ſure to excite a hearty and indelible contempt and abhorrence for the inflictor.

The force of ridicule, on the contrary, brings upon them the cutting ſneers of the other Negroes, and always turns the edge of their contempt and rage from their maſter, to themſelves; and hence they may ſmart more ſeverely under ſuch reprehenſion, than they would

under

under the fcourge. Every overfeer has not the patience, or talents, to qualify him for this mode of governing, but all fhould endeavour at it; and, for this purpofe, it is neceffary for each of them to ftudy well the temper of every Creole Black under his particular command, to learn fomewhat of their private hiftory, and never betray any fign of heat or paffion in his admonitions.

The firft and chief requifite therefore is to know how to command his own temper; for, without having gained this advantage, he is totally unfit to be a manager of other mens; but having once gained this point, he need not doubt of paffing through a fuccefsful adminiftration.

It is certain, that the Negroes, fo far from fuffering any inconvenience, are found to labour with moft alacrity and eafe to themfelves in the very hotteft part of the day. The chilinefs of the morning air in this ifland feems to caft a damp upon their fpirits, and renders them for a time feeble and torpid; one fees them creeping flowly out of their huts, bundled up with thick cloathing, fhivering, and uneafy; but as the day advances, they grow more and more active and alert. The opennefs of their pores gives a free tranfpiration to bad humours; and they would enjoy robuft health, under the hardeft toils expedient here, if they were lefs prone to debauch, and venereal excefs. They love warmth in the night, and never fleep without a fire in their hut; the watchmen too, in the open air, lay themfelves upon a board, by a rouzing fire, and fometimes fo near, as to fcorch their very fkins; for it is to be obferved, that thefe nocturnal guards, like thofe of London, after a comfortable repaft in the evening, have no objection to amufe themfelves, for the remainder of the night, with a dog's fleep. They account fhoes and ftockings very ufelefs incumbrances; and the foals of their feet, by conftant expofure, acquire the callofity and firmnefs of a hoof; but fome, who are to take a journey over very rocky roads, prepare themfelves with fandals, cut from an ox-hide, which they bind on with thongs. They dread rain upon their bare heads almoft as much as the native Africans; perhaps, their woolly fleece would abforb it in large quantity, and give them cold. When they are caught in a fhower, it is very common to fee them pull off fhirt and jacket, and fometimes their breeches or trowfers, all which they wrap up in a bale, and place upon their heads. They are fond
of

of covering this part of their bodies at all times, twisting one or two handkerchiefs round it, in the turban form, which, they say, keeps them cool, in the hottest sunshine. The same custom prevails among the Eastern nations, and probably from the like reason; even the free Mulatto women here think themselves not compleatly drest without this tiara, and buy the finest cambric or muslin for the purpose, if their pockets can afford it. The Creole white ladies, till lately, adopted the practice so far, as never to venture a journey, without securing their complexions with a brace of handkerchiefs; one of which being tied over the forehead, the other under the nose, and covering the lower part of the face, formed a compleat helmet. The Negroes use their heads, instead of their shoulders, or backs, for carrying all sorts of burthens; with a dried plantain leaf they plait a circular pad, which they call a *cotta*; upon this, the load rests, and preserves their wool from being rubbed off. This custom enlarges, and strengthens, the muscles of their necks, in an amazing degree; and it is really wonderful to observe, what prodigious loads they are able to carry in this manner, with the greatest apparent ease; insomuch, that they will even run with them, and affirm, at the same time, with a laugh, that they feel no weight; perhaps, the perpendicular position of the load, and the equilibre which, from habit, they know well how to give it, produce this facility of carriage, while the incumbent pressure is diminished in proportion to the velocity of their progressive movement under it; this, however, is no more than happens every day with the London porters, some of whom will carry 300 lb. weight. The cotta serves likewise for another purpose; on the voluntary divorce of man and wife, it is cut in two, and each party takes half; as the circle was a symbol of eternity, and the ring of perpetual love or fidelity, so this ceremony, perhaps, is meant to express the eternal severance of their mutual affection. Their diet consists generally of pulse, herbs, plantains, maize, yams, or other roots, prepared with pork, and fish, fresh or salt; salted beef, herrings, jerked hog, or fowls. Salt fish they are extremely fond of, and the more it stinks, the more dainty; they make likewise a kind of pudding, with pounded maize; and sometimes of the sweet potatoe, which they call a potatoe-pone; their broths, or pots (as they are termed), are well seasoned with the country peppers; *ochra* is a principal ingredient; and they are

extremely

extremely relishing, and nutritive; but they come doubly recom
mended by the cleanliness of preparation, their cooks usually washing
their hands three or four times, whilst they are about it: I mean the
Creole Blacks, and better sort of the Africans; for as to the rest, they
feed with all the bestiality peculiar to the genuine breed of Guiney.
Cane rats are much in esteem, and, when roasted and stuffed, are said
to have a delicate flavour; but, to see them impaled before the fire
with their goggle eyes and whiskers, is enough to turn an European
stomach; the Creoles wash their mouths, as soon as they awake in the
morning.   About noon is their usual time of bathing, in some river
open to the sun.   They first wet their bodies all over, then roll in the
sand, and plunge into the water; this method serves to cleanse their
skins, as well as soap, or a flesh brush.

They are all married *(in their way)* to a husband, or wife, *pro
tempore,* or have other family connexions, in almost every parish
throughout the island; so that one of them, perhaps, has six or more
husbands, or wives, in several different places; by this means they
find support, when their own lands fail them; and houses of call and
refreshment, whenever they are upon their travels.   Thus, a general correspondence is carried on, all over the island, amongst the Creole
Blacks; and most of them become intimately acquainted with all affairs of the white inhabitants, public as well as private.   In their
houses, they are many of them very neat and cleanly, piquing themselves on having tolerably good furniture, and other conveniencies. In
their care for their children, some are remarkably exemplary. A Negroe
has been known so earnest and sincere in the tuition of his child, as
to pay money out of his own pocket for smith's work, to keep a
truant son employed, during his apprenticeship to that business, that
he might not become remiss in acquiring a proper knowledge of it,
for want of work.   They exercise a kind of sovereignty over their
children, which never ceases during life; chastizing them sometimes
with much severity; and seeming to hold filial obedience in much
higher estimation than conjugal fidelity; perhaps, because of the whole
number of wives or husbands, one only is the object of particular
steady attachment; the rest, although called wives, are only a sort of
occasional concubines, or drudges, whose assistance the husband claims
in the culture of his land, sale of his produce, and so on; rendering

to

to them reciprocal acts of friendfhip, when they are in want. They laugh at the idea of a marriage, which ties two perfons together indiffolubly. Their notions of love are, that it is free and tranfitory.

This is well known to their white gallants, for even the authority of a mafter muft bend to the more abfolute empire of Cupid; nor is the fable beauty (except a very common hack) to be won, without fome previous addrefs and courtfhip; in the progrefs of which the powerful charms of gold muft generally lend their aid, to make the moft paffionate fuitor fuccefsful; thefe belles allowing nothing more of their perfons than their head, hands, and feet, to be at their mafter's difpofal. Their propenfity to lazinefs is chiefly confpicuous among the domeftic fervants, who are never more happy than when they can find a commodious poft, pillar, or corner of a houfe, to loll againft, whilft they are taking a nap. I have even feen them fall faft afleep, whilft attending at table, behind a gentleman's chair. Like fome other animals, they are fond of caterwauling all night, and dozing all the day. If they indulge in fleep at night, one muft fuppofe they are very little difturbed with anxious thoughts. Their repofe is perfectly found; infomuch that fometimes they are rouzed with the utmoft difficulty; the loudeft clap of thunder, or the repert of a cannon at their ear, would not wake them. On the plantations I have feen fome, but they are moftly Africans, fo exquifitely indolent, that they have contracted very bad ulcers on their feet, by fuffering multitudes of *chiegos* to neftle and generate there, rather than give themfelves the trouble of picking them out.

Although fome domeftics are very trufty fervants; the greater number are fo, merely becaufe they have no fit inducement to be otherwife, or no means of bettering their condition. But when occafion offers, of ferving themfelves by a roguifh fhift, adieu fidelity! You may confide a fum of money to a Negroe's charge, and he will deliver it punctually; but, beware of leaving any fum cafually in his way, for he would not be able to refift the temptation of ftealing it; his fidelity, in the former cafe, arifes from his defire to imprefs you with the beft opinion poffible of his honeft dealing, in order that you may afford him more convenient opportunities of pilfering from you, without immediate detection. It reflects no great honour on their difpofition, that the freed Blacks and Mulattos are obferved to treat

their

their flaves with extraordinay harfhnefs, and fometimes even barbarity; a fure characteriftic of a vindictive, bafe, and cowardly mind.

The domeftics are remarkably adroit in the negociation of all intrigues, and affairs of gallantry; and fhew a peculiar delight on being entrufted *plenipos*, to affift at thefe congreffes of love. Upon thefe occafions, the brain of a Spanifh enamorato, or an Italian cecifbeo, cannot be more fruitful of expedients. The fuperftition of thefe Blacks is carried to very fingular lengths, although the more polifhed among them believe in a future ftate of reward and punifhment; they do not confider certain acts to be criminal, which are ufually reputed fuch among true believers.—Murder is with moft of them efteemed the higheft impiety.—Filial difobedience, and infulting the afhes of the dead, are placed next. But as for petty larcenies, affairs of gallantry, fornication, &c. they are reputed only peccadilloes, which are fufficiently punifhed in this world, with the baftinadoe, or the diftempers occafioned by them. The greateft affront that can poffibly be offered a Creole Negroe, is to curfe his father, mother, or any of his progenitors. This generally provokes a fpeedy revenge on the aggreffor, after every other mode of provocation has failed. They firmly believe in the apparition of fpectres. Thofe of deceafed ftiends are *duppies*; others, of more hoftile and tremendous afpect, like our rawhead-and-bloody-bones, are called *bugaboos*. The moft fenfible among them fear the fupernatural powers of the African *obeah-men*, or pretended conjurers; often afcribing thofe mortal effects to magic, which are only the natural operation of fome poifonous juice, or preparation, dexteroufly adminiftered by thefe villains. But the Creoles imagine, that the virtues of baptifm, or making them Chriftians, render their art wholly ineffectual; and, for this reafon only, many of them have defired to be baptized, that they might be fecured from *Obeah*.

Not long fince, fome of thefe execrable wretches in Jamaica introduced what they called the *myal dance*, and eftablifhed a kind of fociety, into which they invited all they could. The lure hung out was, that every Negroe, initiated into the myal fociety, would be invulnerable by the white men; and, although they might in appearance be flain, the obeah-man could, at his pleafure, reftore the body to life. The method, by which this trick was

carried

carried on, was by a cold infufion of the herb *branched colalue* [*u*] ; which, after the agitation of dancing, threw the party into a profound fleep. In this ftate he continued, to all appearance lifelefs, no pulfe, nor motion of the heart, being perceptible ; till, on being rubbed with another infufion (as yet unknown to the Whites), the effects of the colalue gradually went off, the body refumed its motions, and the party, on whom the experiment had been tried, awoke as from a trance, entirely ignorant of any thing that had paffed fince he left off dancing. Not long ago, one of thefe myal men, being defirous of feducing a friend of his to be of their party, gave him a wonderful account of the powerful effects produced by the myal infufion, and particularly that it rendered the body impenetrable to bullets ; fo that the Whites would be perfectly unable to make the leaft impreffion upon them, although they were to fhoot at them a thoufand times. His friend liftened with great attention, but feemed to doubt the truth of it exceedingly ; but, at length, propofed to the other, that, if he was willing to ftand a fhot, he fhould be glad to make the experiment ; and, if it turned out as he pretended, he himfelf would then moft readily confent to be a myal man. To this the other agreed, not imagining, perhaps, that matters would come to extremity ; or elfe convinced in his own mind of the reality of what he afferted. Having prepared himfelf, he ftood up to receive the fhot. His

[*u*] This herb is a fpecies of *folanum*, and is the *aquaraguia* of Brafil. Pifo, 223. Browne, 174. It is very common in the lowlands of Jamaica. It is alfo called the *folanum fomniferum officinale*. The Negroes make ufe of it daily for food in their broths ; and it is found, by long experience, to be a pleafant and wholefome green. Barham fays, he was furprized to fee the Angola Negroes eat it as we ufe fpinnage in Europe, without any prejudice, it has fo ftrong a refemblance to the deadly nightfhade. Pifo fays, " that the rind of it, bruifed and fteeped in water, intoxicates fifh " fo, that they may be eafily taken, but does not kill them." The juice is cooling and reftringent ; the leaves, applied to the head in phrenctic fevers, give eafe. It is probable, its narcotic qualities are deftroyed by the fire in boiling ; but that the crude juice, or a cold infufion of the bark and leaves, would be found to poffefs them in a high degree ; which agrees with Pifo's account of the effects on fifh. The myal gentry make the infufion with rum. In regard to the other infufion, which puts an end to its operation, we can only conjecture. It is poffible, that, by frequent trials, the Negroes have found pretty accurately the length of time which the fleep may laft, and fo take care to proportion the dofe. Befides, it has lately been difcovered, that vegetable acids, fuch as lime-juice, vinegar, &c. are antidotes to the effect of opium, and all vegetable poifons, taken internally : their external application has not been tried ; but might probably anfwer the fame purpofe, efpecially towards the decline of the fleepy fit ; and I think it is not unlikely, that thefe Negroes ufe them to revive their myal men.

friend fired, and killed him dead. This accident, with the circumftances leading to it, were foon made known; and, for fome
time, brought the priefts and their art into great difrepute among
all their converts. The dexterity of thefe priefts, or conjurers,
in the preparation of poifons, has been mentioned by many authors.
Kalm obferves, that this art is known to the Negroes of North-
America, in the provice of Pennfilvania; and that they frequently
practife it on one another. This poifon does not kill immediately;
for fometimes the fick perfon dies fome years after: but, from the
moment he receives the poifon, he falls into a decline, and enjoys
but few days of good health. Kalm fays, they commonly employ
it on fuch of their brethren who behave well; are beloved by their
mafters; and feparate, as it were, from their countrymen, or do
not like to converfe with them. There are likewife other reafons
for their enmity; but there are few examples of their having
poifoned their mafters. Perhaps, the mild treatment they receive
keeps them from it; or they fear a difcovery, and that in fuch cafe
their punifhment would be very fevere [w]. Sir Hans Sloane
gives one or two inftances of this practice in Jamaica. And Dr.
Barham tells us, that the favannah flower, which grows exceedingly common in all the lowlands of that ifland, has been made ufe
of for this purpofe. It is a fpecies of dog's bane; the *apocynum
erectum* of Sir Hans Sloane, p. 206; the *nirium* of Browne, p. 180.
It is one of the rankeft poifons in the world. Barham fays, he faw
but two drachms of the expreffed juice given to a dog, which
killed him in eight minutes; but that it may be fo ordered, that it
fhall not deftroy a perfon in many days, weeks, months, or years.
Some call it the Spanifh gilly-flower. Some years paft (continues
he) a practitioner of phyfick was poifoned with this plant by his
Negroe-woman, who had fo contrived it, that it did not difpatch
him quickly; but he was feized with violent gripings, inclination
to vomit, lofs of appetite, and afterwards fmall convulfions in feveral parts of his body, a hectic fever, and continual wafting of
his flefh. Upon application to Dr. Barham for advice, he gave him
fome *nhandiroba* kernels, to infufe in wine, and drink frequently;
which cured him in time; but it was long before the convulfive

[w] Kalm's Travels into North-America.

symptoms left him. This plant is an ever-green; and it is re-marked, that no animal will meddle with it, although in the greatest drought, and when no other green thing appears. The root, dried and powdered, is purgative. The milky juice of the plant is a severe cauftic, and takes away warts and ring-worms. Barham gives another inftance of its deleterious effects. A Negroe, having some rum in a jar, ignorantly ftopped the mouth of it over-night with some leaves gathered from this plant, one or two of which fell in, and so imparted their noxious quality to all the liquor. The next morning, he drank some of it himself, and diftributed drams to feveral of his countrymen; but, in lefs than two hours, they were all feized with violent vomiting, and tremors all over their bodies. Upon the alarm being given, a furgeon was fent for; but, before he could arrive, three of them expired, and another lay at the point of death. Some Indian arrow-root was imme-diately got, bruifed, and the exprefled juice adminiftered. The firft glafs revived the Negroe that appeared to be dying; the fe-cond brought him to the ufe of his fpeech; and, upon repeated dofes, he continued mending till he was perfectly recovered. The *nhandiroba* is a climbing plant. Pifo, p. 259, calls it likewife *acaricobo, ambuyaembo,* and *caapeba*; and thus defcribes it. It is a fpecies of climbing ivy. Its leaves are difpofed like the ivy; fomewhat roundifh; and, as it were, terminating in three points, green, fmooth, and glofly; the flowers fmall, of a dufky pale hue; the fruit round, green, fhining, about the fize of a large apple, the upper part appearing with a circular indentation, and at the centre three lines uniting together at the extremity in an obtufe angle. The fruit on the infide is difpofed fomewhat like the walnut, but in three diftinct cavities, appearing, upon taking off the rind, per-fectly white, and containing an oily kernel, of a pale yellow colour, inclofed in a pellicle. From this kernel an oil is ex-tracted, which may be ufed for lamps, and holds a long time in burning; but it is of no ufe for food, becaufe it is extremely bitter, as well as the fruit. Barham fays, the firft time he met with this plant was in St. Thomas in the Vale; where he faw it climbing and running up to the top of very high trees. It happened to be in fruit. Its leaf much refembles the Englifh ivy; but the fruit

is

is like a green calibafh; only it has a circular black line round it, and two or three warts or little knobs. The infide of the fhell is full of white, flattifh beans, inclofed in a white membranous fub-ftance; and, when thoroughly ripe, the fruit turns of a brownifh caft, like a ripe calabafh. The beans or nuts are then of a lightifh brown colour, covered with a thin, hard cruft, in which is a whitifh kernel full of oil, and exceffively bitter. The nuts are ge-nerally ten or twelve in a fhell, clofe and compreffed; fo that, after being taken out, they cannot be replaced. He fays, the Spa-niards call it *avilla*; and the Negroes, that he employed to gather it, called it *fabo*. It feems to be a fpecies of the *fevillea foliis cordatis angulatis*, Linnæi, Sp. Pl. Angl. " antidote cocoon of " Jamaica;" whofe kernels yield a great deal of oil, of a bitter tafte, and ufed here for burning. The Negroes infufe thefe kernels, when dried and fcraped into a powder, in rum, to relieve pains in the ftomach. They alfo efteem them antidotes to poifon. But the pod feldom contains above three, or at moft four, feeds; and therefore it cannot be the fame as Barham's. Browne mentions very imperfectly, p. 373, a plant which he faw growing, on the windward part of Montferrat, at the fide of Kaby's Gully; which bore white bloffoms, fucceeded by many large apples, containing a number of large compreffed feeds, difperfed in the pulp of the fruit; which probably is the fame as that defcribed by Barham.

But to return. The Negroes wear the teeth of wild cats, and eat their flefh, as a charm for long life; for they hold the vulgar opinion, that a cat has nine lives. Thus, by affimilation of the cat's flefh and juices into their own, they imagine they can enfure longevity, and a power of fuftaining great fatigues. Many a poor grimalkin has fallen a victim to this ftrange notion. Bits of red rag, cats teeth, parrots feathers, egg-fhells, and fifh-bones, are fre-quently ftuck up at the doors of their houfes when they go from home leaving any thing of value within (fometimes they hang them on fruit-trees, and place them in corn-fields), to deter thieves. Upon converfing with fome of the Creoles upon this cuftom, they laughed at the fuppofed virtue of the charm, and faid they prac-tifed it only to frighten away the falt-water Negroes, of whofe de-predations they are moft apprehenfive. Their funerals are the very

reverfe

reverse of our English ceremony. The only real mourners are the husband, wife, or very near relations of the deceased; yet even these sometimes unite their voices to the general clamour or song, whilst the tears flow involuntarily down their cheeks. Every funeral is a kind of festival; at which the greater part of the company assume an air of joy and unconcern; and, together with their singing, dancing, and musical instruments, conspire to drown all sense of affliction in the minds of the real mourners. The burthen of this merry dirge is filled with encomiums on the deceased, with hopes and wishes for his happiness in his new state. Sometimes the coffin-bearers, especially if they carry it on their heads, pretend that the corpse will not proceed to the grave, notwithstanding the exertion of their utmost strength to urge it forwards. They then move to different huts, till they come to one, the owner of which, they know, has done some injury to, or been much disliked by, he deceased in his life-time. Here they express some words of indignation on behalf of the dead man; then knock at the coffin, and try to sooth and pacify the corpse: at length, after much persuasion, it begins to grow more passive, and suffers them to carry it on, without further struggle, to the place of repose. At other times, the corpse takes a sudden and obstinate aversion to be supported on the head, preferring the arms; nor does it peaceably give up the dispute, until the bearers think proper to comply with its humour. The corpse being interred, the grave is but slightly overspread with earth. Some scratch up the loose mould, with their backs turned to the grave, and cast it behind them between their legs, after the manner of cats which have just exonerated. This, they say, is done, to prevent the deceased person from following them home. When the deceased is a married woman, the husband lets his beard remain unshaved, and appears rather negligent in his attire, for the space of a month; at the expiration of which, a fowl is dressed at his house, with some messes of good broth, and he proceeds, accompanied by his friends, to the grave. Then begins a song, purporting, that the deceased is now in the enjoyment of compleat felicity; and that they are assembled to rejoice at her state of bliss, and perform the last offices of duty and friendship. They then lay a considerable heap of earth over the grave, which is called *co-*

vering

vering it; and the meeting concludes with eating their collation, drinking, dancing, and vociferation. After this ceremony is over, the widow, or widower, is at liberty to take another spouse immediately; and the term of mourning is at an end.

The Negroe funeral calls to mind the *late-wake* of the highlands in Scotland, thus described by Mr. Pennant. The evening after the death of any person, the relations and friends of the deceased meet at the house, attended by bag-pipe and fiddle. The nearest of kin, be it wife, son, or daughter, opens a melancholy ball, dancing and greeting (*i. e.* crying violently) at the same time. This continues till day-light, but with such gambols and frolics among the younger part of the company, that the loss which occasioned them is often more than supplied by the consequences of that night. If the corpse remains unburied for two nights, the same rites are renewed. Thus, Scythian-like, they rejoice at the deliverance of their friends out of this life of misery. The *coranich*, or singing at funerals, is still in use in some places. The songs are generally in praise of the deceased, or a recital of the valiant deeds of him or his ancestors.

Cambden, in his account of the antient Irish, mentions their custom of using earnest reproaches and expostulations with the corpse, for quitting this world, where he (or she) enjoyed so many good things, so kind a husband, such fine children, &c. There seems a striking conformity between this antient rite and that in use among the Negroes.

The Negroes strew grave-dirt on the highway when any thing is stolen from them, intimating this curse: " May the thief be re-" duced to the same state and condition as the corpse which lies bu-" ried in the grave whence this dirt was taken! may his existence " be short! may he not live to enjoy his theft! but be crumbled " and trampled under foot, like the soil of a public road!"

This dirt is a material ingredient in their solemn oaths, which are administered in the following manner. A small quantity of the earth is mixed with water in a calibash. The person who tenders the oath dips his finger into the mixture, and crosses various parts of the juror's naked body, repeating the following imprecation as he touches each part, the juror assenting at the close

of

of every fentence; after which, he drinks up the refidue of the mixture, and may therefore be faid literally to *fwallow the oath*, which is to this effect. If I have (ftolen this hog, fowl, corn, or—as it may happen to be the cafe), may the grave dirt make my bowels rot! may they burft and tumble out before my face! may my head never ceafe to ach! nor my joints to be tortured with pain! &c. Regularly, the oath ought to be adminiftered by an obeah man; but their fuperftition makes them hold it in great reverence and horror, even when adminiftered by any other Black, efpecially by an old man or woman: but they do not apprehend any ill confequence will arife from breaking it, when tendered by a white perfon.

They have good ears for mufic; and their fongs, as they call them, are generally *impromptus*, without the leaft particle of poetry, or poetic images, of which they feem to have no idea. The tunes confift of a *folo* part, which we may ftyle the recitative, the key of which is frequently varied; and this is accompanied with a full or general chorus. Some of them are not deficient in melody; although the tone of voice is, for the moft part, rather flat and melancholy. Inftead of choofing panegyric for their fubject-matter, they generally prefer one of derifion, and not unfrequently at the expence of the overfeer, if he happens to be near, and liftening: this only ferves to add a poignancy to their fatire, and heightens the fun. In the crop feafon, the mill-feeders entertain themfelves very often with thefe *jeux d'efprit* in the nighttime; and this merriment helps to keep them awake.

Their *merry-wang* is a favourite inftrument, a ruftic guitar, of four ftrings. It is made with a calibafh; a flice of which being taken off, a dried bladder, or fkin, is fpread acrofs the largeft fection; and this is faftened to a handle, which they take great pains in ornamenting with a fort of rude carved work, and ribbands.

The *goombah*, another of their mufical inftruments, is a hollow block of wood, covered with fheep-fkin ftripped of its hair. The mufician holds a little ftick, of about fix inches in length, fharpened at one end like the blade of a knife, in each hand. With one hand he rakes it over a notched piece of wood, fixed acrofs the inftrument, the whole length, and croffes with the other alternately,

7   ufing

ufing both with a brifk motion; whilft a fecond performer beats with all his might on the fheep-fkin, or tabor.

Their tunes for dancing are ufually brifk, and have an agreeable compound of the *vivace* and *larghetto*, gay and grave, purfued alternately. They feem alfo well-adapted to keep their dancers in juft time and regular movements. The female dancer is all languifhing, and eafy in her motions; the man, all action, fire, and gefture; his whole perfon is varioufly turned and writhed every moment, and his limbs agitated with fuch lively exertions, as ferve to difplay before his partner the vigour and elafticity of his mufcles. The lady keeps her face towards him, and puts on a modeft demure look, which fhe counterfeits with great difficulty. In her paces fhe exhibits a wonderful addrefs, particularly in the motion of her hips, and fteady pofition of the upper part of her perfon: the right execution of this wriggle, keeping exact time with the mufic, is efteemed among them a particular excellence; and on this account they begin to practife it fo early in life, that few are without it in their ordinary walking. As the dance proceeds, the mufician introduces now and then a paufe or reft, or dwells on two or three *pianiffimo* notes; then ftrikes out again on a fudden into a more fpirited air; the dancers, in the mean while, correfponding in their movements with a great correctnefs of ear, and propriety of attitude; all which has a very pleafing effect.

In the towns, during Chriftmas holidays, they have feveral tall robuft fellows dreffed up in grotefque habits, and a pair of oxhorns on their head, fprouting from the top of a horrid fort of vizor, or mafk, which about the mouth is rendered very terrific with large boar-tufks. The mafquerader, carrying a wooden fword in his hand, is followed with a numerous croud of drunken women, who refrefh him frequently with a fup of anifeed-water, whilft he dances at every door, bellowing out *John Connu!* with great vehemence; fo that, what with the liquor and the exercife, moft of them are thrown into dangerous fevers; and fome examples have happened of their dying. This dance is probably an honourable memorial of John Conny, a celebrated cabocero at *Tres Puntas*, in *Axim*, on the Guiney coaft; who flourifhed about the year 1720. He bore great authority among the Negros of that diftrict. When

the

the Pruſſians deſerted Fort Brandenburgh, they left it to his charge; and he gallantly held it for a long time againſt the Dutch, to whom it was afterwards ceded by the Pruſſian monarch. He is mentioned with encomium by ſeveral of our voyage-writers.

In 1769, ſeveral new maſks appeared; the Ebos, the Papaws, &c. having their reſpective Connus, male and female, who were dreſſed in a very laughable ſtyle.

Theſe exerciſes, although very delightful to themſelves, are not ſo to the generality of the white ſpectators, on account of the ill ſmell which copiouſly tranſudes on ſuch occaſions; which is rather a complication of ſtinks, than any one in particular, and ſo rank and powerful, as totally to overcome thoſe who have any delicacy in the frame of their noſtrils. The Blacks of Afric aſſign a ridiculous cauſe for the ſmell peculiar to the goat; and with equal propriety they may well apply it to themſelves. They ſay, " that, " in the early ages of mankind, there was a ſhe-divinity, who uſed " to beſmear her perſon with a fragrant ointment, that excited the " emulation of the goats, and made them reſolve to petition her, " to give them a copy of her receipt for making it, or at leaſt a " ſmall ſample of it. The goddeſs, incenſed at their preſumption, " thought of a method to be revenged, under the appearance of " granting their requeſt. Inſtead of the ſweet ointment, ſhe pre- " ſented them with a box of a very fœtid mixture, with which " they immediately fell to bedaubing themſelves The ſtench of " it was communicated to their poſterity; and, to this day, they " remain ignorant of the trick put upon them, but value them- " ſelves on poſſeſſing the genuine perfume; and are ſo anxious to " preſerve it undiminiſhed, that they very carefully avoid rain, and " every thing that might poſſibly impair the delicious odour." This rancid exhalation, for which ſo many of the Negroes are remarkable, does not ſeem to proceed from uncleanlineſs, nor the quality of their diet. I remember a lady, whoſe waiting-maid, a young Negroe girl, had it to a very diſagreeable exceſs. As ſhe was a favourite ſervant, her miſtreſs took great pains, and the girl herſelf ſpared none, to get rid of it. With this view, ſhe conſtantly bathed her body twice a day, and abſtained wholly from ſalt-fiſh, and all ſorts of rank food. But the attempt was ſimilar to wafhing the Black-a-moor white; and, after a long courfe of endeavours to no purpofe, her miftrefs found there was no remedy but to change her for another attendant, fomewhat lefs odoriferous.

The labouring Negroes are all allowed, by their mafters, a frock and trowfers for the men, and the women a jacket and petticoat of ofnabrig, befides woollen ftuff; but tradefmen, and the better fort, are generally fupplied likewife with checks, handkerchiefs, hats, and caps; and the laws of the ifland oblige every owner to give his Negroes proper cloathing. What they receive annually in this manner compofes their working drefs: but there are few of them who do not acquire fufficient profit, by their huckftering traffic, to furnifh themfelves with a wardrobe of better cloaths for holiday-wear; upon thefe they beftow as much finery as their circum-ftances will permit, invariably preferring the gaudieft colours.

They fupply their ignorance of letters by a kind of technical memory. Few of them can afcertain their own age, or that of their children; but, when queftioned about any event that has happened in the courfe of their lives, they recur to a ftorm, a par-ticularly dry or wet feafon, and the like, and reckon by the number of Chriftmafes they recollect fince thofe periods. Thus, if you afk a Negroe how long ago it was that he left Africa, he anfwers, eight, ten, twelve Chriftmas, according as the cafe happens to be, or according to his remembrance. They have no computation for the fractional parts of a year; and confequently can never fix any fact or event nearer than about a twelvemonth before or after the time when it occurred. They reckon the ages of their children, their horfes, and dogs, in the fame manner. They give their dogs as many names as a German prince; or more frequently call them by a whole fentence, as, *Run-brifk-you-catch-'um-good*, &c. The Africans fpeak their refpective dialects, with fome mixture of broken Englifh. The language of the Creoles is bad Englifh, larded with the Guiney dialect, owing to their adopting the African words, in order to make themfelves underftood by the imported flaves; which they find much eafier than teaching thefe ftrangers to learn Englifh. The better fort are very fond of improving their language, by catching at any hard word that the Whites happen to let fall in their hearing; and they alter and mifapply it in a

ftrange

ftrange manner; but a tolerable collection of them gives an air of knowledge and importance in the eyes of their brethren, which tickles their vanity, and makes them more affiduous in ftocking themfelves with this unintelligible jargon. The Negroes feem very fond of reduplications, to exprefs a greater or lefs quantity of any thing; as *walky-walky, talky-talky, wafhy-wafhy, nappy-nappy, tie-tie, lilly-lilly, fum-fum*: fo *bug-a-bugs* (wood-ants); *dab-a-dab* (an olio, made with maize, herrings, and pepper); *bra-bra* (another of their difhes); *grande-grande* (augmentative fize, or grandeur), and fo forth. In their converfation, they confound all the moods, tenfes, cafes, and conjugations, without mercy: for example; *I furprize* (for, I am furprized); *me glad for fee you* (pro, I am glad to fee you); *how you do* (for, how d'ye do?); *me tank you*; *me ver well*; &c. This fort of gibberifh likewife infects many of the white Creoles, who learn it from their nurfes in infancy, and meet with much difficulty, as they advance in years, to fhake it entirely off, and exprefs themfelves with correctnefs.

Many of the plantation Blacks call their children by the African name for the day of the week on which they are born; and thefe names are of two genders, male and female; as for inftance:

Male.	Female.	Day.
Cudjoe,	Juba,	Monday.
Cubbenah,	Beneba,	Tuefday.
Quâco,	Cuba,	Wednefday.
Quao,	Abba,	Thurfday.
Cuffee,	Phibba,	Friday.
Quamin,	Mimba,	Saturday.
Quafhee,	Quafheba,	Sunday.

There are fome other words, that are remarkable for the different fenfes in which they are ufed; viz.

	Original Import.	Common Import.	Dia'ect.
Mungo,	Bread,	Negroe's name,	Mundingo.
Bumbo,	Alligator,	*Pudendum muliebre,*	*Idem.*
Coffee,	Goodmorrow,	Name of a plant, the berries of which yield an agreeable morning repaft to many of the Negroes,	Fûli.
Guinnay, Guinee,	Devil,	Name of the flave country,	Jaloff, Fûli.
Sangara,	Brandy,	Sangree, or Strong Negus,	*Idem*
Tate,	The Pofteriors,	Tête, the head in French,	Jaloff.
Kenne-kénne,	Small-fand,	Κονις, Græc. *Cinis,* Lat.	Mundingo.
Buaw,	Devil,	Bullock (Negroe phrafe),	*Idem.*

Some

Some good perfons have expreffed their wifhes, that the planta-tion Negroes might be all converted to the Chriftian faith. The planters would be the laft to oppofe fuch a fcheme, if it were thought practicable; well knowing, that their becoming true Chriftians would work no change of property, and might poffibly amend their manners. But few, if any, of the African natives will liften to any propofition tending to deprive them of their fa-vourite fuperftitions and fenfual delights. The Portuguefe mif-fionaries at Congo, perceiving, upon experience, that a religion, in culcating rigid precepts of morality, felf-denial, honefty, and ab-ftinence from women and drunkennefs, was not at all relifhed, contrived to form a medly of Paganifm and Chriftianity; which was more acceptable, and has gained them many converts; only the exterior ceremonies and facraments being indifpenfably en-forced; while, in other refpects, they are left to the antient modes of their country. I have known fome Creole flaves defire to be baptized; but they had no other motive than to be protected from the witchcraft of obeiah-men, or pretended forcerers; which af-fords a plain proof of the influence which fuperftition holds over their minds. But the mere ceremony of baptifm would no more make Chriftians of the Negroes, in the juft fenfe of the word, than a found drubbing would convert an illiterate faggot-maker into a regular phyfician. The Rev. Mr. Hughes fupports the fame opinion. " To bring them," fays he, " in general, to the know-" ledge of the Chriftian religion is undoubtedly a great and good " defign, in the intention laudable, and in fpeculation eafy; yet, I " believe, for reafons too tedious to be mentioned, that the diffi-" culties attending it are, and I am afraid ever will be, infurmoun-" table." This will appear lefs extraordinary, when we confider, that very few of the North-American Indians, who are far more civilized and enlightened people, have as yet been perfuaded to embrace Chriftianity, notwithftanding the inceffant and indefati-gable labours of French and Englifh miffionaries for fo many years. Not many of thefe pious men have crowned their apoftle-fhip with any other iffue than by becoming enrolled in the ho-nourable lift of martyrs. No perfuafion, I am induced to think, can wholly recall them from purfuing the favourite bias of their

minds

minds towards their prefent fyftem; which lays no penalty or penance on their fenfual pleafures, impofes no reftraint of decorum, and which tolerates their unlimited indulgence in thofe vices and delightful abfurdities which are exprefsly reprobated by the Chriftian doctrines. The laws of Jamaica require the planters to do their utmoft for converting their Negroes, and caufing them to be baptized, fo foon as they can be put into a fit capacity of fentiment to admit of it. But their general inappetency to become converts, together with their barbarous ftupidity, and ignorance of the Englifh language, which render them incapable of underftanding or reafoning upon what is faid to them, would foil the moft zealous endeavours. Befides, the planters are averfe to exert an authority and conftraint over their minds, which might wear the appearance of religious tyranny. They do not think the caufe of Chriftianity at all honoured by adding involuntary profelytes; they hold it rather for a fhameful hypocrify and infult to the true worfhip. But, when any of their Negroes have made requeft to be baptized, I never knew, nor heard, of a planter's having refufed compliance with it. The Creole Negroes are the fitteft fubjects to work upon; and, with fome pains (as they have better knowledge of the Englifh tongue), they might probably be brought to retain fome of the elements of Chriftianity. It would certainly be productive of good confequences, if the more fenfible part of them were to be baptized, and occafionally inftructed, as far as they can be made to underftand, in the morality and fundamental points of our holy faith. In order to this, the baptifmal fees payable for Negroes ought to be fixed, by the juftices and veftry in each parifh, at a very low rate; the prefent ordinary rate of 1 *l.* 3 *s.* 9 *d.*, paid by the owners, being enormoufly high. A Popifh miffionary would perform the ceremony *gratis*, and be happy at the occafion; but, in fome other eftablifhments, we too often find, that it is, *no fee, no holy water; no pay, no Swifs.* Bofman fhrewdly obferves, " that, if it were " poffible to convert the African Negroes to Chriftianity, the " Roman Catholics would probably fucceed much better than any " other fect; becaufe they agree in fome points, fuch as abftinence " from particular kinds of food on certain days, &c. and in their " mutual attachment for ceremony and fuperftition." In fact,

the

the vulgar herd is much more affected by those things which ftrike the eye, than what are directed to the heart. Negroes are the apteft fubjects in the univerfe to be kept in fubordination and difcipline by the awful ceremonies, the indulgencies, injunctions, mummery, and legerdemain, of the Romifh church and its minifters. Hence it is, that, in the French fettlements, we find them as much, if not more, reftrained by the fuperftitions of that communion, than by the rigour of edicts and codes. I have feen many of them provided with ftore of croffes, relicks, and confecrated annulets ; to which they paid the moft fincere veneration, though wholly uninformed of any thing more than the efficacy of thefe baubles, the neceffity of adoring the Bleffed Virgin and a few chofen faints, the power of their prieft to abfolve fins, and the damnable ftate of all heretics. They had alfo acquired a *Pater Nofter*, a few *Ave Maria's*, and the right method of croffing themfelves, and counting their beads, morning and evening.

I doubt not but that, in the French churches belonging to their iflands, they have images of *black faints*, like the Portuguefe at Madeira, for the particular devotion of thefe poor wretches. Thefe arts our eftablifhed church difdains and abhors, it being founded on the principles of reafon, and therefore adapted only to rational minds ; which, by their own natural ftrength, are capable to judge of its rectitude, and embrace it on account of its purity and refinement from that very grofsnefs which pleafes, while it enflaves, other minds, that are clouded with ignorance. Next to the Romifh forms, perhaps thofe fyftems, which are fet off with abundance of enthufiaftic rant and gefticulation, would operate moft powerfully on the Negroes; fuch as Quakerifm, Methodifm, and the Moravian rites. The Romifh practices we find at leaft beneficial in the French iflands, co-operating with ftate-policy, and contributing ftrongly to maintain their flaves in peaceable fubjection. In our colonies, we are in want of fo potent a co-adjutor to our municipal laws; and, from this caufe, one fhould think, are more liable to be difturbed by infurrections, than the French iflands; to which end alfo another local difference would feem much to conduce. The Negroes in the foreign colonies are habituated to the fight of a defpotic frame of government, which controuls their

masters

masters from highest to lowest, and assimilates their condition nearer to that state of servility under which they live themselves. But, in our islands, the word *liberty* is in every one's mouth; the assemblies resound with the clamour of, " liberty and property;" and it is echoed back, by all ranks and degrees, in full chorus. The Whites are nearly on a level; and the lowest can find the way of bringing the highest to public justice for any injury or oppression. The Negroes here grow habitually familiar with the term; and have that object ever obvious to their sight, which is wholly withheld from, or at least but dimly seen by, the French Blacks. To the same effect is the remark of Montesquieu: " The multitude " of slaves has different effects in different governments. It is no " grievance in a despotic state, where the political slavery of the " whole body takes away the sense of civil slavery. Those, who " are called freemen, are in reality little more so than they who " do not come within that class. This makes it therefore a matter " of indifference, whether, in such states, the slaves be few or nu- " merous. But, in moderate states, it is a point of the highest im- " portance, that there should not be a great number of slaves. The " political liberty of those states adds to the value of civil liberty; " and he, who is deprived of the latter, is deprived also of the for- " mer. He sees the happiness of a society, of which he is not so " much as a member: he sees the security of others fenced in by " laws; himself, without any protection: he sees his master has a " soul which can enlarge itself; while his own is constrained to " submit to a continual depression. Nothing more assimilates a " man to a beast, than living among freemen; himself a slave. " Such people as these are the natural enemies of the society; and " their number must be dangerous. It is not therefore to be won- " dered at, that moderate governments have been so frequently di- " sturbed by revolts of slaves; and that this so seldom happens in " despotic states!"

It has been a matter of surprize to some, that the Negroes in our colonies do not increase in that natural proportion which is observed among mankind in other countries, and to a remarkable degree among the Blacks of Afric. Some writers, perceiving the large and continual importations made every year, and which are

found

found expedient for the carrying on our plantations in thefe parts, attribute this wafte to the too fevere labour and oppreffion they are forced to undergo. But this is an erroneous conjecture: the authors, not having refided in thefe colonies, were not fufficiently informed, to attend to other caufes, which prove more deftructive than the fevereft toil; nor to thofe which throw impediments in the way of a regular propagation.

It was computed formerly, that fix new Negroes were required annually to every hundred, to keep up the ftock in Barbadoes. The prefent import at Jamaica does not exceed, upon an average, fix thonfand *per annum*; which is about the rate of four to one hundred.

In the year 1761, when a draught of two thoufand Negroes was made here, to be fent on the Havannah fervice, the whole number of flaves in the ifland, according to the account then taken, was ———— ———— ———— ———— 146805

I do not exactly know the number that returned from that expedition. Several deferted, and fome were killed; but I fuppofe the non-returned, from the beft enquiry I can make, amounted to about eight hundred; which, being deducted from the above total, there remained about - 146000

In 1768, by an account taken, there were found —— —— 166904

So that the whole ftock was augmented, in feven years, 20904

The import, at the average of 6000 *per ann.* [x], was ⠀⠀ 42000

From which deducting the augmentation, ⠀——— ⠀ 20904

There appears a dead lofs of ⠀ ———— ⠀ ———— ⠀ 21096

which is equal to about 3000 *per annum*; and, at 35 *l.* fterling *per* head, makes 105000 *l.* annual lofs in value; a moft aftonifhing fum! Upon moft of the old fettled eftates in this ifland, the number of births and deaths every year is pretty equal, except any malignant diforder happens. The deaths, which conftitute the

[x] I have put the average at 6000, though perhaps it is too fmall a number, confidering the brifknefs of the African trade during part of the time, and that a great many French Negroes were brought in from the conquered iflands. The average for fome of the years in this feries was 9000; but others fell fhort. In the prefent computation, the greater the average is proved to have been, the higher muft the lofs appear. But I have chofen rather to be under than over.

major

major part of the above annual balance, are of native Africans. Hence therefore appears the miftake of the writers before-mentioned; for it is well known, that thefe new Negroes are always much indulged during the firft two or three years after their arrival, being put to the gentleft work, that they may be gradually feafoned to the change of climate, and trained by a flow and eafy progrefs to undergo the fame degree of labour as the reft. If then all this care and preparation be neceffary, and not only neceffary, but actually attended to, it may be afked, by what means it comes to pafs, that we obferve fo great a decreafe among them? In reply to this, feveral reafons may be given.

Thefe Negroes are few of them exempt from a venereal taint; and very many have, at the time of their arrival, that dreadful diforder, the *yaws*, lurking in their blood. It is faid (I know not with what truth), that the furgeons on board the Guiney fhips ufe methods to repel it, by a mixture of iron-ruft with gun-powder and lime-juice, in order to remove all external fymptoms of it before they are expofed to fale. There is fome reafon for believing that fuch wicked frauds have been practifed; becaufe it is no uncommon thing to fee a whole parcel of new Negroes, within a few weeks after they are brought on a plantation, break out all together with this diforder, and especially if they have drunk the cane-liquor in the boiling-houfe, which is very efficacious in throwing the venom out of the habit.

The plantation furgeons have depended chiefly on mercurial preparations for a cure; but it is found, that fuch medicines break and impoverifh their blood, and fubject them to catch violent colds, which often ftrike the matter in upon the nobler parts, and bring on the joint-evil. Sometimes they fall into dropfies, which generally prove mortal; for this diforder requires a very nutritious diet; and experience proves, that, when left to nature, and the ufe of flour of brimftone, to keep the humour in a conftant elimination towards the fkin, it gradually wears off in about three years. Mercurials interrupt this natural crifis, and, inftead of curing, generally either fix the diforder more rootedly in the habit, or give rife to others of the moft dangerous kind.

VOL. II. K k k I have

I have had occafion, in the courfe of feveral years, to mark the fate of many hundred new Negroes; and am pofitive, that a third part of them have perifhed, within three years after their arrival, by this difeafe, through a miftaken method of treating it, and the too eager defire of their owners, or an affectation of extraordinary fkill in their doctors, to make a fpeedy cure of it by fome mercurial *noftrum*. Another miftake has arifen, by judging from the appearance of an acrimonious humour, fo copioufly difcharged, that the patients required to have their juices corrected by proper fweeteners of the blood, and a low, abftemious diet. This error has but ferved to haften their death. Inftead of oatmeal gruel, and fuch weakening meffes, they ought to have their ftrength fuftained, during the progrefs of the eruption, and whilft it continues, with hearty food, nourifhing broths, and the like ; which preferve the blood in a balfamic, vigorous ftate, and enable nature to throw out the latent *virus*. This diftemper, there is reafon to believe, holds a near affinity with the fmall-pox ; at leaft, it has been remarked, that the natural fmall-pox, in thofe afflicted with the yaws, is commonly very mild.

Mercury has, in this climate, a great propenfity to falivate; and moft of the Negroes, by frequently taking mercurials for venereal complaints, have their fluids fo impregnated with them, that the utmoft caution is neceffary in adminiftering fuch medicines. For this reafon too, they cannot bear frequent repetitions of ftrong purgatives ; the confequence of fuch copious evacuations being, almoft always, a tendency to a dropfy.

The fmall-pox has frequently made great ravage among them. Sometimes they have been landed with this difeafe upon them; and this has proved fo fatal, that I have known feven in ten die of it, which is equal to feventy in a hundred, or fifty-fix more than the computation made of thofe who die in England by this diforder taken in the natural way. The late method of inoculation, happily practifed in this ifland, promifes fair to put an end to fuch dreadful examples of mortality ; and I therefore only mention this, as one principal fource of depopulation which exifted here before inoculation was brought into general ufe, which was not long ago.

The

The removal of Negroes from a dry to a damp fituation, from a South fide to a North fide parifh, has often been fatal to many. New Negroes, fent into the mountains immediately after their importation, efpecially during a wet feafon, are almoft fure of being afflicted with fevere colds, pleurifies, fluxes, and other diftempers, which prove their bane. Even the Creoles do not bear thefe removals from places where, perhaps, they have refided from the time of their birth. And it is inconceivable what numbers have perifhed, in confequence of the law for recovery of debts; which permits Negroes to be levied on, and fold at *vendue*. By this means, they are frequently torn from their native fpot, their deareft connexions, and transferred into a fituation unadapted to their health, labouring under difcontent, which co-operates with change of place and circumftances to fhorten their lives.

Some planters think it good policy to quarter their new Negroes among the old fettled ones: but thefe hofts generally make their guefts pay dear for their lodging and maintenance, forcing them to be their " hewers of wood, and drawers of water;" and, in fhort, impofing on their ignorance without meafure or mercy, until they fink under the oppreffion; whilft the owner, a ftranger to what paffes, is furprifed to fee them continually on the decline, and gradually confuming, without any fufpicion of the real caufe.

The introduction of too many recruits at once has fometimes proved fatal to them. It is very evident, that a fmall number can be much eafier and better provided for, lodged, fed, and taken care of, than a multitude. The planter therefore, who buys only eight or ten at a time, will in the end derive more advantage from them, than the planter who buys thirty; for, by the greater leifure and attention in his power to beftow upon them, he will greatly leffen the ordinary chances againft their life, and the fooner prepare them for an effectual courfe of labour. The comparifon, indeed, founded upon fact and obfervation, is, that, at the end of three years, the former may poffibly have loft one fifth, but the other will moft probably have loft one half, of their refpective numbers.

The women do not breed here as in Africa; for, in fhort, it has never been the planter's care to proportion the number of females to males: upon fome eftates there are five men to one

woman.

woman. Now, the population of Afric, as has been fhewn, is partly imputable to their larger proportion of women; infomuch that, although the greateft man among their provinces may have fifty, fixty, or more wives or concubines, yet the meaneft man is fure of one at leaft. The women here are, in general, common proftitutes; and many of them take fpecifics to caufe abortion, in order that they may continue their trade without lofs of time, or hindrance of bufinefs; and, befides, their admitting fuch promifcuous embraces muft neceffarily hinder, or deftroy, conception. We may add to this the venereal difeafe; which, together with the medicines taken, either to repel, or carry off the *virus*, frequently kills the fœtus, and fterilizes both men and women.

Worms are extremely fatal to children in this climate, and deftroy more than any other difeafe. Others frequently perifh, within nine or ten days of their birth, by what is called here *jaw-falling*; which is caufed by a retention of the *meconium*: by not keeping the infant fufficiently warm; or by giving it rum, and aliment of hard digeftion.

Moft of the black women are very fubject to obftructions; from what caufe I will not prefume to fay; but, perhaps, they may be afcribed, in part, to their ufing reftringent baths, or wafhing themfelves in cool water at improper periods. Child-birth is not fo eafy here as in Afric; and many children are annually deftroyed, as well as their mothers, by the unfkilfulnefs and abfurd management of the Negroe midwives.

Thus we find here are various caufes which prevent the multiplication of Negroes on the plantations; not but that unfeafonable work may fometimes be added to the lift; yet, in general, as it is happy for thefe people, that the planter's intereft concurs with the obligations of humanity in moft cafes that relate to the care of them; fo it is unneceffary to fay, that in the time of geftation, they are treated with more than common indulgence, to prevent any fuch accidents.

The knowledge of the caufe of any difeafe conducts us to the method of cure. To augment our Negroes therefore by procreation, we muft endeavour to remedy thofe evils which impede or fruftrate its natural effect. And, to conclude, if the wafte of thefe men ſhould become leſs, the price of them would fall; and the ſame annual demand might be kept up, by extending our plantations, which is now produced by the mortality of theſe people; eſtates would be gradually well-ſtocked, and rendered more flouriſhing; and the circumſtances of the planters totally changed for the better. The purchaſe of new Negroes is the moſt chargeable article attending theſe eſtates, and the true ſource of the diſtreſſes under which their owners ſuffer; for they involve themſelves ſo deeply in debt, to make theſe inconſiderate purchaſes, and loſe ſo many by diſeaſe, or other means in the ſeaſoning, that they become unable to make good their engagements, are plunged in law-ſuits and anxiety; while, for want of ſome prudent regulations in the right huſbanding of their ſtock, and promoting its increaſe by natural means, they entail upon themſelves a neceſſity of drawing perpetual recruits of unſeaſoned Africans, the expence of which forms only a new addition to their debts and difficulties.

I will not deny that thoſe Negroes breed the beſt, whoſe labour is leaſt, or eaſieſt. Thus the domeſtic Negroes have more children, in proportion, than thoſe on penns; and the latter, than thoſe who are employed on ſugar-plantations. If the number of hogſheads, annually made from any eſtate, exceeds, or even equals, the whole aggregate of Negroes employed upon it, but few children will be brought up on ſuch eſtate, whatever number may be born; for the mothers will not have ſufficient time to take due care of them; and, if they are put under charge of ſome elderly woman, or nurſe, as the cuſtom is in many places, it cannot be ſuppoſed that they meet with the ſame tenderneſs as might be expected from their parent. But, where the proportion of the annual produce is about half a hogſhead for every Negroe, there they will, in all likelihood, increaſe very rapidly; and not much leſs ſo, where the *ratio* is of two hogſheads to every three Negroes, which I take to be a good *meſne* proportion; agreeably to which, an eſtate, making, *communibus annis*, two hundred hogſheads, ought to muſter on its liſt, old and young, three hundred Negroes; and, if it makes three hundred hogſheads, four hundred and fifty ſuch Negroes: and ſo on. An eſtate, ſo handed, *may* not only, *cæteris paribus*, ſave the expence of buying recruits, but *may* every year afford ſome addition to the

2   firſt

firſt number, of which I have known inconteſtable examples in Jamaica; and although the nature of the ſoil here and there may
cauſe ſome difference in reſpect to hard or eaſy labour, yet it will
ſtill hold for a good general rule. There are very few plantations,
whoſe ſoil is uniform throughout; and, where the ſoil is moſt ſtiff
and laborious, perhaps the yielding in ſugar is equal on the whole;
which works no objection to the rule. For example: if we ſuppoſe a North ſide eſtate of very ſtiff land, and compare it with one
on the South ſide, whoſe ſoil is of a free texture, and that each of
them yields, upon average, one hogſhead *per* acre round; the South
ſide eſtate contains three hundred acres in canes, yields three hundred hogſheads, muſters four hundred and fifty Negroes; and the
North ſide eſtate, three hundred acres, yields three hundred hogſheads, and muſters four hundred and fifty Negroes. Although the
North ſide land is far more laborious, yet the annual plant being
far leſs, on account of the rattoon canes, which ſtand ſeveral
cuttings, the *meſne* proportion of labour upon both, for a given
number of years, may be found very even; the South ſide eſtate
being obliged, perhaps every year, to hole and plant double the
quantity of ground.

The proportion, according to the before-mentioned rule, is one
hundred and fifty Negroes to one hundred hogſheads. An eſti-
mate was made, not long ſince, on this ſubject, with reference to
the produce of each diſtinct pariſh. I know not how far it may
be depended on in regard to exactneſs; but, if it comes any thing
near the truth, it proves that ſome have more, but very few leſs,
than the rate propoſed. For better comprehending the table, I
ſhall claſs the different pariſhes according to the general condition
of their ſoils. The firſt claſs contains thoſe whoſe ſoil is, comparatively, the moſt ſtiff and heavy; the ſecond, ſuch as have the
lighteſt; the third, thoſe whoſe ſoil may be eſteemed between
both.

Firſt Claſs.		Negroes to 100 Hhds.		
St. Mary,	———	150	at *par*	0
St. John,	———	168	exceeds by	18
Portland,	———	182	ditto	32
St. George,	———	158	ditto	8
			Weſtmoreland,	

First Clafs.		Negroes to 100 Hhds.		
Weftmoreland,	——	141	lefs	9
Hanover,	——	142	ditto	8
Second Clafs.				
St. Catharine,	——	171	exceeds	21
St. Dorothy,	——	200	ditto	50
St. Thomas in the Vale,		180	ditto	30
Vere,	——	138	lefs	12
St. Anne,	——	200	exceeds	50
St. Andrew,	——	162	ditto	12
Port Royal,	——	250	ditto	100
St. David,	——	172	ditto	22
St. Elizabeth,	——	204	ditto	54
Third Clafs.				
Clarendon,	——	127	lefs	23
St. Thomas in the Eaft,		120	ditto	30
St. James,	——	132	ditto	18

Thus, of the whole number, only fix appear deficient. I muft own, that fuch general calculations are not entirely to be relied on; becaufe, in any individual parifh, upon a furvey of the eftates comprehended in it, fome will appear to have more than their complement, and others to fall very fhort of it. Much likewife depends on favourable or unfavourable feafons, good or bad management. In regard to births, they are probably as many as can be expected, under the obftacles which I have before enumerated; and, when I fay that any eftate, having the juft proportion of hands to the average quantity of its produce, may require no purchafed recruits, I muft be underftood with an exception to fome or other of thofe obftacles; for, if its women are not numerous enough, or if they are rendered unprolific by difeafe or their own bad practices, or their children precluded from reaching to maturity, no fuch population can of courfe enfue. It is worth every planter's attention, to encourage the mothers, by little helps, to take good care of their children. Some mark of diftinction, or a reward, fhould always be allowed to thofe who have fhewn the moft affiduity in refpect to their cleanlinefs and health. A premium might be affigned for every new-born child; and a fmall annuity to be con-

tinued

tinued until its attaining the fourth or fifth year. Thefe politic gratuities would not only endear the owner to the parents, but prove a conftant incitement to their care, and at the fame time enable them to provide better, the feveral little neceffaries wanted to keep their infants cleanly and decent. If thefe meafures fhould operate, as probably they would, to the increafe of their families, the expence attending them would be amply repaid.

I have obferved, in feveral accounts of our Weft-India colonies, comparifons drawn between the condition of the flaves in them and in the French iflands, very much to the difadvantage of the former. It is faid, that the Negroes in the French colonies are not left fo much to the planter's difcretion; that their mafters are obliged to have them inftructed in the principles of the Chriftian religion; that there are methods taken, at once to protect them from the cruelty of their mafters, and preferve the colony from any ill effects that might arife from treating them with a lenity not confiftent with their condition; that the *Code Noir*, or fet of regulations, purpofely framed for the Negroes, and eftablifhed by the royal edict, as well as other ordinances relative to thefe poor creatures, fhew a very juft and fenfible mixture of humanity and fteadinefs; and that thefe regulations have given the French, in their colonies, a reputation for good difcipline and clemency; which degrades the Englifh planters, when their laws are brought into comparifon. The Fench are thus held out as a pattern well deferving the imitation of the Britifh owners, and very properly, if all thefe encomiums are founded in truth. But there is fome reafon to doubt their good effects; and to believe, that, however they may glow with humanity and maxims of prudence, they are not efficacioufly obeyed. Monf. Boffu, a French officer, who was at Hifpaniola in 1751, gives fome right to draw fuch a conclufion; and I muft fay, that his teftimony is of the greater weight, as the French are well known to be very cautious of revealing whatever can tend to difhonour their countrymen. He condemns the brutal avidity of fome French planters; " who," he tells us, " force their " wretched flaves to fuch hard labour, that they refufe to marry, in " order to avoid generating a race of beings to be enflaved to fuch " mafters, who treat them, when old and infirm, worfe than their

" dogs

" dogs and horfes. I have feen, adds he, a planter, whofe name
" was *Chaperon*, who forced one of his Negroes to go into a heated
" oven, where the poor wretch expired; and his jaws being fhri-
" veled up, the barbarous owner faid, " I believe the fellow
" laughs," and took a poker to ftir him up. Since this event, he
" became the fcarecrow among all the flaves, who, when they do
" amifs, are threatened by their mafters to be fent to *Chaperon*."
What are we to think of the edicts and ordinances of any country,
where fo horrid a monfter is fuffered to live with impunity; and
of how little efficacy is the celebrated *Code Noir*, in giving protection to the French Negroes? Such acts of wanton, diabolical
cruelty, are a ftanding reproach to the laws of any country; the
fact might have feemed incredible, had it been related by any other
than a Frenchman; and, I think, we are fairly warranted to judge
from it, that what we have been told of their regulations is not
entirely true; for how does it appear that their Negroes are protected from the cruelty of their mafters, whilft fuch atrocious examples of the contrary are to be feen in their colonies? This
queftion is impartially deduced, and proves, that fo far as refpects
the perfonal well-being of the Negroes, thefe boafted laws are fpecious perhaps in their complexion, but ineffectual and feeble in their
real operation. It is not enough to make laws; it is alfo neceffary
to provide for their execution.

However, we are fo fond of depreciating our own colonies, that
we paint our planters in the moft bloody colours, and reprefent
their flaves as the moft ill-treated and miferable of mankind. It is
no wonder therefore that Jamaica comes in for a large fhare of
abufe; and even our common news papers are made the vehicles
of it. I read in one of them not long fince, " that the cruel ufage
" inflicted on Negro flaves in Jamaica by their mafters, is the
" reafon why infurrections there are more frequent than in the
" French or other fugar-iflands." The firft enquiry to be made
in anfwer to fo invidious a charge is, whether the fact here afferted
be really true? and, 2dly, whether this frequency may not have
been owing to fome other caufe?

Within a few years paft, we have heard of them at Hifpaniola, at Cuba, at the Brafils, at Surinam, and Berbice, and at the Britifh iflands of Tobago, Dominica, Montferrat, and St. Vincent. If they fhould happen oftener at Jamaica than in the fmaller iflands, it would not be at all furprizing, fince it has general'y contained more Negroes than all the Windward Britifh ifles put together; and its importations in fome years have been very great.

For inftance, in the year 1764, the importation was,   10,223.
And from January 1765 to July1766, one year and an half, 16,760.
So large a multitude as 27,000 introduced in the fpace of two years and an half, furnifhes a very fufficient reafon, if there was no other, to account for mutinies and plots, efpecially as no fmall number of them had been warriors in Afric, or criminals; and all of them as favage and uncivilized as the beafts of prey that roam through the African forefts.

A general accufation can only deferve a general reply If the author of it had particularized any certain fpecies of barbarity tolerated by law or cuftom, or in conftant ufe at Jamaica, it would be incumbent on its advocates, either to difprove, or admit, the exiftence of fuch particular facts.   But a charge, which involves a whole country, ought to be well founded, and fupported by evidence taken from notorious practice, or the fyftem of laws by which that country is regulated. If a foreigner, being told of a mother in England, fo void of natural feeling, as to fhut up her own children in a dungeon, ftarve and cruelly beat them; of others, who ftrangle their infants, cut their throats, or confume them in ovens; of mafters and miftreffes fo brutal as to whip their appren tices to death; of daughters poifoning their fathers; nieces their uncles; wives butchering their hufbands, and hufbands their wives; with many other examples of barbarity, which the public chronicles have recorded from time to time; fhould we not think the foreigner extremely void of impartiality and good fenfe, if for this reafon he was to charge all the people of England with being a moft bloody, inhuman and unfeeling race? Yet there is full as much caufe for it in this cafe, as in the former. The truth is, that ever fince the introduction of Africans into the Weft-Indies,

insurrections

7

infurrections have occurred in every one of the colonies, Britifh as well as foreign, at times. But the calumniator has not been more erroneous in bringing the charge, than in the reafons affigned to fupport it; becaufe a faulty indulgence has been one leading caufe of the difturbances that have occurred in Jamaica; which is evidently proved by what is fet forth in many of the laws paffed in confequence of them, reftricting feveral fports, and prohibiting certain feftive affemblies, which the Negroes had freely enjoyed before, but were made fubfervient to the forming and carrying on of dangerous confpiracies. They were formerly allowed to affemble with drums and mufical inftruments; to dance, drink, and be merry. This was permitted, becaufe it was thought an inoffenfive mode of recreation for them. But when thefe games were afterwards converted into plots, they were with great juftice fuppreffed, as riotous affemblies of people are in England, and for the like reafon; that, being perverted from their original intention to wicked and unlawful ends, they became inconfiftent with the peace and fafety of the community. Such prohibitions (of which there are feveral) prove undeniably, the great latitude of indulgence, that has been given to the Negroes of this colony; and fhew the propriety, and indeed neceffity, there has been of laying them under reftrictions, when that liberty was abufed. The innocent, it is true, were unavoidably involved with the guilty in thefe reftraints; but they have ftill fufficient paftimes and amufements to divert them, without offending againft the public welfare. In every country under the fun the like commotions muft happen, where licentioufnefs among the moft ignorant and profligate of the people is not repreffed by the difcipline of laws, and the energy of good government; and where drunkennefs and luft, thofe great incentives to violence among this order of men, are fuffered, as in Jamaica, to reign without controul.

The heedlefs practice formerly of keeping large ftands of firearms and cutlaffes upon the inland plantations, having only three or four white men upon them, became a ftrong temptation to any difaffected or enterprizing Africans. It might well be expected, that throwing fuch magazines and ftores of ammunition in their way, was a direct invitation to them to rebel. The turning fo

many

many indefenfible houfes into arfenals for arming mutinous favages, was doubtlefs the very height of imprudence, tending not only to generate projects of hoftility, but to afford the means of conducting them with probable hope of fuccefs.   Add to this, that many fhop-keepers, from a ftrange fpirit of avarice, have been known to fell gunpowder privately to fuch confpirators, although they muft have forefeen the ufe to which it might be applied; and, to gain a few fhillings, even hazarded their own deftruction; incredible as this may feem, yet it is certain that fuch a practice has been carried on, as two laws were paffed, one in 1730, the other in 1744, to put a ftop to it.

Another caufe of confpiracy may have been, a remote hope of fome Negroes, who, having heard of the freedom granted to the Marons after their obftinate refiftance of feveral years, expected, perhaps, that by a courfe of fuccefsful oppofition they might obtain the like terms in the end, and a diftinct fettlement in fome quarter of the ifland.

The vulgar opinion in England confounds all the Blacks in one clafs, and fuppofes them equally prompt for rebellion; an opinion that is groffly erroneous. The Negroes, who have been chief actors in the feditions and mutinies, which at different times have broke out here, were the *imported Africans*; and, confidering the numbers of them who were banifhed their country for atrocious mifdeeds, and familiarized to blood, maffacre, and the moft deteftable vices, we fhould not be aftonifhed at the impatient fpirit of fuch an abandoned herd, upon being introduced to a life of labour and regularity. The numbers imported would indeed be formidable, if they continued in a body; but they are foon difperfed among a variety of different eftates many miles afunder, by which means they remain a long time ignorant of each other's place of fettlement. They often find themfelves mixed with many ftrangers, differing from them in language; and againft others they hold a rooted antipathy.   But they are chiefly awed into fubjection, by the fuperior multitude of Creole Blacks, with whom they dare not confederate, nor folicit their concurrence in any plan of oppofition to the white inhabitants

The

The ringleaders of confpiracy have been the native Africans, and of thefe the *Coromantins* ftand the foremoft. The Jamaica planters are fond of purchafing the Negroes who pafs under this name, in preference to thofe of the other provinces; but the French, and fome other Weft-India colonies, will not knowingly admit them; being fenfible of their dangerous tempers and unfitnefs for the peaceable walk of hufbandry.

As the infurrections which have happened in our ifland have been mifreprefented, I fhall give a fummary account of them, which may ferve to illuftrate what has been advanced, and explain the motives of them not to have been founded in the manner they have been generally fuppofed, by perfons ill informed, or but little acquainted with Jamaica.

The *Maron* or wild Negroes, of whom I have given the hiftory, were improperly called *rebellious*. The compilers of the *Modern Univerfal Hiftory*, in their account of the ifland, have fallen into this miftake, and, giving a detail of the infurrection that happened in 1761, they fpeak of it as " a revolt of thofe Negroes, who, fince the " late treaty with them in Mr. Trelawny's government, *not having* " *been fufficiently watched*, had become fo numerous and ftrong, that " they now meditated no lefs than the extirpation of all the white " men in the ifland."

It is not an eafy matter to difcover what is meant by " their be " coming too numerous and ftrong, for want of being *watched*;" nor how the watching of them could either thin their numbers, or weaken them : however, the whole is erroneous, and the very reverfe is the truth; for thefe Negroes have, as far as we have any certain information, always adhered to the treaty, and were the principal inftruments employed in fuppreffing that very infurrection. The Jamaica laws have from the beginning termed them *rebellious*; but they did not deferve the appellation, becaufe they were the free defcendants from the aboriginal Spanifh Negroes, who had never come under any fubmiffion or allegiance to the Britifh government. The rebellions (properly fpeaking) are confined to thofe Negroe flaves, who have at different periods renounced obedience to their Britifh mafters, and fought to refcue themfelves from a life of labour by force of arms; and all thefe difturbances are extremely remarkable, in that they have been planned and conducted by the

Coromantin.

Coromantin Negroes, who are diftinguifhed from their brethren by their averfion to hufbandry, and the martial ferocity of their difpofition. The firft rebellion of importance, on record, happened in the year 1690, when between three and four hundred flaves, belonging to Mr. Sutton's plantation in Clarendon, forced their way into the dwelling-houfe, killed the white man entrufted with the care of it, and feized upon a large ftore of fire-arms, powder and ball, and four fmall field-pieces, with fome provifions: at this time, the interior fettlements, of which this was one, fituated near the woods, were furnifhed in this manner with implements of defence to withftand the affaults of the *Marons*, who frequently fallied out in the night to attack them. The rebels, after this exploit, proceeded to the next plantation, and murdered the overfeer, but were difappointed of being joined by the flaves belonging to it, who all betook themfelves to the woods; upon this they returned to Mr. Sutton's houfe, where they put every thing into a pofture of defence. By this time the white inhabitants of the neighbourhood, having taken the alarm, collected about fifty horfe and foot, marched to beat up their quarters; and, being joined by the way with frefh fuccours, they increafed to a formidable body. On the next day the militia began their attack, upon which the rebels withdrew to the cane pieces, and fet fire to them, in order to cover their retreat; but a detachment of the militia having fetched a little compafs, found means to affault them in flank, whilft the reft advanced upon them in front; unable to withftand this double fire, the rebels immediately fled, but were fo brifkly purfued, that many were killed, and two hundred of them threw down their arms, and begged for mercy; the reft were afterwards either flain, or taken prifoners; and the ringleaders of the confpiracy hanged. I find no rebellion of any confequence for feveral years fubfequent to this; one reafon for which ceffation probably was, that the Marons were endeavouring, by every means in their power, to bring over the flaves in different parts of the ifland to their caufe; fuch therefore as were difcontented with their condition, deferted to the Marons; but, feveral who took this ftep, performed fome previous act of outrage, by way of recommending themfelves to their new friends; none was more horrid than what was committed on Mr.

B—

B— of St. Anne; a gentleman diftinguifhed for his humanity towards his flaves, and in particular to one of his domeftics, on whom he had beftowed many extraordinary marks of kindnefs. Yet this ungrateful villain, at the head of a gang who were equally difpofed to revolt, affaulted his mafter whilft he was in bed; Mr. B— defended himfelf for fome time with his broad fword, but being overpowered by numbers, and difabled by wounds, he fell at length a victim to their cruelty; they cut off his head, fawed his fkull afunder, and made ufe of it as a punch-bowl; and, after doing as much further mifchief as they were able, they retreated into the woods.

After the pacification made with governor Trelawney, no infurrection of moment occurred for many years. Some trifling difturbances happened, and fome plots were detected, but they came to nothing; and indeed the feeds of rebellion were in a great meafure rendered abortive, by the activity of the Marons, who fcoured the woods, and apprehended all ftraggling and vagabond flaves, that from time to time deferted from their owners. But in the year 1760, a confpiracy was projected, and conducted with fuch profound fecrefy, that almoft all the Coromantin flaves throughout the ifland were privy to it, without any fufpicion from the Whites. The parifh of St. Mary was fixed upon, as the moft proper theatre for opening their tragedy. It abounded with their countrymen, was but thinly peopled with Whites, contained extenfive deep woods, and plenty of provifions: fo that as the engaging any confiderable number heartily in the fcheme, would depend chiefly on the fuccefs of their firft operations, they were likely to meet with a fainter refiftance in this parifh than in moft others; and fhould the iffue of the conflict prove unfavourable to them, they might retreat with fecurity into the woods, and there continue well fupplied with provifions, until their party fhould be ftrengthened with fufficient reinforcements, to enable their profecution of the grand enterprize, whofe object was no other than the entire extirpation of the white inhabitants; the enflaving of all fuch Negroes as might refufe to join them; and the partition of the ifland into fmall principalities in the African mode; to be diftributed among their leaders and head men. A principal inducement

ducement to the formation of this scheme of conquest was, the happy circumstance of the *Marons*; who, they observed, had acquired very comfortable settlements, and a life of freedom and ease, by dint of their prowess. On the night preceding Easter-Monday, about fifty of them marched to Port Maria, where they murdered the storekeeper of the fort (at that time unprovided with a garrison), broke open the magazine, and seized four barrels of powder, a few musquet-balls, and about forty fire-arms. Proceeding from thence to the bay, which lies under the fort, they met with some fishing-nets, from which they cut off all the leaden sinkers, made of bullets drilled. These Negroes were mostly collected from Trinity plantation, belonging to Mr. Bayley; Whitehall, and Frontier, belonging to Mr. Ballard Beckford; and Heywood Hall, the property of Mr. Heywood. Mr. Bayley had been called up by one of his domestics, and, mounting his horse, rode towards the bay, in hopes that, by expostulating calmly with the rebels, he might persuade them to disperse and return to their duty; but their plan was too deeply laid, and they had conceived too high an opinion of it, to recede.

Upon his nearer approach, he perceived they were determined to act offensively, and therefore galloped back with great expedition; a few random-shots were discharged after him, which he fortunately escaped, and rode directly to the neighbouring estates, alarming them as he went, and appointing a place of rendezvous. In this he performed a very essential piece of service to the white inhabitants, who before were entire strangers to the insurrection, and unprepared against surprize; but this notice gave them some time to recollect themselves, and to consult measures for suppressing the insurgents. In the mean while, the latter pursued their way to Heywood-Hall, where they set fire to the works and cane-pieces, and proceeded to Esher, an estate of Mr. William Beckford, murthering on the road a poor white man, who was traveling on foot. At Esher they were joined by fourteen or fifteen of their countrymen. The Whites on that estate had but just time to shut themselves up in the dwelling-house, which they barricadoed as well as they could; unhappily they were destitute of ammunition, and therefore incapable of making any resistance. The rebels, who knew
their

their fituation, foon forced an entrance, murthered the overfeer and another perfon, and mangled the doctor, till they fuppofed him dead; in this condition they drew him down feveral fteps by the heels, and threw him among the other murthered perfons: his limbs ftill appearing to move, one of the rebels exclaimed, that " he had as many lives as a *pufs*;" and immediately difcharged four or five flugs through his back, fome of which penetrated the bladder. This gentleman was fo dreadfully wounded, that the two furgeons, who afterwards attended him, were every day fatigued with the multiplicity of bandages and dreffings, neceffary to be applied upon almoft all parts of his body; fo that his recovery was next to miraculous.

After this exploit, they ravifhed a Mulatto woman, who had been the overfeer's kept miftrefs; but fpared her life, at the requeft of fome of the Efher Negroes, who alledged, in her favour, that fhe had frequently faved them from a whipping, by her interceffion with the overfeer; confidering the hands into which fhe had fallen, this was thought an act of very extraordinary clemency; and, in fact, not owing really to any merit on her part, as the overfeer had only chofe to let his forgivenefs appear rather to come through the importunity of another, than from the lenity of his own difpofition. The doctor, notwithftanding his wounds, recovered afterwards. Yankee, a trufty flave belonging to this eftate, behaved on the occafion with fignal gallantry; he was very active in endeavouring to defend the houfe, and affift the white men; but, finding they were overpowered, he made his efcape to the next eftate, and there, with another faithful Negroe, concerted meafures for giving immediate notice to all the plantations in the neighbourhood, and procuring auxiliaries for the white inhabitants. The rebels, after this action, turned back to Heywood Hall and Ballard's Valley, where they picked up fome frefh recruits, fo that their whole party, including women, increafed to about four hundred. The fatigues of the opening their campaign had fo exhaufted their fpirits by this time, that they thought proper to refrefh themfelves a little before they renewed their hoftilities; having therefore a good magazine of hogs, poultry, rum, and other plunder of the like kind, they chofe out a convenient fpot, furrounded with trees, and a little retired from the road, where they fpread their provifion, and began to carouze. The white inhabitants, alarmed by Mr. Bayley, had affembled in the mean time about 70 or 80 horfe, and had now a fair opportunity of routing the whole body; they advanced towards the place where the rebels were enjoying themfelves, and luckily difcovered them by their noife and riot, or they might have fallen into an ambufcade. The Coromantins did not exhibit any fpecimen of generalfhip upon this occafion; on the appearance of the troop, they kept clofe in the wood, from whence they poured an irregular fire, which did no execution. The drilled bullets, taken from the fifhing nets, defcribed an arch in their projection, and flew over the heads of the militia. After keeping their ranks for fome time, it was propofed that they fhould difmount, and pufh into the wood; but on examining their ammunition, the militia found their whole ftock, if equally divided, did not amount to more than one charge each man; they therefore held it more advifeable, for the major part to ftand their ground on the referve, while their fervants, and fome others well armed, advanced into the wood clofe to the rebels, feveral of whom they killed; a Mulatto man was faid to have flain three with his own hand, and a brave North Briton about the fame number. The rebels, intimidated with this bold attack, retreated; but it was not judged proper at that time to purfue them.

During all thefe tranfactions, two Negroes, belonging to Mr. Beckford, having taken horfe at the firft alarm, were on the road to Spanifh Town, and traveled with fuch expedition through very bad ways, that they brought the intelligence to lieut. governor Sir Henry Moore, by one o'clock the fame day, who immediately difpatched two parties of regulars, and two troops of horfe militia, by different routs, to the parifh; orders at the fame time were fent to the *Marons* of Scot's-Hall Town, to advance by another road from the Eaftward, and a party from the Leeward Towns were directed to enter by the Weft. All thefe detachments were in motion as early as poffible, and no meafures could have been more effectually taken. The lieutenant governor happily poffeffed, in addition to great abilities, uncommon prefence of mind, prudence, and bravery, a moft confummate knowledge of the geography of the ifland, and of every road and avenue in its feveral diftricts. By this means, he was enabled to take every fit precaution, and form the moft proper difpofition of the forces, as well for reducing the infurgents, as protecting the eftates in thofe parts,

2   where

where the flame might be expected to kindle afrefh. Thefe detachments, by forced marches, foon made their appearance in St. Mary,
and damped at once all the ideas of conqueft, which at firft had elevated the rebels. They kept in the woods, rambling from place to
place, feldom continuing many hours on one fpot; and when they
perceived themfelves clofe befet on all fides, they refolved to fell their
lives as dear as poffible. The *Marons* of Scot's-Hall behaved extremely ill at this juncture; they were the firft party that came to the
rendezvous; and, under pretence that fome arrears were due to them,
and that they had not been regularly paid their head-money allowed
by law, for every run-away taken up, they refufed to proceed againft
the rebels, unlefs a collection was immediately made for them; feveral gentlemen prefent fubmitted to comply with this extraordinary demand, rather than delay the fervice; after which they marched, and
had one engagement with the rebels, in which they killed a few. A
party of the 74th regiment lay quartered at a houfe by the fea fide, at
a fmall diftance from the woods; in the night the rebels were fo bold,
that they crept very near the quarters, and, having fhot the centinel
dead, retired again with the utmoft agility from purfuit. Not long
after this accident the regulars, after a tedious march through the
woods, which the fteepnefs of the hills, and heat of the weather, con-
fpired to render extremely fatiguing, came up with the enemy, and an
engagement enfued, in which feveral of the rebels were killed, and
lieut. Bevil of the regulars wounded. The different parties continued
in chafe of the fugitives, and fkirmifhes happened every day; but in
the mean while, the fpirit of rebellion was fhewing itfelf in various
other parts of the ifland, there being fcarcely a fingle parifh, to which
this confpiracy of the Coromantins did not extend. In St. Mary's
parifh a check was fortunately given at one eftate, by furprizing a famous obeiah man or prieft, much refpected among his countrymen.
He was an old Coromantin, who, with others of his profeffion, had
been a chief in counfeling and inftigating the credulous herd, to whom
thefe priefts adminiftered a powder, which, being rubbed on their bodies, was to make them invulnerable: they perfuaded them into a belief, that Tacky, their generaliffimo in the woods, could not poffibly
be hurt by the white men, for that he caught all the bullets fired at
him in his hand, and hurled them back with deftruction to his foes.

This

This old impoftor was caught whilft he was tricked up with all his
feathers, teeth, and other implements of magic, and in this attire fuffered military execution by hanging: many of his difciples, when they
found that he was fo eafily put to death, notwithftanding all the
boafted feats of his powder and incantations, foon altered their opinion of him, and determined not to join their countrymen, in a caufe
which hitherto had been unattended with fuccefs.   But the fame of
general Tacky, and the notion of his invulnerability, ftill prevailed
over the minds of others, as that hero had efcaped hitherto in every
conflict without a wound.   The true condition of his party was artfully mifreprefented to the Coromantins, in the diftant parifhes; they
were told that every thing went on profperoufly, that victory attended
them, and that nothing now remained but for all their countrymen to
be hearty in the caufe, and the ifland muft fpeedily be their own.
Animated with thefe reports, the Coromantins on capt. Forreft's eftate,
in Weftmoreland, broke into rebellion.   They furrounded the manfion-houfe, in which Mr. Smith, attorney to Mr. Forreft, with fome
friends, was fitting at fupper; they foon difpatched Mr. Smith and the
overfeer, and terribly wounded captain Hoare, commander of a merchant fhip in the trade, who afterwards recovered.   Three other Negroes belonging to this eftate made their efcape privately, and alarmed
the neighbouring fettlements, by which means the white perfons upon
them provided for their lives, and took meafures which prevented the
Negroes on three contiguous eftates from rifing.   A gentleman, proprietor of one of thefe eftates, remarkable for his humanity and kind
treatment of his flaves, upon the firft alarm, put arms into the hands
of about twenty; of whofe faithful attachment to him, he had the utmoft confidence: thefe were all of them Coromantins, who no fooner
had got poffeffion of arms, than they convinced their mafter how little
they merited the good opinion he had entertained of them; for having
ranged themfelves before his houfe, they affured him they would do
him no harm, but that they muft go and join their countrymen, and
then faluting him with their hats, they every one marched off.   Among
the rebels were feveral French Negroes, who had been taken prifoners
at Guadaloupe, and, being fent to Jamaica for fale, were purchafed by
capt. Forreft.   Thefe men were the more dangerous, as they had been
in arms at Guadaloupe, and feen fomething of military operations; in
which

which they acquired fo much fkill, that, after the maffacre on the
eftate, when they found their partifans of the adjacent plantations did
not appear to join them, they killed feveral Negroes, fet fire to buildings and cane-pieces, did a variety of other mifchief, and then withdrew into the woods, where they formed a ftrong breaft-work acrofs
a road, flanked by a rocky hill; within this work they erected their
huts, and fat down in a fort of encampment; a party of militia, who
were fent to attack them, very narrowly efcaped being all cut off.
The men were badly difciplined, having been haftily collected; and
falling into an ambufcade, they were ftruck with terror at the difmal
yells, and the multitude of their affailants. The whole party was
thrown into the utmoft confufion, and routed, notwithftanding every
endeavour of their officers; each ftrove to fhift for himfelf, and whilft
they ran different ways, fcarcely knowing what they were about, feveral were butchered, others broke their limbs over precipices, and the
reft with difficulty found their way back again. This unlucky defeat
raifed the fpirits of the Coromantins in this part of the country, and
encouraged fo many to join the victorious band, that the whole number very foon amounted to upwards of a thoufand, including their
women, who were neceffary for carrying their baggage, and dreffing
their victuals. This confequence fhewed, how ill-judged it was, to
make the firft attack upon them with a handful of raw, undifciplined
militia, without advancing at the fame time a party in referve, to fuftain their efforts, and cover their retreat. In fuppreffing thefe mutinies, the firft action has always been of the utmoft importance, and
therefore fhould never be confided to any except tried and well-trained
men. The winning the firft battle from the rebellious party, ufually
decides the iffue of the war; it difconcerts the confpirators, not as yet
engaged, and who keep aloof, irrefolute whether to join or not; and it
intimidates all that are in arms, and moft commonly plunges them
into defpondency: the reverfe is fure to follow a defeat of the Whites
on the firft encounter; and nothing can add greater ftrength to rebellion, or tend more to raife the authority of the priefts and leaders who
have fet it on foot. Thefe remarks have been fully verified, in courfe
of the prefent, and every other infurrection that has occurred in this
ifland. The infurgents in St. Mary, who opened the campaign, were
repulfed in the firft conflict, and from that time grew difheartened,

and

and diminishing in their numbers; their confederates in that parish looked upon their rout as ominous, and would not venture to associate with them in the undertaking, whilst those of Westmoreland, who would probably have given up the cause, if they had met with a severe check at their first outset, were now become flushed with a confidence in their superiority, and gathered reinforcements every day. However, they were not suffered to remain long in this assurance of success; a detachment of the 49th regiment, with a fresh company of militia, and a party of the Leeward *Marons*, marched to attack them. The regulars led the van, the militia brought up the rear, whilst the *Marons* lined the wood to the right and left, to prevent ambuscades. The rebels collected behind their fortification, made shew of a resolution to defend their post, and fired incessantly at their opponents, though with no other injury than wounding one soldier. The officer, captain Forsyth, who commanded the detachment, advanced with the utmost intrepidity, ordering his men to reserve their fire, till they had reached the breast work; at which time, they poured in such a volley, that several of the rebels immediately fell, and the rest ran as fast as they could up the hill. A Mulatto man behaved with great bravery in this action; he leaped on the breast-work, and assaulted the rebels sword in hand. Having gained a lodgement, the troops declined a pursuit, and carelessly entered the huts, where they sat down to refresh themselves with some provisions, of which they found a large store; the rebels, perceiving this, discharged several random shot from the hill above them, which passed through the huts, and had very near been fatal to some of the officers: the *Marons*, upon this, penetrated the wood at the foot of the hill, and ascending it on the opposite side, and spreading themselves, suddenly assaulted the rebels in flank, who were instantly routed, and a great number killed, or taken prisoners. During the attack at the breast-work, Jemmy, a Negroe belonging to the late Mr. Smith, gave proof of his fidelity and regard to his master, whose death he revenged by killing one of the rebels, and other services, for which he was afterwards rewarded with his freedom, and an annuity for life, by the assembly. After this overthrow, the Westmoreland rebels were never able to act any otherwise than on the defensive; several skirmishes happened, in which they were constantly put to flight; their numbers were gradually reduced, and

many

many deftroyed themfelves. About the time of their breaking out, feveral other confpiracies were in agitation: in the Vale of Luidas, in St. John's, the Coromantins had agreed to rife, ravage the eftates, and murther the white men there; they fixed a certain day for commencing hoftilities, when they were to break open the houfe at Langher's plantation, *and feize the fire arms lodged there*; after which, they were to flay all the Whites they could meet with, fire the houfes and canepieces, and lay all the country wafte. Three Negroes, who were privy to this machination, difclofed it to their overfeer, in confequence of which, the ringleaders were taken up, and, upon conviction, executed; others, who turned evidence, were tranfported off the ifland: and thus the whole of this bloody fcheme was providentially fruftrated.

In the parifh of St. Thomas in the Eaft, a Negroe, named Caffee, who had been preffed by fome Coromantins there to join with them in rebelling, and deftroying the eftates and white inhabitants, declined at firft being concerned; but recollecting that fome advantages might be gained to himfelf by a thorough knowledge of their intentions, he afterwards pretended to have thought better of their propofals, and, profeffing his zeal to embrace them, he affociated at their private cabals from time to time, till he became mafter of the whole fecret, which he took the firft opportunity to difcover, and moft of the confpirators were apprehended.

Confpiracies of the like nature were likewife detected in Kingfton, St. Dorothy, Clarendon, and St. James, and the partizans fecured.

In Kingfton, a wooden fword was found, of a peculiar ftructure, with a red feather ftuck into the handle; this was ufed among the Coromantins as a fignal for war; and, upon examining this, and other fufpicious circumftances, to the bottom, it was difcovered, that the Coromantins of that town had raifed one Cubah, a female flave belonging to a Jewefs, to the rank of royalty, and dubbed her *queen of Kingfton*; at their meetings fhe had fat in ftate under a canopy, with a fort of robe on her fhoulders, and a crown upon her head. Her majefty was feized, and ordered for tranfportation; but, prevailing on the captain of the tranfport to put her afhore again in the leeward part of the ifland, fhe continued there for fome time undifcovered, but at length was taken up, and executed. Thefe circumftances fhew the great extent of the confpiracy, the ftrict correfpondence which had been carried on by the Coromantins in every quarter of the island, and their almost incredible secresy in the forming their plan of insurrection; for it appeared in evidence, that the first eruption in St. Mary's, was a matter preconcerted, and known to all the chief men in the different districts; and the secret was probably confided to some hundreds, for several months before the blow was struck.

Some persons surmised, that they were privately encouraged, and furnished with arms and ammunition, by the French and Spaniards, whose piccaroons were often seen hovering near the coast; but there seems no just foundation for such an opinion: it is certain, the rebels found an easier means of supplying themselves with large quantities of powder, ball, lead, and several stands of arms, on the different estates where they broke out; on some of these, they found two or three dozen musquets and cutlasses, which were not guarded by more than two or three white men. The planters, as I have before remarked, very imprudently kept these magazines, which were by far too many for their necessary defence, and attracted the notice of the Coromantins, who are practised in the use of arms from their youth in their own country, and are at all times disposed for mutiny.

A fresh insurrection happened in St. James's, which threatened to become very formidable, had it not been for the activity of brigadier Witter of the militia, and lieut. colonel Spragge of the 49th, who dispersed the insurgents, and took several prisoners; but the rest escaped, and, uniting with the stragglers of the other defeated parties, formed a large gang, and infested Carpenter's Mountains for some time. Another party of twelve Coromantins in Clarendon, whom their master, from a too good opinion of their fidelity, had imprudently armed, at their own earnest intreaty, and sent in quest of a small detached band of rebels, of whose haunt he had gained intelligence, deserted to their countrymen, but were soon after surprized, and the greater part of them killed or taken. Damon, one of the Westmoreland chiefs, with a small gang, having posted himself at a place called Mile Gully in Clarendon, a voluntary party, under command of Mr. Scot and Mr. Greig, with three or four more, went in quest of them. They had a long way to march in the night, through the woods, and across a difficult country; but, having provided themselves with a trusty guide, they came up to the haunt about midnight, attacked the rebels without

loss

lofs of time, killed the chief, and one of his men, wounded another, and took two prifoners; for which fervice, the affembly made them a genteel recompence, befides a good reward to the Negroes who affifted them in this enterprize.

The rebels in St. Mary's, under general Tacky. ftill maintained their ground. Admiral Holmes had difpatched a frigate to Port Maria, which proved of great ufe for the fafe cuftody of prifoners, who were too numerous to be confined on fhore, and required too large a party of militia to guard them; but after they were removed on board, where they were well fecured, the militia were ready to be employed on more active fervice: no meafure, therefore, could be more feafonable and judicious; and it was one good effect of the harmony then fubfifting between the commander of the fquadron and the lieutenant governor. The rebels now thought only of concealing themfelves, and made choice of a little glade, or cockpit, fo environed with rocky fteeps, that it was difficult to come at them; but, in this fituation, a party of militia and *Marons*, with fome failors, affaulted them with hand grenades, killed fome, and took a few prifoners. Soon after this, they fuffered a more decifive overthrow; the *Marons* of Scot's-Hall, having got fight of their main body, forced them to an engagement; the rebels foon gave way, and Tacky, their leader, having feparated from the reft, was clofely purfued by lieut. Davy of the *Marons*, who fired at him whilft they were both running a full fpeed, and fhot him dead. His head was brought to Spanifh Town, and ftuck on a pole in the highway; but, not long after, ftolen, as was fuppofed, by fome of his countrymen, who were unwilling to let it remain expofed in fo ignominious a manner. The lofs of this chief[y], and of Jamaica, another of their captains, who fell in the fame battle, ftruck moft of the furvivors of their little army with defpair; they betook themfelves

[y] He was a young man of good ftature, and well made; his countenance handfome, but rather of an effeminate than manly caft. It was faid, he had flattered himfelf with the hope of obtaining (among other fruits of victory) the lieutenant governor's lady for his concubine He did not appear to be a man of any extraordinary genius, and probably was chofen general, from his fimilitude in perfon to fome favourite leader of their nation in Africa. A gentleman, feveral years fince, having fet up in a confpicuous part of his plantation a bronzed ftatue of a gladiator, fomewhat larger than the natural fize, the Coromantins no fooner beheld, than they were almoft ready to fall down, and adore it. Upon enquiry, the gentleman learnt, that they had difcovered a very ftriking likenefs between this figure and one of their princes, and believed that it had been copied from him.

themfelves to a cave, at the diftance of a mile or two from the fcene of action, where it was thought they laid violent hands on one another, to the number of twenty-five; however, the *Marons*, who found them out, claimed the honour of having flain them, and brought their ears to the lieutenant governor, in teftimony of their death, and to entitle themfelves to the ufual reward. A few miferable fugitives ftill fculked about the woods, in continual terror for their fate; but at length, they contrived to fend an embaffy to a gentleman of the parifh (Mr. Gordon), in whofe honour they repofed implicit confidence, and expreffed their readinefs to furrender upon the condition of being tranf-ported off the ifland, inftead of being put to death. This gentleman had a congrefs with their leaders unarmed, and promifed to exert his endeavours with the lieutenant governor; on their part, they feemed well pleafed to wait his determination, and gave affurance of their peaceable demeanour in the mean while. The lieutenant governor's confent was obtained; but under an appearance of difficulty, to make it the more defireable; and, upon intimation of it at the next private congrefs, they one and all fubmitted, and were fhipped off, purfuant to the ftipulation. The remains of the Weftmoreland and St. James's rebels ftill kept in arms, and committed fome ravages. In September therefore (1760) the lieutenant governor convened the affembly, and in his fpeech informed them, " That the various fcenes of diftrefs, occafioned by the infurrections which broke out in fo many different parts of the country, would have engaged him fooner to call them together; but he was obliged to defer it, as their prefence was fo neceffary in the feveral diftricts, to prevent the fpreading of an evil fo dangerous in its confequence to the whole ifland.

" That he had the fatisfaction to acquaint them, his expectations had been fully anfwered, by the vigilance and bravery of the troops employed during the late troubles; that the many difficulties they had to encounter, only ferved to fet their behaviour in a more advantage-

---

Two of the St. Mary's ringleaders, Fortune and Kingfton, were hung up alive in irons on a gibbet, erected in the parade of the town of Kingfton. Fortune lived feven days, but Kingfton furvived till the ninth. The morning before the latter expired, he appeared to be convulfed from head to foot; and upon being opened, after his deceafe, his lungs were found adhering to the back fo tightly, that it required fome force to difengage them. The murders and outrages they had committed, were thought to juftify this cruel punifhment inflicted upon them *in terrorem* to others; but they appeared to be very little affected by it themfelves; behaving all the time with a degree of hardened infolence, and brutal infenfibility.

ous light; and the plan now propofed for carrying on their operations, had the faireft profpect of totally fuppreffing, in a very fhort time, all the difturbers of the public repofe.

" That the ready affiftance he had received from rear-admiral Holmes, in tranfporting troops and provifions, and in ftationing his majefty's fhips where they could be of moft fervice, enabled him to make ufe of fuch vigorous meafures, and employ to advantage fuch a force, that, notwithstanding the formidable number of rebels which had appeared in arms, and the many combinations which were formed among the flaves throughout the ifland, *their projects were rendered abortive*, and tranquillity again reftored, where total deftruction had been threatened.

" That nothing had been omitted to render the martial law as little grievous as poffible to the inhabitants, although the long continuance of it could not fail of being feverely felt by the community in general; but the public fecurity required it; and to that, every other confideration gave place.

" That the care which had been taken to introduce a proper difci-pline among the militia, had now put them on fo refpectable a footing, that they only required the aid of legiflature, to make them truly ufeful. The great defects of the laft militia law were never more apparent than during the late misfortunes, when the private foldier was fupported in difobedience of his commanding officer's orders; and, when called upon for his country's fervice, empowered, on the payment of an inconfiderable fine [z], to withdraw that affiftance, for which he was enlifted."

The latter part of the lieutenant governor's fpeech alludes princi-pally to the conduct of feveral privates in the militia, and particularly the Jews, who refufed to turn out and appear under arms on their fab-bath, and other feftivals or fafts, making a religious fcruple of confci-ence their pretext, though it was well known that they never fcrupled taking money and vending drams upon thofe days; others wilfully abfented themfelves, and paid the fine, which came to much lefs than their profits amounted to by ftaying at home, and attending their fhops. I muft not here omit a little anecdote relative to thefe people: one of the rebel leaders, having been taken prifoner in Weftmoreland,

[z] Ten fhillings for non-appearance at mufter.

was

was confined in irons, in the barrack at Savannah la Mar, to wait his trial. It happened that, on the night after his captivity, a Jew was appointed to ſtand centry over him: about midnight the rebel, after reconnoitering the perſon of his guard, took the opportunity of tampering with him, to favour his eſcape. " You Jews, ſaid he, and our " nation (meaning the Coromantins), ought to conſider ourſelves as " one people. You differ from the reſt of the Whites, and they hate " you. Surely then it is beſt for us to join in one common intereſt, " drive them out of the country, and hold poſſeſſion of it to ourſelves. " We will have (continued he) a fair diviſion of the eſtates, and we " will make ſugar and rum, and bring them to market. As for the " ſailors, you ſee they do not oppoſe us, they care not who is in poſ- " ſeſſion of the country, Black or White, it is the ſame to them; ſo " that after we are become maſters of it, you need not fear but they " will come cap in hand to us (as they now do to the Whites) to " trade with us. They'll bring us things from t'other ſide the ſea, " and be glad to take our goods in payment." Finding the Jew's arguments, in objection to this propoſal, not ſo difficult to ſurmount as he had expected, he then finiſhed his harangue with an offer, that, " if he would but releaſe him from his irons, he would conduct him " directly to a ſpot, where he had buried ſome hundred of piſtoles, " which he ſhould have in reward." The Jew was very earneſt to know whereabouts this hidden treaſure lay, that he might firſt ſatisfy his own eyes, that what he had been told was true, before he ſhould take any further ſtep; but the priſoner flatly refuſed to let him into the ſecret, unleſs he was firſt ſet at liberty; which condition the Iſraelite was either too honeſt or too unbelieving to comply with, but the next day reported what had paſſed, to his officers.

The lieutenant-governor recommended to the houſe, the putting the iſland into a better poſture of defence, and the paſſing ſuch new regulations for remedying thoſe defects in the laws, which the late calamities had pointed out, as might beſt ſeem adapted to prevent future attempts of the like nature.

The aſſembly immediately addreſſed him, to proclaim martial law, in order to put an end to the rebellion ſtill ſubſiſting in the Leeward part of the iſland. They tranſmitted the thanks of their houſe to admiral Holmes for the aſſiſtance he had given; who returned a very

polite

polite anſwer, and aſſured them, "that his greateſt pleaſure would " confiſt in the execution of his duty againſt his majeſty's enemies, " and in giving the utmoſt protection in his power to the trade and " commerce of the iſland."

They likewiſe expreſſed their moſt grateful ſentiments of the lieutenant-governor's vigilance and conduct, which had ſo happily contributed to the reduction of the rebels in one part, and would, they hoped, very ſhortly effect their total ſuppreſſion. For this end, they applied their deliberations, and received the propoſals of William Hynes, a millwright by trade, who had been uſed to the woods, and very ſerviceable againſt the rebels in St. Mary's. He propoſed that he ſhould be empowered by the lieutenant-governor to beat up for volunteers, and raiſe among the free Mulattos and Negroes a party of one hundred ſhot; with which he would march againſt the rebels in Weſtmoreland, and do his utmoſt to reduce them.

He deſired to have two lieutenants and one enſign to be in ſubordinate command; that the reward for their ſervice ſhould be equal, and that his party ſhould be furniſhed at the public expence with ſuitable arms and accoutrements, money to provide neceſſaries, and a ſtated premium for every rebel they ſhould take or deſtroy. This ſcheme was approved of, and a bill paſſed for carrying it into immediate execution. At the ſame time ſeven companies, of thirty men each, were draughted from the militia, and fifteen baggage-Negroes allotted to each company, making in all three hundred and fifteen, who were ſtationed by the lieutenant-governor in the moſt advantageous poſts; and troopers were diſpoſed in ſuch a manner, as to carry diſpatches to and from them, with the beſt expedition. The aſſembly granted 450 l. to be divided among the Marons of Trelawny and Accompong Towns, in payment of their arrears due to them, and to encourage their future ſervices. Captain Hynes, with his party, went in ſearch of the rebels, and was four months on the ſcout; at laſt, after a tedious purſuit, he ſurprized them in their haunt, killed and took twelve, and the remainder were afterwards either ſlain or taken priſoners by other parties, or deſtroyed themſelves, which latter was the cataſtrophe of numbers; for the parties of militia frequently came to places in the woods, where ſeven or eight were found tied up with withes to the boughs of trees: and

previous

previous to thefe felf-murders, they had generally maffacred their
women and children. The affembly ordered 562 *l.* 12 *s.* 6 *d.* to be
paid captain Hynes, for his difburfements, and as a recompence for
his fervices. Thus terminated this rebellion ; which, whether we
confider the extent and fecrefy of its plan, the multitude of the confpirators, and the difficulty of oppofing its eruptions in fuch a variety of different places at once, will appear to have been more formidable than any hitherto known in the Weft Indies ; though happily
extinguifhed, in far lefs time than was expected, by the precaution
and judgement of the lieutenant-governor in the difpofition of the
forces, the prompt affiftance of the admiral, and the alacrity of the
regulars, feamen, militia, and Marons, who all contributed their
fhare towards the fpeedy fuppreffion of it. The lieutenant governor, under whofe prudent conduct this inteftine war was fo fuccefsfully brought to a conclufion, was a native of the ifland, and
had a property in it at ftake ; but if this may detract any thing
from the merits of his exertion, it proves at leaft, how much more
may reafonably be hoped from the affiduity of a gentleman of the
ifland, who is interefted in its welfare, and in whom a perfect knowledge of the country is fuperadded to natural ability and public
fpirit, than from others, who, having nothing to lofe in it, may be
lefs anxious for its prefervation. There fell, by the hands of the
rebels, by murder, and in action, about fixty white perfons; the
number of the rebels who were killed, or deftroyed themfelves, was
between three and four hundred. Few in proportion were executed,
the major part of the prifoners being tranfported off the ifland [a].
Such as appeared to have been involuntarily compelled to join them,
were acquitted ; but the whole amount of the killed, fuicides, executed and tranfported, was not lefs than one thoufand ; and the
whole lofs fuftained by the country, in ruined buildings, cane-pieces,
cattle, flaves, and difburfements, was at leaft 100,000 *l.* to fpeak
within compafs.

[a] Moft of them were fent to the Bay of Honduras, which has long been the common receptacle of Negroe criminals, banifhed from this ifland ; the confequence of which may, fome time or
other, prove very troublefome to the logwood cutters ; yet they make no fcruple to buy thefe outcafts, as they coft but little. It is difficult to find a convenient market for fuch flaves among the
neighbouring foreign colonies ; but, if poffibly it could be avoided, thefe dangerous fpirits fhould
not be fent to renew their outrages in any of our own infant fettlements.

The

The affembly, upon the lieutenant governor's recommendation, proceeded to frame and pafs an act, to remedy the evils arifing from irregular meetings of flaves; to prevent their carrying arms, or having ammunition, or going from place to place without tickets; to prohibit the practices of *obeiah* (or the arts of pretended conjurors); to reftrain overfeers from leaving eftates under their management on certain days (Sundays and holidays); and to oblige all free Negroes, Mulattoes, and Indians, to regifter their names in the veftry books of their refpective parifhes, and carry about them a certificate, and wear (the crofs) a badge of their freedom; and, laftly, to prevent any captain, mafter, or fupercargo, of any veffel, from bringing back convict tranfported flaves. All thefe regulations were extremely prudent and neceffary; but they explain the *defects* hinted in the lieutenant governor's fpeech to the houfe, and evince the abufe which has been made by the Negroes of the indulgencies hitherto allowed them. The affembly further voted, that the feveral flaves, fent out againft the rebels during the late rebellion, fhould receive the fame rewards for killing, or taking them alive, as the *Marons* were entitled to, upon producing a certificate to the commanding officer, of their having effected fuch fervice. They alfo paffed an act, for purchafing from their owners, and granting freedom, to about twenty Negroe flaves, for their fidelity to the public; they fettled upon each of them an annuity for life, and gave them a circular badge, or medal of filver, on which was engraved the date of the year, with the words, " *Freedom for being Honeft,*" on one fide, and on the reverfe, " *By the Country.*"

As thefe infurrections and confpiracies had, for the moft part, appeared upon eftates belonging to perfons refident in England, and the expences attending their fuppreffion occafioned a very enormous fum to be levied in taxes, it was thought but equitable, that the proprietors, who, by their abfence, had left their flaves in want of a due controul, and the perfonal influence of a mafter, and their eftates to be defended by the perfonal fervices and hardfhips of other men, while they themfelves were repofing in eafe and affluence, beyond the reach of danger, ought to compenfate for their non-refidence, by paying a larger fhare of the public charges, incurred in fome meafure through their means. They accordingly refolved to double the deficiency tax for the year 1761; and allow every proprietor refident within

the

the ifland to fave his own deficiency for 30 flaves, or 150 head of cattle; and all proprietors, under twenty-one years of age, fent off for the benefit of their education, to fave half a deficiency. By this meafure they threw an extraordinary weight of taxation, for that year, upon the abfentees. They likewife addreffed his majefty, that he would be pleafed to give directions, that the company of the 49th regiment, ftationed at the Mofquito fhore, and four companies of the 74th, at the coaft of Africa, might repair to, and join, their refpective regiments in Jamaica. They reprefented, that many gentlemen, of large eftates in the ifland, were non-refidents, whofe influence over their flaves, if refident, would, in all probability, contribute much to the prevention of the mifchiefs arifing from rebellious confpiracies and infurrections; and that they found themfelves under indifpenfable ne-ceffity of foliciting his majefty for another regiment, for the better fecurity of the ifland; and the rather, as they had paffed a bill, oblig-ing the inhabitants of the feveral parifhes to erect barracks for the re-ception and accommodation of more troops. They voted a large fum for ftrengthening the fortifications, ordered a fupply of ftores for the forts, and directed a powder magazine to be built at Spanifh Town.

On the 12th of October, 1761, the affembly met again; when the lieutenant governor, in his fpeech, informed them, that he had delayed their meeting beyond the ufual time, in order that every meafure might be enforced, which could tend to the prefervation of the general tranquillity, at that time happily reftored again, *by the total fuppreffion of the rebellion*, and to give them opportunity of fupporting, by their prefence in their feveral diftricts, thofe refolutions, which were taken for the internal fecurity of the ifland, and the prevention of future attempts, to involve them again in calamities of the like nature. That the advantages which muft attend the erection of barracks in the differ-ent parifhes, and the cantoning his majefty's troops according to the plan then laid down, were fo evident, that no one, interefted in the welfare of that community, could difapprove of fo prudent a meafure.

Thus, every meafure that could be fuggefted, either for remedying the diforders under which the ifland had fuffered fo much, or for baf-fling the machinations of future infurgents, or putting the forts and fortifications into a refpectable ftate of defence againft foreign enemies, was

was profecuted as far as the lieutenant governor's authority could give it fanction, or the affembly fecond his recommendations. Mr. Lyttelton arrived as governor the following year (February, 1762); and the public tranquillity remained undifturbed by infurrections for fome time. It was however well known, that feveral Coromantins, who had actually been in arms during the late commotion, whilft their caufe wore a promifing afpect, flunk away afterwards, and returned again again to their duty, affecting great abhorrence at the behaviour of their countrymen, and even pretending that they had been exerting themfelves in oppofition to the rebels. With good reafon therefore it was fufpected, by many perfons in St. Mary's, that thefe deferters, who had taken the *fetifhe*, or oath, which they regard as inviolable, would diffemble their genuine fentiments for the prefent, and wait a favourable opportunity to execute their bloody purpofes. Some time in July, 1765, there was a private meeting in that parifh, of feveral Coromantin headmen, who entered into a confpiracy for a frefh infurrection, to take place immediately after the Chriftmas holidays; they bound the compact with their fetifhe, according to cuftom, and received affurances from all or moft of the Coromantins in the parifh, that they would join. But the impatience of fome among them to begin the work, hurried them on to rife before the day appointed, and difconcerted their whole plan; for, on the 29th of November, at night, a Coromantin, named Blackwall, belonging to Whitehall plantation, who had been tried formerly on fufpicion of being concerned in the rebellion of 1760, and acquitted for want of fufficient evidence, having previoufly feduced to his party nine Coromantins on the fame eftate, but a little before imported from Africa, fet fire to the works and trafh houfes, with a view to decoy the overfeer, and other white perfons there, from their beds, to extinguifh it; and then to cut off their retreat to the dwelling-houfe, fecure the arms lodged there, and proceed to murther them, without fear of refiftance.

Upon the firft alarm of fire, the overfeer and white fervants repaired to the works, as had been forefeen; where they met with Blackwall (who held a poft of fome authority on the eftate), bemoaning the fad accident, and fhewing great alertnefs in fetching water to fupply the Whites, whom he advifed to get upon the roofs, where they might throw it on the flames with the best advantage; the overseer, not having the smallest distrust of him, and wholly employed about extinguishing the fire, readily pursued his advice. In the dwelling-house were Mr. B——, and his sister Mrs. B——d, who had hastily slipped on their cloaths, and were standing in the piazza, at the front of the house, and looking towards the conflagration; when, all at once, the nine confederates broke through the back-door, all stark-naked, with the most hideous yells, and sharpened bills in their hands; Mr. B—— was unfortunately very infirm, and had no chance of escaping; while therefore he turned to expostulate with them, they surrounded and hacked him into a thousand pieces. The pleasure they enjoyed in mangling the body of this unhappy gentleman (who had only lodged here, by accident, in his way to Spanish Town) afforded Mrs. B——d an opportunity to jump out of the piazza, and run towards the bottom of the hill on which the house stood; but, before she could reach so far, she fell down; in this situation she was seen by two faithful Negroe men, her domestics, who flew to her assistance; upon their coming up to her, she concluded no less than that she was in the hands of the rebels, and destined for immediate butchery; but, whilst she was imploring for mercy, the servants seized her in their arms, and, with great presence of mind, hastened with her as fast as they could to the side of a neighbouring river, where they concealed her amongst the sedge and grass, that grew very thick, injoining her to lie close, whilst they were gone to look for more assistance. The rebels, in the mean time, dispatched another gentleman, who, upon the cry of fire, had come from the next estate, and fell into their clutches. But the overseer, and other Whites, on hearing the groans of Mr. B——, and the shouts of his murtherers, fled to Ballard's Valley, which estate joins Whitehall; where they called up the white men to secure themselves, and prepare for their defence. The flames, which were seen at a great distance, served as a signal to other conspirators; so that their number was now augmented to fifty or sixty; who, with the most horrid acclamations, (having got possession of all the arms at Whitehall, with powder and ball) began their march, passed close by the place of Mrs. B——d's concealment, without perceiving her, and proceeded on to Ballard's Valley. When they were got to a sufficient distance, one of her trusty servants returned, with great

caution,

caution, to the ftable, where, finding a horfe, he fixed on a pillion, and, coming to his miftrefs, carried her through bye-ways to another eftate, and brought to the white people there the firft intelligence of what had happened. Confidering the great danger to which that lady was expofed, and that the moft trifling noife, at the time when the rebels paffed her retreat, might have betrayed it, her efcape appears almoft miraculous; and it feems as if the hand of Providence had interpofed, to protect her life, and make her two fervants the inftruments of prefervation, whofe fidelity and addrefs cannot be too highly extolled. The rebels, being arrived at the valley, laid clofe fiege to the overfeer's houfe, which was garrifoned with about ten white men. This houfe was erected upon a ftone foundation, raifed fome height from the ground, and furnifhed with loop-holes. The little garrifon made proper difpofitions for defence, and placed fome of their party at the loop-holes below. The rebels were joined by feveral of their countrymen on this eftate; and, furrounding the houfe, began to ufe the moft infulting language in their power, to provoke the Whites to come forth, that they might enjoy the fatisfaction of killing them; but finding this ineffectual, they prepared for burning the houfe about their ears; for this purpofe they collected a parcel of dry trafh, which they faftened to the extremity of a long pole, and one of their leaders fetting his back to a loop-hole, kindled the trafh, and applied it to the wood-work of the roof. At that inftant he was perceived by one of the centries pofted below, who difcharged his piece at him; the ball ftruck againft the lock of a gun, which the rebel had in his hand, and recoiling into his body, killed him upon the fpot. His fall threw the reft of the confpirators into difmay, for he was one of their chiefs; upon which the garrifon, taking advantage of their fufpence, fallied out with great fpirit, killed two or three, and difperfed the reft, who immediately fled into the woods. Blackwall, the principal of the gang, finding how matters were likely to end, detached himfelf from his brethren, and a few hours afterwards prefented himfelf before his overfeer in feeming terror, pretending he had narrowly efcaped being put to death by his countrymen; to avoid whofe fury, he had crawled into a cane-piece, and there hid himfelf till that inftant. Parties were fpeedily collected, who purfued the rebels into the woods, and reduced them with but little difficulty.

Sufpicion

Suspicions arising, that this conspiracy was more extensive than at first appeared, and upon recollection that there had been a merry meeting of the Negroes at Ballard's Valley two nights preceding the insurrection, and that the Coromantins had separated from the rest, a strict inquiry was entered into; and upon examining some Coromantins, who were most suspected, they impeached several of their countrymen; fresh evidences produced further discoveries, and at length the plot was partly unraveled. It appeared that the Coromantins on no less than seventeen estates in that parish were engaged in the confederacy; that Blackwall was the principal instigator; and that the premature rising at Whitehall was owing to the impetuosity of one Quamin, belonging to their gang, who would not wait the appointed time; so that it is probable, if they had not met a repulse soon after their first outrage, the insurrection would have been general, from the encouragement their better success would have given to the rest of the conspirators. Some among them regretted exceedingly the precipitate eagerness of Quamin, and threw out insinuations that the *Marons* were in the secret, and that the insurrection was intended to have opened at once in three different places, at a certain day soon after Christmas; that three days previous notice was to be given of the exact hour of rising; and as they hoped to find the white people off their guard, and to get possession of sufficient arms and powder, in the several dwelling-houses, they had full confidence, that, by their precautions, and secrecy, they should carry all before them, and make amends for their former disappointment; they knew, that a large stock of fire arms and ammunition would be absolutely necessary; one of their first attempts therefore was to be, the surprize of the fort at Port Maria, which was garrisoned by only a small number of sickly soldiers, whom they supposed incapable of making any resistance; these they were to drive into the sea with their bill-hooks, and then proceed to massacre all the Whites in that neighbourhood. A second party were to ravage the Eastern quarter of the parish, quite down to the very coast; whilst a third band should take their route through the Southern district, and penetrate by the woods to Sixteen-mile-walk, where they pretended to have several associates in readiness; then, uniting their forces, they were to slaughter, or force the white inhabitants to take refuge on board the ships, after which they were to divide the conquered coun-

try

try with the *Marons*, who, they alledged, had made choice of the woody uncultivated parts, as being moſt convenient for their hog-hunting; the Coromantins were to enjoy all the remainder, with the cattle and ſheep, and live like gentlemen; at leaſt they flattered themſelves, that the governor would apply to the king of the white men, to put the Coromantins upon the ſame eſtabliſhment as the *Marons*, who, they ſaid, were diſguſted at the little reſpeſt ſhewn them, and wanted the Coromantins to be incorporated with them, in order to become of more conſequence in the eyes of the white inhabitants.

This account of the defeſtion of the *Marons* was ſo improbable, that the white people would not give any credit to it: in the firſt place, it appeared not at all likely that the *Marons*, who had always received the higheſt encouragement from the legiſlature and private perſons, would hazard the loſs of their liberty and lives, by a treaſonable breach of the treaty; and upon the uncertain iſſue of an inteſtine war, by the event of which, if ſucceſsful to them, they could gain nothing more than what they already enjoyed; ſecondly, they were to admit a dangerous ſet of confederates, diſtinſt in intereſt, and ſuperior to them in number, by twenty to one, who would undoubtedly give the law to, and hold them in perpetual ſubjeſtion. The ſtory was therefore ſuppoſed to be either the reſult of a deep-laid policy, to ſtir up a jealouſy and difference between the *Marons* and white people, from which ſome advantage might accrue to the Coromantins in ſome future inſurreſtion; or elſe, if the *Marons* did really aſſociate in any ſuch plan, they muſt have done ſo, from a wicked deſign of embroiling the Coromantins in freſh rebellion, in the ſuppreſſion of which they might reap a conſiderable emolument, as they had heretofore experienced, by killing or taking priſoners. Something like ſuch a projeſt uſed to engage the frontier Indians in North America, who were never ſo happy as when the French and Engliſh were at war, becauſe they were ſure of employment and reward, on one ſide or other; and for this reaſon alone, many of their tribes were exceedingly out of humour with the laſt treaty of peace, which gave the finiſhing blow to theſe contentions for the maſtery, and to their mercenary artifices. If therefore the *Marons* had any concern in the plot, it is moſt reaſonable to believe that ſuch muſt have been their true deſign. The importance of this evidence naturally made the

pariſhioners

parifhioners defirous of examining ftill further, in order to get addi-tional lights, and guard themfelves againft a repetition of thefe horrid attempts, which it appeared they had juft grounds to apprehend; but the number of their militia was fo inconfiderable, that, after providing the proper guards for the different eftates moft expofed to danger, they had fo few left to take charge of the Negroe prifoners, that the latter were treble their number; fo that the magiftrates, whilft they were fitting on the trial of the rebels, were not without fear for their own fafety, as they had no protection againft any fudden infurrection made in favour of the prifoners; and, from the teftimony already given, it was certain, that a very confiderable body of the Coromantins had en-lifted in the confpiracy, befides thofe who were in cuftody. Remon-ftrances were repeatedly made upon this head, and the expediency ftated of fending round a fhip of war to Port Maria, as had been done in the former rebellion, to receive the prifoners, there being no gaol in the parifh, and only eighteen foldiers at the fort, who were in too feeble a condition to render them any fervice. At this time, there were no lefs than four companies quartered in Spanifh town, befides what lay in the different forts adjacent, fo that it was thought a detach-ment might very well have been fpared; but the commander of the fquadron fent no fhip, nor was a fingle man detached to reinforce the parifhioners, who were therefore left to take care of themfelves; and, defifting from further examination, through a regard to their own imminent danger, what remained to be known of this black affair was fmothered at once, to the no fmall joy of the confpirators [b].

A committee of the affembly, appointed to enquire into the rife and progrefs of this rebellion fome time afterwards, reported, That it had originated (like moft or all the others that had occurred in the ifland) with the Coromantins; whofe turbulent, favage, and martial temper was well known:

That their outrages had tended very much to difcourage the ef-fectual fettlement of the ifland; and, as a remedy in future, they pro-pofed " that a bill fhould be brought in for laying an additional higher " duty upon all Fantin, Akim, and Afhantee Negroes, and all others " commonly called Coromantins, that fhould, after a certain time, be " imported, and fold in the ifland."

[b] Thirteen were executed, thirty-three tranfported, and twelve acquitted.

Such

Such a bill, if paffed into a law, would doubtlefs have ftruck at the very root of the evil; for by laying a duty equal to a prohibition, no more Coromantins would have been brought to infeft this country; but, inftead of their favage race, the ifland would have been fupplied with Blacks of a more docile, tractable difpofition, and better inclined to peace and agriculture; fo that, in a few years, the ifland might in all likelihood have been effectually freed of all fuch dangerous combinations. Whether the conceit of fome few planters, in regard to the fuperior ftrength of the Coromantins, and greater hardinefs to fupport field labour, ought to outweigh the public tranquillity and fafety, or fhould be thought to atone for the blood of murthered white inhabitants, the ruin of others, the defolation of eftates, and the intolerable charges of taxation thereby thrown upon the public, not to fpeak of the obftruction of all trade and bufinefs during the martial law, muft be left to the ferious confideration of a difpaffionate legiflature; the fuppreffion of the Coromantins, in 1760 and 1761, coft the ifland 15,000 *l* I have before eftimated the expence of making good loffes fuftained, &c. at 100,000 *l*.; and the erecting of parochial barracks, in confequence of that infurrection, coft as much more. In the whole, the ifland expended not much lefs on that account than appears from the earlieft accounts to have been difburfed on the reduction of the *Marons*; for this was no more than 240,000*l*.

No bill however was paffed, the meafure was oppofed, and it dropped; but the firft fruits of this oppofition burft forth the very next year (1766), in a frefh difturbance, that happened on a gentleman's eftate in Weftmoreland; where thirty-three Coromantins (for no other were concerned), moft of whom had been newly imported, fuddenly rofe, and, in the fpace of an hour, murthered, and wounded, no lefs than nineteen white perfons; but they were foon defeated, fome killed, and the remainder executed or tranfported. So that the owner fuftained a very confiderable lofs, and would himfelf have fallen a facrifice, had he been on the eftate; for they entered his dewelling-houfe, and hacked every thing they found in it to pieces. If fuch reiterated examples will not convince men of their errors, we muft fay, with an old Latin author, that,

Quos Deus vult perdere, prius dementat.

It

It is worthy our remark, that the ringleaders of the St Mary's rebellion, in 1760, belonged to a gentleman diftinguifhed for his humanity, and excefﬁve indulgence towards his flaves in general, and thofe in particular; his lenity. fo far infiuenced him, that, upon their complaint, he never failed to difcharge their overfeer, and employ another more agreeable to them. No pretence of ill ufage was alledged by any of the prifoners, in any of thefe infurreﬁions, by way of extenuating their mifconduﬁ; the fole ground, and objeﬁ of their taking arms, as they *unanimoufly* concurred in acknowledging, was, the vain-glorious defire of fubduing the country; and they wanted neither ambition nor felf-confidence, to doubt their ability, or fuccefs, in accomplifhing this projeﬁ. It muft be allowed, that confpiracies fo extenfive could not have been conceived, me. thodized, and concluded upon, without various meetings of the confpirators, in different parts of the ifland; and hence, there muft appear to have been a very culpable inattention among the white inhabitants, who negleﬁed to keep a vigilant eye over the Coroman. tins in general, during their hours of leifure or recreation; for a feafonable regard to their private cabals and feparate affociations might have proved the means of deteﬁing their plot, long before it was ripe for execution; and to prevent, is always better, as well as eafier, than to remedy fuch evils. They fhould remember the dying words of one of the Coromantins executed in 1765, who repented his having been concerned in the rebellion, and cautioned the white perfons prefent, " never to truft any of his countrymen." Much having been faid of this clafs of Negroes, who have indeed been the heroes of my tale, it may not be unacceptable to give fome account of their origin, and qualities.

The Negroes who pafs under this general defcription are brought from the Gold coaft; but we remain uncertain, whether they are natives of that traﬁ of Guiney, or receive their feveral names of Akims, Fantins, Afhantees, Quamboos, &c. from the towns fo called, at whofe markets they are bought. That diftrict is populus and extenfive; and may therefore afford a confiderable number of cri- minals every year for tranfportation; however, whether they are brought from fome diftance inland, or are the refufe and outcaft of the feveral provinces whofe names they bear; it is certain they are marked

with

with the fame characters, which authors have given to the natives of this part, who are faid to be the moft turbulent and defperate of any on the coaft of Guiney; and that, were it not for their civil divifions, they would become dangerous neighbours to all the furrounding ftates. *Bofman* fays, " they are bold, hardy, and ftick at nothing, " where revenge or intereft is concerned; they are lazy, rapacious, " cunning, and deceitful; much addicted to theft, drunkennefs, " gluttony, lying, flattery, and luft; vain and haughty in their " carriage; envious and malicious in the higheft degree, diffembling " their refentments, for many years, until a fit opportunity offers of " gratifying their thirft of revenge; they are the moft treacherous " villains, and confummate knaves, yet known on that continent."

War and contention are their favourite amufements; inured very early to the ufe of fire arms, they are good markfmen; they go naked, and their bodies by this means acquire a furprizing degree of hardinefs, and ability to undergo fatigue; but they have an invincible averfion to every kind of labour, and particularly agriculture, which they leave to their women. Their priefts, or *obeiah-men*, are their chief oracles in all weighty affairs, whether of peace, war, or the purfuit of revenge. When affembled for the purpofes of confpiracy, the obeiah-man, after various ceremonies, draws a little blood from every one prefent; this is mixed in a bowl with gunpowder and grave dirt; the fetifhe or oath is adminiftered, by which they folemnly pledge themfelves to inviolable fecrecy, fidelity to their chiefs, and to wage perpetual war againft their enemies; as a ratification of their fincerity, each perfon takes a fup of the mixture, and this finifhes the folemn rite. Few or none of them have ever been known to violate this oath, or to defift from the full execution of it, even although feveral years may intervene. If defeated in their firft endeavours, they ftill retain the folicitude of fulfilling all that they have fworn; diffembling their malice under a feeming fubmiffive carriage, and all the exterior figns of innocence and chearfulnefs, until the convenient time arrives, when they think it practicable to retrieve their former mifcarriage. If at length their fecret defigns are brought to light, and that hypocrify can no longer ferve their turn, they either lay violent hands on themfelves, or refift till they are difabled.

To their other illaudable qualities, they add thofe of ingratitude, and implacable anger. Not the mildeft treatment, the moft condefcending indulgence, can make the fmalleft impreffion upon them, conciliate their friendfhip, or divert their avidity for revenge, after they have received what they think an injury; they are utterly incapable of forgetting or forgiving; the higheft marks of favour produce in them no fenfe of obligation or gratitude. Prompted by thefe qualifications, and this infernal difpofition, they are always foremoft in plotting, and heading mutinies; and the fame caufes generating the fame invariable effects, there is no doubt but they will ever fupport an uniformity of character, and be found, by repeated experience, the moft unruly, infolent, ftubborn, and difaffected fet of labourers, that can poffibly be introduced upon our plantations.

Their language is copious, and more regular than any other of the Negroe dialects; their mufic too is livelier, and their dances entirely martial, in which they refemble the North Americans; like them too they defpife death (more through ftupidity than fortitude), and can fmile in agony [c]. Their perfons are well made, and their features very different from the reft of the African Negroes, being fmaller, and more of the European turn. Their dances ferve to keep alive that military fpirit, for which they are fo diftinguifhed; and the figure confifts in throwing themfelves into all the pofitions and attitudes, cuftomary to them in the heat of an engagement. Is it not then a very injudicious and impolitic obftinacy in the planters, who perfift, in defiance of reafon and experience, to admit thefe dangerous fpirits among them? Nature does not inftruct the farmer to yoke tigers in his team, or plough with hyænas; fhe gives him the gentle fteed, and patient ox: but it would be no lefs abfurd for him to make ufe of wild beafts for thefe purpofes, than it is for the planter fo vainly to attempt the taming of fuch favage minds to peaceful induftry, and humble fubmiffion to his authority. But, if he will perverfely continue to employ them, fome effectual regulations ought to be provided, in order to break that fpirit of con-

---

[c] Barbarians always die without regret: what attachment have they to life? They feel not the pleafures of fociety, the ties of affection, or of nature; their faculties are in fuch a perpetual ftate of infancy, that the fpace between their birth and death is fcarcely perceptible.

Voltaire, Les Sauvages d'Europe.

federacy,

federacy, which keeps thefe Negroes too clofely affociated with one another. On many eftates, they do not mix at all with the other flaves, but build their houfes diftinct from the reft; and, herding together, are left more at liberty to hold their dangerous cabals, without interruption. Their houfes ought to be intermixed with the reft, and kept divided from one another, by interpofing thofe of the other Negroes, who by this means would become continual fpies upon their conduct. A particular attention fhould alfo be had to their *plays*, for thefe have always been their rendezvous for hatching plots, more efpecially whenever on fuch occafions any unufual refort is obferved of their countrymen from other plantations; and very particular fearch fhould be made after their obeiah-men, who, whenever detected, fhould be tranfported without mercy. The employers of this deteftable race owe thefe cautions at leaft to the public, who have fuffered fo much in times paft from the total neglect of them. From the foregoing detail, which I have given upon the moft credible and authentic teftimonies in my power to procure, every candid perfon may judge, with how little regard to truth the infurrections, that have happened in Jamaica, are afcribed to extraordinary cruelties exercifed over the flaves in that ifland; I think it will appear from inconteftable proofs, that fo impudent a calumny could have no other foundation than malevolence, complicated with ignorance.

C H A P. IV.

FRANCIS WILLIAMS.

I Have forborne till now to introduce upon the ftage a perfonage, who made a confpicuous figure in this ifland, and even attracted the notice of many in England. With the impartiality that becomes me, I fhall endeavour to do him all poffible juftice; and fhall leave it to the reader's opinion, whether what they fhall difcover of his genius and intellect will be fufficient to overthrow the arguments, I have before alledged, to prove an inferiority of the Negroes to the race of white men. It will by this time be difcovered, that I allude to *Francis Williams*, a native of this ifland, and fon to John and Dorothy Williams, free Negroes. Francis was the youngeft of

three

three fons, and, being a boy of unufual lively parts, was pitched upon to be the fubject of an experiment, which, it is faid, the Duke of Montagu was curious to make, in order to difcover, whether, by proper cultivation, and a regular courfe of tuition at fchool and the univerfity, a Negroe might not be found as capable of literature as a white perfon. In fhort, he was fent to England, where he underwent a regular difcipline of claffic inftruction at a grammar fchool, after which he was fixed at the univerfity of Cambridge, where he ftudied under the ableft preceptors, and made fome progrefs in the mathematics. During his abode in England, after finifhing his education, it is faid (I know not with what truth) that he compofed the well-known ballad of " Welcome, welcome, brother debtor,&c." But I have likewife heard the fame attributed to a different author. Upon his return to Jamaica, the duke would fain have tried his genius likewife in politics, and intended obtaining for him a privy feal, or appointment to be one of the governor's council; but this fcheme was dropped, upon the objections offered by Mr. Trelawny, the governor at that time. Williams therefore fet up a fchool in Spanifh Town, which he continued for feveral years, where he taught reading, writing, Latin, and the elements of the mathematics; whilft he acted in this profeffion, he felected a Negroe pupil, whom he trained up with particular care, intending to make him his fucceffor in the fchool ; but of this youth it may be faid, to ufe the expreffion of Feftus to Paul, that " much learning made him mad." The abftrufe problems of mathematical inftitution turned his brain ; and he ftill remains, I believe, an unfortunate example, to fhew that every African head is not adapted by nature to fuch profound contemplations. The chief pride of this difciple confifts in imitating the garb and and deportment of his tutor. A tye perriwig, a fword, and ruffled fhirt, feem in his opinion to comprehend the very marrow and quinteffence of all erudition, and philofophic dignity. Probably he imagines it a more eafy way of acquiring, among the Negroes, the reputation of a great fcholar, by thefe fuperficial marks, which catch their eye, than by talking of Euclid, whom they know nothing about.

Confidering the difference which climate may occafion, and which Montefquieu has learnedly examined, the noble duke would have

2   made

made the experiment more fairly on a native African; perhaps too the Northern air imparted a tone and vigour to his organs, of which they never could have been fufceptible in a hot climate; the author I have mentioned will not allow, that in hot climates there is any force or vigor of mind neceffary for human action, " there is (fays " he) no curiofity, no noble enterprize, no generous fentiment."

The climate of Jamaica is temperate, and even cool, compared with many parts of Guiney; and the Creole Blacks have undeniably more acutenefs and better underftandings than the natives of Guiney. Mr. Hume, who had heard of Williams, fays of him, " In Jamaica indeed " they talk of one Negroe as a man of parts and learning; but 'tis " likely he is admired for very flender accomplifhments, like a parrot " who fpeaks a few words plainly." And Mr. Eftwick, purfuing the fame idea, obferves, " Although a Negroe is found in Jamaica, or " elfewhere, ever fo fenfible and acute; yet, if he is incapable of moral " fenfations, or perceives them only as beafts do fimple ideas, without " the power of combination, in order to ufe; it is a mark that diftin- " guifhes him from the man who feels, and is capable of thefe moral " fenfations, who knows their application, and the purpofes of them, " as fufficiently, as he himfelf is diftinguifhed from the higheft fpecies " of brutes [d]." I do not know, if the fpecimen I fhall exhibit of

[d] The diftinction is well marked by Bifhop Warburton, in thefe words:

" 1ft, The MORAL SENSE: (is that) whereby we conceive and feel a pleafure in *right*, and a " diftafte and averfion to *wrong*, prior to all reflexion on their natures, or their confequences. This " is the firft inlet to the *adequate idea of morality*; and plainly the moft extenfive of all. When in- " ftinct had gone thus far, 2d, The REASONING FACULTY improved upon its dictates; for re- " flecting men, naturally led to examine the foundation of this *moral fenfe*, foon difcovered that there " were real, effential differences in the qualities of human actions, eftablifhed by nature; and, con- " fequently, that the love and hatred, excited by the *moral fenfe*, were not capricious in their opera- " tions; for that the effential properties of their objects had a fpecific difference." Hence arofe a fenfe of moral obligation in fociety, &c. *Divine Legation, vol. I. p. 37.*

It is this inftinct which difcriminates mankind from other animals who have it not, whereas in other inftinctive impulfes *all agree.* But the queftion is, whether all the fpecies of the human kind have this inftinctive fenfe in equal degree? If the brutal inftincts impel the African to fatisfy his appetites, to run from danger, and the like; why does he not exhibit equally the tokens of this *moral inftinct*, if he really poffeffes it? would it not infenfibly have gained admittance into their habits of living, as well as the other inftincts, and have regulated and directed their general man- ners? But we have no other evidence of their poffeffing it, than what arifes from the vague conjec- tural pofitions, " that all men are equal, and that the difparity between one man and another, or " one race of men and another, happens from accidental means, fuch as artificial refinements, edu- " cation, and fo forth." Certain however it is, that thefe refinements muft neceffarily take place, where the moral fenfe and reafoning faculty are moft abundant, and extenfively cultivated; but cannot happen, where they either do not exift at all, or, are not diftributed in fuch due portion, as to work the proper afcendancy over the more brutal fpecies of inftinct.

his

his abilities will, or will not, be thought to militate againſt theſe poſitions. In regard to the general character of the man, he was haughty, opinionated, looked down with ſovereign contempt on his fellow Blacks, entertained the higheſt opinion of his own knowledge, treated his parents with much diſdain, and behaved towards his children and his ſlaves with a ſeverity bordering upon cruelty; he was fond of having great deference paid to him, and exacted it in the utmoſt degree from the Negroes about him; he affected a ſingularity of dreſs, and particularly grave caſt of countenance, to impreſs an idea of his wiſdom and learning; and, to ſecond this view, he wore in common a huge wig, which made a very venerable figure. The moral part of his character may be collected from theſe touches, as well as the meaſure of his wiſdom, on which, as well as ſome other attributes to which he laid claim, he had not the modeſty to be ſilent, whenever he met with occaſion to expatiate upon them. Of this piece of vanity, there is a very ſtrong example in the following poem, which he preſented to Mr. Haldane; upon his aſſuming the government of the iſland; he was fond of this ſpecies of compoſition in Latin, and uſually addreſſed one to every new governor. He defined himſelf " a *white* man acting under a *black* ſkin." He endeavoured to prove logically, that a Negroe was ſuperior in quality to a Mulatto, or other caſt. His propoſition was, that " a ſimple white or a ſimple black complexion was reſpectively perfect: but a Mulatto, being an heterogeneous medley of both, was imperfect, *ergo* inferior."

His opinion of Negroes may be inferred from a proverbial ſaying, that was frequently in his mouth; " Shew me *a Negroe*, and I will ſhew you *a thief*." He died, not long ſince, at the age of ſeventy, or thereabouts.

I have ventured to ſubjoin ſome annotations to his poem, and particularly to diſtinguiſh ſeveral paſſages in the claſſic authors, to which he ſeems to have been indebted, or to have had alluſion; there may be other paſſages which have eſcaped my notice; I have added an Engliſh tranſlation in verſe, wherein I have endeavoured to retain the ſenſe, without wilfully doing injuſtice to the original.

Integerrimo et Fortiſſimo

Viro

GEORGIO HALDANO, Armigero,

Inſulæ *Jamaicenſis* Gubernatori;

Cui,

Cui, omnes morum, virtutumque dotes bellicarum,
    In cumulum accefferunt,

CARMEN.

DENIQUE venturum fatis volventibus annum [*e*]
    Cuncta per extenfum læta videnda diem,
Excuffis adfunt curis, fub imagine [*f*] clarâ
    Felices populi, terraque lege virens.
[*g*] Te duce, [*h*] quæ fuerant malefuadâ mente peracta
    Irrita, confpectu non reditura tuo.
Ergo omnis populus, nec non plebecula cernet
    [*h*] Hæfurum collo te [*i*] *relēgāſſe* jugum,
Et mala, quæ diris quondam cruciatibus, infons
    Infula paffa fuit; condoluiffet onus
Ni victrix tua Marte manus prius inclyta, noftris
    Sponte [*k*] ruinofis rebus adeffe velit.
Optimus es fervus *Regi* fervire *Britanno*,
    Dum gaudet genio [*l*] *Scotica* terra tuo :
Optimus herôum populi [*m*] fulcire ruinam ;
    Infula dum fupereft ipfe [*n*] fuperftes eris.
Victorem agnofcet te *Guadaloupa*, fuorum
    Defpiciet [*o*] meritò diruta caftra ducum.
Aurea vexillis flebit jactantibus [*p*] *Iris*,
    Cumque fuis populis, oppida victa gemet.

[*e*] *Afpice venturo lætentur ut omnia* Sæclo. *Virg*. E. iv. 52.

[*f*] *Clara* feems to be rather an improper epithet joined to *Imago*.

[*g*] *Te duce*, fi qua manent fceleris veftigia noftri
Irrita, perpetua folvent formidine terras.   *Virg*. E. iv. 13.

[*h*] Alluding perhaps to the conteft about removing the feat of government and public offices from *Spanifh Town* to *Kingfton*, during the adminiftration of governor Kn——s.

[*i*] Pro *rēlēvāſſe*.

[*k*] Quem vocet divûm populus *ruentis*
    Imperî *rebus*.   *Hor*. Lib. I. Od. ii.

[*l*] Mr. Haldane was a native of North Britain.

[*m*] Tu Ptolomæe potes magni *fulcire ruinam*. Lucan. *Lib*. viii. 528.

[*n*] This was a promife of fomewhat more than antediluvian longevity. But the poet proved a falfe prophet, for Mr. Haldane did not furvive the delivery of this addrefs many months.

[*o*] Egerit *jufto domitos* triumpho. *Hor*. Lib. I. Od. xii.

[*p*] *Iris*. Botanic name of the *fleur-de-luce*, alluding to the arms of France.

I   Crede,

Crede, [q] meum non eft, vir *Marti* chare! [r] *Minerva*
　　Denegat *Æthiopi* bella fonare ducum.
Concilio, caneret te *Buchananus* et armis,
　　Carmine *Peleidæ* fcriberet ille parem.
Ille poeta, decus patriæ, tua facta referre
　　Dignior, [s] altifono vixque *Marone* minor.
[t] Flammiferos agitante fuos fub fole *jugales* [u]
　　Vivimus; eloquium deficit omne focis.
Hoc demum accipias, multâ fuligine fufum
　　Ore fonaturo; non cute, corde valet.
Pollenti ftabilita manu, ([w] Deus almus, eandem
　　Omnigenis animam, nil prohibente dedit)
Ipfa coloris egens virtus, prudentia; honefto
　　Nullus ineft animo, nullus in arte color.
Cur timeas, quamvis, dubitefve, nigerrima celfam
　　Cæfaris occidui, fcandere [x] *Mufa* domum?
[y] Vade falutatum, nec fit tibi caufa pudoris,
　　[z] *Candida quod nigrâ corpora pelle geris!*
Integritas morum [a] *Maurum* magis ornat, et ardor
　　Ingenii, et docto [b] *dulcis in ore decor;*

[q] *Phœbus,* volentem prælia me loqui
　　Victas et urbes, increpuit lyra
　　Ne.　　　　　　　　　*Hor.*

[r] Invitâ Minervâ. 　*Hor. de Art. Poet.*

[s] *Maronis altifoni* carmina. 　*Juv. Sat.* xi. ver. 178.

[t] *Flammiferas* rotas toto cælo *agitat.*

[u] I apprehend Mr. Williams miftook this for *jŭbără,* fun beams.

[w] This is a *petitio principii,* or begging the queftion, unlefs with Mr. Pope,
　　　" All are but parts of one ftupendous whole,
　　　" Whofe body nature is, and God the foul."
　　　But,
　　　" Far as creation's ample range extends,
　　　" The *fcale* of fenfual *mental* powers afcends."

[x] Mr. Williams has added a *black Mufe* to the Pierian choir; and, as he has not thought proper to beftow a name upon her, we may venture to announce her by the title of madam *Æthiopiffa.*

[y] *Vade falutatûm* fubitò perarata parentem
　　Litera. 　　*Ovid.*

[z] See his apophthegms before-mentioned.

[a] *Maurus* is not in claffic ftrictnefs proper Latin for a *Negroe.*

[b] *Mollis in ore decor. Incert.*

Hunc,

" The general *order*, fince the whole began,
" Is kept in *nature*, and is kept in *man*.
" *Order* is heaven's firft law; and, this confeft,
" *Some are*, and *muft be, greater* than the reft."

C H A P. V.

S E C T. I.

An Abftract of the Jamaica *Code Noir*, or Laws affecting Negroe and other Slaves in that Ifland.—And, firft of, PENAL CLAUSES.

Anno

1696 N° 1. Straggling flaves, apprehended without a ticket (or pafs), are to be punifhed with *moderate* whipping.

2. Striking or doing violence to a white perfon (except by command of their mafter or employer, or in defence of his perfon or goods), punifhable at difcretion of two juftices and three freeholders, according to circumftances.

3. Stolen goods found in the cuftody of a flave—fuch flave on conviction of receiving, knowing them to have been ftolen to fuffer death, tranfportation, difmembering [*h*], or other punifhment, at the difcretion of two juftices and three freeholders.

4. Wilfully returning from tranfportation, *death*.

5. Compaffing or imagining the death of a white perfon, and being attainted thereof by *open deed* (or *ouvert act*), before two juftices and three freeholders, *death*.

6. [*i*] On complaint made to a juftice of any felony, burglary,

[*h*] This inhuman penalty is entirely obfolete, and never of late inflicted. It is, however, reproachful to the laws, and ought to be expunged. Fugitives were formerly punifhed here with amputation of their toes. This execrable barbarity hindered them from *running* away, but it prevented them likewife from rendering effectual fervice to their owner; and for this reafon, perhaps, more than from a juft fenfe of its impropriety, it was difcontinued. Men are too often difpofed to be cruel, of their own depraved hearts; and it becomes a Chriftian legiflature not to inflame and encourage, but to reprefs as much as poffible, this fanguinary difpofition, by giving example throughout its penal ordinances, of *juftice in mercy*.

[*i*] The reafon of not allowing a jury, inftead of this mode, probably was, the fcarcity of Whites fpread over the country, and that, in a time of infurrection and rebellion, the proceedings could not be too fummary. The fummoning twenty or thirty Whites, in order to make fure of 12 appearances on the panel, would have required too much time and delay, and have often been impracticable. Add to this, that the Whites never confidered themfelves as the *pares* of the Blacks. The prefent mode, by two juftices, and three freeholders, five perfons in all, of whom the party immediately interefted can never be one, who are indifferent and unbiaffed, and upon oath to judge uprightly, according to evidence, is perhaps fufficient to anfwer all the ends of impartial judicature with refpect to thefe people.

robbery,

robbery; burning of houses, canes; rebellions; confpiracies; or other capital offences; the juftice is to iffue his
warrant to apprehend the offenders, and for fummoning
the evidence before him. The evidence of one flave to
be admitted againft another flave; and if, upon examination, it appears, *primâ facie*, that the offenders are guilty,
he is to commit them to prifon, certify accordingly, and
affociate himfelf with another juftice. Thefe two are then
to cite three freeholders, intimating the caufe, and appointing a certain day and place for the trial to be held;
and if, upon full and due hearing of the matter (the freeholders being firft fworn, by the juftices, to judge uprightly, and according to the evidence), they deem the cul-
prits guilty, judgement is then forthwith to be given, of
death, tranfportation, or other punifhment, as they, in
their judgement, fhall think meet to inflict.

7. All *petit* crimes, trefpaffes, and injuries, committed by a
flave, are to be heard and determined by any of his
majefty's juftices within the ifland.

1711   8. Slaves, deftroying fifh by poifoning, ufing nets of mefhes
lefs than one inch and a quarter, or deftroying turtle eggs,
or killing pigeons, in the months of May, June, or
July, are punifheable with [*k*] *thirty-one lafhes* on the
bare back, on conviction before a juftice of the peace.

9. To put a ftop to the wanton flaughter of old breeding
cattle and marked young ones, with other abufes of the
like fort, no flave to keep any horfes, mares, mules,
affes, or cattle, on penalty of forfeiting the fame.

10. No flave to hire himfelf out to work to another, without
confent of his owner, or employer. Penalty, upon conviction before a magiftrate, whipping at the magiftrate's
difcretion, not exceeding *thirty-one lafhes* [*k*].

11. Hawking about and felling goods [*l*] (except provifions,
fruits, and other enumerated articles) to be punifhed,

[*k*] By the Jewifh laws, a wicked man, worthy to be beaten, was to be beaten before the judge,
according to his fault: *forty* ftripes might be inflicted; and not to exceed. Deut. xxv. 3. In
another place, we are told, the punifhment was *forty* ftripes, *fave one*. Numb. xxv.

[*l*] This reftraint is conftrued to extend only to beef, veal, mutton, and falt-fifh; and to manufactures, except bafkets, ropes of bark, earthen pots, and fuch like.

on

on conviction before a magiftrate, by whipping, not exceeding *thirty-one lafhes*.   See N° 20.

12. Selling, or giving away, fugar or fugar-canes, without a ticket; on conviction, whipping as above.

13. Free perfons, or flaves [m] buying fuch goods, to forfeit 10*l*, and fuffer punifhment by whipping, not exceeding *twenty lafhes*.

1749 14. [n] A flave of eighteen years of age, or upwards, being a native of the ifland, or refident in it three years from the time of importation, running away and abfenting himfelf for fix whole months, is to be tried as for a capital offence; and, upon due proof and conviction, is to fuffer *death*, or fuch other punifhment as the court fhall think fit to adjudge; provided that profecution be commenced within three months after his being taken or returned; and, further, that no owner fhall be repaid for any flave fo executed, but that the lofs fhall fall upon fuch owner [o].

15. A

[m] Some Jews, however, have been known to accumulate feveral cafks of fugar in a year, purloined, in fmall quantities at a time, by the Negroes, who were handfomely rewarded for robbing their mafters.

[n] There feems a great degree of hardfhip on the face of this claufe, in fubjecting flaves to the penalty of a capital crime, who perhaps may be ignorant of the penalty they incur.   The policy on which it is founded is, that all penal laws are made *in terrorem*, and for prevention: fo is this.   If one flave might elope into the woods, there abide with impunity, and form a fettlement; fo might ten thoufand, to the ruin of the colony.   A law to the fame effect, paffed thirty-two years before, fet forth, " that many crimes, committed by flaves, which were punifhable with " death, often remained undetected, by omiffion of their owners to profecute."   The owner is neceffarily the profecutor; and the provifo, which fubjects him to the entire lofs of the value of his flave, if he profecutes to conviction, effectually prevents fuch profecutions from being commenced; for which reafon, this claufe is *felo de fe*, and utterly non-effective.   And, confidering the feverity which it breathes, it is beft it fhould be fo; or elfe be repealed, and the punifhment altered to tranfportation: for to inflict *death* on a poor wretch, for a tranfgreffion, committed perhaps through mere ignorance of the law, or enormous ill ufage, is highly tyrannical and cruel.

[o] It feems to be an imperfection in thefe claufes, that the punifhment is, in many cafes, left undefined and arbitrary.   The plain meaning of the legiflature in the ftructure of them, where an alternative is admitted, was to give room for a mitigation, or commutation of the penalty expreffed, according to the circumftances of each cafe, and the greater or lefs degree of guilt that might appear.   This was commendable, and confonant to the penal claufes which govern the navy and army of Great-Britain.   But it is a great defect in them, not to require thefe reftrictions, and penalties, to be duly promulgated among the Negroes; for how can they reafonably be condemned upon laws which they never fee or know?   Unlefs they are duly apprized of what
they

15. [*p*] A slave, harbouring, concealing, or entertaining, a runaway slave, *knowing him to be such,* upon due conviction and proof before two justices and three freeholders, to suffer *death,* or be otherwise punished at the discretion of the court; provided that the prosecution be commenced within one month next after the discovery of such offence.

16. [*q*] Slaves, hunting cattle, horses, mares, &c. with lances, guns, cutlasses, or other instruments of death, unless in company with their master, &c. or other white person by him or them deputed, on conviction before two justices and three freeholders, to be adjudged guilty of felony, and be transported.

17. No slave to carry fire-arms about the island without a ticket from his owner or employer, under penalty of such corporal punishment (not extending to life or limb) as two justices shall think meet to inflict.

18. [*r*] A person killing a slave in the fact of stealing, or running away, or found in the night out of his owner's or employer's estate, or on the road, and refusing to submit, such person not liable to action or damage for the same.

they are to do, and what they are not to do, and are admonished of the certain punishment they will incur by doing so and so; these unlettered savages might as well be condemned on the laws of Japan or Crim-Tartary. I should, however, have excepted this particular act, which the *custos* of every parish is directed to take the most effectual methods for making public.

[*p*] So, Exod. xxi. 16, " He that stealeth a man, and selleth him, or if he be found in his hand, " he shall surely be put to death." This, I presume, extended as well to stealing another Jew's slave, as stealing a fellow-Jew, in order to sell him for a slave to a Gentile nation. By ver. 8, it appears, that a Jew might sell his own daughter for a slave, except to a Gentile or strange nation. Deut. xxiii. 15. " Thou shalt not deliver unto his master the servant which is escaped from his " master unto thee." " He shall dwell with thee." This must be understood of a slave belonging to a stranger, or Gentile, and not to a brother Jew; for, otherwise, it would be repugnant to the sense of the preceding statute.

[*q*] By act 14 George II. cap. 6, stealing of sheep and cattle is made felony without benefit of clergy. And 15 George II. cap. 34, explaining the former act, declares sheep and cattle to extend to any bull, cow, ox, steer, bullock, heifer, calf, and lamb. So horse-stealers are excluded from clergy.

[*r*] So, Exod. xxii. 2, 3, " If a thief be found breaking-up" in the *night,* " and be smitten that " he die, there shall no blood be shed for him." But, if in the *day-time,* such killing is murder. The penalty on the thief, in this case, is restitution of the things stolen, or the value; or, having not wherewithal to pay the value, then to be sold for a slave.

19. A

19. A flave, *malicioufly* giving poifon to any free perfon, or flave, and being convicted thereof before two juftices and three freeholders, to be adjudged guilty of murder, and to fuffer death.

20. A flave, felling in any public place, or market, any other goods than fuch as properly belong to his owner, or for his owner's ufe, and that are not expreffed in a ticket, upon complaint and conviction before a juftice, to be *whipped* by order of fuch juftice. See Nᵒ 11.

1760 21. [*s*] *Obeiah-men*, pretended conjurors, or priefts, upon conviction before two juftices and three freeholders of their practifing as fuch, to fuffer death, or tranfportation, at the difcretion of the court.

22. Slaves, convicted before two juftices and three freeholders of having in their cuftody fire-arms, gun-powder, bayonet, fword, or other military offenfive weapon (except in company with, or under the direction of, a white perfon, or having a ticket, or licence, in writing, from their owner, overfeer, or employer), to fuffer *death*, or other punifhment, at the difcretion of the court.

1768 23. Slaves, attempting to defert from the ifland in any fhip, boat, &c. and being convicted before two juftices and three freeholders, to fuffer *death*, or other punifhment, at the difcretion of the court.

1769 24. Slaves, taking ftones or ballaft from the *Pallifadoes, imprifonment*, not exceeding three months.

25. Slaves, found felling frefh-fifh in any part of Kingfton, except at the fifh-market, within the market-hours of eight in the morning and two in the afternoon, punifhable at the difcretion of any of the magiftrates in that parifh; and fuch fifh to be forfeited, and diftributed to the poor.

[*s*] Many of thefe incendiaries, called marbûts, or marabouts, on the coaft of Guiney, are banifhed from their own country for mal-practices.

S E C T. II.

Diſtributive and Munerary.

Anno.
1696   1. Male ſlaves are to have jackets and drawers; and female
ſlaves, jackets and petticoats; ſupplied them once a year,
under penalty of five ſhillings, to be paid by the owner or
maſter for every default [*t*].

2. Conſtables are to preſent all ſuch defaulters every year
to the juſtices; and ſuch conſtables to be charged on
oath, by the juſtices, to do their duty herein.

3. All maſters, owners, &c. are to have [*u*] one acre of
ground, well planted with proviſions, for every *five* ſlaves
belonging to them, under penalty of 40 *s.* for every ſuch
acre deficient.

4. Gaol-keepers, having cuſtody of run-away ſlaves, are to
ſupply them with convenient food, water, and dry
lodging, on penalty of 40 *l.* for every default.

5. A ſlave, taking up a run-away, and bringing to the
owner or to the next gaol, ſhall receive one ſhilling *per*
mile for the firſt five miles, and eight-pence *per* mile for
every other, ſo that the whole does not exceed 40 *s.* And
any perſon, depriving or defrauding the ſlave of ſuch reward, ſhall forfeit *treble* the value.

6. A ſlave, taking priſoner or killing a rebellious ſlave, to
receive 40 *s.*, and a coat with a red croſs upon it. By
a ſubſequent act, the reward is raiſed to 10 *l.*

7. Female convicts, pregnant, to be reſpited from execution until after their delivery.

[*t*] On every well-regulated plantation they are allowed, beſides a ſuit of warm woollen cloaths,
hats, caps, checks, handkerchiefs, working aprons to the boilers, beads, needles, thread, knives, ſciſ-
ſars, pipes, tobacco, iron pots, ſalt, ſugar, rum, &c. As to holiday-ſuits and finery, the ſettled
Negroes are very able to afford them out of their own profits. Tradeſmen and chief Negroes
receive a ſtated weekly allowance of beef, herring, or ſalt-fiſh; the reſt occaſionally. Every ſuch
eſtate has a convenient hoſpital for the ſick; where they are duly provided with medicines, nurſes,
and ſuitable diet, and neceſſaries.

[*u*] In England one acre of good land is deemed ſufficient to maintain four perſons, or three
oxen, or two aſſes, or twelve ſheep. The ſuperior fertility of the Weſt-India land makes a confiderable difference.

8. All masters, mistresses, owners, employers, &c. are to endeavour, as much as possible, the instruction of their slaves in the principles of the Christian religion; and facilitate their conversion; and do their utmost to fit them for baptism; and, as soon as convenient, cause all such to be baptized as they can make sensible of a Deity, and the Christian faith [*w*].

9. The justices, at their first session in every year, are to appoint the number of holidays to be given to slaves at Christmas, Easter, and Whitsuntide [*x*].

1735

[*w*] All the Creole slaves ought to be baptized, under a high penalty on their owners for neglecting it; and the baptismal fees should be fixed by law at a low rate; for example, at six-pence each; which, supposing there are now one hundred thousand unbaptized Creoles in the island, would bring in to the clergy there 2500 *l.*

" In all civilized states two things may be observed, which may be considered as the great foun-
" dation and support of political society : the first of these, the ceremonies that accompany the
" union of a man with a woman, which fix and regulate the ties of marriage, and the state of chil-
" dren ; the second, the ceremonies of public worship solemnly paid to the Deity. These two
" have been found, by legislators, the wisest and most effectual means for the support and good go-
" vernment of states." Goguet.

[*x*] The Negroes are so sensible of their right to these, and their leisure-hours of each day in the intervals of work, that they call them emphatically *their own time*. Nor is it ever borrowed from them but in some very particular emergency, when they are either paid for it, as may be agreed upon, or allowed an equal portion of time on some other day. They generally begin work at six in the morning, and leave off at six in the afternoon, having half an hour at breakfast, and on most estates two hours at noon. Thus their day's work is nine hours and a half in general. Their leisure-times, on most estates, are Saturday afternoon, except in case of very urgent business ; every Sunday throughout the year; three days at Christmas, two at Easter, and two at Whitsuntide ; and, at some estates, a jubilee-day, on finishing crop : so that the whole number of days, they have to themselves in the course of the year, is about eighty-six. The Jews allow their slaves Saturday (which is their sabbath), and Sunday (which is the Christian's) : their slaves have therefore about one hundred and eleven holidays in the year at least ; which amount to more than three months out of the twelve. The usual gross value of a Negroe's labour, hired *per diem*, being about two shillings ; a Christian's Negroe (supposing him not more conscientious than barbers, tavern-keepers, inn-keepers, stable-keepers, and many shop-keepers, are on the Lord's-day in England) gains for himself 8*l.* 12*s.* in value of his labour, and a Jew's slave 11*l.* 2*s.*, *per annum.* But it is well known, that many of them gain infinitely more, since the produce of one day's labour for themselves will turn out more worth than a fortnight's hire.

An ingenious writer observes hereupon, " The principal time I would have reserved, for indul-
" gence to the slaves, is Sunday, which is prophaned in a manner altogether scandalous in our co-
" lonies. On this day some pains should certainly be taken to instruct them, to the best of their
" comprehension, especially the children, in some of the principles of religion and virtue, parti-
" cularly in the humility, submission, and honesty, which become their condition. And, if one
" whole day in the week, or two half-days at proper distance, were allowed for their private labour
" in their grounds, in lieu of Sundays, they would more chearfully bear fatigue during the other

" five

1735 10. Slaves may carry about, and fell, all manner of provifions, fruits, fresh fish, milk, poultry, and other small stock of all kinds, having a ticket from their owner, or employer.

11. No flave to be difmembered at the will and pleafure of his owner, mafter, or employer, under penalty of 100 *l.* payable to the informer.

1751 12. To prevent the bloody, inhuman, and wanton killing of flaves, any perfon, fo offending, to be adjudged, for the firft offence, on conviction, guilty of felony, and have benefit of clergy; and fuffer the further punifhment of imprifonment, as the court fhall award, not exceeding the term of twelve months; and, for the fecond offence, fuch perfon to fuffer death, but not to work corruption of blood, nor forfeiture of lands, chattels, &c. [*y*].

SECT.

"five days; and, by means of thefe intervals, have time to recruit their ftrength, fo as, on the "days appropriated to their mafters labour, to go through more work, and perform it better, than "they commonly are able to do under their prefent regulations; for it is eafy to conceive, that, "with moderate intervals of reft, any man will better, and with lefs hurt to his body, execute a "given quantity of work, than he can poffibly perform without them; fo that, at the week's end, "the fame quantity of labour, at leaft, would be gone through, with no injury to their healths, "nor wafte of fpirits, which is now poffibly performed with injury to both. With a tincture of "religious precepts, as far as can be adapted to their capacity, they would grow more honeft, "tractable, and lefs of eye-fervants; unlefs it can be proved (contrary to univerfal experience), "that the fanctions of religion, and doctrines of morality, and all the habits of an early inftruc-"tion, are of no advantage to mankind." Thefe opinions are founded in policy and truth; but difficulties would attend the adoption of them in practice, although far from being infurmountable. It is certain, that the fabbath-day, as at prefent it is paffed, is by no means a day of refpite from labour: on the contrary, the Negroes, either employing it in their grounds, or in traveling a great diftance to fome market, fatigue themfelves much more on that day, than on any other in the week. The forenoon of that day, at leaft, might be given to religious duties; but I think it rather defirable than othèrwife, that the after-part of it fhould be fpent in their grounds, inftead of being ufelefsly diffipated in idlenefs and lounging, or (what is worfe) in riot, drunkennefs, and wickednefs. If fuch an alteration fhould take place, Thurfday might be affigned for the market-day, inftead of the fabbath, and prove of great advantage to all the Chriftian fhop-keepers and retailers; the Jews now engroffing the whole bufinefs of trafficking with the Negroes every Sunday, at which time there is a prodigious refort of them to the towns, and a vaft fum expended for drams, neceffaries, and manufactures. This alteration would therefore place the Chriftian dealers upon an equal, fair footing, which they do not at prefent enjoy. The whole number of Negroe holidays in the year would then amount to one hundred and eleven, which is no more than the Jews at prefent allow to their flaves; and, by this divifion of the time, they would probably grow improved in their behaviour, as well as in their ability and willingnefs to ferve their Chriftian owners.

[*y*] So, Exod. xxi. 20, 21. "If a man fmite his fervant with a rod, and he die under his "hand, he fhall furely be punifhed." But in what manner the text does not explain; though it is

evident

SECT. III.

Remarks on the Negroe Regulations.

THE Negroe code of this iſland appears originally to have copied from the model in uſe at Barbadoes; and the legiſlature of this latter iſland, which was the firſt planted by the Engliſh, reſorted to the Engliſh *villeinage* laws, from whence they undoubtedly transfuſed all that ſeverity which characterizes them, and ſhews the

evident no *capital puniſhment* is here meant. But, " If he continue a day or two" *alive*, " he ſhall " not be puniſhed; for he is his money." Strange (ſays Monteſquieu), that a civil law ſhould thus relax the law of nature.!

One Lockwood (who was afterwards proved to be a lunatic) inhumanly butchered his ſlave; which gave riſe to this act. I remember one inſtance of a man convicted upon it; and, it being his firſt offence, he was burnt in the hand.

By the law of Pennſylvania, a white owner, who kills his Negroe ſlave with malice prepenſe, is liable to ſuffer *death* for it. There is not, however, any example there of an owner having been executed for this crime. A few years ago, a maſter murdered his ſlave; upon which, his friends, and even the magiſtrates, ſecretly adviſed him to leave the country, as, otherwiſe, they could not avoid apprehending him; in which caſe, he muſt be adjudged to die, according to the law, without any hope of ſaving him. This lenity (ſays Kalm) was employed, that the Negroes might not have the ſatisfaction of ſeeing a maſter executed for killing his ſlave; for this would lead them to dangerous deſigns againſt their maſters, and to ſet too high a value upon themſelves. I muſt beg leave here to differ a little in opinion from this writer. An impartial execution of juſtice, and the law, upon thoſe who wantonly ſhed innocent blood, muſt inevitably attract a high veneration to ſuch a law from the Negroes, and induce them to regard *murder* in the moſt atrocious light, when they ſee it puniſhed with ſuch exemplary ſeverity without reſpect of per-ſons; for, ſurely, no pretence can juſtify ſuch execrable deeds: the guilty perſon puts himſelf out of all protection of human law, when he commits the crime; he ceaſes to be conſidered as a man; he becomes a ſavage beaſt; and, whatever may be his complexion, the good of ſociety and ſound policy require he ſhould ſuffer *capitally*, as an example of terror to Black as well as White At preſent, a Negroe ſees only what may juſtify him in retaliation. The law of the Whites plainly tells him, " If a white man murders a white man, he ought to *die* for it; but, if a white " man murders a black man, he ought to be *acquitted!*" Is not the Negroe led to eſpouſe the very ſame principle and creed *ex converſo?* " I believe," he may ſay, " that it is a very great " crime for a Negroe to murder a Negroe; but for a Negroe to murder a white man is no crime " at all; at leaſt, I infer as much from the law of the Whites, which meaſures the extent of guilt, " not according to reaſon, but according to the tincture of the ſkin; they favour the White, and " we the Black, with equal propriety and juſtice."

It was, I think, very much to the honour of government, that the following inſtructions were given to ſome of the firſt commanders in chief of this iſland:

" You ſhall endeavour to get a law paſſed for reſtraining of any inhuman ſeverity, by reaſon of " ill maſters or overſeers, that may be uſed towards their Chriſtian ſervants, or other ſlaves. And " you are alſo, with the aſſiſtance of the council and aſſembly, to find out the beſt means to faci-" litate and encourage the converſion of Negroes to the Chriſtian religion."

" And

the abject flavery which the common people of England formerly laboured under. In the 34th of Edward III, for example, a labourer, or flave, fleeing from his mafter's fervice into any town or city, the chief officer of the place was required to deliver him up to his mafter; fo, if he eloped into another country, he was to be burned in the forehead with the letter F. Whoever ferved in hufbandry till the age of twelve, was to continue in that ftation ever after; and not be bound or put out to any trade, or artifice. By another act, 12 Richard II, *anno* 1388, no artificer, labourer, or fervant, was allowed to pafs from one hundred to another, without a permit under the king's feal, unlefs fent on bufinefs by his lord, or mafter, on pain of being fet in the ftocks, and compelled to return. But the moft remarkable badge of fervility was impofed, in the 1ft of Edward VI, by the ftatute againft vagabonds; which adjudges them abfolutely and exprefsly flaves; inflicts feveral violent punifhments, by beating, chaining, &c. to force them to work for their owner; punifhes run-aways, for the firft offence, by branding on the cheek with a red-hot iron; and, for the fecond offence, by *death*. This law likewife empowers the mafter to put an iron ring about his flave's neck, arm, or leg, for fafer cuftody; and lays a penalty of 10 *l.* on any perfon taking it off without the mafter's confent. A man, detaining or harbouring another's run-away flave, knowing him to be fuch, is made liable to an action of trefpafs, and 10 *l.* damages. The fervice of fuch flaves might be hired out, fold, or bequeathed, as any other moveable goods and chattels. And any fuch flave, confpiring to murder, kill, or maim, his mafter or miftrefs, or to burn their houfes, barns, or corn, lying in wait with a weapon, or committing any overt act leading to fuch effect, was to fuffer death as a felon. If the father, mother, nurfe, or bearer about, of a child

"And whereas, amongft other laws paffed in Jamaica the 5th of April, 1683, an act for regu-
"lating flaves was tranfmitted unto his late majefty, who did not think fit to confirm the fame, by
"reafon of a claufe therein contained, whereby fuch, as wantonly and wilfully kill a Negroe,
"are only liable to a fine and three months imprifonments; which penalties, not being equal to
"the guilt, might encourage the wilful fhedding of blood; for which it is neceffary fome better
"provifion be made, to deter all perfons from fuch acts of cruelty; you are therefore to fignify
"the fame unto the next affembly, and further propofe to them the enacting a ftricter claufe in
"that behalf, which may be fit for our royal confirmation." The law is certainly not yet fevere
enough in this refpect.

adjudged

adjudged a flave, fhould fteal, or entice, away fuch child from its mafter; fuch father, mother, &c. were to be adjudged flaves to fuch child's mafter for ever. I think the word *flave* occurs no lefs than *thirty-eight* different times in the courfe of this ftatute. But this is not the only inftance of legiflative barbarity at home. In the 13th of Elizabeth, 1571, upon reading a bill then before the houfe for fuppreffion of vagabonds, Mr Sandys endeavoured to prove the above-mentioned law of Edward VI. to be too fharp and bloody, ftanding much on the care which is to be had for the poor. Wilfon, mafter of the requefts, argued thus: that poor, of neceffity, we muft have; and as true it is, that beggars by God's word might not be among his people, *ne fit mendicans inter vos*; that it was no charity to give to a ftranger; and that even as thieves did the Greeks judge of them. In the following year, the law paffed which enacted, " that every perfon above the age of *fourteen*, " being taken begging, or going about as a vagrant, fhould, for the " firft offence, be grievoufly whipped, and burned through the " griftle of the right ear with an hot iron of an inch compafs; " and, if of *eighteen* years of age, if he afterwards fall into a " roguifh life, to be adjudged a *felon*." A ftatute of 8 Elizabeth, c. 3, enacted, that perfons, bringing, delivering, fending, receiving, or taking, or procuring to be brought, &c. into any fhip, or bottom, to be carried out of the kingdom, any ram, fheep, or lamb, alive, fhould, for the firft offence, forfeit all their goods for ever, fuffer a year's imprifonment, and at the year's end have their left hands cut off in a market-town, to be there publickly nailed up; and, for the fecond offence, fhould fuffer death. The modes of punifhment in thefe ftatutes, and the general provifions contained in the ftatute of Edward VI, have fo near an affinity to the Barbadoes law refpecting Negroe flaves, as to leave fcarcely any doubt but that the legiflature of that ifland tranfcribed from thefe precedents, which they found in the mother ftate. At the time we firft entered on the fettlement of Barbadoes, the idea of flavery could hardly be extinguifhed in England; the firft emigrants to the Weft-Indies, it is natural to think, carried with them fome prejudices in favour of the villeinage fyftem, fo far as it might feem to coincide with the government of Negroe-labourers. They

perceived

perceived very strong traces of it in the before-cited statutes; and the expediency and propriety of rigorous penalties, were pointed out to them, from time to time, after the reign of Elizabeth, by the star-chamber judgements. Many other vestiges besides remained still fresh in the mother-country, which were supported by law; in the regulation, discipline, and punishment (for example) of vagabonds, of labourers, of apprentices, of soldiers, seamen, the workers in coal and saltmines; all which favoured much of the antient coercions under which they had lain, and which indeed to the present hour have been little more relaxed, except by mitigating the cruelty of some punishments, and giving a protection in life and limb against wanton violences, which in truth is no contemptible triumph over the extreme severity of their primitive bondage. The penal laws in England were always sanguinary, and still retain this savage complexion; which has given occasion to an ingenious author to assert, " that they seem " rather calculated to keep *slaves* in awe, than to govern *freemen*; " they seem to contradict all notions of justice, and confound all " distinctions of morality. By the ignominy they impose in many " cases, they bend the mind to the lowest state of servitude; by the " rigour thay indiscriminately inflict, they adopt the principles of " despotism, and make *fear* the motive of obedience [z]."

One of the greatest imputations against the Negroe laws is, that, in many cases, they leave the punishment to be inflicted arbitrarily by their judges. This is precisely adopted from the law-martial, enacted for the discipline of the fleet and army, which leaves the punishment to be invented, as well as proportioned, by the court. The Negroes in our colonies might, perhaps, have fared better, if their masters had taken the Athenian slave code for their guide, instead of ransacking the statute-law of England for modes of judging and chastizing them. But the idea of assimilating to the practice of the mother-state influenced them to this conformity in those points, which perhaps less merited their imitation than any other. It was a further disadvantage, that the first form of government, exercised in these colonies, was of the military kind; whose sanctions did not tend in the least to diminish their judicial aspe-

[z] Considerations on Criminal Law.

rity.

rity. The Africans, firſt imported, were wild and ſavage to an extreme: their intractable and ferocious tempers naturally provoked their maſters to rule them with a rod of iron; and the earlieſt laws enacted to affect them are therefore rigid and inclement, even to a degree of inhumanity. By what means it happened, that, from the firſt colonization in the Weſt-Indies, this race of men were ſo degraded as we find them, is not entirely clear. The Engliſh, probably, did no more than follow the ſteps of the Portugueze and other nations, who had begun, long before, to trade in Negroes as a commodity, and to hold them as mere chattels and moveables. Perhaps the depravity of their nature, much more than their colour, gave riſe to a belief of their inferiority of intellect; and it became an eſtabliſhed principle to treat thoſe as brute beaſts, who had ſo little pretenſions to claim kindred with the human race, except in the ſhape of their bodies, and their walking upon two legs inſtead of four. However it might be, certain it is, that the planters of that age thought it no greater crime to kill a Negroe, than to knock a monkey on the head.

So ſoon as the African trade became a national concern, from its importance, the parliament of Britain fell in with the general idea, and conſidered Negroes, purchaſed from that continent, as a lawful commercial property; and this in ſo ſtrong a ſenſe, that the greateſt oppreſſion, under which our Negroes in the iſlands at preſent labour, ariſes materially from the ordinance of that ſtatute [a], which declares them to be as houſes, lands, hereditaments, aſſets, and perſonal eſtate, transferrable, and amenable to payment of debts due to the king or his ſubjects. Since the *major* part of theſe Negroes, eſpecially in the older colonies, by having been born and trained up in them, have appeared more humanized than their anceſtors, the laws in theſe places have worn a milder aſpect: yet, as thouſands are every year introduced from Guiney, who differ not at all from the earlieſt imported in barbarity of manners; ſo the ſeverity of the firſt inſtitutions has ſtill been retained in ſeveral reſpects, which chiefly affect the Blacks of this claſs, although all are equally bound by them without exception. This obſervation leads me to enquire, whether ſome diſtinction might not be taken,

[a] 5 Geo. II. c. 7. and likewiſe 13 Geo. III. c. 14.

by our colony-laws, between the native or Creole Blacks and the imported favages; and whether the laws might not be mitigated in favour of the former clafs, and (without a weak or effeminate indulgence) be fo tempered, as to make their fervitude approach near to a well-regulated liberty. This would confift in giving them fuch a fecurity for life and limb, and fuch an attachment to the place of their birth, as may ferve to fweeten their toils, and engage them by the ftrongeft ties to be faithful fervants and defenders of the country. All punifhments by *mutilation* fhould be utterly abolifhed and prohibited, becaufe they are fcandaloufly cruel, not warranted by neceffity, nor juftified by utility; for it cannot be proved, that they are more effectual than more humane methods; and, when the laws of any country either dictate fuch inhumanities, or connive at them, they lend encouragement for individuals to feed a bloody and vindictive fpirit, which is difgraceful to the members of a civilized fociety.

The punifhment by *whipping* fhould be brought within fome limit; fo that overfeers might not with impunity tranfgrefs, through the heat of rage, a fit degree of juft correction; and as the degree, fo the *inftrument*, fhould be afcertained, and none permitted which may lacerate or disfigure the body.

A white perfon, found guilty of wantonly *murdering* a Negroe, fhould be adjudged a felon, and fuffer *death*. If convicted of wantonly maiming or difmembering (death not enfuing), and the owner be the offender, the flave fo maimed fhould be adjudged to enjoy his freedom, befides a compenfation for his maintenance, if he fhould be fo difabled as to be incapable of earning a livelihood. But, if the offence fhould be committed by another perfon, fine and imprifonment, with an adequate fatisfaction in money to the owner, may be thought no inequitable punifhment.

The penalty of *death* for *running away*, or abfenting for a certain fpace, fhould be commuted to fome milder for the firft offence; and, for the fecond, tranfportation: but the inveigling, harbouring, and concealing, fuch fugitives, might remain under the fame rigorous penalties as at prefent.

The fevereft punifhments ought, in juftice and policy, to fall on rebels, murderers, confpirers againft the public tranquillity, in-

cendiaries,

cendiaries, and rioters; runaways, found carrying unlawful weapons; and fuch as ftubbornly and wilfully refufe to labour; for it
is in confiftent with the general welfare, that any fhould be rebellious,
guilty of outrage and violence, idle, or vagrant.

Lenity in fome points, rigid feverity in others, protection to the
well-difpofed, and difcouragement to the abandoned and difaffected,
might prove the means of polifhing their manners, inciting them to
induftry, and enfuring their voluntary obedience. But nothing
would more effectually operate to thefe purpofes, than the admitting
fome alteration in the prefent laws for recovery of debts.

I have already pointed out, that making Negroes liable to be
feized for bond and fimple contract debts, and hurried from one part
of the ifland to another, conftitutes the chief oppreffion under
which they labour; renders their fervitude more bitter, and intolerable; and produces a very great annual lofs to the public, by the
mortality which it occafions.

I am fenfible, that the exigency of commercial contracts, and the
mixt nature which the laws of commerce have affigned to Negroes,
combat ftrongly againft an alteration. But the law of humanity,
and the general intereft of the ifland, plead more forcibly in favour
of it; and fince the utmoft a creditor can defire, is the payment of
his debt, or as good fecurity for it as his debtor can give, no injury
is done him, by changing an oppreffive mode, for one that is
not fo.

If, for example, Negroes were made *glebio adfcriptitii*, affixed
to the foil, and only liable to pafs with it; it is evident, they ftill
might pafs in defcent, or payment of contracts, or in fale. If bonds
and fimple contracts were left to take their remedy folely againft
other perfonal affets, or againft the produce of the Negroes labour;
or, thefe proving deficient, that then the whole eftate, land, and
Negroes, were liable to be fold collectively, for yielding full fatif-
faction; would the bond or fimple contract creditor be put into any
worfe fituation than a mortgagee, who has at prefent identically
the fame remedy? Perhaps no fcheme might anfwer the intention
better, than the committing debtors eftates *in truft*, as I have propofed in the courfe of this work: a variety of plans indeed might be
formed, for faving the creditor harmlefs; none however could be

carried

carried into execution, unlefs the act of parliament, before cited, was firft new modeled, and Negroes, more efpecially the natives of our iflands, diftinguifhed fome degrees above fheep and oxen. To make this improvement in the fyftem of our colony laws, were furely not unbecoming that liberal fpirit, which dignifies the prefent age : but the reform fhould begin *at home*; and doubtlefs would without difficulty be affented to by parliament, if the provincial affemblies were, upon the conviction of its utility, to facilitate their concurrence, by fubftituting an equivalent fecurity to the creditor. The circuity of action and delay, that attend recovery of mortgage debts, might probably be abridged, and mortgage deeds be made as negotiable in commerce, and as fummary in their procefs, as common bonds ; nor is there any juft reafon to be affigned, why that mode of fecurity fhould not then be given for a debt of fifty pounds, as well as for five hundred pounds ; in the colonies, many obftacles, that prevail in the mother country, are removed at once by the office where fuch contracts, and their affignments from hand to hand, are duly regiftered. So long as Negroes are feverable from the land, every colony is retarded in its progrefs ; for, as I have before remarked, it matters not (in a general view) how often the ownerfhip of a Weft-India eftate changes hands, *provided the Negroes pafs with the land*; but it is their feverance from it, which is effentially a depreciation of both, and extremely hurtful to the progrefs of induftry and fettlement in thefe iflands, particularly in Jamaica, where property

" puncto mobilis horæ

" Nunc prece, nunc pretio, nunc vi, nunc morte fuprema,
" Permutat dominos, et cedit in altera jura [*b*]."

" Shifting every hour,

" By gift, by purchafe, force, or fate's commands,
" Changes its lord, and falls to other hands."

To afcertain the Negroes who fhould pafs in this manner, would not be difficult ; fince every planter and landholder might be compelled to deliver annually to the juftices and veftry upon oath, a lift of the Negroes *bonâ fide* belonging to, and fettled upon, his refpective lands ; and where any doubt or difpute might arife, the *onus probandi*

[*b*] Hor. lib. II. Epift. ii.

might

might lie on the landholder. It is true, it may be faid, that every landholder has the remedy at prefent in his own hands; he has only to make his contracts by mortgage, inftead of bond or note; but the prolixity of mortgage deeds, which enumerate all the parcels of property, and contain a multitude of covenants and claufes, make them lefs convenient for ordinary tranfactions in borrowing and lending, efpecially for fmall fums; perhaps fuch deeds might be fhortened without lofing their efficacy; but, if this be impracticable, we muft then turn back to the firft propofition, in regard to bonds, and give them effective operation againft the planter's cattle, furniture, and implements, or (thefe failing) againft the annual produce, by fequeftration, until they are fully fatisfied. The iniquitous advantages which have been taken of the laws, as they now ftand, are innumerable: among the multitude of planters, fome will be found, whofe hearts are petrified with avarice, and rapacity; whofe views all center in felf; and who foar around with the keen appetite of vultures, feeking whom they may devour. I remember one of thefe harpies, who, in order to ftock his eftate with feafoned Negroes, went fyftematically to work. He engaged the deputy marfhal in his intereft, and having bought up judgements, extant againft feveral inferior fettlers in his neighbourhood, caufed their flaves to be levied on, and fold; he himfelf was the underhand purchafer, and thus found means to advance his own fortune, upon the certain ruin of many induftrious fettlers, who threw up their lands after being ftripped of their labourers; and this furnifhed him with a further opportunity of driving advantageous bargains, by engroffing the contiguous acres at a cheap rate.

The fallacy of their opinion, who fuppofe, that no harm is done by the fhifting of property, may be demonftrated in numberlefs inftances more than I have already given; and they all tend to prove thefe maxims: " That changing the property of lands from one " owner to another, can be of no injury to this ifland, in hindering " the fettlement and improvement of thofe lands, fuppofing the fkill " in hufbandry pretty equal at an average.

" But changing the property of labouring Negroes from one " owner to another, living in different places, obftructs the fettle- " ment of lands; turns thofe already fettled into ruinate; leffens the

" number

" number of planters, diminifhes the ftock of labouring Negroes,
" and produces a certain lofs to the community in various ways."

There is every year a certain number of thefe negroes, whofe labour (if I may fo exprefs myfelf) is in *abeyance*, from the time of heir being taken upon a writ of *venditioni*, to the time of their being being brought to a regular courfe of work again, at the place to which they are removed by their purchafer. The number of flaves fo levied on, one year with another, I compute, upon the beft grounds, four hundred ; and that their lofs of labour is equal at leaft to one month each in the year, without taking into account the time frequently fpent in their concealment, to prevent their falling into the marfhal's hands. In feven years the account will therefore ftand thus :

| Levied | } Negroes | 2,800 | { Value of lofs, computed at leaft at 84,000 *l.* currency. |
| Lofs of labour; | } Months | 7 | |

Of thefe Negroes, it is not eafy to difcover how many perifh by change of place, nor the lofs on the fale fuftained by their owners; but the latter muft be confiderable ; for, at an average, the Negroes, thus fold, have not yielded above 26 *l.* to 30 *l.* trett, which probably was not more than one third of their real worth, or what they would have been appraifed at, upon their fale with the land.

To conclude ; fince Negroes are the finews of Weft-India property, too much care cannot be taken of them ; and it well becomes a Chriftian legiflature, at the fame time that it conforms its policy to what may refpect their health, and ability for labour, to foften by every reafonable means the obduracy of their fervitude, fo as to make them forget the very idea of flavery ; together with this, I acknowledge that ftrict juftice and equitable inftitutions ought to guarrantee all legal contracts entered into either by the planter, or the merchant, or other individuals : but if the rigorous exactions of payment can admit of any alleviating meafures; if lands can be made more transferable by writ of *elegit*, or other fcheme of *extent*, or bonds and fimple contract debts be payable by other means, than hauling the Negroe labourers from one part of the country to another, tearing them from their fettlement and family, aggravating the hardfhip of their condition, and obftructing the population and culture of the ifland ; it well deferves the interpofition of legiflative wifdom and humanity, to amend the law, to let juftice flow in a fmooth eafy

current,

current, or to reſtrain, where it tranſgreſſes its bounds. It has been the opinion of very ſenſible writers, that the intereſt of our colonies demands, that the Negroes ſhould be better treated, and even raiſed to a better condition; this, however, muſt be underſtood with ſome exceptions againſt the imported Blacks, whoſe ſavage manners render them incapable of thoſe benefits conſiſtent with the ſafety of the colonies, which perhaps might be granted to the natives or Creoles, to a certain limit, without any ill conſequence. Some *medium*, it is ſaid, might be ſtruck, between liberty, and that abſolute ſlavery which now prevails; in this *medium* might be placed *all Mulattos,* after a certain temporary ſervitude to their owner; and ſuch *native Blacks,* as their owners, for their faithful ſervices, ſhould think proper to enfranchiſe. Theſe might have land allotted to them, or ſome ſort of fixed employment, from either of which they ſhould be obliged to pay a certain moderate rent to the public. Whatever they acquired beyond this, to be the reward of their induſtry. The neceſſity of paying a rent, would keep them employed; and when once men are ſet to work through neceſſity, they will not ſtop there; but will gradually ſtrive for conveniencies, and ſome even for ſuperfluities. All this muſt add to the conſumption of manufactures, and the cultivation of lands; and the colonies would be ſtrengthened by the addition of ſo many men, who have an intereſt of their own to fight for.

It becomes the gentlemen of Jamaica to ſet the example, and raiſe their iſland to the ſame rank of ſuperiority in the wiſdom and mildneſs of its laws, as it already enjoys in its extent and opulence, above the other Britiſh territories in the Weſt-Indies; let them boldly purſue every meaſure, which will tend to multiply their people, or to ſtrengthen their country againſt foreign enemies; let them, in order to prevent domeſtic ones, conciliate the attachment of their Negroes by protection and encouragement, rather than ſeek to exact an involuntary obedience by auſterity and terror. In the diſtribution of our gratitude, we are bound to beſtow ſome ſhare on thoſe, whom God has ordained to labour. The juſt ſubordination, within the line of which our Negroes muſt be kept, does by no means diſpenſe with our loving, and treating them humanely. We are obliged to it, both from reaſon and ſelf-intereſt; bodily ſtrength,

5   and

and their adaptation to the climate, would enable them to pass from the lowest to the highest stations, and give the law to their masters, if they were willing unanimously to attempt it; but when those who fill the lowest rank, are used with equity and benevolence, so far from becoming dreadful, by flocking together in order to trample upon us, they comply with whatever we require of them; they offer themselves willingly to be our defenders, and are themselves the instruments made use of to restrain one another within the bounds of their allotted condition. Among all the nations of antiquity, slaves were no where treated with greater humanity than at Athens, so celebrated for the wisdom of its laws, and the refined manners of its inhabitants.

Their slaves had an action against their owners, for acts of outrage and ill usage; if the fact was proved, the owner was obliged to sell his slave, who while the process depended, might retire into an asylum appointed to secure him from all intermediate violence [c]. The liberty of which the Athenians were so jealous was not interdicted to their slaves; the latter were authorized to purchase their freedom, in despite of their owners, whenever they had amassed the sum which the law had fixed for that purpose. It was not even unusual for a patron, who was content with the services of his slave, to grant him his liberty for a reward; this was a state of servitude so mildly regulated, that it differed but little in essentials from absolute freedom. Let the planters copy from this bright example, as far as prudence, and the disposition of Negroes, can admit; if the native slaves in our colony can with safety be brought under an enlarged degree of protection, and secured by rational provisions from violence and barbarity; or be permitted to redeem themselves from perpetuity of servitude, with the fair and honest earnings of their private industry; it seems highly just, humane, and politic, to favour them; that their allegiance to the country and white inhabitants, may be more firmly engaged; after obtaining their freedom, it still remains by legal regulations to enforce their employing themselves in some honest course of livelihood; they will then contribute largely not to the strength alone, but to

[c] This resembles the process under the antient English writ *de libertate probanda*, pending which, the villein, laying claim to freedom, was protected from the vexation of the suitor who challenged him.

the

the wealth and profperity of the ifland, and to the profits of Great Britain.

CHAP. VI.

REGULATIONS for preferving HEALTH in JAMAICA.

SECT. I.

PLACE of HABITATION and AIR.

OBSERVATION of the effects which the change from a cold to a hot climate produces on hard inanimate fubftances, fuch as wood, iron, and the like, muft naturally teach us to expect, that the human body, a fyftem of tubes and glands, or matter delicately organized, cannot pafs rapidly from the one to the other, without being affected in a proportionate degree.

As the heated air between the Tropics acts upon metals by expanfion; fo, when it acts upon the human body, it relaxes the folid parts, and rarefies the fluid, increafes the velocity of the blood's circulation, caufes an unufual difcharge of the bile, and a regurgitation of it into the ftomach, violent acute pains in the head, loathing of food, and ficknefs; hence feverifh diforders may enfue, which would be foon and eafily cured, if no other predifpofing caufes fupervened.

The authors, who have treated on this fubject with moft difcernment, agree pretty uniformly, in afcribing the malignancy of Weft India fevers to a vitiated air, either at fea, or on fhore.

At fea, occafioned by noxious exhalations, raifed during long continued calms, when the water, not being agitated as ufual by the trade winds, is fubject to become corrupt near the furface, where it is lefs charged with falt, to preferve it from ftinking.

On fhore, by the like exhalations, excited by the heat of the fun, from foul, oozy fhores, the naufeous ftagnant water of lagoons, and the fetid mud or foil of low, fwampy grounds.

This morbid air, admitted into the lungs and circulation, may induce a difpofition to putrefcency, and render thofe diforders of the frame malignant, which otherwife, perhaps, the efforts of nature alone, or but flightly affifted, might have thrown off.

Such an air may therefore be confidered truly poifonous to the hu- man conftitution; for which reafon, a firft and principal caution is, to avoid it as much as poffible; or, at leaft, to correct its baneful quality, or tendency, as much as may be, by fuitable antifeptic re- medies.

As we remark, that water, whether on fhore, or in the ocean, will grow corrupt in this climate, if, for any length of time, it is not put in motion; fo the fluids in the human body will become putrefcent, if due exercife is too long neglected: hence we may conclude, that habitual indolence and inactivity are likewife to be reckoned among the predifpofing caufes of bad fevers, in a hot climate. There are practical irregularities in regard to the reft of what phyficians have called the *non-naturals*, which may tend either co generate or exafpe- rate fuch fevers, and which I fhall occafionally advert to. Men who commit thefe, fin with their eyes open: but from the evils of a nox- ious atmofphere; numbers cannot fly, by reafon of the duties of fer- vice, and the exigencies of bufinefs. I fhall therefore give a firft atten- tion to the injuries deriveable from this fource; and, bringing together fuch general remarks on the means of fhunning or counteracting them, as gentlemen of the faculty, the moft eminent for their fkill and know- ledge in the fubject, have beneficently given to the public, apply them more particularly to this ifland. In this detail I fhall endeavour to fecond the humanity of their defign; claiming indulgence, at the fame time, for thofe fupplemental precepts and ftrictures which may be inter- fperfed, and meant to correfpond to the fame view.

The ingenious Doctor Lind remarks, that every country has its healthy and unhealthy fituations; and he inftances, in refpect to the former clafs, the ifland of Portfea, near Portfmouth, and the town of Brading, in the ifle of Wight; he might have added the marfhes of Kent, Effex, Lincolnfhire, and Cambridgefhire, and perhaps fome other fpots in England. In the Weft Indies fuch low fwampy fpots are ftill more fatal; and they are infefted with mufkeetos, which feem as if placed there by the hand of Providence, to affault with their ftings, and drive away, every human being, who may ignorantly ven- ture to fix his abode among them. It is moft dangerous to pafs the night in fuch places, and it is at fuch time that thefe infects collect in fwarms, and make war on every daring intruder. In fome parts of the

3   South

South American continent the torments they inflicted were so intolerable, that many houses, and even whole villages, were obliged to be deserted by the Spaniards and Indians; of which Ulloa gives an account, who, in his passage from Guayaquil to Caracol, suffered inexpressibly from the multitudes which infested the marshy banks of the river of Guayaquil, insomuch that their stings penetrated through all his cloathing, and would not permit him to take one moment's repose. Such places in Jamaica are to be deemed unfit for residence; but, in so extensive an island, we meet with few of them in proportion, nor does it abound with situations that can be justly stigmatized for a natural insalubrity.

There are various reasons to be assigned, why the inhabitants of this island were formerly afflicted with frequent visitations of epidemic sickness. When Europeans resorted hither in great numbers, they were crowded into two towns, and inconveniently accommodated. A buccaneering intercourse subsisted with the baleful coasts about Carthagena and Porto Bello. In 1671, when the fleet commanded by Sir Henry Morgan returned from that coast, his crews brought with them the malignant fever of Porto Bello, and the greater part of them died of it; the contagion spread to those on shore, where it produced a terrible mortality. In 1741, a very great sickness prevailed here from a similar disorder, imported by the troops, on their return from the Carthagena expedition; and the like had happened before in 1704, when admiral Neville's squadron was on this station. The houses were inconveniently built, the diseases of the West Indies were very little understood, and such contagious distempers were often fatal, for want of those remedies which were afterwards invented. Many lives must have been lost, by these putrid fevers, before the Jesuits bark was brought into general use, or copious bleeding exploded; hundreds perished by the ravages of the small pox, before the art of inoculation grew into practice; multitudes have been formerly stifled to death in this climate, by confinement in close hot rooms, under loads of bed-cloaths, and poisoned with their own atmosphere, while the fresh air, which was their best remedy, was most industriously excluded. Nor is Jamaica singular in having suffered great depopulations by pestilential maladies, imported into it from other parts. In 1691, the island of Barbadoes was invaded with a contagion, brought by an English

T t t 2   fleet,

fleet, which continued to rage there more or less for twelve years, and swept off above a third part of the white inhabitants. In the year 1740, the South Sea galleons, having touched at Guayaquil, in order to secure their treasure, on account of the war between Spain and Great Britain, brought with them a putrid malignant fever, which had never been known at that place before, and numbers died of it: it is needless to multiply examples of what must have happened to every country carrying on any confiderable trade; this cause is very diftinct from local maladies, excited and nourifhed by fomething pernicious to human health, in the foil or atmofphere. In regard to the latter, a foreigner, fays Lind, who fixes his abode on a fickly fpot in England, as for inftance at *Hilfea Barracks*, muft not call the climate of England unhealthy, becaufe he fuffers from the difadvantages of a bad fituation; fo, to apply this remark to Jamaica, an European, who fixes his refidence at Greenwich near Kingfton, or in the near neighbourhood of a lagoon, ought not to reckon the climate of this ifland unhealthy, becaufe he has fuffered by an injudicious choice. The fact really is, as before has been ftated, that healthy as well as unhealthy fituations are to be found in all countries; but that the Englifh, for the convenience chiefly of their trade, and fometimes through ignorance, have generally fixed on the moft unwholefome fpots, for the fituation of their towns in the Weft Indies. The healthy air of Barbadoes is owing to that ifland's being entirely cleared of wood; but the principal town there is fixed on a fwamp, and therefore perhaps incurably unhealthy. Bafle-Terre in St. Kitts, St. John's in Antigua, are not lefs fo, and, as I am informed, from the like reafon [a].

The

[a] In the year 1766, fixteen French Proteftant families, confifting of *fixty* perfons, were fent, at the expence of government, to *Weft Florida*; the ground allotted for their refidence was on the fide of a hill, *furrounded with marfhes*, at the mouth of the river *Scambia*. Thefe new fettlers arrived in winter, and continued healthy till the fickly months, which in that country are thofe of *July* and *Auguft*; during thefe two months the annual fever of that climate proved fo fatal to them, that, of the *fixty*, only *fourteen* furvived; and even this fmall remnant were all in a bad ftate of health in *September*, and moft of them died in a few months afterwards. Such cataftrophes are fhocking; efpecially when we confider, that if thefe induftrious people had been fixed on a healthy fpot, not incommoded with the malignant vapours of a fwampy foil, they might have lived many years, and covered a large diftrict with their offspring. *Kalm* gives another inftance of fuch fatal fituations, in the little town of *Salem*, in Penfylvania, adjacent to which are fome very low fwampy meadows. They who come hither from other parts acquire a very pale fickly look, although they

enjoy

The general proofs of an unhealthy fituation, in this climate, are,

Firft, Sudden alterations in the evening air, from ftifling heat, to a chilling cold; this is perceived foon after funfet, and is accompanied with a very heavy dew, which indicates a fwampy unwholefome foil.

Secondly, Thick noifome fogs, arifing after funfet, from mud, flime, and other impurities, having fomething of the fcent of a new-cleanfed ditch.

Thirdly, Innumerable fwarms of large mufkeetos, flies, and other infects, which attend putrid air and low unventilated places, where they delight to breed.

Fourthly, Where butchers meat is foon corrupted, and in a few hours becomes tainted and full of maggots; and where wounds, nearly brought to heal, fuddenly break out afrefh, attended with great pu-trefaction of the parts.

Fifthly, Where a dead corpfe becomes intolerably offenfive in lefs than fix hours.

Sixthly, Where, by the fubfidence of the water in dry weather, the channel of any river is left bare to the fun, and emits a difagree-ble fmell, by night as well as by day, from putrid flime, dead fifh and infects, and other corrupted fubftances.

In fummer nights, the body is moft liable to fevers, becaufe of the alterations of the air; for, in the beginning of the night, it is fultry; in the middle, more temperate; and, towards the morning, cool: by which, the accuftomed flow of perfpiration is checked in time of fleep, by throwing off the cloaths. This is confirmed by all who travel in hot climates; fudden cold, after warmth, makes a change in the habit, by repelling the tranfpiring fteams, which were copioufly rifing; in thefe climates, therefore, it may be neceffary to cover the body, when the nocturnal dews happen, left the pores fhould be too fuddenly clofed; which might produce fevers of the worft kind.

The dew, which is moft unwholefome and dangerous, is that which rifes imperceptibly from the earth after funfet. This may eafily be

enjoy ever fo perfect health, and lively colour, at their firft arrival. In the month of May a moft difagreeable ftench annoys it from the fwamps; the putrid vapours are wafted upon the inhabitants, and are inhaled into their bodies together with the air which they breathe. At the end of every fum-mer they are fure to be afflicted with intermittent fevers. A young couple, who came paffengers with *Kalm*, went, foon after their arrival at Philadelphia, in perfect health to *Salem*; but in a few weeks they both fell fick, and died before the winter was half over. A hot atmofphere, fo impregnated with putrid particles and watery vapours, cannot fail of producing diarrhœas, dyfenteries, and various kinds of putrid and malignant fevers.

collected,

collected, by inverting a bowl, or glafs tumbler, and placing it on a stick, with the mouth about half an inch from the surface of the ground. After fixing it thus at funfet, if it be examined about midnight, it will be found entirely covered within with watry globules, like the cover of a boiling kettle, while the outfide perhaps is barely moift. But if fuffered to remain the whole night in this pofition, the condenied vapour of the earth precipitating towards morning, in the cool hours before fun-rife, will cover the outfide alfo with the like appearance.

I have frequently obferved, that, in Kingfton, there is fometimes no dew at all perceptible in the morning; at other times, after heavy fhowers in the Liguanea mountains, and a brifk land wind, it has been very copious. In the former cafe, which happened in dry weather, there either was no reek or perfpiration from the earth of the ftreets, or the atmofphere above continued in too warm a ftate during the night to condenfe any vapours which might afcend. In general, I think it may be concluded, that it is not wholefome to be much abroad in this climate after dark, at leaft without due precaution of putting on additional cloathing.

The beft prefervative againft the mifchievous impreffions of a putrid fog, a fwampy or marfhy exhalation, is a clofe, fheltered, and covered place, fuch as the lower apartments in a fhip, or a houfe which has no doors nor windows facing the fwamp. If, in fuch place, a fire be kept either at the doors or other inlets, as is practifed in fome unhealthy countries during their rainy or noifome foggy feafon, thefe fires, together with the fmoak, prove an excellent fafeguard to thofe within, againft the injuries of a vitiated atmofphere.

The cuftom of the Negroes in this refpect, perhaps, may conduce as much as any thing to their enjoying health in fuch marfhy foils, when white perfons are affected by the malignant effluvia, and contract ficknefs; few of their huts have any other floor than the bare earth, which might poffibly tranfmit noxious exhalations in the night, if they did not keep up a conftant fire in the center of their principal room or hall; the fmoak of which, though intended to difperfe the mufkeetos, has another good effect, the correcting the night air, and difarming it of its damp and chill, which might be prejudicial to their healths [b].

In

[b] Doctor *Trapham* fpeaks to the fame effect: "Though water is a moft neceffary conveni-"ency, and its plenty and goodnefs a great accommodation to thefe fettlements; yet, as the air "itfelf is very moift, we ought to covet as dry a living as may be; and therefore not to lodge "ourfelves

In fuch low fpots, even in this climate, the chill and denfity of the air is fuch, as to render the breath vifible early in the morning, a circumftance which is not obferved in other parts of the lowlands.

Unwholefome fogs in Jamaica are, fuch as emanate from lagoons and marfhy foils ; but they are not common. The fogs of Sixteen-mile-malk, and fome other places among the mountains, are not unhealthy, nor have they any ill fmell. Thofe who inhabit places where falt or unwholefome marfhes are formed by frequent inundations of the fea, or where the fhores are lined with ftinking ooze or mud, and aquatic plants of a noxious quality, ought, during the fickly feafons, to retire into the country at fome diftance. The fafeft retreats are to be found on the fides of hills or mountains, where there are no moraffes within three miles ; preferring alfo thofe fituations which are not affected by vapours fpringing from the circumjacent valleys, at leaft in their perpendicular afcent. Experience confirms the fact, that in fuch elevated fituations, where the foil is dry, and clear from wood and ftagnant water, Europeans enjoy good health, in the very hotteft climates, during all feafons of the year: but, if perfons will obftinately run the hazard of their life and health, by remaining all night, or fleeping in unhealthy places, they cannot expect to reap the benefit of fafety and fecurity from a healthy air in their neighbourhood.

In every ifland, perhaps, fuch afylums may be found, where the air proves healthy, and reftorative to European conftitutions.

The ifland of Dominica is in moft places woody and unhealthy; yet there were feveral French families in it, who, by fixing their refidence on the fides of hills, lived exempted from the attack of agues and fevers, the difeafes common there ; and thus enjoyed as good a ftate of health and conftitution, as if they had been in France.

The beft fituation for a change is, where the heat of the day feldom exceeds 70 on Fahrenheit's thermometer, and where the cold of the night is not more than 16 degrees lower on the fame fcale,

" ourfelves or fervants receptive of additional water from ponds or rivers; for I have obferved
" it matter of fact, where fuch care hath been omitted, more lives than elfewhere have been
" flooded into *Styx*. Befides its great prefervation in this refpect, a dry lodging, *removed at leaft*
" *one ftory from the ground,* is approved the beft fecurity of our white fervants ; as for the Negroes,
" though their lodging be near the ground, they force' off the moifture of the earth by their con-
" ftant fires, and thereby become healthy." P. 27.

or at 54 ; where the ground is cleared from wood and bushes.; has
no stagnating water upon or near its, surface.; where the soil is
fertile, and favours the cultivation of European plants, and the
health of European animals; and, lastly, where sheep, brought from
England or North America, still retain, without inconvenience, a
fleecy covering.   There are spots of ground, in all the mountains
and hills adjacent to the towns in Jamaica, which, by industry and
cultivation, might be converted into the most healthy and delightful rural retirements.   In such places, on those eminences where
at present the chillness of the evening renders a fire comfortable,
and requisite to an European constitution, the improvement of the
soil would gradually mend the quality of the air.   Gentlemen,
who can afford to keep a horse or carriage, after doing business
in Kingston, or other maritime towns, might, before sunset, return
to such a healthy and pleasant country seat as is here recommended,
taking the precaution of never sleeping elsewhere during a sickly
season.   Those, whose circumstances and business will permit, should,
retire, especially in the night-season, to such places for health, until they grow inured to the climate ; and others, who cannot afford
this precaution, or whose affairs will not admit of it, should be
immediately removed thither when taken ill.   Should the change
of air not produce an instantaneous recovery, it will at least miti-
gate the symptoms of the disorder ; and, the use of medicines being
attended with more efficacy, a patient will more speedily regain a
vigorous state of health.   When a person is seized with a fever, proceeding from the bad air of any place, his illness, whilst he continues there, is daily, nay hourly, aggravated, and reinforced, by a
constant application of the morbid cause.   In this situation, the best
medicines, even the bark, have been ineffectual in relieving the patient, whilst thus incessantly exposed to the sources of his disease.
They who labour under fevers, fluxes, and other diseases of the like
violent nature, may be removed with the greatest safety for change
of air.   Such, therefore, as are taken ill during the rage of any epidemic sickness, should be carried immediately into a purer air, to
some distance beyond the reach of infection ; and frequently, in these
cases, this is a certain and immediate cure of itself: so in 1765,
when a mortal sickness raged on shore at Pensacola, the crews of
the

the men of war, lying at a mile's diftance from the town, enjoyed the moft perfect health ; and fuch patients, who, after their being feized with the fever on fhore, were carried on board fhip, prefently recovered ; the diforder, by change of air, foon loft its alarming fymptoms, and was eafily fubdued ; nothing is more certain, than that the fea air, and fea breezes, in this part of the world, are fpecifics for the removal of malignant diforders contracted from a vitiated atmofphere on the land.   I fhall now apply thefe remarks more particularly to Jamaica.   The fituation of Spanifh Town is healthy ; it has no marfhes about or near it ; and the rain water that falls upon it is drained into the river by a pretty rapid defcent.   Nothing more is needful to preferve this natural falubrity of its air, than a well-regulated police, under the controul of the magiftrates, who fhould provide, that the ftreets and environs be kept clear from filth, and all putrid fubftances, which might breed annoyance.   The air of all the Tropical countries is moft impure, *immediately* before and after the periodical feafons ; and, at fuch times, the greater caution muft be ufed to avoid catching colds, which may produce intermittent, or fometimes remittent, fevers.   At fuch times, or when any epidemic diftemper of a contagious nature is by accident brought into the town, the adjacent hills afford a convenient and fecure retreat. The town of Port Royal, being almoft furrounded with the fea water, is juftly commended for the falubrity of its air, a certain proof of which is the longevity of its conftant inhabitants.

The town of Kingfton, lying on a gravely flope, and open to the fea breeze, would probably be a healthy place, if it was not expofed to infectious diforders, brought into it from the fhipping ; yet, when any fuch malady begins to rage, the fick might always find a falutary retreat among the Liguanea Hills.   I have already fpoken of the barrack at *Stoney Ridge,* in St. Andrew's ; the neighbourhood of this place would doubtlefs be very well adapted for a retreat from contagion,. or for the recovery of convalefcents ; nor might it be a lofing project perhaps for a builder to purchafe land here, and erect a certain number of commodious houfes, to be lett for this purpofe.   Society might allure thofe to try the experiment, who would otherwife be averfe to it, from a diflike to folitude ; and, indeed, nothing more alleviates the diftrefs and dejection incident to fevers of the putrid clafs, than chearful company. The fituation of the other towns is but indifferent ; but the inhabitants of all have their places of retreat, if they could but refolve to make ufe of them. For Old Harbour there are the Goat Iflands, and the Hills of St. Dorothy. Savannah la Mar is at no great diftance from hills and rifing grounds ; Lucea and Montego Bay are furrounded with high lands ; at the latter place, in particular, the flat fpace for build-ing is fo circumfcribed, that, as the town enlarges, the houfes muft be built on higher ground, along the fides of the contiguous hill; which circumftance will one day contribute to render it populous and flourifhing. The lower part of Kingfton, next the harbour, having been founded upon foil recovered from the water, is too much pent up with the fhipping that lie near the wharfs, and with warehoufes and goods, to be eligible for pafling the night. Befides, the mud near this quarter, whenever it is difturbed, either by the violence of the furge in high breezes, or by the oars, poles, or boat-hooks of navigators, is apt to emit a very putrid and unwholefome ftench ; fuch fituations may either generate bad fevers, or exafperate the fymptoms of thofe diforders which otherwife might eafily be conquered.

Throughout this ifland, wherever we turn our eyes, it appears fo crowded with hills and rifing grounds, ventilated always with a free and falubrious air, that we cannot but condemn thofe perfons, who chufe low, damp, and fultry hollows, for their conftant refidence ; and who often fuffer from the ill effects caufed by fuch fituations, without difcerning the real fource of their bad health : but in time, perhaps, when the importance of this matter comes to be more ferioufly attended to, the planters will allow more weight to thofe particulars in the œconomy of health; which reafon and experience combine to recommend.

Thofe whom fortune has bleft with abundance, fhould be ftudi-ous to preferve the lives of their dependents, whofe poverty perhaps is their greateft crime. The cruelty of expofing the lives of men to ficknefs or death, by reftricting them to dwell in wretched hovels, and on unhealthy fpots, needs only to be pointed out, inorder to be relieved. The natural generofity, and benevolent difpofition, of the planters will immediately lead them to adminifter the certain remedy,

although

although it may be attended at firft with fome extraordinary expence to them. The habitations of their white fervants fhould be fixed on airy, dry, and elevated, fpots, raifed fome feet above the furface of the earth, floored, and conftructed either of timber and plaifter, or brick, but never (if poffible to avoid it) of ftone ; which is a very improper material in this climate for dwelling-houfes, on account of the damp and chill which it ftrikes in rainy weather; but, whenever it is unavoidably ufed for fuch buildings, the effects may be rendered lefs pernicious, by furrounding them with a fhed or piazza, or lining the walls with boards, or lath and plaifter, fet off to fuch a diftance as to let the air circulate between.

The like precautions muft be ufed in the eftablifhment of white families, if the fpirit fhould ever revive of introducing and fettling them in the ifland. The place allotted for their habitation fhould be ftony, gravely, or at leaft dry, open to the wind, and remote from the annoyance of vapourifh fwamps, or ftagnant waters.

It may happen, that many perfons, from the urgent nature of their employment and circumftances, may be obliged to remain in unhealthy fituations; in this cafe they muft ufe the beft means in their power to guard themfelves from the local mifchiefs to which they may be occafionally expofed. Such perfons fhould fleep in the higheft apartments of their houfe, whofe doors and windows ought to be fo contrived as not to front or open towards a damp foil or marfh. At thofe feafons of the year when fwampy exhalations are moft to be dreaded, as after heavy rains, and great heats fucceeding, fires made in the evening, and early in the morning, with lignum vitæ, cafcarilla, candlewood, and other refinous woods, or fubftances, would be very ferviceable. A Guiney merchant of Kingfton, whofe Negroes were feized with the fmall-pox, then raging malignantly in the town, put them all into a warehoufe, in which was lodged a confiderable quantity of pimento, for exportation, whofe odour was fo powerful as to fubdue the offenfive ftench of the diforder, and refrefhed the patients fo much, that they all got through it fafely. But of all *antifeptic* vapours, none is fo powerful as the acid fteam of burning brimftone, for correcting putrid air, and checking contagion.

In many parts among the mountains I have known houfes upon elevated fpots not unhealthy, though furrounded with woods. The greater coolnefs of the air, in fuch places, and their diftance from any ftagnant water, or fetid ooze, may contribute to their falubrity; the clearing away fuch woods, which fcreen the lower fituations, and increafe their fultrinefs, by excluding the free air from them, will render them more habitable, but perhaps not add much to the healthinefs of the former; for the reafon why the mountain woods are lefs injurious than the clofe thickets of the low lands, is, that the trees ftand further afunder, fo as to give a freer paffage to the winds and vapours; and confift, for the moft part, of the aromatic kinds, which ferve to correct any noxious exhalations, with their fragrancy and perfume. Their leaves in general are thick and firm; their pores extremely minute, and filled with a refinous or glutinous juice; by which means they perfpire lefs, and are enveloped with a lefs baneful atmofphere, than the trees of moift and low grounds. Pimento walks are remarkably healthful for refidence. Perfons, obliged to refide upon or near marfhy, unhealthful fpots, fhould avoid expofing themfelves, when fafting, to the chills of the morning and evening air, and never go abroad with an empty ftomach; but, previous to their labour, or amufement abroad, they fhould take either a glafs of wine, with a flice of bread, or drink a fmall quantity of chamomile or bark tea, or of an infufion of garlic, bark, and rhubarb in brandy; which may be taken either alone, or diluted a little with fome water, before they venture out in the morning.

In all fuch humid fituations fmoaking tobacco is beneficial; as alfo a more plentiful diet of flefh, with wine, and the peppers of the country. The pit of the ftomach, the feet, and the back bone, are more particularly to be guarded by coverings of flannel or cotton; a fquare piece of thick dimitty, with a tape ftrap to put round the neck, may be worn next the fkin, to cover the cheft and ftomach. This has been experienced very conducive to health, in fuch places, and a good preventative againft thofe colds and rheumatifms, which are apt, in thefe climates, to fall on the bowels, and caufe the belly-ach; and, to thefe precautions the daily ufe of bathing may be added, in the forenoon, when the ftomach is empty. Strangers newly arrived at fuch places, or thofe who are conftitutionally fubject to agues, fhould, during the fickly feafons, take, every other night, two or three fpoonfuls of *tinctura facra*, or a few grains of *pilulæ rufi*, not fufficient to

purge,

purge, but only to keep the body gently open; and, for further prevention, a wine glass of the [c] infusion of bark and orange-peel, in water; or a table spoonful of a strong [d] tincture of bark, in spirits, may be taken, diluted with water, occasionally, in a morning before breakfast. When a person is attacked with a fit of shivering, or the chills of an ague, he ought to go to bed; and, mixing about two ounces of white-wine vinegar with a quarter of an ounce of finely powdered chalk, should drink them immediately, while in the state of effervescence. This draught generally shortens the cold fit, brings on a profuse sweat, and may be repeated in the subsequent paroxysms. A mixture of salt of wormwood with lime or lemon juice, taken in its effervescent state, is administered for the same intention; but the best cure for an ague is the preparation subjoined in the note [e], which has rarely been found to fail in carrying it off.

For persons on the recovery from these and other debilitating maladies in the West Indies, no food whatever contributes more or sooner to the restoration of strength, than a turtle, or fish-diet, or nourishing fish-soup, warmed with the spices of the country; and, if necessary, rendered more palatable by the addition of a little juice of ripe limes.

It has been a received opinion, that, upon change of air from a cold to a hot climate, the first fever or fit of sickness alters the constitution of the body, so as to season it in the change; and that such a sickness is absolutely necessary to season and accommodate an European to it. But this is fallacious.

Sickness, though often primarily caused by the alteration of climate, does not always adapt the body, nor season it; nor is it absolutely necessary for that purpose. For many persons, either from some constitutional ailment, some latent predisposing source in their habit, as a scorbutic taint, may suffer reiterated fits of illness, without perceiving themselves better reconciled to the change, than they were after

[c] ℞. One ounce of bruised bark, half an ounce of sour orange peel, half a pint of boiling water; infuse these ingredients, and, after suffering them to settle for some time, pour off the liquor so long as it runs clear.

[d] ℞. One ounce of pounded or bruised bark, eight ounces of French spirit of wine; let it stand in a warm place four days, then strain off, and bottle it for use; it may prove more efficacious with a slight addition of rhubarb; or, in hot temperaments, a very little nitre. Linde.

[e] ℞. Three drachms of bark, finely powdered, one drachm and half of Venice treacle, the juice of one and half common-sized lemons, and six table spoonfuls of sound red Port wine; mix the ingredients well, and divide into three equal parts; one whereof to be taken at morning, noon, and evening, of the well day, on an empty stomach. This dose is for a grown person, and may be proportionably lessened for those of tender years.

the firſt attack ; many others ſuffer no illneſs at all from the change, but bear it well ; which proves, that ſickneſs or a fever was not required to prepare or adapt them to it. The thorough and proper ſeaſoning to ſuch a climate is brought about effectually by remaining in it for ſome length of time ; and all *ſudden changes* from cold to heat, or heat to cold, produce nearly ſimilar effects. Thus, if 500 ſeamen or ſoldiers paſs from England to the Weſt Indies, ſetting out in very cold weather, and arriving there after a quick voyage, many of them will be ſeized with a diarrhœa, and with violent and mortal fevers, if they indulge, ſoon after their arrival, in *rum newly diſtilled.* But, if the ſame men are kept at ſea, and the ſhip does not put into any unhealthy port, during the ſickly ſeaſon of the year, theſe men, after being twelve months in the Weſt Indies, will become perfectly ſeaſoned to the climate, and enjoy as good a ſtate of health, as if they were in England.

So, if the ſame men, after being ſome years in the Weſt Indies, are relieved, and arrive on the Engliſh coaſt, in the winter time, they will be again ſeized with diarrhœas ; the cure and removal of which will intirely depend on keeping the patients *warm.* On their change to the hot climate, the humours, unable to paſs off faſt enough by the outlets of perſpiration, fall on the bowels. On their return from a hot to a cold climate, the outlets by perſpiration being ſuddenly cloſed, the humours are repelled, and driven again upon the ſame parts ; and the keeping the patients warm is no more than recalling their bodies to the ſame glow to which they had lately been accuſtomed, and thereby promoting a free diſcharge by the ſkin.

It has been obſerved, that muſkeetos are intolerably numerous in thoſe places in the Weſt-Indies, which are leaſt adapted to human habitation. They are found in the greateſt ſwarms among lagoons, and ſwamps on the ſea coaſt, and in little creeks ſheltered with mangrove trees ; in gullies which contain any ſtagnant water; in puddles on the flat country after the rainy ſeaſons, and in rivercourſes in dry weather, where the water reſts in detached hollows, and becomes corrupted from the fermentation of aquatic weeds, and ſubſided ſcum. Sometimes, I have known them driven from their ſkulking holes, by the violence of ſtrong ſea breezes, to a conſiderable diſtance up the country; but in general among the mountains,

tains, they are scarce, very diminutive and feeble. They are principally troublesome, and in swarms, after the periodical rains, when the lowlands are drenched with water, and full of little puddles, where these insects deposite their eggs, and multiply the breed.

They are therefore no positive harbingers of unhealthy spots, except where they are found at *all seasons of the year*, in the *greatest abundance*; such are the places, where they can enjoy a warm atmosphere, and water undisturbed by rude winds. They are found in the most healthy situations; they swarm in all the provinces of North America, and even in Canada in the summer time; but it is very certain, that in those countries, as well as the West-Indies, they are most numerous in the least healthful parts; and that the summer season is the most sickly time of the year in North America. These insects cannot exist long, nor propagate their species well, without stagnant water. Dry weather, dry exposures, and a cool air, are equally obnoxious to them; their favourite haunts therefore, and such as seem most to promote their multiplication, are to be rejected as the least fit (in proportion) for mankind to inhabit, at least during those months in the year when they appear most vigorous and numerous.

Butchers meat does not ordinarily grow tainted, in the lowlands of Jamaica, under 30 to 36 hours (unless exposed to the sun). When hung up in an airy shaded place, and protected from flies, it will keep longer. In the mountains, I have eat beef corned and boiled, very good and sweet, after five or six days keeping; and pork pickled here of a twelvemonth old. Corpses are kept, on the South side of the island, in general, twenty-four hours or more, according to the nature of the disease, and season of the year, before interment, without becoming offensive.

The effects observed here on metals exposed to the air, is no criterion of an unhealthy state. This rusting, or corrosion, particularly remarked on iron or steel, is thought to be occasioned by a muriatic acid, or by nitrous particles, with which the air of this island is impregnated. I have seen iron work upon one of the highest ridges of the mountains, in as healthy a situation as any on the globe, corroded in as great a degree as in any part of the lowlands. I observed, on a large iron scale beam suspended close by the

sea,

fea, that the fide next the water was cankered with ruft in the courfe of a few weeks after being hung up; but the oppofite fide remained perfectly found, and the paint as frefh as at firft

Tranfient fhowers here, though fometimes very heavy, do not leave the air affected with moifture; and thefe metals ruft leaft here during rainy weather.

May not fuch irrigations dilute, conduct, or carry off, thofe particles floating in the atmofphere, which at other times act as *menftrua* upon iron? or, may they not render them lefs active?

Fixible or mephitic air acts very powerfully upon iron but has not any effect upon copper. But copper is corroded in this climate, though not fo violenly as iron. The volatile vitriolic acid diffolves both; this latter fubftance has been conjectured to be plentifully diftributed throughout the univerfe, in the fubterraneous regions, and even in the atmofphere; it is conftantly prefent in the *electrical fluid* which is diffufed in fuch great abundance between the Tropics; and from the fuppofed exiftence of it in the air, it has been called, the *fal acidum vagum univerfale* [*f*]. We may therefore venture, perhaps, to afcribe the effect obferved to this caufe, until fome more probable, or powerful, agent fhall be difcovered.

Having now laid down general rules for diftinguifhing a good from a fickly fituation I proceed to another effential article, which merits attention from all Europeans, coming to refide in this climate, viz.

S E C T.   II.
C L O A T H I N G.

Fafhion and cuftom, fays Dr. Hilary, are two prevailing things, which enflave the greater part of mankind, though often in oppofition both to reafon and convenience, and particularly in our *drefs*; for no doubt but the loofe, cool, eafy drefs of the Eaftern nations, their gown or banyan, is much eafier and better fitted for ufe in a hot climate, than the Englifh drefs, which is clofe and tight. All who have tried both, find it fo: but, fuch is the influence of fafhion and cuftom, that one may fee men loaded, and half melting under a ponderous coat and waiftcoat, richly bedaubed with gold lace or

[*f*] Falconer.

embroidery

embroidery on a hot day, fcarcely able to bear them, and little confidering how much they injure their conftitutions by a fweltering
load of garments, of whofe inconvenience they cannot but be fenfible;
and under whofe preffure, they cannot but feel the moft uneafy
fenfations.

A banyan is the drefs of the mandarins at the courts of China
and Japan, of the nobility and gentry at Indoftan and Perfia; and
why it fhould not be adopted in other hot countries, can only be
attributed to the tyranny of cuftom, which is ever perverfe, and
whofe councils refemble the laws of the Medes and Perfians, which
altered not. If a Chinefe mandarin was to be crammed into a fuit
of Englifh cloaths, he would look like a hog in armour, and feel as
much diftrefs. But wrap an Englifhman, under the torrid zone, in a
Chinefe banyan, and he would efteem it luxurioufly delightful;
cuftom arbitrarily forbids him to enjoy fo much blifs, and commands
him to drefs in the modes of London and Edinbugh. It is not however unwife to borrow fo much from the fafhions of other nations,
as we may practife ourfelves with equal advantage. To come
nearer therefore to Jamaica, let us obferve a little the management
of our Spanifh neighbours. All their cloaths are light; their
waiftcoat and breeches are of *Bretagne* linen, and their coat of fome
other thin ftuff. *Wigs* are not much worn among them; only the
governor and chief officers appearing in them, and that moftly on
public occafions. *Neckcloths* are likewife very uncommon; inftead
of thefe, the neck of their fhirt is adorned with large gold buttons,
or clafps, and thefe are fuffered to hang loofe. On the head, they
wear a cap of very fine, thin, and white linen. Others go entirely
bare headed, having their hair cut from the nape of the neck
upwards. *Fans* are very commonly worn by the men, made of a
thin branch of the *palmeto*, in the form of a crefcent, with a ftick of
the fame wood in the middle for a handle. Their *women* wear a
kind of a petticoat, which they call a *pollera*, made of thin filk,
without any lining; and on their body a very thin white jacket;
but this is only put on, in what they call their winter, during the
rainy feafon; for, in the hot months, they think it infupportable.
Although this attire is fo fimple and loofe, yet it is decent; for they

always

always lace in such a manner as to conceal their breasts. When they go abroad they wear a mantlet or short cloak. The richness of their dress does not consist, as with the English ladies, in a multitude of things piled one upon another; but in the finest linen, laces, and jewels, so disposed as to add very little to incovenience, and to produce the most ornamental effect.

On the head, they wear a cap of fine linen covered with lace, and worked into the shape of a mitre; which, being plentifully starched, terminates forward in a point, not easily discomposed. This they call *panito*, and it is worn by the ladies, and other native Whites, as an undress; nothing can be more becoming, and, having used themselves to it from their infancy, it sits upon them with a better air. Our English belles in Jamaica differ very widely from these madonas. They do not scruple to wear the thickest winter silks and sattins; and are sometimes ready to sink under the weight of rich gold or silver brocades. Their head-dress varies with the *ton* at home; the winter fashions of *London* arrive here at the setting in of hot weather; and thick or thin caps, large as an umbrella, or as diminutive as a half crown piece, are indiscriminately put on, without the smallest regard to the difference of climate; nay, the late preposterous mode of dressing female hair in London, half a yard perpendicular height, fastened with some score of heavy iron pins, on a bundle of wool large enough to stuff a chair bottom, together with pounds of powder and pomatum, did not escape their ready imitation; but grew into vogue with great rapidity, and literally might be affirmed, *to turn all their heads*; for it was morally impossible to avoid stooping, and tottering, under so enormous a mass. Nothing surely can be more preposterous, and absurd, than for persons residing in the West-Indies, to adhere rigidly to all the European customs and manners; which, though perhaps not inconvenient in a cold Northern air, are certainly improper, ridiculous, and detrimental, in a hot climate. How perverse is an attachment to thick bushy periwigs (the fit antidotes to frost and snow), under a vertical sun; or complete suits of thick broadcloth, laced from top to bottom, in a country where there is not the least occasion to force a sweat! The proper coats for this climate are of the lightest English broadcloths, commonly known

by.

by the name of *kerfeymeres*, made without any lining or lace, eafy and loofe. The waiftcoat and breeches fhould be of cotton (corded or India dimity for example), in preference to linen, as it prevents catching cold; a circumftance not well to be avoided in a linen drefs, which is no fooner moift, than it ftrikes a very fenfible chill, fo as frequently to obftruct perfpiration. The fame fubftance is alfo proper for ftockings. Moft men however, in this ifland, wear linen drawers in preference to linings, for the fake of cleanlinefs; and prefer the Ruffia drab for breeches, as it is very durable, and has a neat look.

White hats are beft adapted to this climate, on account of their being light and cool. The black hats abforb the fun's rays, and are fometimes extremely inconvenient. All white fervants there-fore, foldiers, and others, whofe employments may neceffarily oblige them to be often expofed to the fun in the heat of the day, fhould be furnifhed with white hats inftead of black; the former repelling, the latter imbibing, the heat [*f*]; and experience convinces, that light-coloured cloathing is by far the cooleft in this part of the world, and black or dark-coloured the hotteft; for the fame reafon a full mourning, or black fuit, is improper here; becaufe, in fuch cloaths, the body is more heated by the fun in walking abroad, and heated at the fame time by the exercife; which accumulated fervour may occafion dangerous illneffes. They are prudent, who, inftead of this, wear a fcarlet, with black cuffs and button holes, by way of mourning; for nothing is more likely to fubject a perfon to catch cold, and a fit of ficknefs, than a fudden change from an habitual light and cool drefs, to one twice as hot; and as fudden a return again, after a time, to his former mode. On the fame princi-ple, the ladies hats or bonnets fhould be lined with black, as not reverberating on their faces thofe rays of the fun, which are reflected upwards from the earth and water, and occafion freckles, or tan. And hence alfo it appears, that putting a bit of white paper *within*

[*f*] This is illuftrated by Dr. Franklin's experiment, who took a number of little fquare pieces of broadcloth of various colours, and laid them all out upon the fnow, in a bright fun-fhiny morning. In a few hours, the *black cloth*, being moft warmed by the fun, funk fo deep as to be below the action of the folar rays. The dark blue, almoft as deep. The lighter blue not quite fo much as the dark. The other colours ftill lefs, in proportion as they were lighter; and the white remained on the furface of the fnow, not having funk at all.

the

the crown of a black hat will not keep out the heat, though it would, if placed *without* [g].

Travelers in this climate fhould be careful always to change their cloaths after getting wet by riding in the rain. It is a common practice here, as in the Eaft-Indies, to cool bottled liquors by wrapping cloths dripping-wet round the bottles, the warmth which the liquors had contracted evaporating with the water as it paffes from the cloths; and the operation is greatly facilitated by fetting them in a fhaded place, where they are acceffible to the wind [h]. A traveler, caught in rain, is much in the fame fituation as one of thefe bottles, and, by the quick evaporation of his natural warmth, perceives his body chilled and aguifh. It is ufual here to ftrip, and rub all over with rum, and then put on dry cloaths; which prevents any ill confequence.

Having nothing more material to add on the fubject of drefs, I fhall next fpeak of,

S E C T. III.

Diet *and* General Regimen *of* Life.

A learned phyfician [i] has given it as his opinion, that, as the time approaches for feamen to enter hot climates, their diet fhould, by pofitive inftitutions, be varied from what is ufual at land, or at fea, in Europe; that inftinct has taught the natives between the Tropics, and in all hot climates, to live chiefly on vegetable diet and fubacid fruits; for which reafon, devouring large quantities of flefh-meats, and ufing the fame hard indigeftible food as might pafs off in cold weather, or more Northerly regions, muft alone have proved the caufe of the deftruction of many Englifh lives. He, therefore, recommends for trial, in hot climates, that the feamen on board men of war fhould not have falt meat of any kind above once a week, or twice; beef and pork alternately; and that every other fpecies of allowance fhould be provided in much greater abundance than is commonly done for fea-voyages:

[g] Franklin.
[h] If thefe cloths were wetted with rum; query, if they would not render the liquors ftill cooler?
[i] Brocklefby.

by

by which regulation, he thinks, many of the ordinary mifchiefs, attending the conftant ufe of putrefcent falted meats, may be prevented.

The example of fome people in the Eaftern part of the world has been quoted, by many writers, to fhew that vegetables are the natural appropriated food for hot climates; but there are fome circumftances attending it, in thofe Eaftern climes, which efcaped obfervation, or were not known. The truth feems to be, that the animal food, in fome of thofe Eaftern parts, is naturally unfit for food; of which Mr. Ofbeck mentions inftances, The Gentoos at Surat eat nothing but milk, butter, and vegetables. They have flefh in great plenty, but fuch as probably is not very wholefome, efpecially to thofe who come on fhore after a voyage, and indulge their appetites. They are fubject to vomitings and diarrhœas, and are in danger of lofing their lives. On this account, Mr. Ofbeck is of opinion, that Brama, or whoever at firft gave law to thefe people, had difcovered that thefe meats were very unwholefome to the Malabarians. "If all the Malabaric oxen (continues he) "were like thofe which we got, it is no wonder that the Gentoos "will not eat their flefh; the meer defcription of them would "make the moft hungry lofe their appetites." And he attributes to this meat, that many of the Swedifh failors were afterwards exceedingly tormented with intolerably bloody ulcers. This gentleman's conjecture on the origin of their total vegetable diet feems, therefore, well-grounded; efpecially as the Jewifh law-giver prohibited the ufe of fwine's flefh, which in Paleftine, perhaps, had a particular ill quality, and was thought to have firft produced that horrid difeafe the leprofy, with which the inhabitants were fo much afflicted.

It is by no means certain, that a total vegetable diet is proper in hot climates, at leaft not in all of them, nor at all times indifcriminately. Although vegetables in thefe climates are better concocted and matured by the heat of the fun, and therefore more nutritious, and in general wholefomer, than in Europe; yet, after violent rains, the vaft quantity of water that defcends upon the earth renders all forts of roots, plants, and fruits, for fome time, crude and unwholefome. This more efpecially happens, if a courfe

of

of hot dry weather has preceded; for the heavieft rains **always**
follow fuch weather; and all vegetables then imbibe the water in
a prodigious quantity, till they are faturated.   At fuch times, they
are very improper food, and often caufe very dangerous fluxes
among fuch of the Negroes as make too free with them.   A vegetable diet, from its extreme flatulence, occafions other diforders,
inflates the body into an immoderate fize, and may thus give an
appearance of fatnefs; as Mr. Ofbeck obferved of the Gentoos.
Some of the Negroes have the like tumefactions, which would
more frequently occur, if they did not ufe falt and the country
peppers very liberally.   The flefh of fowls and cattle comes fooner
to maturity here than in Europe.   The texture of it is loofer, and
the mufcular and tendinous parts lefs rigid.   Their flefh, therefore,
is not fo grofs, heavy, and hard of digeftion, as in Northern climates; but approaches nearer to vegetable food in its nature.   A
total abftinence from animal food, in Jamaica, would probably
increafe the relaxation already promoted by the climate, and debi-
litate the bodily vigour to a very dangerous excefs.   Even the
Gentoos, we find, do not wholly abftain; for they ufe milk and
butter (perhaps no fmall portion of their meal), which are nu-
trimental, and help to qualify the deleterious effects of their
vegetables.

The moft appropriated diet, in my opinion, for the Weft-Indies,
is a conftant mixture of animal and vegetable food, (if any thing)
inclining to the vegetable; that is, if an equal proportion be exceeded, it ought to be in favour of the vegetable [k].   And fuch is the
variety and multitude of this clafs, moft of which are adapted to

[k] It is certain, that, fo long as men have plenty of vegetables, and will ufe them, they are
never troubled with the fcurvy, whether they live in moift, warm, or cold climates.   On the contrary, where there is a total want of them, all writers agree, that this diforder (or tendency of the
animal juices to putrefaction) is the immediate confequence.

Dr. Falconer has a very judicious remark in refpect to the preparation of flefh-meats in hot
climates.   " Meats *little done*," fays he, " are certainly eafieft foluble; but they are, at the fame
" time, exceedingly *alcalefcent*, and run quickly into putrefaction; fo that it is much to be que-
" ftioned, whether they are to be chofen for thofe who eat a large proportion of animal food, as
" fuch diet would be apt to induce a habit of body highly fcorbutic, or tending to putrefaction,
" except taken with a large proportion of vegetables."   On this account, he fufpects, that the
French (who, for a warm climate, eat a large quantity of animal food) eat their meat fo much
roafted, or boiled, from a kind of natural inftinct, in order to obviate its feptic tendency, which is
much augmented by the greater heat of the climate.

nourifh, or refrefh the body, that the daintieft perfon need not be at a lofs in felecting fuch as are moft palatable to him. The olios, or pepper-pots, here (which conftitute the ordinary food of the Negroes, were the moft efteemed difhes among the Spaniards, and are equally relifhed by our natives or Creoles) confirm the propriety of fuch a diet as I have propofed; for they confift of flefh or fifh, greens, roots, plantains, okra-pods, and pulfe, differently mingled and prepared; fo that there is a great variety in their preparation and flavour; and every change in fucceffion of the ingredients prefents fome novelty, which is certainly no fmall recommendation; for they can be fo altered in tafte, by putting in fome vegetable or animal ingredients, and omitting others, as to feem entirely a new difh; and they are unqueftionably a moft wholefome kind of food for Europeans newly arrived, provided they are not too highly feafoned with pepper.

Inftead of attending to what reafon points out, moft Europeans, after their arrival here, perfift in devouring vaft quantities of animal food, with very little (if any) mixture of vegetable: they indulge in bad butter, cheefe, falt-beef, ham; and wafh them down with deluges of porter, ale, bad cyder, and all forts of wines. The butter imported hither is often in a ftate of putrefcence when it arrives; in general, it is rancid. So acrimonious an ingredient in diet is noxious to health, diforders the ftomach, and, oftener than is fufpected, gives rife to thofe terrible fevers, whofe fource is a vitiated bile [l].

[l] The nourifhment is extremely hurtful which is drawn from fubftances difficult to be diffolved, which tend to putrefaction, and cannot eafily be affimilated; fuch as dried-fifh, and particularly cheefe, which is often putrid, bacon, and old oil. Butter, in warm climates, by being kept a fhort time on board fhip, grows rank and fetid; for it frequently happens in fhips, particularly thofe bound to the Weft-Indies in a warm feafon, that it melts away, like oil, in the firkins, by which it lofes great part of its falt; and, the inteftine motion being increafed by the heat, it becomes bitter and ftinks. Such grofs food not only refifts the powers of digeftion very much; but the juices, drawn from them, are of a very acrid nature. Rouppe.

Many particles of flefh, though carefully falted, will in time grow putrid, as appears from Dr. Addington's experiment; who put a fmall piece of falted beef into water, and at the fame time a like piece of frefh, unfalted beef into another like quantity of water, and found the falted flefh to ftink firft; which proves the tendency of it to putrefaction, though the falt keeps it from offending the tafte or fmell: fo that falted flefh, as well as putrid air, has a tendency to occafion the fcurvy, as well as other putrid diftempers.

Chocolate

Chocolate is wholesome, and well-adapted to repair the loss sustained by liberal perspiration; but it ought not to be too freely used by Europeans at their first arrival at least, unless it is well diluted with milk and water, in which way many of the Creoles prefer it.

All those substances should be cautiously shunned which dispose the blood to putrefaction. Such are all rancid fats and oils; tainted flesh or fish; a flesh or fish diet, diluted with simple water alone; and excess in all spirituous liquors. Instead of this, such a diet should be observed as tends to acescency; for this intention are all the varieties of vegetables, combined with found fresh meat of flesh and fish; and the subacid fruits, as lemons, oranges, shaddocks, &c. and wine, particularly Madeira, which, diluted with water, is one of the wholesomest drinks in the West-Indies; it is highly antiseptic, strengthens the stomach and organs of digestion, and far preferable to the French wines. Next to this is weak punch, made with ripe fruit, and rum of at least a twelvemonth's age. The vast abundance of mild, vegetable acids, as well as the various species of peppers, distributed to these climates by the hand of nature, is a most benevolent provision. The moderate use of them, considering the tendency of the solids and fluids to be relaxed, and contract a putrescency, is absolutely necessary; and we find the natives, white and black, covet them with a singular avidity.

The biscuit and flour, imported from North-America, are very apt to harbour weevils, especially when they are kept for any length of time. These insects have such a caustic quality, that, when applied to the skin in form of a poultice, they will raise a blister like *cantharides*. How baneful then must their effects be on the tender coats of the stomach and bowels! The best means of driving them away, or destroying them, is by exposing the flour, or biscuit, to the sun, in the heat of the day, before it is used, or heating it in a hot oven: the former method compels these insects to shift their quarters; the latter kills them, and takes away the musty smell they have occasioned: care, however, must be used to pick out all the dead, which ought never to be mixed with food.

Disorders of the putrid class are the most to be dreaded by Europeans in this climate. Persons, indeed, living in England and

colder

colder climates, are not exempt from thefe maladies; and they happen in both, moſt commonly, from irregularity of diet, want of proper exercife, or from debauched habits of life.

An European, on arriving in Jamaica in good health, muſt refolve, immediately after he is landed, to purſue a regimen of diet, fomewhat different from what he had been accuſtomed to at home. He ſhould eat leſs fleſh-meat, and increaſe his allowance of vegetables. This diet requires wine; but even wine ſhould be moderately taken, and chiefly confidered as a mixture neceſſary to qualify and counteract the putrefactive tendency of plain water. On the voyage to this iſland, he ſhould not gorge in ſalt-meat; but, laying in a ſtock of European vegetables, particularly onions, pickled-cabbage, and the like, eſtabliſh fome or other of them as a part of his daily meals. It is perhaps much owing to the conſtant diet upon onions, that the Portugueſe at Madeira enjoy ſuch good health and vigour. What theſe men eat through neceſſity, others may by choice; fince the object to be obtained is worthy their purſuit, found health, and the poſſeſſion of ſtrength and faculties.

But as an Engliſhman, who has been uſed to a plentiful diet of fleſh during the former part of his life, might ſuffer by a too ſudden or unlimited abſtinence from it; fo it is moſt adviſeable for them to change and qualify it gradually, abating a little of their fleſh-meat every day, until they can bring themſelves to a due proportion of animal and vegetable dinners, without ſuffering any fenſible inconvenience. Their greateſt danger is, that, on firſt landing, they find their appetite unuſually keen, after the *tædium* of ſhip-fare, for five or fix weeks at ſea, and ſtimulated by the fight of feveral dainties they have been before unacquainted with; thus ſtrongly ſolicited to gratify their palates, they may fall into hurtful exceſſes, if they are not on their guard. A proper diet, with exerciſe in moderation, and the avoiding exceſſes in eating and drinking, particularly the former, will procure and preſerve a good ſtate of health; and a man, who regulates his life by a due conformity to this regimen, need not doubt of enjoying it in as great a degree here, as he might have done in other parts of the world.

Inflammatory fevers are not common in the Weſt-Indies; nor a buffy appearance of the blood. The reafons aſſigned for this ex-

emption are, the warmth and moifture of the climate, copious
perfpiration, and acidulated drinks. Excefs in eating, drinking,
and exercife, between the Tropics, neither corroborates the folids,
nor increafes the denfity of the blood: thefe errors in the non-naturals may render the Weft-India blood acrid; but they certainly
render the bile *peccant* both in quantity and quality. This is the
paffport to all the fevers in the Weft-Indies ; for it may well be
doubted, whether ever the blood is the primary feat of a fever,
unlefs in perfons newly arrived in the Torrid Zone. Of courfe,
the impropriety of frequent bleedings, as always practifed by the
French, and too often by the Englifh furgeons, muft be obvious;
and the neceffity of carrying off the *peccant* matter by vomit and
ftool, no lefs apparent.   This opinion is ftrengthened by experience of the almoft conftant fuccefs which attends the treatment
of them in this way ; and the great mortality which has followed
the free ufe of the lancet: and hence likewife appears the great
efficacy of antimonial preparations, and of James's powder in particular, which operate in the manner recommended, and feldom
fail of making a cure, if reforted to in time [*m*].

Fevers in the Weft-Indies feldom put on the appearances of in-
flammation beyond the firft twenty-four hours ; after that, they
become putrid, or malignant, and nervous. In the firft ftage only
of the difeafe, blood may be let, and even then in a very fmall

[*m*] The firft change, caufed by the tranfition from a cold into a hot climate, is a rarefaction of
all the humours in the body, and of the blood among the reft ; and, when the containing veffels
do not expand fufficiently to give it a free circulation, the confequence muft neceffarily be a feverifh heat, anxiety about the *præcordia*, a difficulty of breathing, violent pains in the head, and
uneafinefs. Thefe fymptoms are fometimes relieved by a fpontaneous bleeding at the nofe, which
anfwers the end of venefection : and it is to be underftood, that I do not mean to condemn
bleeding in all cafes, becaufe, where the party is young, vigorous, and contracts a fever immediately afrer his coming to the Weft-Indies, moderate bleeding, in the beginning of the diforder,
may often be not only fafe, but neceffary ; and, for this, the particular fymptoms are the beft indication. But it fhould be ufed in the Weft-India fevers with great caution, and ftrict regard had to
the age and habit of body, the time that the patient has refided in the Weft-Indies, his general
diet, and fuch other circumftances as may lead to the forming a competent judgement whether
opening a vein be proper or not. Where there is a very ftrong pulfe and great heat, which is often
obfervable in young, florid perfons, newly arrived from a cold climate, venefection is often found
ferviceable, to check the too rapid motion of the fluids, and gain more time to treat the diforder
properly. But fuch fymptoms rarely occur, after an European has been a twelvemonth in the Weft-
Indies ; unlefs it may happen in Jamaica, by a fudden check of the perfpiration, on the firft
fetting-in of the cold Northerly winds.

quantity.

quantity. When the bilious matter has once entered the blood (which it will foon do, if fweats are incautioufly ufed at firft), vomits and acid purges become lefs ufeful; and the morbid matter muft be thrown out upon the fkin by wild-fage tea, weak punch, or other liquors which promote a flight diaphorefis. In this difcorder it often happens, that a weak purgative, or emetic, will produce uncommon evacuations. This fhould not alarm; and the patient's ftrength fhould be well fupported with Madeira whey. This fever often fubfides into a remittent, and then into an intermittent, whofe beft remedy is the bark, which not only produces a wholefome bile, but invigorates the whole habit. Fluxes and dyfenteries proceed often from the fame caufe, a corrupted bile, and fometimes from a fuppreft perfpiration, or too free indulgence in crude, watery vegetables. Of all the fubftances known, the bark, and ripe orange or lemon juice, deferve, for their excellence, the name of fpecific againft putrefaction. I knew an European gentleman in Jamaica, who regularly drank every day a fmall tumbler full of fweet or four orange juice, ufing them indifferently, immediately after dinner, and enjoyed conftant health. I remember another who cured himfelf of a bilious putrid fever with no other remedy than the juice of ripe Seville and other oranges. And fo many inftances have been noticed of their antifeptic quality in thefe cafes, that the utmoft confidence may be repofed in their falutiferous effects.

Much more might be added on the fubject of thefe diftempers, their caufes, fymptoms, and method of cure; but, as I mean not to enter into an elaborate and medical inveftigation of them, I refer to the writings of Pringle, Huxham, Lind, Biffet, Hilary, Rouppe, and De Monchy, who have treated of them with the greateft ability.

Moft Europeans, on firft coming within the Tropics, are affected with an eruption upon their fkins of fmall red pimples, which goes by the name of the *prickly heat.* This is looked upon to be falutary, unlefs it is repelled; and it is remarkable, that it returns periodically every year, about April or May, on perfons who have refided a long time in the Weft-Indies[n]. It is, probably, caufed

[n] At leaft in Jamaica.

by

by an extraordinary flow of perspiration, and the current of the
humours towards the skin, promoted by the heat of climate. It
must not be unnoticed, that the peristaltic motion of the bowels
being here perhaps more languid than in Europe, persons newly
arrived are often subject to constipations; and sometimes the *faeces*
are so hardened, as to be excreted with great difficulty. The retention of them too long may therefore not only cause an acrimony
to lodge in the intestines, productive of belly-ach, or other spas-
modic complaints; but give rise to bad fevers, by the absorption of
such an acrid and putrid humour into the veins. It is necessary,
therefore, to keep the body always open. Chocolate tends to this
effect; and it is observed by Ulloa, that, at Carthagena, where it is
to be had extremely cheap, there is not a Negroe slave but allows
himself constantly a regale of it after breakfast and dinner; but
they never use it *fasting*, nor without eating something with it. I
have, in another place, cautioned Europeans, newly arrived, from
indulging too much in it, especially when made thick. I alluded
to the costlier sort of chocolate, manufactured here with cinnamon,
and other hot spices, which are the ingredients that render it improper for them. But the common sort, chiefly used among the
free Negroes, and others of the natives who love it plain, is mixed
up with maize; and this may be safely used by such Europeans,
diluted with milk and water: in this state it will be found rather
cooling than heating; and the addition of sugar makes it the more
aperitive. *Sedes figuratæ* are seldom observed in this climate;
which may be ascribed to the weaker peristaltic motion above
remarked, as well as to the diet pursued by most of the inhabitants,
consisting chiefly of vegetables and soluble substances.

In all hot countries it has been observed, that healthy people generally perspire very much; and this (from the greater disposition
of the humours to putrefcence) may be accounted one of the principal conservators of health. It is therefore surprizing to find Mr.
Reaumur assert, "that perspiration impairs the longevity of all
" animals, by discharging, not only the useless, but nutritious, parts
" of the animal fluids; and that an excess of perspiration seems to
" be the reason why the inhabitants of hot climates live a shorter
" term than those who inhabit the temperate zones;" for, in fact,

this

this effect, by a waste of actual substance, can only happen when the body is kept unreplenished, by supplies of nutriment, to repair the loss of what may be carried off by this means. Hence those, who are most healthy, are known to dilute more frequently and plentifully than others; their perspiration chiefly eliminates aqueous particles, which are speedily replaced; they do not grow emaciated, but plump; and gain, instead of losing, weight; which would not be the case, if the fact was as Mr. Reaumur supposes. Neither is it proved, that the native inhabitants of hot climates are shorter-lived than those of the temperate zones; since there are many instances to the contrary, both in the islands, and on the continent of South-America.

The reapers in Pennsylvania, who work in the open fields, in the clear, hot sun-shine, common in their harvest-time (about the end of June, or beginning of July), find themselves very able to go through that labour, without being much incommoded by the heat, while they continue to sweat, and while they supply matter for keeping up that sweat, by drinking frequently of a thin, evaporable liquor, water mixed with rum; but, if the sweat stops, they drop, and sometimes die suddenly, if a sweating is not brought on again by drinking that liquor, or (as some rather chuse in that case) a kind of hot punch, made with water mixed with honey, and a considerable proportion of vinegar. Hence Dr. Franklin very properly concludes, that the quicker evaporation of perspirable matter from the skin and lungs of Negroes, by cooling them more, enables them to bear the sun's heat so much better than the Whites can do; though, abstracted from this, the colour of their skins would, otherwise, make them more sensible of that heat [o] From the same cause, perhaps, it is, that they do not bear cold weather so well, and are more apt to have their limbs frost-bitten in the Northern parts of America; their greater evaporation contributing to chill them more severely. However this hypothesis may be, it is certain, that Europeans, coming to reside in the West-Indies, are never known to enjoy their health and spirits, unless they perspire freely; and those, who continue to do so, are not afflicted with sickness so long as it continues: that regimen thefore of diet,

[o] Franklin's Papers on Philosophical Subjects.

of

of exercife, and cloathing, which anfwers beft for fupporting this regular flow, without carrying it to extreme, is the moft falutary for European ftrangers to purfue. The natives, black and white, are not fubject, like Europeans, to bilious, putrid, and malignant fevers: they are not only habituated to the climate, but to a difference in refpect to diet and manners; which works no fmall change in mens conftitutions. A Creole, if he was to addict himfelf to that kind of diet which is known to have a tendency to produce putrid diforders, or an acrid, corrupt bile, would no more be exempt from them, than an European. I knew a Creole boy, of about fix years of age, who, being reftrained by his mother from eating any fort of fruit or vegetables (the former, left they fhould generate worms; and the latter, through fear of acidities and gripes) made his principal meal every day on butchers meat, fowl, or fifh, without falt, feafoning, or any bread, except now and then a very fmall quantity, and wafhed it down with plain water. The boy, after perfifting for fome months in this regimen, was feized with a very violent, bilious, remittent fever, accompanied with a *delirium* and other bad fymptoms, that threatened his life; but, by adminiftering the bark inwardly, applying poultices of it externally to the ftomach and abdomen, and often foaking his feet in a ftrong warm decoction of it, he at length recovered, and doubtlefs owed his life to this noble fpecific, thus thrown into his body by fo many different ways. But the acrimony in his blood was apparent, from the vaft abundance of boils, which broke out afterwards from head to foot. I think it probable, that the luxuriant flefh-diet of Englifhmen at home, together with fome fcorbutic taint in their blood, may be affigned partly as an occafional caufe of their being more obnoxious, generally fpeaking, to bad fevers in the Weft-Indies, than many other Northern nations. This, however, is not the fole caufe, becaufe we find that Englifh women, who are alfo equally flefh-eaters, and liable to the fame fcorbutic taint in a degree, are not fo often feized with thefe dangerous fevers; nor are they attacked fo violently, nor to fuch a degree of malignancy. Perhaps, we may impute this diverfity to the more cool and temperate regimen of the women, their lefs expofure to heat and hard exercife in the fun, lefs addiction to intemperance, and late hours.

There

There may be other reasons suggested for the difference observed between the English men, and those of other countries. First, their excessive indulgence in a promiscuous commerce on their first arrival, with the black and mulatto women; and this, with so little prudence and caution in their amours, that they are almost morally sure of being very speedily infected. The facility with which the milder symptoms of the *virus* are removed, in this warm atmosphere, serves only as an incentive to these persons, and renders them indifferent and careless about consequences; for a *gonorrhœa simplex* yields in a very few days to gentle medicines. Encouraged, therefore, to persevere in this unheeding course, they in due time attain to the highest honours this impure contact is qualified to confer, as a reward for their temerity; the consequence of which is, their being laid under absolute necessity of praying to their god *Mercury* for relief. Not a few also arrive here, who have already passed through many of these fiery trials in London, and other seats of debauchery. It has been remarked by several of the most eminent physicians, and stands confirmed by repeated experience, that *mercurial* medicines are attended with the most pernicious effects upon scorbutic habits, and on such as are disposed to *putrid fevers*. These gentlemen all agree in opinion, that the power of mercurials chiefly consists in weakening and relaxing the solids, and in attenuating and dissolving the fluids; a human body therefore, which has recently undergone a mercurial regimen, is already on the very brink of putrefaction, and very ill prepared to resist the assault of a putrid fever. Thus in the *scurvy*, a very small quantity of mercury is sufficient to bring on a salivation. When this disorder raged among the imperial troops in Hungary, four-hundred soldiers, who took mercury contrary to the advice of their physician, *all* died to a man in a salivation. *Pringle* observes, that persons who have lately undergone a salivation, and whose blood is consequently in a state of dissolution, are much sooner infected by noxious *effluvia* than others; and, that malignant fevers, and the scurvy also, are rendered more severe and dangerous in such circumstances. To the same effect is the remark of *De Monchy*, who found, that, after using mercury in *venereal* disor-

ders,

ders, the *Peruvian bark* lofes a great part of its efficacy, in the moft virulent cafes. Thus, that admirable medicine the bark, which in found habits proves a fovereign antidote againft putrid and malignant fevers, is robbed of its virtue by the putrefactive counteraction of mercurials; thefe noxious effects therefore, conjunctly with any morbid difpofition of the humours, or with a bad air, and improper diet, or too violent exercife in the fun, may eafily and naturally either haften the attack of a putrid diftemper, or promote the exacerbations of it, if already formed; and, fuch being allowed the predifpofing caufes, it is eafy to admit, that a common fever may foon degenerate into a putrid, and even one of the moft malignant fpecies. The female flaves, and even free Blacks, in our plantations, are few of them exempt from this *virus*; but they conceal it by every artifice in their power, that no delay may happen in their bufinefs; for a hindrance in this refpect would be a certain lofs of profit to them. What *Ulloa* mentions of the Spaniards at *Quito*, is applicable to thefe traders: he tells us, " The " venereal difeafe is there fo common, that few perfons are free " from it; even *little children*, incapable by their age of having " contracted it actively, have been known to be attacked with it " in the fame degree as perfons who have acquired it by their " debauchery; the chief caufe of its prevalence, is negligence in the " cure. This difeafe muft naturally be thought in fome meafure " to fhorten their lives; though it is not uncommon, to fee per- " fons live to feventy-five years or more, who have never been en- " tirely free from that diftemper, either hereditary or contracted, " from their early youth." It is probable, that the Scotch and Irifh, who come over with founder conftitutions, lefs impaired perhaps by fcorbutic and venereal taints, are, for this reafon, more healthy than the Englifh; befides, the Scotch, in particular, if not more chafte, are at leaft in general more circumfpect in their amours.

I knew an European gentleman, who, by imprudent connexions of this fort, was infected not only by the *lues venerea*, but with the *yaws* at the fame time; under thefe two diftempers (than which there are few in *Pandora's* box more loathfome), he lingered for a

long

long time; the remedies proper for the one, only ferved to exafperate the other; and therefore not being able, by the powers of mercury, to obtain relief, he was obliged to leave the ifland, in the hope of receiving fome benefit from the advice of phyficians in Great Britain. Another, a young man of a lively but lafcivious turn, for feveral months after his arrival, was fcarcely ever free from venereal infection, having not patience to wait the cure of one taint, before he contracted another; by this infane conduct, a falivation became neceffary; debilitated with this, and his preceding exceffes, he was fuddenly, upon fome little irregularity, feized with a fever, fo flight at firft, that, had not his conftitution been worn down, and his whole habit degenerated, it would have been eafily removed; but, being aggravated by the tabid ftate to which his body was then reduced, it turned by degrees to a highly putrid diftemper, and carried him off.

Cataftrophes of this nature, it is to be feared, have but too often occurred in the ifland, to the untimely deftruction of many an improvident youth; nor are our furgeons wholly to be exculpated, who are but too fond of prefcribing mercurials upon all occafions, without adverting to their fatal operation on fome habits.

Ardent fpirits, particularly brandy, and frefh diftilled rum, *in excefs*, are no lefs injurious in all cafes where the humours have a difpofition to putrefcence; although, when ufed with due moderation, and not too frequently, they are antifeptic, or antiputrefcent. What chance have thofe men for longevity, who act as if they were engaged in a perpetual confpiracy againft their own health; who are inceffantly inflaming and irritating their blood and juices with an acrimony, that is productive of mortal diftempers; who indulge beyond meafure in fiery fpirits; carelefsly hurry about, and ufe violent exercifes in the hotteft part of the hotteft days [p]; fit up late at night, deprive their bodies of refrefhing fleep, and expofe them to the night air; and laftly, who plunge

[p] From a great increafe of corporeal motion, and a want of repofe and fleep, the fame confequences are to be expected as from fevers; the nature of which confifts in an accelerated circulation of the blood, attended of courfe with an exceffive heat; whence proceeds an enfuing putrefcency of the humours: juft as a *hare*, killed after being hard run for a confiderable time, becomes fooner tainted than one that has been killed upon its form. DE MONCHY.

headlong into venereal debauches, and a mercurial regimen! ought the premature fate of such men, to be charged on climate? They who follow such improper courses, must count on their natural consequences; and unless, by the perversion of their intellectual faculties, they can be acquitted as lunatics or idiots, they must expect, in the award of divine justice, to be deemed guilty of self-murder; having willfully, wickedly, and, I am sure, I may add *wantonly*, put themselves to death, by means as effectual, as if they had used arsenic, or a dagger.

Early-rising, which has been spoken of with the greatest encomiums by medical-writers, for its contributing very eminently to the health, vigour, and activity of animal life, as well as rational, is particularly necessary in Jamaica; and no man ever attained to longevity here, who was not an early riser; nor are any so healthy, as those who religiously addict themselves to this practice. It is necessary here, because nothing more relaxes the body than the warmth of a bed, more especially if sleep is indulged at a time when the sun has ascended to some height above the horizon, and renewed the heat of the atmosphere [q]. The morning air is here delightfully cool; and the most agreeable time for exercise is before, or just about, sun-rise; they who exercise at this hour, feel their bodies refreshed and vigorous, so as to suffer no inconvenience from heat during the remainder of the day. The bed should be forsaken by six o'clock at furthest; many there are who rise at five; this supposes an early retreat to rest, the preceding evening; the more common bed-time at night, is from ten to eleven. They who lounge till eight or nine in the morning, and make it an habitual practice, cannot be long free from distemper; it is not only,

---

[q] It is a curious, although not a new remark, that the inhabitants within the Tropics sleep less than those who dwell in the cold, Northern climates; I believe, the difference in this respect, between a healthy person in Jamaica, and another in Britain, may, on a fair calculation, amount at least to thirty days *per annum*. If an inhabitant of England sleeps eight hours a night, at an average the year throughout, the inhabitant of Jamaica will be found to sleep not more than seven; consequently, the latter possesses thirty days, or upwards, of conscious existence more than the former; and, at the end of twelve years, may be said to have outlived the other by a full twelvemonth. How far this difference may tend to free the West-Indian from some distempers, incident to Northern drowsiness, or to irritate his animal spirits, or enliven his faculties, has not yet been examined; but it is probable, that it may obviate, in some degree, the relaxing effects of a warm atmosphere, and sweep away that gloom from the soul, which November weather is so apt to cast upon it in England

that

that an excefs of fleep, inftead of nourifhing and refrefhing, ener-
vates and emafculates, the human frame, but the body gains not
a moment's refpite from heat, or relaxation ; it is heated during
the day, it is heated again by fitting up late ; and, after retiring to
bed, it is plunged into a kind of hot bath ; and lies ftewing in its
own vapours : while, as the fun draws nearer the meridian, the air
grows more fervid every moment. So beneficial indeed is
the cuftom of early rifing in this climate, that it fortifies the organs againft the invafion of ficknefs, and is of more importance
than any other branch of regimen ; more efpecially, if joined to
moderate exercife.

It is difficult to fay, what degree of exercife a man may ufe here
without danger ; it muft perhaps be confidered relatively to mens
different conftitutions, and ftrength. The weakeft are ftrengthened
by it, and the ftrongeft become weak without it. In general, I
believe, the inhabitants, efpecially Europeans, ufe it to a greater
degree every day, than men in general do in England, and with
feemingly lefs fatigue. I have myfelf traveled frequently fifty miles
in a day on horfeback, without fuffering any laffitude, and always
found fuch journies moft fupportable, the earlier I fet out in the
morning [r]. But, confidering the expence of perfpiration and
fpirits, which the body undergoes here daily, efpecially in the
Southern diftricts, we ought to infer, that a lefs degree is requifite
here for health, than in colder climates ; for it feems reafonab
to fuppofe, that we fhould endeavour here, rather to reftrain, than
promote, all violent motions of the blood and humours, and preferve them calm and temperate, at the fame time not fuffering abfolute inaction and floth to poffefs us fo far, as to caufe a ftagna-
tion ; extraordinary exercife is lefs hurtful than fuch an indolent,
motionlefs habit of life. The beft exercife in this climate is geftation, either in a wheel-carriage, or on horfeback ; but the latter
is to be preferred, except in long journies. But walking is too
laborious, and attended with too great a wafte of fubftance and
fpirits. The common practice of many in the towns, who are continually in agitation, and take the fame liberty of buftling about
on foot, at all hours of the day, as if they were in London, is evi-

[r] Sixty miles are ufually reckoned here a day's journey, on horfeback.

dently

dently abfurd. It feems probable, that fo much hurry, which increafes the *momentum* of the blood, and throws the whole body into violent heat, which is augmented by the intenfe ardour of the fun at noon, may bring on fevers of the moft fatal kind. This practice is equally injudicious and unneceffary; the former, becaufe it may be productive of fevere illnefs; the latter, becaufe, by rifing early, much cooler hours might be found for tranfacting all the bufinefs, which any man who values his health can, or at leaft ought to, go through in this climate, during the forenoon. When bufinefs demands attendance abroad, they ought to choofe the morning and afternoon for difpatching it, and keep within doors, or in the fhade, at that time of the day when the folar rays are felt with moft force and inconvenience; but, if they cannot avoid expofing themfelves, they ought to walk flowly, and ufe fome other precautions, to guard againft any bad effects. The Negroes arm their heads with a load of handkerchiefs, carefully twifted about them, in form of a turban. The Eaftern nations ufe the turban, which is not more calculated for ornament, than as a prefervative againft the violent action of the meridian fun upon the delicate, capillary veffels in the head; the obftruction of which occafions obftinate head-achs, and fometimes that fatal apoplexy, called by the French, *coup de foleil.* In the French, Spanifh, and Portuguefe colonies, umbrellas are in general ufe, and found extremely ferviceable to protect the head and body from this unwholefome fultrinefs. But our brave countrymen, defpifing all thefe precautions, as too ridiculous, or too effeminate, courageoufly face the fun at high noon; and will fuffer death rather than put on any armour for their defence. It is not therefore without juft reafon, that the Spaniards, who fit calmly within doors, whilft honeft John Bull is anxioufly trotting about his bufinefs, all befmeared with duft and fweat, fay proverbially, that, " no animal, " except a *dog* and an *Englifhman,* is to be feen walking the ftreets " in the middle of the day."

Doctor Hilary exclaims moft profanely againft *dancing:* " It is, " fays he, too violent an exercife for a hot climate, and many in-
" jure their health very greatly by it; I have known it fatal to
" fome; neither is it ufed in the Eaftern hot countries. But moft
of

" of the ladies are fo exceffively fond of it, that, fay what I will, *they*
" *will dance on*."

The doctor very rightly concludes his foliloquy, in defpair of prevailing on his fair audience to defift from an amufement fo delightful to
them, and, in my opinion, fo innocent, if not carried to excefs. I fear
the doctor forgot his reading, when he afferted that no fuch diverfion
was in ufe in the Eaftern hot countries; there are none of them, perhaps, where it is not in ufe: we find it in Afia, in Africa, and every
part of America. The Indians of South America are particularly fond
of it; even the grave Spaniard here is melted into an affection for it,
and capers in *farabands* and *faldangos*; the natives of Jamaica are dancers from their infancy. The domeftic life of women, which prevents
them from exercifing abroad as much as the other fex, naturally inclines them to love thofe active amufements which may be followed
within doors; dancing therefore, confidered as an exercife, is healthy
and proper for them, promotes the circulation of the blood, and re-
frefhes the fpirits in the moft agreeable manner, by the chearfulnefs
and gaiety which it infpires. In Jamaica, indeed, it is fcarcely to be
called an exercife *within doors*; the windows are all thrown open, and
the dancers enjoy a conftant fucceffion of frefh air. It is very different
here in its effects from what it is in cold countries, where the heat, and
offenfive fmell of fires and lights, and the atmofphere of a clofe apartment, from which the external air is carefully excluded, and which is
further vitiated by the breath and copious perfpiration of a multitude
of perfons crowded together, make it productive of no falutary confequence. It has rarely been prejudicial in Jamaica, except where common prudence was wanting afterwards, and the parties have carelefsly
expofed themfelves, when in a profufe perfpiration, to the damp and
chilling midnight air. They, who are more cautious, cloathe themfelves properly on going home, put on dry, well-aired linen, take a little draught of fome warm liquor at getting into bed, and feldom feel
any bad effect, even after what fome may think an excefs; the principal reafon for which may be, that the pleafure and vivacity, infeparable
from it, in fome meafure counteract the laffitude which fo much motion (mechanically confidered) would naturally bring on, and prepare the body for a found and undifturbed fleep, which reftores very
peedily the wafte of fpirits; infomuch, that I have known in this ifland,

a regular dancing-bout perfifted in for a whole week, not intermitting a fingle night, without any ill confequence to the parties concerned. However, it is certainly more advifeable to ufe it in moderation; and, thus ufed, it will prove, in my humble opinion, a healthful recreation, an excellent antidote to cares, and a happy promoter of nuptial unions.

The utility of *bathing* need not be infifted on, where we find it practifed by the White and Negroe natives fo univerfally, and conftantly. Frequent wafhing the body with water, cleanfes the perfpiratory ducts from that foulnefs that is continually falling upon them from their own condenfed, dewy atmofphere; the middle of the day is fitteft for this operation, in water which has been placed fome hours in the fun-fhine, fo as to acquire a tolerable degree of warmth. The Negroes wafh in the open rivers at that time, and find it moft wholefome, by experience; they have a different opinion of *cold-bathing*; and indeed it feems not proper for this climate, except at a very early hour before fun-rife, and in the cooler mountainous or Northfide parts, rather than the Southern: in the latter, I have known three or four fatal accidents which have followed plunging in cold water in the heat of the day. It fhould feem therefore more eligible to follow that ufage, which experience fhews to be not only healthy, but neceffary to cleanlinefs, than to try experiments which have proved unfuitable to the climate, and are condemned by the native inhabitants, whofe judgement has originally been founded upon trials, of what cuftom was hurtful, and what harmlefs.

The influence of the *paffions* upon health, has been the fubject of many differtations from medical pens; in this country it muft operate with double force, where men are more *feelingly alive* to joy or inquietude; where the nervous fyftem is far more irritable than in a Northern climate. Men of lively imaginations and great vivacity (and fuch are the natives of this ifland) are more liable than others, to fudden and violent emotions of the mind, and their effects; fuch ftrong and fudden tranfports may actually throw men into acute difeafes: but the flow and durable paffions, folicitude, grief, ftifled refentment, and vexation, are more often dangerous and mortal. Thefe confuming enemies to health difturb the functions of the ftomach, and vitiate its juices, fo that no wholefome chyle or nourifhment can enter the blood; the patient languifhes under a bad habit of body, contracted from this caufe,

2

pines

pines with atrophy, and want of refreshing sleep; hence a complication of diseases succeeding each other, from bad to worse; and, unless he can subdue his anxiety, and restore peace to his mind, he gradually sinks under it, and dies, as it is said, of a *broken heart* [s].

Anxiety affects men in this country in proportion to their sensibility, and to its duration. When once it has taken a firm hold, it is generally productive of mortal consequences. Multitudes have expired here under the pressure of this fatal cause. Hurried by levity of disposition or want of thought, into an expensive way of living, or imprudent schemes and pursuits; distress has poured in upon them at once like a deluge. Fretted, and wearied out at length with the conflict, and closely beset on all sides with implacable creditors, they have yielded passively to their fate, and sunk down into the grave, under a load that was too grievous for their mind to support. In such desperate circumstances, a slight indisposition is soon converted into one more formidable; the symptoms become more and more dangerous, and the malignancy increases every day, till, in the end, it has destroyed those, who required the aid of good spirits and chearfulness, to second the efficacy of medicine; every drug has lost its usual virtue; the organs refuse to perform their functions; and thus, the disease in the mind has led the way to a sure conquest over the body. The life of an industrious planter is one continued scene of activity, both of body and mind. He is necessarily engaged in many public duties, as well as private affairs. His slumbers are often disturbed with corroding cares, the failure of seasons, the casualties to which his property may be liable, and the importunity of creditors. The day is often insufficient for the multiplicity of business which he finds himself obliged to allot to it. He ought, therefore, to arrange his various occupations, and make them conform to a certain orderly train and method, that he may proceed in them with the greater ease and dispatch; and, by this means, retrench great part of the perplexity, which must otherwise ensue. The like regular method he should inforce throughout all the inferior departments of his plantation; and, weighing well the uncertainty of all human possessions, and the frequent vicissitudes of fortune, he should determine with himself to confine his annual expences of living within certain positive bounds, so as not to exceed, if possible, *one*

[s] Cadogan on Chronic Diseases.

third

third part of his clear income, computed upon the average of five or seven years preceding. Some caution may likewise be requisite in his dealings with mankind; but there is one, which particularly merits his constant recollection; which is, that more persons in this country have been made unhappy, and even ruined, by *other mens debts*, than by their own. Let him therefore, above all things, keep a strict guard over the liberality or credulity of his own temper, and resolve inflexibly, *Never to be bound for any man*, and to consider *debt* as one of the most substantial evils in life. By a course of even moderate œconomy, he may have some little overplus at the year's end; and let this be applied (if necessary) to supply the wants of his friend, or his dependant. Men are not injured here so much by what they lend, or give away to the necessitous, as by setting their hands and seals to paper too often, and for too considerable sums; which unexpectedly rise up in judgement against them, or their family, after many years have elapsed. By engaging as *collaterals*, they have made themselves *principals*; destroyed their peace of mind; involved their estates, and beggared their children; without essentially benefiting their pretended friend: for such is the strange disposition of a sinking man, that, like one who is in danger of drowning, he catches at every straw within his reach; thinks of nothing but temporary expedients; and, between hope and despair of extricating himself from distress and ruin, he will, even when he knows it will turn out wholly unavailing to his own affairs, insiduously draw his best benefactor into the same abyss, to perish with him.

Misfortunes here, in planting and in trade, are necessarily very frequent, where men often adventure without limits; give, and take credit; are subject to be hurt by misplaced good-nature and confidence; and liable to various calamities and losses. It is difficult for men to reason themselves into a calm composure under afflictions, or vexatious circumstances, by all the arguments that philosophy or religion can furnish:

" Durum: sed levius *patientiâ*,
" Quidquid corrigere est nefas."
" 'Tis hard: but *patience* must endure,
" And soothe the woes it cannot cure."

This is the remedy which philosophy suggests, as the best means of alleviating those ills, that vexation only serves to render more sharp
and

and intolerable. The heathen moralifts called it, for this reafon, " *portus miferiarum*; the afylum of miferies:" but *Chriftian* patience brings infinitely more comfort and fupport. This inftructs us to believe, that nothing befals us, except by the permiffion, or the direction, of Divine Providence; it attracts our dependence upon that Being, who can enable us to bear what, otherwife, the frailty of our nature muft fink under; it informs us, that difeafes, pain, lofs of friends, ingratitude, difappointments in our affairs, and *all the various ills that flefh is heir to*, fall to the lot of the good, as well as the wicked: the Divine Being exercifes our virtue with fuch trials; corrects our vices and miftakes by thefe examples; leads us to foberer purfuits and councils; and excites us to repofe our future thoughts on his care for our happinefs, by fubmitting to his wife and provident difpenfations, with ferenity and fortitude. Thefe trials, in a greater or lefs degree, every mortal muft expect to meet with, in the courfe of his life; he fees continual inftances of them, if he will but turn his eyes to view what befals the reft of mankind; he ought then to prepare to meet them himfelf; never to be too confident under good fortune, nor too defponding under the common mifchances to which all are equally liable. Inftead of giving way to thofe corroding thoughts, which keen fenfibility, when too much indulged, is fure to aggravate with frefh tortures every moment, he fhould apply himfelf to meditate on the means of leffening his torment, by fubmiffion to the Father of all men, and frequent fupplications to him for affiftance and relief: books, exercife, bufinefs, chearful fociety, any innocent amufements, fhould be reforted to, for unbending the mind, and breaking the iron chain of forrowful reflection. Too many have flown to the bottle, or to *laudanum*, to quaff the fweet oblivion[t]; fuch men are cowards, who have neither courage to bear up againft their misfortunes, nor to end a painful exift-

ence

[t] I cannot avoid taking fome notice of the abufe committed by many perfons here, male as well as female, in their daily potations of this baneful mixture; feveral of both fexes love to become inebriated with it, and make their boaft, that, of all liquors, it is not only the fpeedieft and cheapeft, but the pleafanteft, to get drunk with. This vice (for a notorious vice it is) has ruined, and ftill ruins, the beauty of many a fine woman in this ifland, both in complexion and conftitution; for it fo poifons the whole corporeal mafs, as to render the lips of a deadly pale or livid hue, and the face cadaverous. After frequent repetitions of it, fo importunate and ftrong are its folicitations, as to admit of no denial, till, in the end, it conftrains even its debauchees to abufe it. One morning I paid a vifit to an elderly gentleman, whom I had frequently feen, and talked with be-

ence by one bold ſtroke; to end it indeed in ſuch a manner, were but a temporary cure, for this world only; and the means, perhaps, of making that miſery eternal, which otherwiſe would have been, at the worſt, of ſhort duration.   To combat with ſteadineſs againſt adverſity, and resolve

fore, at other places.   I found him ſitting in a chair in his hall, and, accoſting him as uſual in as civil a manner as I could, I perceived that, contrary to his former polite and friendly manner, he ſat regardleſs of me, and every thing elſe about him, except that his eyes were fixed upon me with a ghaſtly ſtare.   Upon this, I appeared to take no further notice of him, but, addreſſing myſelf to the other company preſent, ſat down, and diſcourſed on different ſubjects.   Soon after, he withdrew into an adjoining room, and, ſtaying there not half long enough for me to be informed what his diſorder was, he returned alert and chearful, with a bottle and a ſpoon, and kindly aſked me if I would take a cordial with him; which I declined doing, as I did not know the liquor; but he frankly told me, it was liquid laudanum of his own preparing, of which he had juſt drunk one ſpoonful, and ſhould at leaſt twice repeat the draught in courſe of the day, according to a cuſtom he had practiſed for ſome years paſt.   It was ſurpriſing to me, to ſee how ſuddenly and powerfully it had operated upon him; for, inſtead of the torpid, ſpiritleſs creature, whom I firſt ſaw, he was, in the ſpace of five minutes, fluſhed in his countenance, gay, talkative, animated throughout, and univerſally changed in mind and body.

This puts me in mind of the account which travelers have given of the Perſians, who, like other Eaſtern nations, take pills of ſolid opium, which ſome of them gradually increaſe to a doſe that would deſtroy half a dozen Europeans.   Within half an hour after taking the pill it begins to operate, and a thouſand vagaries delight their imagination; they laugh, ſing, and talk extravagantly, like men in a delirium, or *maddened* with wine; but, after the effect is gone off, they find their ſpirits exhauſted, and grow penſive and melancholy, till they repeat the doſe again: by this means, ſome make it ſo neceſſary to them, that they cannot live without it.

I have known a whole company of men in Jamaica, at table, pledge one another in this liquor. The women, in general, are more moderate in the quantity they take at once; but, although they ſip it drop by drop, it is repeated ſo frequently, that the whole they take in a twelvemonth is pretty near as much, as what others drink, who recur to it ſeldom, but in larger doſes at a time; and its effects, in both caſes, are equally fatal.   Some ladies are never without a bottle of it in their pocket, with ſome lumps of ſugar; and ſwallow it with great privacy, and by ſtealth, twice or thrice every day, increaſing the doſe ſo high, as to eighty or one hundred drops.   They pretend it is their " *curarum dulce levamen*," and abſolutely requiſite for their comfort and happineſs.

" Their only labour is to kill the time,
" And labour dire it is, and weary woe.
" They ſit, they loll, turn o'er ſome idle rhyme;
" Then riſing ſudden to the *dram* they go,
" Or ſaunter forth with tottering ſteps, and ſlow;
" This ſoon too rude an exerciſe they find;
" Strait on the couch their limbs again they throw,
" Where hours on hours they, ſighingly reclin'd,
" *Embrace* the vapoury god, ſoft-breathing in the wind."

THOMSON.

The Turks, and other diſciples of Mahomet, betook themſelves to this mode of inebriation, becauſe their religion forbad the uſe of wine.   The Aſiatic Indians are ſaid to indulge in it, not ſo much to make them ſleep, as from a notion, that it is a great provocative, and qualifies them the better for libidinous exerciſes.

Sottiſhneſs

refolve to conquer it, is the higheft teft of a good mind, true courage, and found underftanding; in other things, men will perfevere through every difficulty, and fucceed in defiance of every obftacle; nothing more is required, than the like fpirit of perfeverance and fortitude, to furmount the greateft ills of life, and trample upon thofe diftreffes, which ceafe to be burthenfome, when we have learned to bear them; but ever redouble their preffure upon us, when we bear them with impatience and timidity.

Sottifhnefs then and luft being the chief founders of its ufe among thefe Eaftern people, what opinion are we to form of thofe ladies in our Weftern hemifphere, who are bewitched to the fame deteftable cuftom? If drunkennefs is fo difgraceful to the fair fex in particular, they furely ought to reflect, that it makes not the leaft difference, in point of difhonour, whether they fuddle themfelves with laudanum, or with brandy; neverthelefs, there are too many among them, who, if a dram was to be offered them in public company, would confider it a high affront put upon them, and yet take the firft convenient opportunity to beaftialize themfelves with their favourite liquor, till they are deprived of their reafon, and driven into the moft incoherent ravings in their converfation, and the wildeft extravagancies in their conduct; thus facrificing fenfe, beauty, health, fame, and even virtue, to this pernicious habit. All phyficians agree, that it is exceedingly hurtful to thofe of weak and delicate habits, and brings on prematurely the infirmities of old age; for, among the Eaftern nations, it has been obferved, that fcarcely any, who begin this practice while they are young, live to be above fifty. It produces paralytic diforders, and palfies; hinders digeftion, and palls the appetite. It likewife is charged with caufing a relaxation of the lower jaw, and a ftammering fpeech; in regard to the latter bad effect, I am morally fure, we may afcribe the drawling, faltering pronunciation of many women and men in this ifland, to their exceffive ufe of laudanum.

In fome cafes, and in the hands of a difcreet phyfician, it is a noble remedy, and particularly in the diftemper called the locked jaw, fo frequent in the Weft Indies; and not feldom, as a palliative in the colic, and belly-ache: but thofe perfons, who make it a part of their daily diet, receive all the injury it is capable of producing; and preclude themfelves from all hopes of relief from it, in thofe maladies, where it might otherwife have proved their certain friend.

The firm hold which fo horrid a fafhion has taken in this ifland is really unaccountable, unlefs we fuppofe that the force of example, and the alluring perfuafion of inveterate female tipplers, have combined with the deluding charms of this *Circean* draught:

" Offering to every weary *vifitor*
" Their *magic* liquor in a cryftal glafs,
" To quench the drought of Phœbus; which as they tafte,
" (For moft do tafte through fond, *and curious* thirft)
" Soon as the potion works, their human count'nance,
" Th'exprefs refemblance of the gods, is chang'd
" Into fome brutifh form of wolf, or bear,
" Or ounce, or tiger, hog, or bearded goat,
" All other parts remaining as they were;
" And they, fo perfect in their mifery,
" Not once perceive their foul disfigurement,
" But boaft themfelves more comely than before,
" And all their friends, and native home forget,
" To roll with pleafure in a fenfual ftye."

MILTON.

4 A 2

SECT.

SECT. IV.

Of Sugar, confidered Medicinally.

There is no better prefervative, perhaps, againft thofe difeafes which owe their rife to a putrefcency of the humours, than the juice of the fugar-cane, and its various preparations. The effects they produce on debilitated Negroes, and on brute animals, whom they reftore to health and vigour, rendering the moft emaciated plump and lively, are extremely remarkable. There cannot be a ftronger recommendation of any fubftance proper for aliment, than to fay, that it is eagerly devoured by all animals, and offenfive to none; more efpecially, as they, who are governed by unerring inftinct, are never known to delight in any fpecies of food, which is inimical to their health: but human reafon and experience correfpond with this inftinct, in recommendation of thefe mild, nutritious, and falutary effects.

It has been obferved, that, fince fugar and acefcent fubftances have come into vogue, all putrid difeafes, the fcurvy no lefs than putrid malignant fevers, the dyfentery, and even the plague itfelf, are much abated. The ableft writers on thefe difeafes mention fugar or melaffes as neceffary ingredients in the diet of patients afflicted with them; and that their virtue confifts in the efficacy with which they refift, and counteract, all putrid humours. The Spaniards in the Weft Indies, fenfible of this effect by long experience, ufe it univerfally; it forms a part of all their collations, and they never drink even a glafs of water without previoufly eating fome conferve, or fweetmeat. In the putrid yellow fever, Doctor Mc Bride recommends very ftrenuoufly the juice of the *fugar-cane* before it is thoroughly ripe, diluted and acidulated with the frefh juice of limes or Seville oranges. Let our men (fays he) in the navy be as well cloathed as in the army, and let them be allowed, whilft at fea, a daily portion of *fugar*; and, I will venture to promife that, in a time of war, we fhall annually fave fome thoufands of very ufeful lives.

To the ufe of this, and frefh vegetables, which now make up fo great a part of the diet of the European nations, it is to be afcribed, that we at this day fo feldom hear of the dreadful putrid difeafes which formerly fwept off fuch multitudes, every thirty or forty years, under the name of plagues.

The

The diet moſt fit to preſerve health in hot climates muſt conſiſt (for the greater part) of vegetables, and of thoſe ſubſtances, which produce the greateſt quantities of air, in order to afford a ſufficient quantity of antiſeptic vapour, to make up for the extraordinary waſte of air, which is carried off from the fluids by inſenſible perſpiration; and thoſe perſons muſt inevitably fall into putrid diſeaſes, who eat much animal food, which produces but little air; who drink much of ſpirituous liquors, which contain no air in themſelves ſcarcely, and prevent the ready extrication thereof from the aliment, during the digeſtive proceſs; and who incautiouſly expoſe themſelves to a moiſt atmoſphere, which hinders any thing but the aërial part of the perſpirable matter from being carried off.

The great efficacy of vegetables conſiſts partly in their containing a large quantity of this fixed antiſeptic air or vapour, and their impregnation with a very ſweet juice, or mixture of ſaccharine oil and ſalt, which doctor Tiſſot obſerves is highly ſalutary. All the culinary roots, even in Europe, are full of this kind of ſugar, which may eaſily be extracted from them. Experiments to this effect have been tried on ſeveral; and, in particular, eight ounces of the juice of ſkirret yielded one ounce and an half of ſugar [u]. This ſaccharine juice predominates in moſt of the fruits and eſculent roots in Jamaica in a very ſurpriſing degree, as if the Divine Being h d meant peculiarly to adapt them as neceſſary correctives of thoſe putreſcent humours, which a diet on animal food is apt to generate in this climate. Thus we find, that the Iriſh potatoe, when tranſplanted into this ſoil, acquires a ſweetiſh taſte, which ſhews its impregnation with ſaccharine principles; the ſweet potatoe, the native of this climate, is largely ſupplied with the like impregnation; ſo are the yams, eddos, cocos, moſt of the different ſorts of pulſe, and almoſt all the fruits. The plantain, when ripe, and dried in the ſun, is a perfect conſerve, without the aid of any more ſugar, than what is naturally contained in it; the banana is ſtill more luſcious, but with a ſlight aſtringent quality, which has made it extremely remedial in fluxes; correcting the putrid humour by its antiſeptic virtues, ſheathing the acrimony with its balſamic oil, rendering the bowels gently ſoluble, and yet ſtrengthening their tone by its mild aſtringency. The China oranges here, when full ripe, and in a good

[u] Margraff's Mem.

foil, are frequently incrufted over with a palpable integument of white fugar, concreted on their rind, and hardened by the fun. How benevolent and gracious is this ample provifion of fo wholefome and neceffary a fubftance, which is fo copioufly lodged in the foil, to be imbibed, prepared, refined, and duly adapted, by all thefe vegetable productions, for the ufe, fuftentation, and health, of the inhabitants! The fugar prepared from the cane contains thefe virtues in abftract, which are found lefs copioufly diftributed to the culinary roots, and efculent fruits; it therefore prefents itfelf as a portable remedy, always at hand, to fupply the occafions of thofe perfons who are not able to procure other vegetable productions, endowed with the like properties; or to be mixed with thofe aliments, which contain too little, or none at all, of them; it feems therefore peculiarly of ufe, as a neceffary part of feaftore, for the ready fervice of thofe, who are too diftant from the land to come at frefh vegetables, and the nature of whofe flefh diet requires fuch a conftant corrector. The warrant and petty officers on board a fleet are fcarcely ever feized with *acute* putrid difeafes, excepting by meer infection; and they are very feldom known to become fcorbutic in any violent degree, unlefs the general caufe (exceffive moifture) be of a remarkably long continuance. The diet of this clafs of men is, in general, the fame with the reft of the crew, but they are well clad for the moft part, and never want a little ftore of *fugar*.

The expence of allowing fugar, or melaffes, as a part of fea provifions, even taking it at the higheft, is too trifling, when put in competition with preferving fo valuable a part of the community as our feamen, at leaft, for all that they might have occafion for, when at fea.

The efficacy of this medicine, in preferving the health of feamen, is far from being a recent difcovery; fo early as the reign of Charles the Firft fugar had been found eminently ufeful in fcorbutic cafes, as appears by *Woodall's* Treatife, re-publifhed in 1639. But Great Britain had at that time no colonies to fupply her with a fufficient quantity of it; and it is worthy remark, that the plague almoft uninterruptedly raged in London till towards the Revolution, when confiderable remittances of fugar began to arrive from Barbadoes, Nevis, Jamaica, and other iflands, belonging to Britain. This affluence

rendered

rendered it much [*w*] cheaper than ever it had been before; confequently the ufe and confumption became far more extenfive, particularly in London, than in preceding times; and the vifitations of the plague gradually became lefs frequent, till at length they ceafed intirely. Thofe medical writers, who have entertained very fanguine expectations from new *wort* in the cure of the fcurvy, feem neverthelefs to be of opinion, that fugar is equally efficacious; the fame reafons which lead to expect fuccefs from the one, holding good, in moft effential circumftances, in regard to the other; and their opinion is founded on this doctrine, that fuch vegetable fermentable fubftances are difcovered, by experiment, to have the power of preferving animal fluids from corruption, and of even reftoring them after having undergone fome degree of putrefaction.

The hot liquor taken from the *tache*, or laft copper, in the Weft India boiling houfes, during crop, and mixed to a fufficient dilution with water, makes a moft agreeable drink, having fomewhat of the tafte of new wort, but more pleafant; of this both the Negroes and Whites in general are extremely fond, and it ought to be the principal drink of Europeans newly arrived. From this caufe it happens, that the imported Negroes, purchafed during the crop, are more likely to do well than thofe who are introduced at other times of the year; for they are freely indulged with a daily allowance of this liquor, and it is found to recover the languid and diftempered, and make them grow fat, fleek, and vigorous. In its operation it is cooling, gently moves the body, and throws any latent acrimony or putrid humour, which may be lurking in the blood and juices, upon the furface of the fkin, as many Europeans experience on drinking it; but, on perceiving boils, or cutaneous eruptions, about the lips, or other parts of the body, to follow the ufe of this beverage, they ignorantly fancy, that thefe falutary fymptoms are a real diforder, caufed by fome noxious quality in the liquor; and fome have difcontinued it

---

[*w*] When the Portuguefe fupplied England with fugar, the price of this commodity was from 7 *l*. to 8 *l*. fterling *per* cwt. a moft exorbitant rate in thofe days As the Englifh plantations increafed, they reduced the price to 3 *l*. and 2 *l*. 10 *s*.; and, fince that period, to 2 *l*. and 1 *l*. 10 *s*. *per* cwt. But the merchants were obliged to bring it down as low as even to feven or eight fhillings, before they could force the Portuguefe out of the market.

for

for this reafon, at the very time, when it has been doing fuch effential fervice, by driving out fuch foul and corrupt humours, which, when retained in the habit, produce fevers, and other dangerous maladies. Nor are its good effects confined to the human race.   It is the common practice, on the plantations in Jamaica, to feed the working horfes and mules in crop-time with chopped cane-tops, and the fkimmings of the boiling-houfe liquor, which anfwer better than corn, in preferving them plump, ftrong, and healthy.   Hogs, poultry, and, in fhort, all the animals belonging to a plantation, thrive on this juice.   Even the dogs in this ifland, although qualified by nature not only to relifh, but to digeft, putrid food, are not lefs fond of fugar.   I have known a well-fed animal of this fpecies, who was commonly dieted from a plentiful table, and never tafted carrion by way of *bon bouche* without fuffering feverely for it ; on thefe occafions he ufed a quantity of what is called here *dog-grafs*, fufficient either to make him difgorge, or compofe, his ftomach, probably, by the fixed air contained in that plant ; at other times he would greedily devour the avogato pear, clammy cherry, ripe plantains, yams, bananas, &c. ; but, when introduced to the boiling-houfe, he never failed to regale himfelf without intermiffion ; and, from being in a ftate of miferable leannefs, was fure to become plump, and full of life and agility.

I have feen the good effects of it on Negroes afflicted with the yaws, even after the diforder (by catching colds after a mercurial regimen) had fallen upon their joints ; it threw the venom out on the furface in a plentiful eruption, and thus brought on a crifis, which no other known remedy could have produced fo defireably.

In worm diforders there is not a more powerful remedy than the juice of ripe canes, to expel thefe vermin [x]. The Negroe children (as if prompted by inftinct) fuck them with the utmoft avidity, and are always relieved. When powders and other vermifuge medicines are adminiftered, melaffes or fyrup ufually forms a part of the compofition, and perhaps contributes more than is generally imagined to

[x] Doctor Grainger obferves, that fugar is commonly fuppofed to favour worms ; that, however, he knows this, from repeated experiment, to be a *vulgar error.* That perhaps no one thing in the *materia medica* is more deadly to worms than *cane-liquor*, unlefs we except *mufcovado*, mixed with an equal quantity of fweet oil, efpecially what is made by expreffion from the cocoa nut.

their

their fuccefs. I have known many old white perfons in this ifland, extremely fond of the refined fugar, eating it frequently in a morning, and with a fingular *goût*, from a firm affurance (eftablifhed by long experience) of its mild, balfamic, and falubrious, operation.

Some (fays Brookes) are great enemies to fugar, and affirm, that it produces I know not what bad effects ; but, as thofe who have ufed it very freely have never received any detriment from it, we may conclude, that it is intirely harmlefs. It does not produce confumptions, as fome pretend, becaufe an apothecary, who had that diftemper, almoft lived upon fugar of rofes, and was cured by it. Some have affirmed, that it produces the fcurvy, and was the original caufe of it ; whereas it is well known, that the fcurvy appeared long before fugar was in ufe : befides, the pooreft people, who eat much lefs fugar than the rich, are moft afflicted with the fcurvy. This is likewife true of common failors, who eat more falt provifions, and lefs fugar, than their officers. Some affert, that it turns four upon the ftomach, but give us no argument to prove it. An acid may indeed be extracted from fugar, and fo there may from all forts of corn, as well as wine ; but then it muft be performed by art, and turned into an ardent fpirit firft, by fermentation. Befides, fugar is a natural foap, and will readily mix with any fort of liquor ; and therefore it is not probable that it fhould turn four on the ftomach [*y*]. The officinal compofitions of fugar are allowed on all hands to be good in diforders of the breaft ; and, mixed with oil of fweet almonds, it is good in coughs, hoarfeneffes, and the like. Externally applied, it is a very great vulnerary, efpecially when mixed with a little brandy, whofe ftyptic quality, joined to the balfamic virtues of the fugar, makes a compofition, which will heal wounds, cleanfe ulcers, and *prevent putrefaction*. Doctor James concurs in the fame opinion. When duly ufed (fays he) it is not fo offenfive to the blood as is vulgarly

[*y*] I am apt to fufpect, that the other ingredients, fuch as rancid butter, and other greafe, unfermented flour, and crude fruits, &c. with which fugar is generally combined by paftry-cooks and confectioners, may occafion fuch effects, and deferve the whole blame, which has been wrongfully afcribed to the fugar alone, from ignorance of its principles. This probably is the only wholefome ingredient belonging to fuch compofitions, and may prevent much of the bad confequences they would otherwife produce, efpecially in the weak ftomachs and bowels of children, who are the principal fufferers.

thought. It is daily taken to a degree of excefs by fome, who, inftead of being injured by it, live in a found and perfect ftate of health. It is a mild and fweet falt, which is far from being unfriendly to the mixture of the fluids, becaufe it *corrects acid, bilious* humours, and renders the body foluble.

Every teftimony, in fhort, agrees in pronouncing it to be one of the beft adapted prefervatives of health in cold as well as hot climates, from its nutritious, healing, and antifeptic qualities. Thofe who reject punch, from an opinion that lime or lemon-juice is offenfive to their bowels, which often is the cafe in gouty habits, would do well to mix fugar and fyrup with their rum and water; at the fame time being very moderate in the ufe of that fpirit; they may be affured, that fuch a beverage will be far wholefomer for them than the liquor called *grog*, which is a mixture of rum and water only; for, although rum is far preferable to any other fimple diftilled fpirit, yet it may be advifeable in the Weft Indies to mix it with fome fermentative ingredient; and none is more proper than fugar or melaffes.

For the fame reafons on which the caufe of the plague's decreafe in many parts of Europe has been fuppofed, it may be juftly concluded, that putrid and malignant fevers neither originate fo frequently, nor (when brought by infection) ravage fo extenfively in the Weft Indies now as formerly they did. A proof of this declenfion is not only the comparative healthinefs of Jamaica, formerly deemed a fickly ifland, but the greater health of the feamen employed in this trade, who ftill drink as hard, and expofe themfelves to all extremities of the climate as much, as they did one hundred years ago. Yet the merchant fhips feldom lofe any of their crew by thefe diftempers, and moft of them lofe none. Some will attribute this to the more extenfive cultivation of the country, the cutting down its thick woods in feveral parts, and melioration of its atmofphere; but there is fuperadded to all this the much greater quantity of fugar manufactured throughout the ifland; and the greater facility which the feamen have found in getting at fupplies of it for their private ufe, whilft they wait in port the loading of their fhip, as well as during the voyage home; for, when they cannot procure it *gratis*, they either buy of the Negroes for a little tobacco, or other trifling confideration, or get it by theft. There is now near fixty times as much fugar made in the ifland,

ifland, as there was an hundred years ago; and a large quantity falls to the fhare of the Negroes, not only in what is given to them, but what they fteal, which it is impoffible to prevent, as they are the conductors of it to the fhipping-place, as well as manufacturers. The fuperfluity, or what they do not referve for their own ufe, is chiefly difpofed of to the failors, and poorer Jews; the failors likewife, who come afhore to the wharfs, find many opportunities to fill their hats or pockets from the packages that lie there. Befides this, they are generally allowed fugar on their voyage home, to mix with their tipple; and, when it is denied them, they make no ceremony in pur-loining it; and, by this means, eftablifh a pretty regular article in the Britifh factor's account with the planter, which goes under the name of *plunderage.* From this caufe we do not hear of the crews of Weft India men fwept off, or indeed hardly afflicted at all with the fcurvy, or thofe malignant difeafes, which fo commonly depopulate the Eaft India fhips in their paffage homewards; although fome of the former, in wet and fevere winter voyages to England, are often, by contrary winds and bad weather, detained at fea for a fpace of eleven or twelve weeks, and without any difference to their crews in point of diet from thofe employed in other trades, except that they have the ufe of fugar and melaffes; and rum, inftead of brandy.

Thefe facts feem to be confirmed by the confent of the ableft of the faculty, who acknowledge this change to have been actually wrought; and fome among them have thrown further light on the caufe of it, by infifting, that the very *fame prefervatives,* in *Weft India* voyages, an-fwer as well againft *malignant, remittent,* and *intermittent, fevers,* as againft the *fcurvy.* Grounding our judgement therefore on the con-current evidence of obfervation, and the opinions of fo many learned and intelligent phyficians, who have adopted their fentiments, upon certain experience, and moft accurate enquiry, we are well fupported in recommending the plentiful ufe of the cane-liquor, and its prepa-rations, to all thofe who pafs from Europe to refide in Jamaica; and may venture to affert, that it is perfectly inoffenfive in its principles, and fingularly conducive to health in its effects on the human body in that climate. The Spaniards in our neighbourhood are very liberal in their ufe of fugar and honey; their fweetmeats they eat chiefly with wheat bread, which they referve for thefe and chocolate only. The

honey

honey they fpread on caffava cakes; the affinity between thefe two fweet fubftances need not be infifted on.

That malignant and terrible difeafe, called the *black vomit*, was unknown at Carthagena (as it is faid) till about the year 1729. It was fufpected to have been firft brought thither from Porto Bello. It made its appearance in that year on board the guarda coftas and galleons lying in the harbour, and deftroyed almoft the whole of their crews. The Spanifh phyficians attributed it to the falt meat on which the feamen were fed, as it was obferved to rage more among them, than thofe who had been able to live on more wholefome food; they confidered falt meat as tending to bring on this diftemper, and that the humours it generated, together with the labour and hardfhips of duty, inclined the blood to putrefaction; but it is certain, that the failors alone were not its only victims; for even paffengers, who had not tafted any falt meat during the voyage, felt is effects; it was therefore, with more appearance of truth, imputed to the peftilential air of Porto Bello. It is remarkable, however, that the *natives* of *Carthagena*, and thofe who had lived there fome time, were not, nor ever are, affected by it; but enjoy an uninterrupted health, amidft the dreadful havock it makes among others; it feems rational to fuppofe, that this diforder has its fourcce at firft in a high degree of the fcurvy, which, from the baleful influence of the fwampy *effluvia* at Porto Bello, degenerates into a putrid fever of the worft fpecies. This is confonant to the idea of our Englifh writers on the fubject, who affert, that fuch as have any *fcorbutic* fymptoms are in porportion more fubject to the *dyfentery*, and *malignant putrid fevers*; and likewife are the moft feverely handled by thefe diftempers. A proof of this theory, was the memorable deftruction of the feamen belonging to admiral *Hofier's* fquadron, at the *Baftimentos*, which began with the fcurvy, and was compleated by a malignant putrid fever, and dyfentery, contracted from the fatal air of that place. The diet of the *native* Spaniards, and others, who naturally fall into their cuftoms at Carthagena, preferves them free from any fcorbutic acrimony, or difpofition in their humours to breed cr admit the entrance of putrid difeafes. The fame good confequence would probably enfue at *Kingfton* in *Jamaica*, if the inhabitants of that town would adopt a diet, and regimen of life, fimilar to thofe of the Spaniards at Carthagena. For although this

difeafe

difeafe has made but little ravage, at any of our Jamaica fea ports, of late years, in comparifon with anterior times, which is to be afcribed to the greater abundance of vegetable food, fugar, and fruits, in common ufe; it feems likely, that the inhabitants would be equally proof againft its attacks, as the Spaniards are found to be, if they would but depart a little more from a too plentiful flefh diet, and ftrong liquors, and regale more frequently on chocolate, and fugared preparations; ufe none but rum of due age, with the fubacid fruits, not green, but thoroughly ripened; with fuch other materials, in their ordinary refrefhments, as, by the confent of experience, and medical precepts, appear beft calculated to refift the venom of this, and fuch like putrid diftempers. That *Carthagena* is not a very unhealthful climate (though in a low fituation, and intenfely hot), is manifeft from the good old age which feveral of its inhabitants attain, many of whom enjoy fo confirmed a ftate of health, as to reach their 80th year. This, indeed, is not an extraordinary thing in Jamaica, which is much cooler, and where there are now, and have at all times been, feveral perfons exceeding that period; but, in order to make this longevity a more univerfal blefling, thofe means and habits of life muft be practifed, and refolutely attended to, which are found to be the moft conducive and favourable to the end propofed. I fhall next confider, as another ingredient in the common diet of perfons in the Weft Indies, the article of

R U M.

SECT. V.

I do not know of any author, who has treated this fubject in a manner fo fcientific and elaborate, as the ingenious Mr. *Dofjie*; as his pofitions, relative to the analyfis and properties of this fpirit, have not been controverted, and appear to be the refult of experiments, joined to an eminent degree of chemical knowledge, I fhall readily adopt, and endeavour to illuftrate their truth, by other obfervations. From thefe, a judgement may be formed, why rum in fome circumftances is to be confidered an unwholefome article of diet; why under others it is quite the reverfe, when ufed in moderation; why it is to be preferred to other fimple-diftilled fpirits, whether it be drank in moderation or to an excefs; and hence will appear the means moft certain,

7

to

to difarm it of noxious qualities, and adapt it with greateft fafety to common ufe.

1. Ardent fpirits, in their pure ftate (*i. e.* not dulcified by union with fome corrective), have a violent aftringent action upon the folid parts of animals, coagulate the fluids, and diminifh the power of the nervous fyftem

From thefe caufes they produce fuitable effects:

A tabidnefs, or wafting of the extremities,

A nervous weaknefs, or tendency to palfy,

Deftroy the appetite and fecretions,

Render the liver fchirrous, and occafion dropfies.

On diffecting the bodies of perfons, who have died of exceffive dram-drinking, the whole liver has been found converted into a fchirrus of peculiar hardnefs, fo as to be altogether incapable of its office, of *fecreting the bile*; and the mefentery fometimes aftonifhingly enlarged and tumefied.

§ To this may alfo be added, Doctor Macbride's pofition, that fuch fpirits contain little or no air *per fe*; and that they prevent the ready extrication of it from alimentary fubaftnces during the digeftive procefs. From all which caufes it is evident, that perfons, who indulge in fuch drink, generate nothing but crudities in the ftomach: and are fubject to dyfenteries, wafting of the flefh for want of nourifhment, all forts of nervous diforders by the continual irritation of acrid matter, and to dangerous fevers; from the want of that aërial principle, which is neceffary to ferment and prepare the aliment for concoction. Rum is therefore leaft wholefome, when it comes neareft to fuch pure ardent fpirit in its properties; and hence, new or frefh diftilled rum, which is in this predicament, appears to be in its moft unwholefome ftate.

2. The fubftances, which, by uniting with pure ardent fpirit, counteract its noxious qualities, are, *volatile oils*, generated either in the fermentation or diftillation; and *acids*, either fuch as were natives in the particular vegetable matter which was the fubject of fermentation, or fuch as are generated in the courfe of the fermentation.

3. Thefe corrective fubftances are, in part, combined with the fpirit before diftillation, and rife united with it; and, in part, uncombined

with

with it before the diftillation, but, rifing with it then, unite themfelves gradually with it *afterwards*.

4. It is from the *latter* union, which takes place *after the diftillation,*
that rum is fo much improved by time, and efpecially in a cafk. Where
a large quantity of it is kept together, the inteftine motion being
greater, and at greater liberty to act, than in a fmall confined fpace,
the particles are more fpeedily brought within the fphere of each other's
attraction, and the union more quickly compleated. Hence, when
kept in bottles, a very great length of time is required to perfect it;
but when kept in cafks, the fpirit becomes gradually milder, and lofes
that violent aftringency, which manifefted itfelf before this change,
in a fiery fenfation in the mouth and throat of thofe who have drunk
it.

§ I have tafted rum in Jamaica, which had been bottled 30 years,
but ftill retained this pungent, fiery quality, and a moft difagreeable
twang; which fhewed, that the oil was not thoroughly united with the
fpirit. But, when it is kept in a cafk fix or eight, to twelve months
time, is generally fufficient to perfect it; thofe planters who keep
their ftock rum in large butts, which hold three or four hundred gallons, find this union perfected in a ftill fhorter time; and the rum
fo packed is of a far fuperior quality to what is ftowed in fmall
cafks.

I am apt to fufpect, that there is likewife, in all frefh diftilled rum,
a certain etherial volatile fpirit, of a very cauftic and pernicious quality, which *evaporates* by keeping for fome time in cafks, but cannot
entirely efcape when fuch frefh rum is put into bottles well ftopped,
and laid on their fides.

It fhould be the practice, on all the plantations in this ifland, to lay
up one or more puncheons of rum every year, that they might fupply their white men with what is of due age, inftead of poifoning them
with that fiery, unwholefome fpirit, juft drawn from the ftill. A
neglect of this humane œconomy, either through a pitiful avarice, or a
brutal indifference, has deftroyed many hundreds. The like caution
may be offered, in refpect to the foldiers and feamen on this ftation.
The way to have it wholefome, and potable, is to lay up, in large
tight buts, a fufficient ftock to ferve two years; the one-half new, the
other at leaft a year old; by this method, there would be a con-

ftant fupply of good fpirits; and whatever fuperfluity might remain, upon leaving the ifland, would certainly produce much more than the prime coft, whether it fhould be difpofed of at that market, or brought to Great Britain.

5. Where an *acid* abounds, the fpirit gains by time, in confequence of this dulcification, a grateful flavour and odour.

Where *volatile oil* abounds, the feeming ranknefs of fmell and tafte gradually goes off, or is converted into a fpecies of perfume.

6. The wholefomenefs is alfo improved by time, as it caufes a privation of thofe ill qualities, which render the frefh diftilled fpirits fo noxious.

7. The melaffes fpirit, diftilled in *Britain* and *North America*, is fo defective in the *volatile oil*, which is the great corrective, and gives the charactriftic to rum, that it is moft palpably different from it in tafte and flavour, as well as in its moft falubrious qualities.

§ For this reafon the North American fpirit is better than the Britifh; the former being made from the firft-drawn melaffes, which generally contains a portion of fugar, and a large fhare of this oil. The French melaffes indeed is impoverifhed very much, by their boiling it over again, to make their *paneel* fugars; but in Jamaica this piece of œconomy not being practifed, the melaffes fold here to the North Americans is twice as rich as what they purchafe at the French iflands; and their diftillers probably find it fo in the yielding.

In Britain the melaffes is proportionably jejune, and deprived of its richnefs; as the mufcovado fugars, by the time they fall into the *baker's* hands, have been pretty well drained; fo that what is drawn in the refining procefs, and afterwards fold to the diftillers, muft be very much impoverifhed.

Some diftillers buy up the dark uncured fugars, which yield a fpirit of better quality; but it is impoffible for them to produce the fame fpirit as Jamaica rum, where the liquor for diftillation is compounded of various mixtures, not to be obtained by the Britifh diftiller.

This liquor, for example, confifts of

1 — part fkimmings,
1 — part wafhings,
1 — part cool lees.

To

To thefe varioufly compounded, according to the particular judgement of the manufacturer, and other circumftances, the melaffes is added during their fermentation in the cifterns, and in the proportion of about fix gallons of melaffes to every hundred gallons of liquor.

Sometimes it is made wholly of crude cane-liquor and melaffes, run into fermentation together.

So that not only the ingredients are various and differently compounded; but the melaffes, which is the principal or only fubftance ufed in Britain and North-America, bears in Jamaica but a very fmall proportion to the other ingredients, being only as 6 to 100, or thereabouts.

8. The fpirit, when meliorated by union with thefe corrective fubftances, and by age, is reduced to a mild and gentle ftate; and, when taken *in moderation*, is not only fafe and wholefome, but even in fome cafes falutary and medicinal.

Its aftringency, when duly reftrained, renders it invigorating and cordial; and its power of checking the animal ferments, renders it opponent to a putrid difpofition. In hot countries, therefore, it prevents that extreme relaxation which is generally fo incommodious and debilitating; and, by its antifeptic power, that tendency to a putrid habit, which induces the moft fatal difeafes.

§ The effential points, to make it become medicinal and wholefome, are then, 1ft, the keeping it to a due age; 2dly, the ufing it in moderate quantity. The ufe of it in the Weft-Indies, under thefe precautions, is fo far from being injurious, that it adapts the body to fuftain the heat of the climate with lefs inconvenience, and checks the humours from running into putrefcency. This feems confirmed by obfervation, and the cuftomary practice of the inhabitants in hot climates.

Among the Spaniards at Carthagena, the ufe of fpirits is fo common that the moft regular and fober perfons never omit drinking a fmall glafs every forenoon about eleven o'clock, alledging that it ftrengthens the ftomach, weakened by copious, conftant perfpiration, and fharpens the appetite. *Hacer las once, To do the eleven*; that is, to drink a glafs of fpirit, is the ordinary invitation. But this cuftom, which is not efteemed pernicious when ufed with *moderation*, has degenerated into vice; many being so fond of it, that they do nothing the whole day but *Hacer las once*. Persons of distinction use Spanish brandy, but the lower sort a kind of rum distilled from the sugar-cane.

Jobson remarks, that the common people in Guiney eat only *once* a day, which is after sun-set. They hold, that eating seldom, and in the cooler part of the day, is a good preservative of health. He adds, that the natural moisture being drawn outwards to refresh the external parts when parched by the sun's heat, the stomach is then cold, and fitter to receive a dram than to digest solid food; in proof of which opinion, he asserts to have found by experience, that he and his men could drink as much brandy in the middle of the day, at a time, as in England *would have burnt out their very hearts*; that is his expression.

The sweating, which happens in consequence of overmuch relaxation in *some* hot climates, seems to be of the colliquative kind, resembling that which accompanies putrid distempers in their advanced stage, when there is an utter prostration of strength, and when the blood is hastening into a total dissolution; a moderate dram of some spirituous liquor, at such times, operates by its bracing or astringent quality, and suppresses the immoderate flow of perspiration; hence those persons who drink this liquor moderately, when they are almost overcome with the debilitation of heat and moisture, perceive a sensation of coolness, and cease to sweat so profusely. But the wholesomer way of using it would probably be with a due mixture of water, like the reapers of Pennsylvania, mentioned by Mr. Franklin. In this way likewise admiral Vernon, when he was at Jamaica, caused the crews of his squadron to be served, and it caused a wonderful change in their health; for with this caution they became less subject to bad fevers, and were able to go through the fatigues of their duty without inconvenience.

The most wholesome proportion of rum to water, in this climate, is as 1 to 16, or half a pint of rum to a gallon of water, and the allowance to soldiers, seamen, and white servants, should rarely or ever exceed it, for their ordinary beverage; the price of half a pint of rum is seldom above $1\frac{3}{4}d.$ Jamaica currency, or $1\frac{1}{4}d.$ sterling; the navy allowance of beer is one gallon to each common feaman *per diem*, the price of which cannot be rated lower than 3 *d*. whence it appears, that, without any extra charge to government, the feamen on this ftation might be fupplied with a daily allowance of fugar or melaffes, *viz.* a pint of melaffes, or half a pound weight of mufcovado fugar, the coft of either of which would not exceed one penny fterling, and in general it would be found to fall fhort of the expence of beer, about ¼ *d* fterling *per* gallon, and conduce infinitely better to keep the men in good health.

The liquor called *grog*, or a mixture of rum and water, is often rendered noxious by putting in an over-proportion of rum. For although the drinkers of it fet out at firft with a moderate quantity of the fpirit; yet, as by habit it grows more and more taftelefs, they are induced gradually to add a little and a little more, till they bring their mixture to equal parts of half rum, half water, and fometimes hree parts fpirit to one of water, for their common dilution at meals, nd in the heat of the day. I have known feveral perfons deftroy themfelves in this manner, who at firft were extremely fober and temperate; but it was a work of fome time before they arrived at that degree of excefs which was neceffary to bring on a dropfy, or other bad habit of body. Without a large proportion of water, or the correction of a fubacid, as the juices of fruits, melaffes, fugar, *cremor Tartari*, tamarinds, and the like, it promotes, inftead of allaying, thirft; and every draught, that is fwallowed, ferves but to provoke the fwallowing another, till the faculties are ftupified.

After being heated in this climate with exercife in the fun, I know not a more excellent remedy than a bafon of warm green tea, fweetened with fugar or fyrup, with the addition of a fpoonful of found old rum. This prefently reftores the perfpiration, takes off the fenfation of fatigue, and is cooling and refrefhing. But cold liquors, as punch, &c. drank at fuch a time, are apt to fupprefs the perfpiration, increafe heat, and bring on violent pains in the head, and fometimes a fever.

9. The faccharine matter fermented in order to the making rum, produces in hot climates a copious quantity of *volatile oil*, which unites with the fpirit *during fermentation*.

Part of this oil then combines with the fpirit, and comes over in the courfe of diftillation united with it.

The

The other part rifes uncombined, but unites by *flow degrees afterwards*. A proportion of volatile oil is likewife produced in the procefs of diftillation, by the action of the fire upon that faccharine matter in the diftilling liquor, which has continued unchanged by fermentation, and adheres to the ftill, *in form of what is generally called dunder.*

10. The volatile oil, which comes over uncombined, imparts to frefh diftilled rum that ranknefs of fmell and tafte, which are almoft always found in it. And the aftringent quality of the pure fpirit, as yet not united in due proportion with this oil, caufes that fiery pungency, which it remarkably poffeffes at that time.

11. But the union being afterwards perfected and matured, by due age, the rank tafte, fmell, and acrid pungency, are then converted into fuch as are grateful. The aftringent and coagulating powers of the fpirit, of courfe, are materially corrected, infomuch that they ceafe to be detrimental to thofe perfons who drink it in fit moderation.

12. This dulcification is verified by an eafy experiment. A piece of raw flefh being fteeped in brandy, another in rum, it is found, that the plumpnefs and foftnefs of the flefh is much longer retained under the action of rum, than under that of brandy. Although brandy will harden it ftill lefs than rectified fpirit of wine, or alcohol.

13. Brandy is united with fome portion of *acid*, but no *volatile oil*. It comes therefore nearer to *pure* ardent fpirit, has not its noxious qualities corrected, and confequently is very inferior to rum in falubrity.

14. There are inftances where the frefh diftilled rum has all the fenfible good qualities that, in general, are only to be gained by the improvement of time and long keeping. This peculiarity has its caufe in the volatile oil being of fuch a nature, that the whole of it unites immediately with the fpirit in the proceffes of fermentation and diftillation, and thus renders the rum perfect at the firft.

§ This muft be underftood only in a certain degree. For the beft fpirit that can be made, when firft drawn, is not without that fiery, pungent, acrid tafte before defcribed, though it becomes divefted of it in a much fhorter time.

15. This

15. This materially depends on the right management of the diftilling procefs, taking care never to draw off the fpirit or *runnings* too low; for whenever this happens, the concreted matter at the bottom of the ftill will be apt to burn, and an *empyreumatic oil* comes over, which requires great length of time to make it unite with the fpirit, and fometimes it cannot be cured of this depravity by the longeft keeping.

§. The beft method for preventing fuch an effect will be, to keep up an equal, and not too violent, fire, and to draw off the runnings for marketable ufe not a moment longer than while they continue perfectly limpid, colourlefs, or clear from any whitifh cloud or tinge; a fmall quantity of which is fufficient to fpoil the flavour of a whole puncheon of the fpirit.

§ This milky tinge is the fure criterion, to fhew that a burnt or naufeous empyreumatic oil is rifing, and that the rum is what is commonly called *ftill-burnt*. It afcends commonly towards the end of the operation. Some planters draw the runnings too long, from a miftaken thrift of making the moft they can, and thus perhaps depreciate the whole of their diftillation. What firft comes over is always the beft, and, when diluted to the ftandard proof with pure fpring water, it makes the fineft rum. In Jamaica, they generally mix the whole of the firft runnings together, and diftil or rectify them over again, referving alfo the low wines, or latter runnings, for the fame purpofe.

16. This empyreumatic oil is apt to difagree with fome ftomachs, and caufe the heart-burn. But the effect is rather an inconvenience than any injury. It only gives rife to an unpleafing fenfation, but does no real prejudice to the health.

17. No fpirituous liquor digefts more kindly, or affifts digeftion more efficacioufly, than *good rum*, fufficiently diluted with water, and drank in *proper quantity*. The ufe of it has even been found effectual in fome chronical cafes of bad digeftion, where all other means of relief have failed.

The comparative effects of rum and brandy on the health have been noted at fea, where they are particularly diftinguifhable; when it has happened, that, in failure of being able to procure the former,

the

the latter has been fubftituted. The decline of health that has followed has been exceedingly confpicuous on this change, from the
ufe of rum to that of brandy; numbers of feamen contracting diforders they were free from before.

§ Mr. *Kalm* mentions, that, in the North-American provinces,
rum is efteemed much wholefomer than brandy; and he was told
by *Major Rutherforth*, that, being upon the *Canada* expedition, he
had obferved that fuch of his men as drank brandy for fome time,
died of it; but thofe who drank rum were not hurt, though they
got drunk with it every day, and oftener than the others.

The caufe of this great difference is obvious from the foregoing
remarks.

19. It is proper however that this fpirit fhould always be drunk in
moderation. Whatever quantity infringes on fobriety, and brings
on any diforder, ought to be diminifhed. It is always proper likewife, that in the daily conftant ufe of this fpirit, it fhould be diluted with water or other fmall liquor, which will render it more
mild and inoffenfive in its action on the ftomach, and organs of
fecretion.

The too copious ufe of thofe very aftringent acids, the juice of
limes and lemons along with fpirits, has greatly promoted the injury done to the health of thofe who have drunk them to excefs,
and in moft habits they are apt to do mifchief. But the juice of
oranges, and milder fruits, taken with fuch fpirits, is lefs noxious.
Lemons and limes ought always to be admitted fparingly and with
the greateft caution.

§ It is a very wrong and injudicious cuftom in Jamaica, in taverns
as well as private houfes, to ufe green limes in making punch; for
lemons or Seville oranges are feldom made ufe of. The juice of
green limes is of a very corrofive nature; and hence its efficacy in
cleanfing foul ulcers. There is ftrong reafon to believe, that this
moft noxious ingredient is often productive of cramps and other
fpafmodic complaints; and that its bad effects would be more
feverely felt, if it were not that they are in fome meafure corrected
by the fugar which makes a part of the compofition. The acid of
this unripe fruit is fo fharp, that it excoriates the inteftines, and

caufes

caufes bloody ftools, if fwallowed without any corrector [y]. But when they are ripe, their juice, having been thoroughly concocted by the fun, becomes mild and inoffenfive, if ufed with a due proportion of fugar; and experience fhews, that all fruit may be more fafely eaten, the more fugar it contains.

The fafer way is, to fubftitute the Seville orange, which grows wild in every part of this ifland, and might eafily be propagated in fufficient quantity on every plantation, or in the neighbourhood of the towns, for fupplying the inhabitants.

It is a queftion whether the addition, of the cafhoo fruit, which poffeffes an highly ftyptic acid, be proper in punch? It communicates a pleafant flavour; and perhaps the roafting before it is ufed for this purpofe may abate much of its aftringency, which is fo great in the crude fruit, that it has often performed a cure in dropfical complaints, occafioned by the immoderate ufe of fpirituous liquors; I fhall not therefore haftily condemn, what may poffibly operate as an antidote in fome degree to the bad effects of thofe fpirits.

It was a long time a vulgar prejudice, that the diforder called the belly-ache was caufed by drinking rum mixed with dark uncleanfed fugar in punch. But it is morally certain that this was an erroneous opinion, and that the juice of unripe fruit, which was fuppofed the moft harmlefs ingredient, was in fact the primary caufe of this mifchievous confequence in *many cafes* [z].

[y] If a fowl juft killed, or a piece of butchers meat juft flaughtered, is fteeped before it is put on the fpit, in the juice of unripe limes for fome little time, or if the juice of three or four is fqueezed into the water wherein fuch flefh is intended to be boiled, it will become fo foftened as to be thoroughly dreffed in an hour's time. The Negroe cooks, who are to drefs what is called here a *furprized fowl*, or one which is required to be roafted or boiled with great expedition immediately after it is killed and plucked, pour lime-juice down the throat, and at the vent, to make the flefh tender and eatable. The fame effect is caufed by the juice of the unripe papaw fruit, which is known to be highly cauftic. An eminent phyfician for this reafon advifed, that the limes ufed for making punch fhould be fliced thin, and boiling water poured on them, to extract mucilage out of the feeds, which may prevent the acid from fhutting up the neck of the gall-bladder; and he affirmed that it might be drunk with much more fecurity by being fo blended.

[z] Dr. Cheyne declares it the *fole* caufe. " In the *Weft-Indies* (fays he) where, from the neceffity of drinking much, and from the *want of proper liquors*, they are forced to drink much *punch*, though lemons and oranges be in their full perfection, they are *univerfally* afflicted with nervous and *mortal* dry belly-aches, palfies, cramps, and convulfions, which *cut them off in a few days,* entirely owing to this *poifonous* mixture." The doctor was fadly miftaken in thefe pofitions, and fo he was told by a cotemporary writer. " If the Weft-Indians are *univerfally* afflicted with thefe diforders, and are *cut off in a few days,* how can any inhabitants remain alive? But if

the

This diforder is a fpafmodic affection of the bowels, which may proceed from the irritation of fuch a corroding acid, or from a fudden repulfe of the perfpiration after the body has been violently heated

" the *punch-drinkers* alone are meant, the doctor has been mifinformed; for the people in the
" Weft-Indies have plenty of wines from all the countries producing that commodity, and ale
" and cyder from England, and are under no neceffity of drinking punch for want of other liquors.
" They make Madeira wine and water ferve the common purpofes of drinking, as we do fmall
" beer in England; nor is it to to be fuppofed that an opulent people, whofe commerce obliges
" them to have dealings with almoft every country in Europe, would want any conveniency that
" Europe can afford; nor can we imagine, without infulting the good fenfe of thefe people, that
" they would indulge themfelves in a liquor fo poifonous and deftructive to them, as the doctor
" defcribes punch to be, when they have fo great a variety of other liquors that anfwer all the
" ends of drinking. The dry belly-ache, which is fo peculiar to that part of the world, attacks
" the women as well as the men; yet the women there are particularly remarkable for their
" temperance, and abftinence from ftrong liquors; and many of both fexes, who never tafted
" punch, or indulged in any ftrong liquor in their lives, are afflicted with this diftemper. Nor
" is it true that it is mortal; going to a colder climate never fails to produce a cure, without
" taking any other remedy; and this difeafe is fo far from cutting them off in a few days, that
" they who live foberly, when they are fo afflicted, generally recover in a very little time; and it
" will hold thofe who continue the exceffive ufe of ftrong liquors many months, and even years,
" before they are either killed by it, or cured of it." The laft point is in regard to the fruit,
lemons and oranges, which, the doctor fays, are found in the utmoft perfection in thofe places;
and of courfe he fuppofed, they were ufed only in that ftate: but herein he was greatly miftaken
again; for whatever mifchievous effects thefe fruits have produced, have been owing entirely,
either to the eating too large a quantity of them at a time, or to the ufe of fuch as were not half
ripe, and confequently not in that ftate of perfection which he has fuppofed. Dr. Trapham, in
remarking on this diforder, ingenioufly obferves, that the Eaft-Indians, though living under much
the fame temperament of climate, are not afflicted with it; which exemption he afcribes to their
conftant ufe of baths and unctions; by which the cutaneous pores are kept open for a free
difcharge of the perfpirable matter, and the origin of thefe fpafms thus fet loofe, inftead of being
locked up. And upon this principle he ftrongly recommends the ufe of warm and refrefhing
baths, fweetened with orange-flowers and the aromatic leaves of the country; more particularly
after a journey, or other hard exercife; to which may alfo be joined dry-rubbing with flannel or
a coarfe towel. This advice is ftrongly fupported by an obfervation which every one here muft
have made, *viz.* that the Negroes, and the white natives, who bathe every day, are rarely or ever
ubject to this diforder; and that warm bathing has generally procured relief and eafe to patients
labouring under it, when other remedies have failed. Trapham mentions a fpecific for it, which
had been proved efficacious by a vaft number of trials; this is a fpecies of *tithymalus*, Br. p. 234.
called by Pifo, *Cajacia*, p. 102. fnake-weed, or creeping-hairy-fpurge. It is a fmall, creeping,
milky plant; its leaves not unlike thofe of mint, but longer and narrower, of a dark-green colour;
its ftalk inclining to a reddifhnefs, with fmall fibres or hairy radicles; between its leaf, at the
joints of the ftalk, the flowers come out in fmall bunches, and of a green colour. It is common
in all the dry favannahs of Jamaica.

A drachm of the dried herb is given powdered in any convenient liquor, and repeated once in
three or four hours till the ufual fymptoms abate; or it may be made into a fyrup, and given from
one ounce to three, *pro re natâ*; likewife in decoctions and clyfters. He recommends it alfo to
be infufed or boiled in the medicated baths prepared for cafes of this nature.

with

with motion or hard drinking, by which fome acrimonious humour is lodged upon them. Sailors who tope half rum, half water, till they are fweating at every pore, and tumble almoft naked on the open deck, or in a ftreet, and there fleep, expofed to the damps of the night air and dew; or white fervants on plantations, who follow the like fottifh practice; or others who are obliged to travel in the night, and after riding hard till a fweat is excited, come on a fudden to a fteep hill, or a river, which conftrains them to walk their horfes a gentle pace; or thofe who are chilled by a fudden rain; or who are too carelefs after violent dancing; all thefe perfons are liable to be afflicted with fuch fpafmodic diforder. Hence it appears, that it may proceed from a variety of caufes, and affect even the moft fober and temperate perfons, as is well known it does in Jamaica; and the *oleum ricini,* or *nut-oil,* which is ufed with fo much fuccefs in giving relief to thofe afflicted with it, owes perhaps its efficacy to the opening, foothing, lubricating nature of its operation, by which it fweeps away the acrid matter that was perpetually ftimulating, fupplies the want of *mucus,* to the abraded parts, and recompofes the nerves, in confequence of which the fpafm or convulfion ceafes.

Let me now juft recapitulate, for it cannot be repeated too often, the deftructive effects of fpirituous liquors *immoderately ufed;* for rum, though lefs pernicious than any other, is not lefs noxious in the end, when drank in excefs for any confiderable time.

When drank in this manner, they render the fibres of the body too rigid and tenfe. They communicate an acrimony to the animal fluids, and, not mingling freely with them, thicken, coagulate, and obftruct their circulation, efpecially in the fmaller veffels. They caufe the liver and mefenteric glands to become fchirrhous, render the bile tenacious and vifcid, deftroy the appetite, hinder the excretion of the urine, and produce difeafes that terminate in untimely death [a]. The dropfy was formerly fo common in Jamaica,

[a] Their corrofive action on the ftomach and bowels may be imagined, from the effects obferved on the hogs in Germany fed with the diftillers wafh; their guts are fo rotted, that the inhabitants cannot make hogs-puddings with them. To the fame caufe it is owing, that the flefh of fuch hogs becomes fo tender that it will not keep by falting.

It is a known obfervation of expert dealers in hair for wigs, that they can diftinguifh the dram-drinkers hair by the touch, finding it dry, harfh, dead-ended, and unfit for ufe: and in the fame maica, that it went by the name of the *country difeafe*; it drew its origin from the practice of inebriating with raw rum, which in thofe days was almoft the only fpirituous liquor the inhabitants were able to procure. It is now grown uncommon; the inhabitants are not only more temperate, but provide themfelves with Madeira wine, and a variety of other vinous liquors; drink lefs rum, and more diluted; perhaps too they are much improved in the art of diftillation, and have produced fome amendment in point of quality.

One of the beft of all drinks for this climate is good water, mixed with a moderate quantity of found wine, as I have had before occafion to remark; but as fome cautions are neceffary to direct the choice of fuch water as is beft accommodated to health and digeftion; or to inftruct the means of purifying and correcting it, when impregnated with noxious mineral or other particles; I fhall confider them in a feparate fection.

WATER.

manner it is that it fpoils the ftomach and bowels, the liver and lungs, and the whole body, of thofe unhappy perfons. Their ftomachs are contracted into half the common natural fize, and hardened like leather that has been held to the fire; the confequence of which is a lofs of appetite, and a wafting confumption.

The rage of mankind is fuch for thefe liquors, that it is almoft dangerous to fay any thing in their behalf, left it fhould be miftaken for an encouragement to perfevere; and indeed it avails but little to preach up moderation in the ufe of them, to thofe who will fet no bounds to their fottifh habits from any fenfe of their ill confequence to health; fuch beafts muft be reftrained by meer force and authority, and debarred from the means of procuring fo much as may do them injury, for they cannot or will not judge for themfelves within the line of common prudence.

It appeared from admiral *Knowles's* orders, when he commanded a fleet at *Bofton*, that his men got drunk with New-England rum at the rate of a *thoufand in a day*; and that 1400 New-England men were killed by it in two months; and in New Jerfey, where it is fold very cheap, the people are fo attached to it, that in harveft-time they make it their bargain to have every man a *pint* a day, befides wages.

Thofe commanders therefore cannot be too much applauded, who have the prudence and humanity to oblige their men to drink fpirits largely diluted with water; which, as I have before taken notice, was practifed with the happieft effect by admiral *Vernon*. Captain *Ellis* attributed to the fame wife precaution, the uncommon fuccefs he had in bringing home, in the years 1753 and 1755, all his white men, which were thirty-four, and thirty fix in health, from a *Guiney* voyage of fifteen months. Hales on Ventilators.

The fame precaution fhould be ufed by the commanders of the regular troops, and the overfeers of plantations in Jamaica. Nothing can more plainly evince the fatal effects of thefe exceffes, than the general appearance and untimely end of moft of the white men and Negroes employed in the diftilling-houfes, who, as they can fupply themfelves freely and without reftraint, fo they will immoderate quantities of frefh diftilled rum, piping hot from the worm; for they cannot

WATER.
SECT. VI.

Water, in its natural ftate, is no where to be found entirely fimple and pure; but it is generally treated of by authors, under two heads, common, and mineral. Common water admits of all thofe various impregnations, which are not obvious to the fmell or tafte, and have no fenfible action on the human body. The impregnations in mineral waters will affect the body, and health, according to the properties of the fubftances diffolved, or contained in them; and in proportion as the quantity of fuch heterogeneous particles be greater or lefs. But it is to be obferved, that this definition is not compleatly fatisfactory: there is a middle clafs of water, which is uncompounded with any mineral or foffile fubftance, and yet may contain particles imperceptible to the eye or tafte, different from what are ufually found in common water. It may, for example, contain the fubtile *ova*, or *exuviæ*, of various infects, or a volatile gas,

fo well procure any better. They are bloated, pallid, emaciated, without appetite, and generally die of dropfies or confumptions.

The overfeer fhould never deliver an allowance of rum to the white fervants to ufe at their pleafure, unlefs he can rely on their difcretion and fobriety; it ought to be ferved to them every day ready mixed with water; at leaft this might be the conftant fure penalty of their being ever found inebriated.

The beft way of leaving off a habit of dram-drinking is, by degrees to mix water with the drams; to leffen the quantity of fpirit every day, and keep to the fame, or an encreafed quantity of water, till, in about the courfe of a week, no fpirit, or but very little, is ufed.

By this means the party will fuffer no inconvenience, hut reap great benefit, as has been experienced by many.

If any gnawing is left in the ftomach, a little warm broth is a good remedy.

The appetite always increafes after leaving off this cuftom of fwilling raw fpirit, unlefs by too long a continuance the tone of the ftomach is deftroyed.

In this melacholy ftate,

Take One ounce of elixir proprietatis.
Three drachms of elixir of vitriol.
One drachm of Minficht's elixir of fteel: mix together.

A teafpoonful of this mixture in a fmall wine-glafs of white-wine, or a cup of carduus or chamomile tea, every morning and evening taken fafting, is recommended for the benefit of thofe who have wifdom or refolution enough left to defift from a pernicious *Excefs* in thefe liquors, which cannot be long perfifted in, without the greateft mifchief to health; for fuch perfons only it is meant; and not for thofe infatuated wretches, who are blind to felf-prefervation, and wilfully rufh into their grave.

* Hales

4 D 2

injurious

injurious to health. It is of confequence therefore, to have fome *criteria*, whereby to diftinguifh any noxious qualities contained in water, that fuch may be chofen as is beft adapted to preferve health. Philofophy and experiment have inftructed us in the means of making the difcovery, in moft refpects; and likewife have pointed out thofe waters, which deferve a preference before others, for their lightnefs and falubrity.

Of all waters the atmofpherical, or rain water, is the moft light and fimple; yet even this is found to contain fome impregnations, difcoverable by a chemical procefs. Next to this, is fpring water; which varies in purity and goodnefs, according to the nature of the foil through which it percolates; what rifes amidft a rocky, gravelly, or chalky *ftratum*, is generally moft efteemed. The water of wells, if fed by a fubterraneous current, comes next in order; and improves, by ftanding for fome time expofed to the air before it is drank. River water is not much to be recommended, unlefs fome previous cautions are ufed in depurating, and preparing it for ufe; but of all waters, fuch as is ftagnant, found in lakes, ponds, or ditches, is the very worft. I fhall now apply thefe diftinctions more particularly to Jamaica. The rain water here is experienced to be extremely light, pure, and wholefome, collected in thofe mountainous places where no fprings are at hand; provided it is carried in clean gutters, into fome refervoir, or fhaded place, which is not expofed to the fun at any time, nor open to infects for depofiting their eggs. When I was at St. John's Town in Antigua, fome years ago, 1 obferved moft of the houfes were provided with cifterns, for receiving the rain water which fell on the roofs; this water, from the multitude of mufkeetos which bred in it, the lizards, cockroaches, and other animals, that had fallen in, and the dirt wafhed down from the houfe tops, was feculent, and almoft putrid. Such water, even boiling can fcarcely accommodate to health. The water of many of the rivers in Jamaica is turbid, from the frequent heavy fhowers that fall in the uplands, and flood them; in general therefore, their water ought to be kept for fome days, until the clayey and other impure particles are entirely fubfided, or that it is otherwife purified. The water of lagoons is

fo

ſo fetid, that the ſenſes will ſufficiently caution againſt the admitting any of it into the ſtomach.

The moſt common impregnations in the Jamaica waters are,

On the South ſide — a foſſile muriatic ſalt, terrene particles, and particularly lime-ſtcne.

On the North ſide — Terrene, argillaceous, ſtalactite matter, and chalk.

There are likewiſe, of the mineral claſs, ſuch as are known to be impregnated with iron and ſulphur; and others, that are ſuſpected to contain copper, lead, or allum.

1. BRACKISH, or Water impregnated with a Muriatic Salt,

Is diſcovered, by letting fall two or three drops of ſolution of ſilver (in *aqua fortis*) into a glaſs of it; when, if there is ever ſo ſmall a quantity of that ſalt, it will unite with the *aqua fortis,* and cauſe it to ſeparate from the ſilver, which will fall ſlowly in the form of a white cloud; and if the proportion of the ſalt be large, the cloud will have a curdled appearance, and a cœrulean caſt.

2. TERRENE Impregnation.

A few drops of oil of tartar will diſcover a ſuperabundance of earthy matter, by cauſing it to precipitate to the bottom of the glaſs, in a whitiſh cloud or ſediment.

3. CALCARIOUS and STALACTIC Matter.

Syrup of violets detects alcaline as well as acid particles; communicating to the water a greeniſh tinge, if an alcali, and red, if an acid predominates.

4. VITRIOLIC, CHALYBEATE, or IRON.

The milder acids, as vinegar and lemon-juice, poured into a chalybeate water, give it a ſweetiſh taſte. But the principal teſt of the iron impregnation, is the black colour it ſtrikes with a vegetable aſtringent, as tincture of galls; and the purple caſt when an alcaline ſalt, or lime water is added to the aſtringent; and which is of deeper hue in proportion to the larger mixture of the alcali. The galls of which the tincture is made, for purſuing this experiment, ſhould be blue, of the ſtrongeſt kind, freſh and ſound.

5. SULPHUR

is diſtinguiſhed by the taſte, and inflammability of the ſediment; and by the waters ſtriking a black colour, with a few drops of solution of *saccharum saturni* in water; or solution of lead in the nitrous acid; by its sudden tarnishing of silver; and by the fetid smell resembling a rotten egg, or scowerings of a foul gunbarrel, on dropping in solution of alcalis.

6. COPPER.

This is discovered by spirit of sal ammoniac, made with quick-lime; which, if the smallest particles of copper are present in the water, cause it to assume a very beautiful blue colour. Iron precipitates this metal. A plate of iron laid in water, impregnated with copper, will soon be covered with an incrustation of it.

7. LEAD

is not a native impregnation of mineral waters; it is generally found in the earth united with sulphur in form of an ore. Waters, impregnated with its rust or mineral vapour, strike a pink or red colour with *aqua fortis*, and are highly poisonous; for which reason, on liquor should ever be kept in leaded cisterns or other vessels, either for drink or preparing food. That lead, when dissolved by fire, or corroded by an acid, emits poisonous *effluvia*, is sufficiently shewn by the diseases incident to plumbers and painters. But much less heat than is required for melting lead, is capable of detaching such pernicious *effluvia*. The heat in the bowels of the earth in this climate may be justly suspected, especially in Liquanea, and other parts where lead ore has been found to work this effect; so far at least as to impregnate any springs of water, which circulate among this ore. Water alone, if not perfectly pure, is a sufficient agent to cause a solution of the metallic poison; and has been found by experience to imbibe it largely. The noted colic of Amsterdam, which for a long time eluded the search of physicians with respect to its cause, took its rise from this poisonous impregnation of the rain water, which was collected in leaden reservoirs, after first lodging on flat leaded house roofs, upon which the leaves of trees had fallen in great abundance about autumn. These excited a fermentation, which corroded the lead, and contaminated the water. *Tronchin* relates that whole families were seized with this dreadful colic: eleven persons fell ill with it at once in one house; who, upon new covering the roof with other materials, and changing their water, recovered. Dr. Baker suspects, that the lead used about the

works

works in our plantations, where fugar and rum are made, is a principal caufe of the Weft-India colic, or belly-ache. But in this conjecture he feems to be greatly miftaken; for, if this was true, the effects would always be certain and invariable; and thofe only would be fubject to that malady, who fwallowed rum and fugar in the largeft quantities, which does not agree with obfervation or experience; fince many are fubject to it, who never drink any rum, and eat but very little fugar. The drinkers of new rum are the moft fubject to it, the reafon of which I have endeavoured to explain. Befides, the caufe is not proportioned to the fuppofed effect. It is true the mill-bed is covered with lead; but the metal fuffers no abrafion, as in a Devonfhire cyder-mill, to which the Doctor's idea perhaps compared it. The cane liquor does not reft upon it long enough, or with preffure enough, to act upon the metal; it falls in fmall quantities, and keeps on its progrefs, in a gentle fmooth current to the gutter, which is commonly made of folid wood hollowed; and where one gutter joins another, the joint is fometimes covered for the fpace of two or three inches with a piece of lead, though more generally with clay. Two or three fuch gutters at moft are commonly long enough to reach the receiver in the boiling houfe, which is made entirely of wood; and there the liquor remains to fettle, till it is wanted for the copper. If any ill effect can be fuppofed to arife from this metal in the procefs, it can only happen from what is laid round the rim of the coppers, where it undergoes a conftant great heat; and might poffibly communicate its *effluvia* to the liquor, whenever it is fuffered to boil fo high as to come in contact with it. This the boilers in fome meafure prevent, by beating it conftantly down with their fkimmers; however it might be advifeable, never to lay the lead low in the coppers. In the diftilling houfe, this metal is never ufed in any fhape; and, therefore, the rum cannot be fufpected to be impregnated with any of its *effluvia*, except what may come in the fkimmings, which are but a fmall part of the liquor ufed in diftilling rum. Whether the fkimmings have any fuch impregnation is a fact very queftionable, and not very probable; but againft a partial degree of impregnation, the oleaginous and laxative principles of fugar appear to be a fufficient prefervative; and hence it is found, that they who

5

eat

eat *pan sugar*, which is the hard cruft formed about the mouth of the *tache*, and which cannot well be taken off without fcraping at the fame time into the very fubftance of the lead, do not fuffer any of thofe fpafmodic fymptoms in their bowels after eating it, which the ruft or *effluvia* of this metal are apt to caufe, when combined with things which are not qualified to correct their natural effects. Dr. *Cremer* obferved, that the potters at Ofterhout near Breda, though conftantly employed in glazing earthen veffels, were rarely affected with any diforder in their bowels; which exemption he attributes to the large quantities of butter and fat bacon, which are their ordinary food; fo experience has taught the labourers in lead mines, to fortify their ftomach, and inteftines, with fat broths, and fuch like unctuous aliments, which are antidotes to this poifon.

The vapour arifing from the fmelted ore at the mines in Mendip Hills, in Somerfetfhire, is fo poifonous, that if it fweeps the ground adjacent, it affects the grafs in fuch a manner, as to deftroy cattle or fheep that browze on it. There is a *flight*, or light fubftance, which floats in the fmoak; and this, if it chances to mix with the water in which the ore is wafhed, and carried away with the ftream, is faid to have deftroyed cattle, that have drunk of it after a current of three miles.

The diforders to which the workmen are fubject, are pains in the ftomach, violent contorfions of the bowels, obftinate coftivenefs, afthmas, and fhortnefs of breath, vertigos, paralytic affections, lofs of appetite, ficknefs, and frequent vomitings.

The foil about thefe mines is red and ftoney; and the ftones wafhed by the brooks and fprings, are of a reddifh caft and very ponderous: I cannot precifely anfwer, whether the foil about the Liquanea lead mines has a conformity in this refpect. It feems, from the foregoing account, that a ftrong degree of heat is required to difengage this pernicious fume; the fubterraneous heat is fufficient for fuch an effect in fome places, where there are *ftrata* of particles qualified to produce it by their fermentative action. No doubt too, but ftones containing this mineral, if lying upon and very near the furface expofed to a Tropical fun, may caufe this poifonous vapour to be emitted or perfpired in fome degree; and, mixing with the air, may render it unwholefome; but we have no certain proof, that

2

any

any fuch effect happens about the lead mines of Liguanea. This merits a further inveftigation; and likewife the fprings, or ftreams, which pafs among them, ought to be carefully examined. It appeared, from Mr. Mufchenbrock's experiment, that lead is the fooneft rarefied of all metals; its expanfion with the fingle flame of a lamp being (compared with iron) as one hundred and fifty-five to eighty: which is nearly double; fo that its parts are evidently liable to be affected by a very fmall portion of heat. And we find, that milled lead, when expofed to the action of the fun in Jamaica, by being improperly made ufe of, inftead of fheet-lead, for covering gutters and valleys on the roofs of buildings, very foon blifters, cracks, and becomes leaky.

8. ALLUM.

Waters which contain it difcover themfelves, on evaporation, by their auftere, aftringent tafte. They change vegetable blues (as fyrup of violets frefh-made) to a red colour; but, if the fyrup is old, to a green. An addition of lime-water deepens the green. They alfo coagulate milk. Bricks harden the fofteft water, and give it an alluminous impregnation. The practice therefore of lining wells with brick is fuppofed improper.

But, on the other hand, about a quarter of an ounce of allum, powdered, and thrown to every fix or feven gallons of turbid, muddy water, will, in about an hour or two, render it perfectly pure and tranfparent. Nor does any inconvenience refult from the allum. It is not only an excellent purifier of fuch water, but is thought, in hot climates, to cool the body, and brace up its relaxed fibres.

There are other methods likewife recommended for purifying water. In Jamaica, the people of Spanifh Town keep their river-water in feveral large jars, where it fettles and depofites a fediment in about twenty-four or thirty-four hours. Some families have three, or more; which, being taken in turn, well cleanfed, and replenifhed regularly, fupply them with a very pure and light water inferior to none.

Very foul water may be purified by letting it percolate through fand ftowed in half-puncheons, or tubs made on purpofe; with fmall holes two or three inches above their lower end, guarded with a piece of hair-cloth, doubled on the infide, to prevent any

of the fand from dripping out with the water, which may be collected in a receiver placed underneath. The fand ufed for this
purpofe fhould be fhifted now and then, perfectly clear from dirt,
and free from all mixture of fea-fand. Several of thefe fand-
ftrainers might be provided where a large fupply is required. And
thus any perfon may have no bad fubftitute, where a natural fpring
is not to be met with. Brackifh water might be very much depurated, if not wholly corrected, by this method : but, fhould this
fail, a very pure element may be obtained with a common ftill,
even from fea water; and, for this procefs, Dr. Hales advifes
powdered chalk, in the proportion of half an ounce to a gallon of
water, to be from time to time put in at a hole in the upper part
of the ftill, below the head, to prevent the rifing of the fpirit of
the bittern, which would caufe a difagreeable tafte; this hole to
be immediately clofed, to prevent any abatement of the quantity
diftilled. The fame ingenious gentleman invented the tin air-box,
full of holes; by blowing through which, with a pair of common
bellows, the moft ftinking water may be fweetened; the frefh
ftreams of air thus thrown in, and difperfed throughout the ventilated water, caufing the putrid vapour to afcend, and efcape from
it: and, by this method, a whole butt of ftinking water has been
corrected in the fpace of an hour. Nothing is more likely to difpofe
the body for the reception of diforders, than water filled with putrid
particles. It is worth the experiment, whether even lagoon water
may not be rendered potable, after being firft well ftrained, by
tranfmitting fhowers of frefh air through it. The failors, belonging to the merchant-fhips which load at this ifland, will very frequently, out of meer lazinefs or ignorance, fill their cafks with
brackifh water, taken up at the mouth of a river, or even with
lagoon water; rather than be at the pains to procure what is fweet
and wholefome. There is fcarcely a harbour in the ifland, indeed
I do not know of above one, where a fupply may not be had of
good water. This carelefs practice, and the want of cleanfing
their cafks before they are filled, may probably have often bred
fluxes and other diforders among the crews of thefe fhips.

The lagoon water, being the conftant feminary for mufkeetos,
is loaded with the eggs and dead bodies of thefe infects. It fwarms,

befides, with numbers of other *animalculæ*; and is further corrupted with ftinking aquatic plants and filthy ooze [r].   It is
difficult to exclude mufkeetos from water referved for ufe, without keeping the mouth of the jar covered with a piece of ofnabrig,
or other cloth, which may hinder them from penetrating, at the
fame time not wholly excluding the admiffion of frefh air.   They
depofite their eggs in river-water, and in cifterns.   I have even
known them hatch in lime-water : but, when the eggs are hatched,
the young ones are very confpicuous to the eye, and appear like
little tad-poles.   Whenever the water is fufpected to contain them,
it is carefully ftrained, for drinking, through a clean linen cloth
three or four times doubled.   The Spaniards generally made ufe
of percolating ftones ; and, indeed, many perfons now ufe them
in Jamaica.   They tranfmit an exceeding pure, and very cool
water ; but the procefs is rather tedious, where a large quantity is
every day wanted.   Moft people here put out of doors, in a fhaded
place (the more open to the wind, the better), feveral fmall unglazed jars, with water ; which is always cooleft in thofe whofe
texture is fo loofe as to admit part of the water to penetrate through,
and appear in a conftant moifture on their outfide ; the evaporation,
no doubt, contributing greatly to the coolnefs of the fluid within,
by carrying off the heated, rarefied particles inceffantly.

Cool water may juftly be regarded in this climate as medicinal,
and neceffary either to preferve health or reftore it.   Many perfons,
afflicted with putrid fevers, have even recovered by no other remedy ; and, in thefe diforders, it is remarkable with what eagernefs and pleafure the patient will drink cold water in preference
to fubacid liquors, or any other.   The natives drink it almoft univerfally.   Sir Hans Sloane mentions it as the cuftom, when he was
here, to take a glafs of it every morning at getting out of bed;
and he judges it extremely conducive to health, as it not only may
cool the inflamed blood, creating a rheumatifm (very often taken
for, and almoft always joined with, the belly-ach), but it may
alfo clear the bowels of fome four or fharp matter, which may
happen to lodge in their cells.   He therefore efteems good water to

[r] A dead lizard being put into a tub of frefh rain-water, the water became putrid in about
twelve hours.

be the moft wholefome drink of any ; obferving, very juftly, that fpirits, wine, beer, ale, cyder, and all other vinous and fermented liquors, inflame the blood, and load the ftomach with phlegm, caufing hiccoughs with their fharpnefs, and difordering the head. It muft be underftood, however, that, when water is ufed as the only beverage in a hot climate, it ought to be as pure as poffible; and that acefcent fubftances, fuch as vegetables, fhould make a conftant part of the water-drinker's food, in order to avoid that putrefcency of the bodily humours which a total water and flefh diet, without the correction of vinous acids, or the antifeptic air of vegetables, would probably generate. We find, accordingly, that although the natives in this climate feldom drink any other liquor, except cool, pure water; yet they make their principal daily meal confift chiefly of vegetables in their pepper-pots; eat plantains, yams, and cocos, inftead of bread; and are fond of fallads, fruits, and fugared preparations.

The great axiom of health among the natives of the Weft-Indies (as Roupro well obferves) is, " to keep the body open, to drink " water, and not to indulge in exceffive venery." But I muft re- mark, that, of thefe three cautions, the laft is the leaft attended to

S E C T.   VII.

HAVING now confidered the beft means of preferving health in this climate under the feveral general heads propofed, it may be neceffary, perhaps, that I fhould make fome apology for having trefpaffed thus far upon the province of phyficians. Some, who obferve that I have founded the rules prefcribed on the opinions of many among the ableft of the faculty, will acknowledge the weight of authority from whence they come recommended. Others will, at leaft, have the candour to allow, that any inaccuracy, or error, betrayed in the afforting of them, may be pardoned, for the fake of their utility, and the object in view, which is no other than that of promoting the health and happinefs of this colony. For the reft, I fhall gratefully be one of the foremoft in offering my thanks and applaufes to any gentleman of the faculty refident here, who fhall bend his thoughts to this important fubject, and give the public a more elaborate and ufeful detail of the means whereby the

diforders, incident to the climate, may beft be prevented, or remedied. For what can be a more praife-worthy tafk, than the
God-like difpenfation of health to the fick, life to the dying, relief
to the miferable? It is not a little extraordinary, that, among all
the gentlemen eminent and learned in the medical profeffion,
who have practifed in this ifland, not one of them fhould have
publifhed his fentiments on its difeafes, and the remedies found
moft efficacious in the cure of them, at leaft not within thefe
fixty or feventy years paft. The only treatife, I ever faw, was
compofed by Dr. Trapham, who refided here long ago. Dr.
Patrick Brown, who printed a natural hiftory of the ifland in the
year 1756, gave his fubfcribers affurance of a fecond volume,
which was to contain differtations upon climates, atmofpheres,
and difeafes, the yellow and remittent fevers, and worm-diforders;
with a particular application of thefe fubjects to Jamaica: but this
gentleman has not hitherto thought proper to comply with his
engagement. Is it becaufe feveral celebrated phyficians, as Hillary,
Biffet, Lind, and others, have publifhed their opinions already,
that our Jamaica profeffors of the healing art have, through modefty, been filent? If it be a modeft reluctance, we may defervedly
call it a *pudor malus*, a blameable diffidence, which brings fome reproach on their underftanding, if not on their humanity; for,

Scire tuum nihil eft, nifi te fcire hoc fciat alter.

And although thefe learned precurfors mentioned may have handled the fubject with much fkill and accuracy; yet it cannot be
denied but much ftill remains to be faid: for the fcience of phyfic,
like other human ftudies, is far too complex in its nature, and admits too comprehenfive a variety of obfervation and experience, to
derive more than a partial, progreffive improvement from the practice of many phyficians, even applying their thoughts to it inceffantly during their lives. After a feries of ages, it is perceived ftill
very fhort of perfection; but it may be gradually brought nearer
and nearer to that ftate, by the concurrent obfervation, practice, and
experiment, of a *multitude* of intelligent men, rather than of two
or three. Befides, although the *genera* of the difeafes, moft mortal
in the Weft-Indies, may perhaps be well defined and diftinguifhed;
yet, in the extenfive range of atmofpheres, and countries comprehended

hended within that part of the globe, there muſt neceſſarily happen a diverſity in the ſpecies, a deviation of ſymptoms, and a conſequential obligation to treat them differently, according to the various ſeaſons and ſituations.

Thus, for example, the putrid fevers of the Weſt-Indies may appear with different ſymptoms at Jamaica, than have been obſerved at Barbadoes, at Tobago, at Surinam, at Porto Bello, or the Havannah. It may be requiſite, according to the ſeaſon of the year, to vary the precautions in avoiding, as well as the precepts for removing, them. In the Northernmoſt parts of the Torrid Zone, theſe and other diſeaſes may differ from, and call for a mode of treatment materially altered from what might be abſolutely proper in, ſituations under or very near to the Equator. That ſuch a publication is much wanted is, in no reſpect, more conſpicuous than in the ill ſucceſs (too often the child of ignorance) which, to the deſtruction of many inhabitants every year, has accompanied the practice of ſome *homicides* in this country.

If every phyſician here, of good education and ability, was to publiſh the fruits of his knowledge and practice, his work would fall into many hands, and prevent much of the miſchief likely to happen from thoſe, who, wanting ſuch a guide, are continually in error. But, inſtead of this, we obſerve with regret, that, when an experienced gentleman of the faculty has died here, or removed from the iſland, his treaſure of experimental knowledge has been buried with him, or paſſed away to another country, where, from difference of climate, it becomes uſeleſs.

If to reſcue one man only from impending death can yield unſpeakable pleaſure to a benevolent heart ; how infinitely ſuperior muſt be his ſatisfaction, who, whilſt he communicates the means by which thouſands, perhaps, of his fellow-creatures may be ſaved from extremity of torture and diſtreſs, reflects a moment, that, by ſo doing, he builds a monument that will tranſmit his name with eulogy to future generations ! that the happy reſult of his ſkill does not periſh with him ! but that, after his body ceaſes from exiſtence, he may continue ſtill the author of health, life, and eaſe, to lateſt poſterity !

To

To lay the foundation of unceafing benefit to mankind in this way, is a work of the nobleft ambition that can infpire the human mind. How applauded is the patriotifm and benevolence of thofe princes, who have erected bridges, formed roads, cut navigable canals, made fecure harbours, and executed other plans of great public utility! They are defervedly ftyled the fathers and friends of their country. Nor lefs fo the phyfician; who is really a father to thofe who enjoy their life through his means.

Opifer per orbem dicor was thought an epithet the moft honourable of any to be conferred on the fabulous god of phyfic; and not undefervedly; for, if there is a being upon earth to whom divine honours could, without impropriety, be offered, it is a learned, virtuous, and communicative phyfician.

To defcribe the ftate of phyfick in this ifland, would be an invidious tafk. It is happily fupplied with feveral men of great ability. But, as every plantation requires what is called *a doctor*, it is needlefs to obferve, that there are too many pretenders to the fcience, as in other countries, the practice not being as yet put under any regulation by law. It may be fome amufement to my reader to be prefented with the hiftory of a Jamaica *quack*; not that he is to regard it as an epitome of all the practitioners. *Qui capit, ille facit.* To a few it may be applicable; but, for the credit of human nature, I declare it is not applicable to any confiderable number. Mr. *Apozem*, the hero of my narrative, was the fon of a houfe-carpenter in London. At the age of twelve, he was put to a grammar-fchool; and, at fifteen, removed from thence, and apprenticed to an apothecary, of mean circumftances, and very little bufinefs; but he was an old acquaintance of the father, and a member of a weekly porter-club, where they had regularly met each other for twenty years, and contracted a ftrict friendfhip. During the firft three years of apprenticefhip, Mr. Apozem had no other employment except to *fcrape* and *fweep out* the fhop every morning, *clean his mafter's fhoes*, and *go on errands*; and, when he had juft attained his nineteenth year, his mafter unfortunately dying by one of his own naufeous compofitions, inadvertently fwallowed, he returned to his father's houfe, where he continued perfectly idle for about a twelvemonth; when an opportunity offered

fered of getting him provided for, that he might no longer lie a burthen on his father's hands, who was extremely poor, and had a numerous family to maintain. This was effected through the good office of another member of the club (which shews the utility of such institutions); who, on being appointed captain to a Guiney trader, readily offered to take Apozem with him, in quality of surgeon. This being chearfully assented to, the young *doctor* was properly equipped for the occasion, and soon after entered on the voyage. They took in three hundred slaves, and sailed from the coast, bound to the Jamaica market. The first great exploit, performed by Mr. Apozem, was in diminishing the number of *mouths* on board; and so effectually did he exercise his skill, that, by the time they had reached their destined port, he registered no less than eighty Blacks, and nine white seamen, on his dead list. This wonderful dispatch made the captain extremely anxious to look out for something on shore more proportioned to his great abilities; for he wisely apprehended, that a longer continuance on board might probably leave the ship without hands to navigate her. He therefore gained the interest of the merchant to whom he was consigned. The merchant had a proper regard for the ship-owners, and soon found means to engage Mr. Apozem in the service of an honest planter who dealt with him; and who, conceiving the highest opinion of Mr. Apozem's skill and knowledge, from the many encomiums that were lavishly given both by the captain and merchant, stipulated so handsome a salary, that Apozem quitted the sea without the smallest hesitation.

Mr. Apozem, soon after his entering upon this new scene of business, disdained to confine his carnage merely to the family with whom he resided. The first step he took, after looking about him a little, was to extend his practice, as much as he could, among other families and plantations; some of which were not less than thirty miles distant from his employer's habitation: so that, in about six or eight months, he was continually upon the high-trot, riding post, and spreading depopulation far and wide. His principal instruments of death were mercury and *opium*, ever mistakenly applied, and injudiciously combined. Liquid laudanum was his ready help in time of need, and stood his ignorance in great stead.

Whenever

Whenever at a lofs to find out the caufe, or nature, of a diftemper (which generally was the cafe), a dofe of laudanum was the firft piece of artillery he brought into the field, to begin the attack. If the fymptoms ftill left him doubtful, *repetatur dofus!* laudanum again, either *per fe*, or jumbled with a new mixture, to raife the credit of his fkill, and prevent detection. Thus the fiege went brifkly on, with laudanum, to the end of the campaign, until the patient's life, or conftitution at leaft, was fairly fapped, and compelled to furrender at difcretion. As *opium* was his grand fpecific for all hyfterical and nervous ailments, as well as others where the fymptoms puzzled the doctor's imagination; fo mercury was lugged in by the head and fhoulders, to fave his credit, in all cafes of cuticular eruptions, belly-achs, and topical inflammations. If mercury failed, after a bill of one or two hundred piftoles, " The de- " vil's in this obftinate difeafe !" cried Apozem ; " it is not, fure, " in the power of phyfic to conquer it ! There's no remedy left, " Sir, but to flee to Bath, or change the climate !" This was the laft refource of his art ; for he reafoned thus : " I fhould be a con- " fummate blockhead, indeed, to put the finifhing ftroke to this " bufinefs, and fo blow myfelf up at once. No ! let my patient " perifh at Bath, or on the road thither ! or fail for Britain, and die " in his hammock ! If death fhould lay hold of him, after he is " difcharged out of my hands, *thou canft not fay I did it!*" Thus argued Mr. Apozem ; and thus did he extricate himfelf from many a troublefome fcrape. It was a great misfortune to the public, that his father had not kept him long enough at fchool to acquire a fmattering of Latin : it was, indeed, no lefs inconvenient to himfelf, and multiplied his difficulties on many occafions. But true genius leaps over every ftumbling-block ; and, what he could not conftrue with the help of Cole's dictionary, he always gueffed at as well as he was able. No man, furely, could have done more. It is needlefs to fay, that he never boafted his fkill in decyphering a common *formula*, or Latin prefcription. He condemned the folly of writing receipts for health in an unknown tongue ; and one might as well have fent him an infcription taken from one of the ruins at Palmyra. After puzzling his brain for half an hour in vain, to difcover the meaning, he ufually mixed up fome horrid *hotchpot* of his own invention, in order to comply with vulgar prejudice, and leave no room to fufpect that he had not compleated a grammatical and claffical education. It was enough for him, if he could but luckily explain the laft words of a prefcription, to diftinguifh a *fiat bolus* from a *fiat hauftus*. Under the aufpices of thefe qualifications, the following efcape of a patient may be confidered as almoft miraculous. A certain gentleman was troubled with an eruption on his fkin; and, having a fmattering of medical knowledge, he took upon him to be his own phyfician, wrote a Latin prefcription for a liniment, in which *fulph. vivum* was the principal ingredient; and difpatched it to be made up by Mr. Apozem. Our hero pored over it for fome time with great attention; and, concluding at length that *fulph. vivum* and *argent. vivum* were coufin-germans, compounded a mercurial ointment; with which the patient unthinkingly befmeared himfelf from head to foot: but, in a fhort time, he became convinced of his error; the eruption ftruck in; he gave himfelf up for a dead man; and, indeed, did not come off without a violent fit of illnefs, which had nearly coft him his life. I cannot, without horror, reflect on the multitudes who have quietly defcended into their grave, leaving the frauds impofed upon them undetected. It was always a maxim with Mr. Apozem, "that the dead tell no tales."—"My reputation," (thought he) "is fafe, under the authority of a diftemper which "is often known to be mortal. But, if that won't ferve my turn, "I'll fay the patient was *fulky*, and determined not to live; or "that he was *faint-hearted*; or had a bad habit of body; or had "lived too free in his youth; or wanted a *ftamen*; or that fome- "*thing* broke within him; or—any other reafon why." Under fuch prudent *falvos* did Mr. Apozem, "not having the fear of "God before his eyes, but moved and feduced by the inftigation of "the Devil," go on to ravage and deftroy the human fpecies, with as little remorfe and fhame as Alexander the Great, or the greateft flaughterers of antiquity. His utmoft dread was the decline of fuch bloody bufinefs; his principal wifh, the quick fale and confumption of his drugs, which were rotten or fophifticated: though, bad as they were, he generally made a profit of one thoufand *per cent.* upon them in the retail way. The fale of thefe poifons

formed

formed the moſt gainful part of his buſineſs; though he was, occaſionally, a phyſician, apothecary, ſurgeon, man-midwife, dentiſt,
phlebotomiſt, farrier, &c. He profeſſed every branch, knew as
much of one as of another, underſtood none: and, thus accoutred,
he was ready at all calls, and engaged in the cure of diſtempers,
whoſe names he had never heard before. He had a happy manner
of diſcuſſing the *rationale* of any diſeaſe, of which I ſhall give a
ſpecimen that does him honour. He was ſitting one day by the
bed-ſide of his patient, whom the hero had over-doſed with a purgative, which cauſed fifteen evacuations in a few hours; and, the
irritation ſtill continuing, the very *mucus* of his bowels came away
The patient, alarmed at this appearance, languid and almoſt ſpent,
having taken no ſuſtenance all the day, for want of ſome reſpite
from his agony, requeſted the doctor to inform him of the cauſe
of the laſt mucilaginous diſcharge. "Oh," quoth Apozem, with
an air of moſt ſolemn ſagacity, "it is nothing more than the ſuper-
"fluous juices of the blood, Sir, which are following the operation
"of the *bolus*, Sir; 'tis a ſure diagnoſtic that the medicine has
"worked critically, and that the morbid acrimony of the *primæ*
"*viæ* is depurated from the abdominal emunctories." Mr. Apozem
continued in this ſtrain till he had talked his patient faſt aſleep by
dint of hard words; in which comfortable ſtate he ſoftly left him,
to recruit his waſted ſpirits.

Mr. Apozem was a profeſſed enemy to regular phyſicians, becauſe none, who valued their good name and reputation, would be
concerned with him; for they never could have the ſatisfactory
aſſurance, that a ſingle ingredient of their preſcriptions would ever
enter into Mr. Apozem's manufactures. It was impoſſible they
could meet with ſucceſs; for, when they preſcribed one thing,
Apozem was ſure to compound and adminiſter ſomething very different: ſo that, in deſpight of all their learning and aſſiduity, the
patient was morally ſure of dying. When the manner of the
death came to be the ſubject of converſation, Apozem laid it, with
a ſhrug of his ſhoulders, at the phyſician's door: "the poor man
"died *regularly!*" After a few ſuch examples, the preſcriber loſt
his buſineſs; and Apozem was ſent for in his ſtead. I have often
thought, that, conſidering the deſolation which Apozem ſpread

through

through the country, and the many hundred victims which he facrificed every year, there arifes a very ftrong evidence of the falubrity of
the climate, which of itfelf is pregnant with but few endemial difeafes;
and thefe are pretty well underftood by phyficians of any tolerable
education and experience; fo that, had it not been for the activity of
Mr. Apozem, the proportion of fuch as might have owed their *exit*
fairly and truly to the climate, during the time he flourifhed here,
would have been too infignificant to caufe the fmalleft furprize.

Mrs. Apozem (for our hero thought meet to take unto him a wife,
in hopes of making fome reparation to fociety for the thoufands he had
fent out of the world) was a religious, good fort of a woman, and
would very often give him wholefome admonition. " I would ad-
" vife you, my dear Mr. Apozem, faid fhe, to turn from your evil
" ways, and honeftly confefs your ignorance, by refufing to prefcribe
" for diforders, to which you know you are as much a ftranger as
" myfelf. Surely this would be more humane in you, than to go on
" at this rate, wilfully and confcioufly adminiftering your flops to the
" deftruction of your fellow creatures. Ignorance is never criminal,
" except when it does mifchief; and then, if it is unchecked, God only
" knows where it will ftop. It is true, you think to fupprefs your
" qualms of confcience by alledging, that you do not difpenfe your
" ftuff with a downright direct intention to wound or kill; but, if the
" effect is generally hurtful, what does your intention fignify in the
" fight of God? If you was to ftand in the middle of a crowd with a
" loaded gun in your hand, and difcharge it with your eyes fhut,
" would this acquit you of the damage that enfued; you might fay,
" I took no aim, I pofitively did not fire at any particular perfon, and
" therefore did not intend to kill the poor man who happened to be
" ftruck with the ball: but, I am afraid, this excufe would not fatisfy
" a jury, they would moft undoubtedly call it *murder*, and, after all
" the logic of your diftinction, you certainly, my dear, would be
" hanged, which heaven forbid! for in fhort, although you did not
" pofitively intend to kill Dick or Tom, yet you confcioufly did an
" act, which, your own mind muft have fuggefted, was not perfectly
" innocent, confidering the fatal effect it would in all human probabi-
" lity occafion." Mr. Apozem ufed to hear thefe harangues pretty
frequently, and fometimes he would even promife amendment; but fo

4

flinty

flinty was his breaft become by inveterate habit, that the dying groans of a patient never coft him a fingle pang; and he grew more hardened in proportion as he fuffered no lofs, either in bufinefs or chara&ter, from fuch misfortunes; fo fertile was his invention, in fhifting the blame from his own hands. Thus, like a fkilful archer, he dealt his arrows from behind a bufh, whilft,

"Sævit atrox *Volfcens*, nec teli confpicit ufquam
"Au&orem."

"*Volfcens* ftorm'd, nor found
"The daring author of the diftant wound."

He never voted the calling in a phyfician, till his patient lay at the very laft gafp, drenched with his deadly potions beyond the falvation of medicine; and hence always drew the advantage of proclaiming "that death and the phyfician generally came into a fick room toge-"ther." His rule for vifiting, is not the leaft curious part of his œconomy: whenever he was fent for, his maxim was, to meafure the delay of fetting out, and the length of the vifit, "according to the "ftrength and length of the patient's purfe." If he faw reafon to ex-pe& a handfome gratuity, or a long bill, he ufed to fcud upon the wings of the wind, and was at the patient's wrift in a trice. He held, that "putting any interrogatories to fick perfons, was only perplexing "their minds, already too much difcompofed with illnefs; and im-"peached the dignity of thofe who are born do&ors, and fo compre-"hend every branch of the art, by natural intuition." Any enquiry therefore, into the paft habits of living, diet, exercife, irregularities, and the general ftate of health and conftitution, "were utterly fuper-"fluous to a man of true penetration." Apozem was fatisfied to fay no more, than "l'll fend you fomething dire&ly;" and he never was known to break his promife; phials, boxes, and gallipots, followed by dozens, whilft, repofing in his elbow chair, he fat down to enter £. s. d. His vifits were repeated three or four times *de die in diem*, more or lefs, according to the patient's rank and fortune. If his applications were unable to interrupt the laborious efforts of nature, and the difeafe be-gan to lofe ground, it was very well; there was, however, no want of regular fupplies, of pe&orals, emenagogues, febrifuges, and vermi-fuges; paregories, and fudorifics; laxatives, and alteratives; fomenta-tions, and embrocations; draftics, and epifpaftics, to be fwallowed, or
applied,

applied, every fifteen minutes, night and day; none of which, we may be sure, were unnoticed in Mr. Apozem's manuscript, commonly called a Journal.

To conclude my narrative; since the best precautions cannot at all times guard the most temperate and careful; since all flesh is subject to pay the debt of nature, and even doctors themselves are not exempted from the common lot of mortality; so it fell out, that Mr. Apozem was taken, by surprize, with a malignant distemper, which laid hold of him with so much violence, that he was very near calling out for help of the faculty, if he had not been restrained by a riveted opinion, that such auxiliaries were like the Saxons and Normans, who (upon invitation) first drove out the intestine enemy, and then fell upon the intestines themselves: consigning himself therefore to despair, he soon fell a victim to his own drugs, which had inflicted the same fate on many a worthier man. Such were the life and opinions of Mr. Apozem, who might boast of having sent more souls to the banks of Styx in one year, than the yellow fever ever did in ten.

The science of physic, when taken out of the hands of such poison-mongers, is truly noble. We find the Saviour of mankind employed himself in this godlike office; his miracles were medicinal, he "went "about doing good," and his divine power was exerted in healing the sick, restoring sight to the blind, and vigour to the infirm. It certainly merits the greatest encouragement in all inhabited countries, but more especially in colonies and new settlements, where unusual diseases are observed. This exalted art, if duly cultivated, is capable of producing very important effects in such places. If nothing more was to be expected from it, than the augmentation of commerce, this alone is a sufficient motive for a trading people to give it the most honourable distinctions among them; since commerce stands so largely indebted to physic, and its sister botany, not only for materials of import and export, but the abilities of men employed in collecting those materials.

Nor must we pass over the happy consequence accruing to a new settlement, from having its endemial diseases thoroughly understood, and the lives of the settlers preserved or prolonged, by medical skill and sagacity.

The number of hands in such a place is generally so inconsiderable, that a sudden mortality, and the loss of a very few inhabitants, may nip
the

the moſt hopeful projeƈt in the bud, and deter other adventurers from going to reſide in it; for, if once the charaƈter of any remote ſettlement is eſtabliſhed for unhealthineſs, it is always found a very difficult taſk, and a work of long time, to diſpel the popular prejudice, and convince mankind that ſuch a place is habitable. Beſides, it may happen, that the perſons firſt carried off by the attacks of ſickneſs in ſuch a country, for want of proper medical aſſiſtance, have been the chief promoters or undertakers of the ſettlement; they may be men of the moſt capacity and ability among the inhabitants; and, in ſuch caſe, the loſs is irreparable.

But, in a colony already formed and provided with a legiſlative power, it is the higheſt reproach, it is even an impiety, that a tribe of *Apozems* ſhould be tamely permitted to over-run and depopulate it, preying on the purſes and lives of innocent men, with an impudence, ignorance, and rapacity, that is unparalleled. If the woods were peſtered with tigers or rattle-ſnakes, like the foreſts on the American continent, with what terrors ſhould we not reflect on the deſtruƈtion they might cauſe! with what zeal and ſolicitude would not the legiſlature promote rewards and encouragements to extirpate them! Yet, in ſome colonies, they have been known to ſuffer with impunity a much more lethiferous race of ſavage animals in human ſhape, who have ſtifled the emotions of humanity and conſcience, whilſt they poiſoned, and tortured to death, the bodies of their very friends and benefaƈtors.

The dignity of the ſcience of healing (not of *murthering*) ought ſurely to be placed on the firmeſt baſis in ſuch a country; that, whilſt the inhabitants confide their very exiſtence to the phyſician's care, he may be enabled, by proper regulations, to aſſure himſelf, that his patients will not be forced to ſwallow any other mixture than what he has preſcribed; and that the varying, or adulterating, his preſcription, will be puniſhed by the laws, in the ſevereſt and moſt exemplary manner; and ſurely, if we conſider a moment, that ſuch deceit is no leſs than a clandeſtine attempt againſt the life of one party, and the reputation of another, it muſt appear an offence of the moſt capital nature, and worthy of capital puniſhment.

As a foundation for this, we may recommend the plan, which that good man colonel Codrington found means to carry into execution, from the opulence of his fortune, and liberality of his ſentiments. He, no doubt, had long deplored the calamitous circumſtances of Barba-does, unprovided with a ſufficient ſtock of practitioners, regularly trained to the knowledge of phyſic. He was ſenſible, that a colony, ſurrounded with enemies, and liable to internal inſurrections of ſlaves, required a conſtant ſupply of white inhabitants; and that, if the pro-portion of thoſe annually imported did not counterbalance the number annually ſwept off by diſtempers, the colony muſt inevitably decline; for, it is the multitude of uſeful hands which conſtitutes the vigour and proſperity of every ſettlement; and the greater the mortality is, the greater, and heavier, muſt be the labour that falls upon the ſurvi-vors: if 500 men only are employed to garriſon a country, which, from its extent and circumſtances, requires 2000, the inſufficient body may harraſs themſelves to death, and yet be unable to maintain their ground againſt an enemy; ſo if, by judicious practice, only 500 lives *per annum* are retrieved, which, by erroneous practice, would have in-fallibly been loſt to the community, no man ſurely will deny the im-portance of ſuch an acquiſition to a Weſt India colony; the ſaving thoſe lives may introduce, perhaps, an increaſe of many hundred more to the ſtock by procreation; add to this, that the death of a principal planter, on whoſe well-being twenty white perſons are probably de-pendent for bread and employment, is equal to the loſs of twenty-one perſons; becauſe theſe diſcarded ſervants, who have attained to no fixed property, may remove to ſome other country in ſearch of a pro-viſion. Nor does the loſs entirely reſt here; if he was a virtuous man, ſuſtained a public employment with integrity, and diffuſed happineſs and utility from the greatneſs of his ſtation, his ability, and benevolent ſpirit, ſuch a chaſm becomes ſtill more extenſive, and difficult to be re-paired. Colonel Codrington, who enjoyed the government of Barba-does, deviſed by his will in 1710, two plantations in that iſland, and likewiſe a part of Barbuda, another of the Carribbee iſlands, in value about 2000*l. per annum*, or upwards, to the ſociety *de propaganda fide*, for the purpoſes of inſtructing Negroes belonging to Barbadoes, and the other Carribbees, in the Chriſtian religion, and for erecting and en-dowing a *college* in Barbadoes, in which the liberal arts ſhould be taught, particularly *phyſic and ſurgery*. A college was accordingly erected there, the good effects of which may be traced, not only in the greater number of white inhabitants in proportion to the other Britiſh

iſlands,

illands, but in the fuperior fkill of the phyficians refiding in it; for, it has been in no fmall degree owing to the practitioners of Barbadoes [*s*], that we have any tolerably fcientific account of difeafes incident to the Weft Indies, their treatment, and method of cure. We muft not expect, perhaps, to fee a tolerable performance on this fubject, compofed by a Jamaica phyfician, until the legiflature, in commiferation of the fufferings, and lofs of inhabitants, fhall take vigorous and effectual meafures, for excluding all thofe from commencing phyficians, who do not bring with them authentic and fufficient credentials, certifying their qualification for fo arduous a bufinefs.

It is true, a diploma from Glafgow does not always confer fenfe, neither fhould the want of that *venal honour* deprive any man of the efteem and deference due to real merit. If a furgeon or apothecary has got the education and knowledge required in a phyfician, he is a phyfician to all intents and purpofes, and ought to be refpected accordingly [*t*]; but fome line fhould be drawn, in order to refcue the practice out of the hands of low and illiterate perfons, who are a fcandal to the profeffion. The difeafes of the human body are fo intimately combined, that it is impoffible to underftand fome of them perfectly, and be entirely ignorant of the reft; and equally impoffible to underftand any of them without a proper knowledge of *anatomy*, and the *animal œconomy*, both in its found and morbid ftate. To excel in this profeffion, requires a greater compafs of knowledge than is neceffary in any other art. A knowledge of the mathematics, at leaft of the elementary parts of them, of natural hiftory, and natural philofophy, are effentially connected with it; as well as the fciences of anatomy, botany, and chemiftry, which are deemed its immediate branches. There are likewife fome pieces of knowledge, which though not abfolutely neceffary to the fuccefsful practice of medicine, are yet fuch ornamental acquifitions, as no phyfician, who has had a regular education, is found without; fuch is, an acquaintance with the Latin, Greek, and French languages; to which may be added, fome knowledge of the world, of men, and manners [*t*]. All thefe qualifications we look for in a regular-bred phyfician; but when the three branches, of the prefcriber or phyfician, the furgeon, and the apothecary, all mix in one man,

[*s*] Viz. Towne, Warren, Bruce, Hillary, and others.

[*t*] Gregory's Lectures.

which

which is more generally the cafe in Jamaica, we may difpenfe with many of thefe attainments, fo rcquifite in an accomplifhed phyfician, provided fuch a practitioner is well acquainted with the fciences of anatomy, botany, and chemiftry ; for, without a competent knowledge in thefe, he cannot underftand properly the principles of any drug or medicine, nor in what manner to apply it to a difeafed body.   The animal machine will be, in his hands, like a watch in the hands of an Indian; he will fee it move without knowing the caufe ; and when it is difordered, he may break it to pieces by his unfkilful attempts to rec-tify it.   Perhaps, no fcheme might be apter to eftablifh the practice on a proper footing in Jamaica, than the erection of a college, endow-ed with a library, lecturers on phyfiology, pathology, anatomy, bo-tany, and the *materia medica*; with licenfed infpectors of apothecaries fhops and drugs.   Teftimonials of a regular apprenticefhip fhould be required from every apothecary, furgeon, or man-midwife, and an oath for the honeft and confcientious difcharge of his refpective func-tion, before he could be admitted to open fhop, or practife in the ifland.

From fuch an inftitution might be hoped the beft effects, in refpect to the health of the inhabitants, the triumph of ability and learning over impudent empiricifm, and a large fund of information to guide fu-ture practitioners; here is the nobleft field for botanical enquiries, and the readieft helps to anatomical knowledge.   In procefs of time, the commerce of the ifland might expect to participate the advantages re-fulting.   The fpices of the Eaft, the bark tree of Peru, the balfam trees of Mexico, and many other valuable plants and productions, might be introduced under the aufpices of a learned fociety, and propagated in this fertile foil.

Providence has accommodated every region with fpecific remedies for its endemial diftempers : but the medicinal virtues of the Jamaica plants are as yet but little known to any of its practitioners.   It is attended with lefs trouble to find a medicine in the next drawer, or gallipot, than ramble into woods for it, or enter upon a laborious courfe of experiments.   And, in truth, very few here underftand any thing of botany, or chemiftry.   Yet as the American difeafes differ in many refpects from thofe of Europe, fo they feem to require a differ-ent *materia medica*; and none can be fo appropriated, as the native productions of the country to which thofe difeafes are endemial. The practice of phyfic then, where necessarily deviating from the European (refpect being had to the diftinctions occafioned by climate) would become eftablifhed upon more rational, and certain grounds; many lives would annually be faved, and the profeffion, which is now difgraced by illiterate dabblers, would refide in hands, from whofe fkilfulnefs the inhabitants might expect more fecurity to their life and welfare, whilft the ifland, thus relieved from one principal caufe of mortality, would fee its people multiply, its trade and exports enlarge, its ftrength and opulence augment. From the neceffary connexion of caufes with effects, it is reafonable to think, that all thefe advantages would happen, in confequence of a thorough *purgation* of abufes from the practice of phyfic in this ifland.

A moderate fhare of induftry, with health, has laid the foundation of many a great fortune in Jamaica; this place is, therefore, juftly an object of attention to thofe, whofe flender patrimony, or indigent circumftances, render them unable to gain a competent provifion in their native country. It is the afylum of the diftreffed and unfortunate, where all may enjoy fuftenance, and where a beggar is unknown. They who arrive now have an advantage, unknown to our anceftors, of coming to an eftablifhed fociety, which, from the number of towns and fettlements, has every accommodation and convenience that can be defired. Here is ftill ample room for man young beginners, fince much of the beft land has hitherto, by reafon of its central fituation, lain neglected and uncultivated. The daily improvements that are making in the roads will foon (with the public aid) render thefe lands of the middle diftricts extremely valuable, and convenient for fettlers; the chief difficulty which always attends new fettlements, in hilly or woody countries, being the want of good carriage roads, affording an eafy communication with towns and fea-ports. It is a further inducement, that thefe diftricts are as healthful as any part of Great Britain; which circumftance feems fully evinced by the undiftempered lives of thofe perfons who have already refided in them. The purity and mild cool temperature of their air, at all times of the year, are propitious to human health, whilft the fruitfulnefs of the foil is inexhauftible, and affords abundant fupplies of food more than anfwerable to the labour beftowed upon it. What may be further conducive to population, muſt depend on wiſe laws and fit regulations, calculated for the protection of property, the encouragement of induſtry, the abo‑ lition of tyranny, the diſcountcnancing of ſelfiſh monopolies, and the *conſervation* of *health*. Theſe demand aſſiſtance, from a legiſlature in‑ fluenced by public ſpirit, a liberal judgement, and perfect knowledge of their country's beſt intereſt. Such a legiſlature need not to be inform‑ ed, that the advantages of a thorough population and ſettlement are of ſuch vaſt importance to this iſland, as to be well worth their pur‑ chaſe, by every ſuitable proviſion and encouragement in their power to frame or beſtow. Convinced of this truth, the means are obvious.

APPENDIX

APPENDIX *to the* SECOND VOLUME.

JAMAICA is divided. p. 1.] My opinion in regard to the Indian origin of the name of this ifland, as hinted in the former volume, p. 353, is ftrengthened by the account we have from Peter Martyr, in his Decades; who fays, that it was called Jamaica by the Indian inhabitants when the Spaniards firft difcovered it.

Indian natives, who fell victims to the barbarity of their Spanifh conquerors, p. 153.] Peter Martyr mentions, that it was exceedingly populous; and the Indian natives far more lively, acute, and ingenious, than any the Spaniards had met with in the other iflands.

Known by the name of Curtin's fpring, p. 138.] This water, I am informed, has been examined, with ftill greater accuracy, by Dr. Turner; but I have not been fortunate enough to meet with his ingenious remarks upon it.

P. 207. To the account of Weftmoreland parifh I am enabled to add the following particulars:

Its metropolis was formerly Queen's Town (now Crofs-Path), which contained a church and many inhabitants. But, in the year 1729, fhipping began to refort to the harbour of Savannah la Mar; and, in the following year, the parochial meetings were removed thither, and houfes began to be built. Thefe changes brought on a fpeedy declenfion of the old town. The ftructure of the fort was firft begun in 1733; and it was judicioufly fituated for commanding the feveral channels leading into the harbour; but the town, inftead of the low, fwampy foil on which it now ftands, might have been placed, with far greater advantage, about a mile more to the Eaftward, on an elevated, dry fpot, through which a rill of good water conftantly runs. This fcite would likewife have been more commodious for carrying on mercantile bufinefs; not only becaufe there is a greater depth of water near the fhore, but that fmall veffels may pafs to and fro with any wind. The inhabitants of Savannah la Mar lie under the further inconvenience of being obliged to fetch their water, for domeftic ufes, from a great

diftance

distance across the bay; except immediately after the rainy seasons, when, by the flooding of some gullies, they gain a temporary supply in their neighbourhood. The sum of thirteen hundred pounds has been lately expended on repairs to the fort, which the parishioners intend to furnish with cannon.

The town contains near one hundred houses: Beckford-town consists of about thirty; and the remainder of the savannah has about as many more. The number of vessels loaded here, at an average of the last four years, amounts to about eighty *per annum* (not including coasters, or droguers); and their burthen has been computed at eleven thousand five hundred and eighty-five tons; which calculation allows about one hundred and forty-five tons to each vessel. Hence some opinion may be formed of the consequence and value of the trade carried on at this port. And, that an estimate may likewise be made of the improved state of the plantations in this parish, the following may suffice.

Anno.	Negroes.	Hhds. of Sugar.	Number of Sugar Estates.
1770,	17237	7915	72

which the reader may compare with the state I have before given of it for the year 1768.

Manning's free-school maintains only six or seven boys. This is attributed to some inattention in the trustees; for it is asserted, that the fund is improveable, and very capable, if judiciously managed, of supporting many more. I know not what truth there may be in this charge; but, if it is fairly adduced against the trustees, there is evidently some defect in the law which was passed for regulating this foundation.

Mineral Waters.

The chalybeate spring at Ricketts Savannah has been already found of singular benefit in obstructions, and other disorders accompanying a lax fibre. It appears to contain volatile-vitriolic-acid, selenitic-earth, and a portion of fixible air. This spring, if it was properly attended to, and guarded from the access of rain and other mixtures, might prove highly serviceable to the inhabitants. There is also a hot-spring lately discovered in the mountains lying between this parish and Hanover; in all probability it is sulphureous, and has affinity in its principles and operation to the hot bath of

St. Thomas

St. Thomas in the Eaſt. As yet it has not undergone any analyſis: But there is every reaſon to believe, that it will prove, upon experiment, not to differ much from the Eaſtern medicinal ſtream; and, in this event, that it will be of the utmoſt utility to the pariſhioners, and indeed deſerving of every public and private encouragement in order that its ſalutary effects may be rendered more acceſſible and diffuſive.

The other articles proportionably, p. 229.] Dr. Campbell, in his Political Survey of Great-Britain, &c. vol. II. p. 666, has favoured us with a liſt of the exports from this iſland in the year 1770, with their value. The latter, however, is rated arbitrarily; which muſt always be the caſe in ſuch calculations, though probably not varying much from the truth. If the rates ſhould be judged too high, it will be at the ſame time conſidered, that the articles of

       Indigo,
       Tortoiſeſhell,
       Zebra-wood,
       Lignum-vitæ,
       Braſiletto,
       Fuſtic,
       Logwood, and ſome few others, beſides
       Bullion,

are not enumerated, though a large allowance is due to them.

Exported from Jamaica, *A. D.* 1770.

		£. Sterling.
2249	bales of cotton, at 10 *l. per* bale,	22,490
1873	cwt. of coffee, at 3 *s.* 5 *d. per* cwt.	6,068
2753	bags of ginger, at 2 *l.* 5 *s. per* bag,	6,194
2211	hides, at 7 *s. per* hide, — ——	774
15,796 {	hhds. of rum, for Great-Britain, at 10 *s. per* hogſhead, —— }	157,960
679	ditto Ireland, at 10 *s. per* hogſhead,	6 790

16,475

15,675 } pieces, 8,500 } feet, }	Mahogany, ——	50,000
2,089,734 lb. wt. of pimento, at 6 *d. per* lb.		52,243

                                                     61,970

61,970 hhds. of fugar, at 17*l.* 10*s. per* hhd.   1,086,620
205 bags f farfaparilla, at 10*l. per* bag,   2,250

Total exports to Great-Britain and Ireland,   1,391,408
Ditto to North-America, —— —— 146,322
Ditto to other parts, —— —— 1,000

                      £ 1,538,730

In 1763, the exports to Great-Britain and Ire-}£ 1,076,155
    land were rated at —— ——}

The advance therefore in feven years, *i. e.* to 1770, is — £ 315,253

    In the above detail, the export to North-America is certainly put a great deal too large ; and the export to other parts, as difproportionably too fmall ; the reafon for which is very obvious : and, befides, it is probable, that many veffels, which were deftined to other parts, took out clearances for North-America. I fhall add to the foregoing the eftimated value of exports in the fame year (1770) from the other Britifh fugar-iflands, and ftate their aggregate in comparifon with that of Jamaica, omitting fractions, as in the former example.

		£
Grenades,	——	506,709
Antigua,	——	465,990
Barbadoes,	——	436,013
St. Kitt's,	——	427,454
St. Vincent,	——	110,501
Montferrat,	——	102,540
Tortola,	——	71,828
Dominica,	——	62,856
Nevis,	——	57,982
Anguilla,	——	5,857

                                 £

Total from the Windward Ifles, —— 2,243,730
Total from Jamaica, —— —— 1,538,730

Grand total, —— —— —— 3,782,460

THE END OF VOL. II.

Lightning Source UK Ltd.
Milton Keynes UK
UKHW030429070720
366136UK00007B/90

CORRIGENDA.

VOL. II.

Page.	Line.	
26	23	r. which *prevent.*
31	(penult.)	r. *acacia.*
33	13	del. *and* (before) " the Conflux."
39	20	r. and *faftneffes* of.
45	15	r. were *even* known.
49	1	r. or *Echinite.*
50	25	r. *Montano.*
15	22	r. *Cudjoe.*
61	19	r. *have* encouraged.
63	17	r. quite dry, *although* at.
65	18	r. *Indian.*
69	28	r. *in width.*
Id.	(4th from the bottom)	r. the channels dangerous to.
75	29	r. *is* extremely.
80	1	after *St. Anne,* place a *comma.*
87	2	r. *detainer.*
107	11	after *dry,* place a *comma.*
115	33	r. exhalation.
118	21	del *Men.*
138	5	place a *comma* (after) *acid.*
149	7	r. 30,900 lb. wt.
197	7	r. *Commiffions.*
202	26	r. *furely* opulent enough.
223	9	r. *cultivable.*
226	18	r. *Morfe's.*
227	15	r. *Burthen,* fifty thoufand.
233	(penult.)	r. tranfmiffion *of.*
236	35	r. fuppofed *in this cafe.*
238	24	place a *comma* (after) *Governor.*
250	10	r. *are* barely.
261	2	r. *en el Ayre.*
254	7	(Note) r. after feven years, *and* 10 s. *on every Patent of Naturalization.*
298	31	r. for *Inftance.*
299	3	r. *to* make.
305	22	r. *may* be.

Page.	Line.	
319	(Note, 3d from the bottom)	r. or *Broth.*
323	11	del. *to* (after) *than.*
325	5	r. *could* be.
328	5	place a full ftop (after) *Miftrefs.*
339	5	r. *had* taken.
343	34	del. *were.*
353	7	place a *comma* (after) *been.*
360	10	r. *Loango.*
403	21	r. and *Law.*
407	25	r. the ''race.
414	17	r. in *as many* different.
458	19	(after) *Stipulation* place the † reference to the *Note.*
465	29	r. perfons *thither.*
468	3	r. *making* at.
470	19	r. *thofe that* lay.
473	27	r. *horrid* rite.
475	5th of Chap. IV.	r. to the *opinion of my readers.*
484	5th from the bottom,	r. *through* an exact.
Id.	3d Id.	r. reafoning *then.*
494	(4th Note)	r. *Imprifonment.*
499	25	r. *Glebæ.*
502	18	r. 30 *l. nett.*
527	(8th Note) r. from *it.*	
542	26	r. *they* muft.
562	1	r. *a* vice.
Id.	29	r. *produced* a wonderful.
569	21	r. *they* cannot.
574	14	r. *no* liquor,
Id.	20	*et fequent.* r. *Liguanea.*
576	29	r. it *fhould feem.*
577	13	r. *Alum.*
589	21	r. perfons, *only perplexed.*
593	5	r. fee *any equal* performance.
*599	Appendix.	r. in two places — 10 *l. per* hogfhead.